LOTUS® 1-2-3® RELEASE 5

Related titles of interest from Wiley:

ADVANCED LOTUS 1-2-3 RELEASE 3, Yu and Harrison

LOTUS 1-2-3 RELEASE 2.2, Williams

LOTUS 1-2-3 RELEASE 2 A.S.A.P., Williams

USING LOTUS AGENDA, Goodman

MACROS, MENUS, AND MIRACLES FOR LOTUS 1-2-3, Lunsford

BUSINESS STATISTICS USING LOTUS 1-2-3, Kilpatrick

LOTUS 1-2-3 QUICK REFERENCE HANDBOOK, CPCE

DESIGNING INTELLIGENT FRONT ENDS FOR BUSINESS SOFTWARE, Shafer

INSIDE ALLWAYS, Sandler and Badgett

Lotus® 1-2-3® Release 3

Andrew T. Williams

John Wiley & Sons, Inc.
New York   Chichester   Brisbane   Toronto   Singapore

Editor: Therese A. Zak
Managing Editor: Ruth Greif
Editing, Design, and Production: Impressions, Inc.

This publication is designed to provide accurate and authoritative information in regard to the subject matter covered. It is sold with the understanding that the publisher is not engaged in rendering legal, accounting, or other professional service. If legal advice or other expert assistance is required, the services of a competent professional person should be sought. FROM A DECLARATION OF PRINCIPLES JOINTLY ADOPTED BY A COMMITTEE OF THE AMERICAN BAR ASSOCIATION AND A COMMITTEE OF PUBLISHERS.

Copyright © 1989 by John Wiley & Sons, Inc.

All rights reserved. Published simultaneously in Canada.

Reproduction or translation of any part of this work beyond that permitted by section 107 or 108 of the 1976 United States Copyright Act without the permission of the copyright owner is unlawful. Requests for permission or further information should be addressed to the Permission Department, John Wiley & Sons, Inc.

Library of Congress Cataloging-in-Publication Data

Williams, Andrew T., 1943–
   Lotus 1-2-3 release 3 / Andrew T. Williams.
     p. cm.
   ISBN 0-471-61847-0
   1. Lotus 1-2-3 (Computer program)   2. Business—Data processing.
 I. Title.
HF5548.4.L67W523 1989
005.369—dc20   89-22406
                                                                         CIP

Printed in the United States of America

89 90 10 9 8 7 6 5 4 3 2 1

This one's for Erin

Contents

Acknowledgments *xxiii*
  Trademark Acknowledgments *xxiii*

CHAPTER 1: Mastering the Basics *1*

Objectives *1*

Introduction *1*

Getting Started *2*
  Running the INSTALL Program *2*
  Starting 1-2-3 *3*

Screen Tour *3*
  The 1-2-3 Spreadsheet *3*
  The Control Panel *8*

Working in 3-D: Sheets, Files, and Stacks *10*
  Creating Multisheet Stacks *13*
  Stack Versus Current File *13*
  Making a Sheet the Current Sheet *14*

Mastering 1-2-3 Basics *14*
  Cursor Control Keys *14*
  Perspective View *19*
  Scrolling the Screen *19*
  Function Keys *20*
  Types of Entries: Values and Labels *20*
  Getting Out of Trouble *23*
  Getting Help *24*

Slash Commands 25
　Using a Command Menu 26
　Correcting Mistakes with ESC 28
　Correcting Mistakes with Undo 29
　Group Mode 29
　Ending a Work Session 30

How to Read This Book 30
　Straight Through 31
　Skipping Around 31
　Two BIG Tips 31

CHAPTER 2: Worksheet Commands 33

Objectives 33

Introduction 33

Command Overview 33
　The Range Commands 34
　Default Settings 35

The Worksheet Global Command 36
　The Global Format Command 38
　The Global Label Command 43
　The Global Col-Width Command 45
　The Global Recalculation Command 46
　The Global Protection Command 48
　The Global Default Command 50

The Worksheet Insert Command 56
　Inserting Rows and Columns 56
　Inserting Sheets 58

The Worksheet Delete Command 59
　Deleting Rows and Columns 59
　Deleting Sheets 60
　Deleting Files 61
　Caution: ERR 61

The Worksheet Column Command 62
　Set and Reset 63
　Hide and Display 64
　Controlling the Width of a Range of Columns 65

The Worksheet Erase Command 65

CONTENTS

The Worksheet Titles Command *67*

The Worksheet Window Command *70*
  Splitting the Screen into Windows *71*
  Perspective on a Stack *74*
  Graph Window *75*
  Map View *76*
  Using Windows *76*
  Display *79*

The Worksheet Status Command *79*

The Worksheet Page Command *81*

Hands On: Using the Worksheet Commands *82*

Tips & Traps *85*
  Tips *85*
  Traps *86*

CHAPTER 3: The Range Commands *88*

Objectives *88*

Introduction *88*

Home, Home on the Range . . . *90*
  Specifying a Range *92*
  Lotus' Marvelous, One-Size-Fits-All Expanding Cursor *93*

Commands Common to Range and Worksheet *96*
  Format *96*
  Label *100*
  Erase *101*

Commands Unique to Range *102*
  Name *102*
  Justify *113*
  Prot and Unprot *118*
  Search *120*
  Input *123*
  Transpose and Values *125*

Hands On: Using the Range Commands *125*
  Widening a Column *127*
  Range Format Date *128*
  Range Format Fixed *128*

CONTENTS

    Range Format Currency *128*
    Range Labels *129*
    Range Justify *130*
    EDIT/F2 to Center Long Labels *130*
    Worksheet Insert Row *130*
    Conclusions: Making Range and Worksheet Commands Work for You *131*

Tips & Traps *131*
    Tips *131*
    Traps *132*

CHAPTER 4: The Copy, Move, System, and Quit Commands *134*

Objectives *134*

Introduction *134*

The Copy Command *135*
    Using the Copy Command *136*
    The Relationship Between FROM and TO Ranges *139*
    Copying Formulas and Functions *143*
    Relative Cell References *144*
    Absolute Cell References *146*

The Range Value and Range Transpose Commands *149*
    Range Value *149*
    Range Transpose *150*

The Move Command *151*
    Using the Move Command *153*
    Caution: Named Ranges *153*

The System Command *154*
    When Not to Use the System Command *155*
    Warning *156*

The Quit Command *156*

Hands On: Using the Copy Command *157*
    Constructing the Individual Retirement Account Worksheet *157*
    Using the Individual Retirement Account Worksheet *160*

Tips & Traps *160*
    Tips *160*
    Traps *162*

CHAPTER 5: The File Command 163

Objectives 163

Introduction 163
    The Need to Save 163
    The File Command Options 165

Filenames 166
    Good and Bad Filenames 166
    Filename Extensions 167
    Organizing Your Worksheet Files 169

The File Save and File Retrieve Commands 170
    Formatted Diskettes 170
    The File Save Command 171
    The File Retrieve Command 176

The File Xtract and File Combine Commands 179
    The File Xtract Command 179
    The File Combine Command 181

The File New and File Open Commands 185
    Using the File Open Command 185
    Using the File New Command 187

The File Import Command 188
    The .PRN Extension 188
    Position Cursor Before Entering File Import Command 189
    Text or Numbers 189
    Using the File Import Command 190

The File Admin Command 190
    The Admin Reservation Command 191
    The File Admin Seal Command 193
    The File Admin Table Command 194

The File Erase, List, and Directory Commands 196
    Erase 196
    List 197
    Dir 198

Hands On: The FILE_TBL.WK3 Worksheet 199
    Create FILE_TBL.WK3 199
    Name the Ranges 200
    Use the File Combine Command 201
    Complete the Table 202

CONTENTS

Tips & Traps *202*
   Tips *202*
   Traps *203*

CHAPTER 6: The Print Command *205*

Objectives *205*

Introduction *205*
   The Print Command *207*
   The Printer/File/Encoded Options *207*
   The Suspend/Resume/Cancel Choices *209*

The Print Sample *210*

Printing Plain and Printing Fancy *211*
   Trial and Success *211*

Printing Plain: Using the Print Command Default Settings *212*
   An Example *212*
   The Default Page *215*
   Problems with the Default Print Settings *218*
   Forcing a Page Break *221*
   Stopping the Printer *221*
   Additional Print Commands *222*

Printing Fancy: Using the Print Command Options *224*
   Page Parameters *226*
   Headers and Footers *227*
   Borders *230*
   Setup Strings *231*
   Other *234*
   Name *236*
   The Options Advanced Commands *237*

The Print File and Encoded Commands *241*
   Creating an Encoded File *241*
   Creating a Print File *242*

Hands On: Printing in Compressed Type *244*
   Without Compressed Type *245*
   Printing in Compressed Type *246*
   Line-Spacing Compressed and Orientation Landscape *248*

Tips & Traps *248*
   Tips *248*
   Traps *249*

CONTENTS   xiii

CHAPTER 7: 1-2-3's Built-In Functions and the Add-In Command   251

   Objectives   *251*

   Introduction   *251*
      Operators   *252*
      Built-In Functions   *252*
      Cell References   *252*
      "What If..." Analysis   *253*

   Arithmetic Operators   *254*
      Order of Operations   *255*
      Examples of Arithmetic Operators   *255*

   Logical Operators   *256*

   String Operators   *257*
      Simple String Functions   *258*
      Using Quotation Marks in String Functions   *259*
      Writing Sentences with String Functions   *259*
      Combining Numbers and Text   *259*
      Tips   *260*

   General Rules for Using Built-in Functions   *260*
      Begin with @   *260*
      Use NAME/F3 to Paste Function Names   *261*
      Arguments   *261*
      Use HELP/F1 to Get Information About Arguments   *261*
      Point to Arguments   *261*
      Use Range Names   *262*
      Multiple Arguments   *262*
      Correct Mistakes as You Go   *263*
      Close All Open Parentheses   *263*

   Statistical Functions   *263*

   Logical Functions   *265*
      The @IF Function   *265*
      Nested Functions   *267*

   Time and Date Functions   *267*
      Entering a Specify Date   *268*
      Attributes of Date/Time Numbers   *269*
      Using Date/Time Numbers   *269*

   Financial Functions   *270*
      Uses of Financial Functions   *270*

CONTENTS

  Calculating Your Mortgage Payment   *270*

Mathematical Functions   *272*
  Using the @MOD Function   *273*
  Using the @ROUND Function   *274*

Special Functions   *275*
  Constructing Lookup Tables and @LOOKUP Functions   *275*
  How the Lookup Function Works   *279*
  Always Test Your Lookup Functions   *279*
  Using @CELL, @CELLPOINTER, and @INFO   *280*

String Functions   *283*
  Combining Text and Values with the @STRING Function   *283*
  Tips for Including @STRING Functions in Paragraphs   *285*

Relative and Absolute Cell References   *285*
  Absolute Named Ranges   *286*

The Lotus Add-in Command   *286*
  The Add-in Menu   *287*
  Loading an Add-in   *287*
  Running an Add-in   *288*
  Add-in Types   *288*
  Conclusions   *289*

Tips & Traps   *290*
  Tips   *290*
  Traps   *291*

CHAPTER 8: Data Fill and Data Table Commands   *292*

Objectives   *292*

Introduction   *292*

The Data Fill Command   *293*
  Using the Data Fill Command   *295*
  Warning: Data Fill Overwrites Cells in Fill Range   *296*
  Filling Ranges with Dates and Times   *296*
  Canceling Proposed Fill Ranges   *296*

The Data Table Command   *297*
  The Assumption Space   *297*
  Advantages of Assumption Spaces   *299*

One-Way Data Table   *299*

CONTENTS

    Constructing a One-Way Data Table *300*
    Table Range *301*
    Input Cell *301*
    Using the One-Way Data Table Command *301*

Two-Way Data Table *302*
    Constructing a Two-Way Data Table *303*
    Using the Two-Way Data Table Command *304*

Three-Way Data Table *304*
    Constructing a Three-Way Table *305*
    Entering the Third Variable *306*
    Specifying the Formula *307*
    Using the Three-Way Data Table Command *307*

Tips for Using Data Tables *309*
    Canceling Remembered Ranges *309*
    Modifying a Data Table *309*
    The TABLE/F8 Key *310*
    Using Range Names *310*

Data Table Labeled Command *311*
    Terminology *312*
    Using the Data Table Labeled Command *314*
    Verifying Variable Ranges and Input Cells *316*
    Advanced Labeled Data Tables *316*
    Conclusion *318*

Tips & Traps *319*
    Tips *319*
    Traps *320*

CHAPTER 9: The Database Commands *321*

Objectives *321*

Introduction *321*

Overview *322*
    What Is a Database? *322*
    What Can You Do with a Database? *324*

The Data Sort Command *325*
    Using the Data Sort Command *326*
    Problems with Blanks, Brackets, and Formulas *329*
    Restoring the Original Order *332*

CONTENTS

Setting Up the Data Query Command *333*
 Construct the Database *334*
 Construct the Criteria Range *335*
 Relative Criteria *337*
 Multiple Criteria *341*
 Summary *344*

The Data Query Find Command *345*
 Specifying the Input Range *346*
 Specifying the Criteria Range *347*
 Using the Data Find Command *347*

The QUERY/F7 Function Key *349*

The Data Query Delete Command *350*
 Specifying the Range for Deletion *350*
 Undoing the Delete Command *351*

The Data Query Extract Command *351*
 Constructing the Output Range *351*
 Specifying the Output Range *352*
 Extracting Records *353*
 Calculated Fields *354*
 Omitted Field Names *355*
 Rearranged Field Names *355*

The Data Query Unique Command *357*

The Data Query Modify Command *358*
 Inserting New Records *359*
 Modifying Existing Records *359*
 Canceling the Data Query Modify Command *360*

The Database Statistical Functions *360*
 Using Database Statistical Functions *361*
 Database Statistical Functions in Action *363*

The Data Distribution Command *363*
 Constructing the Bin Range *363*
 Using the Data Distribution Command *366*

Hands On: Using the Data Command *367*
 Constructing the Data Table *368*
 Using the Data Table *368*

Tips & Traps   *371*
   Tips   *371*
   Traps   *372*

CHAPTER 10: Multiple Input Ranges and External Databases   *373*

Objectives   *373*

Introduction   *373*

Using Multiple Input Ranges   *374*
   The Implied Database   *375*
   Joining Input Ranges   *378*
   Using Identical Field Names   *382*

Using External Databases   *383*
   The Database Driver   *384*
   Connecting to an External Database   *386*
   Data External List   *388*
   Using an External Database Table   *392*
   Data Query Extract   *392*
   Summary   *394*

Creating a New Table in an External Database   *395*
   Creating the Table Definition   *396*
   Naming the External Database Table   *397*
   Creating the External Table   *398*
   Modifying a Table Definition   *400*
   External Delete   *400*
   Alternate Ways to Generate a Table Definition   *401*
   Adding Records to an External Table   *402*

Other Data External Commands   *404*
   Refresh   *404*
   Command   *406*
   Translation   *406*

Ending the Connection to an External Table   *406*

The Data Regression, Parse, and Matrix Commands   *407*
   The Data Regression Command   *408*
   The Data Parse Command   *409*
   The Data Matrix Command   *411*

Tips & Traps   *412*
   Tips   *412*
   Traps   *413*

CHAPTER 11: The Graph Commands 415

Objectives 415

Introduction 415
   A Word About Hardware 417

The ABC's of Creating a 1-2-3 Graph 418
   Create the Worksheet First 418
   Specify the Graph 418
   View the Graph 421
   Understand the X Range 421

The ABC's of Printing a 1-2-3 Graph 422

Titles and Legends 423
   Legends 423
   Titles 426

Alternative Ways to Specify Data Ranges 428
   The Correct Spreadsheet 428
   Group 429
   Automatic Graphing 430

Graph Types 432
   Line Graph 432
   Bar Charts: Horizontal, Vertical, and Multiple 432
   Stacked-Bar Chart 434
   Mixed Graph 435
   High-Low-Close Graph 436
   XY Graph 437
   Pie Charts 438

Features 440
   Features Options 440
   Logarithmic Scaling 444

Displaying Graphs and Spreadsheets Simultaneously 445

Building a Library of Named Graphs 447
   Using Named Graphs 448
   Removing Named Graphs 448
   Modifying Named Graphs 449
   Tabling Named Graphs 450

Canceling Graph Settings 451
   Reset Graph 451

CONTENTS

Reset Data Range *451*
Reset Ranges *451*
Reset Options *451*

Options *452*
B&W and Color *452*
Data Labels *452*
Grid *454*
Scale *455*
Format *457*
Advanced *458*
Quit *461*

Using Graphs with Multiple Active Files *461*
Data Ranges *462*
Names Across Files *462*
Current Graph *462*

Using Graphs with Other Programs *463*

Printing Graphs *463*
What You See May Not Be What You Get *464*
Defaults *464*
Printer or Encoded *465*
Printing the Current Graph *465*
Printing a Named Graph *466*
Combining Graphs with Other Print Ranges *466*
Options Advanced Image *469*
Conclusion *471*

Hands On: Using the Graph Command *471*
The Worksheet *471*
Creating a Horizontal Bar Chart *472*
Adding Titles *473*
Adding Y-Axis Labels and Legends *474*
Naming the Graph *476*
Modifying the Database and Redrawing the Graph *477*
Conclusion *478*

Tips & Traps *479*
Tips *479*
Traps *479*

CHAPTER 12: Macros: The Hidden Power of 1-2-3 *481*

Objectives *481*

Introduction *481*

CONTENTS

What Is a Keyboard Macro? *482*

Six Rules for Creating and Using Keyboard Macros *483*
    Rule 1: Text Only *483*
    Rule 2: Use a Single Column *484*
    Rule 3: Name the First Cell *484*
    Rule 4: Turn Off Automatic Recalculation *485*
    Rule 5: Position the Cursor *485*
    Rule 6: Run the Macro *486*

How a Macro Works *486*

The Single Step Command *487*

Special Key Names *488*
    The ENTER Key *489*

Advanced Macro Commands *489*
    The Pause Command *489*
    The /X Commands *496*

Custom Menus *496*
    Creating the Menu Text *498*
    Using a Custom Menu *501*
    Modifying a Menu *501*

Additional Macro Commands, Keywords, and Features *503*
    Automatic Macros: \0 *503*
    Autoloading Worksheets *504*
    Branching Commands *504*
    Input Commands *505*
    If/Then Command *505*
    Additional Advanced Macro Commands *506*

Working with Several Active Files *507*
    Range Names *507*
    Running Macros Across Active Files *508*
    Creating a Macro Library *508*

Using the Keystroke Recorder *509*
    Erase *510*
    Playback *510*
    Copy *511*

Macro Hints *513*
    Always Use Range Names in Macros *513*
    Know Your Action *514*

CONTENTS

    Place Logically Separate Actions in Separate Cells *514*
    Easy HELP *515*
    Use Subroutines *515*
    Give All Macros Titles *515*
    Place All Macros on a Separate Sheet *516*
    Use Uppercase Only for Range Names and Advanced Macro Commands *516*
    Select Easy-to-Remember Names for Macros *516*
    Enter Macro Name as Text to Left of Macro *517*
    Use Custom Menus *517*
    Test Macros for Errors *517*
    Use Blank Cells for Macro Testing *517*

Summary *517*

Hands On: Self-Modifying Macros *518*
    Constructing the Menu Screen *518*
    Constructing the Macro *518*
    Name the Ranges *520*

Tips & Traps *521*
    Tips *521*
    Traps *522*

Index *525*

Acknowledgments

Many people contributed directly or indirectly to this book, and it is a better book for their help. I would particularly like to thank Audrey Keesing for her aid in preparing the index and an early draft of the manuscript. I would also like to thank Linda Williams for her continuing writerly support and for her dedication to the proposition that two writers can meet simultaneous deadlines without bloodshed or divorce.

Special thanks to my editor at John Wiley & Sons, Therese Zak, for her support and patience, and to Susan Earabino and Mary Beth Retteger at Lotus Development Corporation for the right stuff at the right time. And finally, my deep appreciation to my copy editor, Lynn Brown. The errors that remain are my own, but there are fewer of them for Lynn's good-humored attention to consistency and detail.

TRADEMARK ACKNOWLEDGMENTS

Allways is a trademark of Lotus Development Corporation.
dBASE, dBASE II, dBASE III, and dBASE IV are registered trademarks of Ashton-Tate Corporation.
Epson and Epson FX-85 are registered trademarks of Epson America, Inc.
Lotus and 1-2-3 are registered trademarks of Lotus Development Corporation.
Microsoft and MS-DOS are registered trademarks of Microsoft Corporation.
Paradox and Sidekick are registered trademarks of Borland International.
RBase is a trademark of Microrim, Inc.
WordPerfect is a registered trademark of WordPerfect Corporation.

1 Mastering The Basics

OBJECTIVES

After mastering the content of this chapter, you will be able to

☐ start Lotus 1-2-3 Release 3 and perform basic spreadsheet construction tasks.

☐ distinguish between single worksheets, sheets in a stack, stacks, and active files.

☐ use Lotus 1-2-3's special function keys for obtaining help, moving to specific locations, and editing entries.

☐ use the cursor movement keys to navigate around a spreadsheet and from spreadsheet to spreadsheet and file to file in a three-dimensional stack.

☐ construct spreadsheets out of value and label entries.

☐ master the techniques for correcting mistakes in spreadsheet construction and use.

INTRODUCTION

There are a number of important tasks to perform and concepts to master before you can use 1-2-3 effectively. These include installing and starting the program, understanding the meaning of the different elements of the 1-2-3 screen, moving the cursor from cell to cell and from sheet to sheet, and using the function keys. These and other basic but necessary topics are covered in this chapter.

If you are just learning to use Lotus 1-2-3 Release 3, read this chapter carefully and refer to it often. The information contained in this chapter is used with every spreadsheet you construct. Come back and reread this chapter after you have worked with 1-2-3 for awhile. At that point, a quick review of the basics will remind you of important and powerful features you may have overlooked or forgotten.

If you have already worked with earlier versions of Lotus 1-2-3, it is still important that you read this chapter. In addition to information about new features such as three-dimensional stacks of worksheets, the chapter also contains a quick, complete review of the 1-2-3 basics. If you are self-taught, you probably missed some commands and features that can be applied to spreadsheets constructed with any version of 1-2-3. You will also relearn important, time-saving features that you may have forgotten since you first learned to use the program.

GETTING STARTED

Running the INSTALL Program

To copy program files to your hard disk and to prepare 1-2-3 to run on your computer, place the diskette labeled Install in the A drive, type **INSTALL**, and press **ENTER**. Then follow the instructions as they appear on the screen. The install program creates a subdirectory on your hard disk to contain the program files and copies the appropriate files to that subdirectory. The default name for the subdirectory is 123R3. In this book it is referred to as the LOTUS or 1-2-3 subdirectory.

You also use the install program to select printers to use with 1-2-3, to specify the monitor type you are using, and to generally configure 1-2-3 to work with your particular microcomputer system. Installation isn't difficult, but you must do it in order to have 1-2-3 work properly with your computer. If you need help, consult the manual or press the HELP/F1 key. (Here and throughout, I show the name of a hot key followed by a slash and the function key you press for that action.)

Once installation has been completed, you won't need to repeat this step unless you change your printer or monitor. If necessary, consult the "Setting Up 1-2-3" section of the Lotus 1-2-3 manual for step-by-step instructions for copying the program to your hard disk and running the install program.

Starting 1-2-3

To start 1-2-3, make the LOTUS subdirectory on your hard disk the current directory and then type either **LOTUS** or **123** at the system prompt and press **ENTER**. After a few moments, 1-2-3 loads into your microcomputer's memory and is ready to use.

SCREEN TOUR

Figure 1–1 shows how your screen looks after you have loaded 1-2-3. The screen is divided into two parts. The lower, larger part is a small portion of the 1-2-3 *worksheet* (or spreadsheet or sheet, for short). The upper, smaller part is called the *control panel*. The worksheet part of the screen is discussed first, then the control panel.

The 1-2-3 Spreadsheet

Before exploring the concept of a 3-D stack of spreadsheets, you must understand a single spreadsheet. A spreadsheet—manual or electronic—is a blank work space divided into *columns* and *rows*. This is what you

Figure 1–1 1-2-3 Release 3 worksheet screen.

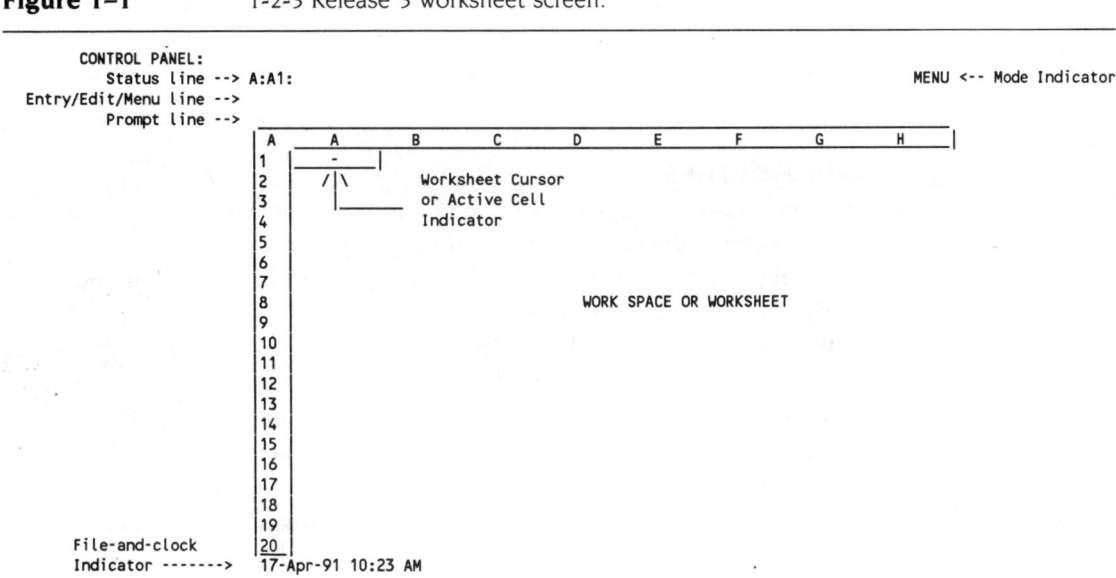

see in the lower part of the screen. In 1-2-3 the columns are labeled across the top with letters and the rows are numbered down the left side. In Figure 1–1, 8 columns (A to H) and 20 rows (1 to 20) are displayed. This is the standard screen size. Some screens in some modes can display more than 8 columns and 20 rows.

Size of the Worksheet

In Figure 1–1 the 20 rows and 8 columns form 160 cells, but this is just the very tip of the iceberg. Each Lotus 1-2-3 sheet actually has 8192 rows and 256 columns.

Sheet Indicator

Lotus 1-2-3 Release 3 can assemble a stack of up to 256 spreadsheets in memory at one time. Each spreadsheet is similar to the one in Figure 1–1. The letter *A* in the upper left corner of the inverted *L* is called the *sheet indicator*. In Figure 1–1 it shows that sheet A is the sheet currently on the screen. There may or may not be additional sheets in this stack.

Cell

The fundamental unit of an electronic spreadsheet is the *cell*. A cell is formed at the intersection of a column and a row. Everything you do with 1-2-3 is done in cells. You enter words into cells to label worksheets. You enter numbers and formulas in cells to create tables. Think of the cells as cubbyholes in your desk and the process of constructing an electronic spreadsheet as organizing the desk by placing your business materials in different cubbyholes. Unlike a desk, with 1-2-3 you have plenty of cubbyholes to work with, because the 256 columns and 8192 rows intersect to form more than 2 million cells!

Cell Address

Each of 1-2-3's 2 million cells has a unique name or *cell address*. The *minimum* cell address is formed out of the column letter and row number that intersect to form the cell. For example, B3 is the cell at the intersection of column B and row 3.

If there is no sheet letter before the cell address, it is assumed that the cell is on the current sheet. If it is necessary to specify the sheet, the sheet letter followed by a colon can precede the cell address. Thus, C:B3 is cell B3 on sheet C. Looking at Figure 1–1, identify cells A:A1, A:B7, and A:E20.

When you deal with stacks of sheets, sometimes you need to provide more information to correctly identify an individual cell. As you saw, to specify a cell on a particular sheet, you precede the cell address with the

MASTERING THE BASICS

sheet letter and a colon. When two or more *files* are in a stack, both may have several sheets in common. For example, every file must contain at least one sheet—sheet A. To distinguish cell A:A1 in one file from A:A1 in another, Lotus adds the path and filename to the cell address. For example, the complete cell reference to cell A1 on sheet A in a file named BUDGET.A1 stored in the C:\FINANCE subdirectory would be

<<**C:\FINANCE\BUDGET.WK3**>>**A:A1**

Note that the filename is enclosed in double less than and greater than symbols. (The distinction between sheets, stacks, and files is discussed later in the chapter.)

When you omit the path, 1-2-3 assumes the file is in the default directory. When you omit the filename, 1-2-3 assumes the file is the current file. And when you omit the sheet letter, 1-2-3 assumes the cell address is a cell on the current sheet.

To summarize, the parts of the complete cell address

<<**C:\FINANCE\BUDGET.WK3**>>**A:A1**

are

Part	Meaning
<<**C:\FINANCE\BUDGET.WK3**>>	*Filename*; the complete path is optional
A:	Sheet indicator
A1	Column letter followed by row number

Specify the filename and sheet indicator only when you are referring to cells in different files or on different sheets. If you do overspecify a filename, however, 1-2-3 accepts your specification and drops the unnecessary information. Lotus also has some convenient ways of supplying the cell address information so you don't have to do a lot of tedious typing. (See Pointing with the Cursor in Chapter 3.)

Active Cell

Of all the 2 million cells on a 1-2-3 worksheet, one cell—the *active cell*—is special. It is the cell that currently contains a bright bar of light and the flashing underline character. This bar of light is called the *worksheet cursor*. In Figure 1-1 the worksheet cursor is located on cell A:A1 and is shown as an underline within a rectangle (actually, you see a highlight on your screen). Thus, cell A:A1 is the current or active cell.

What makes the active cell special is that anything you type and enter into the spreadsheet appears in the active cell. It is where your electronic "pencil" touches your electronic worksheet.

In a moment you learn how to move the cursor to activate any one of 1-2-3's more than 2 million cells.

File-and-clock Indicator

At the bottom left of the worksheet area is the File-and-clock indicator. When you first load 1-2-3, the date and time stored in your computer system appear there. (Many computers set the date and time automatically. Others require you to provide this information as part of the computer's startup procedure.)

When you load a worksheet file into memory or add a new file to the stack, the name of the file appears in the File-and-clock indicator. For example, when you retrieve the file named SALESTOT.WK3, SALESTOT.WK3 replaces the date and time at the bottom of the screen. See Figure 1–2.

Status Indicators

Status indicators also appear from time to time at the bottom of the screen. Many indicators relate to the actions of specific keys. For example, **END** appears when you press the END key and **CAPS** appears when you press

Figure 1–2   Sales by Division worksheet.

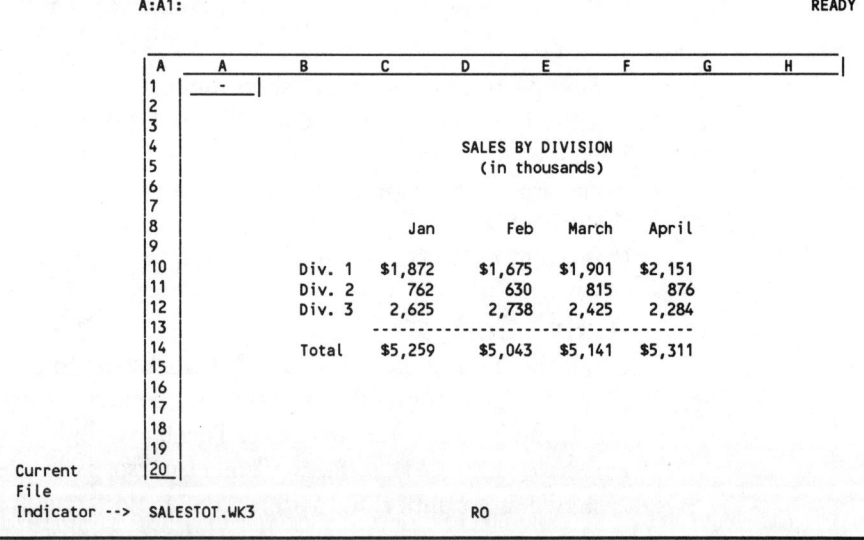

MASTERING THE BASICS

the CAPS LOCK key. Other indicators such as CALC, GROUP, RO, and CIRC signal important information about 1-2-3's current operating state.

In Figure 1–2, for example, the RO status indicator appears to indicate that the SALESTOT.WK3 file is a read only file. See Table 1–1 for a list of the status indicators and their meanings.

CALC

The CALC indicator indicates that the formulas in the spreadsheet may not be displaying the correct results. If **CALC** displays in white, the recalculation status has been set to manual. This shows you that numbers

Table 1–1 Status indicators that appear at the bottom of the screen.

Status Indicator	Explanation
CALC	Formulas require recalculation
CAP	Uppercase letters will be entered
CIRC	Circular reference has been created
CMD	Information is being retrieved
END	END pointer keys will be used
FILE	Pointer keys are being used to move between files
GROUP	Group mode is active
MEM	Memory available has fallen below 4096 bytes
NUM	Numeric keypad will enter numbers rather than move the cursor
OVR	Overwrite mode is active
RO	Read only status is active; you can view but not change the document
SCROLL	Arrow keys are active so you can scroll the worksheet
STEP	Step mode is active
SST	A macro is being run in Step mode
ZOOM	Full window display was activated from perspective display

on the screen haven't been recalculated after a change to the spreadsheet and may be incorrect. Before you trust the numbers (or print out your worksheet), press the **CALC/F9** key to force a recalculation of all of the formulas on the spreadsheet. (The CALC/F9 key and the other commands stored in function keys are discussed later in the chapter.) If a flashing **CALC** appears, 1-2-3 is currently recalculating the spreadsheet. Even on very large spreadsheets it takes only a few moments to complete a recalculation, because of Lotus' very efficient recalculation routine. You can continue working with your spreadsheet while **CALC** flashes, but you shouldn't trust the displayed numbers until **CALC** disappears.

GROUP

The GROUP indicator means that all of the worksheets in the current file (up to 256) are treated as a group for certain commands, such as Worksheet Insert and Delete and Range Format. For example, when GROUP is active, inserting a row into one worksheet inserts the corresponding row into all spreadsheets. See Chapter 2 for a detailed discussion of the possibilities and problems of using GROUP.

RO

The RO indicator only appears when you are using 1-2-3 on a network. It means that the file you have retrieved is a "read only" file. You can retrieve and view the file, but you can't save any changes you make to it. An RO file is only for reading (viewing), not for saving. (See Chapter 5 for a discussion of the File Admin command and read only files.)

CIRC

The CIRC indicator appears whenever a formula or function refers to itself either directly or indirectly. This creates what is called a "circular reference." See the Worksheet Status command in Chapter 2 for a discussion of circular references and how to find them.

The Control Panel

The small area above the column letters is called the *control panel*. Constructing a 1-2-3 worksheet is a two-step process. First, you position the worksheet cursor on the cell where you want to make an entry. Then you type the entry.

What you type appears first in the control panel where you can review it for accuracy, change it, or cancel it. When you are satisfied, press the **ENTER** key, and what you have typed is transferred (or "entered") into

MASTERING THE BASICS

the cell underneath the worksheet cursor. If your entry is longer than 72 characters (the width of the typing area on the screen), the control panel expands to 9 rows so that all of your typing can be viewed at one time.

Think of the control panel as a scratch pad where you work out and verify your entries before transferring them to the current, active cell.

Status Line

The top line of the control panel is called the *status line*. On the right side of the status line is the *Mode indicator*. In Figures 1–1 and 1–2, the Mode indicator displays the word **READY** to show that 1-2-3 is ready to begin work. The Ready mode is the starting point for all 1-2-3 operations. When you take an action, the Mode indicator changes. When you finish, 1-2-3 returns to the Ready mode, ready to begin work on your next instruction.

Lotus switches modes automatically to reflect what you are doing. When you are entering a label, 1-2-3 switches to Label mode to accept it. When you press the **EDIT/F2** key, 1-2-3 switches to Edit mode. See Table 1–2 for a list of 1-2-3's modes.

At the other end of the status line is the *Active Cell indicator*. In Figures 1–1 and 1–2 the indicator shows **A:A1**, the address of the current active cell. To the right of the cell address is the content of the active cell. In Figures 1–1 and 1–2, the active cell is empty, so nothing is displayed to the right of A:A1:. In Figure 1–3, the cursor has been moved to cell C13. This cell contains a formula, which is displayed after A:C13 on the status line.

Entry/Edit/Menu Line

The second line of the control panel has a different name, depending on the function you are performing. When you type information it is called the *Entry line*, because what you are entering appears there. When you are editing an entry it is called the *Edit line*, because the cell contents you are editing appear on the line. Finally, when you are using a menu it is called the *Menu line*, because menu choices are displayed on the line.

The Mode indicator changes to **Value** or **Label** when the line is used as the Entry line; to **Edit** when you are editing; and to **Menu** when menu choices are displayed. In Figure 1–4 the program is in Edit mode. The content of the active cell is now displayed on the Edit line, and the Mode indicator has changed from **READY** in Figure 1–3 to **EDIT** in this figure.

Prompt Line

The bottom or third line of the control panel is the *Prompt line*. When you are making menu choices, two types of information appear on the

Table 1–2	Mode indicators that appear at upper right of the screen.
Mode Indicator	**Explanation**
EDIT	Permits entry to be edited
ERROR	Indicates an error. Press HELP/F1
FILES	Displays list of filenames
FIND	Highlights data selected
HELP	Displays a Help screen
LABEL	Enters a label
MENU	Displays a menu of commands
NAMES	Displays names of ranges, graphs, databases, etc.
POINT	Specifies a range or creates a formula
READY	1-2-3 is ready to continue
STAT	Displays Status screen
VALUE	Enters a value
WAIT	Completes an action, asking you to wait during processing

Prompt line. If a particular choice leads to submenus, the submenu choices are listed on the Prompt line. Otherwise, the Prompt line displays a brief description of the action to be taken when you select a particular menu item. The prompt changes as you use the SPACE BAR or LEFT and RIGHT arrow keys to move the highlight from menu item to menu item.

WORKING IN 3-D: SHEETS, FILES, AND STACKS

As you know, 1-2-3 provides a 2 million-plus grid of cells for building spreadsheets. You can think of this as a large, single sheet of electronic paper to be manipulated by the electronic tools that 1-2-3 provides. This may seem to be a large enough work area for any project, but 1-2-3 can also provide a stack of electronic spreadsheets, each as large and powerful as the one you have learned about.

This three-dimensional stack of worksheets, or *stack* for short, is an entirely new Lotus concept introduced with Release 3. You can think of

MASTERING THE BASICS

Figure 1-3   Status line showing the actual contents of cell under worksheet cursor, A:C13.

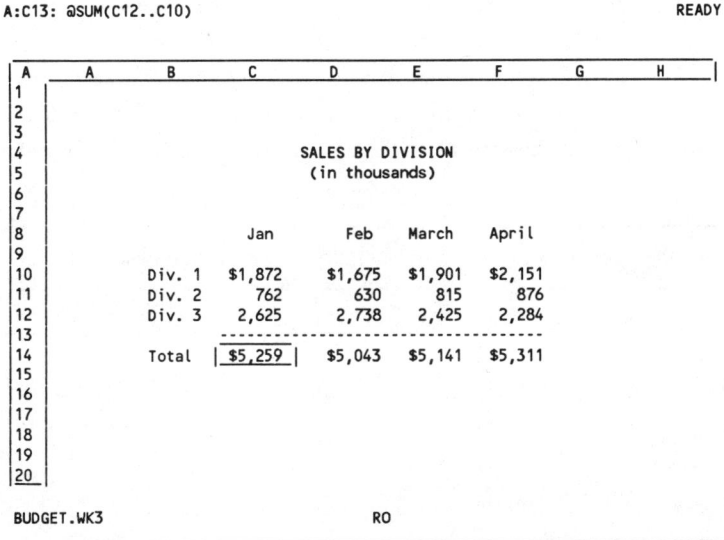

Figure 1-4   Worksheet in Edit mode, contents of A:C13 displayed in control panel ready for editing.

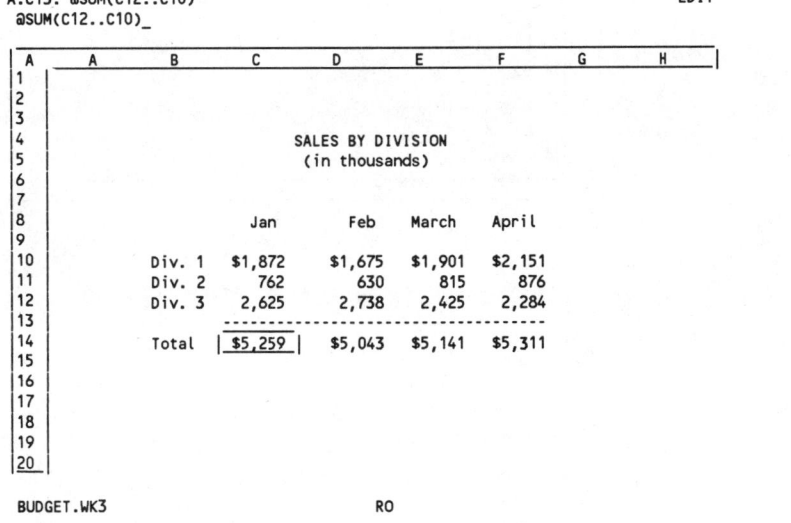

a stack of worksheets as a "pad of paper" in which each sheet or page represents an individual 1-2-3 worksheet. When you need a new worksheet, you just turn to a new page in your stack. Organizing the spreadsheets associated with a project now becomes a simple matter of placing all the worksheets for the project into the same stack (or pad or binder). Figure 1–5 contains a representation of a stack in memory, where the stack consists of three sheets in a single worksheet file.

Figure 1–5 Single file in memory containing multiple worksheets.

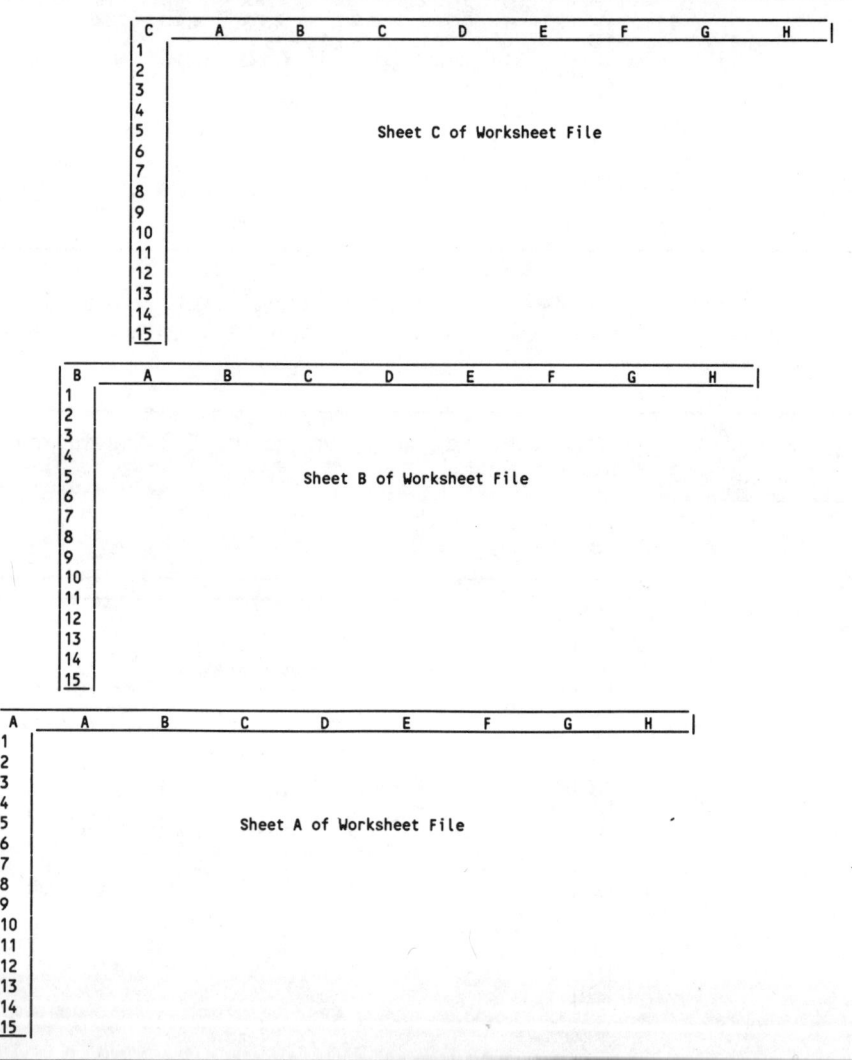

Each stack can contain up to 256 worksheets or pages, with all of the worksheets in a stack residing in your computer's memory at one time. Each sheet or page in a stack is a complete 1-2-3 worksheet—256 columns wide by 8192 rows deep.

Stacks of worksheets can be stored and retrieved as a unit (as in Figure 1–5) or they can be made up of worksheets loaded from separate files. Two or more files can be combined in a single stack as long as the total number of worksheets in memory at one time doesn't exceed 256. The amount of random access memory (RAM) in your computer may also limit the number of sheets that can be in memory at any one time.

As you know, when a file is retrieved, the File-and-clock indicator at the bottom of the screen displays the current filename. When there is no current filename, it displays the date and the time. Keep an eye on this indicator to tell which file you are currently working in.

Creating Multisheet Stacks

The stack consists of a single sheet when you first load 1-2-3 or after you use the Worksheet Erase command (discussed in Chapter 2) to erase the worksheet's contents. To build a multisheet stack, use the Worksheet Insert command (also discussed in Chapter 2) to add blank sheets to the current file or the File New or File Open command (discussed in Chapter 5) to add additional files to the stack.

Stack Versus Current File

When all of your worksheets are contained in a single file, you won't have to worry about the distinction between the *current file* (sometimes called *current active file*) and the stack. They are the same thing. When you use the File Open or File New commands to add additional files to the stack in memory, however, the concept of the current file becomes very important. Most actions you can take are confined to the current file. However, some actions extend to all of the files currently in the stack.

To identify the current file, look at the File-and-clock indicator at the bottom of the screen. It displays the filename for the current file. If the filename changes as you move from one sheet to the next, you have moved from one current file into another current file. See Figure 1–6 for an example of a stack made up of three different files. The sheet containing the worksheet cursor is the current file. Its filename appears in the File-and-clock indicator at the bottom of the screen.

Figure 1-6 Three files in memory at the same time, each containing one worksheet.

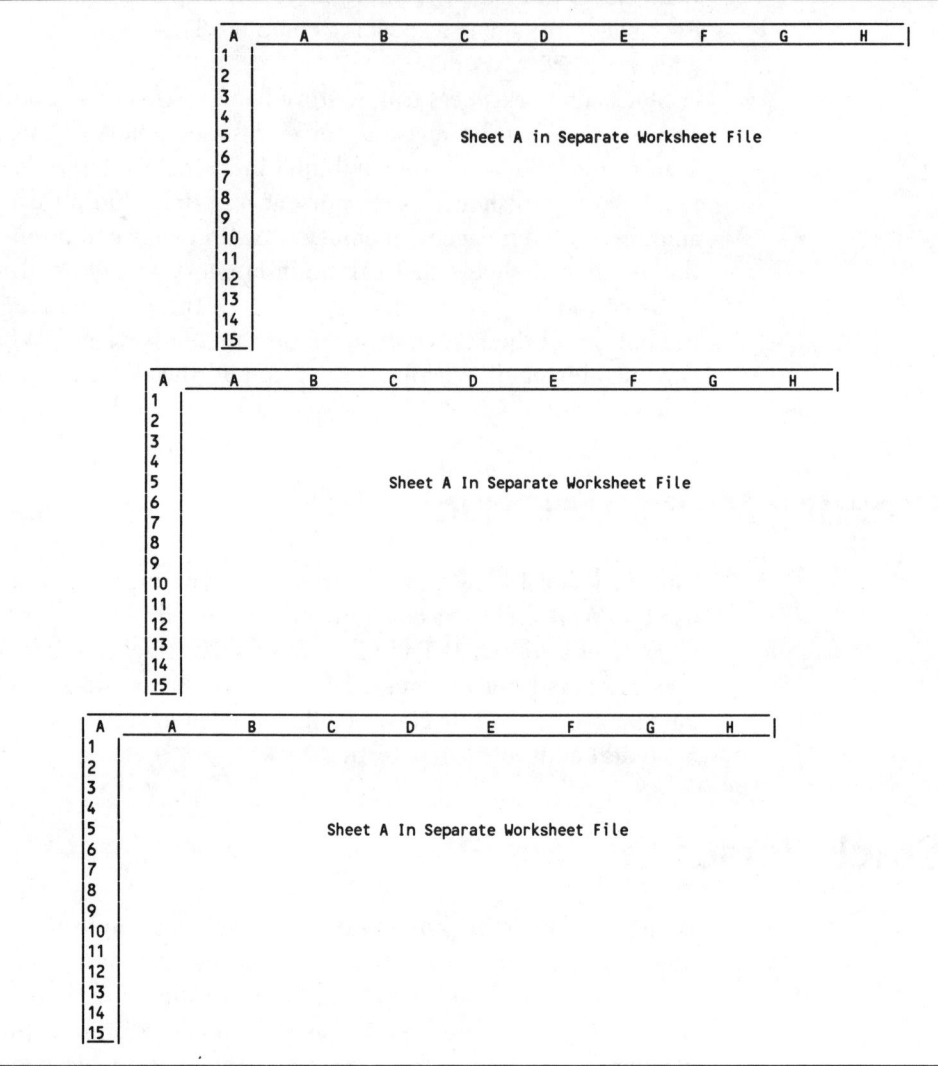

Making a Sheet the Current Sheet

The worksheet currently containing the worksheet cursor is called the *current worksheet*. It is also a sheet in the current file. To apply a command to a worksheet other than the current worksheet or to a file other than the current file, you must move the cursor to a cell on that sheet—thus making it the current sheet—or to a sheet in that file—thus making it the current file. The commands for moving around a single sheet as well as the commands for moving from sheet to sheet in a stack are discussed later in the chapter.

Remember: When a stack is made up of more than one file, keep an eye on the File-and-clock indicator to discover in which file the cursor is currently located and, consequently, which file is the current file.

MASTERING 1-2-3 BASICS

Now you know your way around the 1-2-3 screen and understand the important concepts of current sheet, current file, and stack. You are now ready to see the fundamental actions of the program at work. The following actions are used during the construction and use of *all* 1-2-3 worksheets, regardless of how complicated or simple your spreadsheets are.

Cursor Control Keys

First, to construct a worksheet you must be able to position the worksheet cursor on the cell where you want to make an entry. Table 1–3 lists the ways you can move the worksheet cursor around the worksheet. In a moment you'll learn how to move from sheet to sheet and from file to file in a stack.

In Table 1–3 and throughout this book, a hyphen separating two keys, as in **SHIFT-TAB**, means press and hold down the first key while you press the second key. When no hyphen appears between two keys, as in **END RIGHT**, press the first key, release it, and then press the second key.

Try each of the cursor movement commands in Table 1–3 and observe what happens as the cursor moves from cell to cell. Particularly notice that the Active Cell indicator changes to reflect the address of the cell currently underneath the worksheet cursor.

Arrow Keys

Usually you press the *arrow keys* to position the worksheet cursor. On most microcomputers the arrow keys are located on the right side of the keyboard on the numeric keypad. Enhanced keyboards—those on newer computers—contain a second set of arrow keys between the typewriter keys and the keypad. Both sets of arrow keys work the same in 1-2-3. Pressing an arrow key moves the cursor one cell in the indicated direction.

Table 1-3 Cursor movement keys for moving the cursor on a single worksheet.

Keystroke	Worksheet Cursor Moves
RIGHT (arrow)	One cell to the right
LEFT (arrow)	One cell to the left
UP (arrow)	One cell up
DOWN (arrow)	One cell down
HOME	To cell A1
PGUP	Up one full screen
PGDN	Down one full screen
TAB or CTRL-RIGHT	Right one full screen
SHIFT-TAB or CTRL-LEFT	Left one full screen
END HOME	To last activated cell
END RIGHT, END LEFT, END UP, END DOWN	In indicated direction; if next cell is blank, stops on last blank cell before next cell containing an entry; if next cell contains an entry, stops on last entry cell before the next blank cell

Try the arrow keys and notice how the worksheet cursor moves. You can move the cursor in any direction, but if you try to move it above row 1 or to the left of column A, 1-2-3 beeps. You've tried to move the cursor off the worksheet, and 1-2-3 lets you know that you can't do that.

Big Move Keys

The PGUP, PGDN, TAB, and SHIFT-TAB keys are the next most frequently used method of moving the cursor. They are called the *Big Move keys.* Pressing one of these keys moves the cursor one screen up, down, left, or right. Again, if you attempt to move the cursor above row 1 or to the left of column A, 1-2-3 beeps to indicate that you have given an invalid command.

Going to a Specific Cell

To move the cursor to a particular cell, press the **GOTO/F5** function key. The function keys are usually located across the top of the keyboard (on

MASTERING THE BASICS

enhanced keyboards) or in a double row down the left side. 1-2-3 uses them for many important, frequently used tasks. One of these tasks is to move the cursor to a particular cell. The most important function keys and their uses are discussed later in this chapter.

When you press GOTO/F5, a prompt appears at the top of the screen asking for the address to go to. Respond by typing the cell address, such as G56 or ih7000. No spaces are legal, and upper- and lowercase letters are interchangeable. Then press **ENTER** to move the cursor to the designated cell.

The next section shows how to use the GOTO/F5 key to move to a particular sheet in a stack.

Moving from Sheet to Sheet

When a file contains two or more sheets, you can move from one sheet to another by pressing the appropriate combination of keys. Note that some of these keys move the cursor across files as well as from sheet to sheet within the current file. Others stop at the last sheet in the current file. See Table 1-4.

The most frequently used sheet movement keys are CTRL-PGUP to move to the next sheet and CTRL-PGDN to move to the previous sheet. These keys move you one sheet forward and one sheet backward through the current file and across active files. Where the cursor appears in each sheet depends on a number of things.

Table 1-4	Cursor movement keys for moving from sheet to sheet in a stack or in the current file.	
	Movement/Keystroke	Worksheet Cursor Moves
	END CTRL-PGUP	Backward through stack. Movement similar to END arrow on one sheet
	END CTRL-PGDN	Forward through stack. Movement similar to END arrow on one sheet
	CTRL-HOME	To cell A:A1 in current file
	END CTRL-HOME	To lower right corner of current file's active area
	CTRL-PGUP	To next worksheet
	CTRL-PGDN	To previous worksheet

When you use Point mode (which specifies ranges for functions and formulas and is discussed in detail in Chapter 7) the cursor moves to the corresponding cell in each worksheet. That is, if you begin work in A:GB75 in Point mode, the cursor moves to B:GB75 when you press CTRL-PGUP. If you aren't in Point mode, where the cursor appears as you move to a sheet depends on whether the cursor has been in that sheet previously in this work session. If it has, it moves to the location it last occupied in that sheet. If it hasn't, the cursor moves to cell A1. See Table 1–5 for a list of the keystrokes that move the cursor between active files.

Using GOTO/F5 to Move from Sheet to Sheet

The GOTO/F5 function key is an extremely useful key for navigating through a stack of spreadsheets. When you press GOTO/F5 and specify a complete cell address, such as <<BUDGET.WK3>>G:A5, the cursor moves to that cell of that spreadsheet. Omit the filename and 1-2-3 assumes you want to go to the specified cell in the current file, G:A5.

Specify only G: and the cursor moves to sheet G: and occupies the cell it last occupied during this work session on that sheet. If the cursor hasn't been in the sheet, specifying only G: moves the cursor to A1 on the sheet. Finally, specify only the filename, <<BUDGET.WK3>>, and the cursor moves to the last cell occupied by the cursor in the specified file.

Hint: You can save a lot of typing when you move between files in a stack by pressing NAME/F3 twice after you press GOTO/F5. When you do, a list of all of the current named ranges (see the Range Name command in Chapter 3) and the names of active files appear on the screen. You can use the arrow keys to highlight the desired filename and select it by pressing ENTER.

Table 1–5	Cursor movement keys for moving to first and last and next and previous active files.	
	Movement/Keystroke	**Worksheet Cursor Moves**
	CTRL-END HOME	To cell you last highlighted in first active file
	CTRL-END END	To cell you last highlighted in last active file
	CTRL-END CTRL-PGUP	To cell you last highlighted in next active file
	CTRL-END CTRL-PGUP	To cell you last highlighted in previous active file

MASTERING THE BASICS 19

You receive an error message if you try to move to a file that isn't currently in memory. Press **HELP/F1** for an explanation of the error or press **ENTER** to edit your response and try again. Alternatively, you can press **ESC** the required number of times to cancel the Go To command and return to the Ready mode.

Perspective View

Using adjacent sheets and moving to them is made easier when you can see several sheets on the screen at one time. To do this, use the Worksheet Window Perspective command (discussed fully in Chapter 2), to display a few rows from each of three adjacent spreadsheets on the screen at one time. See Figure 1-7 for an example of a screen in Perspective view.

Scrolling the Screen

If you haven't already done so, try moving the cursor beyond the rightmost column or below the bottommost row. These movements cause new columns or rows to appear. The technique is called *scrolling the screen*. It is how you move the window represented by your screen so that you can view any one of 1-2-3's more than 2 million cells.

Figure 1-7   Stack displayed in Perspective view.

```
A:A6:                                                                    READY

           C |   A        B        C        D        E         F       G       H       |
           6 | 2004     2005     2006     2007     2008      2009            TOTALS
           7 |
           8 | $61,545  $69,899  $79,089  $89,198  $100,318  $112,550        $126,005
           9 | $2,000   $2,000   $2,000   $2,000   $2,000    $2,000          $40,000
          10 | $6,354   $7,190   $8,109   $9,120   $10,232   $11,455         $86,005
          11 |
         B |   A        B        C        D        E         F        G         H       |
         6 | 1996     1997     1998     1999     2000      2001     2002      2003
         7 |
         8 | $16,974  $20,872  $25,159  $29,875  $35,062   $40,769  $47,045   $53,950
         9 | $2,000   $2,000   $2,000   $2,000   $2,000    $2,000   $2,000    $2,000
        10 | $1,897   $2,287   $2,716   $3,187   $3,706    $4,277   $4,905    $5,595
        11 |
       A |   A               B        C        D       E        F        G        H       |
       6 |                            1990     1991    1992     1993     1994     1995
       7 |
       8 | Balance Forward            $0       $2,200  $4,620   $7,282   $10,210  $13,431
       9 | Deposits                   $2,000   $2,000  $2,000   $2,000   $2,000   $2,000
      10 | Interest                   $200     $420    $662     $928     $1,221   $1,543
      11 |
FIG_2-20.WK3
```

When you scroll the screen in Perspective view, all three windows scroll together. They are said to be "synchronized." If you wish to scroll only one window, leaving the display of the other two unchanged, unsynchronize the windows with the Worksheet Window Unsync command discussed in Chapter 2.

Function Keys

You have already been introduced to the GOTO/F5, HELP/F1, and NAME/F3 function keys. 1-2-3 uses many other function keys to perform specific actions. Function keys are located either across the top of your keyboard or in a double row down the left side. Their designations—F1, F2, and so on—are printed on them. On enhanced keyboards, which contain 12 function keys, 1-2-3 only uses the first 10 function keys. Table 1–6 contains a list of 1-2-3's function keys and their actions.

The most frequently used function keys are GOTO/F5, EDIT/F2, and HELP/F1. They move the cursor to a particular cell, edit what is on the entry line or the contents of the cell under the worksheet cursor, and enter the help facility. The Go To command was discussed in detail earlier. The Edit and the Help commands are discussed later in the chapter.

Types of Entries: Values and Labels

The first guideline for constructing a 1-2-3 worksheet is that you make either a *value entry* or a *label entry*. This is just a fancy way of saying that each entry is a word (a label) or a number or formula (a value).

Label entries are used to label rows or columns or to write messages on your worksheets. Value entries are used for the numbers that make up the body of your tables.

Making Entries

To make an entry on your worksheet, use any cursor movement key to position the worksheet cursor on the cell in which the entry is to appear. When the cursor is on the right cell, type whatever you like. Try typing your name.

As you type, several actions happen. The most obvious is that the letters of your name appear in the control panel as you type them. Also, the flashing underline character in the worksheet cursor jumps to the control panel, where it becomes the *entry line cursor*. In the control panel it indicates where the next character you type appears.

Table 1-6   Function keys and their actions.

Function Key	Action
HELP/F1	Displays Help screens
EDIT/F2	Enters Edit Mode
NAME/F3	Displays range names, file names, graph names, @ functions, and macro keywords
ABS/F4	Designates cell reference as absolute (nonadjusting)
GOTO/F5	Moves cursor to designated cell, sheet, active file, or range name
WINDOW/F6	Moves cursor between active windows
QUERY/F7	Repeats the last defined Data Query operation
TABLE/F8	Repeats the last defined Data Table operation
CALC/F9	Forces a recalculation of the worksheet
GRAPH/F10	Displays the current graph or creates an automatic graph from information near the worksheet cursor
ALT-F1	Composes special characters
ALT-F2	Manages keystroke recorder and turns on Step mode for macros
ALT-F3	Macros run key
ALT-F4	Undoes last action. Undo must be enabled to function
ALT-F5	Unassigned
ALT-F6	Expands sheet to full screen from perspective view
ALT-F7	Runs Application 1
ALT-F8	Runs Application 2
ALT-F9	Runs Application 3
ALT-F10	Displays menu for using Release 3 add-ins

The Mode indicator also changes. Instead of displaying **READY**, it now shows **LABEL**, because the first character you typed was a letter of the alphabet. Most of the characters on the keyboard are label characters, but when you began by entering a number (0–9) or one of the special value characters, +, –, @, $, #, (, or a decimal point, 1-2-3 shifts the Mode indicator to **VALUE** to indicate that you are entering a value.

When you are sure your entry is correct, press the **ENTER** key to transfer your entry into the cell underneath the worksheet cursor. Try moving the cursor to different cells. Type words or numbers and press **ENTER** to transfer what you've typed from the control panel into the active cell.

With Release 3 you can make many value entries by typing what earlier versions of 1-2-3 would either accept as a label or reject altogether. For example, try typing **1-Jan**; 1-2-3 accepts it and converts it to the date number for the first of January of the current year. Other examples are 24-April-90 or 4/24/90 for April 4, 1990, and 10:00 AM for 10 o'clock in the morning. Each of these value entries is automatically converted to the appropriate date or time. You can also enter percents as percentages (such as 10%), and 1-2-3 accepts and converts them to their decimal equivalents. Finally, you can enter dollar amounts such as $1000 or $1,000; 1-2-3 recognizes it as a value and enters 1000. While all these entries are accepted as values and displayed in General format, you can set the Global format to Automatic so 1-2-3 can automatically assign the correct format to the cell as it accepts the number. (See Chapter 2 for a discussion of the Automatic format.)

Value entries can also be annotated. To add a note to an entry, type the value and follow it with a semicolon (;) and the note. Annotated values appear on the screen and are used in formulas and functions just like any other value. To read the note, place the cursor on the cell and read it on the Status line.

Label Alignment Characters

1-2-3 distinguishes label entries from value entries by placing a label alignment character before each label. The following three label alignment characters can be used:

'	Left align (the default label alignment character).
"	Right align.
^	Center align.

These characters are special label characters;

MASTERING THE BASICS 23

	Text following the symbol doesn't print. Used to send instructions to printers.
\	Repeating text. Fills cell with characters following backslash.

1-2-3 automatically supplies the default label alignment character when you begin typing a label. The aligning function only operates when the entry is displayed entirely in a single cell. When the entry is longer than the width of the current cell, the entry is displayed as if it were left aligned. You can begin a particular entry with any of the alignment characters to assign that alignment to the entry.

You must supply a label alignment character when typing literal numbers such as telephone numbers that you want 1-2-3 to display exactly as typed. For example, typing and entering 555-1980 results in -1425 appearing on the screen, because 1-2-3 treats the dash as the subtraction operator! To display 555-1980, begin by typing a single quote or any of the other label alignment characters. This method of forcing 1-2-3 to accept a number but display it as a label is called *forced text entry*.

Getting Out of Trouble

The most important action to learn before you start to construct your first spreadsheet is how to get out of trouble. There are several techniques for correcting mistakes. The one you use depends on whether you have pressed the **ENTER** key. When you haven't, the mistake is still on the Entry line. When you have, the mistake has been entered into a cell.

Correcting Mistakes Before You Press ENTER

When you notice a mistake in an entry before you have pressed the ENTER key, correct it in one of the following three ways.

ESC	Cancels the entry. Enables you to start over.
BKSP	Removes characters to the left of the Entry line cursor. Erases mistakes character by character.
EDIT/F2	Press the F2 function key to enter Edit mode. The RIGHT and LEFT arrow keys move the cursor. The BKSP and DEL keys delete characters. Press **ENTER** to end editing and enter edited contents into cell under the worksheet cursor.

The BKSP key is the natural way to correct typing errors immediately after you make them. If you use the EDIT/F2 key when correcting the mistake, you have to backspace over (erase) a number of correct characters.

Correcting Mistakes After You Press ENTER

When you notice that the mistake has already been entered into a cell, use the following techniques to correct it. Position the cursor on the cell containing the mistake and use one of these techniques.

Type Over	Type a correct entry and press **ENTER** to have the correct entry replace the error.
EDIT/F2	Use the Edit command to edit the entry.
Erase the cell	Use the Range Erase command to erase the cell under the worksheet cursor.

The EDIT/F2 key is the all-purpose mistake-correction method. It works when the mistake is on the Entry line as well as when it is in a cell.

Using the Range Erase command to erase a cell is covered later in this chapter under the discussion of 1-2-3 menus.

Getting Help

You can ask 1-2-3 to describe the current command or situation at any time by pressing the **HELP/F1** key. When you press HELP/F1, the screen blanks and text appears to explain the command or procedure you are using—a system called "context-sensitive help."

Help sometimes extends over several related screens and topics. You can select other topics by using the arrow keys to highlight a key word on the screen. You can also use the **HOME** and **END** keys to move to the first and last topic on the screen. When you have highlighted a topic, press **ENTER**; a new help screen appears. You can also press the **BKSP** key to view the previous help screen and **HELP/F1** to display the first topic displayed when you entered help.

When you are ready to return to your spreadsheet, press the **ESC** key. This returns you to the exact point at which you asked for help.

Type something and try using the **ESC** key to cancel your typing. Now try the **EDIT/F2** key to edit it. Press **HELP/F1** to view the help screens. When you are finished, press **ESC** enough times to return the Mode indicator to **Ready**.

SLASH COMMANDS

So far, everything you have done with 1-2-3 has involved pressing specific keys on the keyboard. To move the cursor to the right, you press the **RIGHT** arrow key. To enter the word *budget,* you press the appropriate letter keys and press the **ENTER** key. Even to perform relatively complicated tasks such as moving the cursor to a distant cell or getting help, you press only one key, either **GOTO/F5** or **HELP/F1**. 1-2-3 can do much more powerful tasks, but to unlock the power of 1-2-3 you must give it *commands* by calling up a command menu and specifying the action.

The commands that place the electronic power of 1-2-3 at your fingertips go by the general name of *Slash commands* because you must press the / key to announce to 1-2-3 that you want to use them. When you type a slash, the Mode indicator in the upper right-hand corner of the screen changes to **Menu** and the Slash commands are displayed in the control panel. Figure 1–8 shows how the control panel looks when you press the slash key.

The *command tree* in Figure 1–9 provides an overview of 1-2-3's Slash commands. A command tree gives you a quick look at a command. It begins with the slash key and the command you select. Lower branches show your options as you work deeper into the command. The command tree in Figure 1–9 shows in general terms what actions are available when

| **Figure 1–8** | Screen after pressing slash key to bring up main command menu. |

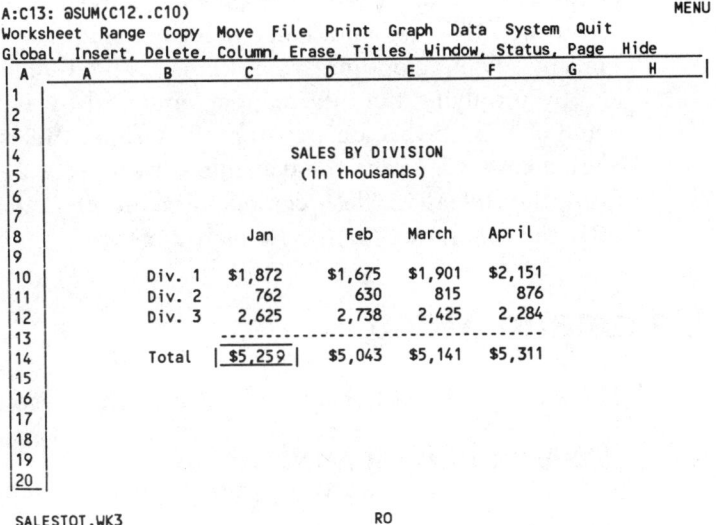

Figure 1-9   Command tree for slash commands.

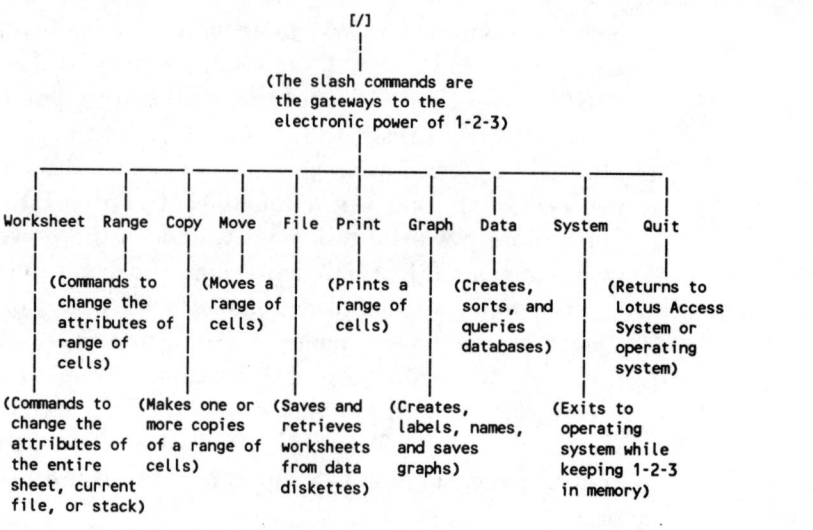

you select each of the Slash commands. In fact, several additional choices must be made to complete each command. Specific options are shown on the detailed command trees that accompany the discussion of each command in later chapters.

The choices on the Slash command menu—Worksheet, Range, Graph, Print, and so on—represent the different tasks you can do with a 1-2-3 worksheet. To graph the numbers on a worksheet, type / and select the Graph command. To save a copy of a worksheet on a disk, type / and select the File command. Once in a command, you complete the instructions by selecting options from submenus (and sometimes sub-submenus) and by supplying the information requested by 1-2-3. Each 1-2-3 command is built in this logical, stepwise fashion. Release 3 adds many new Slash commands to the set available with Release 2. And with few exceptions, the Release 3 Slash command menu offers the same choices in exactly the same order as the Release 2 menu.

Using a Command Menu

There are slow and fast ways to select each choice on a 1-2-3 menu.

Point-and-Shoot Method

The slow way is to use the **RIGHT** and **LEFT** arrow keys to highlight your desired choice and then press **ENTER** to select it. The **SPACE BAR**

MASTERING THE BASICS

can also be used. It is the equivalent of the RIGHT arrow key. The "point-and-shoot" method slows the process down and enables you to read the prompt line before making a selection with the ENTER key.

The following example uses the point-and-shoot method to erase the cell under the worksheet cursor. The keys you press and the prompts 1-2-3 displays are on the left. The actions performed by pressing a key or the meanings of the prompts are on the right.

Position the cursor on the cell you want to erase and type

/	Brings up the Slash command menu.
RIGHT	Moves the highlight to Range.
ENTER	Selects Range. Range submenu choices appear on Menu line.
RIGHT	Moves highlight right; press until highlight moves to Erase.
ENTER	Selects Erase.
Enter range to erase:	Asks for range to erase.
ENTER	Erases cell under worksheet cursor and returns to Ready mode.

Use the point-and-shoot method to learn 1-2-3 or to use an unfamiliar command or menu.

Speed Typing Method

The fast, or "speed typing," method is to type the first letter of the command you want to use. Typing r for example, selects the Range command from the Slash command menu.

Here is an example of using the Range Erase command by the speed typing method.

Again, begin by positioning the cursor on the cell to be erased. Then type

/	Brings up the Slash command menu.
R	Selects Range. Range submenu choices appear on Menu line.
E	Selects Erase.
Enter range to erase:	Asks for range to erase.

ENTER	Erases cell under worksheet cursor and returns to Ready mode.

As your familiarity with 1-2-3 increases, you speed type more and more of your choices, because this method is much faster than the point-and-shoot method. With the speed typing method, erasing a single cell is a simple matter of typing /re and pressing **ENTER**. To encourage you to become a speed typist and to save space, the rest of the examples are given in speed typing form.

Saving Worksheets

One of the most important Slash commands is the File Save command. This command is used to save your worksheets into files on a disk. Once saved, the worksheets can be retrieved with the File Retrieve command for use during later work sessions.

To save the current file, type

/	Brings up the Slash command menu.
F	Selects File.
S	Selects Save.
Enter save file name:	Enters a filename or accepts the default filename of the form **FILEnnnn.WK3**.
ENTER	Executes the command and saves the file.

Chapter 5 contains a complete discussion of all of 1-2-3's commands for saving and retrieving files. Consult that chapter for more details.

Correcting Mistakes with ESC

In many ways Lotus 1-2-3 is like life. When you are in trouble, you want to escape; in 1-2-3 the way out of trouble is often by pressing the **ESC** key. Pressing it clears the entry line and returns 1-2-3 to the Ready mode. Sometimes you have to press it several times, but pressing **ESC** enough times always gets you back to Ready.

To undo a mistake in selecting a command, press the **ESC** key to back up one step in the command tree. This only works if you haven't issued the last keystroke in a command sequence that causes the command to execute (usually ENTER). If you have, the command has already executed and **ESC** won't solve your problem.

Correcting Mistakes with Undo

The Undo command restores your worksheet to the appearance it had when last in the Ready mode. Select it *immediately* after you make a mistake. If you perform additional actions, Undo may not undo what you want it to undo.

To use the Undo command, you must first turn it on, because 1-2-3's default is to have Undo turned off. To turn it on, bring up the Slash command menu by typing a /. Then make the following menu selections: Worksheet Global Default Other Undo (or speed type **WGDOU**). You are then asked whether to Enable or Disable Undo. Select Enable.

When Undo is enabled, press **ALT-F4** and you are given the option of undoing your last modification to the current spreadsheet.

Cautions: You can't undo the Undo command! If you undo something you didn't mean to undo, you must redo it. The greater the action you need to undo, the more random access memory the Undo command uses. This leaves less memory for spreadsheet construction. If you run out of memory in the middle of a command, 1-2-3 suspends the command's operation and gives you the option of temporarily suspending Undo to complete the command, turning off Undo completely, or canceling the command and returning to the Ready mode. Make a selection to proceed.

If your computer doesn't have much memory, you can disable the Undo command by reentering the command and selecting Disable.

Group Mode

When you work with Worksheet or Range commands, it makes a great deal of difference whether you enable Group mode with the Worksheet Global Group command. When you do, the status indicator **GROUP** appears at the bottom of the screen. In Group mode *all sheets* in the *current file* are treated as one for many actions.

For example, if you are in Group mode and you format a cell, the corresponding cells on *all* of the sheets in the current file are assigned the same format. If you insert a column in one sheet, the same column is inserted in *all* of the sheets in the current file. Also, as soon as you enable Group mode the Global format settings and column widths from the current sheet are *automatically* imposed on all of the sheets in the current file. This action can wreck an already constructed file if you use different settings for each sheet.

Using the Group command speeds worksheet construction when all of the sheets in a file are to have the same structure. For example, it is useful when you prepare identical supporting worksheets for a report by departments. However, do not use the command on a file in which the worksheets are not identical. In that situation, it is very easy to destroy data or formulas by performing group actions on unobserved sheets in the current file.

If you are very careful, you can first enable Group to create the identical parts of a set of sheets, then disable Group to customize each sheet. However, *do not* enable Group after you customize the sheets, because it automatically imposes the Range formats from the current sheet on all other sheets in the stack.

Ending a Work Session

To end a work session and leave Lotus 1-2-3, type

/	Brings up the Slash command menu.
Q	Selects Quit.
N or Y	Offers an "escape hatch"; type Y for Yes to quit and return to your computer's operating system.

You must confirm your intention to leave because 1-2-3 doesn't automatically save your worksheet. If you quit without saving, a new worksheet—or the updating you did to an existing one during this work session—is lost forever. In fact, when you select Yes and there is a file in the stack that hasn't been saved, 1-2-3 displays a message about unsaved files and makes you reconfirm your intention to leave.

HOW TO READ THIS BOOK

This chapter has introduced you to the basics of 1-2-3 Release 3. You know about sheets, files, and stacks and how to navigate them. You know how to make value and label entries to construct worksheets, and you know about the electronic power of the Slash commands. You have learned how to correct mistakes, erase cells, and save worksheets. You know the parts of the 1-2-3 screen and the use of the function keys.

You know the basics, but 1-2-3 is far more than the basics. To really get the most out of the program you must master the rest of the material in this book. You can approach that task in two ways: the straight-through approach or the skipping-around approach.

Straight Through

Some people like to learn new techniques from start to finish. If that's you, begin with the next chapter and read to the end. Each chapter discusses a set of related commands, provides keystroke-by-keystroke instructions, and gives numerous examples. Whenever it is appropriate, you are given tips for using a command and warnings about possible problems. The conclusions of most chapters feature Hands On sections that review commands by applying them to a practical worksheet problem. Each chapter concludes with a list of Tips & Traps that apply to the commands discussed in the chapter. Read them carefully for ways to use the tricks and escape from the traps.

Skipping Around

Some people learn best by plunging in and learning what is required to perform the task at hand. If you are that type of person, make use of the index and table of contents to find the particular topics you need to learn at the moment. You should pay particular attention to Chapters 2 and 3 on the Worksheet and Range commands, Chapter 5 on the File command, and Chapter 6 on the Print command. Also, read through the Tips & Traps at the end of each chapter for hints and warnings about the commands.

Two BIG Tips

Whether you are a Straight Through person or a Skip Around person, here are two important tips that will help you get the most out of this book and out of your work with Lotus 1-2-3 Release 3.

The first tip is that you are going to learn to use 1-2-3 by using it, not by reading about it. This book will be indispensable to quickly increasing your skill and understanding, but for your time to be effectively spent there is just no substitute for actually working though the examples, pressing the keys, and watching what happens on the screen. So, whenever possible, read and work on your computer at the same time. If you read about something, don't assume you know it until you have run through the steps on the keyboard a few times.

The second tip is to reread this book after you have been working with 1-2-3 for a few months. When you first learn the program it is difficult to separate the important and useful commands and features from the less important ones. However, after you have worked with the program for a while it is easier to recognize the true gems and to put everything else in perspective.

2 Worksheet Commands

OBJECTIVES

After mastering the content of this chapter, you will be able to

☐ become acquainted with 1-2-3's Worksheet commands.

☐ know when to use Group mode to construct identical worksheets and when to avoid using Group when it will cause harm.

☐ distinguish among single worksheets, sheets in a stack, stacks, and active files.

INTRODUCTION

The commands that place the electronic power of 1-2-3 at your fingertips go by the general name of *Slash commands,* because you must press the / key to announce to 1-2-3 that you want to use them. When you type a slash, the Mode indicator in the upper right hand corner of the screen changes to **Menu** and the Slash commands are displayed in the control panel, the three lines at the top of the screen. See Chapter 1 for a detailed discussion of the 1-2-3 screen.

COMMAND OVERVIEW

The structure of this book mirrors the structure of the Main menu. The first option on the Main menu is Worksheet; the Worksheet commands are discussed in this chapter. The second option is Range; the Range commands are discussed in the next chapter. The other Slash commands are discussed in successive chapters.

Worksheet commands affect the general appearance of your worksheets on the screen and as a printout. (See Figure 2–1 for the Worksheet command tree.) Most of the commands—Column, Titles, Window, Status, and the Global Format command—do not affect the actual contents of any cell. They only change the way the cell is displayed or printed. However, the Insert, Delete, and Erase commands can have a devastating effect on your worksheets. Use them with care.

The Range Commands

It is important to understand the relationship between the Worksheet commands and the second command on the Main menu, the Range command. Both commands have many of the same options—such as Format, Label-Prefix, and Erase—but there is a fundamental difference between a Range command and a Worksheet command.

Range commands only apply to a *range* or group of cells, whereas Worksheet commands apply to *all* of the cells on the current worksheet and, often, to all cells in the current active file. Some Worksheet commands

Figure 2–1 Worksheet command tree.

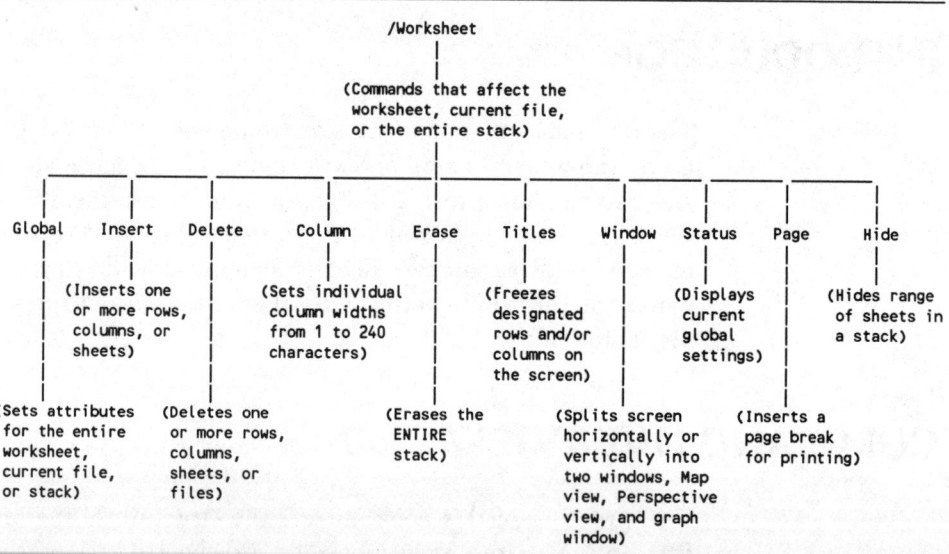

WORKSHEET COMMANDS 35

even apply to all cells in all sheets in the stack. Each time you use the Range command, you must specify the cell or group of cells to which the command applies. Whenever you use the Worksheet command, the action applies to the entire current worksheet, the current file, or the stack, depending on the particular command and whether Group mode is on or off. Group mode is discussed later in this chapter.

Whenever a Range Format or Range Label-Prefix command has been set for a range of cells, that setting overrides any Worksheet settings. Thus, you can set one format at the Worksheet level (Percent, for example) and override it for a particular range of cells with a Range Format command (Currency, for example).

Furthermore, any change you make with the Worksheet command bypasses any cells that have been individually formatted. The exception to this rule is the Worksheet Erase command. It erases all of the sheets in a stack and replaces them with a single blank sheet while returning all formats—Range as well as Worksheet—to those originally in effect when 1-2-3 was first loaded in your computer.

If you use the Automatic format (described later), 1-2-3 accepts what you type and assigns the appropriate range format to the cell. If you type $45.34, for example, 1-2-3 formats the cell to Currency, which formats two decimal places (as "cents") so that $45.34 appears on the screen. Because the cell is assigned a *Range* format, any changes you make to the Worksheet Global Format bypass that cell. To change the format of the cell, you must use one of the Range Format commands. Alternatively, use the Range Format Reset command to return the cell to the control of the Global Format command. These commands are discussed in the next chapter.

Default Settings

A *default* is a setting that a program applies if you don't select another setting. (The word is derived from the financial world, where if you don't pay a loan, you are in default.) 1-2-3 has default settings for all Worksheet commands. You can, in fact, construct many electronic worksheets and never change the defaults. But if you did, you'd be missing some of 1-2-3's most powerful and convenient features.

Here are the default settings:

Label:	Left aligned in each cell.
Value:	General. (Numbers displayed in either decimal form or scientific notation, such as 10,000

	displayed as either 10,000 or 1E+04, depending on the column width.)
Recalculation:	Automatic and natural order. (Recalculation occurs after every change. Formulas are calculated before formulas that depend on them are calculated.)
Column width:	9 characters.
Protection:	Off.
Window:	One.
Titles:	Unlocked.
Group:	Disabled.

You can change each of these default settings with the appropriate Worksheet command.

THE WORKSHEET GLOBAL COMMAND

The first Worksheet command is the Global command (see Figure 2–2 to view all its submenu options). Worksheet Global sets cell attributes for both value cells (Format) and label cells (Label-Prefix). It also sets the universal column width, the method and order of recalculation, the pro-

Figure 2–2   Worksheet Global command tree.

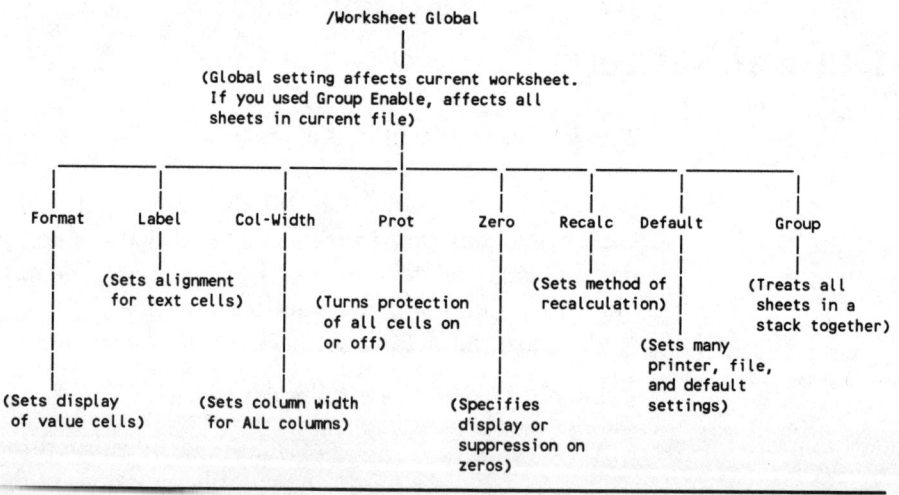

WORKSHEET COMMANDS

tection of all the cells on the worksheet, and certain default printer and directory settings.

To view the defaults in effect for the Global commands or the options that have been selected for those commands, use the Worksheet Status command. To use it, speed type

/W Enters the Worksheet Command.

S Selects Status.

The screen displays the defaults available, as shown in Figure 2–3. Press any key to clear screen and return to Ready mode.

Warning: Global and Group

Whether the Global command affects only the current worksheet or all sheets in the current active file depends on whether you have selected Group mode. You may be very surprised by some of the results, so be careful.

In particular, whenever Group is enabled many of the Global settings from the current sheet (the one containing the cursor when Global is enabled) are *immediately* and automatically imposed on all sheets in the current file. Global settings imposed on all sheets in the current file are Protection, Format, Zero, Label, Col-Width, and Titles. Also, individual column width settings from the current sheet set with the Worksheet Column command are also imposed on all sheets in the current file by Group Enable.

Figure 2–3 Status screen displaying current worksheet default settings, available memory, and math coprocessor status.

```
Available memory: 10800000 of 1501272 Bytes (72%)

Processor: 80286
Math co-processor:   None

Recalculation:
   Method........... Automatic
   Order............ Natural
   Iterations....... 1

Circular reference: (None)

Cell display:
   Format........... (G)
   Label prefix..... '
   Column width..... 9
   Zero setting..... No

Global Protection: Off
```

Furthermore, global settings from the current sheet continue to be applied after Group is disabled. Because of this, be very careful when you enable Group on an already constructed worksheet if you have set different formats, default label alignment, protection status, or global column widths on different sheets.

Warning: Range and Group

The Group command can also produce devastating changes to worksheets whose cells have been formatted with the Range Format command. Enabling Group automatically imposes the Range formats from the current file on the corresponding ranges on all of the sheets in the current file. Furthermore, any unformatted cell on the current sheet causes range formats in corresponding cells on all other sheets to be reset to the current Global Format!

If you are going to enable Group for an already constructed worksheet, be sure to save the worksheet first with the File Save command. If you don't have a saved copy, the actions of the Group command may take years off of your life.

The Global Format Command

Except for Text and Hidden, the Global Format command affects only the display of value entries (see Figure 2-4). It doesn't affect the display of label entries, and, most importantly, it doesn't change the number, formula, or function entered in a cell. For Text and Hidden, both Label and Value cells are affected by the formats. Label cells are displayed left aligned under Text and not displayed on the screen under Hidden.

Table 2-1 shows how the number 33,110.4278 is displayed under different Global Format options. In addition to supplying special characters such as the dollar sign or the percent sign, most format commands enable you to choose the number of decimal places to be displayed (0 to 15).

The table assumes the column is wide enough to display the number under the designated format with two decimal places. To prevent numbers from running together across the screen, 1-2-3 reserves the last character in a value cell as a margin. Thus, value entries under each format setting must be one character narrower than the cell in which they are displayed.

Disappearing Numbers/Appearing Asterisks

The current combination of format and column width may not be sufficient to display a particular number, because setting a format typically adds

WORSHEET COMMANDS

Figure 2-4   Worksheet Global Format command tree.

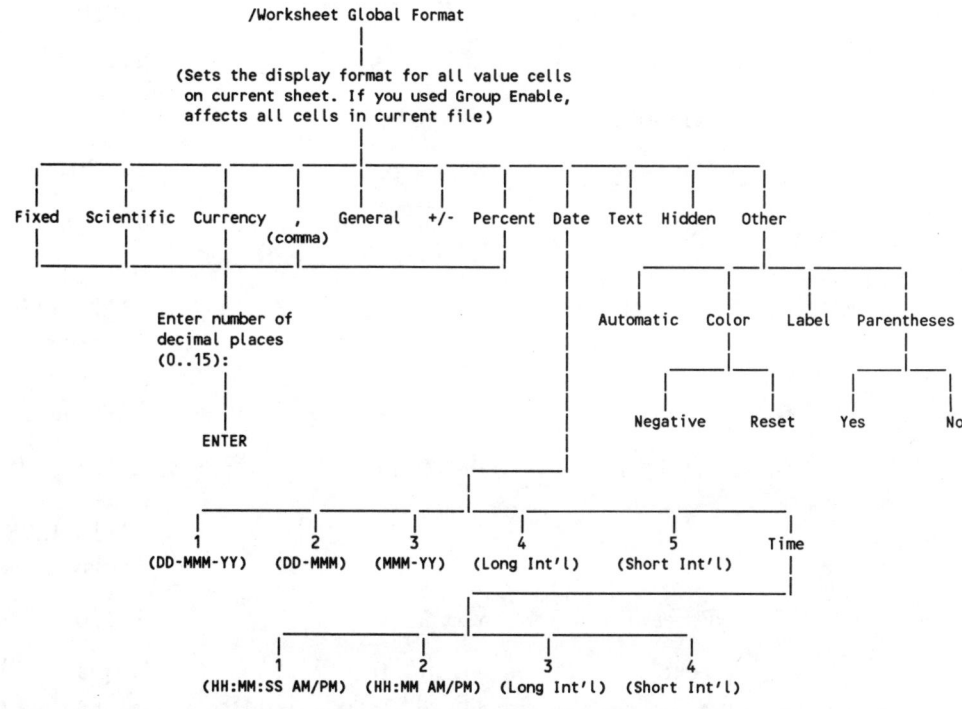

characters to an entry. The Currency format, for example, adds one character for the dollar sign, one for each comma used, one for the decimal point, and trailing zeros for each decimal place designated. When the additional characters cause the value to be too long to display in the current column width, the cell fills with asterisks (********).

For example, 2500 contains only four characters and displays easily in the default column width of nine characters. But under the Currency, two-decimal-place format, it displays as $2,500.00, which contains nine characters, enough to make the stars come out under the default column width.

The asterisks indicate that the cell contains a value that can't be displayed under the current combination of format and column width. However, the number is still in memory and is still used in all calculations.

To remove the asterisks and display the number, use either the Worksheet Column command or the Worksheet Global Col-Width command to expand the column width until the value can be displayed under the designated format. Both commands are discussed later in this chapter.

Table 2–1 The number 33110.4278 displayed under different Global Format commands.

Format Option	Form	33110.4278
Fixed	+x.xx	33110.78
Scientific	+x.xxE+xx	3.31E+04
Currency	$x,xxx.xx	$33,110.43
, (comma)	Commas and negative numbers in parentheses	33,110.43
General	x.xx or x.xxE+xx	33110.4278 (Very large or very small numbers are displayed in Scientific format)
+/−	Bar graph	++++++++++ (+ or − equal to integer value. 33110.4278 would display as asterisks)
Percent	x.xx%	3311042.78%
Text	+G26/34 +F_NAME&L_NAME 33110.4278	Displays cell contents rather than their computed values. Numbers in General format
Hidden	x.xx	No display
Date	33110.4278 (Date Number)	(D1) 25-Aug-90 (D2) 25-Aug (D3) Aug-90 (D4) 8/25/90 (D5) 08/25
Date Time	33110.4278 (Time Number)	(D6) 10:16:02 AM (D7) 10:16 AM (D8) 10:16:02 (D9) 10:16

Rounding Errors

As noted, most Global Format commands give you the option of choosing from 0 to 15 decimal places in each display. The default number of decimal places is two. 1-2-3 rounds 1342.9871 to 1342.99 in Fixed display with two decimal places, and to 1342.987 with three decimal places. No matter what is displayed, the actual number remains in your computer's memory and is used in all calculations.

The fact that the actual number is used in calculations rather than its rounded form can lead to what are called *rounding errors.* For example, if you are adding the contents of three cells that display $0.37, $0.00, and $0.00, the result could equal $0.38 if the numbers in the cells were actually $0.369, $0.004, and $0.004.

If you need to avoid rounding errors, use the @ROUND function discussed in Chapter 7 to actually round the numbers in the cells and not just their display.

Percent

The Percent command multiplies the number by 100, adds the percent sign, and rounds the number displayed to the desired number of places. For example, 0.075 becomes 7.50% under the Percent format, which displays with two decimal places.

+/−

The +/− command displays a row of pluses or minuses equal to the integer value of the number. If the integer part is larger than the current column width, a row of asterisks is displayed. Under the +/− format a period (.) is displayed in any cell containing a zero.

This command can be used to create a simple horizontal bar chart in which each positive integer value is represented by + and each negative integer value is shown with −.

Date Format

The Date format converts the number in a cell to a readable date or time display. A number like 34567 or 0.3456, is usually generated with the @DATE or @NOW functions or from entering a date such as 1-Jan-90 or a time such as 10:45 PM. 1-2-3 has a number of domestic and international time and date formats from which to choose.

You are, however, much more likely to use the Range Format Date command than the Global Format Date command, because the Global command converts all of the values on the current worksheet to date display.

Text Format

The Text format causes the formulas behind each value to be displayed. Use it whenever you want to find out what is really going on behind the scenes. Formulas are usually much longer than the number they generate so you may also have to expand the column widths to see all of each formula.

The Text format is useful to obtain a clear picture of the formulas and functions behind a spreadsheet. You can even print the worksheet this way for a record of its structure. If you split the screen into two windows (see the Worksheet Window command, described later in the chapter), one window can display formulas while the other displays results. When you use the Text format, numbers are displayed in the General format and text is displayed left aligned.

To return to the conventional display, reenter the Global Format command and select another format, such as Fixed or General.

Hidden Format

When you select the Hidden format, 1-2-3 suppresses the display of cell contents, and the worksheet appears empty. You can still see what is in a cell by moving the cursor to it and looking at the Status line. And you can also erase a cell or change it by making a new entry, so be careful. To redisplay the cells, reenter the Global Format command and select another format.

Two other commands are more useful than the Global Format Hidden command. With the Range Format Hidden command, you specify a range of cells to hide. Only those cells you designate appear blank. The other command, Worksheet Hide, hides individual worksheets in a stack. This is a good command for suppressing the display of sheets containing assumptions, data, macros, or other information that you don't currently need to see on the screen.

Global Format Other Commands

Release 3 added several format commands to the Global Format command list available with previous versions of the program. The new formats are found under Worksheet Global Format Other and are

Automatic	Entries that look like numbers formatted as Currency, Fixed, Percent, Scientific, the first four Data formats, or any Time format are accepted and assigned the appropriate format.
Color	Displays negative numbers in a different color, usually red. Uses brighter intensity for negative numbers on a monochrome monitor.

Label   Accepts and stores all entries as labels.

Parentheses   Encloses all numeric values in parentheses.

Of these new formats, the one that is likely to provide the greatest boon to spreadsheet builders is the Automatic format. By selecting the Automatic format, you can have 1-2-3 assign the correct display format to your entries. The action is the same as using the appropriate Range Format command described in the next chapter.

When Automatic Format is set, for example, entering 35.3% is accepted as if you entered a value as .0353, and assigned the Percent Format, with one decimal place.

The Automatic format can be a great timesaver when you create worksheets that consist of a mixture of fixed numbers, currency, percentages, dates, and times. If you need one of the other formats (Scientific or Comma, for example), reformat the desired cells with the Range Format command discussed in Chapter 3.

Once you make an entry in a cell, subsequent entries in that cell inherit the format initially given to the cell by the Automatic format. To change the format, use the Range Format command. If the Automatic format is still active globally, you can use the Range Erase command to erase the cell and the Range Format Reset command to return the cell's format to the control of the Global Automatic format.

The Global Label Command

Just as the Format command controls the display of value cells, the Label command controls the display of label cells. See Figure 2–5 for the command tree.

To understand how the Label command works, you need to understand how 1-2-3 treats label entries. When you type an entry beginning with any character except the digits 0–9, +, –, ., , (, @, $, or #, 1-2-3 interprets the entry as a label and automatically places a label alignment character in front of it.

The label alignment characters are

Single quote (')   Left Alignment (Default)

Double Quote (")   Right Alignment

Caret (^)   Center Alignment

The backslash, \, and the vertical line character, |, are special label characters. The backslash is the repeating text character. It fills the cell

Figure 2–5 Worksheet Global Label-Prefix command tree.

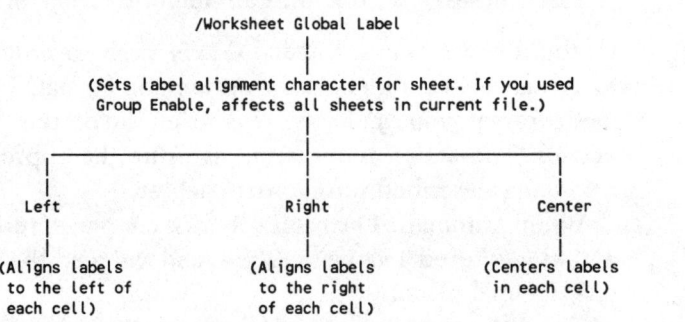

with whatever character appears after the backslash. For example, \- fills the cell with hyphens. The vertical line character is a special nonprinting character. Characters appearing after it are sent to the printer as control codes or ESC instructions (form feed, change font, and so on). The characters you choose to send depend on the characters your printer recognizes as instructions. See Chapter 6 and consult your printer's manual for a list of acceptable instructions.

The label alignment characters and the special label characters appear as part of the entry when you inspect the Status line in the control panel, but they don't appear on the screen or on a printout. (Thus, if you want **word** to appear enclosed in quotation marks you must type ""word" or '"word".)

Right-aligned labels reserve the rightmost character in the cell as a margin. Labels that are as wide or wider than the cell are displayed as if they were left aligned, regardless of the actual label alignment character.

Using the Global Label command, you choose which of the three label alignment characters to automatically assign to labels as they are entered. The default character is the single quote, so left is the default label alignment. When you want to begin a cell entry with one of the special label characters, you must type it.

Changing the Label of Existing Labels

It is very important to understand that the Global Label command *does not* change the alignment of text already entered in the worksheet. Previously entered text continues to have the label alignment character it was given during data entry. Changing the Global Label only affects text entered *after* the change. It has no effect on labels already in a worksheet.

There are three ways to change the label alignment character of a label already entered into a worksheet.

1. Use the Range Label command to change the label prefix for a single cell or a range of cells.

2. Retype an entry, assuming the current Global Label is the one you want.

3. Use the **EDIT/F2** function key to edit the entry by inserting the desired character.

Forced Text Entry

Forced text entry is when you force 1-2-3 to accept a label alignment character other than the default label alignment character. You do this by beginning your entry with the desired character (single quote, double quote, or circumflex.) By typing the label alignment character, you can designate the alignment of labels as you enter them. You can also get 1-2-3 to accept and display as a label something it normally treats as a value, such as a telephone number or a zip code. For example, entering the telephone number 555-8709 without a label alignment character causes 1-2-3 to treat it as a subtraction problem: 555 minus 8709. The result, −8154, appears on the screen instead of the phone number.

The Global Col-Width Command

The Global Col-Width command sets the width for all 256 columns on the current worksheet at one time. If Group mode is active, it sets the column width of all columns in all sheets in the current file. The default width is 9 characters, but you can set the column width to any value between 1 and 240. Figure 2–6 summarizes the process.

To change the Global column width, type

/W	Enters the Worksheet command.
G	Selects Global.
C	Selects Col-Width.
Enter global column width (1...240): 9	Asks for the desired column width.
Arrow keys	Sets the width visually, or you can type a number for the width you want.
ENTER	Sets the Global column width to the designated number of characters and returns to Ready mode.

Figure 2-6 Worksheet Global Col-Width command tree.

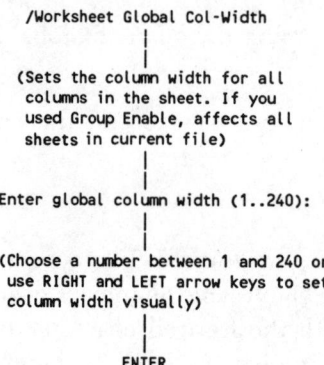

The use of the arrow keys in this command makes it easy to see exactly what effect a given column width has on your worksheet. If, however, you know exactly how wide you want the columns, you can type in the number of characters. It is best to type the number of characters when you are making a large change in the width of a column. If necessary, fine tune the width visually by reentering the command and using the arrow keys.

With narrow columns, you can display more columns on the screen and print more on each sheet of paper. However, if a column is too narrow to display an entry, a row of asterisks appears.

Finally, the Worksheet Global Col-Width command does not change any column widths that have been set with the Worksheet Column command. The Worksheet Column command, discussed later, sets column widths individually.

The Global Recalculation Command

The Worksheet Global Recalc command shown in Figure 2-7 controls the method of recalculation for all of the sheets in a stack even if the stack is made up of *several active files*. Group mode does not affect this command.

The default method of recalculation is Automatic. This means that 1-2-3 recalculates all of the formulas in any cells that need to be recalculated whenever you alter a cell in any way that might change its displayed value.

Most actions—entering a value or a label, or using the Copy, Move, or Range Erase commands—cause a recalculation. On large worksheets

Figure 2-7 Worksheet Global Recalc command tree.

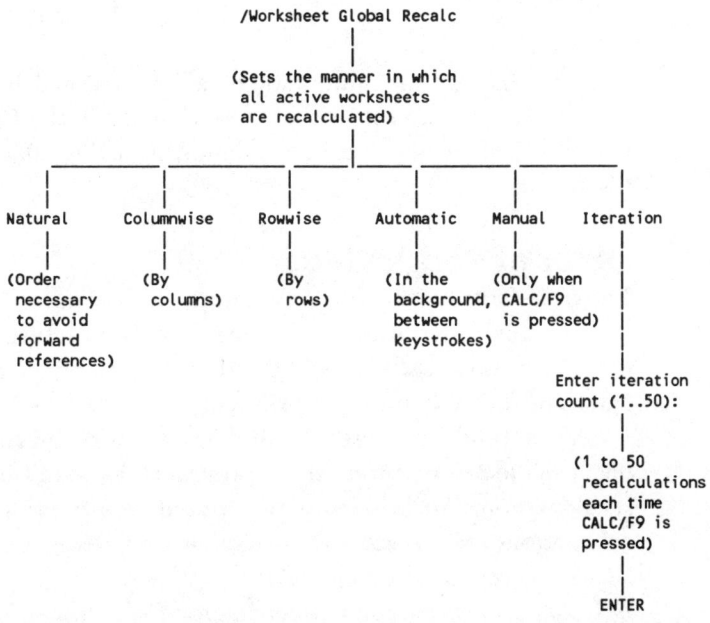

the amount of time required for a recalculation can be significant, but it needn't concern you, because 1-2-3 recalculates the worksheet between keystrokes (in the "background") so that you can continue to work on a spreadsheet as it is being recalculated. While recalculation is taking place, CALC flashes at the bottom of your screen. Unlike in earlier versions of 1-2-3, little is to be gained by turning off automatic recalculation.

Manual Recalculation in Macros

You should turn off automatic recalculation (select Worksheet Global Recalculation Manual) when you run macros because 1-2-3 recalculates the worksheet between the execution of successive macro commands. The result is a considerable increase in macro execution time. When you run macros, use the special macro keywords available to control recalculation of a stack where recalculation has been set to manual. (See Chapter 12.)

CALC and CALC/F9

Whenever recalculation is set to manual and you've made changes that normally require recalculation, 1-2-3 displays the highlighted word **CALC** at the bottom line of the screen. This reminds you a change has been made in the worksheet and the worksheet must be recalculated. To recalculate the worksheet, press the **CALC/F9** function key. You can wait until the worksheet is completed or the updating finished before pressing the **CALC/F9** key.

Unlike background automatic recalculation, which takes place between keystrokes, manual recalculation takes place in the foreground. You can't use the keyboard while recalculation is taking place; wait until CALC disappears.

Order of Recalculation

Lotus' default method of calculating the formulas in a worksheet is to respect the "natural order" underlying its structure. That is, Lotus first calculates those cells on which other cells depend, regardless of the location of the cells on the worksheet.

This method eliminates the problem of "forward references" that often occur in electronic spreadsheet programs that don't include natural order recalculation. Worksheets with forward references may take several recalculations to arrive at the correct answer, because cells depend on cells that have yet to be recalculated.

Lotus also gives you commands for Columnwise or Rowwise recalculation and Iteration. With rowwise or columnwise recalculation, recalculation begins in cell A1 and proceeds either down successive columns or across successive rows. Iteration helps you determine how many times (1 to 50) the worksheet is recalculated. With these options you control the way specially constructed worksheets are recalculated. Iteration is often used with worksheets containing *circular references* (cases where a cell refers to itself either directly or indirectly). Chances are you'll never need the iteration option, but it's good to know it's there.

The Global Protection Command

The Global Prot command activates ("enables") protection for all 2 million cells on the current worksheet when Group mode is off and all of the cells on all the sheets in the current file when it is on. Protection is like stretching a piece of thick plastic over the cells. You can see what is going on, but you can't change anything. Figure 2-8 shows the two options available with Global Prot.

Beware: If there is more than one active file in the stack, the Global Prot command *only* protects the current active file. Other active files remain unprotected unless you make them active by positioning the cursor

Figure 2-8 Worksheet Global Prot command tree.

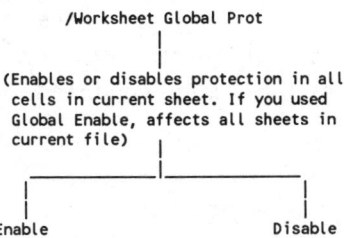

somewhere in the file and then repeat the Worksheet Prot Enable command.

Protection prevents any action (except Worksheet Erase) from changing the contents of the protected cell. Once a cell is protected, you can't erase it with Range Erase or edit it with the EDIT/F2 key. You can't delete a row or column containing a protected cell, nor can you enter new text or values into a protected cell. The protected status of a worksheet is signaled by the letters **PR** on the Status line just after the address of the current, active cell.

Protection provides insurance against the accidental destruction of a worksheet. It is particularly good insurance to have when data is to be entered into your worksheet by someone who is, perhaps, less careful and less knowledgeable than you are. Adding protection is one of the last steps in constructing a worksheet.

If you don't use the Global Protection command, you'll never know it's there because it only affects a worksheet when it is enabled. When it is disabled (the default setting), it's as if global protection doesn't exist.

Changing a Cell on a Protected Worksheet

If you do want to change a cell on a protected worksheet, reenter the command and choose Disable to deactivate protection. Alternatively, you can use the Range Unprotect command to cut "holes" in a protected worksheet. Unprotected cells are often data entry cells. They display in a different color or intensity and **U** appears on the Status line just after the address of the current, active cell. (See Chapter 3 for more information about the Range Unprotect command.)

Super Protection

If you want to prevent any unauthorized use of a spreadsheet, use the File Admin command to seal the file. Enable protection, if necessary designate the data entry cells with the Range Unprotect command, and then seal the file. Sealing requires a password. Once the file is sealed, other users can load the file and make entries into unprotected cells, but they cannot disable protection unless they unseal the file. And to unseal the file they need your—supposedly secret—password. See Chapter 5 for a complete discussion of the File Admin command.

The Global Default Command

The Global Default command is one of those obscure commands that few 1-2-3 users know about. But in many situations, knowing about it can make your life a great deal easier. Figure 2–9 shows the command tree for this command and its many lower-level commands.

Among its various uses, the Global Default command can reset certain default values used by the Print command, specify to which disk drive or directory (on a hard disk) 1-2-3 stores data and temporary files (important if you are using 1-2-3 on a network), and turn on the Undo feature. The screen that appears when you select Global Default Status is shown in Figure 2–10.

Figure 2–9 Worksheet Global Default command tree.

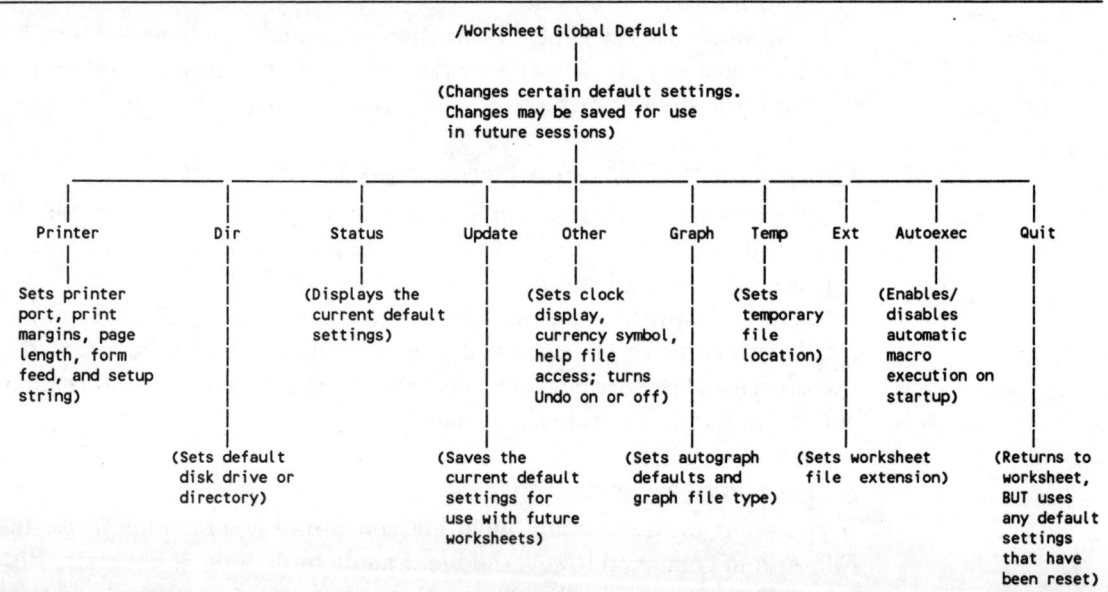

Figure 2-10 Defaults for printer, directory, punctuation, and other settings.

```
Printer:                              International:s
  Interface..... Parallel 1             Punctuation..... A
  Auto-linefeed. No                             Decimal Period
                                               Argument Comma
Margins                                        Thousands Comma
    Left  4      Top    2             Currency........ $ (Prefix)
    Right 76     Bottom 2             Date format D4.. A (MM/DD/YY)
                                      Date format D5.. A (MM/DD)
Page length... 66                     Time format D8.. A (HH:MM:SS)
Wait.......... No                     Time format D9.. A (HH:MM)
Setup string..
Name.......... Epson Series MX-80
                                      Negative........ Parentheses
Automatic graph: Columnwise           Release 2....... LICS
                                      File translate.. Country
File list extension: W*
File save extension: WK3              Clock on screen: Standard
Graph save extension: CGM             Undo: Yes    Beep: Yes
                                      Autoexec: Yes
Default directory: C:\123
Temporary directory: C:\123\TEMP
```

Print Command Defaults

With the Global Default command you can reset the default margins and page length for printed worksheets. The factory-set margins are at 4 characters on the left and 76 on the right. This assumes you print your worksheets on 8½-inch-wide paper in standard type.

If your paper is longer than 11 inches, reset the page length. If your printer requires a line feed at the end of a line (or doesn't) select the correct setting with AutoLF. If you always print on a wide printer (15 inches) or if you frequently print in compressed type to get more information on a single line (132 characters per line on 8½-inch-wide paper, 233 on 15-inch-wide paper), you may have to reset the print margins before you print each worksheet.

Instead of resetting the parameters each time you print, use the Global Default command to reset the print margin defaults and the setup string that signals your printer to print in compressed type.

Global Default Other Commands: International, Clock, Undo, and Beep

The Global Default Other command is a grab bag of options, some of which you'll probably never need; at least one, Undo, can save your sanity.

You use the International choice to change the date and time display to one of the international formats. You can also select the combination of decimal symbols and thousands separators appropriate to your culture. To make these changes, select Other International and then either **Date** or **Time**.

If you are working in Japanese yen, British pounds, or other currency you can change the currency character to represent the currency symbol. Following are sample symbols you can assemble. Select Currency from the Other menu and type

Alt-F1	Enters the compose command you use to compose nonstandard keyboard characters.
For yen, **Y -**	The letter **Y** followed by the dash character.
For pounds, **L -**	The letter **L** followed by the dash character.

Press **ENTER** and designate whether the currency symbol should appear before or after the number.

1-2-3 provides additional choices under International. Negative determines whether under the Comma and Currency formats cells containing negative values are placed in parentheses (default) or preceded by a minus sign (the alternative).

Release-2 sets the way Release 2 (.WK1) files are saved and retrieved.

File-Translation sets whether 1-2-3 uses your country-specific setting (default) or the international character translation table when you import and create text files.

With the Clock option, you designate what is displayed in the File-and-clock indicator. The default is time and date when the current file hasn't been saved to disk, and the filename when it has. Alternatively, you can designate that nothing displays or always display the time and date without the filename.

The Beep option turns the beep that sounds when you make an error off. The default is to have the beep on, but if frequent beeps fray your nerves or cause uncomfortable stares from your co-workers, turn it off.

The Undo option is so important that it is discussed at length next.

Undo

Lotus' Global Default Other Undo command is wonderful, but it can also consume a lot of memory. Consequently, when you first load 1-2-3 Undo is turned off. To turn on the Undo command, type

/WGD	Enters the Worksheet Global Default command.
O	Selects Other.
U	Selects Undo.
Enable Disable	Select Enable to turn Undo on.

WORKSHEET COMMANDS

To use Undo, press **ALT-F4** at any time. When you do, a Yes/No choice appears in the control panel. Select Yes to undo all actions taken since you last were in the Ready mode. Select No to leave the worksheet unchanged.

Limits to Undo

Whereas Undo may save your neck in many situations, there are some serious limitations to the way Undo works. Perhaps the most serious is that Undo does not undo the actions of the Undo command! If you make a mistake and use Undo, you must repeat the action you have undone. As a rule, you can only undo actions that actually change the content of cells; the structure of the worksheet, such as Row Insert or Delete, Move, or Copy; or the display format. Consequently, some common 1-2-3 commands can't be undone. Specifically, the File Erase and File Save commands that affect files on disk or Print Line, Page, and Go commands that initiate printer activity but have no effect on an active worksheet can't be undone. Neither can Data External commands that operate on external databases. Also, Undo won't return the cursor to its original position after you use a cursor movement key or the GOTO/F5 key, because these do not affect spreadsheet cells.

Sometimes Undo may undo more than you expect. Because the command returns the stack to the way it was when you were last in the Ready mode, commands that you use to take actions without returning to the Ready mode may have more than one action undone. Examples are the Graph, Data, and Print commands. Using Undo after the Graph command cancels everything you have specified since you were last in the Ready mode—not just the last action you took in the Graph command. The same is true when you use the Data Find command to edit entries in a database. Undo undoes all changes since you were last in the Ready mode, not only the most recent change.

The general principle here is that Undo restores the stack to its appearance when you were last in the Ready mode. Undo views multiple actions taken without returning to the Ready mode as *one* action and undoes them all.

If you have enabled Undo and the memory needed to perform a particular task causes available memory to fall below about 4K, 1-2-3 suspends the operation and gives you the following three choices:

Proceed	Turns off Undo, completes the command, and turns Undo back on.
Disable	Turns off Undo, completes the command, but does not turn Undo back on.

Quit   Returns to Ready without completing the command, but any partial action completed is kept. Undo remains turned on.

Proceed and Disable only complete the command if there is enough memory available after Undo is disabled.

To find the memory available for spreadsheet construction, check the Worksheet Status screen. If memory is low, turn Undo off.

Dir

When you want to change the default directory 1-2-3 searches whenever you use the File command, select Dir and type in the full path to the directory. When 1-2-3 is first installed, it automatically uses the directory containing the program files as the default directory. This is not a place to store data files, so one of your first tasks is to change directories (usually with the File Dir command discussed in Chapter 5). To set 1-2-3 so it always uses your designated directory as the default directory, specify the directory you want here and then save the changes with the Update option, discussed later in this chapter.

Temp

When you are using 1-2-3 on a network, you can speed up 1-2-3's operation by designating a directory on the machine you are using as the location for the temporary files 1-2-3 creates as it works. To specify a new location for the temporary files, use the Worksheet Global Default Temp command. Enter the command and supply the full path to the directory where you want the temporary files stored.

Autoexec

This command determines whether 1-2-3 automatically executes macros assigned the name \0 (zero) when the file containing the macro is loaded into memory. The default is to execute the macro, but you can turn off that feature with this command. See Chapter 12 for an example of a macro application that makes use of the \0 feature.

Graph

Use this command to set the direction in which 1-2-3 divides automatic graph ranges into data ranges (columnwise is the default, rowwise the alternative); the format 1-2-3 uses when you create files with Graph Save (.CGM is the default, .PIC the alternative); and the extension 1-2-3 searches for when you select File List Graph or File Erase Graph (.CGM is the default, .PIC the alternative).

Group

The concepts of a group of sheets and Group mode have already been introduced in Chapter 1. To turn Group mode on, type

/W	Enters the Worksheet command.
G	Selects Global.
G	Selects Group.
E or D	Asks to Enable or Disable Group mode.
E	Selects Enable.

When Group mode is enabled, the word **GROUP** appears at the bottom of the screen. Now most Worksheet Global commands act on the group of worksheets contained in the current file and not just on the current worksheet. Worksheets in other files in the stack are unaffected by these commands.

When Group is enabled, the Range commands Format, Prot and UnProt, and Label affect corresponding cells on all sheets in the current file. This makes it easy to construct a group of *identical* worksheets. But this same feature makes it dangerous to enable Group mode when the worksheets are not identical. Unless you are sure that you want to treat each and every sheet in the current file in the same way, it is best to disable Group mode and construct each sheet separately.

Zero

When you enable it, the Worksheet Global Zero command causes any cell displaying a zero to appear blank or to display text that you specify. This command is particularly useful on worksheets containing formulas that display zero before data entry. Instead of having to view a screen filled with zeros or to make printouts containing large numbers of zeros, you can select Worksheet Global Zero and only display those cells with non-zero values.

Alternatively, you can display a text message, such as **Data Missing**. But unlike other long labels, this text is truncated at the edge of the cell, so select a message that fits in your column widths.

Note that some zeros occur as the result of a particular display format and not because the cell actually contains a zero. For example, a cell containing 0.04 displays as 0 under the fixed format 0 decimal places. Zeros that result from display formats are *not* suppressed by this command, but continue to display as zeros.

To suppress the display of zeros, type

/WG		Enters the Worksheet Global command.
Z		Selects Zero.
No Yes Label		No redisplays zeros, Yes suppresses zeros, and Label specifies text to be displayed in cells displaying zeros.
Y		Selects Yes to suppress the display of zeros and returns to Ready mode.

To display zeros, reenter the command and select N for No. To specify text, reenter the command and select L for Label. Then type the text you want displayed in cells that would otherwise display zeros.

Saving the New Defaults

Any defaults you change are only in effect for the *current* work session. To make them the default settings to use each time you begin a 1-2-3 session, use the Update command on the Global Default menu to save the new default settings.

THE WORKSHEET INSERT COMMAND

The Worksheet Insert command is one of those electronic worksheet commands that can bring tears of joy to the grouchiest of analysts. With this command, you can insert one or more blank rows or columns into the center of an already constructed worksheet while all existing references and built-in functions automatically adjust to accommodate to the new rows or columns. If a few rows or an additional column or two aren't enough for your needs, you can use the Insert command to insert entirely new sheets into the current file.

Keeping track of everything is one of those tasks computers do so well. The result is that you won't have to redo a table because you left out a line item or because someone suggested more detail to include. No longer do you have to resort to microscopic writing to add another row of numbers. Figure 2–11 gives the command tree for Worksheet Insert.

Inserting Rows and Columns

The location of the worksheet cursor is used to tell 1-2-3 where to insert columns or rows. New rows are inserted above the cursor, and new columns are inserted to the left of the cursor. You can position the cursor

WORKSHEET COMMANDS

Figure 2-11 Worksheet Insert command tree.

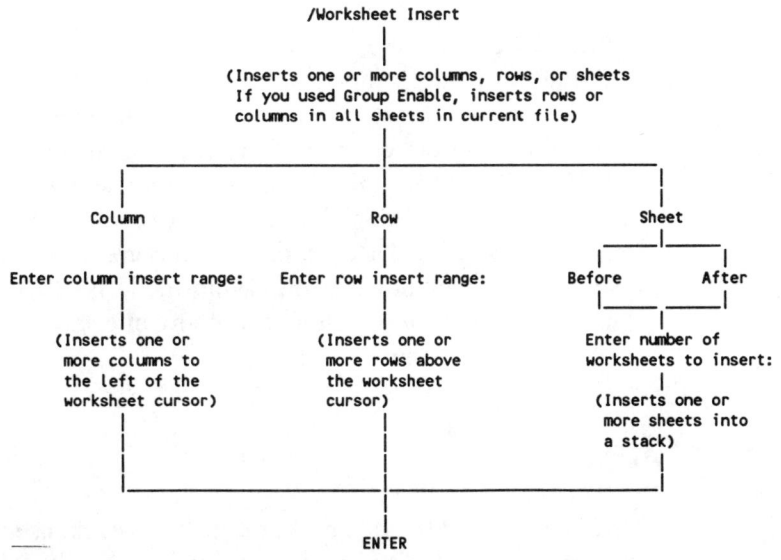

before or after you enter the command. When Group mode is on, the Insert command inserts rows or columns into every worksheet in the current file.

To insert rows or columns position the cursor below the row or to the right of the column you intend to insert and type

/WI	Enters the Worksheet Insert command.
C or R	Selects Column or Row insert.
Enter column (or row) insert range:	Use the arrow keys to expand the cursor to cover two or more rows or columns.
ENTER	Executes the Insert command.

Unsticking the Cursor

If you want the rows or columns inserted somewhere other than the current cursor location, press the **ESC** or **BKSP** keys. These keys "unstick" the worksheet cursor. You can then use the arrow keys to move the cursor around the worksheet.

To insert a single row or column, position the cursor correctly (remember rows are inserted above, columns to the left of the cursor) and press **ENTER**. If you want a range of rows or columns, "stick" the cursor back down by typing a period, ., and use the arrow keys to expand the cursor to the desired size. Press **ENTER**. The rows or columns are inserted, and the worksheet cursor jumps back to its original location.

Inserting Across Sheets

In addition to inserting rows or columns in the current worksheet, you can insert rows or columns across several sheets at the same time. For example, to insert columns F and G into sheets M, N, and O, specify M:F1..O:G1 as the range of columns to insert by either typing the cell addresses or stretching the cursor across the sheets. Because the range extends across three sheets, the columns are inserted into each sheet. You can use this technique when Group mode is off. With Group mode on, inserting one or more columns into any one sheet inserts them into all of the sheets in the current file.

Inserting Sheets

When you need to add another sheet to a stack, use the Worksheet Insert Sheet command. The stack in memory may have been retrieved from storage and already contain several sheets, or you may just be beginning a work session, in which case the stack contains only one sheet. In either case, you can add sheets to the stack until you reach the limit of 256 sheets or run out of RAM, whichever occurs first. As with inserted rows and columns, any formula that extends across the inserted sheet adjusts to include cells from the inserted sheet in its ranges. Any formula that refers to a cell on an existing sheet adjusts to reflect the addition of the new sheet.

As with the Insert Column and Insert Row commands, the position of the cursor determines where the new sheets are inserted.

To add a blank sheet to the stack in memory, position the cursor on a sheet *next* to where you want the new sheet to appear and type

/WI	Enters the Worksheet Insert command.
S	Selects Sheet
B or **A**	Inserts the sheet before or after the current sheet.
Enter number of worksheet to insert:	Default is 1. Type number or use **RIGHT** and **LEFT** arrow keys to increase or decrease number.
ENTER	Executes the command.

Each blank sheet you insert requires about 800 bytes of memory, and you get an error message when you try to insert more sheets than your available RAM can handle. To free up memory, use the Worksheet Delete command to remove unneeded sheets or active files. Use the File Save command (Chapter 5) to save unneeded active files before you delete them. You can also free up a considerable amount of memory if you turn off the Undo feature by selecting the Worksheet Global Default Other Undo Disable command. If you insert too many sheets, use the Worksheet Delete command to remove the extra ones.

THE WORKSHEET DELETE COMMAND

The Worksheet Delete command (Figure 2–12) is similar in form but opposite in action to the Worksheet Insert command. It deletes one or more rows or columns from a worksheet. You can also use it to delete one or more sheets from a stack or one or more active files from a stack.

Deleting Rows and Columns

Again, the location of the worksheet cursor tells 1-2-3 which rows or columns to delete. In this case, the selection is the column(s) or row(s)

Figure 2–12   Worksheet Delete command tree.

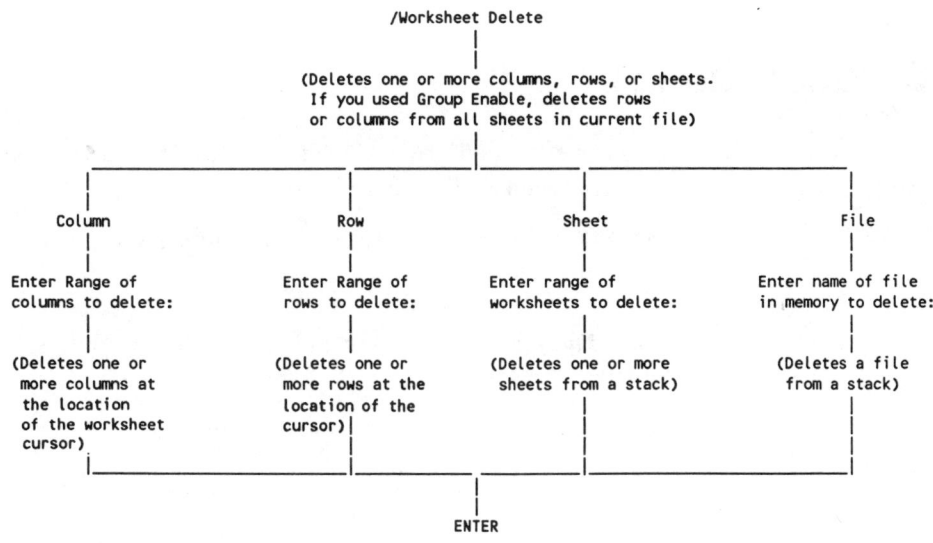

containing the expanded cursor. Beware of the Delete command when you are using Group mode, because deleting rows or columns from one sheet deletes the corresponding rows or columns from *all* sheets in the current file.

To delete rows or columns, position the cursor and type

/WD	Enters the Worksheet Delete command.
C or R	Selects Column or Row delete.
Enter column (or row) delete range:	Use the arrow keys to expand the cursor to cover two or more rows or columns.
ENTER	Executes the command.

Be sure you have correctly specified the rows or columns you want to remove before pressing **ENTER** the final time in this process. If you make a mistake and Undo is enabled, you can press **ALT-F4** to restore the worksheet, provided you take no intermediate action after pressing **ENTER**.

The command deletes rows or columns from one edge of the worksheet all the way to the opposite edge of the worksheet. Be careful not to unintentionally delete information that is off the screen, but in the same row or column.

As with the Insert command, you can unstick the cursor with either the **ESC** or **BKSP** key, reposition it, and stick it down again with the . key.

Deleting Sheets

To remove a sheet from a stack, position the cursor on any cell in the sheet you want to delete and type

/WD	Enters the Worksheet Delete command.
S	Selects Sheet.
Enter range to delete:	Asks for range of sheets to delete.
CTRL-PGUP or **CTRL-PGDN**	Stretches cursor over desired range of sheets.
ENTER	Deletes specified range of sheets.

WORKSHEET COMMANDS

Be careful when you delete sheets. In particular, verify that the sheet contains nothing you want to keep before using the command. If you have the slightest doubt, use the File Save command to save the file before you use the Delete command. If you do make a mistake, you can retrieve the stored file. If Undo is enabled, you can undo the damage by pressing **ALT-F4**, provided you haven't taken any additional actions on the worksheet.

Deleting Files

In addition to deleting rows, columns, and sheets, you can use the Worksheet Delete command to delete active files from a stack.

Unlike the other commands, with Worksheet Delete you don't have to position the cursor in the active file to be deleted. The operation can be performed regardless of the cursor's location.

To delete an active file, type

/WD	Enters the Worksheet Delete command.
F	Selects File as the Delete action. A list of current active files is displayed on the screen.
Enter name of file in memory to delete:	Asks for name of file to delete.
Arrow keys	Highlight name of file to delete.
ENTER	Executes the command.

The file is removed from memory, but it remains on the disk. However, any changes you made to the file after loading it into memory are lost. If there have been changes, use the File Save command to save the current version of the active file before you delete it. If Undo is enabled, pressing **ALT-F4** restores the deleted file.

Caution: ERR

In previous versions of 1-2-3, when you deleted the end of a range designation that was used in a formula or built-in function the letters **ERR** appeared on the screen and other formulas that depended on the formula displayed **ERR**. This would occur, for example, when a spreadsheet contained the formula @SUM(A1..A10) and the Delete command was used to delete row 1. Such actions caused the heart of many a 1-2-3 user to skip a beat—deleting a row turned the screen to a field of **ERR**s.

Fear no more. One of the improvements in Release 3 is that deleting the end point of a range no longer generates **ERR**. Instead, the range shrinks back to the last column or row before the Delete command was executed. Lotus assumes you intended to snip off the deleted rows or columns and wanted to have the formulas apply to the remainder of the range.

ERR still appears when you delete a column or row containing a single cell reference in a formula or function. In that case, 1-2-3 has no idea what to substitute, so **ERR** is the result. **ERR** also appears when you define a formula that divides by zero or contains a reference to a blank cell in the denominator of some function. Using an undefined range name also generates the message. To make **ERR** disappear, redefine the formula or function, supply a value to the blank cell, or define the range name.

THE WORKSHEET COLUMN COMMAND

The Worksheet Column command sets or resets the width of individual columns or ranges of columns. See Figure 2–13 for a command summary. Worksheet Column is one of the most frequently used Worksheet com-

Figure 2–13 Worksheet Column command tree.

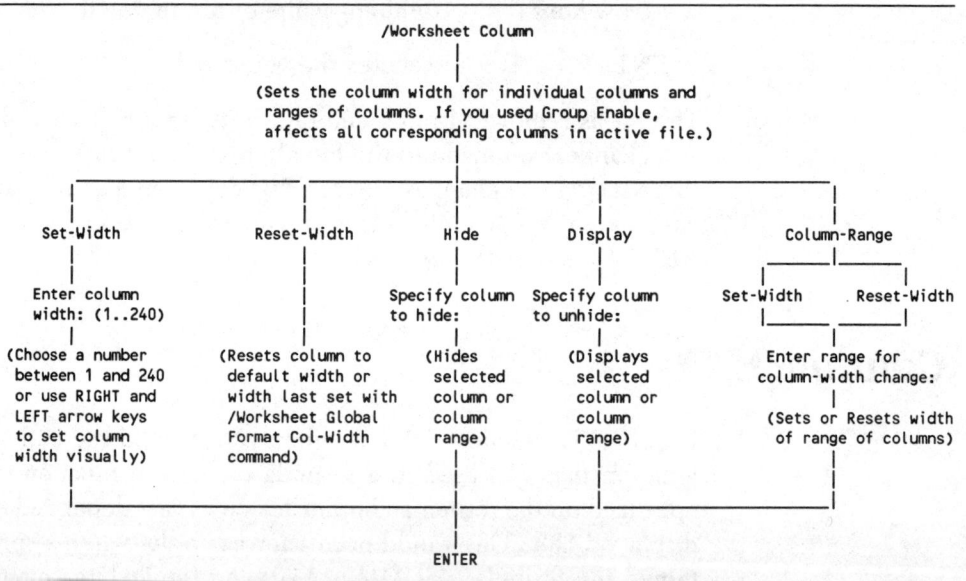

mands, because it helps you to tailor each column width to the contents of the column.

A column containing the row labels, for example, can be made wider, whereas a column containing small numbers can be made narrower. You can also insert columns (often just a few characters wide) to separate one column of numbers from another. This additional space often greatly improves the appearance and clarity of a worksheet. When Group mode is used, the action extends to the corresponding columns in all of the sheets in the current file.

Set and Reset

The Worksheet Column command operates exactly like the Worksheet Global Col-Width command, except that only the width of the columns *containing* the expanded worksheet cursor are changed. If you are changing the width of a single column, be sure to position the worksheet cursor in the correct column before entering the command since you cannot move it once you start the command. If you are changing the width of a range of columns, position the cursor in the first column of the range to be changed. Alternatively, you can specify the column range by typing the appropriate range.

To use the command, position the cursor on any cell in the column whose width you are going to change and type

/WC	Enters the Worksheet Column command.
S	Selects Set-Width.
Enter column (1..240):	Type a number or use the **RIGHT** or **LEFT** arrow key to visually set the column width.
ENTER	Completes the command and sets designated column to the width you specify.

Using the **RIGHT** and **LEFT** arrow keys is the best way to change a column's width, because you can see the effect the change has on the worksheet. If you know how wide you want the column to be, you can type in the desired number in the range 1 to 240. It is also faster to use the number method when you change the width by a large amount. Estimate the appropriate change, reenter the command, and use the arrow keys for additional fine adjustment.

The Reset option resets the column containing the worksheet cursor to the last column width set by the Global Col-Width command or, if one has not been set, to the default column width (9 characters).

Hide and Display

You can hide a column or group of columns and display them when you want to.

To hide or display a column, simply point to the column you want to hide by positioning the cursor in it. You can also tack the cursor to a column with the period key and then expand it over a range of columns.

To hide one or more columns, position the cursor and type

/WC	Enters the Worksheet Column command.
H	Selects Hide.
Specify column to hide:	Move cursor to column to hide. To hide more than one column, tack the cursor to first column to hide with . and use arrow keys to expand the cursor over two or more columns.
ENTER	Completes the command and hides the designated columns.

Once hidden, columns disappear from the screen, but you can tell that a particular column has been hidden, because its letter is missing from the list at the top of the screen. When, for example, column C is hidden, the screen indicates that column B is next to column D.

To display a hidden column, reenter the Column command and select the Display option. Then designate the column or range of columns to display.

Viewing Hidden Columns

Because the Worksheet commands Insert and Delete and many Range commands—such as Move, Copy, and Erase—can affect the contents of hidden columns, 1-2-3 displays all hidden columns whenever you use one of these commands. The columns designated as hidden are displayed with an asterisk after their column letter (such as **C*** for hidden column C).

You can use this feature as an easy way to inspect the contents of hidden columns without actually displaying them. Simply enter the Copy command by typing /c, for example, and the hidden columns display. After you inspect the contents, press the ESC key the required number of times to return to the Ready mode and the columns are rehidden.

Using Hidden Columns

Hidden columns can be the answer to several common worksheet problems. If, for example, you have several columns that perform intermediate calculations, but which you neither need to see on the screen nor print with your printer, just hide them. This conserves display space and allows you to view more of the important parts of your spreadsheet.

Likewise, if you only want the summary columns to appear on a printout, you can hide all other columns just before printing. You can't rearrange the order of the columns, but you can suppress the printing of intermediate columns that are unimportant or unnecessary.

Controlling the Width of a Range of Columns

Changing the width of a range of columns is much like using the Hide and Display commands discussed earlier. If you select Set-Width, you get to specify the width of all of the columns in the range. If you select Reset-Width, the column widths in the range are returned to the current Global Col-Width setting. When Group is on, this command affects the corresponding columns in all of the sheets in the current file.

To set the width of a range of columns type

/WC	Enters the Worksheet Column command.
C	Selects Column-Range.
Set-Width **Reset-Width**	Select Set-Width to set the width of a range of columns.
Enter range for column-width change:	Cursor is tacked to current cell. Use arrow keys to expand the cursor over two or more columns. Press **ESC** to untack cursor.
Enter column width:	Type number from 1 to 240 or use arrow keys to visually adjust column width.
ENTER	Completes the command and sets widths of the designated columns.

THE WORKSHEET ERASE COMMAND

The Worksheet Erase command is another command you are likely to use every time you work with 1-2-3. Use it after you have saved the current stack and when you are ready to begin constructing the next worksheet. Use it whenever you decide that the project you are constructing is beyond repair, and you want to start over with a clean slate. Figure 2–14 shows the simple—but potentially destructive—Erase command.

| **Figure 2–14** | Worksheet Erase command tree. |

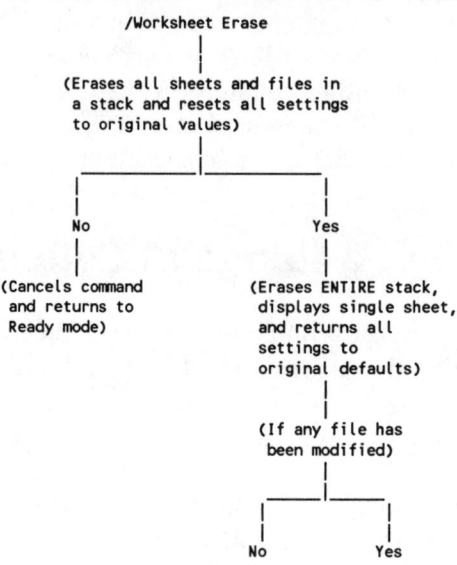

The Erase command erases the *entire stack*—not just the current worksheet—and resets all options (column width, protection, and so on) to their original default settings. The only settings not changed by the Erase command are those set with the Worksheet Global Default command.

Warning: The Erase command is devastating in its impact. It overrides all other commands, including worksheets protected with the Protection Enable command and files sealed with the File Admin command. Consequently, 1-2-3 requires you to confirm your intention to erase a worksheet *twice*. First, you must either move the command line cursor to the word **YES** and press **ENTER**, or you must type **Y**. This procedure is called a "sanity check." It alerts you to the fact that you are about to wipe the worksheet from your computer's memory forever (and, therefore, go insane). It gives you a chance to stop and save your worksheet with the File command. If you have made modifications to any file in the stack, a second **Yes/No** message appears. It tells you a file has been changed and suggests you save it.

However, if the Undo feature is active and you accidentally erase important data, you can immediately press **ALT-F4** before taking any other action to restore the stack to memory.

Finally, remember that the Worksheet Delete command discussed earlier in this chapter is the command to use to remove sheets or active files from a stack. The Range Erase command discussed in Chapter 3 is the

THE WORKSHEET TITLES COMMAND

appropriate command to send the contents of only a few cells, and not the entire stack, to electronic never-never land.

As you know, 1-2-3 has many more cells than it can display on the screen at any one time. In fact, tables of even modest size (more than 20 rows and 10 or 15 columns) do not display on the screen in their entirety. To help deal with worksheets larger than the screen, 1-2-3 provides two worksheet commands: Titles and Window.

The Worksheet Titles command, discussed here, "freezes" designated rows or columns, usually those holding row or column titles, on the screen so that other cells can be scrolled past the frozen titles. See Figure 2–15 for the command tree.

When Group mode is used, the Worksheet Titles command freezes corresponding rows and/or columns on all sheets in the current file.

The Worksheet Window command, discussed in the next section, splits the worksheet into two different windows to display cells at widely different locations on the same sheet or from different sheets in a stack. The Window command is unaffected by the Group mode.

The Titles command can best be explained with an example. Figure 2–16 contains a table to calculate the balance in a bank account over a 20-year period from 1990 to 2009. It assumes a deposit of $2,000 is made on the first day of each year, and the interest rate over the period is a constant 10 percent.

Figure 2–15 Worksheet Titles command tree.

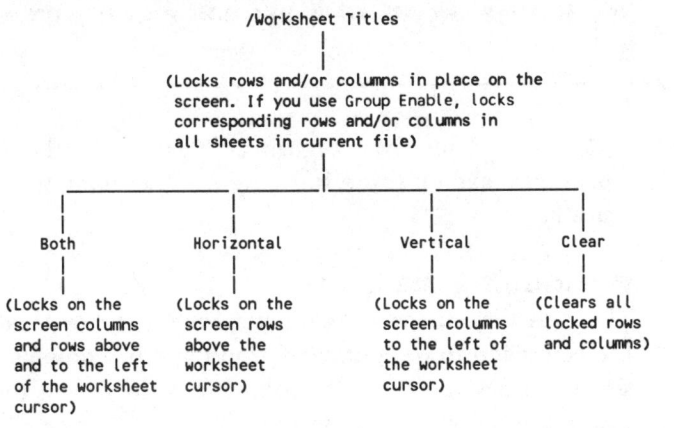

Figure 2-16 Compound interest table stretching over 24 columns, which takes three separate screens to display all the information.

	A	B	C	D	E	F	G	H
1	Assumption Space							
2								
3	Interest:	10.00%						
4	Deposit:	$2,000						
5								
6			1990	1991	1992	1993	1994	1995
7								
8	Balance Forward		$0	$2,200	$4,620	$7,282	$10,210	$13,431
9	Deposits		$2,000	$2,000	$2,000	$2,000	$2,000	$2,000
10	Interest		$200	$420	$662	$928	$1,221	$1,543
11								
12	Total		$2,200	$4,620	$7,282	$10,210	$13,431	$16,974
13								
14								

	A	I	J	K	L	M	N	O	P
1									
2									
3									
4									
5									
6		1996	1997	1998	1999	2000	2001	2002	2003
7									
8		$16,974	$20,872	$25,159	$29,875	$35,062	$40,769	$47,045	$53,950
9		$2,000	$2,000	$2,000	$2,000	$2,000	$2,000	$2,000	$2,000
10		$1,897	$2,287	$2,716	$3,187	$3,706	$4,277	$4,905	$5,595
11									
12		$20,872	$25,159	$29,875	$35,062	$40,769	$47,045	$53,950	$61,545
13									
14									

	A	Q	R	S	T	U	V	W	X
1									
2									
3									
4									
5									
6		2004	2005	2006	2007	2008	2009		TOTALS
7									
8		$61,545	$69,899	$79,089	$89,198	$100,318	$112,550		
9		$2,000	$2,000	$2,000	$2,000	$2,000	$2,000		$40,000
10		$6,354	$7,190	$8,109	$9,120	$10,232	$11,455		$86,005
11									
12		$69,899	$79,089	$89,198	$100,318	$112,550	$126,005		$126,005
13									
14									

As you can see from Figure 2-16, the 24 columns that make up the worksheet take up three full screens—too much to view on the screen at one time.

Positioning the Cursor

The Titles command uses the worksheet cursor location *before* entering the command to designate the rows and/or columns to be locked on the screen. Rows *above* and/or columns to the *left* of the current cursor location are locked on the screen.

WORKSHEET COMMANDS

You cannot reposition the cursor once you are using the command. If the cursor is in the wrong place, you must return to the Ready mode in order to move it.

Example: Locking Columns on the Screen

In Figure 2–16 move the cursor to cell C6 before entering the command. Because you are going to lock columns containing the row labels on the screen, any cell in column C would be appropriate. Then type

/WT   Enters the Worksheet Titles command.

V   Selects Vertical and locks on the screen all columns to the *left* of the current cursor location. (No ENTER is required.)

Now scroll the cursor to the right to view successive columns of your table while you keep the row labels in columns A and B on the screen. See Figure 2–17 where column S is displayed next to column B.

Locking Both Rows and Columns on the Screen

The Titles command is particularly useful when your table has many rows and many columns. You can set the Both option so the appropriate column headings *and* row labels are always displayed.

Figure 2–17   Columns A and B locked with the Title command while the rest of the worksheet is scrolled to reveal columns S through X.

```
A:S8: +A:R12                                                    READY


  A        A           B         S        T        U         V    W     X
  1    Assumption Space
  2
  3    Interest:   10.00%
  4    Deposit:    $2,000
  5
  6                              2006     2007     2008     2009       TOTALS
  7
  8    Balance Forward         $79,089  $89,198 $100,318 $112,550
  9    Deposits                 $2,000   $2,000   $2,000   $2,000     $40,000
 10    Interest                 $8,109   $9,120  $10,232  $11,455     $86,005
 11
 12    Total                   $89,198 $100,318 $112,550 $126,005    $126,005
 13
 14
 15
 16
 17
 18
 19
 20
      SAVINGS.WK3
```

To use the command, position the cursor at a point where the rows above *and* the columns to the left are the ones you want to keep on the screen. If you want to keep both the row containing the years and the columns containing the row labels on the screen in the spreadsheet in Figure 2–16, position your cursor on cell C7 before entering the command. Then type

/WT   Enters the Worksheet Titles command.

B   Selects Both and locks on the screen columns to the left and rows above the current cursor location. (No ENTER is required.)

Now when you scroll around your spreadsheet both the row labels in columns A and B and the column headings in rows 1 through 6 remain on the screen. Titles settings are stored with the worksheet and are in force when the worksheet is retrieved with the File command.

Clearing Titles

To gain access to the locked rows or columns, unlock the titles by typing

/WT   Enters the Worksheet Titles command.

C   Selects Clear. (No ENTER is required.)

Limitations

You can't use the Titles command and the Print command to print a worksheet with column B next to column S. You can, however, use **SHIFT-PRTSC** to print the screen as it appears, or you can achieve the same result with the Worksheet Column Hide command discussed earlier. Also, the Borders option of the Print command prints column headings and row labels on every page of a multiple page printout. (See Chapter 6.)

THE WORKSHEET WINDOW COMMAND

The Worksheet Window command is the other feature 1-2-3 has to compensate for the limited number of rows, columns, or sheets that can be displayed on the screen at one time. (See Figure 2–18 for the command tree.) The Window command performs several actions relating to the display screen.

First, it can split the screen into two windows. The split is either horizontal or vertical, and one row or column is lost to the new line of column letters (horizontal split) or row numbers (vertical split). Two parts of the

WORKSHEET COMMANDS

Figure 2-18 Worksheet Window command tree.

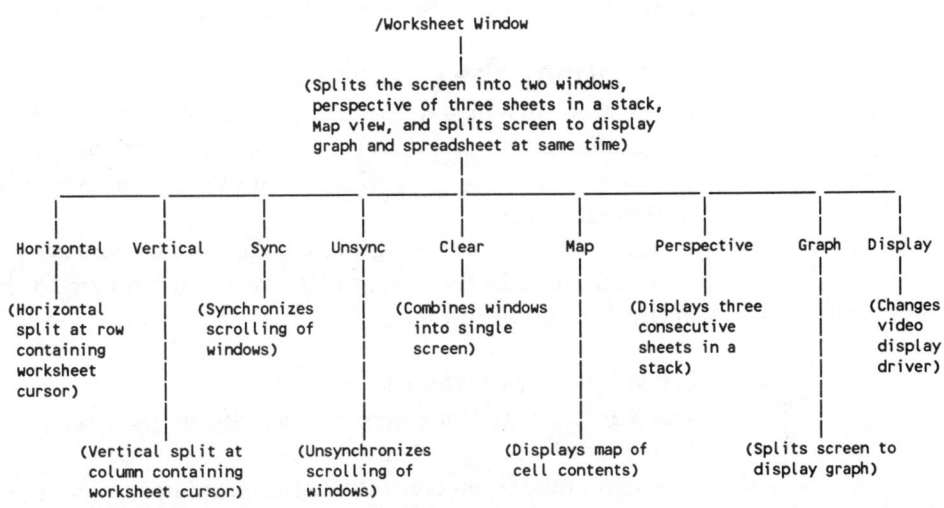

same worksheet or parts of two different sheets can be viewed in each window. Keep an eye on the sheet indicator (the A:, B:, and so on) in the upper left corner and the file indicator in the lower left corner. These indicators change when the cursor moves from sheet to sheet and file to file.

The Worksheet Window command also provides a Perspective view of three adjacent sheets in a stack and a Graph window in which a graph can be drawn at the same time you view your spreadsheet in the other window.

The command also has an option called Map that displays a map of your spreadsheet where each column is two characters wide and the contents are represented by **f** for formula, **#** for number, and **"** for label. With Map you get a quick overview of the structure of your spreadsheet, which is useful for detecting errors in structure. Finally, the Display option is used to switch between different video display drivers, provided you installed two during the initial installation procedure.

Splitting the Screen into Windows

The Window command is often used to split the screen into two windows in order to view both the beginning of a table where assumptions are entered and the end of the table. You can also view two entirely different sheets in each window. With the Window command, you can quickly do a "What If . . ." analysis where you vary the assumption to see what happens if, for example, the interest rate is 15% or if the deposit is $1,500.

Positioning the Cursor

The Window command, like the Titles command, uses the worksheet cursor location *before* it enters the command to designate the row or column where the split is to occur. Horizontal splits occur above and vertical splits to the left of the cursor.

Again, you cannot reposition the cursor once you are in the command. If the cursor is in the wrong place, you must return to the Ready mode in order to move it.

Example: Vertical Window

The Vertical Window command can also be used with the worksheet in Figure 2–16.

To split the screen vertically between columns B and C, move the cursor to C7—actually, any cell in column C will work—and type

/WW   Enters the Worksheet Window command.

V   Selects Vertical and splits the screen to the left of the current cursor location. (No ENTER is required.)

The screen is split to the left of the cursor location and the cursor is positioned at the left-hand window.

Moving Between Windows: WINDOW/F6

The cursor can be in only one window at one time. To move it from one window to another press the **WINDOW/F6** key.

In Figure 2–19 the cursor has been moved to the right-hand window and the window was scrolled until the end of the table (columns T to Y) appears. You can press **WINDOW/F6** to move to the left-hand window to make a change in either the Deposit rate or the Interest rate. Then press **WINDOW/F6** to move the cursor back to the right-hand window.

When you are viewing the same worksheet in both windows (as in Figure 2–19) it is important to understand that when you are viewing cell B3 in both windows you are looking at two copies of the same cell, one in each window. If you erase B3 in the left-hand window, it also disappears from the right-hand window.

ZOOM

When your screen is split into windows and you want a full-screen display of one of your windows, move the cursor to that window with the

Figure 2-19 Compound interest table with screen split vertically so both the Assumption Space in columns A and B and the Totals in column X can be viewed at the same time.

```
A:Y7:                                                           READY

  A      A         B     A    T        U        V       W    X        Y
  1   Assumption Space   1
  2                      2
  3   Interest:  10.00%  3
  4   Deposit:   $2,000  4
  5                      5
  6                      6    2007     2008     2009         TOTALS
  7                      7
  8   Balance Forward    8    $89,198  $100,318 $112,550
  9   Deposits           9    $2,000   $2,000   $2,000       $40,000
 10   Interest          10    $9,120   $10,232  $11,455      $86,005
 11                     11
 12   Total             12    $100,318 $112,550 $126,005     $126,005
 13                     13
 14                     14
 15                     15
 16                     16
 17                     17
 18                     18
 19                     19
 20                     20
SAVINGS.WK3
```

WINDOW/F6 key and press the Zoom key, **ALT-F6**. The window currently containing the cursor expands to full size, and the word **ZOOM** appears at the bottom of the screen. When you are ready to restore the split screen, press **ALT-F6** again, and the split is restored.

Windows in Stacks

If you have a stack of two or more worksheets, you can view different sheets in different windows using the **CTRL-PGUP** and **CTRL-PGDN** keys to move forward and backward in a stack. Consult the Sheet indicator in the upper left corner and the File indicator at the bottom of the screen to see which sheet and which file the cursor is in at any particular moment.

It is easy to coordinate Copy and Move commands when you are viewing different worksheets in each window or to construct formulas or functions that use cell references from different spreadsheets.

To Synchronize or Not to Synchronize

The Window command also gives you the option of having the two windows scroll together (synchronized) or scroll independently (unsynchronized). When the split is horizontal, synchronized windows show the same columns in each window. When you scroll the columns in one window, columns in the other window also scroll. When the split is vertical, the same rows appear in each window.

Unlike earlier versions of Lotus 1-2-3, when you split the screen into two windows the default is to have the windows unsynchronized when first split. This is true even when you use the **CTRL-PGUP** and **CTRL-PGDN** keys to move to other sheets in a stack. However, when you use Perspective view (discussed next) the three windows are synchronized.

To synchronize the windows, type

/WW Enters the Worksheet Window command.

S Selects Sync. The rows (vertical split) or columns (horizontal split) now scroll together in each window. (No ENTER is required.)

Perspective on a Stack

The Window command also helps solve the problem of managing a stack of sheets by displaying parts of three adjacent worksheets in a stack. When the three parts of Figure 2–16 are placed on three consecutive sheets, you can use Perspective view to see all of the cells at one time.

To enter the Perspective view, type

/WW Enters the Worksheet Window command.

P Selects Perspective view and executes the command. (No ENTER is required.)

See Figure 2–20 for a Perspective view of the worksheet in Figure 2–16 when the contents of Figure 2–16 are placed on sheets A, B, and C.

Scrolling forward and backward in the stack with **CTRL-PGDN** and **CTRL-PGUP** and the other stack cursor movement commands adds and removes sheets from the display. You can move from window to window by pressing the **WINDOW/F6** key. If you want a full-screen display of one of the windows move the cursor to the window and press the Zoom key, **ALT-F6**. To restore the Perspective view, press the Zoom key a second time.

To leave Perspective view, use Worksheet Window Clear by typing

/WW Enters the Worksheet Window command.

C Selects Clear, executes the command, and returns the screen to normal display. (No ENTER is required.)

Figure 2–20   Perspective view of Compound Interest worksheet.

```
A:A6:                                                              READY

     C     A         B         C         D         E         F         G      H
     6    2004      2005      2006      2007      2008      2009           TOTALS
     7
     8  $61,545   $69,899   $79,089   $89,198  $100,318  $112,550         $126,005
     9   $2,000    $2,000    $2,000    $2,000    $2,000    $2,000          $40,000
    10   $6,354    $7,190    $8,109    $9,120   $10,232   $11,455          $86,005
    11
       B    A         B         C         D         E         F         G      H
       6   1996      1997      1998      1999      2000      2001      2002   2003
       7
       8 $16,974  $20,872   $25,159   $29,875   $35,062   $40,769   $47,045  $53,950
       9  $2,000   $2,000    $2,000    $2,000    $2,000    $2,000    $2,000   $2,000
      10  $1,897   $2,287    $2,716    $3,187    $3,706    $4,277    $4,905   $5,595
      11
         A   A         B         C         D         E         F         G      H
         6                      1990      1991      1992      1993      1994    1995
         7
         8 Balance Forward        $0    $2,200    $4,620    $7,282   $10,210  $13,431
         9 Deposits           $2,000    $2,000    $2,000    $2,000    $2,000   $2,000
        10 Interest             $200      $420      $662      $928    $1,221   $1,543
        11
        FIG_2-20.WK3
```

Graph Window

If you want to see a graph and your spreadsheet on the screen at the same time, then the Worksheet Window Graph command is what you are looking for. It works exactly like the Vertical Window command except that a graph is displayed in the right-hand window and the current sheet in the left-hand window. When you make changes to the data presented in the graph, the graph changes.

This feature requires a system that can display both graphics and text on the screen simultaneously. Some systems can display only text. In this case, the window is created, but nothing is displayed in it. To view a graph, you must use either **GRAPH/F10** to create an automatic graph or the Graph View command, which is discussed in Chapter 11.

To set a graph window, begin by moving the cursor to any cell in the column where you want the split to take place and type

/WW   Enters the Worksheet Window command.

G   Selects Graph and splits the screen to the left of the current cursor location and draws the current graph in the right-hand window. (No ENTER is required.)

To change the size of the graph window, first clear the split with the

Worksheet Window Clear command. Then reposition the cursor and repeat the steps just listed to create a graph window of a different size.

Map View

When you select Map from the Worksheet Window menu, the display changes to show a view of the structure of your spreadsheet. Columns are two characters wide, and the contents of cells are represented by a # for numbers, a + for formulas, and a " for labels. By providing a good overview of your spreadsheet's structure, Map view helps you spot construction errors. You can view the actual contents of a particular cell on the Status Line by moving the cursor to that cell. When you are ready to return to conventional view, press the **ENTER** key. See Figure 2–21 for the Map view representation of the contents of Figure 2–16.

Using Windows

The two main uses of split windows have already been discussed. They help you to see widely separated parts of the same worksheet such as the Assumption Space and the "bottom line," and they help you to simultaneously view two different worksheets in the same stack.

Figure 2–21 Map view of Compound Interest worksheet.

```
A:A1: 'Assumption Space                                                READY

A   A B C D E F G H I J K L M N O P Q R S T U V W X Y Z AAABACADAEAFAGAHAIAJ
1   "
2
3   " #
4   " #
5
6       # # # # # # # # # # # # # # # # # # # #   "
7
8   "   # + + + + + + + + + + + + + + + + + + +
9   "   + + + + + + + + + + + + + + + + + + + +   +
10  "   + + + + + + + + + + + + + + + + + + + +   +
11
12  "   + + + + + + + + + + + + + + + + + + + +   +
13
14
15
16
17
18
19
20
Fig_2-21.WK3
```

WORKSHEET COMMANDS

In addition, you can use the split screen to display more columns or rows than you could normally view on the screen at one time. This is illustrated in Figure 2–22, where twice as many columns can be displayed by splitting the screen horizontally. Notice that the Titles command has also been used to freeze the row titles on the screen in both windows.

Because each window of a split screen can act as an independent copy of the same worksheet, another use of windows is to view the same cells in both windows. When you do you can set different formats, label-alignments, and column widths in each window. However, when you merge the windows to unsplit the screen, the settings in the top or left window become the settings for the entire worksheet. This is true even if you are looking at *different* sheets in *different* active files in each window.

Perspective view works differently. Changes made to each window remain after the view is cleared. And if Group mode is enabled, many changes (column width, format, label prefix, and so on) are made to sheets in the current file, whether they are displayed in a window or not.

In Figure 2–23 the window is split vertically, and the same cells are displayed in each window. In the right-hand window, the Global Format Text command has been used to display the formulas behind the numbers in the left-hand window. The columns in the right-hand window have also been expanded so the longer formulas can be displayed.

Figure 2–22 Screen split horizontally to display columns at both the beginning and the end of the table.

```
A:B3: (P2) [W7] 0.1                                              READY

   A     A          B       C        D        E        F        G        H      |
   1     Assumption Space
   2
   3     Interest:  10.00%
   4     Deposit:   $2,000
   5
   6                        1990     1991     1992     1993     1994
   7
   8     Balance Forward    $0       $2,200   $4,620   $7,282   $10,210
   9     Deposits           $2,000   $2,000   $2,000   $2,000   $2,000
   10    Interest           $200     $420     $662     $928     $1,221
   11
   12    Total              $2,200   $4,620   $7,282   $10,210  $13,431
   A     A          B       S        T        U        V        W    X       Y  |
   6                        2006     2007     2008     2009          TOTALS
   7
   8     Balance Forward    $79,089  $89,198  $100,318 $112,550
   9     Deposits           $2,000   $2,000   $2,000   $2,000        $40,000
   10    Interest           $8,109   $9,120   $10,232  $11,455       $86,005
   11
   12    Total              $89,198  $100,318 $112,550 $126,005      $126,005
   SAVINGS.WK3
```

Figure 2–23 Different formats, column widths, and displays for each window of a split screen. Global Format Text displays in the right-hand window the formulas behind the numbers in the left-hand window. The column width is expanded in the right-hand window. Text format displays numbers in General format.

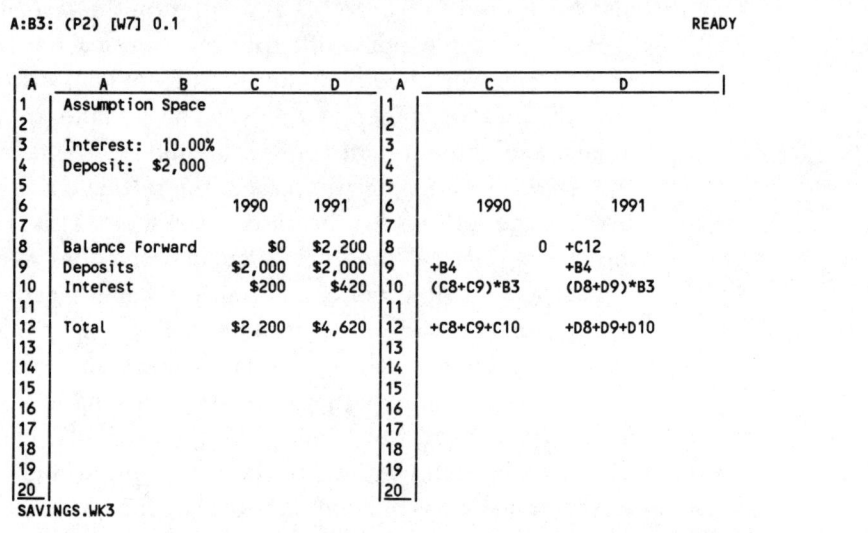

When you save a worksheet with a split screen or in Perspective view, the screen is split or Perspective view is in force when you retrieve the worksheet. Also, when you add a file to a stack with the File Open command, the window settings *in that file* are used to control the windows in the stack. For example, if the stack is in Perspective view and the file you are loading is in full-screen display, the stack is automatically converted to full-screen display as soon as the file is loaded. Surprise!

You can only print the split screen with the SHIFT-PRTSC key. This command, which exists on most IBM® and IBM-compatible microcomputers, prints an exact copy of your computer screen, control panel letters, numbers, and all.

Clearing Windows

To clear any Window command setting and restore the screen to its original appearance, type

/WW   Enters the Worksheet Window command.

C   Selects Clear. Window is restored to original appearance. (No ENTER is required.)

WORKSHEET COMMANDS

Remember, for horizontal and vertical splits, the formats and column widths set in either the upper or left window remain in effect after the split is cleared. Those set in the right or lower window are not in effect. However, if you were using the Perspective view, any change you make to any sheet remains after full-screen display is restored.

Warnings

Because there is only one underlying cell when viewing the same worksheet in both windows, anything you do to change the contents of a cell in one window changes the contents of the cell in both windows. For example, erasing, editing, or moving the contents of a cell in either window erases, edits, or moves it in both.

Beware the Worksheet Erase command; it erases the *entire* stack, not just the window currently containing the cursor. To erase some of the cells in the window currently containing the cursor, use the Range Erase command described in the next chapter. If the window displays a different sheet or a sheet from a different file, use the Worksheet Delete Sheet command to remove it entirely. But remember, if the same cell is displayed in both windows, erasing it from one window simultaneously erases it from the other. Finally, use the Worksheet Hide command described later in the chapter if you want to suppress the display of a window without removing it from the stack.

Display

The final command under the Worksheet Window command is Display. If you specified two screen modes in the Install program, this command switches between them. If, as is most common, you selected only one display mode, this option doesn't apply to your situation.

THE WORKSHEET STATUS COMMAND

The next worksheet command on the command line is the Status command, summarized in Figure 2–24. This command displays the current global settings for the worksheet. Use it to check the values you have set with the Worksheet commands. In addition, it tells how much memory is available for constructing your worksheets and the location of the most recently constructed circular reference.

To display the Status command screen, type

/WS   Selects the Worksheet Status command. (No ENTER is required.)

Figure 2–24 Worksheet Status command tree.

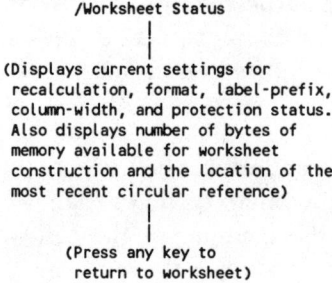

The worksheet screen is replaced by the display in Figure 2–3, which you saw early in this chapter. When you have finished viewing the display, press any key to return to the Ready mode.

CIRC: Circular Reference

A *circular reference* is a formula or function that refers to itself. Whenever you create a circular reference, the **CIRC** indicator appears at the bottom of the screen. The status screen shows the location of the most recently created circular reference.

To create a circular reference, make the following entries:

1	In cell A:A1
2	In cell A:A2
+A1+A2+A3	In cell A:A3

Because the formula in cell A3 includes itself, the **CIRC** message appears at the bottom of the screen. Now each time the worksheet is recalculated (by pressing the **CALC/F9** key, for example), the number displayed in cell A3 changes. If recalculation is set to Automatic, the number in cell A3 changes whenever an entry is made anywhere in the stack or whenever the Copy, Move, or Range Erase command is used.

To find the location of the circular reference, type

/WS   Enters the Worksheet Status command.

The circular reference message now shows **A:A3**. If the file has been saved so that it exists on disk, the cell containing the circular reference is preceded by its filename (such as <<BUDGET.WK3>>A·A4). If the file hasn't

WORKSHEET COMMANDS

been saved, <<>> appears before the cell to indicate the reference is in a sheet in the unsaved part of the stack.

Even though there are some legitimate uses of circular references, most occurrences are out-and-out mistakes and need to be corrected. Whenever **CIRC** appears, bring up the status screen, find the address of the cell containing the circular reference, verify the formula, and, if necessary, change it. If your worksheet is set to manual recalculation, you must press **CALC/F9** to recalculate the worksheet and clear the **CIRC** message.

If your worksheet contains more than one circular reference, the status screen shows only the last occurrence. If **CIRC** is still displayed after you press **CALC/F9**, check the status screen for the location of the next circular reference.

THE WORKSHEET PAGE COMMAND

The Worksheet Page command solves a very common printing problem, but because it isn't part of the Print command many 1-2-3 users don't know it exists. What the command does is to help you control the location of page breaks in a printed worksheet with what are called *forced page breaks*.

If you don't use the Page command, you must either carefully specify several different print ranges when you print a table spanning a number of pages, or you must accept 1-2-3's standard page breaks. If you accept the standard page breaks, the result is often the unsatisfactory division of a table at arbitrary points.

To insert a page break into a worksheet, begin by properly positioning the worksheet cursor.

The cursor must be (1) in the row where you want the new page to begin and (2) in the left-hand column of the range of cells to be printed. If the cursor isn't in the correct spot, the forced page break will not work. Note that if you change the print range, you may have to change the location of the forced page break. Also note that when Group mode is on, a page break is inserted in each sheet in the current file.

With the cursor correctly positioned, type

/WP Selects the Worksheet Page command. (No ENTER is required.)

A new row is inserted at the location of the worksheet cursor, and the Page Break indicator, ::, appears in the cell. The indicator is actually the split vertical line character, ¦, followed by two colons. The vertical line character doesn't display; rather it signals 1-2-3 that what follows is a command to the printer and not text to be printed.

When the range is printed, a new page begins with the row immediately below the :: symbol. Furthermore, *nothing* in the row beginning with :: is printed.

Manually Inserting a Forced Page Break

You can bypass the Worksheet command and insert the Page Break indicator directly by moving the cursor to the cell in the left-hand column of your print range where you want the page break to occur.

To insert the Page Break indicator, type the vertical line character, **SHIFT**-\, followed by two colons, so the indicator looks like |::. The vertical line character doesn't display; rather, it signals 1-2-3 that what follows is a command to the printer and not text to be printed. If you use the direct method, make sure there is nothing else in the row except for the Page Break indicator and that you have entered it into a cell in the rightmost column of your print range.

Removing a Forced Page Break

To remove a Page Break indicator, use the Worksheet Delete Row command to delete the row containing the indicator. This removes the row that was inserted when you created the page break, as well as the indicator. If you don't want to remove the row, erase the indicator with the Range Erase command described in Chapter 3.

Finally, to get the full use of the Page command, you must be familiar with the printing of 1-2-3 worksheets. If you are not, read the information in Chapter 6. Pay particular attention to 1-2-3's default page so you can correctly position page breaks to achieve the type of printout you desire.

HANDS ON: USING THE WORKSHEET COMMANDS

You can get a good idea of the power of the 1-2-3 worksheet commands by comparing Figures 2–25 and 2–26. Both figures contain the same information—average weekly and hourly earnings in a number of representative industries—but the "Before" worksheet in Figure 2–25 is crowded and hard to read. The "After" worksheet shows what a few Worksheet commands can do to improve a worksheet's appearance.

Begin by looking at Figure 2–25. A number of Worksheet commands should be used to improve its appearance. First, the elements are too close together. The title, column headings, and body of the table are

WORKSHEET COMMANDS

Figure 2-25 Table before using worksheet commands to improve presentation.
Source: *American Averages* by Mike Feinsilber and William B. Mead (New York: Dolphin Books, 1980), p. 235.

```
A      A         B          C       D        E     F      G
1
2
3              MAKING MONEY MAKING THINGS
4                           Weekly   Earnings
5              Industry     Earnings Per Hour
6      Steel, Copper, and   430.62   10.25285
7      Petroleum            377.1     8.38
8      Automobile           369.27    8.450114
9      Transportation Equ   320.67    7.689928
10     Chemicals            292.18    6.989952
11     Paper                279.48    6.529906
12     Printing             244.02    6.489893
13     Leather Working      231.42    6.1712
14     Food Processing      231.42    5.8
15     Electrical Equipme   228.71    5.790126
16     Lumber               228.71    5.732080
17     Furniture Manufact   180.96    4.64
18     Textiles             172.43    4.3
19     Clothes Manufactur   140.76    3.91
20
```

Figure 2-26 Data and labels from Figure 2-25 after using Worksheet Insert, Delete, Column, and Format commands.
Source: *American Averages* by Mike Feinsilber and William B. Mead (New York: Dolphin Books, 1980), p. 235.

```
A      A              B          C    D      E        F
1                 MAKING MONEY MAKING THINGS
2
3                              Weekly      Earnings
4           Industry           Earnings    Per Hour
5
6      Steel, Copper, and Aluminum  $430.62   $10.25
7      Petroleum                    $377.10    $8.38
8      Automobile                   $369.27    $8.45
9      Transportation Equipment     $320.67    $7.69
10     Chemicals                    $292.18    $6.99
11     Paper                        $279.48    $6.53
12     Printing                     $244.02    $6.49
13     Leather Working              $231.42    $6.17
14     Food Processing              $231.42    $5.80
15     Electrical Equipment         $228.71    $5.79
16     Lumber                       $228.71    $5.73
17     Furniture Manufacturing      $180.96    $4.64
18     Textiles                     $172.43    $4.30
19     Clothes Manufacturing        $140.76    $3.91
20
```

almost on top of one another. Adding a few blank rows and columns would make the table easier to read.

Position the cursor on the row below where you want to insert a row and type

/WIR	Enters the Worksheet Insert Row command.
ENTER	Inserts one row immediately above the current worksheet cursor location.

Repeat this step for each row you want to insert. After you have inserted rows into the worksheet, you'll find that the last line of the table has disappeared off of the screen. To bring it back into the screen display, you need to delete the two extra rows at the top.

Position the cursor on any cell in row 1 and type

/WDR	Enters the Worksheet Delete Row command.
DOWN	Stretches the cursor over rows 1 and 2.
ENTER	Deletes the two rows (1 and 2) that contain the expanded worksheet cursor.

The table moves up and all of the rows are once again visible on the screen.

The numbers in columns C and D would be easier to read with more space between them. To insert a column between column C and D, position the cursor on any cell in column D and type

/WIC	Enters the Worksheet Insert Column command.
ENTER	Inserts one column between columns C and D.

You can achieve the same effect by expanding the original column D and right aligning the labels.

What about the row labels in Figure 2–25? What is **Steel, Copper and** . . .? Something is missing. Indeed, several row labels are truncated because they are too long to display in the 18 characters allotted to columns A and B by the default column width. Column A needs to be expanded.

Position the cursor on any cell in column A and type

/WC	Enters the Worksheet Column command.
RIGHT	Widens column A by one character for each press of the **RIGHT** arrow key.
ENTER	Sets column at selected width.

Finally, the numbers that make up the body of the table are hard to read. The Weekly Earnings figures aren't too bad, but the Earnings Per Hour, which are the result of dividing Weekly Earnings by the average number of hours worked per week, have from one to eight digits to the right of the decimal point. It would be much better to display them in

WORKSHEET COMMANDS

standard form—two places to the right of the decimal with a dollar sign to indicate currency.

To change the Global Format to Currency, two decimal places, type

/WGF	Enters the Worksheet Global Format command.
C	Selects the Currency format.
2	Selects 2 as the number of decimal places to display.
ENTER	Executes the command.

It takes less than a minute to turn the Before into the After worksheet. (Even Clark Kent takes that long in a phone booth.)

Thanks to the Worksheet commands Insert, Delete, Column, and Format, the table in Figure 2–26 has an easy-to-understand, professional appearance. The use of these and other Worksheet commands will become second nature to you as you continue to master worksheet construction with 1-2-3.

TIPS & TRAPS

Tips

Keep Track of the Row Labels and Column Headings.
On even relatively small tables, row labels and column headings frequently scroll off the screen when you examine distant portions of the table. Use the Worksheet Titles command to lock the row labels, the column headings, or both on the screen. Once locked, the headings remain on the screen while the body of the table scrolls by.

Lost in a Stack?
A stack can contain up to 256 sheets, and navigating through a large stack can present some problems. Here are two hints.

If your work has a logical structure, it's a simple matter to divide it into parts, place each on its own sheet, and then page through the stack to find what you need.

If the structure isn't obvious or the stack contains a large number of sheets, use the Range Name Create command discussed in Chapter 3 to name cell A1 on each sheet. Supply a descriptive name. Then press the

GOTO/F5 key followed by the NAME/F3 key. Highlight the appropriate sheet name and press ENTER to move the cursor to cell A1 on that sheet.

What Is a Print Command Doing on the Worksheet Command Tree?

The Worksheet Page command inserts a row and a forced page break into your worksheet. No one knows what it is doing on the Worksheet command tree.

Forced Page Break Doesn't Work.

For the force page break to work it must be in the *left-hand* column of the print range. If it isn't, :: appears on the printout as text. Check your print range and the location of the forced page break. You can move the four dots, reenter them with the Worksheet Page command or simply type |:: in the appropriate location.

Changed Defaults Keep Changing Back.

When you change a default with the Worksheet Global Default command, the change only remains in effect until the end of the current work session. To make changes permanent, you must select Update from the Worksheet Global Default menu. When you do, a new default file is written to the subdirectory containing your 1-2-3 system files. The new defaults are in effect until you change them again.

Traps

Don't Confuse the Worksheet Erase Command and the Range Erase Command.

The Worksheet Erase command erases the stack and replaces it with a single blank sheet. The Range Erase command (discussed in Chapter 3) only erases a designated range of cells.

What to Do When the Stars (******) Come Out.

Asterisks (or stars) appear whenever the current value in a cell cannot be displayed under the current format command. Format commands lengthen value entries because they supply special characters, such as dollar signs or percent signs, embedded commas, a decimal point, and a specified number of digits after the decimal.

The solution is to use either the Worksheet Global Col-Width command to widen all of the columns on the current sheet or the Worksheet Column

WORKSHEET COMMANDS

command to widen a single column or a range of columns. Use the arrow keys to visually adjust the column width until the stars disappear and the numbers appear.

Do You Want to Join the Group?

Be careful when working with already constructed worksheets, because enabling the Worksheet Global Group command immediately imposes the global settings from the current sheet as global settings on all sheets in the current file. Be careful.

What Does It Mean, CALC?

CALC appears at the bottom of the screen when a change has been made to a worksheet after the Worksheet Global Recalculation Manual command has been set. To recalculate the worksheet (and make **CALC** disappear) press the CALC/F9 function key.

The manual recalculation setting is stored with the worksheet and CALC can appear as soon as the worksheet is loaded into memory.

CIRC???

CIRC signals the presence of a circular reference. It appears at the bottom of the screen when the worksheet contains a formula that refers either directly or indirectly to the cell containing the formula. Unless the circular reference is intentional, **CIRC** signals a structural error in your worksheet.

Use the Worksheet Status command to display the status screen. That screen displays the cell address containing the most recently created circular reference.

If **CIRC** doesn't disappear after you correct the formula, press **CALC/F9**. If it still doesn't disappear, check the status screen for another circular reference.

Memory Full . . . of What?

Memory Full appears as an error message when you've run out of RAM. You can free up memory by deleting unused sheets in a stack, deleting active files, constructing tables compactly in the upper left corner of each sheet, using the Range Format Reset command (discussed in Chapter 6) to remove range formats assigned to empty cells, and turning off the Undo command with the Worksheet Global Default Other Undo command. After performing these actions, you may need to save and retrieve the worksheet to actually free up the memory.

Check the Worksheet Status screen for the memory remaining for worksheet construction. In extreme cases, break a stack up into individual worksheets by using the File Xtract command discussed in Chapter 5.

3 The Range Commands

OBJECTIVES

After mastering the content of this chapter, you will be able to

☐ distinguish between Range and Worksheet commands that perform similar tasks and know when to use each.

☐ learn to use 1-2-3's expanding cursor in two and three dimensions to specify ranges for use with Range commands and with many other Lotus commands and functions.

☐ master the use of the most important Range commands: Format, Label-Prefix, Erase, Name, Justify, and Search.

INTRODUCTION

The Range commands are among the most useful—and, thus, most often used—of all Lotus 1-2-3 commands. See Figure 3–1 for the Range command tree.

Several Range commands have the same options and functions as Worksheet commands of the same name. You will have little difficulty applying what you learned in Chapter 2 to the Range Format, Label-Prefix, and Erase commands. Other Range commands—Name, Justify, Input, Search, Values, and Transpose—are unique Range commands. Two Range commands—Prot and Unprot (short for "Protect" and "Unprotect")—are used in conjunction with the Worksheet Prot (Protect) command.

THE RANGE COMMANDS

Figure 3–1 Command tree for all Range commands.

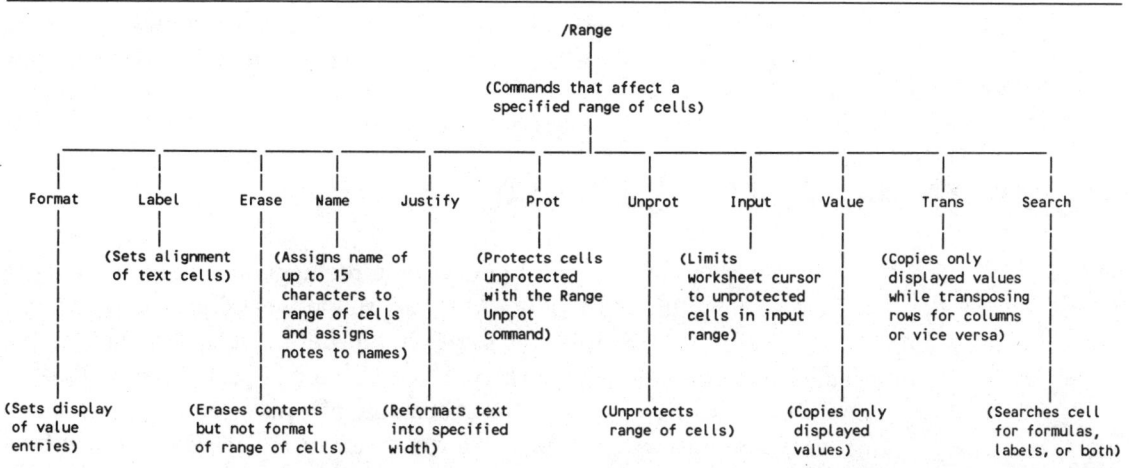

The major difference between Worksheet commands and Range commands is their scope of action. Worksheet commands operate on an entire worksheet, and, depending on the command and the status of the Group mode, all the sheets in the current file. Range commands operate on a specified range of cells, which may be on a single worksheet or can extend across several in the current file. When you use Group Enable, some Range commands (Format, Unprot, and Prot) act on the corresponding cells in every sheet in the current file. The other Range commands only operate on the range you actually specify. In any case, the action of the Range commands is limited to sheets in one file. They never extend across files in a stack.

There are other differences. The Worksheet Label command doesn't change the alignment (left, right, or center) of labels already entered in the worksheet. It only affects the assignment of label alignment characters to labels as the labels are entered. The Range Label command, on the other hand, only affects the alignment of labels already entered in the worksheet.

The Range Value and Transpose commands work much like 1-2-3's Copy command and are, therefore, discussed along with the Copy command in the next chapter. The difference between the commands is that the Range Value command copies only the displayed values and not the underlying formulas or functions. The Transpose command, as its name implies, copies row information into columns or column information into rows.

Because Range commands—as well as most other 1-2-3 commands and built-in functions—operate on a range of cells, your first task is to master the techniques for specifying a range. The next section shows how to do this. Later, this chapter explores specific Range commands and shows how and when to use them.

HOME, HOME ON THE RANGE . . .

In 1-2-3 a range of cells must always be a rectangle or, when working in 3-D, a rectangular solid (a *block*). On a single worksheet the rectangle can be made in four different ways. It can be a single cell. This is the smallest possible range. It can be part of a column or part of a row. Finally, on a single sheet a range can be a rectangle of cells stretching across two or more columns and two or more rows. Across sheets, a range can be a block of cells. See Figure 3-2 for an illustration of the four types of ranges on a single sheet and Figure 3-3 for the ranges across sheets.

All 1-2-3 ranges, whether on a single sheet or across sheets, must meet two conditions:

- They must be rectangular or a rectangular solid. No parts can protrude or hang inward from the edges.

- All of the cells in a range must be next to one another. You cannot specify a few cells, skip some cells, and then continue to specify a range.

Figure 3-2 Four types of ranges usable in a single worksheet: a single cell, part of a row, part of a column, or a rectangular block of cells.

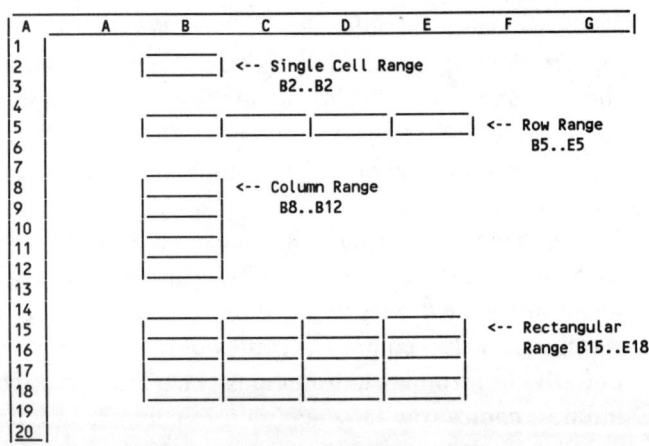

Figure 3–3   Across sheets Lotus recognizes four block ranges.

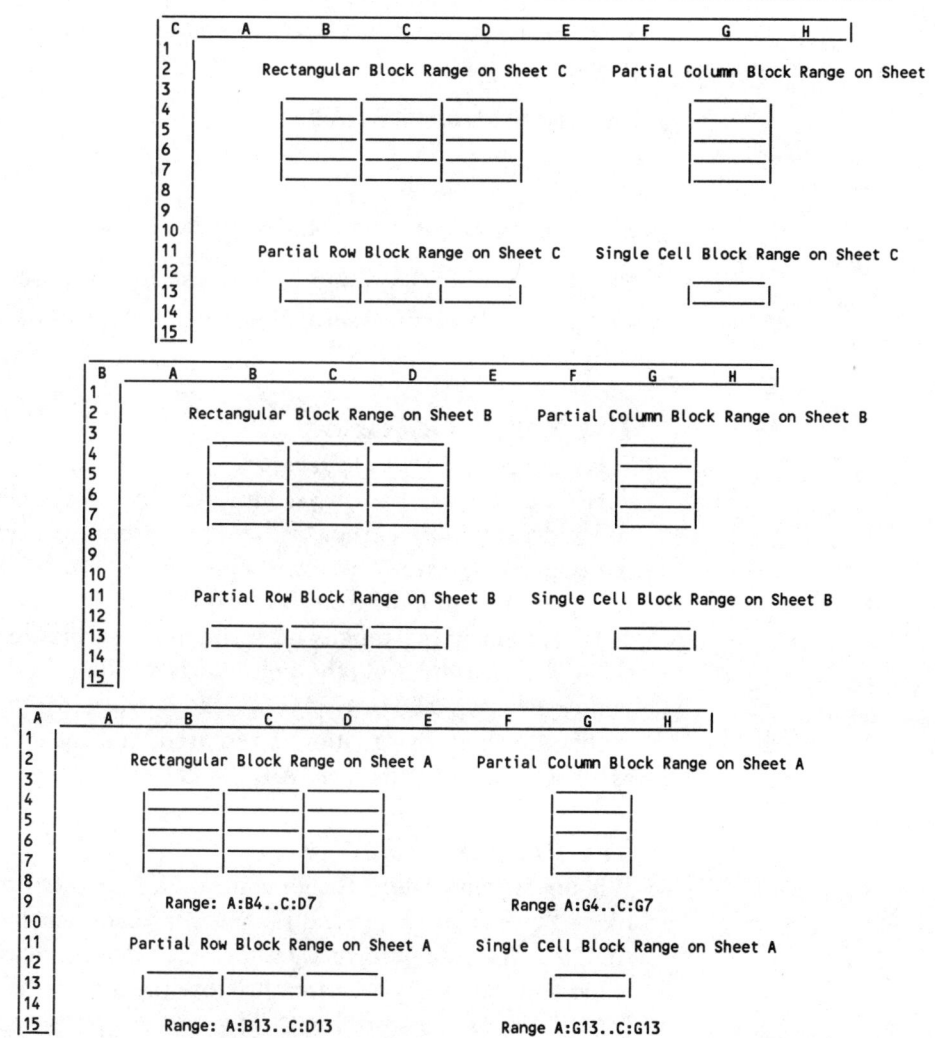

Other than these two restrictions, on a single sheet a 1-2-3 range can be any rectangle of cells from a single cell to the entire worksheet. In 3-D, a range can be any rectangular solid from two cells on two sheets to all of the cells in the current file.

Specifying a Range

Whenever you need to specify a range for a command, Lotus displays a prompt, such as

Enter range of labels: A:B3..A:B3

or

Enter range to format: A:G25..A:G25

The first part of the prompt is clear enough. It simply asks you to specify a range. The last part is a *proposed range* and shows the form your response is to take.

The Range Operator: ..

Lotus ranges are always specified by two cell addresses separated by two dots. The dots are known as the *range operator.* They separate the first cell address, at one corner of the range, from the second cell address, at the opposite corner. The range operator is read as "from . . . to . . ." as in "The range of cells from B3 to C4."

When specifying ranges on a single sheet the default is to drop the sheet designation from the cell address. When both addresses are the same, such as B3..B3 or G25..G25, the range refers to a single cell. Across sheets the sheet designation is required, and the range operator is read as "The range of cells *from* A:B3 *to* G:C4."

The Proposed Range

Whenever you enter a Range command, it always uses the currently activated cell as the proposed range; A:B3 above in the case of labels and A:G25 in the case of format. Other commands, such as the Database command and the Print command, propose the most recently specified range. (These ranges are stored with files and are proposed the next time the file is used.) If no range has been specified, the proposed range for all commands is the current, active cell.

How to Specify a Range

Ranges for the Range commands must be contained entirely within the current file. You receive an error message if you try to specify a range that extends beyond sheets in the current file. With that qualification in mind, there are three ways to specify a 1-2-3 range:

POINT: Use the worksheet cursor to point to the range.

TYPE: Type the range designation (such as **B3..B7** or, across sheets, **A:B3..C:B3**).

NAME: Supply a name previously assigned to a range of cells with the Range Name command.

If you want to use the proposed range, press **ENTER** to select it.

The easiest way to specify a 1-2-3 range, and the one least likely to result in mistakes, is to use the worksheet cursor to point to the range.

Lotus' Marvelous, One-Size-Fits-All Expanding Cursor

Lotus has a powerful feature for specifying ranges. When you are prompted for a range, one corner of the range is usually anchored or tacked to the active cell. This cell is called the *anchor cell*. The other end of the range, the *free cell*, is free to move. The free cell is easy to spot because it contains a flashing underline character. You can use the cursor control commands to stretch the cursor over the range of cells that you want to specify. You can also use the commands that move the cursor from sheet to sheet such as **CTRL-PGDN** to stretch the cursor across the sheets in a stack.

When you first press a cursor movement key, 1-2-3 shifts into Point mode. As you use the cursor movement keys to expand the range, all the cells in the range are highlighted in reverse video so you can see exactly what you have chosen. This visual display of the expanding cursor minimizes errors in specifying ranges. (See Figure 3–4.)

As the cursor expands, the second cell address, the free or pointing cell, in the prompt changes. The first remains as the anchor cell. The address of the free cell changes as you move it around the worksheet with the cursor control commands. See the command line in Figure 3–4.

Stretching the Cursor

There are many ways to stretch the 1-2-3 cursor. Of the options available, the four arrow keys are most useful when the range you want to specify is small or when you want to make small adjustments to the size of a range.

In addition to these keys, you can stretch the cursor over a range by using any of the cursor movement keys listed in Tables 1–3, 1–4, and 1–5 in Chapter 1. Consult those tables to refresh your memory about all of your cursor movement options.

You can adjust the range until you have highlighted exactly the cells you want to include. Remember, however, that you cannot specify a range that extends beyond the current file.

Figure 3–4 Lotus' expanding cursor makes it easy to tell which cells are in a range by displaying them in reverse video. The Range Format Currency command prompt is **Enter range to format** and the range B8..D19 has been highlighted.

```
A:D19:  11.05                                                       POINT
Enter range to format: A:B8..A:D19

  A         A         B         C        D    E    F         G         H
 1
 2                            ACME
 3                       LEMONADE AND
 4                       HOT CIDER STAND
 5
 6                  SALES    EXPENSES   PROFIT   REMARKS
 7
 8   JANUARY        13.75       8.94     4.81   ONLY ONE BLIZZARD!!
 9   FEBRUARY       16.2        8.91     7.29   CIDER PRICE INCREASE
10   MARCH          10.01       5.71     4.30   RAIN!!!!
11   APRIL           7.2        2.88     4.32   USED UP CIDER CONCENTRATE
12   MAY             3.1        1.77     1.33   TOO MUCH SCHOOL. TOO MUCH RAIN.
13   JUNE           12.75       7.27     5.48   FIRST HEAT WAVE
14   JULY           17.8       10.15     7.65   4TH OF JULY
15   AUGUST         27.5       15.68    11.83   HOTTEST ON RECORD
16   SEPTEMBER       6.3        3.59     2.71   BACK TO SCHOOL: RAIN
17   OCTOBER         7.34       4.18     3.16   MORE RAIN
18   NOVEMBER       15.75       8.98     6.77   FIRST GOOD SNOWS
19   DECEMBER       25.7       14.65    11.05   WORKING FOR CHRISTMAS
20
31-Dec-89 10:23 AM
```

When you finish specifying a range, press the **ENTER** key; the range is accepted. If you are specifying a range for a Range command, the ENTER key also causes the command to execute.

Tacking Down the Cursor

Several 1-2-3 keys have special functions when you are expanding the cursor. When you enter a Range command, the position of the active cell is usually where you want the anchor cell to be. Thus, 1-2-3 automatically anchors the range to this cell.

In some situations you don't want the active cell to be a corner of the range. This is particularly true of the built-in functions, and, therefore, the active cell is not anchored. When you first enter Point mode with a built-in function, the cursor is free to move around the worksheet, but it doesn't stretch over a range. When you have positioned the active cell at one corner of a desired range, tack it down by typing a period (.). (Think of the dot as the *point* of a tack.)

Untacking the Cursor

If you don't like where the anchor cell has been tacked, you can untack it any time by pressing the **ESC** key. This has two effects. The range shrinks back to the location of the anchor cell, and the anchor cell is untacked. You are still in Point mode where you are free to move the active cell around the screen or through the current file with the cursor control commands. When you get to a cell that you want to make one corner of the range, anchor the worksheet cursor to it by typing a period (.) there. Then use the cursor control keys to expand the cursor to point to the range.

Canceling Proposed Ranges

If you have expanded the cursor and wish to cancel it, or you wish to cancel a range proposed by any 1-2-3 command such as the Print command, press either the **ESC** key (as just described) or the **BKSP** key.

When you press the **BKSP** key, the proposed range disappears, and the worksheet cursor is positioned on the active cell. This is the cell that contained the worksheet cursor immediately before you entered the command. In many situations it is in a different location than the anchor cell of the proposed range. After you press **BKSP**, the active cell won't be tacked down, and you are free to move it with the cursor commands. When it is in the right spot, tack it by typing a period and proceed to expand the cursor.

When you press the **ESC** key, the proposed range disappears and the worksheet cursor is positioned on the anchor cell of the proposed range. This may be a quite different location from where the **BKSP** key positions the cursor, which is where the cursor was before entering the command. Again you can reposition the cursor, tack it down with the period, and proceed to highlight a new range.

When canceling a proposed range, decide where you want to begin pointing. Choose the **ESC** key when you want the anchor cell; choose the **BKSP** key when you want the active cell.

Moving the Anchor Cell

Once a range has been expanded into a rectangle or a block, you can continue to expand the range in only a few directions from the free cell. This can be frustrating when a particular situation calls for expanding the range in one of the other directions.

To solve this problem, press the period key. Each time you press it, the anchor cell moves to another corner of the range. Moving the anchor cell repositions the free cell, and once it is repositioned, you can use the arrow keys to expand the range in a different direction. The anchor cell usually moves clockwise, though the actual direction depends on how the range was specified.

You can also use this technique of moving the anchor cell as a way to view the corners of a rectangular range that is too large to fit on the screen. This is particularly useful for verifying correct print ranges and other proposed ranges.

COMMANDS COMMON TO RANGE AND WORKSHEET

Now that you know how to specify a range, you are ready to learn how to use 1-2-3's Range commands. You'll begin with the commands that are common to both the Range and Worksheet commands. They are

Format	Changes the appearance of cells on the screen and on a printout.
Label	Changes the alignment of existing labels.
Erase	Erases a range of cells.

Format

Most Range Format commands modify the display of numeric information in the designated range. The Text and Hidden formats change the display of both label and value cells. As noted, setting a Range Format overrides the Global Format setting for that range of cells. See Figure 3–5 for the Range Format command tree.

With the exception of Reset, the options available under the Range Format command are the same as those available under the Worksheet Global Format command listed in Table 2–1 in Chapter 2. The Reset command cancels any Range Format assigned to the range and returns display to the control of the Global Format currently in force. If no format has been set globally, the default Global format, General, is used.

The Range Format commands customize the different cells on a worksheet to display their contents in the clearest, most accurate manner. You format cells containing dollar amounts with the Currency format. Format cells containing percentages with the Percent format. Use the Date format to display cells containing Date functions in a readable form (such as 4-June-90).

Use the Other Automatic format to prepare the formats in a range of cells to adjust automatically to the type of entry made into the cells. Remember that as soon as an entry is made into an Automatic format cell, 1-2-3 assigns the appropriate range format to that cell.

Figure 3-5   Range Format command tree.

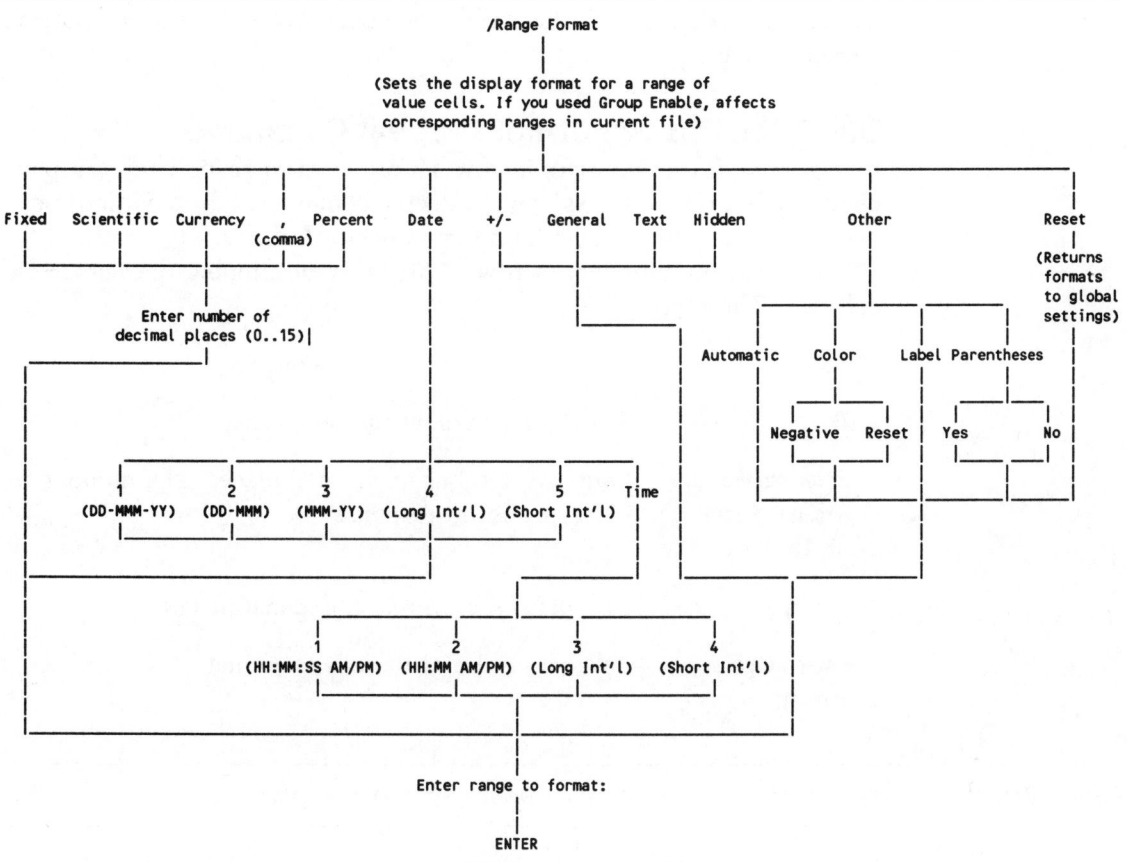

Finally, it is important to remember that when Group is enabled formatting a range of cells on one sheet in a stack automatically assigns the range format to the corresponding cells on all of the sheets in the current file. Be careful because enabling Group causes the range formats from the current sheet to be automatically imposed on corresponding cells on all the sheets in the current file. Unformatted cells in the current sheet are treated as Range Format Reset cells and *reset* the corresponding cells on all other sheets to the default format!

Selecting Commands

As with all 1-2-3 commands, you can select a format choice by speed typing, using only the first letter of the choice, such as **/RFF** for Range Format Fixed. You can also position the command line cursor over your format choice, press **ENTER**, then respond to the prompts.

LOTUS 1-2-3 RELEASE 3

Use the first letter or speed typing method for commands you are familiar with. Use the slower point-and-shoot method for commands that you are less familiar with, because it slows the process down so you can consider each step.

Using the Range Format Percent Command

In Figure 3–6 the numbers in row 12 are hard to read. They are percentages, but they are displayed in decimal equivalent form without percent signs and with varying numbers of decimal places.

To format the numbers in row 6, begin by positioning the cursor on cell B12. Then type

/RF	Enters the Range Format command.
P	Selects the Percent format.
Enter number of decimal places (0..15): 2	Requests number of decimal places. The number 2 is the proposed response.
ENTER	Accepts the proposed 2 decimal places.
Enter range format:	Asks you to point to cells to format.

Figure 3–6 Worksheet with percentages in row 12 displayed as decimals.

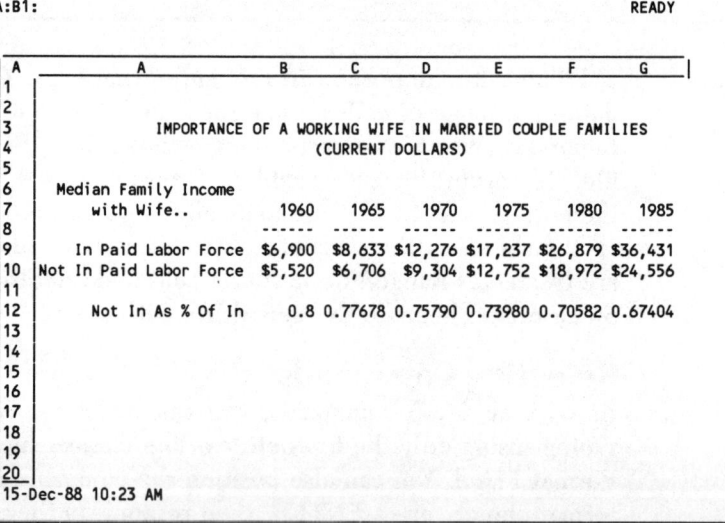

THE RANGE COMMANDS

END RIGHT   Stretches cursor to cell G12 at right end of the row of numbers.

ENTER   Executes the command and formats cells B12..G12 to Percent, 2 decimal places.

Figure 3-7 shows the result of your work with the format command. A working wife certainly is an asset!

The Range Format Command and the Status Line

The status line at the top of the screen displays the Range Format status for the currently active cell. In Figure 3-7 **(P2)** appears on the status line to indicate that cell B12 has been formatted to Percent, two decimal places. A Fixed format, two decimals would display **(F2)**; a Currency format with zero decimals, **(C0)**; the Hidden format, **(H)**, and the Other Automatic format **(A)**. However, when the Automatic format is set, 1-2-3 automatically assigns the appropriate range format as soon as an entry occurs. For example, entering $35.98 automatically converts the cell format to **(C2)**.

Changing Formats

There are two ways to change a range format once it has been assigned to a cell. You can either reformat the cell with a new format or use the Reset option to cancel range formatting for the designated cell or range of cells. When you use Reset the cells return to the control of the Global

---

Figure 3-7   Range Format Percent with two decimals applied to row 12.

```
A:B12: (P2) 0.8                                                    POINT

        A              A         B       C       D       E       F       G

   1
   2
   3              IMPORTANCE OF A WORKING WIFE IN MARRIED COUPLE FAMILIES
   4                                 (CURRENT DOLLARS)
   5
   6       Median Family Income
   7           with Wife..         1960    1965    1970    1975    1980    1985
   8                              ------  ------  ------  ------  ------  ------
   9        In Paid Labor Force  $6,900  $8,633 $12,276 $17,237 $26,879 $36,431
  10    Not In Paid Labor Force  $5,520  $6,706  $9,304 $12,752 $18,972 $24,556
  11
  12         Not In As % Of In   80.00%  77.68%  75.79%  73.98%  79.58%  67.40%
  13
  14
  15
  16
  17
  18
  19
  20
15-Dec-88 10:28 AM
```

Format setting. If no Global Format has been set, the Global Default format (General) is used.

Label

Lotus 1-2-3's Range Label command and the Worksheet Global Label command work in opposite ways. The Worksheet command only affects labels entered after you use the command. It has no effect on existing labels. The Range command changes only the label-prefix of those cells in the range that already contain labels. It has no effect on labels subsequently entered into these or other cells in the range. Their alignment is governed by the label-prefix set at the global level. See Figure 3–8 for the command tree.

The Range Label command performs a "mass edit" on the labels in the specified range in the current file. If, for example, you select centered, the command replaces the existing label alignment characters with the circumflex, the center label alignment character.

Use the Range Label command whenever you want to realign existing labels. This is best done after all the labels in a range have been entered. Otherwise, you have to reset the label-prefix several times. If you find that you want most of your labels to be right aligned or center aligned use the Worksheet command to change the default alignment of labels yet to be entered.

Like the Range Format commands, when Group is enabled, using the Range Label command simultaneously changes the label alignment char-

Figure 3–8 Range Label command tree.

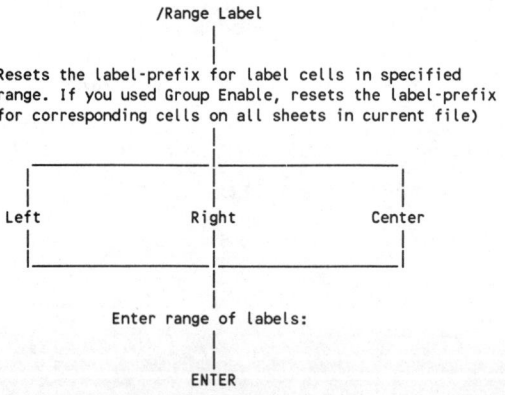

THE RANGE COMMANDS

acter in all of the corresponding cells on all sheets in the current file. However, unlike formatted cells, the label alignments of cells in the current worksheet are not imposed on corresponding cells in other worksheets when Group is enabled.

Erase

The Worksheet Erase and the Range Erase commands work quite differently. Recall that the Worksheet Erase command erases the entire stack and resets all formats, label-alignments, column widths, range names, and remembered print ranges, and so on, to their default values. You get a single, clean worksheet with the Worksheet Erase command.

The Range Erase command is less sweeping in its actions. It only erases text or values from designated worksheet cells in the current file. It does not change the format setting or the column width nor can you extend its action across active files. It does, of course, wipe out the label-alignment character because that is part of each label. The Erase command isn't affected by the Group command. So even when you use Group Enable, the only cells erased are those you specify. See Figure 3–9 for the command tree.

Think of the Range Erase command as the eraser on your electronic pencil. Use it to clean up a worksheet by removing incorrect or unneeded information.

CAUTION

Beware: As with all 1-2-3 Range commands, 1-2-3 does not ask you to confirm your intention to erase a range once you have specified it. Pressing

Figure 3–9 Range Erase command tree.

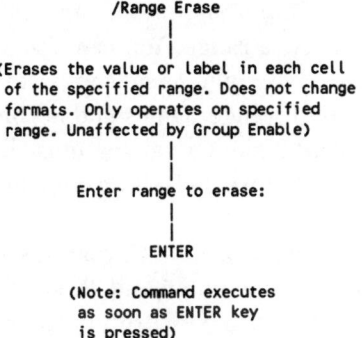

ENTER after choosing a range executes Range Erase, and the contents of the cells in the range are immediately erased.

If Undo is active, you can press **ALT-F4** to restore the worksheet—provided you have taken no action on the worksheet since erasing the range. However, if Undo is not active, the contents of the range are gone forever.

COMMANDS UNIQUE TO RANGE

Eight Range commands have no counterparts in the Worksheet command:

Name	Assigns names to cells.
Justify	Reformats long text entries into paragraphs.
Prot	Reverses Unprotection.
Unprot	Overrides the Global Protection Enable command, allowing entry into unprotected cells.
Input	Creates data entry forms.
Value	Copies displayed values.
Transpose	Copies and transposes rows and columns.
Search	Finds and/or replaces strings in labels and/or formulas.

Name

The most useful of the eight unique Range commands is the Name command. With it you can assign a name to a range of cells. Once assigned, the name can be used in *any* situation—command, formula, or built-in function—where you can use a range. You can also add explanatory notes (up to 512 characters) to each range name and write to an unused portion of your worksheet a table of range names and accompanying notes. Like the other Range commands, named ranges must be contained entirely within the current file. See Figure 3–10 for a command summary of Range Name.

Range names are particularly useful in situations where you must specify different ranges for the same command. A good example is the Print command. As you work with 1-2-3, you print different parts of a worksheet (or sheets in a stack) for different purposes. A summary section might, for

THE RANGE COMMANDS

Figure 3–10   Range Name command tree.

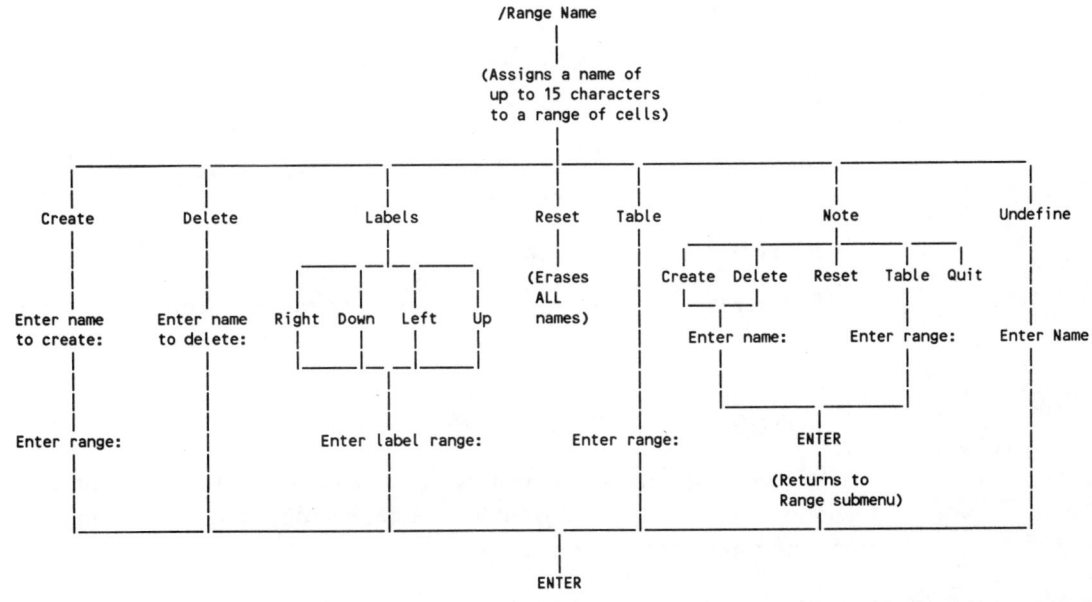

example, go to the office manager, whereas a detailed report goes to accounting. You can name the summary range SUMMARY and the detailed range DETAIL, and when you have to make a printout, simply specify SUMMARY or DETAIL as the range, and leave the rest to 1-2-3.

If you are creating a worksheet that you or someone else may have to modify, you can assign names to ranges so a summation function, for example, reads @SUM(COST) rather than @SUM(B4..B8). With names rather than range references, it is easier to grasp the structure of a worksheet, and, hence, to correct or modify it.

The range name HELP can be used in conjunction with text on your worksheet to create spreadsheet-specific help messages. These messages can contain instructions about using the spreadsheet or information about sources required to update it. To create your own help messages, place the text in an out-of-the-way place or on a separate sheet. Then assign the name HELP to a cell at the beginning of the text. When you want help, press the **GOTO/F5** key and supply the name HELP. When you press **ENTER**, 1-2-3 moves the worksheet cursor to the designated cell and displays your custom help messages.

Assigning Names to Range

To create a range name move the cursor to the cell you want to name or to the first cell if you are naming a range and type

/RN	Enters the Range Name command.
C	Selects Create.
Enter name:	Enter the name you want to use, up to 15 characters.
ENTER	Accepts name.
Enter range:	Stretch the cursor over range of cells to be named. (Or press **ENTER** to assign name to single cell under cursor.)
ENTER	Completes the command.

When naming ranges, you can use any valid 1-2-3 character, but upper- and lowercase letters are treated interchangeably. Thus Sales and **SALES** are the same name to 1-2-3.

Limitations on Range Names

When selecting a range name don't use one such as "FY88," "A1," or "A1..A10," which could be confused with a cell address or range specification. If you do assign a name like FY88 to a cell such as GF36 and then use FY88 in a command or function, 1-2-3 won't know whether you are referring to cell FY88 or to the cell named FY88. Lotus resolves this dilemma by assuming that anything in the form of a cell address *is* a cell address.

Also, don't include the characters +, *, -, /, &, >, <, @, and # in range names. Lotus accepts range names that contain these characters, but because the characters have special meaning in formulas and functions, using them in range names often leads to incorrect results. And don't create range names that begin with a number, such as 25NOV, because you can't include a range name that begins with a number in a formula. Finally, you can use the blank character in range names. However, make it a habit to use either the dash or the underline in place of a blank (for example, TOTAL_COST). Avoid using blanks, because it is easy to incorrectly specify names containing spaces.

Range names must also be unique in each file. You can, however, overlap ranges that are assigned different names, and you can assign different names to the same cells. The same range name can be used on different files in a stack. References to identical range names can be made as long as the filename precedes the reference. If you use the **NAME/F3** key, discussed later in the chapter, to paste range names into formulas and functions, 1-2-3 automatically supplies the required path and filename for any range names outside the current file.

If you assign an already-assigned name to a new range of cells, the new cells are used in any formula, function, or command that previously used the range name.

Unlike their actions in previous releases of 1-2-3, range names are *not* automatically substituted for cell references in existing functions. Cell references continue to be used in existing functions, even though a range name has been assigned to those cells. Also, unlike previous versions of 1-2-3, when you assign a new name to a previously named range, both the old and new names apply to the range. The old range name still exists, and you can continue to use it. Furthermore, formulas and functions using the old name continue to use it instead of converting to the new name, as they did in earlier versions.

Range names used in functions are treated as relative cell addresses. Thus, when a formula containing a range name is copied from one location to another, the reference represented by the range name changes. To use a range name as an absolute reference in a formula precede the range name with a dollar sign. Thus, in @SUM(SALES), SALES is a relative reference to the range named SALES while in @SUM($SALES) it is an absolute reference. If the formula containing a range name has already been entered into a cell you must edit the formula to include the dollar signs that represent absolute references. (For the importance of the distinction between absolute and relative cell references, see the Copy command in Chapter 4.)

Choosing Good Range Names

The best range names are either logically related to their function (such as the DETAIL and SUMMARY examples), or they are taken directly from labels on the worksheet. The best name for a group of cells in a row labeled "Labor Cost" is LABOR_COST. This is much better than VARIABLE1 or some other less descriptive name.

Using the NAME/F3 Function Key

The major problem with range names is that you are likely to forget them. But don't worry. Lotus has a memory an elephant would envy.

Whenever you need to specify a name in response to a slash command prompt or as part of a formula or function, 1-2-3 switches to Point mode. You can then press the **NAME/F3** function key and all the range names you have assigned on the current worksheet appear on the bottom line of the control panel.

The range names are presented in alphabetical order, regardless of the order in which they were created, but only four names fit on a line at one time. You can use the arrow keys and the **HOME** and **END** keys to move the command line cursor through all the names. The **UP** and **DOWN** arrow keys move the cursor one line up or down in the name list and the **HOME** and **END** keys move the cursor to the first and last names in the list, respectively. See Figure 3–11 for a diagram of how the arrow keys work with a list of names.

Instead of using the arrow keys, press the **NAME/F3** key a second time. When you do, the worksheet screen is replaced with a full-screen display of all assigned range names. See Figure 3–12. Use the arrow keys to move the highlight to the desired range name, then press **ENTER** to paste it into the command, formula, or function.

Figure 3–11 Only one row of four names can be displayed at one time on the prompt line in the control panel.
Source: *Lotus 1-2-3 Manual* (Boston, Mass.: Lotus Development Corporation, 1983), p. 61.

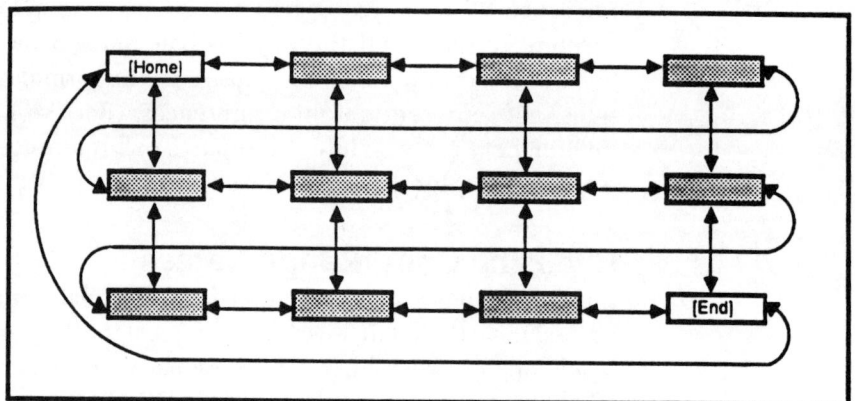

Figure 3–12 Range names from worksheet in Figure 3–13 appear at the top of the screen when Range Name Create is selected.

```
A:A18:  [W21]                                           NAMES
Enter name:
     INTEREST_PAID         B14..D14
     INTEREST_PAID    PRINCIPLE         RATE           WITHDRAWAL
```

Pasting Names Across Files

When you use the **NAME/F3** key to paste range names into formulas and functions, the names of other active files are displayed in file reference format such as <<BUDGET.WK3>>. If the file hasn't been saved, it is designated as <<>>. To use a range name in a file that isn't the current file, highlight its name and press **ENTER**. A list of names in the file then appears. Select the desired range name and press **ENTER**. When the range name is pasted into the formula the full path to the file is included. This establishes a link to the file that supplies information regardless of whether both files are in memory at the same time again.

Assigning Notes to Range Names

Once a range name has been created, you can use the Range Name Note command to add a note (up to 512 characters) to the range name. Notes can be used to tell when the data in the range was entered, who entered it, or where it came from.

The Range Name Note command has four options:

Create	Attaches a note to a range name or edits an existing note.
Delete	Deletes a note.
Reset	Deletes *all* notes in the current file.
Table	Lists the range names and the range name notes in the current file.

Beware of the Reset option. It wipes out all notes in the current file as soon as you press **R** to select it. If you are using Undo (you press **ALT-F4**), you can restore the notes. Otherwise, they are lost. Because of this danger, use the Delete option to remove notes one at a time.

To add a note to a range name, type

/RN	Enters the Range Name command.
N	Selects Note from the menu.
Select Range Name:	Highlight the desired range name or name of other active file to view range names in that file.
ENTER	Selects range name. Type note (up to 512 characters) or edit existing note.
ENTER	Completes command and returns to Ready mode.

Unlike during normal label entry, the control panel doesn't expand when you are entering or editing a note assigned to a range name. If your label is too long to display at one time on the entry line, 1-2-3 scrolls it off of the screen.

Creating a Table of Range Names and Notes

The Table option under the Range Name Note command directs 1-2-3 to write a table to spreadsheet cells listing each range name in the current file, the cell addresses assigned to the range, and any notes you have added to the names. A similar command, Range Name Table, works in exactly the same way except that it omits the notes assigned to the range names.

To get a table of the range names, cell addresses, and notes used in the worksheet in Figure 3-13, type

/RNN	Enters the Range Name Note command.
T	Selects Table.
Enter Range:	Move cursor to A20, the upper left of a blank, three-column-wide area.
ENTER	Executes command.

When the command executes, 1-2-3 writes a three-column table; two columns consist of range names and cell addresses, and the third lists the notes attached to the range name. (See Figure 3-14.) Lotus writes over the cells so be sure you have sufficient room available for the table—three columns and as many rows as range names. If you only want to table the

---

Figure 3-13 Worksheet with cells B5..B7 assigned range names.

	A	B	C	D
1				
2				
3	ASSUMPTIONS			
4				
5	PRINCIPAL	$1,000.00		
6	RATE	10.00%		
7	WITHDRAWAL	$100.00		
8				
9				
10				
11		PERIOD 1	PERIOD 2	PERIOD 3
12	Principal	$1,000.00	$990.00	$979.00
13	Withdrawal	$100.00	$100.00	$100.00
14	Interest	$90.00	$89.00	$87.90
15	Balance Forward	$990.00	$979.00	$966.90
16				
17	TOTAL INTEREST PAID:	$266.90		
18				
19				
20				

THE RANGE COMMANDS

Figure 3-14   Table in cells A20 to C23 of range names, their corresponding cell addresses, and notes from the worksheet in Figure 3-13.

```
   A           A              B          C          D
 1
 2
 3            ASSUMPTIONS
 4
 5         PRINCIPAL      $1,000.00
 6              RATE         10.00%
 7        WITHDRAWAL       $100.00
 8
 9
10
11                         PERIOD 1    PERIOD 2   PERIOD 3
12         Principal      $1,000.00    $990.00    $979.00
13        Withdrawal       $100.00     $100.00    $100.00
14          Interest         $90.00     $89.00     $87.90
15     Balance Forward     $990.00     $979.00    $966.90
16
17  TOTAL INTEREST PAID:   $266.90
18
19
20  RATE                   A:B6..A:B6    From Wall Street Journal.
21  INTEREST_PAID          A:B14..A:D14  Interest paid over all periods.
22  PRINCIPAL              A:B5..A:B5    Enter current balance.
23  WITHDRAWAL             A:B7..A:B7    Per period withdrawal.
24
25
```

range names and their cell address, use the above steps but type **/RNT** to enter the Range Name Table command.

Using Range Names in Commands

Range names can be used with any 1-2-3 command or function that requires you to specify range or cell address. For example, if you have a range named Help on your spreadsheet or on another sheet in the stack, you can move the cursor to the upper left cell of the range by typing

GOTO/F5	Press the F5 function key; enters the Goto command.
Enter cell address to go to:	Either type **Help** and press **ENTER** or press the **NAME/F3** key.
NAME/F3	Press the F3 function key; displays range names.
NAME/F3	Optional second press of the **NAME/F3** key. When you do, all range names are displayed on the screen at one time.
Arrow keys	Highlight the range named **Help**.

ENTER	Selects Help and executes the Goto command.

Viewing Names with Range Name Create

To view the ranges to which names have been assigned, enter the Range Name Create command. When you do, the range names in the current file are displayed, along with the names of other active files. If the list is more than four names long, use the arrow keys to view the names or press the **NAME/F3** key to display all of the range names at one time. When you highlight one of the range names, the name and the range of cells to which it is assigned appear at the top of the screen. (Refer again to Figure 3–12.)

To actually see the cells assigned to a particular range name, go one step further in the Name Create command. Select the name you are interested in, and 1-2-3 highlights the cells assigned to that name. If part of the range is off the screen, press the period key. The anchor cell moves from corner to corner to display the entire range. If the range extends across sheets, pressing the period key only moves the cursor from corner to corner on the first sheet specified.

When you have finished reviewing the range, press **ENTER** to accept it and to exit the command. Alternatively, you can press the **ESC** key the required number of times or press the **CTRL-BREAK** combination to cancel the Range Name command and return to the Ready mode.

Assigning Names with Range Name Label

So far you've assigned range names by directly entering the characters you wanted to use for the range name, but often you may prefer to use labels entered into spreadsheet cells to name adjacent spreadsheet cells. To do this, use 1-2-3's Range Name Label command.

In Figure 3–13, for example, you can use the labels in column A, PRINCIPAL, RATE, and WITHDRAWAL, as names for the cells containing the parameters in column B.

To use the Range Name Label command on the worksheet in Figure 3–13, move the cursor to cell A5 and type

/RN	Enters the Range Name command.
L	Selects Label.
Right Down **Left Up**	Asks for the direction of the cells to be named relative to the cells containing the labels.
R	Selects Right, because cells containing parameters are to the right of cells containing the labels.

THE RANGE COMMANDS

Enter label range:	Asks for range containing labels to be used as range names.
END DOWN	Stretches cursor down to A7.
ENTER	Executes the command and assigns the text in A5, A6, and A7 as range names to the cells B5, B6, and B7.

Using Names in Formulas

As noted, unlike previous releases of the program, 1-2-3 Release 3 does not automatically substitute range names for the corresponding cell references in existing formulas. If you want a range name to appear in a formula or function, you must either type it or use the **NAME/F3** key to paste it into the desired formula or function. However, you can substitute a range name for cell references in existing formulas or functions by using the Range Search command discussed later in this chapter to search for the cell references and replace them with the appropriate range name.

A range name not assigned to a range of cells is called an *undefined range name*. If an undefined range name is used in a formula 1-2-3 accepts the formula but displays **ERR** until you use the Range Name Create or Range Name Label command to assign the name to a range. If an existing range name is undefined with the Range Name Undefine command, the formula also displays **ERR** until the name is reassigned to a range.

Figure 3–15 shows the formulas behind the table in Figure 3–14. The names in the formulas make the formulas easier to understand. Note the use of the name INTEREST_PAID in the @SUM formula. This name combines two words with the underline character.

See the discussion of the Copy command in Chapter 4 for special considerations when you are copying formulas containing named ranges.

Removing Range Names and Notes

Use the Range Name Delete command to remove both range names and any accompanying notes. Use the Range Name Note Delete command to remove only notes from range names.

To remove the range name RATE from the table in Figure 3–15, type

/RN	Enters the Range Name command.
D	Selects Delete. The first four range names are displayed on the bottom line of the control panel.
Arrow keys	Highlight the range name RATE.
ENTER	Deletes the range name RATE.

Figure 3-15 Range names make the formulas used to construct Figure 3-13 easier to understand.

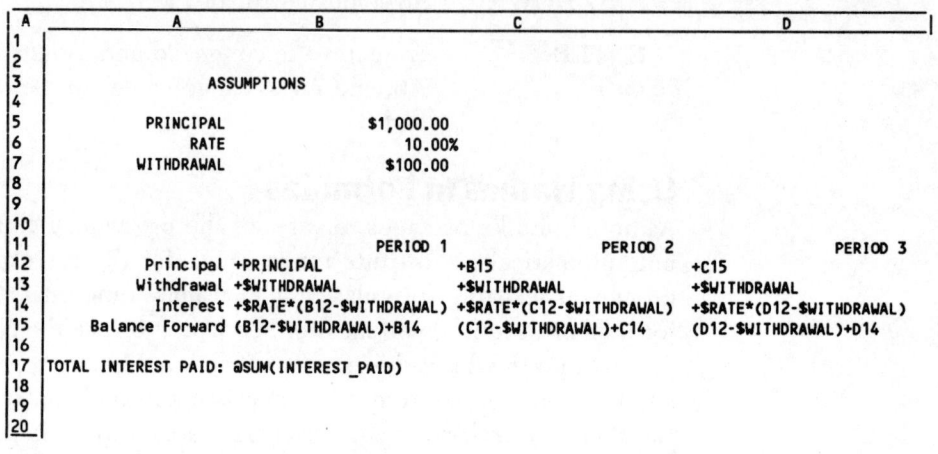

If you know the exact name of the range you want to delete, you can type it in. Otherwise, use the arrow keys to highlight the desired range name. You can also press the **NAME/F3** key to cause the entire list of range names in the current file and the filenames of other active files to appear on the screen at one time. Then highlight the range name you want to delete and press **ENTER**. To delete a name in another active file, highlight the filename and press **ENTER** to see the named ranges in the file.

To eliminate all of the names on a worksheet in the current file, use the Name Reset command. But be careful. This is a dangerous command, because 1-2-3 erases all range names in the current file the moment you select the Reset option by either typing the first letter of the command, **R**, or by positioning the command line cursor over it and pressing **ENTER**. You don't get a chance to reconsider your choice, so before you use the Reset option, be sure you really want to erase *all* the range names. You can, however, use the Undo command, **ALT-F4**, to restore reset range names as long as the Undo command is active and you haven't done anything since you reset the range names.

When you eliminate a range name, 1-2-3 automatically substitutes appropriate cell references in any functions, formulas, or remembered ranges that used the range name. Figure 3-16 shows the functions behind the cells under Period 1 of Figure 3-15 after the Name Reset command has been used. Note that full sheet designations are substituted for the range names.

Figure 3-16 When a range name is deleted, cell addresses replace the name in all formulas, functions, and remembered names. Here, formulas behind Figure 3-15 display after the Range Reset command is issued.

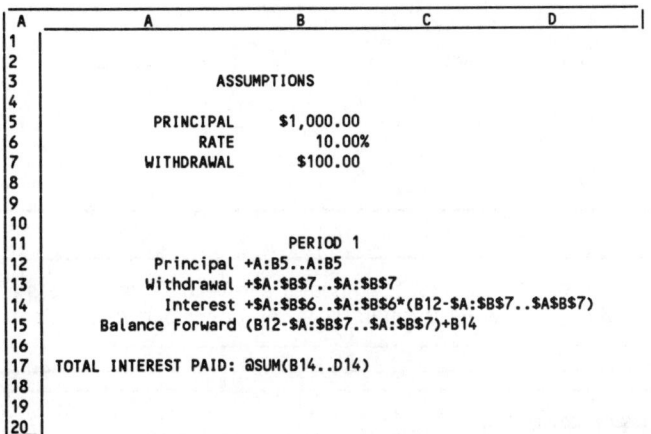

Range Undefine

The Range Undefine command creates an undefined range name by breaking the link between a range name and the cells assigned to it. The range name continues to exist, but it is not associated with a particular group of cells. When an undefined range name is used in a formula, **ERR** displays on the screen until the range name is redefined with either the Range Name Create or Range Name Labels command.

Justify

The Range Justify command is 1-2-3's word processor. With it you can easily add a few paragraphs of explanatory text to a worksheet, write a short memo, or do column oriented word processing. It isn't *WordPerfect,*® but it isn't bad. (See Figure 3-17 for the Range Justify command tree.)

What the Range Justify command does is to reformat long labels into paragraphs. With it you can enter text, up to 512 characters in a single cell, and then reformat the text into a width that looks best on the screen or the printed page.

Lotus begins justifying text at the first cell in the column and continues until it reaches the first nonlabel cell. In practice, this is usually a blank cell, although it can be a value cell or a cell with a string function in it.

Figure 3–17   Range Justify command tree.

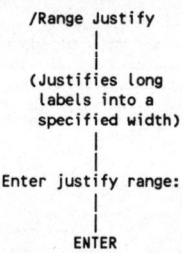

Figure 3–18   The text for the first few lines of the Gettysburg Address are entered as long labels in cells B4 through B7 in the upper part of the figure.

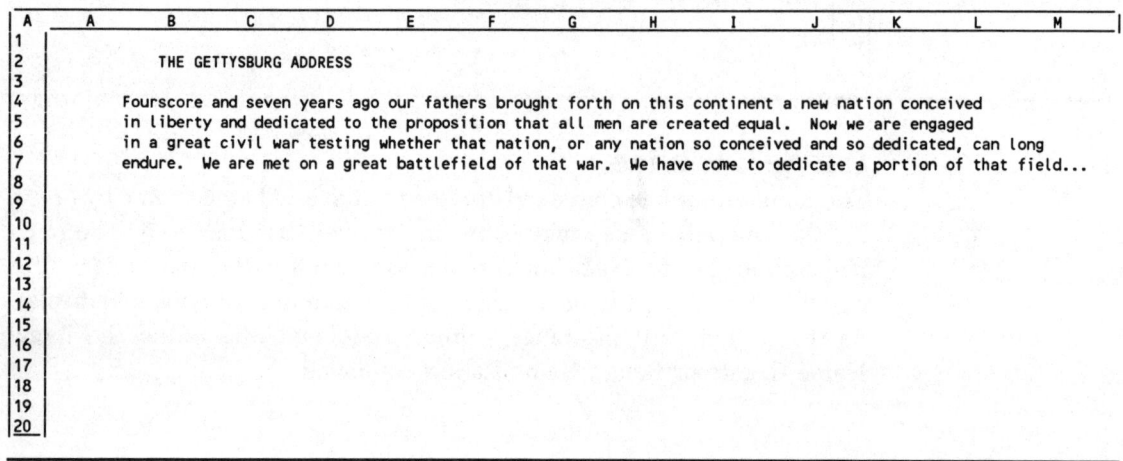

To understand how the Justify command works, look at Figure 3–18, which displays the first part of Abraham Lincoln's Gettysburg Address. It would have been easy for Lincoln to get his ideas down quickly by letting Lotus' soft cell boundaries display characters to the right of each cell in column B. Once the text has been composed, it would look better on the screen and be easier to read if it were justified over just four or five columns.

To justify the Gettysburg Address, position the worksheet cursor on the first text cell in the column (B4 in this case) and type

/RJ   Enters the Range Justify command.

Enter justify range: Asks for desired width in columns.

THE RANGE COMMANDS

RIGHT	Press the **RIGHT** arrow key three times. Cursor expands from B4 to E4.
ENTER	Executes command and justifies text in column B into the combined width of columns B through E.

The justified text appears in Figure 3–19. You can repeat the process with different ranges of columns to widen or narrow the paragraph.

There are two ways to specify the range to justify. Learn both, because each produces a different effect.

Single Row Justify Range

In the preceding example the justify range was specified as a range of cells B4..E4. This range is *one* row deep. This technique is appropriate when the cells below the text cells in column B are either empty or contain additional paragraphs of text. In this case, 1-2-3 adjusts entries down the spreadsheet as needed, moving them up or down when necessary.

However, if there is something below the text that you are justifying, such as a table that you want to remain unmoved, you must use the next technique of specifying the justify range. In particular, be careful when the Justify command moves formulas farther down the worksheet. Cell addresses in the formulas are likely to change in ways that invalidate the formulas.

Multiple Row Justify Range

When the text is justified down the screen in response to a single row justify range, the text writes over the first part of the table. None of the

Figure 3–19 Text for Figure 3–18 justified with the Range Justify command.

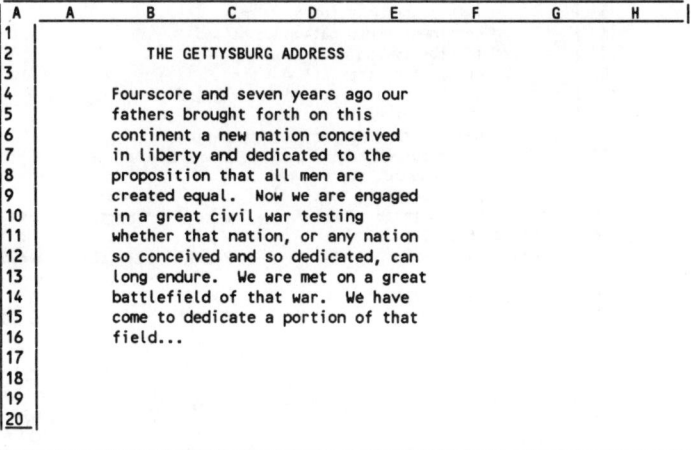

contents of the cells in the table are destroyed, but the table is confusing and difficult to read. See Figure 3–20 for the effect of the Range Justify command when there is information in rows below the text to be justified.

Had the text been in column A, the row labels in the table would have been shifted down the spreadsheet by the action of the Range Justify command.

To prevent the intermixing of different parts of your worksheet or the movement of the contents of cells farther down the spreadsheet, specify the justify range as a rectangle of cells rather than as a single row.

Just as before, the width of the rectangle determines the width of the justified text. But now the number of rows in the rectangle determines the number of rows into which text can be justified.

This method has the important benefit of preventing justified text from moving material below it. Consequently, the multiple-row method is the safest way to specify the justify range.

If the area specified is too small to contain all the justified text in the specified width, Lotus gives the error message:

Justify range is full or line too long

Don't worry. When you respond by pressing **ENTER** or **ESC**, as much text as possible is justified. Only the last few lines remain unjustified. In

---

Figure 3–20   Justified text intermingles with other spreadsheet text.
Source, casualties: *The World Almanac and Book of Facts 1983* (New York: Newspaper Enterprise Association, Inc., 1983), p. 337.

```
    A        B         C         D            E         F          G        H
1
2              THE GETTYSBURG ADDRESS
3
4              Fourscore and seven years ago our
5              fathers brought forth on this
6              continent a new nation conceived
7              in liberty and dedicated to the
8              proposition that all men are
9              created equal.  Now we are engaged
10             in a great civil war testing
11             whether that nation, or any nation
12             so conceived and so dediCIVIL WAR CASUALTIES
13             long endure.  We are met on a
14             great battlef Battle    Other     Wounds
15             have come to  Deaths    Deaths    not Mortal   Total
16  UNION FORthat field...
17    1861-1865           140,414   224,097   281,881      646,392
18
19  CONFEDERATE FORCES
20    1863-1866            74,524    59,297      ---       133,821
21
22
23
24
25
```

Figure 3–21, for example, the justify range, B4..B10, is too small, and the last four lines remain unjustified.

If the justified text won't fit, insert some rows and repeat the Justify command. Usually only one or two trial-and-error adjustments are required to arrive at a correctly justified block of text. See Figure 3–22 for the correctly justified result.

Word Processing with 1-2-3

You can use Lotus' soft cell boundaries and Range Justify command to place extended comments in your worksheets. You can also use 1-2-3 as a simple "memo" word processor by expanding the column width to the number of characters you wish to have on a line. A popular choice is 72 characters, because this is Lotus' default page width to print on 8½-inch-wide paper. It is also the width of a standard screen, so only one column appears on the screen at one time. When all of your text is in a single column, the justification operation is particularly easy to perform.

If your memo has more than one paragraph, use blank lines to separate the paragraphs. That way, 1-2-3 doesn't combine text from two paragraphs

Figure 3–21   When the justify range is a block of cells, 1-2-3 limits justification to the number of rows in the block. If room to justify the text is lacking, the last few lines of text remain unjustified.
Source, casualties: *The World Almanac and Book of Facts 1983* (New York: Newspaper Enterprise Association, Inc., 1983), p. 337.

```
      A       B        C        D         E        F         G         H         I         J        K
 1
 2                THE GETTYSBURG ADDRESS
 3
 4             Fourscore and seven years ago our
 5             fathers brought forth on this
 6             continent a new nation conceived
 7             in liberty and dedicated to the proposition that all men are created equal.  Now
 8             we are engaged in a great civil war testing whether that nation, or any nation so conceived
 9             and so dedicated, can long endure.  We are met on a great battlefield of that war.  We have
10             come to dedicate a portion of that field...
11
12                     CIVIL WAR CASUALTIES
13
14                          Battle    Other     Wounds
15                          Deaths    Deaths    not Mortal    Total
16      UNION FORCES
17        1861-1865         140,414   224,097   281,881       646,392
18
19      CONFEDERATE FORCES
20        1863-1866          74,524    59,297      ---        133,821
21
22
23
24
25
26
27
```

Figure 3–22 Using the Worksheet Insert Row command in conjunction with the Justify command to ensure that justified text and other material fit together properly. Source, casualties: *The World Almanac and Book of Facts 1983* (New York: Newspaper Enterprise Association, Inc., 1983), p. 337.

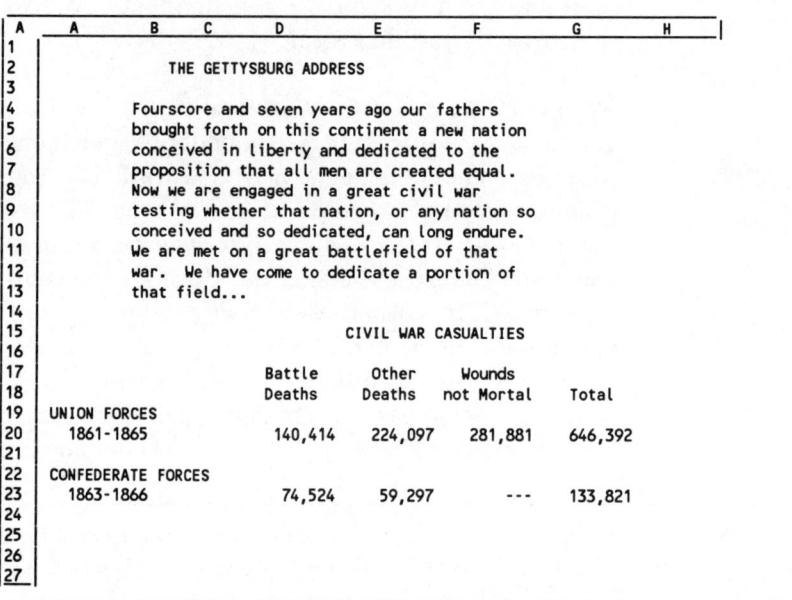

when it justifies columns. Also, if you specify the justify range as a single row, 1-2-3 moves the rest of the text in your memo up or down as required.

The Range Justify command and the Search command discussed in a following section are the only word processing features contained in Lotus 1-2-3. Still, the Justify command in conjunction with soft cell boundaries and the **EDIT/F2** key are adequate for short writing tasks.

Prot and Unprot

The Prot and Unprot commands work in conjunction with the Global Protection and the File Admin Seal commands. When you use Group Enable, these commands work exactly the same way as the Range Format commands discussed earlier. As soon as you enable Group, the Prot or Unprot status of cells in the current sheet is imposed on the corresponding cells on every sheet in the current file. Once Group is enabled, using the Prot and Unprot commands on the current sheet imposes the same action on corresponding cells on all other sheets in the stack.

The Prot ("Protect") Command

The operation of the Range Prot (short for "Protect") command may seem strange at first, because it is not possible to use the command to protect a range of cells! In fact, the Range Prot command is best thought of as an "Un-Unprotect" command, because its only function is to cancel the unprotection status conveyed with the Range Unprot command.

But protection is only reinstated with the Range Prot command when protection has already been enabled with the Worksheet Global Prot Enable command. Only when protection has been enabled can you use the Range Prot command to change a cell's status from unprotected to protected. See Figure 3–23 for the command tree.

The Unprot ("Unprotect") Command

The Range Unprot (short for "Unprotect") command prevents the Global Prot Enable command from locking up all the cells on your worksheet. Think of global protection as a sheet of plastic over your spreadsheet and think of the Range Unprot command as a pair of scissors to cut holes in that plastic. The command is also used to allow entry into specified cells in a sealed worksheet. (See the File Administration command in Chapter 5.)

You can use the command at any time, either before or after using the Global command. However, if you are planning to seal the worksheet, you must use the Range Unprot command before sealing the sheet. Unprotected cells in the current file don't need to be next to one another,

Figure 3–23 Range Prot and Unprot command tree.

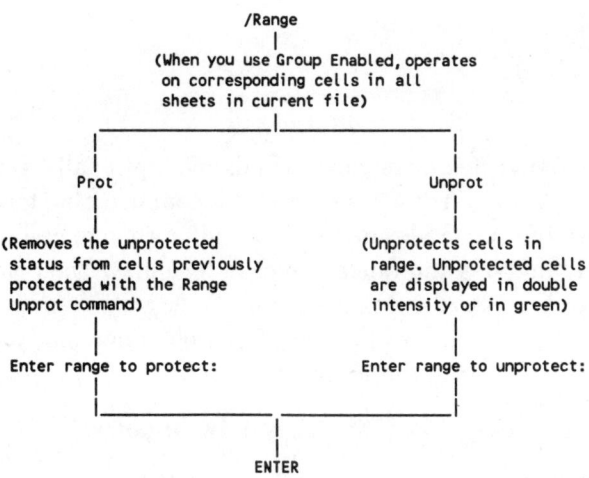

but you do have to enter the Range Unprot command separately for each nonadjacent range of cells.

The cells to unprotect are usually data entry cells where you enter new information during worksheet updates. Global protection prevents formulas and labels in all but the unprotected cells from being changed accidentally.

Once you unprotect a cell, its display changes. On monochrome monitors capable of displaying in two intensities, the contents of unprotected cells are displayed in bright characters. On color monitors, the contents of unprotected cells are displayed in green. In either case, the Status line displays a **U** when the active cell is unprotected.

Using Unprotected Cells on an Unprotected Worksheet

The difference in screen appearance of unprotected cells can be used to draw attention to particular cells on your worksheet. These cells might contain important results, titles, or instructions about the use of the spreadsheet. The green display on a color monitor is a particularly dramatic highlight. Remember that unless you have protected the entire worksheet with the Global Prot Enable command, the only effect of the Range Unprot command is to alter the appearance of the display.

Unprotected Cells and the Range Input Command

Finally, you can use the Input command described later in this chapter to limit cursor movement to only those cells in a specified range that have been unprotected. This makes the process of updating a protected worksheet even easier.

Search

The Range Search command finds and, optionally, replaces all occurrences of a specified string in a range. This command has obvious word processing uses, but it can also be used to find or change cell references in formulas and functions and range names in formulas. The command tree for Range Search appears in Figure 3–24.

When you select the Range Search command, you are presented with a menu offering the following choices:

Formulas   Searches only formulas.

Labels   Searches only labels.

THE RANGE COMMANDS

Figure 3–24 Range Search command tree.

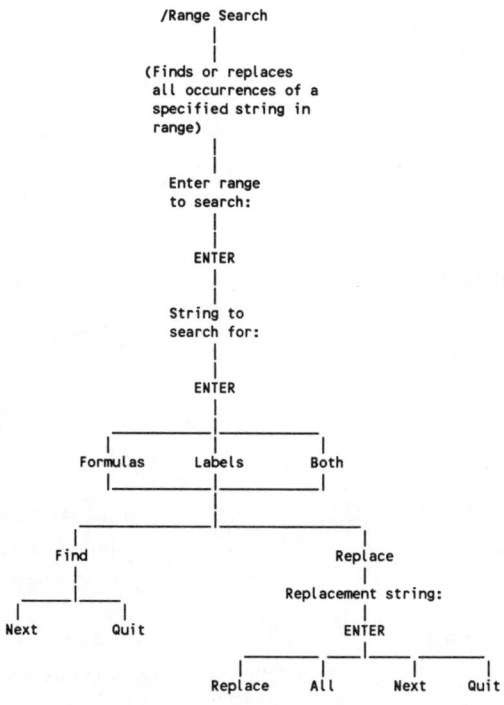

| Both | Searches both formulas and labels. |

Once you make a selection from this menu, you get to choose between Find and Replace. Find locates the next occurrence of the search string; Replace finds and, optionally, replaces the found string with a specified replacement.

If you want to replace the cell reference G35 with P15 in certain formulas on your worksheet, move the cursor to the upper left of the area containing the formulas and type

/RS	Enters the Range Search command.
Enter range to search:	Prompts for range to search. Use arrow keys to highlight range.
ENTER	Selects search range.
String to search for:	Prompts for search string.

G35 ENTER	Type text **G35** and press **ENTER** to accept.
Formulas Labels Both	Asks for location to search.
F	Selects Formulas.
Find Replace	Asks whether to Find only or Find and Replace.
R	Selects Replace.
Enter replace string:	Asks for string to replace.
P15	Replaces G35 as the new string.
ENTER	Accepts replace string. Cursor moves to first occurrence of G35.
Replace All Next Quit	Select Replace and G35 is replaced with P15; cursor moves to next occurrence.
String not found.	Message displayed after last occurrence of G35.

When a match is found, the cell content is displayed on the Status line with the matching string highlighted. Because you selected Replace, at the first occurrence of the search string you are given four choices. Choose the appropriate response. Your choices are

Replace	Replace occurrence and move to next occurrence.
Next	Move to next occurrence without replacing current occurrence.
All	Replace all occurrences. Use only when you are certain there are no occurrences of the search string that you do not want to replace.
Quit	End Search command and return to Ready mode.

Unlike other Range commands, the cursor isn't stuck to the current cell when you first use the command so you must press the period key to stick it down. However, after you have once specified a search range, 1-2-3 remembers it and proposes that you use it the next time you use the command. This feature makes it easy to search the same range several times in order to find and/or replace several different text strings. To unstick the cursor press **ESC** or **BKSP**.

The Search command only searches the range you specify. To search an entire spreadsheet, position the cursor on cell A1 and press **END HOME** in response to the prompt for the search range. This stretches the cursor to the lower right-hand cell of the active area of the current sheet. If you want to search across several sheets in the current file, use **CTRL-PGUP** or **CTRL-PGDN** to stretch the range over several sheets. You can end a long search by pressing **CTRL-BREAK** to cancel the command.

Input

The Range Input command limits the movement of the worksheet cursor to those cells in the input range that have been unprotected with the Range Unprot command. Recall that unprotected cells are displayed in high-intensity (bright) characters on most monochrome monitors and in green on color monitors. The input range must contain at least one unprotected cell. Otherwise you get an error message. See Figure 3–25 for the command tree.

The Input command is used to create data entry forms where the operator (usually someone inexperienced in the use of electronic spreadsheets) is prevented from moving the cursor to any cell other than unprotected data entry cells. In conjunction with the Global Protect Enable command, the Input command provides protection for the worksheet's structure while permitting easy data entry.

Assume you have a range of cells on a worksheet named **DATA_ENTRY**, and you have used the Range Unprot command to unprotect those cells in the range in which data is to be entered.

Figure 3–25   Range Input command tree. (Note: At least one cell in the input range must be unprotected with the Range Unprot command.)

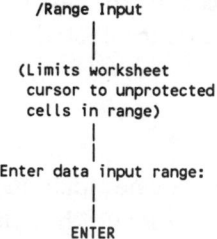

To use the Range Input command, type

/RI	Enters the Range Input command.
Enter data input range:	Asks for input range.
DATA_ENTRY	Either type or press **NAME/F3** and select.
ENTER	Specifies DATA_ENTRY as the input range.

Once the range has been supplied, 1-2-3 takes several actions:

1. It repositions the range DATA_ENTRY so the upper left corner of the input range is placed in the upper left of the screen, thus displaying the largest possible amount of the input range.

2. It places the worksheet cursor on the first unprotected cell in the input range.

3. 1-2-3 limits the worksheet cursor's movement to unprotected cells in the input range.

If you don't want information above and to the left of the first unprotected cell moved off the screen, include those cells in the input range. The size of the range doesn't affect the data entry cells; it just affects where 1-2-3 positions them on the screen.

Moving Around the Input Range

The four arrow keys and the **HOME** and **END** keys are active. The other cursor control keys are disabled. The **RIGHT** arrow key, for example, skips the worksheet cursor to the right to the next unprotected cell. If there is nothing in the first row of the input range, 1-2-3 searches down the rows until the next unprotected cell is found. The other arrow keys operate in a similar fashion.

The **HOME** key moves the cursor to the first unprotected cell in the input range. The **END** key moves it to the last unprotected cell in the range. The cursor does not move to unprotected cells that are not in the designated input range.

Entering Data

When the cursor is on an input cell, type new data and either press **ENTER** or use the cursor movement keys to move the cursor to the next data entry cell.

Ending the Input Command

To end the Input command, press either the **ESC** key or, if you have not pressed any other key, the **ENTER** key. If you have already pressed a key, press either the **ESC** key or the **ENTER** key twice to exit the command.

Input and Undo

You can make many changes to a spreadsheet during one use of the Input command without returning to the Ready mode. Since Undo undoes everything since you were last in the Ready mode, pressing **ALT-F4** cancels all of your changes, not just the latest one. Be sure that is what you want to do before using Undo during the Input command.

Using Macros for Input

Release 3 introduces the specialized macro key word {FORM} that affords you great flexibility in designing data input forms and controlling the data input into a spreadsheet. If you are making extensive use of the Range Input command, check out the {FORM} command in Chapter 12.

Transpose and Values

The Range Transpose command copies information in one range to another location, changing the layout of the data and replacing any formulas with their current values. When you use the Range Transpose command on a single sheet, the command transposes columns for rows, and vice versa. When used on a three-dimensional range the result is rows or columns into sheets or vice versa.

The Range Values command copies only the displayed values and not the underlying formulas. It is, in effect, a way to freeze formulas at their current display values.

These two commands are actually specialized versions of 1-2-3's Copy command. The detailed discussion of these commands is presented where it logically belongs, with the Copy command in Chapter 4.

HANDS ON: USING THE RANGE COMMANDS

The Range commands are powerful tools for modifying the appearance of an electronic spreadsheet and for making it clearer and easier to understand. The Before table, Figure 3–26, shows a hypothetical invoice in which characters in the long labels disappear, date functions appear as

Figure 3-26 The Range commands and the Worksheet Column command can turn a worksheet that is almost impossible to decipher into one that is clear and easy to understand.

```
       A          B        C       D       E       F       G       H
 1
 2
 3                         INVOICE
 4                 Rust, Rot, And Wreckage
 5                 Hardware Store To The Stars
 6                 Rodeo Drive, California
 7
 8     Today's D   32861
 9     Payment D   32891
10
11
12     DESCRIPTI NUMBER    UNITS   $/UNIT  TOTAL
13     Nuts          1232  pieces    0.03   36.96
14     Bolts          281  pieces    0.07   19.67
15     Nails           46  lbs.      1.356  62.376
16     Chains          18  feet      0.45    8.1
17     Whips            3  pairs    27.5    82.5
18     Dog Colla        1  pair      3.56    3.56
19                                          ---------
20                                  TOTAL  213.166
21
22     This month we are featuring our entire line of metallic flecked
23     bathroom sinks. We have a full line of flesh, apricot, umber,
24     olive drab, and chartreuse fixtures. Designer faucet and handle sets are available
25     in mother-of-pearl, gold, and plastic. As a special value, we have
26     one remaining pair of our fabulously popular 14 karat gold plated figures of
27     Marilyn Monroe/Joan Crawford hot and cold water faucet handles!!!
28     This is your last chance to get a pair of these exquisitely jeweled, life-like works of
29     art. What well-appointed WC could be without a pair of Marilyn Joan's?
30
31
32
```

date numbers, and the text at the bottom extends far beyond the right edge of the invoice.

In the After table, Figure 3-27, column widths are expanded. Integer and Currency formats are set where appropriate. The headings under the description are right-justified, and the text is formatted with the Range Justify command. Rows are inserted to open up the table to make it easier to understand, and the date numbers are converted to readable dates in the Day-Month-Year format.

More will be said about 1-2-3's built-in functions in Chapter 8, but for now all you need to know is that the @TODAY function, entered in B8, reads the current system date stored in your system. Whenever you start your computer, either the date and time are read from a system clock, or you are prompted to enter them. It is that date—the system date—that is read by @TODAY.

Payment is due in 30 days, so the Payment Due date in B9 is today's date plus 30. Because 1-2-3 keeps track of dates as numbers, this operation

THE RANGE COMMANDS

Figure 3-27   The After version of the worksheet shown in Figure 3-26.

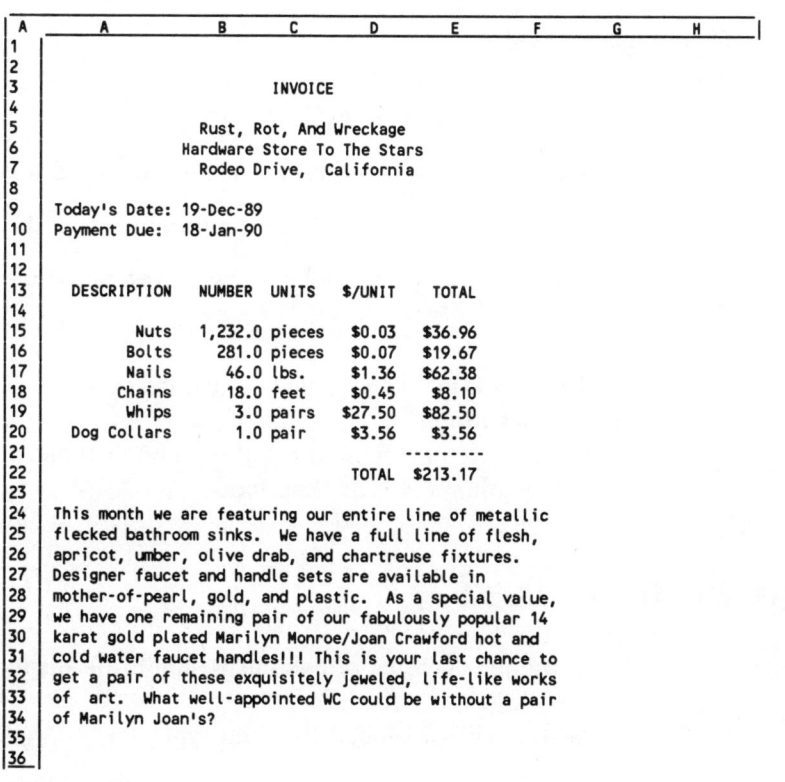

is easy to perform. The Range Format Date command then displays the date numbers in an understandable format.

Widening a Column

Position the cursor in any cell in column A and type

/WC	Enters the Worksheet Column command.
RIGHT	Press this arrow key until all of the labels in column A appear on the screen.

ENTER	Sets column A to desired width.

Range Format Date

Position cursor on cell B8 and type

/RFD	Enters the Range Format Date command.
1 ENTER	Selects and enters format 1, Day-Month-Year.
DOWN	Stretches cursor over range B8..B9.
ENTER	Sets the format.

Notice that asterisks appear in cells, because the column is too narrow for current format.

Position the cursor in any cell in column B and repeat the steps used to widen column A, just described.

Range Format Fixed

The number of items in column B should be displayed with embedded commas and one decimal place.

Position cursor on cell B13 and type

/RF,	Enters the Range Format Comma command.
1 ENTER	Selects and enters one decimal place.
END DOWN	Stretches cursor over range B13..B18.
ENTER	Sets the format.

Range Format Currency

The unit prices in column D and the total in column E should be displayed in currency format, two decimal places.

Position cursor on cell E13 and type

/RFC	Enters the Range Format Currency command.
2 ENTER	Selects and enters two decimal places.
END DOWN	Stretches cursor down to E20.

THE RANGE COMMANDS

RIGHT	Stretches cursor over block E13..D20.
ENTER	Sets the format.

Range Labels

Column headings in row 12 and row labels in column A would look better if they were right aligned. The word **TOTAL** at the bottom of the table would also look better right aligned and the word **INVOICE** at the top would look better center aligned.

To right align the column headings in row 12, position cursor on cell A12 and type

/RL	Enters the Range Labels command.
R	Selects right aligned.
END RIGHT	Stretches cursor over range A12..E12.
ENTER	Sets alignment.

To right align the row labels in column A, position cursor on cell A13 and type

/RL	Enters the Range Labels command.
R	Selects right aligned.
END DOWN	Stretches cursor over range A13..A18.
ENTER	Sets alignment.

To right align the word **TOTAL**, position cursor on cell D20 and type

/RL	Enters the Range Labels command.
R	Selects right aligned.
ENTER	Sets alignment for current cell.

To center align the word **INVOICE**, position cursor on cell C3 and type

/RL	Enters the Range Labels command.
C	Selects center aligned.

| ENTER | Sets alignment for current cell. |

Range Justify

The text below the invoice extends too far to the right. To justify the text, position cursor on cell A22 and type

/RJ	Enters the Range Justify command.
RIGHT	Press **RIGHT** arrow key five times to expand cursor over the range A22..F22.
ENTER	Justifies text in designated column width.

EDIT/F2 to Center Long Labels

The long labels at the top of the invoice would look better centered under the word **INVOICE**, but you can't use the Range Label command because the labels extend beyond the cell boundary.

To center long labels, position the cursor on cell B4 and type

EDIT/F2	Enters the Edit command. Contents of B4 appear at the top of the screen.
LEFT	Moves cursor under first character.
SPACE BAR	Enters spaces to move label to right.
ENTER	Returns edited label to B4.

Centering a long label is a matter of trial and error. You may have to repeat this process several times before the long label is correctly centered.

Repeat the centering procedure for the long labels in B5 and B6.

Worksheet Insert Row

The word **INVOICE** in cell C3 is too close to the text in the next row. Position cursor on any cell in row 5 and type

| /WIR | Enters the Worksheet Insert Row command. |
| ENTER | Inserts row below row 3 and moves the body of the table down one row. |

Conclusions: Making Range and Worksheet Commands Work for You

The Before table, Figure 3–26, and After table, Figure 3–27, dramatically illustrate the power of the Worksheet and Range commands to improve a spreadsheet's appearance. You would, however, be misled if you thought you should wait until worksheet construction was completed to apply these commands. In practice, the Range and Worksheet commands are used interactively to build your worksheets. When you enter a formula or type a label and discover, for example, that the column width is too narrow, press a few keys and change it. Then enter some more labels. If you decide to align them to the right rather than the left, a few keystrokes move the labels where you want them.

There is constant interaction among the formulas, functions, and labels you enter to construct the worksheet and the Worksheet and Range commands you use to improve the worksheet's appearance. Working back and forth between construction and appearance is an easy and natural way to create an electronic spreadsheet.

The Range commands discussed in this chapter and the Worksheet commands discussed in the last chapter make up the bulk of the special electronic tools 1-2-3 has for constructing spreadsheets. As you construct more spreadsheets, commands such as the Worksheet Column, Insert, and Delete commands and the Range Format, Label, and Erase commands become second nature to you. You will quickly type /WC whenever you want to set a column width—you won't even look at the control panel. But when it comes to the less-used commands: Name, Range, or Justify, for example, 1-2-3 stands ready with full-word descriptions and prompts. Should you become stuck at any point, remember to press the **HELP/F1** function key to display an entire screen of information relevant to your current position in a command.

TIPS & TRAPS

Tips

Pointing Is Polite.
Always use the arrow keys to point to the ranges requested by the Range commands. Pointing is faster, and by highlighting the cells to be used in

a function you are less likely to make mistakes. Pointing is always the way to go when you are specifying ranges across sheets.

Pressing the **END** key followed by an arrow key stretches the cursor to the end of a row (**RIGHT** or **LEFT** arrow key) or a column (**UP** or **DOWN** arrow key). This is a particularly easy way to format, erase, unprotect, and so forth, a column or row of contiguous cell entries.

How to See What Is *Really* in a Cell.

Formats change the appearance of cells, and the values displayed in cells may be generated in many different ways. The way to find out the reality behind the appearance on your screen is to position the worksheet cursor in a cell and check the Status line in the control panel for the actual contents of the cell. You can also use the Range or Global Format Text command to display the actual cell contents in each cell.

It's No *WordPerfect*, but It Isn't Bad: Text Editing with 1-2-3.

The Range Justify command makes it easy to add a few paragraphs of text to a 1-2-3 worksheet. Type your text as a column of long labels in consecutive cells and use the command to reformat (justify) the text into a width you specify. The ability to edit the contents of a cell with the **EDIT/F2** key and the Range Search command are the only other word processing features available in 1-2-3 Release 3.

Protect a Range?

It can't be done—directly. The Range Prot command only removes unprotection. You must protect the entire worksheet with the Worksheet Global Protection Enable command. The Range Unprot command can then be used to unprotect any cells you might wish to change.

Seeing the Corners of a Range.

When you point to ranges, often the range is larger than the screen and you need to check the location of each corner to verify that the proper range has been highlighted. To move the free cell (the one with the flashing underline character) to another corner and display it on the screen, press the period key. This doesn't work when the range extends across several sheets.

Traps

GROUP %#$!!@$&!

Always think very carefully when you use Group Enable on a stack of worksheets after you have used Range Format commands. When you do,

THE RANGE COMMANDS

Group automatically imposes the Range Formats from the current sheet onto corresponding cells on *all* other sheets in the stack! This can have a devastating effect on other worksheets. The only way to correct those formats is to reset each one individually.

Watch Out for Reset!

The Reset command (particularly Range Name Reset) is a deadly command. Select it by typing an **R** or pressing **ENTER**; *all* of your range names disappear. Lotus doesn't ask you to verify the action, it simply performs it. Always consider carefully before you use a 1-2-3 Reset command.

Moving Entries with the Justify Command.

If you specify the justify range as a single row of cells, 1-2-3 moves entries farther down the spreadsheet (in the column containing the long labels) up or down as part of the justify process. To keep labels and formulas farther down the spreadsheet from being moved (and possibly invalidated) by the Justify command, specify the justify range as a block of cells. When you do, the Justify command limits its actions to the block.

4 | The Copy, Move, System, and Quit Commands

OBJECTIVES

After mastering the content of this chapter, you will be able to

☐ copy cells, ranges, and blocks with the Copy command while quickly and efficiently constructing electronic worksheets.

☐ understand the distinction between absolute and relative cell references and how the Copy command acts on them.

☐ transpose ranges with the Range Transpose command and copy displayed values with the Range Values commands.

☐ move cells, ranges, and blocks with the Move command to modify electronic worksheets.

☐ exit to the disk operating system with the System command and return from DOS after formatting a data diskette or running another program.

☐ end a Lotus 1-2-3 work session with the Quit command.

INTRODUCTION

Chapters 2 and 3 introduced you to most of the Lotus 1-2-3 commands for constructing and modifying electronic spreadsheets. The Format commands; the Label commands; the Insert, Delete, and Erase commands; and the Col-Width command are used with every electronic spreadsheet you construct. However, the commands discussed in this chapter are, if anything, more important and more frequently used than the commands introduced in the last two chapters. They are productivity commands that magnify your ability to quickly create and modify spreadsheets.

The Copy command copies text and values along with their label-prefix characters and display formats from one range to another. With it you can quickly spread formulas and functions across a table to finish a worksheet or to prepare multiperiod projections. You can also copy text, numbers, formulas, and functions from one sheet to another in the current file or from the current file to any other active file. Because the Range Transpose and Range Values commands are specialized copy commands, they are discussed after the Copy command.

The Move command moves the contents of cells from one location on the worksheet to another or from sheet to sheet within the current file. With it you can easily modify the structure of existing worksheets, but you cannot use the command to move information from one active file to another.

The System command enables you to exit to your computer's Disk Operating System while keeping 1-2-3, and the stack you are working on, in memory. After you have formatted a diskette, used your word processor, or sent a file with a telecommunications program, you can return to 1-2-3 by pressing a few keys.

The Quit command, like the Copy and Move commands, is on the Main menu. The Quit command is used to end a 1-2-3 work session.

Throughout this chapter, full cell references (such as A:A1) are used in the examples to avoid confusion and to allow for taking actions across sheets in a stack. In practice, the sheet designation can be omitted when the reference is to a cell or range on the current sheet. That is, the reference A1 is understood to be a reference to A:A1 when the cursor is on sheet A:.

THE COPY COMMAND

The Copy command is the most important of the six commands discussed in this chapter. It may be the most important worksheet construction command 1-2-3 offers. By copying text, numbers, formulas, functions, and their formats, you can quickly construct a worksheet; spread formulas across columns and rows; and complete other routine, but time-consuming, tedious tasks. You can even copy from the current file into a file stored on disk or from a file on disk into the current worksheet. Figure 4–1 shows how a few keystrokes and the Copy command can spread the contents of one cell across several worksheets.

Figure 4-1 (a) With the Copy command you can copy the information from one cell into many cells. (b) The Copy command can shout your message to the world.

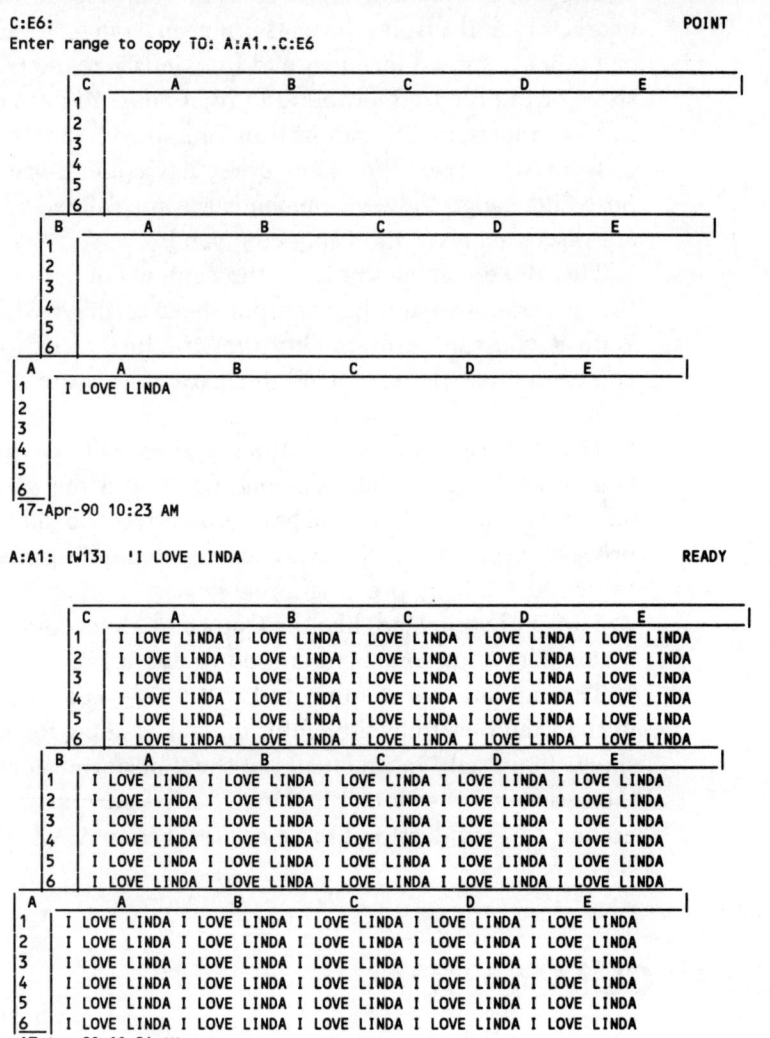

Using the Copy Command

The trick to mastering the Copy command is to realize that you must tell 1-2-3 *two* pieces of information.

The FROM range: The cell or cells to copy.

THE COPY, MOVE, SYSTEM, AND QUIT COMMANDS

The TO range: The cell or cells into which the contents of the FROM range are to be copied.

If the FROM or TO range is in a stored file, supply the path and filename enclosed within double greater than and less than symbols, such as <<C:\123\BUDGET.WK3>>. See Figure 4–2 for the Copy command tree.

To see how Figure 4–1(b) was created by copying the contents of cell A1 in Figure 4–1(a) into the block of cells A:A1..C:E6, position the cursor on cell A:A1 and type

/C	Enters the Copy command.
Enter range to copy FROM:	Asks for the range to copy from. Any valid 1-2-3 range—cell, row, column rectangle, or block—can be used. 1-2-3 proposes to copy A:A1..A:A1, the cell under the worksheet cursor.
ENTER	Selects the cell under cursor as the FROM range.
Enter range to copy TO:	Asks for the upper left corner of range to copy to. Highlights a rectangle or block for multiple copies of a single cell.
.	Tacks cursor to cell A:A1.
DOWN	Press **DOWN** arrow key until cursor is stretched to A:A6.
RIGHT	Press **RIGHT** arrow key until cursor is stretched to A:E6, highlighting rectangle A:A1..A:E6.

Figure 4–2 Copy command tree.

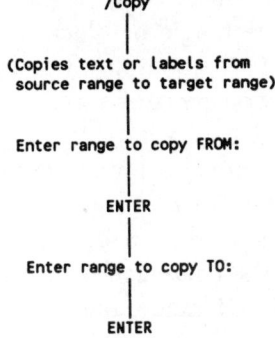

CTRL-PGUP	Press twice. Stretches cursor back to sheets B and C highlighting the block A:A1..C:E6.
ENTER	Executes Copy command.

Changing Ranges: Unsticking the Cursor

Whenever you begin a Copy command, 1-2-3 assumes that you want to begin the FROM range with the current cell. Therefore, the cursor is tacked down to that cell. If you want to start the FROM range from a different cell, press **ESC** to unstick the cursor. Reposition the cursor and tack it down again with the period key. When your FROM range is a single cell, you don't need to tack the cursor to the cell. Just press **ENTER** to accept it.

If you misspecify the TO range, press **ESC** to cancel it. The cursor is unstuck, and you can move it to the correct cell, stick it down with the period key, and specify the correct TO range.

Copying Techniques

To make multiple copies of a rectangle or block of cells, first use the Range Name Create command to name the rectangle or block with a name like AA. Then to make a copy, position the cursor on the upper left corner of the TO range and type

/C	Enters the Copy command.
NAME/F3	Displays the range names. Because range names are displayed in alphabetical order, AA appears first, under the cursor.
ENTER	Selects AA as FROM range.
ENTER	Selects current cell as TO range and completes Copy command.

The technique of copying a named range is particularly useful when you need several copies of a rectangle or block in several different locations on your spreadsheet. This situation often arises when the same row headings are used for several parts of a table or for several related tables on several sheets.

A slight variation on the previous technique is to position the cursor on the upper left corner of the TO range and then copy "backward." That is, enter the command, unstick the cursor, move to the FROM range, and specify it. Then complete the command by pressing the **ENTER** key twice, once to specify the FROM range and once to confirm that the original cursor location is to be the upper left corner of the TO range.

The advantage of copying "backward" is that after the action is completed the cursor is left on the TO range rather than on the FROM range.

Finally, you can split the screen and copy from one window to another. This technique is particularly useful when the FROM and TO ranges are widely separated on a sheet or when you copy from sheet to sheet in a stack.

The Relationship Between FROM and TO Ranges

As you would expect, all TO and FROM ranges must be valid 1-2-3 ranges. On a single sheet a range can be a cell, a row, a column, or a rectangle. Across sheets a range is called a *block* because you can think of it as three-dimensional.

A block can be made up in several different ways. Each way is best thought of as a projection of a range (cell, column, row, or rectangle) from a single two-dimensional sheet onto several sheets in a three-dimensional stack of worksheets.

The simplest block is made up of a single cell from each sheet. It is analogous to a single cell range on one sheet. The cells must be the *same* cell from each sheet, for example, A:A1, B:A1, and C:A1, which are the range A:A1..C:A1. It *cannot* be a diagonal through the stack and, as with other ranges, there can't be any gaps. A block containing only one cell from each sheet is sometimes called a *ray* because a straight line (a ray) can be drawn to pass through the center of each cell.

A block can also be one or more columns or one or more rows from each sheet. A block of this type is simply a projection of the shape from a single sheet onto the other sheets in the range.

Lotus accepts any range of cells as the TO or target range. There is, however, a specific relationship between the shape of the FROM range and the interpretation 1-2-3 gives to the TO range.

If the FROM range is a /	Lotus interprets the TO range as
single cell	whatever is specified (cell, column, row, rectangle, or block)
row of cells	a column (left column of each sheet in a block)
column of cells	a row (top row of each sheet in a block)
rectangle of cells	a single cell (the upper left cell in a row, column, or rectangle or the upper left cell of the top row of each sheet in a block)

block of cells   a single cell (upper left cell in a row, column, rectangle, or upper left cell of first sheet in a block)

Regardless of the target range you specify, 1-2-3 interprets it as listed here. Thus, when the target range is a rectangle, for example, you can specify a row, column, rectangle, or block as the target range, but 1-2-3 ignores everything in the target range except the single cell in the upper left corner of the range or—in the case of a block—the single cell in the upper left corner of each sheet in the block.

The result of the Copy command varies depending on the shape of the FROM and TO ranges. Figures 4–3 through 4–6 show what happens when each of the different types of two-dimensional source ranges are copied into the various target ranges on a single sheet. Each target range produces a particular type of copy.

Study Figures 4–3 through 4–6 until you are familiar with the relationship between FROM and TO ranges. But don't worry. In practice, the relationship is an easy, natural one. In any case, Lotus always makes a consistent determination of the TO range, regardless of the shape you specify.

Copying into a Three-Dimensional Range

Copying across sheets is easy to generalize from the preceding examples but hard to illustrate in two-dimensional form in a book. When you copy

Figure 4–3   When the source range is a single cell, the target range may be any range: a single cell, a row, a column, or a rectangle.

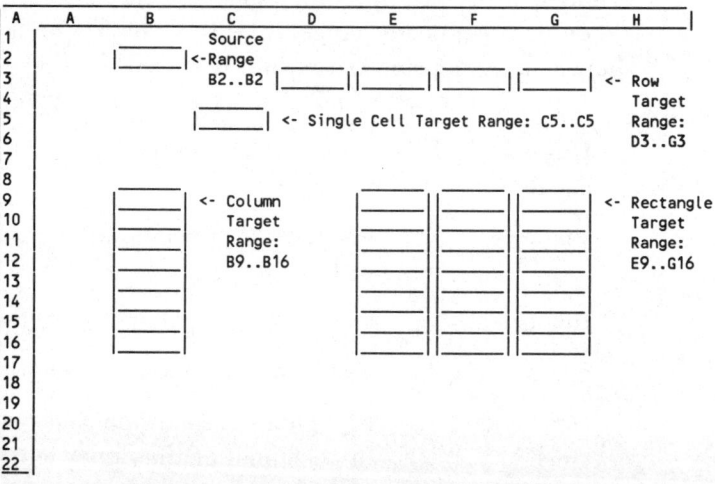

Figure 4-4 When the source range is a row, the resulting range is either a row (when the target range is a single cell or a row) or a rectangle (when the target range is a column or a rectangle).

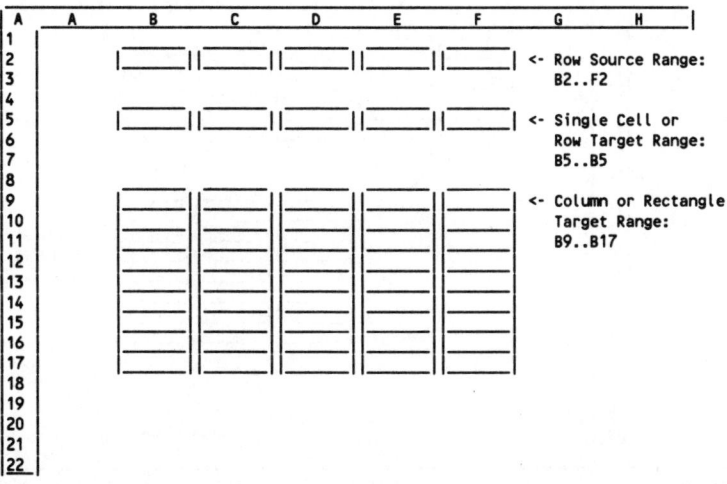

Figure 4-5 When the source range is a column, the resulting range is either a column (when the target range is a single cell or a column) or a rectangle (when the target range is a row or a rectangle).

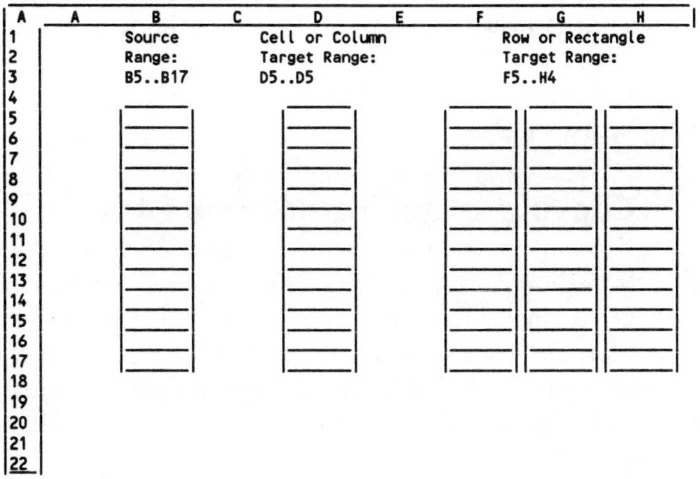

a single cell across several sheets, you get a ray through the sheets when the TO range is a single cell on each sheet. When the TO range is some

Figure 4-6 When the source range is a rectangle, the resulting, range is always a rectangle, regardless of whether the target range is a cell, row, column, or rectangle.

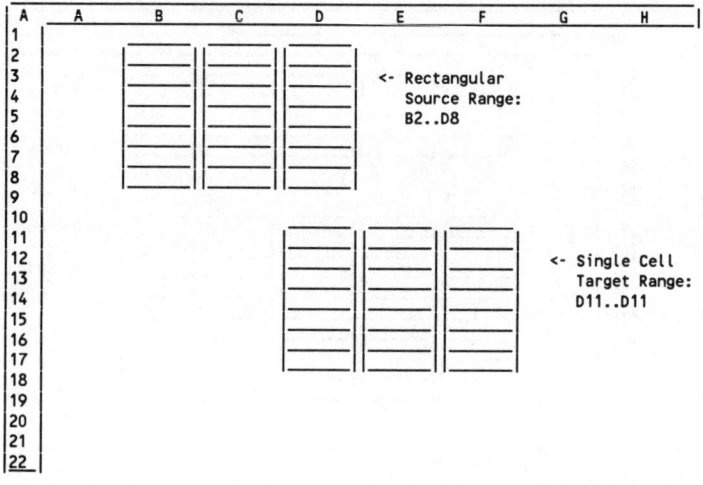

other shape, you get a column, row, or rectangle on each sheet, depending on the shape of the TO range you have specified. When you copy a row or column across sheets, you get as many copies of the row or column as you specify in the TO range. Finally, when you copy a rectangle across sheets, you get one copy of the rectangular area on each sheet.

After you have mastered copying on a single sheet, use the **CTRL-PGUP** and **CTRL-PGDN** keys to stretch the cursor across several sheets. Experiment with the Copy command until you understand how it works across sheets.

Copying to and from Stored Files

You can use the Copy command as a quick and easy way to transfer information from a file on a disk to the current file. Just use the command as previously described but precede the FROM range with the path and filename. To copy a range named DATA from a file named BUDGET.WK3 stored in the 123 subdirectory on the C: drive, position the cursor where you want the copy to appear in the current sheet and type

/C	Enters the Copy Command.
<<C:\123\BUDGET.WK3>>DATA	Specifies the FROM range.
ENTER	Accepts the FROM range.

THE COPY, MOVE, SYSTEM, AND QUIT COMMANDS

    ENTER   Accepts the current cursor location as the TO range and executes the command.

You can use this technique to copy information into a file on disk. When you do, be very careful in designating the TO range; the command overwrites existing cell entries.

Caution: The Copy command copies the formulas and functions in the FROM range to the TO range. These cell references may not work when they are copied to new files. If you only want to copy the displayed values and label entries, use the Range Value command described later in the chapter.

Warnings

Two additional points about the Copy command bear remembering. First, any cells in the TO range already containing text or values have their contents replaced by material from the FROM range. If the FROM range has blank cells, the FROM range erases corresponding cells in the TO range. Be careful when you specify the target range, or you may accidentally erase or overwrite important information. Be particularly careful when the target range extends across several sheets.

Second, you can use the Copy command on a worksheet that you have protected with the Worksheet Protect Enable command. However, you receive an error message if *any* cell in the target range has not been unprotected with the Range Unprot command. If you receive this message, respond by pressing either the ESC or the ENTER key. When there are any protected cells in the TO range, 1-2-3 does not execute the Copy command.

Copying Formulas and Functions

One truly miraculous thing about Lotus 1-2-3 is that as you use the Copy command it keeps track of the cell references in formulas and functions. This means you can create a formula or function in one place on the worksheet and when you copy it to a new location, it refers to the correct cells.

You have already seen how cell references are used to define active cells and ranges of cells in the various slash commands (including the Copy command). Cell references can also be used to create formulas. For example, the simple formula A:B1/A:B4 says, "Take the value in cell A:B1, divide it by the value in cell A:B4, and display the result." Through this technique cell references can be used to create functions in much the same way variables are used in algebra.

Cell references come in two types: *Relative*, which is also called *Adjusting*, and *Absolute*, which is also known as *Unadjusting*. First, you'll see how the Copy command works on Relative or Adjusting cell references.

Relative Cell References

The example in Figure 4–7 shows how the Copy command adjusts a cell reference when it copies it from the source range, cell A:B4, to the target range, A:D4.

The function in cell A:B4, which in the figure is **+A:A1**, is simply a reference to cell A:A1. The function says, "Get the value from cell A1 on a sheet A: and display it in this cell." The meaning of the function is clear enough, but for a real understanding you need to know how 1-2-3 "thinks" about the +A:A1 entered into cell A:B4. It doesn't keep track of cell A:A1 at all. What Lotus does is to keep track of cell references *relative* to the cell into which they are entered.

Thus, when you refer to A:A1 from cell A:B4, 1-2-3 records something like, "Get the value three rows up and one column to the left of the current cell." This, of course, is just another way of identifying cell A:A1 *relative* to cell A:B4. Because the location of A:A1 is defined relative to A:B4, it is said to be a *relative cell reference*.

To see what happens when the contents of cell A:B4 are copied, position the cursor on A:B4 and type

/C	Enters the Copy command.
ENTER	Selects A:B4 as the FROM range.
RIGHT	Press twice to move cursor to A:D4.

Figure 4–7   In this simple worksheet, the reference in cell B4 is +A1.

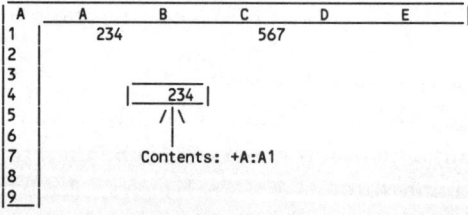

THE COPY, MOVE, SYSTEM, AND QUIT COMMANDS

ENTER | Completes command and copies contents of A:B4 into A:D4.

Observe in Figure 4–8 that the result of copying the contents of A:B4 into A:D4 is a reference to A:C1! The formula in A:B4 (shown as **+A:A1**) is *adjusted*. In A:D4 it becomes a reference to A:C1. However, in both locations it is a reference relative to the cell containing the reference—a reference to "a cell, on this sheet, three rows up and one column to the left of the current cell."

Copying Relative Cell Addresses

Figure 4–9 shows another example of relative cell addresses in action. A formula, **@SUM(B9..B14)** has been entered into cell B16. It adds the 1980 output of the various automobile manufacturers and displays the total. The reference to a range of cells in this formula is a relative reference.

Position the cursor on cell A:B6 and type

/C | Enters the Copy command.

ENTER | Selects cell under worksheet cursor as FROM range.

RIGHT | Moves cursor to A:C16, first cell of TO range.

. | Tacks cursor to cell A:C16.

RIGHT | Stretches cursor over A:C16..A:D16.

ENTER | Copies contents of A:C15 into A:C16..A:D16.

Row 16 of Figure 4–9 shows what happens after the formula in A:B16 has been copied into cells A:C16 and A:D16. The totals for these columns are displayed, and by examining the formulas you can see that the cell references have adjusted so that the correct range of cells is added in each column.

Figure 4–8 When the contents of B4 are copied into D4, the formula adjusts to read +C1.

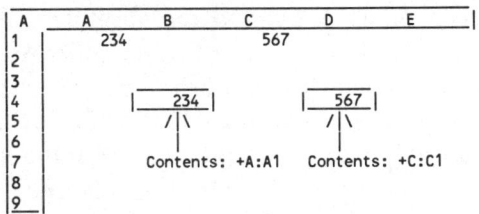

Figure 4-9 The formula in cell B16 contains relative cell references. When it is copied into cells C16 and D16, the references automatically adjust.
Source: *The World Almanac and Book of Facts 1983* (New York: Newspaper Enterprise Association, Inc., 1983), p. 157.

```
 A              A              B          C          D         E
 1
 2
 3                       WHO MAKES THE MOST AUTOMOBILES?
 4
 5                                    PRODUCTION
 6                                                       1982
 7              Company              1980       1981    7 months
 8
 9         American Motors        164,725    109,319     39,927
10          Chrysler Corp.        638,974    748,774    353,053
11         Ford Motor Co.       1,306,948  1,320,197    671,231
12    General Motors Corp.      4,064,556  3,904,083  1,963,263
13    Checker Motors Corp.          3,197      3,010      2,000
14   Volkswagen of America        197,106    167,755     60,160
15
16                  Total:   |6,375,506| |6,253,138| |3,089,634|
17                              /|\         /|\         /|\
18                               |           |           |
19                              B16 --->   /COPY -->  C16 and D16
20                               |           |           |
21                           @SUM(B9..B14) @SUM(C9..C14) @SUM(D9..D14)
```

Absolute Cell References

In the back of your mind you may be thinking: "Do all cell references have to be relative? What if I don't want a cell reference to adjust?" Good questions. In many situations you do not want a cell reference to adjust.

In Chapter 3, Figure 3-13 used an assumption space for the parameters Principal, Rate, and Withdrawal. You certainly want each reference to one of these parameters to be the same in each formula where it's used. Another example is a percentage distribution, in which you want the total to remain the same from formula to formula. In these examples, you want the reference to a cell on a particular worksheet to remain unchanged regardless of where the formula is copied. What you want is an *absolute cell reference.*

To create an absolute cell reference, simply insert a dollar sign ($) into the cell reference before each letter and number. Thus the relative reference to cell A:A1 is A:A1, and the absolute reference to the cell is $A:$A$1. This is a reference to cell A1 or sheet A:. Regardless of where this reference is copied, it continues to refer to A:A1. The dollar signs can be typed in, edited in with the **EDIT/F2** function key, or inserted when creating the function in Point mode with the **ABS/F4** function key.

To illustrate the use of absolute cell references, Figure 4-10 takes Figure 4-9 a step farther and uses a percentage distribution to make it

Figure 4–10 The formulas in row 20 calculate the percentage of total production accounted for by American Motors. The cell references to the total production in each period—$B$16, $C$16 and $D$16—are absolute cell references. They remain unchanged when the formulas are copied down columns B, C, and D to complete the table. Source: *The World Almanac and Book of Facts 1983* (New York: Newspaper Enterprise Association, Inc., 1983), p. 157.

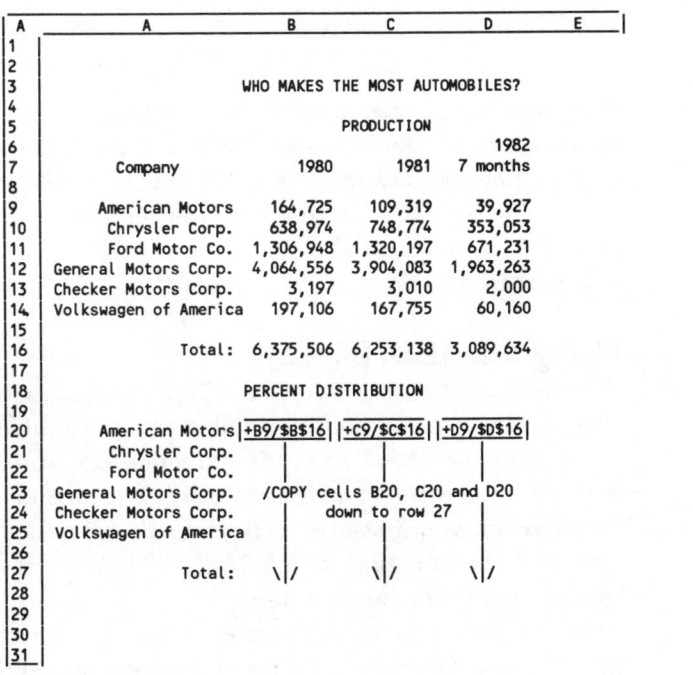

easier to see the relative outputs of different manufacturers and to see what happened to market share over the period.

In row 20 of Figure 4–10 the formulas to calculate the percentage share of American Motors contain an absolute cell reference to the total production by all manufacturers in the appropriate year. The reference to total production must, of course, remain unchanged as the formulas are copied down the column to complete the table. The other part of the formula, production by specific manufacturers, must change from row to row. It does because it is entered in the formula in row 20 without dollar signs.

To complete the table, position the cursor on cell A:B20 and type

/C   Enters the Copy command.

END RIGHT   Highlights A:B20..A:D20 as the FROM range.

ENTER	Selects A:B20..A:D20 as the FROM range.
DOWN	Moves cursor to first cell of TO range.
.	Tacks cursor to A:B21.
Arrow keys	Stretch cursor over TO range, A:B21..A:D27.
ENTER	Completes command and copies contents of A:B20..A:D20 into A:B21..A:D27.

Note that this process also copies a formula to row 26, which you'd like to leave blank. Don't worry. Complete the Copy command, and when you are finished, use the Range Erase command to erase the cells in row 26. Also notice that the row labels in the bottom part of the table were copied from the row labels in the top part of the table and didn't have to be entered again.

Using the ABS/F4 Key

Whenever you create a formula, you can designate a cell reference as absolute by either typing the dollar signs into the appropriate places or by pressing the **ABS/F4** key. The function key works when you are pointing with the cursor to designate cell references or when you are typing them. When you first press **ABS/F4**, the reference is absolute to sheet, row, and column, such as $A:$A$1. This is an absolute reference to a specific cell in the current file.

If you want part of the reference to adjust (relative) and part to be nonadjusting (absolute), continue to press the **ABS/F4** key. The dollar signs cycle through all possible combinations of locations: $A:$A$1, A:$A$1, A:A$1, and so on. If you overshoot your desired combination of dollar signs, keep pressing **ABS/F4** until the correct combination reappears.

To change a relative reference to an absolute reference in an existing formula or function, begin by pressing **EDIT/F2**. Then use the arrow keys to position the edit line cursor under the reference you want to change and press **ABS/F4**.

If you are specifying a range such as A:A1..A:A10, pressing **ABS/F4** while you type the ending cell address or point to it designates the entire range as absolute, such as $A:$A$1..$A:$A$10.

Making Named Ranges Absolute

In a great improvement over previous versions of 1-2-3, you can now create an absolute reference range name by giving it a name that begins with a dollar sign, such as "$NAME." When the name is used in a formula or function the reference is absolute and the references don't change when the Copy command is applied to the formula.

Range names that don't begin with a dollar sign, such as NAME, are treated as relative cell addresses, and thus adjust when copied from one cell to another. To change a range name used in a formula or function from relative to absolute, precede the range name with a dollar sign ($) when you type it into a formula. That is, type @SUM($COST) to make a reference to a range named COST absolute. Alternatively, when you add a name to a function or formula, press **ABS/F4** to convert it to an absolute range name.

You can also create the formula with a relative reference range name and then use the **EDIT/F2** key in conjunction with the **ABS/F4** key to edit in the dollar signs. To convert a range name to an absolute reference, press **EDIT/F2** and position the cursor anywhere under the range name you want to make absolute. Then press **ABS/F4**, and the dollar sign appears. Finally, press **ENTER** to return the edited formula or function to the spreadsheet cell.

THE RANGE VALUE AND RANGE TRANSPOSE COMMANDS

Two Range commands, Value and Transpose, are essentially specialized Copy commands. They have the same steps and similar prompts. But they perform different actions and are put to different uses. These commands work across active files and between active files and files anywhere on disk.

Range Value

The Range Value command operates exactly like the Copy command except that it copies only the displayed values and not the formulas that generated the display. Use this command whenever you want to freeze formulas at a particular value or when you want to give someone a copy of the numbers on your worksheet without revealing the formulas behind them.

To use the Range Value command, begin by positioning the cursor on the first cell of the range you want to copy as values. Then type

/RV	Enters the Range Values command.
Enter range to copy FROM:	Asks for range to copy FROM.
ENTER	Specifies FROM range.
Enter range to copy TO:	Asks for range to copy TO.
ENTER	Specifies TO range and executes command.

If you want to freeze a set of displayed values in their *current* cells by replacing the formulas with their displayed values, you can do so by simply designating the FROM range and the TO range as the same set of cells. This is a common operation in worksheets that calculate a Balance Forward or other summary statistics whose value you want to freeze before you move to the next period. Once you perform the command, the formulas no longer exist. To restore them, press **ALT-F4** if Undo is enabled or load a stored version of the spreadsheet.

Range Transpose

The Range Transpose command transposes the displayed column values (*not* the formulas) from the FROM range into row values in the TO range. The FROM and TO ranges can be on the same sheet or on different sheets.

When you use the command on a single sheet, it is relatively easy to keep track of what is happening; the first column of the FROM range becomes the first row of the TO range, and so on. When the command is used across sheets, however, the results are often hard to visualize. Because the command writes over anything in the target cells, be sure to save your worksheet before you use the Range Transpose command. That way, you can easily recover from any mistakes.

See Figure 4–11 for an example of the Transpose command in action.

The steps in the Range Transpose command are similar to the steps in the Copy Command and the Range Values command described in the preceding section. See Figure 4–12 for the command tree.

To use the Transpose command, begin by positioning the cursor on the first cell of the range you want to transpose. Select the command by typing **/RT** and specify the FROM range. If the TO range is on a single sheet (either current sheet or another in the current file), proceed to point to it. If the TO range extends across two or more sheets, you are asked to choose Rows/Columns, Worksheets/Rows, or Columns/Worksheets.

Figure 4-11 Range Transpose command used to transpose information in columns B and C into rows 17 and 18.

```
   A      A         B        C        D        E        F        G
  1
  2             Transpose FROM Range...
  3
  4             Div. 1    $779
  5             Div. 2    $955
  6             Div. 3    $26
  7             Div. 4    $478
  8             Div. 5    $388
  9
 10             Total     $2,626
 11
 12
 13
 14
 15   Transpose TO Range...
 16
 17       Div. 1    Div. 2   Div. 3   Div. 4   Div. 5            Total
 18        $779      $955     $26      $478     $388             $2,626
 19
 20
```

Transposing Formulas and Functions

Only the *values* displayed by formulas in the FROM range are transposed into the TO range. If you require live formulas in the transposed range, you must reconstruct the formulas after using the Range Transpose command.

THE MOVE COMMAND

The Move command rearranges the structure of an already-constructed worksheet. It has much in common with the Copy command. Like that command, you must specify a FROM range and a TO range. However, unlike the Copy command, the FROM and TO ranges are always the same size, so you only need to specify a single cell in the upper left corner of the target range. (See Figure 4-13 for the command tree.)

Like the Copy, Transpose, and Value commands, the Move command replaces any existing text or labels in the target range with information from the corresponding cells in the source range. Unlike those commands, the Move command *cannot* move information from one open file to another. You can move information to and from an open file and files stored on disk. Also, you can't move protected cells, and you can't move unprotected cells onto protected cells. Furthermore, you can't move unprotected cells into a range containing both protected and unprotected cells. If you attempt this move, an error message appears.

Figure 4–12   Range Transpose command tree.

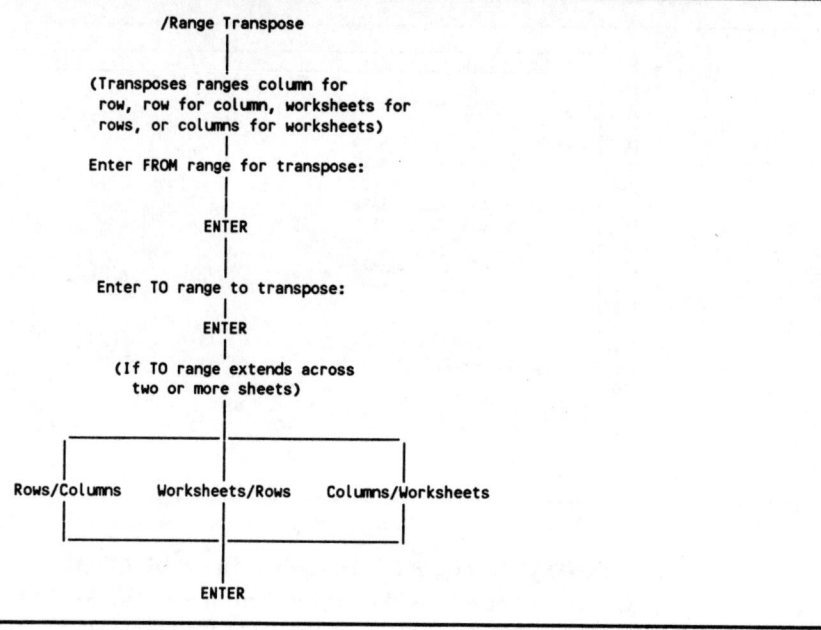

Figure 4–13   Move command tree.

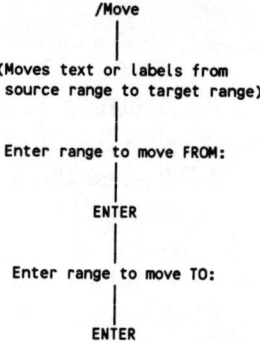

Unlike the Copy command, the moved information no longer exists in the FROM range after the Move command is completed. Relative cell references made to cells in the moved range are adjusted, whereas relative references to cells outside the moved range refer to the same cells as they did before the move.

THE COPY, MOVE, SYSTEM, AND QUIT COMMANDS

Furthermore, any formula, function, range name, or remembered range that refers to moved cells is adjusted so it refers to these same cells in their new location.

The Copy, Insert, Delete, Erase, and Move commands give you a powerful set of tools for constructing and changing electronic spreadsheets. These tools are the electronic scissors, paste, pencils, and erasers that take the tedious drudgery out of spreadsheet construction and analysis.

Using the Move Command

You can use the Move command to rearrange the structure of the automobile worksheet, Figure 4–10, so that the percentage distribution information appears to the right of the table.

To use the Move command, position the cursor on cell A:B20 and type

/M	Enters the Move command.
Enter range to move FROM:	Stretch the cursor over the range A:B20..A:D27.
ENTER	Accepts FROM range.
Enter range to move TO:	Use arrow keys to move cursor to cell A:F9, the upper left corner of the location where you want to move A:B20..A:D27.
ENTER	Completes the Move command.

The percentage distribution formulas are now to the right of rows 9 through 16. Repeat the Move command to move the title **PERCENT DISTRIBUTION** from A:B18 to A:F4. Finally, to complete the transformation of Figure 4–10, use the Copy command to copy the column headings from columns B, C, and D into the appropriate cells of columns F, G, and H and the Range Erase command to remove the unnecessary row labels from A:A20..A:A27. The result appears in Figure 4–14.

Caution: Named Ranges

Named ranges are specified by the cell addresses in the first and last cells of a row or column range and the upper left and lower right corners of the range. For example, if COST is the name of the range A1..A10, the range is a column of cells; if it is the name of A1..B10, it is a rectangle. For blocks that extend across sheets the range is defined by the upper

Figure 4–14 Figure 4-10 rearranged with the Move command.
Source: *The World Almanac and Book of Facts 1983* (New York: Newspaper Enterprise Association, Inc., 1983), p. 157.

```
     A           B         C         D      E     F        G       H
 1
 2                  WHO MAKES THE MOST AUTOMOBILES?
 3
 4                       PRODUCTION           PERCENT DISTRIBUTION
 5
 6                                   1982                         1982
 7        Company      1980      1981   7 months   1980     1981  7 months
 8
 9   American Motors  164,725   109,319    39,927   2.58%   1.75%    1.29%
10   Chrysler Corp.   638,974   748,774   353,053  10.02%  11.97%   11.43%
11   Ford Motor Co. 1,306,948 1,320,197   671,231  20.50%  21.11%   21.73%
12   General Motors Corp. 4,064,556 3,904,083 1,963,263 63.75% 62.43% 63.54%
13   Checker Motors Corp.   3,197    3,010     2,000  0.05%   0.05%    0.06%
14   Volkswagen of America 197,106  167,755   60,160  3.09%   2.68%    1.95%
15
16          Total:  6,375,506 6,253,138 3,089,634 100.00% 100.00%  100.00%
17
```

left cell on the first sheet and the lower right cell on the last sheet, for example, A:A1..C:B2. If you move something onto one of the cells that specifies a named range (A1 or A10 in A1..A10), 1-2-3 deletes the range name. The name still appears in formulas that used it, but because the name is no longer assigned to a range of cells, **ERR** is displayed. To correct this **ERR**, place the cursor on the cell showing **ERR** and reassign the range name to the correct cells.

If you use the Move command to move one corner of a named range, you effectively change the range of cells to which the range name is assigned. This is often an easy way to change a range name, but if you don't intend to stretch or contract a range with the Move command, the result can be disastrous. When you move groups of cells on a worksheet containing many named ranges, you should check the range name assignments after using the Move command to make sure you haven't inadvertently damaged the structure of the spreadsheet.

THE SYSTEM COMMAND

The System command is a way to temporarily invoke your computer's operating system. When you select System from the Slash command menu,

1-2-3 returns you to your computer's operating system and displays the important message:

(Type EXIT and press RETURN to return to 1-2-3)

EXIT and RETURN (the key called ENTER in this book) are your magic keys back into 1-2-3. Don't forget them.

Once you have exited to the operating system, a prompt such as **C>** appears and your computer is waiting for a command. You can now format a diskette, copy files, or copy a diskette. You can also run another program, such as a word processor or a telecommunications program. A typical use of the System command is to alternate between using 1-2-3 and your word processing program. You can do analysis with 1-2-3 and then quickly exit to the word processor to write up your results. In the meantime, 1-2-3 remains in memory so you can return to the worksheet quickly to verify a point or to do further analysis.

When Not to Use the System Command

After you use the System command, you can do any action with your computer that you can normally do, with the following exceptions:

- The number and variety of programs you can run with 1-2-3 in memory depends on how much memory a particular program requires, and how much RAM is left over from the storage of the 1-2-3 program and the current stack in memory. Obviously, this feature works best if your computer contains a large amount of RAM.

- You cannot take an action that causes your computer to clear its memory, such as rebooting the computer by pressing **CTRL-ALT-DEL** or turning the computer off and then on. Actions that clear memory clear 1-2-3 from memory.

- When you are finished running other programs and want to return to 1-2-3, you must first return to an operating system prompt. It doesn't need to be the same drive designator that appeared when you left 1-2-3. Any drive designator will do, but if you are in a program, you must exit that program and return to the operating system.

Once you return to an operating system prompt, type **EXIT** and press **ENTER**. As if by magic, your 1-2-3 worksheet reappears, just as you left it before you selected the System command.

Warning

For the System command to work properly, any program you run after exiting to the operating system must respect 1-2-3's memory allocation. The operating system utilities such as COPY and FORMAT cause no problems, but some programs—particularly terminate and stay resident (TSR) utilities such as SideKick™—write over part of the memory space reserved for 1-2-3 program code or spreadsheet storage. In that case, you won't be able to get back into your spreadsheet. Because unpredictable results may occur when you use the System command, be prepared. If you have modified your spreadsheet during the work session, always use the File Save command to save it before using the command. (See Chapter 5.)

THE QUIT COMMAND

The Quit command is used exactly once each 1-2-3 work session: to end the session. Like the Copy and Move commands, it is a high-level Slash command. You only need type a small number of keystrokes to execute the Quit command, and you have few choices to make along the way. (See Figure 4–15 for the command tree.)

To use the Quit command to end a 1-2-3 work session type

/Q   Enters the Quit command.

No Yes   1-2-3 wants you to confirm your intention to leave the program.

Figure 4–15   Quit command tree.

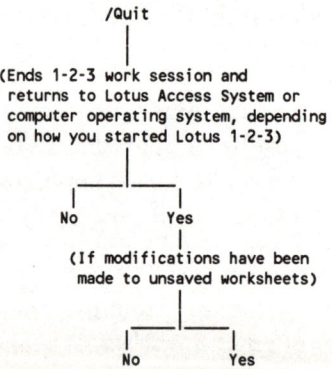

No Yes   If you have modified a worksheet and *have not* saved it, 1-2-3 reminds you and gives you a second chance to end the Quit command and save your work.

Lotus quits the work session only if you press **Y** for yes or if you move the command line cursor to **Yes** and press **ENTER**. If you press any other key, 1-2-3 beeps an error (on those machines with speakers) and waits for you to find the right key. On other machines, Lotus displays an error message and waits. (You can also use **ESC** and **CTRL-BREAK** to cancel a Quit command.)

Anything in your microcomputer's memory at the time you execute the Quit command is lost forever, so 1-2-3 displays a second prompt if any of the worksheets in memory have been modified but not saved. Take the opportunity presented by this second **Yes/No** "sanity check" to be sure that you have saved the current worksheet. If you don't want to save your modified worksheets, you must reaffirm that you don't by typing **Y** a second time.

Leaving 1-2-3 "ungracefully" by simply turning off the power switch or rebooting the computer is not recommended, but unlike some other programs, leaving in this fashion doesn't damage data or program files. Still, make it a habit to leave "gracefully," so that you remember to save the last worksheet you were working on.

HANDS ON: USING THE COPY COMMAND

As noted at the beginning of this chapter, the Copy command is the most useful and most frequently used of all 1-2-3 commands. With the Copy command you can take a few formulas in a few cells and in a few keystrokes create an entire worksheet.

This command is particularly useful for constructing worksheets that project future performance by means of formulas relating successive periods to a base period. Examples include budgets, sales projections, and business plans. They also include the retirement planning worksheet discussed in this Hands On section.

Constructing the Individual Retirement Account Worksheet

In an Individual Retirement Account (IRA), income accumulates tax-free to wage earners in the United States. It can be a powerful tool for accumulating a retirement nest egg, and a spreadsheet is a natural way to project the effects of various choices on the savings available at retirement. The sample spreadsheet developed here can also be used to analyze any savings program—for college, to buy a home, or for a vacation.

Figure 4–16 contains the starting point for the IRA worksheet. To construct the worksheet, enter the labels (set the Worksheet Global Label to Right), and then enter the formulas as shown in Figure 4–16. Notice the use of absolute cell references in some of the formulas.

Set the Global Col-Width to 12 characters and the Global Format to currency. Also set the format for cell B8 to Percent, Two decimals and set the block A:B18..A:C19 to Fixed, Zero decimals.

Certain assumptions must be made. Modify them to fit your circumstances. It is assumed the worksheet is constructed in 1990 and the age of the individual is 35 years.

The assumptions about your starting balance, annual contribution, and interest rate have been entered into an assumption space rather than as elements in the main body of the table. This makes it easy to do a "What If . . ." analysis. An assumption space should be a standard part of every worksheet you construct. When the worksheet is finished, you can enter

Figure 4–16 Formulas for Individual Retirement Account worksheet.

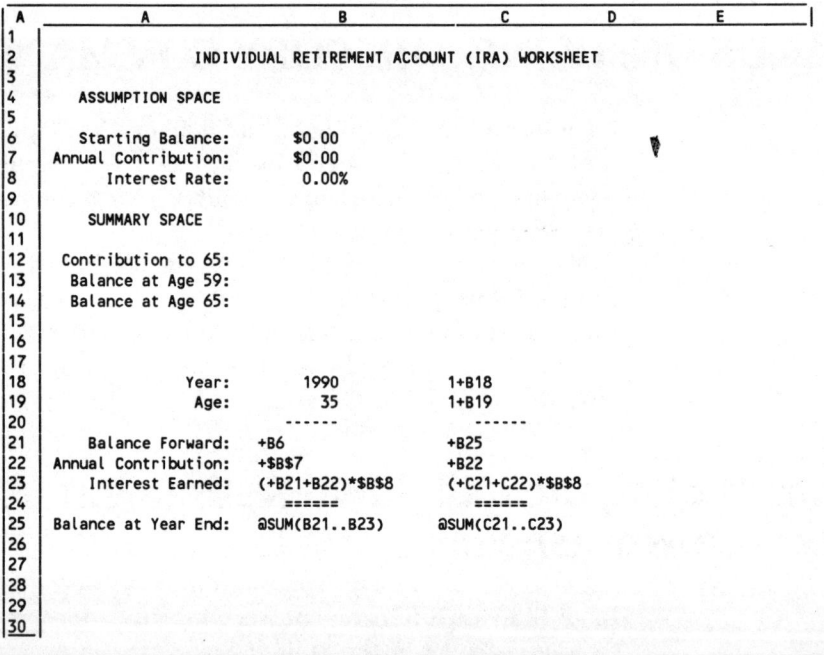

THE COPY, MOVE, SYSTEM, AND QUIT COMMANDS

different assumptions to discover what happens to your retirement nest egg.

Because you are not so much interested in the year-to-year details as you are in the amounts available at age 59 and at age 65, the worksheet is also constructed with a summary space. (The rules allow withdrawals from an IRA account to begin either at age 59½ or at age 65.) The summary space and the assumption space are on the screen at the same time, so you can immediately see the results of a change in one of the assumptions.

Note that the year and the age (rows 18 and 19) are simple counting functions—each cell is one more than the cell to the left. This makes it easy to modify the time span and the age by entering different years and ages into cells A:B18 and A:B19. Alternatively, age and starting year could be included in the entry space. (Sequences of numbers such as age and year can also be entered efficiently with the Data Fill command discussed in Chapter 8.)

To complete the worksheet, position the cursor on cell A:C18 and type

/C	Enters the Copy command.
DOWN	Stretches the cursor over the FROM range, A:C18..A:C25.
ENTER	Specifies the FROM range.
RIGHT	Positions the cursor on first cell of TO range, A:D18.
.	Tacks the cursor to A:D18.
TAB	Stretches the cursor to the left by screenfuls. Press TAB several times.
ENTER	Executes the Copy command.

In performing this exercise you don't need to calculate the number of columns required. The Copy command is so easy to use that trial and error is the most efficient way to complete the table. Copy a number of columns and let 1-2-3 tell you if you have made enough copies. If you have too many, use the Range Erase command. If you have too few, make some more copies. See Figure 4–17 for the result of using the Copy command.

To complete the main body of the table, locate and enter the cell references for the information in the summary space as shown in Figure 4–17. Adjust the cell references for your starting age. The worksheet is now finished.

Figure 4-17 Figure 4-16 after the Copy command has been used to copy the contents of C18..C25 into the range D18..AF18.

```
     A              A              B           C          D          E                  AD         AE         AF
 1
 2                        INDIVIDUAL RETIREMENT ACCOUNT (IRA) WORKSHEET
 3
 4         ASSUMPTION SPACE
 5
 6       Starting Balance:       $0.00
 7     Annual Contribution:      $0.00
 8           Interest Rate:      0.00%
 9
10         SUMMARY SPACE                    Formulas for SUMMARY SPACE
11
12      Contribution to 65:      $0.00   <-- @SUM(B22..AF22)
13       Balance at Age 59:      $0.00   <-- +Z25
14       Balance at Age 65:      $0.00   <-- +AF25
15
16
17
18                    Year:       1991       1992       1993       1994              2019       2020       2021
19                     Age:         35         36         37         38                63         64         65
20                               ------     ------     ------     ------            ------     ------     ------
21        Balance Forward:       $0.00      $0.00      $0.00      $0.00             $0.00      $0.00      $0.00
22     Annual Contribution:      $0.00      $0.00      $0.00      $0.00             $0.00      $0.00      $0.00
23         Interest Earned:      $0.00      $0.00      $0.00      $0.00             $0.00      $0.00      $0.00
24                               ======     ======     ======     ======            ======     ======     ======
25     Balance at Year End:      $0.00      $0.00      $0.00      $0.00             $0.00      $0.00      $0.00
26
27
28
29
30
```

Using the Individual Retirement Account Worksheet

Figure 4-18 shows the worksheet in action. It is a simple matter to discover what happens if you double your annual contribution, begin with a certain balance, or are able to earn a higher or lower interest rate. What would take hours with a pencil, paper, and calculator can be performed instantaneously with 1-2-3.

TIPS & TRAPS

Tips

Split-Screen Copying.

When the screen is split or Perspective view is active, the **WINDOW/F6** key can be used to move the cursor from one window to another during

Figure 4-18   Completed IRA worksheet with assumptions entered into assumption space.

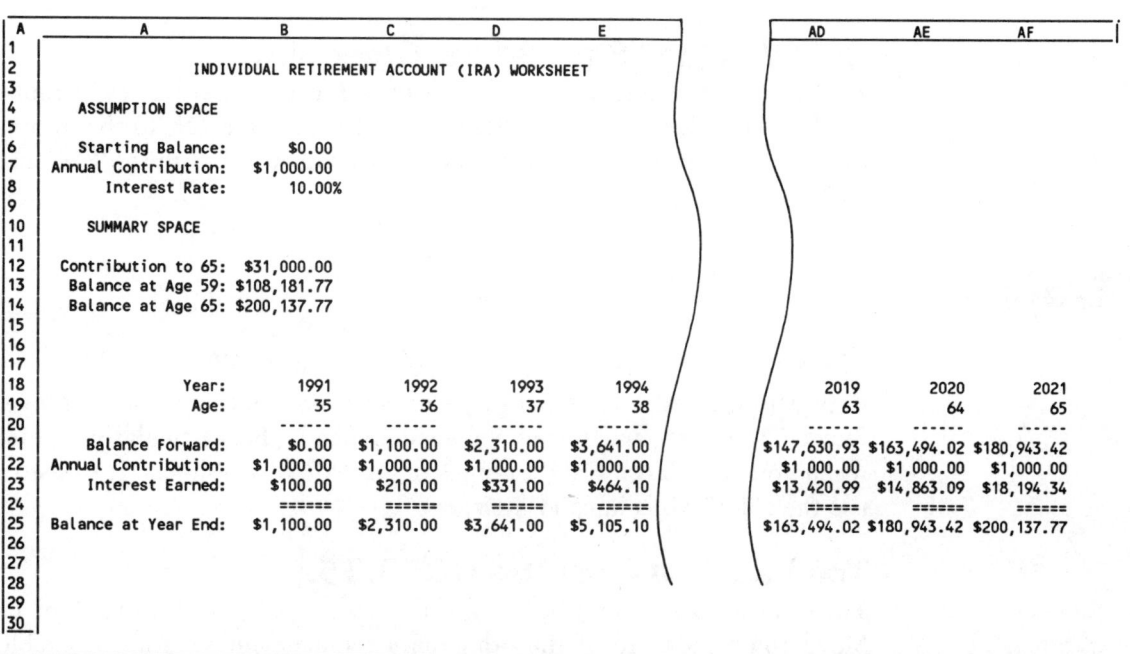

the Copy, Move, Value, or Transpose commands. This technique makes it easy to use these commands on remote parts of the current sheet or on other sheets in a stack. Be sure to split the screen or enter Perspective view *before* you enter one of these commands and to position the appropriate cells in each window.

Multiple Copies Made Easy.

If you have to make multiple copies of the same FROM range, begin by using the Range Name Create command to name the range. Then position the cursor where a copy goes, type /C, and use the **NAME/F3** key to enter the FROM range. Choosing a range name such as AA makes it particularly easy to find the range name on the name list. This tip is particularly useful for copying rectangles or blocks.

Don't Forget How to Point.

All of the cursor control keys can be used when you point at the FROM or TO ranges for any of the commands discussed in this chapter, even when the ranges extend across several sheets in a stack. Don't forget the

Big Move keys such as **PGUP** and **PGDN**, the **END** arrow key combinations, and the stack movement keys, such as **CTRL-PGUP** and **CTRL-PGDN**.

But I Want to "Stretch" the Other Way.
To "stretch" the cursor in another direction, use the period key to move the free cell, denoted by the flashing underline character, to the appropriate corner. If necessary, you can unstick the cursor with the **ESC** and **BKSP** keys.

Traps

"Watch Out, TO Range. Here We Come!"
Entries in the cells of the TO range are overwritten by the Copy, Move, Range Transpose, and Range Values commands. Be particularly careful when you copy large FROM ranges on crowded worksheets. It's best to use the File Save command first.

Too Bad. You Can't Use GOTO/F5.
The GOTO/F5 key can't be used while you are using any of the Copy or Move commands. All of the other cursor movement keys are available and, if the screen is split into windows or is in Perspective view, you can use the **WINDOW/F6** key to move between windows.

Range Transposing with Formulas.
The Range Transpose command doesn't transpose formulas. It only transposes the displayed values of any formulas in the range to be transposed. If you need formulas in the transposed results, you must re-create each formula after the transposition of the displayed values.

5 The File Command

OBJECTIVES

After mastering the content of this chapter, you will be able to

☐ store and retrieve worksheets, stacks, and parts of stacks with the File Save and Retrieve commands.

☐ choose good filenames and organize your library of stored worksheets.

☐ store and retrieve parts of worksheets and combine them with worksheets already in memory.

☐ combine stored files into a stack with the File Open command.

☐ add a new, empty file to a stack with the File New command.

☐ set the reservation status of files, seal files, and generate tables of filenames with the File Admin command.

INTRODUCTION

The Need to Save

The need for the File command arises from the fact that 1-2-3 is an *electronic* spreadsheet. The sheets and stacks you create in your microcomputer's memory are temporary. They exist only as long as a steady supply of electricity is available, and they disappear the instant the power is interrupted. Consequently, you must have a way to store sheets, stacks, and files when you aren't using them and to retrieve them when you want to use them again.

In addition to a complete loss of power, other variations in the electric supply can spell disaster for the contents of your computer's memory. Voltage spikes caused by electrical equipment such as office copiers or elevators and brownouts (slow reductions in the voltage level) have the potential to cause the loss of everything in your computer's memory as surely as turning off the power switch.

To avoid losing valuable information and the time taken to construct a stack, you must save each of the active files in a stack to a diskette or to a hard disk. If you have saved an active file and you do lose the contents of your microcomputer's memory, you still have a copy on a diskette or on a hard disk.

Once stored, a file can be recalled and reused at any time. Stored files become part of an electronic file cabinet into which you place files and from which you retrieve past files for examining, updating, or using as the bases for new worksheets.

Files, Stacks, and Sheets

The elements of a stack that are saved are the active files. If the stack contains only one active file, saving it saves the entire stack. When there is more than one active file, *each* active file must be saved separately.

If the stack contains only one worksheet, it necessarily contains only one file. Then saving the worksheet is the same as saving the file. It is also the same as saving the stack. In this book *saving a worksheet* means saving the active file containing the worksheet. *Saving a stack* means saving all of the active files in the stack.

Save Partially Constructed Worksheets

In addition to storing copies of every active file you want to use again, make it a habit to store files containing partially constructed worksheets. This guards against power failures, as well as any serious mistakes you might make while constructing a worksheet, such as using the Worksheet Erase command at the wrong time. A good rule is to store an active file containing the sheet you are working on whenever you have put in more time and trouble than you'd care to repeat.

Back Up, Back Up, Back Up

Not only must you save worksheets so you can reuse them, but you must also observe the first three rules of microcomputer use: (1) Back up!, (2) Back up!, and (3) Back up!

THE FILE COMMAND

Make backup copies of your data diskettes with the operating system's Copy or Diskcopy command.

Backup copies are necessary because diskettes do wear out, and they are subject to unexpected failure due to stray magnetism (from metal paper clips, for example). The time required to copy a diskette is tiny compared to the time required to re-create the files it contains when the diskette fails.

If you work on a computer equipped with a hard disk, it is particularly important to make regular backup copies of your files on floppy diskettes, a streaming tape, or some other medium. Hard disks can and do fail. When they do, all of your work is lost. A hard disk can store many, many more files than a single floppy disk, so the loss can be catastrophic. Take out the only insurance you have against disk failure: back up, back up, back up.

The File Command Options

Figure 5–1 shows the overall command tree for the File command. The first two options, Retrieve and Save, usually operate on the current file. However, when two or more active files have been modified, selecting File Save gives you the option of saving **ALL MODIFIED FILES** at one time.

Figure 5–1 File command tree.

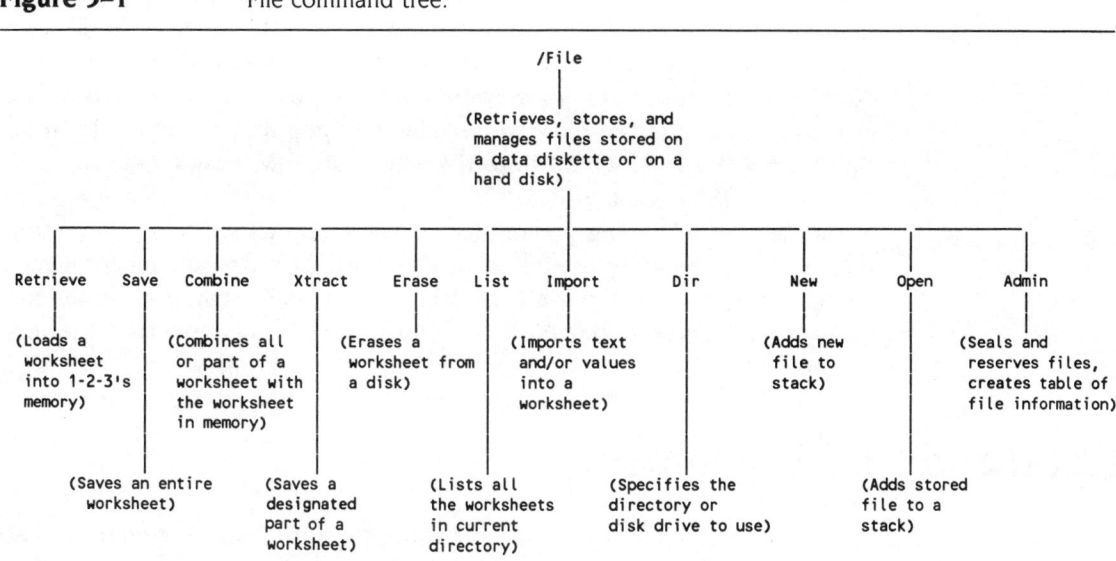

The Retrieve and Save commands are the most often used options on the File command menu.

The Combine and Xtract options operate on a range of cells rather than on the current file as a whole. They are powerful tools for breaking a large worksheet into several parts and for consolidating information from two or more files into a single file. The Import option takes standard text files such as those created with many word processing programs or by downloading from a mainframe computer and (in conjunction with the Data Parse command discussed in Chapter 10) translates them into 1-2-3 spreadsheets.

The options Erase, List, Dir, and Admin are used to manage your library of stored worksheet files and to specify the directory to be used to save and retrieve files. Finally, New and Open are used to add existing files (Open) and new files (New) to a stack. Use these commands when you want to have two or more active files in memory at the same time.

FILENAMES

Before you can use the File command on a worksheet, you must assign a filename to that worksheet. A *filename* is simply a group of letters, numbers, and, sometimes, other characters. Lotus uses filenames to keep track of stored worksheets; consequently, stored worksheets are often called *files*.

The exact characters that can be used in a filename vary from one operating system to another, so check your operating system manual. Most operating systems accept at least the letters (A–Z), numbers (0–9), and the underline character in their filenames. Many computers accept other characters, so check for your system's list of valid filename characters. Because it is one of the most widespread and popular, the examples used throughout this book conform to the Microsoft/IBM Disk Operating System (MS-DOS®), version 3.3.

In addition to having a short list of valid characters, many operating systems limit filenames to eight characters or less and won't accept names containing spaces, the period, or other characters, such as $ or %. You may type letters in either upper- or lowercase; 1-2-3 converts all letters to uppercase.

Good and Bad Filenames

Within the constraints imposed on you, you must choose filenames that (1) give good information about what the file contains and (2) give some indication of how a file is related to similar files. Informative filenames are important, because days or even months may pass between the date you assign a filename and the next time you want to load the file. If the filename doesn't tell you what the file contains, you can waste lots of time loading several different files before you find the one you are looking for.

Examples

With a little care and practice, you can master the art of choosing good filenames. Here are some examples.

Bad filenames	Good filenames
TABLE1	CH6_TBL1
BUDGET	BUD_PROJ
BUDGET	BUD_ACTL
EXPENSES	TRAVL_XP
1ST_QT	SALES_1Q
TEST	TRIAL_BL

The AUTO123 Filename

If you name a file AUTO123 and store it in the default directory, 1-2-3 automatically loads the file when you first run the program at the start of each work session. If you always begin your work sessions with a particular worksheet, this feature saves a few keystrokes. To see an example of how an AUTO123 file can be combined with an autoexecuting macro to provide a startup menu, see Chapter 12.

Filename Extensions

To keep track of the different types of files you can create, Lotus 1-2-3 automatically adds an extension to each filename. The following list shows the extensions automatically assigned to different types of files by Releases 1A, 2, 2.01, and 3 of Lotus 1-2-3.

Filename Extension	File/Program
.WK3	Worksheet file (up to 256 sheets), 1-2-3 Release 3. (This is the default; change with Worksheet Global Default Ext command.)

.WK1	Worksheet, 1-2-3 Release 2 and 2.01.
.WKS	Worksheet, 1-2-3 Release 1A.
.WKE	Worksheet, educational version.
.BAK	Worksheet, backup file, Release 3 only.
.ENC	Worksheet (graphs optional). Encoded file for printing with the DOS command TYPE. Created with the Print command, Release 3 only.
.PIC	Graph files, all versions. Created with the Graph command.
.CGM	Graph file, Release 3. Created with the Graph command.
.PRN	Print (ASCII) files, all versions. Created with the Print command.
.TMP	Temporary file created by Release 3 for use during operations. (Don't erase.)

Graph files (.PIC and .CGM) contain graphs for printing with the PrintGraph utility. Print files (.PRN) are copies of 1-2-3 worksheets stored in a file format that can be used by many word processing programs. You can use print files to incorporate 1-2-3 worksheets into reports. Print files are not created with the File command. Rather, they are created with the Print command, discussed in the next chapter.

The complete filename for a typical Release 3 worksheet file follows the form CH6_TBL1.WK3. There could exist at the same time on the same diskette a graph file named CH6_TBL1.PIC and a print file named CH6_TBL1.PRN. Even though the main part of the filename is the same, 1-2-3 distinguishes between the worksheet file (.WK3), the graph file (.PIC), and the print file (.PRN). Because you can create picture files and print files only after you have created the worksheet, the same filename with different extensions is a good way to make explicit the relationship among a print file, a picture file, and the underlying worksheet file.

Organizing Your Worksheet Files

It won't take you long to generate a large number of 1-2-3 worksheets. If you expect your microcomputer to make your organization tasks easier, you may be in for a big surprise. Generating worksheets is easy, but the result can be as messy and hard to use as many people's hall closet.

You have to organize your worksheets, and the sooner you adopt a system—any system—the sooner you can get the full use of your worksheet library.

Here are some suggestions for organizing your files.

1. Choose informative filenames. As already noted, picking informative filenames is the most important step you can take in organizing your worksheet files.

2. Include the exact filename as a line of text on each worksheet. The filename appears on each printout you make, and you can easily return to the file to modify or update it, or to make additional copies. If you want to omit the filename from a particular printout, erase it with the Range Erase command just before you print the file.

3. Keep printed copies of each worksheet. A printed copy of a worksheet tells exactly what the file contains. This, of course, makes it easier to locate a particular worksheet.

4. Store similar worksheets together on a single diskette or in a single directory on a hard disk. If, for example, all budget projections are on a diskette labeled "Budget Projections," you won't have to sift through personal records, expense accounts, or sales records to find what you are looking for.

5. If your computer doesn't automatically do it, set the system date and time when you first load 1-2-3. The time and date at which each worksheet was saved can be viewed when you use the File commands. This information can help you distinguish between several worksheets with similar filenames.

These suggestions should help you organize your worksheet files. But more important than specific suggestions is that you recognize the need for organization and adopt a system for keeping track of the files. Otherwise, you end up denying yourself easy access to your rapidly growing library of electronic spreadsheets.

THE FILE SAVE AND FILE RETRIEVE COMMANDS

The most frequently used commands under the File command are Save and Retrieve. (See Figure 5-2 for the command tree.) Both operate on an entire file and both enable you to pick an existing filename from the prompt line in the control panel.

Formatted Diskettes

Before you can save a spreadsheet, you must have some place to put it. If you have a hard disk, you probably have adequate room to store your files. If, on the other hand, you use diskettes, you must have a formatted data diskette available before you can save an active file. Diskettes are formatted with the DOS Format command.

Figure 5-2   The File Save and the File Retrieve command tree.

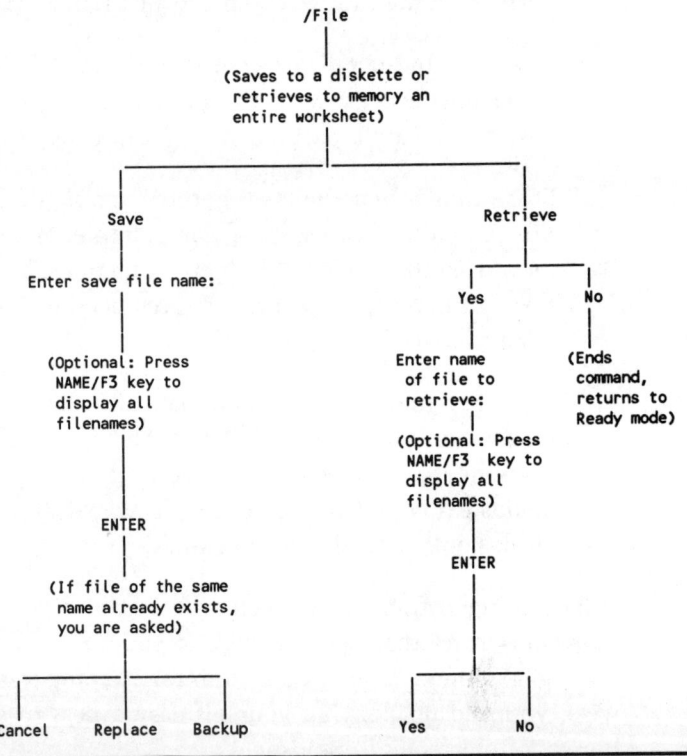

THE FILE COMMAND

You should format your data diskettes before running 1-2-3, but in Chapter 4 you learned how to use the System command to exit to your computer's operating system while leaving your 1-2-3 worksheet intact in memory. Once you've exited to the system level, you can format a data diskette and then return to 1-2-3.

The File Save Command

Active files stored with the File Save command contain all the information necessary to reconstruct all of the sheets in the active file exactly as they were at the moment you executed the File Save command. In particular, the file contains all of the sheets and their assigned column widths, screen splits, named ranges, proposed ranges, protection status, and the location of the worksheet cursor, as well as all Global and Range Format command and label alignment choices you have made.

Saving an Active File

Assuming you have a formatted data diskette or have room on your hard disk, you are now ready to use the File Save command. Because stacks can be made up of more than one active file, you must position the cursor in the active file you want to save. If the stack contains only one active file, the cursor can be anywhere in the stack. If the stack contains more than one active file, move the cursor to any cell on any sheet in the active file you want to save. Then type

/FS	Enters the File Save command.
Enter name of file to save:	If two or more active files have been modified, 1-2-3 suggests you save **ALL MODIFIED FILES**.
ENTER	Saves all modified files.
or	
EDIT	To replace **ALL MODIFIED FILES** with name of current file.
or	
filename	Type a new filename.
ENTER	Execute the command.

Cancel Replace Backup   Displayed if filename already exists. Select **Replace** to save under proposed filename. Select **Cancel** to cancel the File Save command. Select **Backup** to rename the existing file with a .BAK extension.

If you have retrieved a file this work session, the filename of the last file retrieved appears as the proposed filename. This way you can easily perform an updating operation where you load a worksheet, update it, and then save the updated version under the same filename. You can also press **ESC** to clear the proposed filename and display all of the filenames in the current directory.

If you are saving a file for the first time, 1-2-3 assigns it a default filename of the form **FILEnnnn.WK3**. The **nnnn** is replaced by a number such as 0001 or 0002 in sequence, which indicates the first or second default filename assigned this work session. When more than one file is active and you have made modifications to the files, 1-2-3 responds to your request to save a file with **ALL MODIFIED FILES**, as shown in Figure 5–3.

You can press **ENTER** to save all modified files. To save your spreadsheet under a new filename, just start typing. The proposed filename disappears, and the characters you type appear as the new filename. When

Figure 5–3   File Save command with [ALL MODIFIED FILES] displayed.

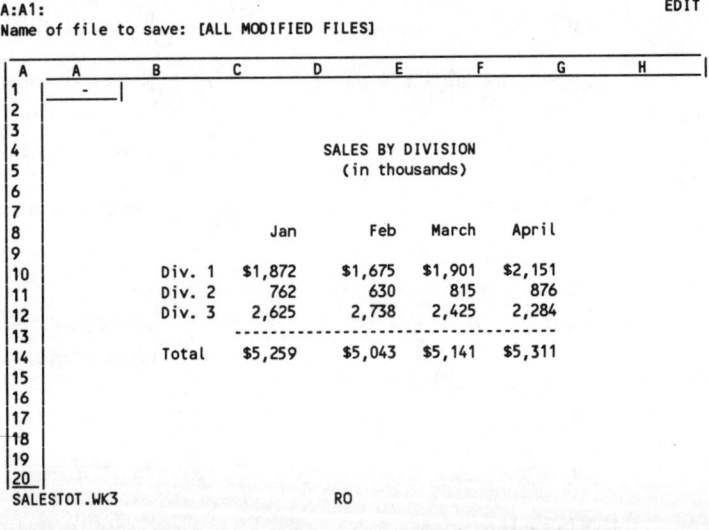

THE FILE COMMAND 173

you are finished, press **ENTER** to save your spreadsheet. If a file is inadvertently saved under a default name, retrieve the file and save it again under a proper filename.

Cancel, Replace, or Backup

If you try to save a worksheet under a filename that already exists, 1-2-3 asks whether you want to cancel the command, replace the existing file, or create a backup file. Filenames must be unique on each diskette or in each subdirectory, so selecting Replace and saving a worksheet under an existing filename erases the worksheet previously stored under that filename.

To prevent the accidental erasure of stored worksheets, 1-2-3 gives you two options. If you want to change the filename, select Cancel or, better yet, press **ESC** to back up one step in the File Save command so you can specify a new filename. If you want to convert the stored file to a backup file, select Backup. The stored file is renamed with a .BAK extension, and the file you are saving is saved with the .WK3 extension. Warning: Any previously created backup file with the same filename is lost.

Be certain you want to eliminate the stored copy of a file before you select Replace instead of Cancel or Backup; once you select Replace, you cannot stop the command. Also, Undo has no effect on stored files.

Beware: If you accept the **ALL MODIFIED FILES** option and then select Replace, each active file replaces its counterpart on disk. Do this only if you are *certain* you want to replace each of the stored files with its current version. It is safer to press **ESC** and save each active file individually. Don't worry about forgetting to save a modified file. If you try to Erase the stack or Quit 1-2-3, a message tells you that there are unsaved files in memory. Just select No and save the files.

Using the NAME/F3 Key

Most of the File commands display filenames on the third line of the control panel at the top of the screen. Only four filenames can appear there at one time. To see all of the filenames on a diskette or in a current subdirectory, press the **NAME/F3** key. See Figure 5-4 for a sample of the screen as it appears when you press NAME/F3.

Once names are displayed, you can move through the list with the arrow keys until you highlight the name you want. Then press **ENTER** to select it. As a bonus, 1-2-3 displays the size of the highlighted file in bytes and the date and time the file was created, all at the top of the filename list.

Figure 5-4 Using NAME/F3 with the File Retrieve command to display all of the filenames on the current data diskette or current subdirectory.

```
A:A1:                                                                    FILES
Enter name of file to retrieve: C:\123R3\FINANCE*.WK*
          ANDYC.WK3      25-July-90      01:20 AM        20480
ANDYC.WK3        AUDREYHRS.WK3     BALDUE.WK3        CLIENTS.WK3
ERINCAR.WK3      EXPENSES.WK3      INCOME89.WK3      IRA.WK3
KNOWCKS.WK3      KNOWHOW.WK3       LETTER.WK3        MEGANCAR.WK3
PHONEBIL.WK3     PHONEDIR.WK3      RENTAL.WK3        TEST.WK3
UCCOURSE.WK3     BUDGET\           FINANCE\          REVENUE\
```

Names of subdirectories below the current directory are displayed followed by a backslash, as in BUDGET\, FINANCE\, and REVENUE\ in Figure 5-4. To select a file from one of the subdirectories, place the cursor on the subdirectory name and press **ENTER**.

When you select a subdirectory, 1-2-3 lists all of the .WK3, .WK1, and .WKS files in that subdirectory. Unlike previous versions of 1-2-3, if you press **NAME/F3** to display all of the filenames in the first subdirectory, Release 3 doesn't continue the full-screen display when you move to a new subdirectory.

To view files in a subdirectory above the current subdirectory, press **BKSP**. 1-2-3 doesn't display any files until you make a selection.

Note: 1-2-3 doesn't remember any directory changes made by selecting subdirectories from the displayed list of files. To change to a new default subdirectory, see the File Directory command later in this chapter. However, when you save a file retrieved from a directory that isn't the current default subdirectory it is automatically saved into the subdirectory from which it was loaded.

Using Wildcards

To display all the files that have .WK3, .WK1, .WKE, or .WKS filename extensions, 1-2-3 essentially executes an operating system Directory command by applying the pattern *.WK*.

This means you can set up your own criteria with the operating system wildcard characters ? and * to view a group of files meeting your criteria. The question mark accepts any single character in the place of the question mark and the asterisk accepts any character in place of the asterisk, *and* any characters can occupy the remaining places in the filename. A couple of examples should make this clear:

What you type   **What 1-2-3 finds**

  *.W??   Any filename with an extension beginning with W.

THE FILE COMMAND

M*.* Any filename beginning with M.

If you have a group of budget files, such as BUDGETIQ.WK3 and BUDGETPJ.WK3, you can use the pattern BUDGET*.* to display only the budget files.

Password-Protected Files

You can assign a personal password to a file so that the file can only be loaded by someone who knows the password. The technique is simple. After specifying a filename, press the **SPACE BAR** once, type a **p** for *password,* and press **ENTER**. Lotus then prompts you to enter a password, which can be up to 15 characters long and can contain any text characters (numbers and letters) but no spaces. As you type, asterisks appear on the screen in place of the characters. When you are finished, press **ENTER**. Lotus then prompts, **Verify Password**. Type your password again and press **ENTER** to save the file.

When someone attempts to retrieve a password-protected file, a message asking for the password appears. The operator can only gain access by providing the correct password.

Warning: Remember your password. There is no way to retrieve a password-protected file without the correct password. Also, the password is case sensitive. That is, *open, Open,* and *oPen* are three separate passwords.

After you have saved a file as a password-protected file, you don't need to respecify the password each time you load the file (with the password, of course) and then save the file again under the same name. When you execute File Save, the message **PASSWORD PROTECTED** appears after the proposed filename. Pressing **ENTER** to save the file under that name saves it as a password-protected file.

Removing Password Protection

To remove the password protection, you must retrieve the file by supplying the password. Then use the File Save command to begin to save it. When the message **PASSWORD PROTECTED** appears, press the **BKSP** key to remove it. With **PASSWORD PROTECTED** gone, proceed to save the file. It no longer is password protected.

Saving Files in Release 2 Format

Release 3 of Lotus 1-2-3 can save a file in a format that can be read directly by Release 2. To share a file with someone who is still using Release 2 or 2.01 or to use the file with a program that can understand Release 2 files, just add the Release 2 worksheet filename extension, .WK1, to the filename when you save the file with File Save. If you don't supply the filename extension, 1-2-3 supplies .WK3 as the extension (unless changed with the Worksheet Global Default Ext command) and saves the file in a format that can only be read by Release 3 versions of 1-2-3.

Note: For a file to be usable with Release 2, you must use the Release 3 File Save command to save the worksheet with a .WK1 extension. You can't simply rename the file with the appropriate operating system command. If you do, you'll still have a file that can only be used with Release 3. Files saved in Release 2 format with the .WK1 extension must

- contain only one worksheet.

- contain no @ functions new to Release 3:
@DUET, @DQUERY, @DSTDS, @DVARS, @D360, @VDB, @ISRANGE, @COORD, @INFO, @SHEETS, @STDS, @SUMPRODUCT, and @VARS.

- contain no formulas linked to data in other files.

- not be sealed with the File Admin Seal command.

- not be a read only file, set with the File Admin Reservation command.

If an active file meets these requirements, supply the .WK1 extension when you specify the filename with the File Save command, and the file can be loaded by Release 2.0 or 2.01 or by other programs that can read worksheet files saved in that format.

If you include one of the new Release 3 @ functions, **NA** appears on the screen when you load the file into Release 2. The function name is replaced with a question mark, but the arguments remain. For example, @INFO("memavail") is a new Release 3 @ function that displays the available memory. When you save a worksheet containing @INFO with a .WK1 extension it is converted to @?("memavail"). All is not lost. If you load the file back into Release 3, the missing function is resupplied and the formula works as before.

You can also use the technique just described with the File Xtract command (discussed later in the chapter) to cut a single sheet out of a multiple sheet stack and save it in a format that can be read by programs that read only Release 2 file formats.

The File Retrieve Command

Once stored, a file can be reloaded into memory at any time. If you want to load an entire file and have it replace the current file, use the File Retrieve command. (Refer to Figure 5-2 for the command tree.) If you

THE FILE COMMAND

want to load only part of a file, use the File Combine command discussed in the next section. If you want to add a file to the stack in memory without erasing the other active files, use the File Open or File New commands discussed later in this chapter. In addition to Release 3 files, all files created by Release 1A, 2.0, 2.01, and Symphony 1.0 and 1.1 can be retrieved using the File Retrieve command.

To replace the stack currently in memory by retrieving an entire file from a data diskette or the current subdirectory, type

/FR	Enters File Retrieve command.
Enter name of file to retrieve:	First four filenames of files on the data diskette or in current subdirectories appear on the bottom line of the control panel.
NAME/F3	Optional. Displays all of the filenames on the screen at one time.
Arrow keys	Use the arrow keys to highlight the desired filename.
ENTER	Accepts the highlighted file.

When you enter the File Retrieve command, the filenames of the first four files on the data diskette or in the current subdirectory on a hard disk appear on the bottom line of the control panel, as shown in Figure 5-5. Only files with the filename extensions that meet the pattern .WK* (.WK3, .WK1, .WKS, and so on) are displayed.

Remember that you can display all of the filenames at one time by pressing the **NAME/F3** key. You can also display a subset of filenames by setting up your own criteria with the asterisk and the question mark. Finally, remember that subdirectories on a hard disk are also displayed and are available selections, just like filenames. Once you've displayed the filenames, either designate a file to load by typing its name or use the arrow keys to move through the existing filenames to highlight the name you want. Then press **ENTER** to retrieve the file.

The retrieved file is an exact copy of the file at the moment it was stored with the Save option.

Read Only (RO) Files

If you retrieve a file and the letters **RO** appear at the bottom of the screen, the file you have just retrieved is a "read only" file. You can view the file and work with it, but you cannot save the file under the same filename with the File Save or File Xtract command. Read only files are used on

Figure 5-5 Results of typing /FR: Lotus displays the first four filenames of the worksheets on the current data diskette or in the current subdirectory.

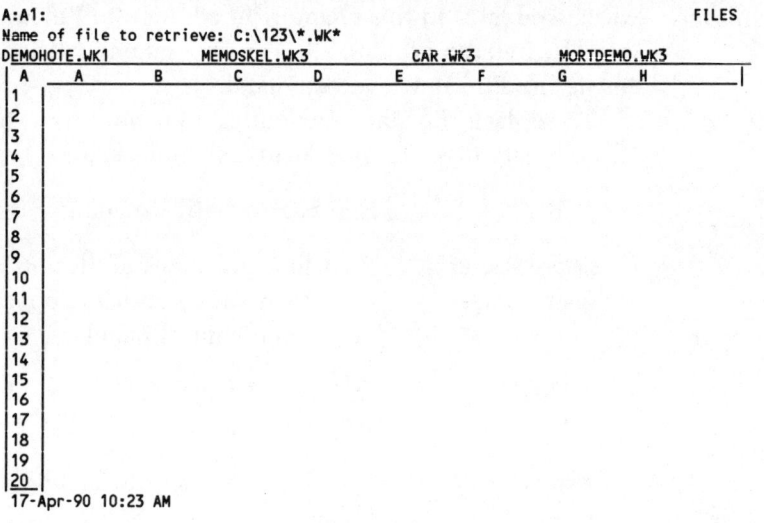

networks to prevent two or more operators from retrieving, changing, and saving the same file without each other's knowledge.

To obtain the right to save changes made to a read only file, use the File Admin Reservation command discussed later in the chapter to get the file reservation. The use of reserved files ensures that an operator on a network can verify that he or she is working with the most up-to-date copy of a file by obtaining the reservation. Without the reservation someone else on the network may retrieve, change, and save the changes without the first operator's knowledge.

Warning

Be careful when you use the File Retrieve command. Once you have selected a file to load, 1-2-3 replaces the current active file (the one containing the worksheet cursor) with the new file in memory. Other active files remain in memory, but the file that was previously the current active file has, in effect, been erased from memory. Use the File Open command discussed later to add a file to a stack without erasing any of the files already in it.

If Undo is active, you can immediately press **ALT-F4** to restore the stack. If Undo is not active and the current active file hasn't been saved, it is lost forever.

When using the File Retrieve command, you can press **ESC** to cancel the command before you press **ENTER** to execute it. Take this escape if you want to save any of the files in memory but forget to do so before you use File Retrieve again.

THE FILE XTRACT AND FILE COMBINE COMMANDS

The Save and Retrieve commands under File act on an entire file. The File Xtract command, on the other hand, saves designated ranges of cells into a file, whereas the Combine command retrieves designated ranges from a file and combines them with a file in memory.

Because the Copy, Move, or Range Value commands discussed in Chapter 4 can transfer information to and from the current file and a file stored on disk, they can do many of the tasks of the File Xtract and File Combine commands. You can also use the File Open command to place the file on disk in the stack or the File New command to create a new file. Then use Copy or Range Value to copy information from the file into the current sheet or vice versa. File New and Open are discussed later in this chapter.

The File Xtract Command

With the File Xtract command you can save part of an active file. The part you save can be a range on a single sheet or it can be a block extending across several sheets. You are also given the choice of saving only the displayed values or saving the underlying formulas.

The command is called *Xtract* rather than *Extract* because another choice on the File command menu, Erase, begins with the letter *E*. Figure 5-6 shows the command tree.

A file created with the File Xtract command is very much like one created with the File Save command. They both have the same extensions, and they can both be reloaded into memory with either the File Retrieve command or the File Combine command. Furthermore, if you choose a filename for the File Xtract command that already exists, the extracted file replaces the existing one. This is true even if the replaced file had originally been saved with the File Save command.

Using the File Xtract Command

To save part of a spreadsheet, position the cursor on the first cell of the range you want to extract and type

Figure 5-6 The File Xtract command tree.

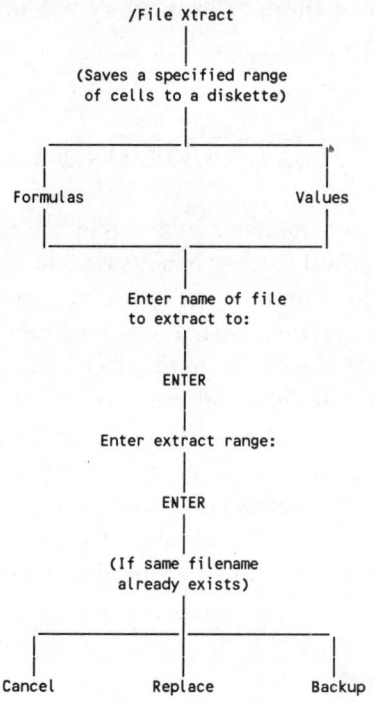

/FX	Enters the File Xtract command.
Formulas Values	Asks whether to save Formulas or only displayed values. Select one.
Enter xtract file name:	Lotus proposed a name of the form **FILEnnnn.WK3**. Optionally, type your own filename or press **NAME/F3** and select an existing filename.
ENTER	Enters proposed or specified filename.
Enter xtract range:	Use arrow keys to highlight range of cells to extract into specified file. Range can be on a single sheet or extend across several sheets in the same file.
ENTER	Executes the Xtract command.

As with the File Save command, if the filename you have assigned already exists on the disk or in the subdirectory, 1-2-3 asks whether you want to

Cancel, Replace, or Backup. Make the appropriate choice to complete the command.

Files created with the File Xtract command can also be password protected. The procedure is the same as that described for files created with the File Save command. For further information, see that discussion.

Extracting Formulas

Be very careful when you use the Formulas option to extract only part of a spreadsheet. If your extract range contains formulas that refer to cells outside the range, the formulas will almost certainly calculate incorrect values when extracted.

Make it a practice to extract all of the cells that are referred to by the formulas. That way, no matter how the extracted material is used, by itself or combined with other worksheets, the formulas calculate and display correct values. If you must extract formulas without extracting all of the cells the formulas refer to, retrieve the extracted worksheet and verify the correctness of each formula.

Removing Unneeded Information from the Extracted File

Files created with the File Xtract command contain *all* of the format commands, Col-Width settings, range names, named graphs, and so on, that the original file contains. Much of the information about named ranges, named graphs, and remembered ranges may no longer be required. You can reduce the size of the stored file by retrieving it and using appropriate commands to delete or reset the unneeded specifications. Then save the file again. Canceling these specifications often greatly reduces the size of the extracted file.

The File Combine Command

The File Combine command combines either an entire file or a named portion or specified cell addresses from it with the stack already in memory. The incoming file supplies text and values or values only to the cells. The file already in memory controls overall worksheet attributes such as column width, Global Format settings, and range names. See the command tree, Figure 5–7, for the File Combine command.

The file or range being combined with the File Combine command can be either two-dimensional or three-dimensional. If it is three-dimensional, there must be enough sheets after the current sheet in the current file to

Figure 5–7   The File Combine command tree.

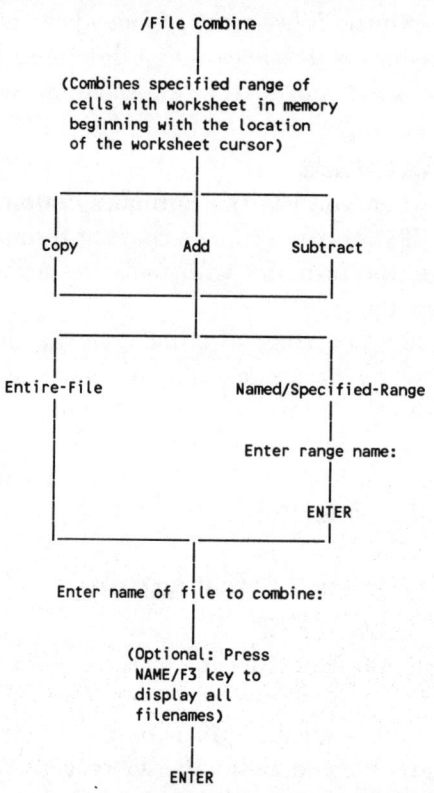

meet the requirements of the block being combined. That is, when you combine a file or range containing three sheets into a file, the file must contain at least two sheets after the current sheet (for a total of three sheets). If there is only one sheet after the current sheet (for a total of two sheets), there aren't enough sheets after the current sheet and an error message is displayed. If this happens, use the Worksheet Insert Sheet command to insert more blank sheets, then repeat the command.

An alternative to using the File Combine command is to use the File Open command to bring the file from disk to the stack. Then use the Copy and/or Range Value commands to transfer the desired information to the current sheet. If you frequently transfer information from the same cells in one file to another file, use formulas to link the files. See Chapter 7 for a discussion of linking formulas across files.

Position Cursor Before Entering File Combine Command

You *must* correctly position the worksheet cursor before entering the File Combine command because the worksheet cursor's location determines where the upper left cell of the incoming range appears. If the incoming range extends across several sheets, the cursor designates the front, upper left cell of the range. If you fail to correctly position the cursor, cancel the command with **ESC** or **CTRL-BREAK**, reposition the cursor, and begin again.

File Combine Options

The File Combine command gives you several ways to combine or merge files. You can combine either an entire file or part of a file in the form of a named or specified range of cell addresses. You can also choose to merge both text and formulas, or only to add or subtract values from existing cell values.

Once you are using the command, you are given two options:

Entire File — Select this option to combine the entire file into the current file.

Named/Specified Range — Select this option to combine only part of the file into the current file.

If you select Named/Specified Range, either supply a range name or designate a range with cell addresses, such as A:A1..G:H20. Range names are easier to use, but, unfortunately, Lotus doesn't have a way to display the names assigned to ranges in the worksheet to be combined. If you can't remember a range name, use File Open to bring the entire file into memory. Move the cursor through the file and use Range Name Table to find the names assigned to ranges in that file. Also, with the file in memory you can use Range Value or Copy to complete the combination.

If you are going to use a range name, either assign easy-to-remember names (for example, **combine** or **update**) or, if the operation is to be repeated, make a note of the range name on the *resident* worksheet. This note should contain both the filename of the incoming worksheet and the name assigned to the range of cells to be merged. If you repeat the combination operation frequently, you can save a great deal of work by putting all of the steps (including the range name) into a keyboard macro. (See Chapter 12 for instructions about creating keyboard macros.)

The File Combine command also gives you multiple ways of performing the combination. The commands under File Combine are

Copy	Everything (values, formulas, labels) is merged. Incoming information replaces resident information.
Add	Only displayed values from cells in specified range are added to value cells in resident sheet. Resident cells containing formulas and labels are bypassed.
Subtract	Only displayed values from cells in specified range are subtracted from value cells in resident sheet. Resident cells containing formulas and labels are bypassed.

You can use the Add option of the File Combine command to convert formulas in the incoming worksheet to displayed values by combining into a blank range in the resident stack. However, if you want to load labels at the same time, you must use the Copy option and then use the Range Values command to convert the formulas to displayed values.

Using the File Combine Command

Position the cursor on the upper left corner of the area where the combination is to take place. If you are selecting the Copy option, be sure there is nothing in the area to be merged to, because this option overwrites existing cell contents.

After you correctly position the cursor, type

/FC	Enters the File Combine command.
Copy Add Subtract	Select the method of combination.
Entire File	If you select this, it combines entire file.
or	
Named/Specified Range	If you select this, it combines specified part of file.
Enter range name:	If you select **Named/Specified**, enter range name or cell addresses of range (such as A:G46, BALANCE_FWD, A:A1..A:A10, or A:A1..G:F10).
ENTER	Accepts Named/Specified Range.
Enter name of file to combine:	Asks for the filename. NAME/F3 optional.

THE FILE COMMAND

ENTER   Completes the command and executes the combination.

Using File Combine to Correct Erased Cells

If you make a mistake and erase a cell on a sheet that you just loaded into memory and the Undo mode isn't active, you can position the cursor on the cell and use File Combine Named/Specified range. You can tell exactly which cell to combine by checking the Status Line.

This technique won't work if you have modified the loaded spreadsheet by inserting or deleting rows or columns or by moving cell contents. Otherwise, it is a simple way to repair a mistake without having to reload the entire file.

If Undo mode is active and you haven't taken any other action, press ALT-F4 to restore the stack to its previous appearance.

Linking Files

As an alternative to using the File Combine command, you can create links between files by referring to cells in different files. When you do, you must use the full cell address, including the filename of the file containing the cell or cells referred to and the complete path to the file if it isn't stored in the current directory. See the discussion in Chapter 7. When information regularly needs to be transferred between two spreadsheets, linking them with formulas is usually more efficient than using the File Combine command.

THE FILE NEW AND FILE OPEN COMMANDS

The File Open command reads an existing file from disk into a stack without erasing the stack. You are given the option of positioning the file either before or after the current file. The File New command creates a new blank file containing a single, blank worksheet and reads it into memory either before or after the current file. Both of these commands are very important in creating and managing 3-D stacks of 1-2-3 spreadsheets.

Using the File Open Command

With the File Open command you can create a stack containing all of the separate files pertaining to a particular project. You can then create formulas that link across sheets and files, copy information across files, and otherwise use the information from all of the files at one time. The only limitations are the standard ones: Your computer must have enough memory to contain the files you want to open and the total number of sheets in memory at one time cannot exceed 256. Figure 5–8 shows the command tree.

Important: To add a file to the stack in memory, you must first position the cursor in an active file that is either before or after the position where you want the new file to appear. The location of the cursor determines where the opened file is positioned in the stack.

Once the cursor is correctly positioned, type

/FO	Enters File Open command.
Before After	Asks whether the file is to be placed before or after the current file. Make your selection.
Enter name of file to open:	Filenames of the files on disk appear on the bottom line of the control panel.
NAME/F3	Optional. Displays all of the filenames on the screen at one time.
Arrow keys	Use the arrow keys to highlight the desired filename.

Figure 5–8   The File New and File Open command tree.

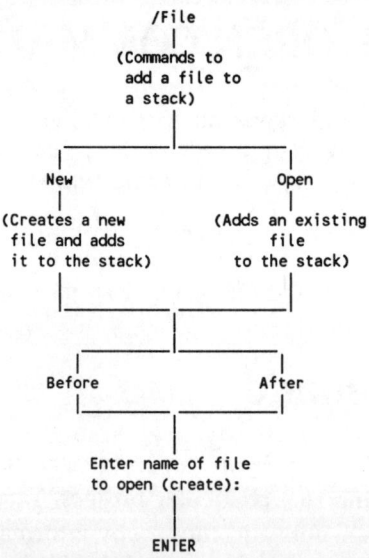

THE FILE COMMAND

ENTER — Accepts highlighted file and reads it into the stack either before or after the current file.

Note: Lotus uses the recalculation and window settings from the file *most recently* added to the stack. Therefore, using the File Open command may change the current recalculation and window settings.

Also, if the **RO** (read only) message appears at the bottom of the screen, the file you just read into the stack should not be changed. You don't have the reservation for the file, and Lotus won't let you save changes you make to the file unless you get its reservation. (See the Admin command described later for more about file reservations.)

When you finish with a stack, use the File Save **ALL MODIFIED FILES** option to save all files in the stack that you have modified during the current work session or save each file individually.

Using the File New Command

The File New command creates a new, blank file on disk and reads it into memory. The new file contains one blank sheet. Use this command to add new blank files to the stack in the same way that you use the Worksheet Insert command to add new blank worksheets to the current file. (Figure 5-8 also shows this command tree.)

To add a new file to the stack in memory, position the cursor in an active file that is either before or after the position where you want the new file to appear. Once the cursor is correctly positioned, type

/FN — Enters File New command.

Before After — Asks whether the file is to be placed before or after the current file. Make your selection.

Enter name of file to create: — Type a filename or accept the default filename of the form, **FILEnnnn.WK1**.

ENTER — Executes the command, creates a blank file on disk, and places it either before or after the current file.

When you execute the File New command, you should always supply a filename. But, if your creative faculties fail, you can have 1-2-3 supply a default filename of the form FILEnnnn.WK3. When the first new, unnamed file is created it is assigned the name FILE0001.WK3, the next is FILE0002.WK3, and so on. When you save the new file, be sure to assign it a descriptive filename, because even elephants can't remember the contents of a file named FILE0008.WK3.

THE FILE IMPORT COMMAND

The File Import command imports information from standard text files into 1-2-3 worksheets. (See Figure 5–9 for the command tree.) Standard text files can be created by many word processing programs, as well as by computer programming languages such as BASIC and FORTRAN. Text files, also called *ASCII files*, are often the form in which information is captured from a mainframe computer. If you plan to use a word processing program to create your text files, consult that program's manual for the exact details. If you plan to convert text to numbers, see the Data Parse command discussed in Chapter 10.

The .PRN Extension

When you use the File Import command, 1-2-3 displays all files with the .PRN filename extension. This is the extension 1-2-3 assigns when it creates a text file with the Print command. (See Chapter 6.) Furthermore, 1-2-3 won't import a file that doesn't have a .PRN extension. Thus, con-

Figure 5–9 The File Import command tree.

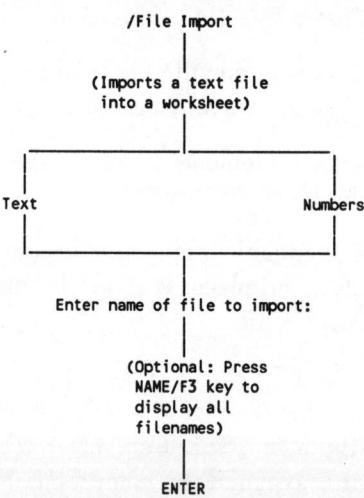

venience dictates that when you create print files to import into 1-2-3 you also choose the .PRN extension. If you can't, you can use the appropriate operating system command to rename the file before importing it.

Position Cursor Before Entering File Import Command

As for the File Combine command, you must properly position the worksheet cursor before entering the command. The cursor's location determines where imported text appears on the resident worksheet. Also be sure the area to be covered by the imported text only contains blank cells, because the imported material writes over the corresponding cells in the resident worksheet.

Text or Numbers

You have to choose whether to import the file as text or as numbers.

When you choose the Text option the file is imported as a *column* of left-aligned long labels beginning at the cursor location. Each line of text is placed in a separate cell in the column. Blank lines in the text result in blank cells (and therefore, blank lines) on the worksheet. If appropriate, you can use the Range Justify command discussed in Chapter 3 to rejustify the long labels into any desired column width.

If you choose the Numbers option, each number in the text file is assigned as a value to a separate cell. Any text enclosed in quotes, "text," for example, is placed in a single cell. Any text not in quotes is ignored by the File Import command.

1-2-3 treats a space as a separator. Thus 123 456 is considered two separate numbers and is placed in separate cells. Lotus also treats commas and the mathematical operators as separators. It, therefore, takes 123,456 and places 123 in one cell and 456 in a separate cell. If you have 1-2-3 in text, the program places the 1 in one cell followed by -2 and -3 in separated cells. Don't use commas in numbers you want to import and be careful about other characters in the file you are importing.

The Numbers option works best with files that are specially created by other computer programs. These are called *structured files* or *comma-separated files* and contain only numbers separated by spaces or commas and text enclosed in quotation marks. If a file you are importing isn't structured and contains a mix of numbers and text, be very careful. For insurance, save the resident worksheet before you use the File Import command. That way, if something unexpected occurs, you can start over without having to rebuild the resident worksheet.

If you are importing an unstructured file that contains both text and numbers, you can save yourself some big headaches by importing the file as text and using the Data Parse command described in Chapter 10. This command divides long text labels into individual cell entries that can be either labels or values. When the Data Parse command is combined with the File Import command, it is a simple matter to convert information captured from remote computers into "live" 1-2-3 spreadsheets.

Using the File Import Command

To use the File Import command, you must first position the cursor at the upper left of the area where the import is to appear. Then type

/FI	Enters the File Import Command.
Text Numbers	Specify **Text** to import a column of long labels; **Numbers** to import only the values and text contained in quotation marks.
Enter name of file to import:	Specify name of import file. **NAME/F3** optional to display all filenames.
ENTER	Executes command and completes the import.

THE FILE ADMIN COMMAND

The File Admin (for "Administration") command sets and changes the reservation status (sometimes called "file locking" status) of files shared on a network; seals files to prevent unauthorized modifications; and writes tables by file type, active, linked, and other characteristics, to spreadsheet cells. This command simplifies the potentially complex task of dealing with files on a network and working with multiple files in memory at one time. See Figure 5–10 for the command tree.

The File Admin command offers three options that perform quite distinct tasks:

THE FILE COMMAND

Figure 5-10 The File Admin command tree.

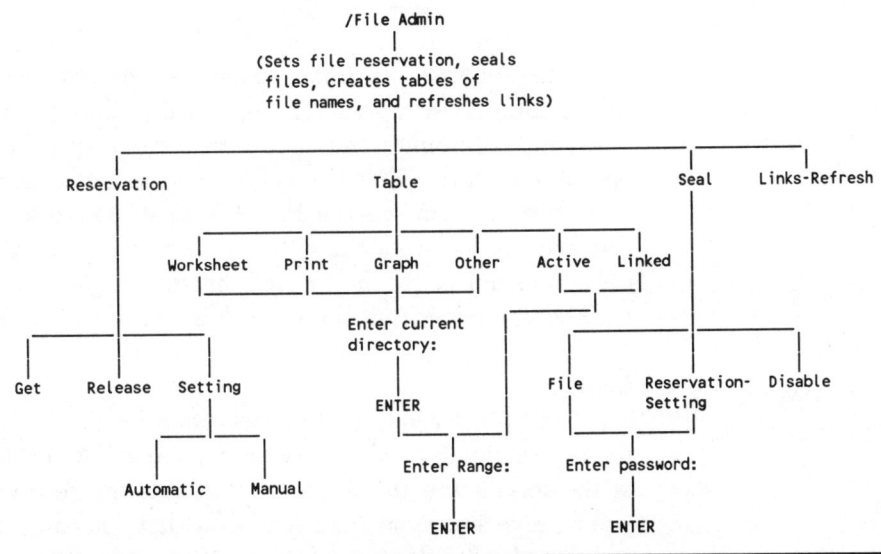

Reservation   Controls who may make changes to the current file. When you share files on a network, only the person who has a file's reservation can save changes to the file, even though several people may be using the file at the same time.

Table   Writes a table of filenames to a range on a worksheet. Files can be selected by type (Worksheet, Print, and so on) or by designations such as active and linked.

Seal   Prevents any changes to a file's reservation status and to the worksheet except to data in unprotected cells. Sealing is password protected and acts like a super Worksheet Protection command.

The Admin Reservation Command

The Admin Reservation command provides a solution to a serious problem that can occur when 1-2-3 files are shared on a network. The problem arises when two or more operators load the file at the same time. If both users make changes to the file and save their changes, neither is aware of the other's changes, and the communication of important information between those using the file may be lost.

The File Admin Reservation command solves this problem by allowing only one operator—the one who has the file's reservation—to save changes to the file. Those operators without the file's reservation can retrieve, view, and manipulate the file but they can't save their changes. Only the operator with the file's reservation can save changes made to the file.

Before you can use the File Admin Reservation command, you must retrieve the file from the network. When you do, the message **RO** (read only) appears at the bottom of the screen. Now enter the File Admin Reservation command. You have three options: Get, Release, and Setting.

Get

The Get option requests the reservation for the file you just retrieved. If the reservation is available, you receive it and **RO** disappears at the bottom of the screen and the file is unlocked. If the reservation isn't available, you receive a message, and you know that you can't save any changes you make to the file. If you do receive the reservation, you can be sure that no one else on the network can change the file and save their changes. The operator with the reservation is the only operator who has the right to save the file.

Release

If you wish to give up the reservation, reenter the File Admin Reservation command and select the Release option. When you do, **RO** again appears at the bottom of your screen. You no longer have the reservation for the file, and any changes you make cannot be saved.

Setting

The final option under the File Admin Reservation command is Setting, which determines whether the reservation is automatically given when you open or retrieve a file or whether you must get it manually. When the setting is Automatic, the reservation is automatically given to the first operator to retrieve the file.

When the setting is Manual (the default setting), each operator must enter the File Admin Reservation command and select Get to obtain a file's reservation.

Automatic is a convenient setting when most operators need to save their changes each time they load the file. It is not a sensible setting when most operators only view the file without making changes. In the latter case, Automatic gives the reservation away to the first person who loads the file whether or not that person needs the reservation to save changes. The reservation then may be unavailable to those operators who do need to save their changes to the file.

To make the Automatic or Manual setting operational, you must save the file with the File Save command after you have completed the File Admin command.

The File Admin Seal Command

The File Admin Seal command seals a worksheet with a password and prevents any changes to the Worksheet Global settings and Range Formats. When Prot is enabled, sealing a worksheet is like a super Worksheet Prot command, because changes can only be made to cells that have been previously unprotected with the Range Unprot command. Once a file is sealed, the password is required to unseal it.

To use the command, load the file you want to seal. If necessary, obtain the reservation for the file. Before you seal the file, use the Range Unprot command to unprotect any cells that you want to be able to change in the sealed file. These cells are often data entry cells. To prevent changes to any other cells, enable Global Prot.

After you have unprotected the appropriate cells and enabled Global Prot, enter the File Admin Seal command by typing **/FAS**. You are presented with three options:

File	Seals the file, including the reservation setting, with a password.
Reservation-Setting	Seals only the reservation setting (Automatic or Manual) with a password.
Disable	After you enter the correct password, unseals the file and the reservation setting.

Select the File option to seal the entire file and prevent changes to cells other than unprotected cells in the file. File also prevents an operator from changing the file's reservation status.

When you select File, you are prompted for a password. Type a password you will remember and press **ENTER**. Lotus asks you to verify your password by typing it again. Type it again and press **ENTER**. Then use the File Save command to make the new settings part of the saved version of this file.

The Reservation-Setting option only seals the reservation setting (Automatic or Manual) for the file. It does not seal the cells, which can still be changed and changes can be saved by the operator with the files reservation. It also requires a password.

The Disable option is how you unseal the file. To use the option, you must supply the password exactly like the original.

Alternative Protection

The File Admin Seal command prevents certain types of changes to a file. Other ways to prevent changes are with the Worksheet Global Prot Enable command and by saving a file with a password.

The Worksheet Global Prot Enable command prevents changes to cells in the current file that have not been unprotected with the Range Unprot command. Unlike a sealed file, the Range Unprot command can be used at any time to gain access to a cell. Furthermore, Worksheet protection can be turned off at any time by entering the Worksheet Global Prot Disable command. (See Chapter 2 for more information about the Worksheet Global Prot command.)

Sealing a file prevents any unauthorized changes to a file but doesn't prevent someone from retrieving the file and viewing it. If you want to prevent unauthorized viewing of a file, save it with a password. Files saved with passwords can only be retrieved by supplying the correct password, and any access to the file is denied to unauthorized operators.

The File Admin Table Command

The final File Admin command, Table, provides a way to record in spreadsheet cells important information about the files on disk or in the current directory. It also tables information about files that are currently active or are linked by formula reference to the current file.

The File Admin Table command creates a table in the current worksheet one, four, or seven columns wide, depending on the option you choose. The table contains as many rows as there are files to be tabled.

Like many 1-2-3 commands, the location of the worksheet cursor before entering the command determines where the table is written, so be sure that there is ample space below and to the right of the current worksheet cursor location. Otherwise, 1-2-3 writes over existing material as the program creates the table. To ensure that you have ample space, insert a blank sheet into the stack with the Worksheet Insert Sheet command and have the table written there.

If you want to view the information provided by this command on the screen but not write it to a table in a spreadsheet, use the File List com-

THE FILE COMMAND

mand. The same options are available, but this command only displays the information; it is not written to spreadsheet cells.

To use the File Admin Table command, position the cursor at the upper left corner of the area where the table is to appear and type

/FAT   Enters the File Admin Table command.

You are given six choices. The files that are written to the table are all from the current directory.

Worksheet	Files with .WK3, .WK1, .WKS, .WRK, and .WR1 extensions, depending on the current Worksheet Global Default Ext List setting.
Print	Files with a .PRN extension.
Graph	Files with a .PIC or .CGM extension, depending on the Worksheet Global Default Graph setting.
Other	All files in the current directory, regardless of extension.
Active	All active files currently in memory.
Linked	All files, whether in the current directory or not, linked by formula reference to the current file.

When you make your selection, 1-2-3 writes a table to the worksheet. The size of the table and the information contained in the columns depends on the type of files you are using in the table.

When you select Worksheet, Print, Graph, or Other, the table is four columns wide and lists the filename, date and time the file was last saved, and the file's size in bytes.

When you select Active, the table is seven columns wide. See Figure 5-11. The first four columns list the filename, date and time the file was last saved, and the file's size in bytes. The fifth column shows the number of sheets in the file (1 to 256), and the sixth column displays a **1** if you have modified the active file since reading it into memory and a **0** if you haven't. The seventh column displays a **1** if you have the file's reservation and a **0** if you don't.

If you selected Linked, 1-2-3 creates a one-column table listing the names of the files linked to formulas in the current file.

The File Admin Table command can provide important information about the files you are using. Use it often to record this information and to print it out for your files. The information about active and linked files is particularly important when you work with complicated models that

Figure 5-11 Table of active files.

```
    A       A           B       C             D      E    F    G
9
10
11       FIG_4-1.WK3   32640  0.4949074074   3170    3    0    1
12       VOTING.WK1    32294  0.2065046296   3192    1    1    1
13       FIG_3-19.WK3  32318  0.2828240741   2360    1    0    1
14       FIG_2-20.WK3  32640  0.3489583333   4202    3    1    1
15
16
17
18
19
```

extend across several files. However, keeping track of the contents of the columns of these tables can be difficult. See the Hands On section at the end of the chapter for a way to handle this problem.

THE FILE ERASE, LIST, AND DIRECTORY COMMANDS

The remaining File command options are Erase, List, and Directory. These commands perform straightforward file management tasks.

Erase

The File Erase command permits you to choose which type of files to erase—worksheets (.WK3, .WK1, or .WKS), graph files (.CGM or .PIC), or print files (.PRN). It then displays the filenames for the file type you have chosen. Alternatively, you can select Other, and 1-2-3 displays all of the files in the current directory.

You can display all filenames of a particular type by pressing **NAME/F3**. Then highlight the file you want to erase. Alternatively, you can type in the name of the file you want to erase. You are asked to confirm your choice before 1-2-3 actually erases the file. You cannot, however, use the File Erase command to erase a file of a worksheet that is currently an active file. First use Worksheet Delete File to delete the file from memory. Then use the File Erase command to erase it from disk. Figure 5-12 provides the File Erase command tree.

THE FILE COMMAND

Figure 5-12   The File Erase command tree.

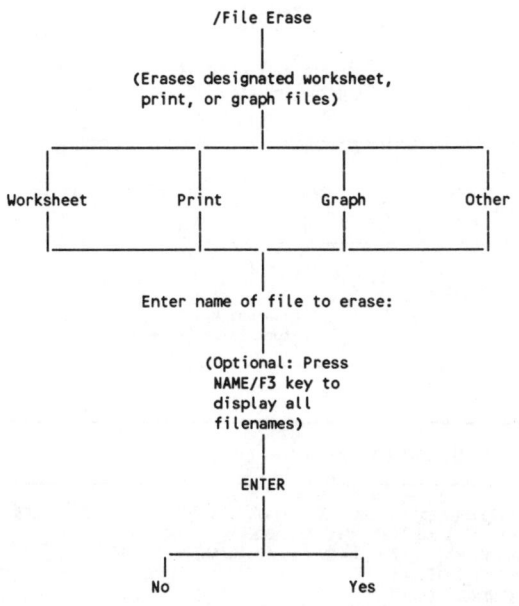

List

The File List command is a convenient way to view all worksheet, picture, or print filenames on the current data diskette or in the current directory on a hard disk at one time. You can also select Other, which lists all of the files regardless of type; Active, which lists the active files currently in memory; and Linked, which lists all files linked to the current file by formula reference. See Figure 5-13 for the File List command tree.

When you select a File List option, the 1-2-3 worksheet screen disappears, and the filenames are listed. You can view the size of the file in bytes and the date and time it was created by moving the highlight to the filename with the arrow keys. See Figure 5-14 for the screen as it looks when you select Linked after entering the File List command.

Should you want the information provided by any of the File List options written to cells on a worksheet, use the File Admin Table command discussed earlier. That command has the same options as the File List command, but it writes the information to spreadsheet cells. Once in a spreadsheet you can save it with the File Save or File Xtract commands, or print it with the Print command.

When you are ready to return to the worksheet, press the **ENTER** key.

Figure 5–13 The File List command tree.

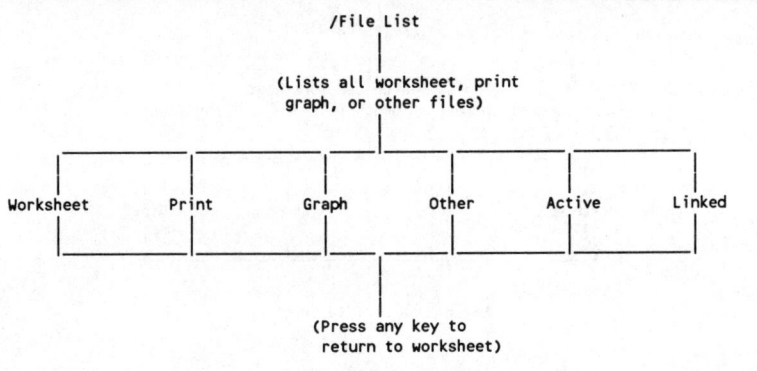

Figure 5–14 Display of files linked to the current file.

```
A:A47: +<<C:\123R3\BOOK\VOTING.WK3>>A:A47..A:A47            FILES
Enter names of files to list: C:\123R3\BOOK\
         GRAPH.WK3     27-jun-89     12:40 AM       2872
C:\123R3\BOOK\FIG_3-13.WK3
C:\123R3\BOOK\WKNGWIFE.WK3
C:\123R3\BOOK\GRAPH1.WK3
C:\123R3\BOOK\BORDERS.WK3
C:\123R3\BOOK\VOTING.WK3
```

Dir

The last option, Dir (for "Directory"), changes the current default directory. This option is particularly important when you store 1-2-3 files in different directories on a hard disk. To make a different directory current, enter the File Directory command, type in the new directory name, including pathnames, and press **ENTER**.

Once you have changed the directory, that directory is used in all subsequent File commands. Furthermore, the new directory won't be changed back to the default directory when you erase a stack with the Worksheet Erase command. The designated directory remains the default directory until you change it or until you end the current work session. The directory then reverts to the default directory chosen with the Worksheet Global Default Directory command, described fully in Chapter 2. See Figure 5–15 for the File Dir command tree.

To change the startup default directory, use the Worksheet Global Default Directory command to designate the new startup directory. To make the change permanent (until you change it again) use Worksheet Global

Figure 5-15   File Directory command tree.

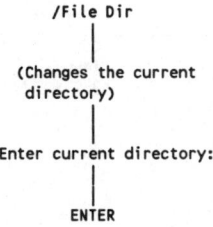

Default Update. See Chapter 2 for more information about these Directory commands.

HANDS ON: THE FILE_TBL.WK3 WORKSHEET

The File Admin Table command provides an effective way to table information about files in a directory, active files in memory, and files linked to the current file. However, much of the information is presented in code or as date or time numbers. Furthermore, there are no column headings to tell you what information appears in the columns. For example, in a table of Active files even the most ardent user may have trouble remembering whether column six contains information about the reservation status of the file or about whether the file has been modified in the current work session.

The solution to this problem is to create a file that contains the appropriate column headings and some convenient named ranges and then to use the File Combine command to combine the column headings into an active file whenever one of the Table commands is to be performed. The named ranges make it easy to respond to the **Enter Range** prompt.

Create FILE_TBL.WK3

To create the FILE_TBL.WK3 worksheet, enter the text to label the columns in the appropriate cell, as shown in Figure 5-16.

Use the Worksheet Column command to widen column A to 15 characters so that all of the Path/Filename headings in A12 in the Linked table can be seen on the screen. Use the Range Label command to center the labels in each column and the repeating text character (\) followed by an equal sign to enter the double dashes into rows 7, 13, and 19.

Figure 5-16 Worksheet containing headings for different File Admin List Table options.

```
      A              B         C       D      E        F         G
 1  Filename: FILE_TBL.WK3                          ACTIVE   A17..G19
 2                                                  LINKED   A12..D13
 3                                                  SHEET    A6..D7
 4  HEADINGS: WORKSHEET, PRINT, GRAPH, AND OTHER
 5
 6     Filename     Date      Time    Size
 7  ==================================================
 8
 9
10  HEADINGS: LINKED
11
12     Path\Filename Date     Time    Size
13  ==================================================
14
15
16  HEADINGS: ACTIVE
17                                           # of    1-Mod    1-Have Res
18     Filename     Date      Time    Size   Sheets  0-Not    0-Don't
19  =================================================================
20
```

Name the Ranges

To make the combination easier, use the name ACTIVE for cells A17..G19, LINKED for A12..D13, and SHEET for A6..A7. These are easy-to-remember range names because they mirror the three types of tables created by the File Admin Table command.

To name the cells A6..D7 SHEET, place the cursor on cell A6 and type

/RNC	Enters the Range Name Create Command.
Enter name to create:	Type **SHEET**.
ENTER	Accepts SHEET as a range name.
Enter range:	Asks for range to name; use arrow keys to highlight A6..D7.
ENTER	Accepts range and assigns the name to it.

Repeat these steps to assign the name LINKED to A12..D13 and the name ACTIVE to A17..G19. This completes the worksheet.

To save the worksheet under the file named FILE_TBL, type

| /FS | Enters the File Save command. |
| **Enter name of file to save:** | Asks for a filename. |

THE FILE COMMAND

FILE_TBL   Type the filename.

ENTER   Completes the command.

The FILE_TBL worksheet is now ready to use.

Use the File Combine Command

When you want to use the File Admin Table command on an active worksheet, begin by positioning the cursor at the upper left corner of an area wide enough to contain the column headings and deep enough to contain the files that will be listed under them. Leave plenty of room or use a separate sheet, because the command writes over anything in the cells.

Now type

/FC	Enters the File Combine Command.
Copy Add Subtract	Select Copy.
Entire File Named/Specified range:	Select Named/Specified range.
Enter range name or address:	Asks for range name.
ACTIVE	Type the range name.
ENTER	Accepts range name.
Enter name of file to combine:	Optional, **NAME/F3**. Highlight FILE_TBL.WK3 filename or type **FILE_TBL**.
ENTER	Completes command and combines the contents of range named ACTIVE into the current file beginning at the worksheet cursor location.

To obtain a table of active files place the cursor on the appropriate cell beneath the Filename column heading and type

/FA	Selects the File Admin command.
T	Selects Table.
A	Selects Active and completes the command.
Enter range	Asks for range for table.

| ENTER | Executes command and writes table beginning with cursor location. |

Complete the Table

Because the column width is determined by the file you are combining into, you may need to adjust some column widths if you can't read all of the filenames or if the columns are too wide. Use the Worksheet Column command. Also, the time and date at which each file in the table was last saved are in time and date numbers. Use the Range Format commands Date and Time to assign appropriate formats to those cells. See Figure 5–17 for an example of a completed File Admin Active table.

Using range names and the File Combine command make it easy to bring frequently used column headings into the current worksheet. Remember to choose easy-to-remember range names and to position the cursor before entering the File Combine command.

TIPS & TRAPS

Tips

There Is Nothing Like a Good Save.
Always save your worksheets—often. Save every few minutes when constructing a new worksheet so you don't lose everything if you make a mistake. Save before you perform an unfamiliar operation.

Figure 5–17 Active worksheet after headings for Active files from FILE_TBL.WK3 are combined, and File Admin Table Active command is executed.

A	A	B	C	D	E	F	G
1					# of	1-Mod	1-Have Res
2	Filename	Date	Time	Size	Sheets	0-Not	0-Don't
3	===
4	FILE0004.	32640	0.606273	0	1	1	1
5	VOTING.WK	32294	0.206505	3192	1	1	1
6	BORDERS.W	32640	0.557477	2905	1	0	1
7	GRAPH1.WK	32321	0.02831	2872	1	0	1
8	WKNGWIFE.	32407	0.303935	2288	1	0	1
9	FIG_3-13.	32640	0.462292	3230	2	1	1
10	FG_10-25.	32321	0.08463	4550	1	1	1

Back Up!
There is simply nothing that can replace a careful program of making backup copies of important worksheet files.

All users think they won't get caught. Everybody does. *You* have been warned.

Don't Forget That You Can Change the Default Directory.
Lotus normally defaults to the subdirectory on a hard disk that contains the program files. You can change the default directory for the current work session with the File Dir command. You can change 1-2-3's startup default subdirectory using the Worksheet Global Default Directory command described in Chapter 2. Using the Worksheet Global Default Update command makes the change permanent—until you want to change it again.

If you use many subdirectories, see the macro in Chapter 12 that helps you switch between them easily.

File Combine Saves RAM.
If your system lacks enough RAM to hold large stacks of worksheets, you can use the File Combine command to bring into memory only those sheets or parts of sheets that are needed for the problem at hand.

I Can't Remember the Active or Linked Files.
The File List and File Admin Table commands display or write to spreadsheet cells all currently active files or all files that are linked to the current file by formula reference. Use the File Admin Table command to obtain a permanent record of this information. Use the File List command when you only want to view it.

Traps

Bloated Xtract Files.
The File Xtract command takes with it all range names, named graphs, and other remembered ranges. Many of these are no longer relevant in the extracted file. Load the file and use the appropriate Reset and Clear commands to get rid of unnecessary settings. Then save the cleaned-up file with the File Save Command. On some spreadsheets this can reduce the size of the stored file by hundreds of bytes.

What Was That Name?

Using named ranges with File Combine command is a great way to combine parts of spreadsheets stored in files into spreadsheets in memory. But to work most smoothly you must know the range names assigned on the stored worksheet. If you don't know a range name, you must load the worksheet to discover it. You can't combine the worksheet into the current stack, because range names aren't combined.

Assign logical, easy-to-remember range names or use the Range Name Table command to make a list of range names assigned to each worksheet. Then, if you have to combine it into a stack, you can tell what range names have been assigned. You can also use the File Open and Copy commands to achieve the same results.

Help! I Forgot My Password.

There is no help. Files saved with password protection or sealed with the File Admin Seal command *cannot* be retrieved or unsealed without the correct password. Select passwords that are easy for you to remember or keep copies of your passwords in a safe place.

What Does RO Mean?

The **RO** message appears at the bottom of the screen and means that the file is a read only file. You don't have the reservation for that file and, therefore, can't save any changes you make to it.

If the reservation setting for the file is automatic, you are automatically given the reservation whenever you retrieve the file and no one else is using it. If the setting is manual, you must request the reservation with the File Admin Reservation Get command. Without the reservation, you cannot save files that you retrieve from a network file server.

RO appears and disappears as you scroll through a stack depending on whether a particular file is a read only file.

6 The Print Command

OBJECTIVES

After mastering the content of this chapter, you will be able to

☐ use 1-2-3's Print command.

☐ print the print Sample to determine the capabilities of your printer.

☐ print a worksheet under the default settings.

☐ pause or end the Print command in the middle of printing a worksheet.

☐ print worksheets in compressed type.

☐ create a print file for later use with a word processing program.

☐ use the advanced features of the Print command to place headers, footers, page numbers, and dates on printed worksheets.

INTRODUCTION

The Print command prints spreadsheets and graphs to a printer, creates encoded files for printing with operating system commands, and prepares print files for combining 1-2-3 spreadsheets with word processing documents. The Print command in Release 3 contains many new features. Among other things, you can now specify multiple ranges, print graphs without leaving the program, print graphs and spreadsheets on the same page, print in the background so you can continue to use 1-2-3 while print jobs are in progress, change typefaces from menus, and change to printing in compressed type without using setup strings.

Partly because of its many features, the Print command is the one most 1-2-3 users find hardest to master. The reason is that there is always a trade-off between the power of a large number of command options and the ease with which that command can be learned and used. The more options, the harder to learn. The fewer options, the easier to use. The 1-2-3 Print command decidedly falls into the "more options" camp. See Figure 6–1 for the Print command tree.

Figure 6–1 The Print command tree.

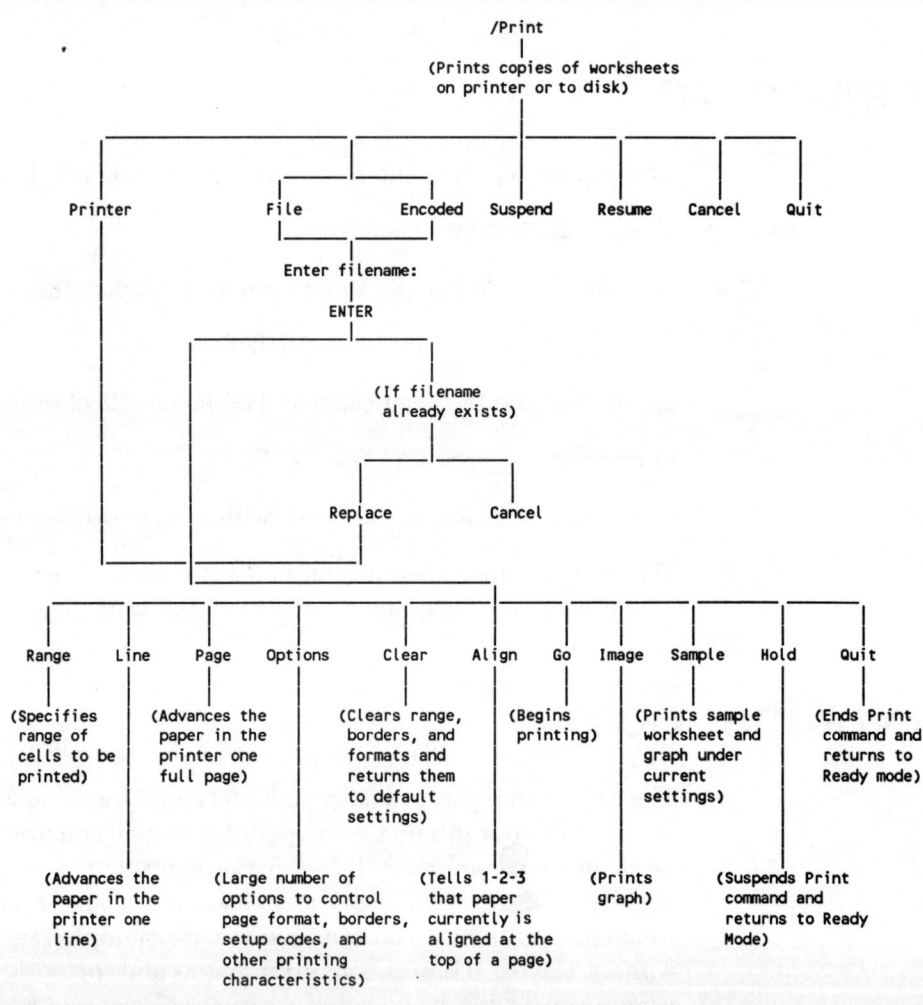

The Print Command

When you first enter the Print command you are presented with the following seven choices:

Printer	Sends output to a printer.
File	Sends output to an ASCII file.
Encoded	Sends output to a file containing all print enhancement commands.
Suspend	Suspends printing.
Resume	Resumes printing.
Cancel	Cancels *all* print jobs.
Quit	Returns to Ready mode.

The first three choices—Printer, File, and Encoded—are the three different types of output that 1-2-3 can create. These choices are discussed in the next section. The last three choices—Suspend, Resume, and Cancel—control the action of your printer. They are discussed after the next section.

The Printer/File/Encoded Options

To print your worksheet or graph you must choose between Printer, File, or Encoded. Your choice depends on the type of printout you want.

Printer
The first choice, Printer, results in the familiar printed, or *hard copy*, version of a 1-2-3 worksheet. You can print all of the worksheet or just a range of cells. This is the most commonly chosen print option. Most users never use the next two options, but you should know they exist in case you need their special features.

File
The second choice is File. This command creates a print file that is an electronic image of the print range stored in a file. The image is exactly like the image sent to the printer by the Printer part of the Print command and, therefore, creating a print file is sometimes called "printing to the disk."

The resulting file is sometimes called a "plain vanilla" file, because it contains no special codes or features—just standard ASCII (American Standard Code for Information Interchange) text characters. Any special font settings are dropped in a print file. Also, Graphs cannot be included in a print file. If there are graphs in the print range, 1-2-3 leaves a blank space as large as the graph would have occupied had it been printed on a printer.

A print file is very different from a file created with the File Save command. First, to distinguish print files from worksheet files, 1-2-3 assigns the filename extension .PRN to all print files. Next, the File Retrieve command cannot be used to reload a print file, because a print file contains none of the information necessary to reconstruct the worksheet. However, you can use the File Import command to load a print file into 1-2-3. (See Chapter 5.)

The most important use of a print file is for export to a word processing program where the worksheet can be combined with text to form a report. This feature greatly extends the usefulness of 1-2-3 worksheets. Depending on your particular word processor, you can improve the appearance of your worksheets by using special characters such as underlining, boldfacing, superscripts and subscripts, and different type fonts.

Encoded

The last choice is Encoded. An encoded file is a cross between a printout and a print file. It is a file on a disk and not a piece of paper, but, unlike the print file, it contains all of the print codes necessary to send special commands to the printer. It can also contain graphs. The file can be printed with the operating system's Print command. A copy of 1-2-3 is not necessary.

One use for an encoded file is to use a modem to telecommunicate the file to a computer at a remote location. The receiving party then uses the operating system's Print command to print the encoded file. Assuming the printer supports all of the print enhancements in the file, the result is exactly the same as if you had made the printout on your own printer. This may be cheaper and faster than sending a printout by overnight express. It is also easier than sending the entire file to the remote location.

Another use is on a "sneaker network." Your office may have only one laser printer, color printer, or plotter. Instead of having to take your 1-2-3 files to these devices, you can create an encoded file on a diskette and then sneaker it (that is, walk it) to the device. For this to work, you must install the particular laser printer, color printer, or plotter as an output device for your copy of 1-2-3. Then don't forget to use the Options Advanced Device command to specify the appropriate device *before* you create the encoded file.

Printing Graphs

While graph printing isn't a main Print command choice, it is the command used to print graphs. You can select either Printer or Encoded to print a graph, but because the creation of a graph and the use of the Graph command options are so tightly interwoven with the printing of graphs, the bulk of the discussion on the printing of graphs is reserved for Chapter 11, the chapter on graphs.

The Suspend/Resume/Cancel Choices

The Suspend, Resume, and Cancel choices you encounter when you select Print actually manage your printer rather than print files.

Suspend and Resume

Suspend causes 1-2-3 to stop sending instructions for the current print job. Resume causes 1-2-3 to resume sending instructions for the current print job. If your printer continues to print after you have selected Suspend, either a print spooler or a print buffer is active.

A *print spooler* collects print jobs and spools them out to the printer at a rate the printer can accept. A *print buffer* is memory in your printer that allows it to accept more instructions than it can print at one time. Both features are designed to return program control to you as quickly as possible. Unfortunately, once the instructions have been sent to a buffer or spooler 1-2-3 considers the instructions printed, and the Suspend option has no effect. All you can do is turn off the printer to cancel the print job.

When you turn off the printer, the error message **Printer error - attention required** appears at the bottom of the screen. The message remains until you respond to it by taking one of two actions. To cancel all print jobs, return to the Ready mode and select Print Cancel. To continue with the print job, fix whatever caused you to interrupt printing and select Print Resume.

Cancel

Be careful when you use the Cancel option, because it cancels the current print job and *all other* print jobs that may have been specified but not yet printed. For example, when you queue several graphs to print, selecting Cancel aborts the printing of the current graph and it cancels all other print jobs as well.

If you have a print spooler or buffer, the printer continues printing until it is empty. You can always stop printing and clear the buffer by turning your printer off. You may be able to clear a print spooler by issuing commands from your keyboard. Consult the instructions that come with the print spooler.

THE PRINT SAMPLE

One of the most important new Release 3 print features is the ability to print a built-in sample that determines which features your printer supports. Consequently, your first task is to print this sample. Keep it handy as a guide to the features available and to the way they appear when printed. Also print the sample any time you change printers to discover the particular set of features supported by the printer.

Before you print, 1-2-3 must be told about the particular printer you are using. You do this during the installation procedure, described in Chapter 1. If necessary, use the Install option from the Lotus Access menu to install your printer, to verify that it is installed, or to install a new printer. Simply select Install and follow the instructions that appear on the screen. If you aren't sure your printer has been installed, repeat the installation procedure. If the Access menu doesn't automatically appear when you begin a 1-2-3 work session, exit to the operating system, make the 1-2-3 directory the default directory, type **LOTUS** and press **ENTER**.

To print the sample, make sure that your printer is turned on, attached to your computer, and loaded with paper. Also, verify that the printer is on line (ready to receive instructions from 1-2-3). Begin by typing

/P	Enters the Print command.
P	Selects Printer to use for output.
S	Selects Sample.
A	Selects Align. Tells 1-2-3 that the print head is aligned at the top of the first page.
G	Selects Go to begin printing.
Q	Selects Quit to return to the Ready mode.

The print sample is four pages long. It begins with a listing of all the current print settings and includes a small spreadsheet, a graph, and samples of the way your printer prints when the various font and pitch choices are made. If your printer cannot support a feature—graphs, colors, or a particular font—the default response is printed. For example, when a printer can't print graphics, a blank space appears where the graph would have been printed.

After the sample has been printed, study the results carefully. Note particularly which of the type fonts are supported by your printer, whether you can print graphs, and whether your printer can print in compressed (smaller) type. You are now ready to explore the mysteries of printing with 1-2-3.

PRINTING PLAIN AND PRINTING FANCY

To help you master the Print command, this chapter is divided into two major parts. In the Printing Plain section you learn to make simple, straightforward printouts under Lotus' default settings for margins and page length. You also learn what happens when your worksheet won't fit on what 1-2-3 considers a standard or "default" page.

The following section, Printing Fancy, discusses how to insert headers and footers, how to change the margins and page length settings, how to send special control codes to your printer, how to create customized settings for your printer, and how to use the other printer options of the Print command. It also explains how to embed print codes in a worksheet so you can print different sections of a worksheet with different type fonts.

Once you understand how to make a straightforward printout and how 1-2-3 views the default page, you can use the Printing Fancy options to enhance the professional appearance of your printed worksheets.

Trial and Success

The most important fact about using the Print command is that almost no one's printout comes out right the first time—or the second time. Printing is a matter of trial and success. Knowing how the Print command works and knowing about 1-2-3's default settings can reduce your frustration, but they can't substitute for trying a printout and adjusting the results.

Most problems arise because people aren't familiar with the basics of the Print command and, in particular, its default settings. So even if you think you know the basics, review the next section before you tackle Printing Fancy.

PRINTING PLAIN: USING THE PRINT COMMAND DEFAULT SETTINGS

The first step in mastering 1-2-3's Print command is to print a worksheet under the default settings for margins, page length, and typesize.

An Example

Figure 6-2 shows a 1-2-3 screen containing a simple worksheet. The entire worksheet fits on a single screen, and, as you can see from the control panel, the Print command has been entered.

To print this worksheet (assuming your printer is hooked up and ready to go) begin by typing

/P	Enters the Print Command.
P	Selects Printer from the menu. Sends output to your printer.
R	Selects Range from the menu. Must specify a range of cells to print.

Figure 6-2   Message and options for the Print command.

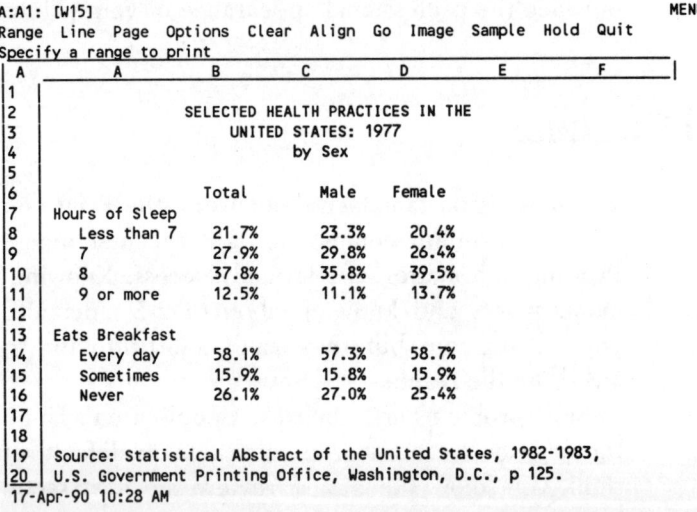

THE PRINT COMMAND

Enter Print range:	Move cursor to upper right cell of print range (A1 in Figure 6–2).
.	Tacks cursor to A1.
Arrow keys	Stretch cursor to highlight to lower right cell of print range (F20 in Figure 6–2).
ENTER	Specifies print range A1..F20.
A	Very important. Selects Align to tell 1-2-3 the print head is at the top of the page.
G	Selects Go to begin printing.
Q	Selects Quit to end Print command and return to Ready mode.

After a range has been printed, 1-2-3 does not return to the Ready mode. Rather, it remains in the Print command where you can specify additional ranges to print. To return to the Ready mode you must explicitly select Quit.

1-2-3 prints spreadsheets in the "background." That is, when you are printing a file you can continue working on your spreadsheet or move to another sheet in a stack and begin working there. You can even erase the spreadsheet you are printing and move on to another project. However, you can't quit 1-2-3 without aborting any unprinted print jobs.

If you try to quit 1-2-3, you receive a message indicating that printing is still in progress and that leaving terminates all remaining print jobs. However, if you are using OS/2 or some other program with a print spooler, you can leave 1-2-3, because as far as Lotus is concerned the print job is actually completed when it is placed in the print spooler.

Print Range

The one thing you must always specify when you use the Print command is a print range. Every other choice of the many in this command is optional. As with any other 1-2-3 range, you can specify it by typing the required cell addresses; by using the cursor control keys to point to it; or if the range is named, by specifying its name. If you print the same range each time you use the worksheet, the easiest way to print it is to name the range and use the **NAME/F3** function key to select it from the list of named ranges.

Ranges can extend across sheets, but not across files. However, you can specify a print range that is not in the current file. If you do, the path and filename are required, so use the cursor movement keys to point to them. You can also specify multiple print ranges at one time. Just separate the print ranges with semicolons. For example,

A1..A7;*COST;<<C:\123\FINANCE\BUDGET.WK3>>REVENUE

specifies two print ranges (A1..A7 and REVENUE) and one graph (*COST). The first print range and graph are from the current file, the last from another active file.

If you attempt to print a worksheet without first specifying a range, 1-2-3 beeps and displays the message **No Print range, Image, or Sample specified -- Press HELP (F1)**. Press ENTER to clear the error message. Specify a print range, graph (image) or sample, then press **A** for Align and **G** for Go to begin printing.

Proposed Ranges

As with other ranges, Lotus remembers the last print range you specified and proposes it the next time you need a print range. Lotus also saves print ranges with worksheets saved with the File Save and File Xtract commands. (It also saves choices you have made under the Options subcommand, described later.) Once the correct range has been remembered by 1-2-3, you can print the worksheet by simply typing **/PPAG**.

Canceling Proposed Ranges

If the proposed range isn't the one you wanted to print, press either **ESC** or **BKSP** to cancel printing. ESC leaves the cursor in the anchor cell of the proposed range. BKSP returns the cursor to its location immediately *before* selecting Range. Press **BKSP** if you have correctly positioned the cursor before entering the Print command.

You can also select Clear from the Print command menu. You are given several options. Select Range to clear the print range or All to clear the print range and restore all settings to their default values.

Align

One of the most frustrating and frequent causes of printing errors is not to select Align before you select Go. Align tells 1-2-3 that the print head of your printer is at the top of a page on line number 1.

Here is how the problem arises. Lotus keeps track of the number of lines it prints by assigning line number 1 to the first line, 2 to the second, and so on. When it prints a table with less than a full page of lines, 1-2-3 remembers the line number of the last line printed. If you now move to the top of the next physical sheet of paper by pressing the form feed button on your printer or by simply using the knob on the side to advance the paper, 1-2-3 and your printer are no longer synchronized. Your printer

THE PRINT COMMAND

is on physical line 1, but 1-2-3's line counter is still on the number of the last line printed.

When you print another copy of the same worksheet, 1-2-3 starts counting with the line it remembered. When it gets to the line number corresponding to the bottom of its page, 1-2-3 inserts a page break (normally 10 blank lines).

If you don't enter the Align command just before printing a worksheet, the result is often a page break where one isn't wanted and no page break where one is needed. Your worksheets end up with blank lines in the middle of text and lines printed across the perforations in continuous feed paper.

To prevent incorrect page breaks and inadvertent printing across perforations, *always* select the Align command before pressing **G** to start printing your worksheet.

The Default Page

Figure 6-3 shows how the worksheet in Figure 6-2 prints if you accept all of 1-2-3's default settings for top, bottom, left, and right margins, number of lines per page, and typesize. To understand and master the Print command, you must look behind the printing process to see exactly what those defaults are.

Page Size

Lotus assumes you are making your printouts on standard 8½ by 11-inch paper. You can print on paper of different sizes by adjusting either the number of lines per page or the number of characters printed per line.

Figure 6-3   Worksheet from Figure 6-2 printed according to 1-2-3's default print settings.

```
                    SELECTED HEALTH PRACTICES IN THE
                          UNITED STATES: 1977
                                by Sex

                    Total        Male      Female
   Hours of Sleep
      Less than 7   21.7%        23.3%     20.4%
      7             27.9%        29.8%     26.4%
      8             37.8%        35.8%     39.5%
      9 or more     12.5%        11.1%     13.7%

   Eats Breakfast
      Every day     58.1%        57.3%     58.7%
      Sometimes     15.9%        15.8%     15.9%
      Never         26.1%        27.0%     25.4%


   Source: Statistical Abstract of the United States, 1982-1983,
   U.S. Government Printing Office, Washington, D.C., p. 125.
```

Line Length
Eighty standard size characters can be printed edge-to-edge on the default 8½-inch-wide page. By adjusting the right and left margins you can specify line lengths from 1 to 1000 characters.

Left and Right Margins
Lotus' default settings are for an 80-character line printed on an 8½-inch wide page. The left margin is set at character 4, and the right margin is set at character 76. To find the maximum number of characters that can be printed on a line, subtract the setting for the left margin from that for the right margin. Thus, under 1-2-3's default settings you can print up to 72 characters in standard type on an 8½-inch-wide piece of paper.

Top and Bottom Margins
Lotus reserves two lines for a top margin and two lines for a bottom margin. It also reserves the third line from the top and the third line from the bottom for header and footer lines. These two lines are reserved whether or not you specify a header or a footer. Finally, 1-2-3 reserves two lines to separate the header line from the top of the printed worksheet and two lines to separate the footer from the bottom of the printed worksheet.

Thus, five lines are reserved at the top of the page for margins and the header line, and five lines are reserved at the bottom for margins and the footer line. Under the default line spacing, the longest print range that can be printed on a standard 11-inch-long piece of paper is 56 rows (or lines). You can also use Options Advanced Layout Line-Spacing Compressed to print "compressed" lines, which places 74 lines on an 11-inch-long page with five-line top and bottom margins. When you select Compressed, 1-2-3 leaves the top and bottom margins in *standard* line spacing so pages printed in compressed lines have the same margins as pages printed in standard lines.

If no header or footer has been specified, you can select Options Other Blank-Header. This shrinks the top and bottom margins to two lines, effectively lengthening the printed page by six lines. This command only works when the header and footer lines are blank.

Changing the Default Settings
Figure 6–4 contains an illustration of the range of 1-2-3's format settings. Note that the right margin is set relative to the left edge of the page. That is, when you set the margin at character 76 it leaves four characters for the right margin.

THE PRINT COMMAND

Figure 6–4 Lotus 1-2-3 page format settings.
Source: *Lotus 1-2-3 Release 3 Reference Manual* (Boston, Mass.: Lotus Development Corporation, 1989), p. 2–19.

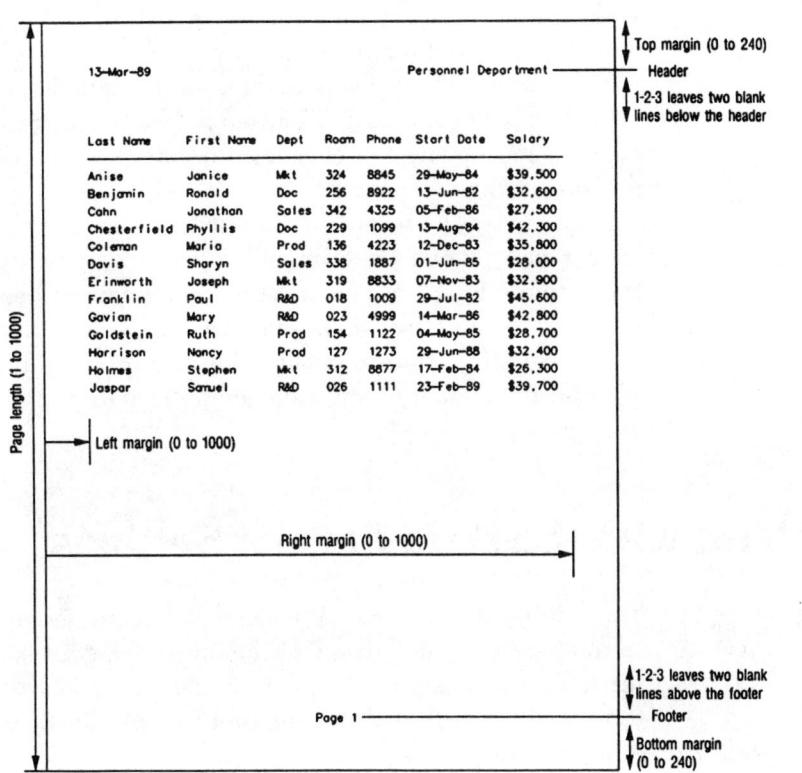

The default settings selected by Lotus are

Lines	Use
1 and 2	Top margin
3	Header (or blank if no header specified)
4 and 5	Blank
6 to 61	Print ranges and graphs
62 and 63	Blank
64	Footer (or blank if no footer specified)
65 and 66	Bottom margin

>   Right Margin   At character 76
>
>   Left Margin   At character 4

If these aren't the settings you use most frequently, you can change the default settings in a number of ways.

One way to change many of the printing defaults is with the Worksheet Global Default command, discussed in Chapter 2. If you change the global defaults and update the changes, they become the default print settings for future work sessions.

Another way is to create a named printer specification, as discussed later. Finally, when you change any setting for a particular worksheet and then use the File Save command to save the worksheet, 1-2-3 remembers your choices and uses them the next time you load that worksheet.

You certainly want to change the default margins if you always make your printouts on 15-inch-wide computer paper rather than on 8½-inch-wide paper.

Problems with the Default Print Settings

The printout in Figure 6–3 works well because none of the default print settings are exceeded. None of the lines is longer than 72 characters, and the table contains no more than 56 lines. If you exceed any default print settings, Lotus prints the worksheet in a predictable, if not entirely satisfactory, way.

Exceeding the Default Line Width

If the worksheet is wider than 72 characters, Lotus prints the worksheet strip-by-strip. Furthermore, the 72 characters must be contained entirely within full column widths, because 1-2-3 won't print part of a column on a page. (See Figure 6–5.) Printing over several pages often results in a satisfactory printout for a large worksheet.

Sometimes, however, only one or two columns are printed on the last page. It is better to print roughly the same number of columns on each page of a multiple-page printout. To accomplish this, adjust the length of the printed line and/or the column width until the results are to your liking.

Getting More Characters on a Line

The easiest way to get more characters on a line is to print on wider paper. On 15-inch-wide paper you can get 135 characters from edge to edge. If

Figure 6-5 When a print range is wider or longer than the current margin or page length settings, 1-2-3 prints it in "strips" according to the order in this figure.

```
┌─────────┬─────────┐
│  First  │ Fourth  │
│  Page   │  Page   │
│ Printed │ Printed │
│         │         │
├─────────┼─────────┤
│ Second  │  Fifth  │
│  Page   │  Page   │
│ Printed │ Printed │
│         │         │
├─────────┼─────────┤
│  Third  │  Sixth  │
│  Page   │  Page   │
│ Printed │ Printed │
│         │         │
└─────────┴─────────┘
```

you do, be sure to select Options Margin Right to reset the right margin to something like character 132.

If you don't have a printer capable of using wider paper, you can use compressed type to print your worksheet in a smaller typesize. In compressed type you can print up to 135 characters from edge-to-edge on an 8½-inch-wide page. If your printer can use 15-inch-wide paper, you can print nearly 250 characters. To print in compressed type, select Options Advanced Layout Pitch Compressed. Note: 1-2-3 automatically prints a full line in compressed characters. You don't need to change the margins.

Landscape printing is printing the long way (sideways or *broadside*) on a page. If your printer supports it, select Options Advanced Layout Orientation Landscape. The actual number of lines and characters you can put on a page longways depends on your particular printer. Do some print tests to determine how much you can get on a page.

Regardless of the method you choose, you must realize that 1-2-3 will not print any characters beyond what is set as the right margin. The default margins allow 72 characters on each line. If your print range is more than 72 characters wide, either adopt one of the alternatives just described or accept 1-2-3's default response, which is to print your print range in "strips." Printing in strips is how 1-2-3 deals with a print range that won't fit on a single page. See Figure 6–5 for a large print range that results in six printed pages. The idea is that you'll be able to tape the pages together to form one giant printout. If you don't want to tape the pages together, accepting printing in strips often results in hard-to-manage printouts. In particular, note that in Figure 6–5 pages 4 through 6 are printed *after* pages 1 through 3 even though they are really extensions of the first three pages. If you accept printing in strips, be sure to adjust the margins so a reasonable number of columns appear on each page. Also, consider using the Border commands discussed later to place copies of the row labels and the column headings on each page.

How can you tell if your worksheet is wider than 72 characters? It's easy! The normal 1-2-3 screen is 72 characters wide (less if you use some combinations of column widths), so if both the extreme left and right columns of your print range can be viewed on the screen at the same time, the worksheet will print within the default margins. If you must scroll the screen to the right to view the last column, the worksheet is wider than 72 characters and won't fit within the default margins.

Note that long labels extending beyond the right margin are printed on the following page. It may appear that 1-2-3 has printed only part of a cell. In fact, it has printed exactly what *appeared* to be in the cell.

Exceeding the Default Page Length

If you specify more than 56 rows in the print range, 1-2-3 prints the additional rows on the next page. The default page parameters reserve a total of 10 lines on the page for margins, headers, and footers.

These lines are reserved whether or not you specify a header and/or a footer. Even if you set the top and bottom margins to zero, you cannot eliminate the 6 lines reserved for the header and the footer. Thus the longest table that can be printed under the default page length of 66 lines is one with 60 lines.

Getting More Lines on a Page

There are three ways to get more lines on a page. The easiest is to select Options Advanced Layout Line-Spacing Compressed. This setting places 74 lines on an 11-inch-long page with 5 standard lines as the top and bottom margins.

Alternatively, you can select Options Other Blank-Header. If both the header and footer are blank, this option adds to the body of the page the 6 lines that would be used by the header and footer and the 2 lines that separate each from the body of the page.

Finally, you can select the Unformatted option under the Print options command. When a page is printed unformatted, all settings for headers, footers, top and bottom margins, and page length are ignored. Each line is printed in sequence, one after the other. However, if you are printing with standard line spacing and the print range contains more than 66 lines it will be printed *across* the perforations of continuous feed paper. You can combine compressed line spacing and unformatted printing to get 88 tightly spaced lines on an 11-inch-long page.

Forcing a Page Break

Lotus 1-2-3 has another solution to the problem of a worksheet that is more than 56 lines long. This option doesn't place more lines on a page, but it does let you select the point where a table is divided between two or more pages. Thus, you can ensure that each section of a multiple-part table begins at the top of a new page, or you can select the logical points to divide a long table. Just remember, the maximum number of lines printed on each page is still determined by 1-2-3's page length setting.

To insert a page break in a worksheet, position your cursor in the cell in the left-hand column of the print range of the row where you want to start a new page. Then type

/WP   Selects Worksheet Page.

There are no further choices to make.

As soon as you complete the command, 1-2-3 inserts a row and places the vertical line character followed by two colons, |::, at the original cursor location. The vertical line character, like other label alignment characters, doesn't appear on the screen.

To function properly, the forced Page Break indicator *must* be entered into the leftmost column of your print range. If it isn't, the indicator isn't treated as an instruction to the printer. Rather, it is printed as two colons.

Finally, nothing in the row beginning with the forced Page Break indicator is printed on the printout. You can, therefore, use this line for nonprinting comments.

To remove a Page Break indicator, either use the Worksheet Delete Row command to delete the row containing the indicator or use the Range Erase command to erase it.

Stopping the Printer

Knowing how to stop printing a 1-2-3 worksheet is almost as important as knowing what keys to press to get the printing started in the first place.

You usually stop the printer when you see it is printing incorrectly because you sent the wrong setup code, set the wrong margins, or specified the wrong range to print. You also pause during printing of a worksheet when you need to answer the telephone or talk to someone.

Unfortunately, if you have a print spooler or a buffer in your printer (memory in your printer), the only way to stop printing is to turn the printer off. Telling 1-2-3 to stop sending characters to the printer isn't enough, because the buffer can contain a large number of characters. When printing continues several minutes after you cancel it, just turn the printer off.

If background printing is still occurring when you turn off the printer, an error message appears across the bottom of the screen. Program operation isn't suspended, but to clear the error message you must select either Print Resume (after correcting the condition that led to the error) or Print Cancel to cancel the print job.

If your printer doesn't have a print buffer, you can stop printing by selecting Print Cancel. Alternatively you can pause the printing process by selecting Print Suspend. The printer stops, and you can inspect the printout or answer the phone. To begin printing again, select Print Resume.

Additional Print Commands

When you select Print Printer, File, or Encoded, the command line reads

Range Line Page Options Clear Align Go Image Sample Hold Quit

The Range, Align, Go, and Sample options have already been discussed. The Options option is the subject of the next section, Printing Fancy. The remaining choices are Line, Page, Clear, Image, Hold, and Quit.

Line and Page

The Line command advances the paper in the printer to the next line, whereas Page advances the paper to the top of the next page. If you use these two commands to advance the paper in your printer, 1-2-3 keeps correct track of the line numbers and the page breaks.

If you are using a laser printer and your print range is less than one full page, you must issue a Page command to tell the printer to eject the page. If you don't, the page remains in the laser printer until you print another page or exit the Print command by selecting Quit or pressing **ESC**. However, if you exit by selecting Hold, the page remains in the printer so you can print more material on it.

Clear

When you choose the Clear option, you are presented with six choices:

All	Clears all print ranges and returns all settings to their default values.
Range	Clears all print ranges.
Borders	Clears border column and row ranges.
Format	Clears margins, page length, fonts, colors, setup strings, layout, and image.
Image	Clears all graphs selected for printing.
Device	Returns to default output device.

Choose All to reset all ranges, borders, formats, and all other choices made under the Options submenu to their default values. Choose Range or Borders to clear either the print range or the borders setting. (Borders are discussed later.) The Formats option resets all options to their default values except the print range and those columns or rows chosen to border the printout. Image removes all graphs selected for printing through the Image option. It doesn't clear graphs specified with an asterisk as part of the print range. To clear those graphs, either edit the print range or use All or Range to clear the print range.

Image

Use the Image option to specify graphs for printing. When you select it, you are given two choices:

Current	Prints the current graph.
Named-Graph	Displays a list of all named graphs in the current file. Optionally, press **NAME/F3** to display all names at once.

Make your selection to print a graph. See Chapter 11 for additional information about printing graphs.

Hold

This command returns you to the Ready mode without closing the current print job. You can retrieve more files and work on active files. When you return to the Print command, the print job is still open and you can add more ranges or graphs to it.

Quit

The last choice on the main Print command menu, Quit, does just that. It ends the Print command and returns 1-2-3 to the Ready mode. Unlike the Hold option, Quit closes the current print job. The next time you enter the Print command you will be working on a new job.

You can also return to the Ready mode by pressing the **CTRL-SCROLL LOCK** combination or by pressing the **ESC** key until **Ready** appears in the Mode indicator. These methods also close the current print job.

PRINTING FANCY: USING THE PRINT COMMAND OPTIONS

Printing under the default options gives acceptable printouts whenever the worksheet is less than 72 characters wide (in full columns) and less than 56 lines long. In other printing situations, you will probably want to change one or more of the default specifications for margins, page length, and typesize. You may also want to add a header, a footer, the current date, or a page number to your printed worksheets.

You can select all these settings and more with the Options command. You can even embed print codes directly in a worksheet in order to have different portions of the same worksheet printed in different type fonts. (See Figure 6–6 for the command tree.)

To select an option from the Print command menu, press **O** for Options. The following choices appear on the command line:

Header	Enters header line.
Footer	Enters footer line.
Margins	Sets top, bottom, left, and right margins. Also sets no margins.
Borders	Sets border rows and columns, turns frame (column letters and row numbers) on and off.
Setup	Enters printer setup strings.
Pg-Length	Sets number of lines per page.
Other	Sets several ways of printing: Formulas, As-Displayed, Formatted, Unformatted, and Blank-Header.

THE PRINT COMMAND

Figure 6-6 The Print Option command tree.

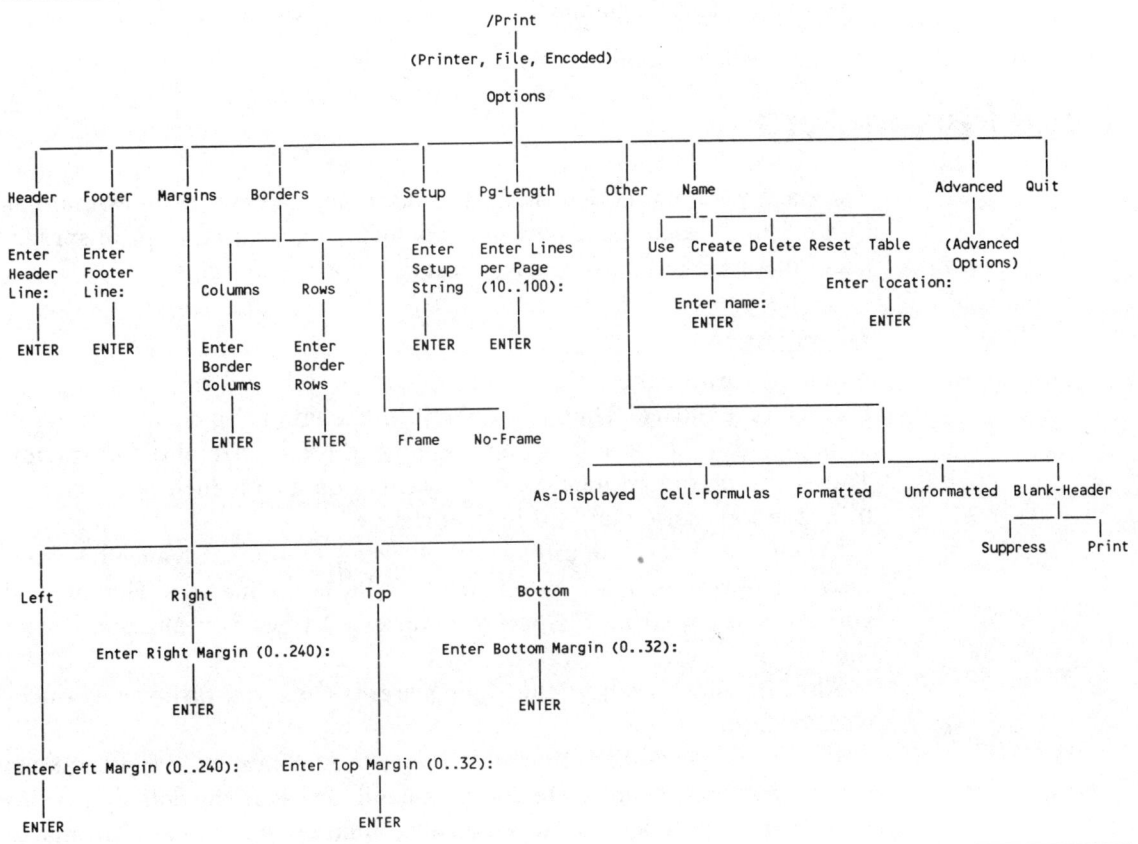

Name	Creates and manages printer setting names.
Advanced	Options for Device, Layout, Fonts, Color, Image, Priority, AutoLF, and Wait.
Quit	Returns to main Print command menu.

When you select an option, you are presented with a submenu. After responding to the submenu prompt either by making a choice or by supplying the requested information (usually followed by **ENTER**), you are returned to the Options menu (not the Print command main menu), where you can make additional choices.

When you're ready to print the worksheet, press **Q** for Quit or **ESC** to move back to the main Print command menu. Printing can then begin when you select Align and Go from the Print command main menu.

Page Parameters

The page parameters determine the maximum number of lines that can be printed on each page, how much of each page is used to print spreadsheet material, and how much is reserved for the margins.

Margins

As noted earlier, the default settings for the left and right margins are characters 4 and 76. Thus, the default line length is 72 characters in full column width. These settings do not depend on the size of the character. To get the maximum number of characters on an 8½-inch page, choose 0 for the left margin and 80 for the right.

When you select compressed type using Options Advanced Layout Pitch Compressed, 1-2-3 automatically adjusts the margins. However, if you use a setup string to specify compressed type, you must also reset the margins.

Also, be sure to adjust the right margin when you print on 15-inch-wide computer paper.

If you customarily print on wide paper or in compressed type you can use the Worksheet Global Default command to change the default margins permanently (or at least until you change them again). You can also change the default setup code to compressed type. See Chapter 2 for more information.

Page-Length

The default page length of 66 lines is based on an 11-inch-long page with 6 lines printed to the inch. This is standard, but you can set the page length to anything from 1 line per page to 1000 lines per page. This enables you to print on odd-sized papers, checks, form-fed note cards, form-fed envelopes, and other uniquely sized paper.

If you want to place more lines on a page, select Options Advanced Layout Line-Spacing Compressed, and 1-2-3 prints 88 lines on an 11-inch-long page. When you use this setting 1-2-3 automatically adjusts the page length.

As with Margins, you can change the default setting for page length with the Worksheet Global Default command. See Chapter 2.

Headers and Footers

Headers and footers are a good way to print common information on each page of a multiple-page printout. You can supply the information—report name or author, for example—or you can call on 1-2-3 to supply the current date or the current page number.

To specify a header or a footer, choose the appropriate option from the Options menu. Then type in the text. Figure 6-7 shows Figure 6-3 printed with headers and footers.

Headers and footers cannot be longer than 512 characters, and they must not be wider than the line defined by the right and left margins. If a header or footer is wider than the line, the remaining characters are truncated. If your header or footer is quite long, use trial and error to adjust them to your margin settings.

Using Text from Spreadsheet Cells

In addition to typing the header or footer, you can use text entered into cells on your spreadsheet to repeat from page to page. To incorporate that text as headers or footers, begin by typing a backslash (\). Then press the **UP** or **DOWN** arrow key to move into Point mode. Highlight the cell you want to use and press **ENTER**.

Figure 6-7   Worksheet from Figure 6-2 printed with headers and footers.

```
           (HEADER)->   This is a table for Chapter 6              18-Feb-90

                        SELECTED HEALTH PRACTICES IN THE
                              UNITED STATES: 1977
                                    by Sex

                              Total      Male     Female
              Hours of Sleep
                Less than 7   21.7%      23.3%    20.4%
                7             27.9%      29.8%    26.4%
                8             37.8%      35.8%    39.5%
                9 or more     12.5%      11.1%    13.7%

              Eats Breakfast
                Every day     58.1%      57.3%    58.7%
                Sometimes     15.9%      15.8%    15.9%
                Never         26.1%      27.0%    25.4%


              Source: Statistical Abstract of the United States, 1982-1983,
              U.S. Government Printing Office, Washington, D.C., p. 125.



           (FOOTER)->                    PAGE 1
```

The advantage of using information from the spreadsheet is that it is easier to change the text in a cell than in the Header or Footer command.

Formatting Headers and Footers

The text of a header or a footer can be located in one of three places on the line: flush left, centered, or flush right. The split vertical line character, ¦, is used to position text.

Text before the first ¦ prints flush left. For example, after the prompt type

Enter Header: This is a draft.

(If the only text in a header or footer is to be flush left, you don't need any vertical lines.)

Text after the first ¦ but before the second is centered. For example, after the prompt type

Enter Header: ¦This is a draft.

Text after the second ¦ is printed flush right. For example, after the prompt type

Enter Header: ¦¦This is a draft.

Cell references (preceded by the backslash) can be substituted for text in any of the foregoing examples.

Printing the Footer on the Last Page

When the last line of a worksheet is printed (not the last line of the *page*), the printer stops rather than proceeding to the bottom of the current page. Because the printer doesn't get to the bottom of the page, the footer for that page is not printed, nor is the page ejected from a laser printer. However, if you issue the Page command from the main Print command menu, the page advances (or is ejected) and 1-2-3 prints the footer when it reaches the bottom of the page. If you are using a footer, be sure to finish printing each print range with the Page command to be sure the footer prints on the last page.

Page Numbers and Time

Lotus provides three special characters for inserting page numbers or date stamps in headers and footers. They are the pound sign, #, double pound sign, # #, and the at symbol, @.

The pound sign prints the current page number in place of the symbol. For example, after the prompt type

THE PRINT COMMAND

Enter Header: ¦Page #

to place **Page 1** in the center of the first page, **Page 2** in the center of the second page, and so on.

The double pound sign followed by a number prints the page number beginning with the specified number. For example, after the prompt type

Enter Header: ¦¦PAGE ##2

This specification places **Page 2** flush right on the first page, **Page 3** flush right on the second page, and so on.

The at symbol, @, reads the system calendar in your microcomputer's memory and places the date (presumably today's) on the printout in the location specified by the symbol. For example, after the prompt type

Enter Footer: @

This specification prints the system date flush left on the footer line.

Example

To create the header and footer lines used in Figure 6–7, type

/PP	Enters the Print Printer command.
O	Selects Options.
H	Selects Header.
Enter Header:	Asks for header line.
This is a table for Chapter 6¦¦@	Type text for header; use vertical line characters to indicate alignment.
ENTER	Sets header.
F	Selects Footer.
Enter Footer Line:	Asks for footer line.
¦PAGE #	Type text for footer; use vertical line characters to indicate alignment.
ENTER	Sets footer.
Q	Selects Quit to return to main Print command menu.

Once the header and/or footer have been specified, proceed to print the worksheet. If necessary, specify the print range and other options.

Borders

A common problem when you print a large spreadsheet is that both the row labels and column headings are only printed on the first page. All other pages contain only row labels, only column headings, or neither column headings nor row labels. Under these circumstances it is extremely difficult to make sense of the printout, because you can't tell which row or column a particular number belongs to.

The solution to this problem is the Borders command on the Print menu. With it you specify one or more adjacent columns and/or one or more adjacent rows to be printed as borders on *each* page of a multiple-page printout. The column headings and row labels appear on each page, and it is easy to make sense of your printout.

The border rows and columns are usually those rows and columns containing the row labels and column headings. But in fact, they can be located anywhere on the worksheet. However, all of the rows and columns must be next to one another.

Note that you specify columns (Border Columns) to contain the *row* labels and rows (Border Rows) to contain the *column* headings. When the worksheet is printed, border columns are printed as the first columns of corresponding rows. Border rows are printed as the first rows of corresponding columns.

You can use named ranges to specify border columns and rows, or you can use the cursor control keys to expand the worksheet cursor over the appropriate rows or columns. See the Hands On section at the end of the chapter for an example of using the Borders option.

Warning: Select the Correct Print Range

A common problem with the Borders command is including the border rows and columns in the print range. When you do, *two* sets of column headings and row labels appear on the first printed page. One set is supplied by the print range, the second by the Borders option. When you use the Borders command, specify as the print range only the body of the table—exclusive of the rows and/or columns specified as borders.

Also, if you are using forced page breaks, they *must* be in the left-hand column of the *print range*. If they are in the columns designated as border rows, move them to the appropriate cell in the print range. See the Worksheet Page command, described earlier.

Frame and No-Frame

The Border command provides two more choices: Frame and No-Frame. When you select Frame, column letters and row numbers are printed on

THE PRINT COMMAND

each page. This is a great help when you are trying to compare a printout with the screen. Select No-Frame to turn off the printing of row numbers and column letters. No-Frame is the default setting.

Setup Strings

In past versions of 1-2-3 you had to specify the appropriate setup string if you wanted your worksheet printed in compressed type. As noted, you can achieve compressed printing in Release 3 simply by selecting Options Advanced Layout Pitch Compressed. Lotus takes care of everything, including adjusting the margins to accommodate the smaller type.

However, printers have other features, such as underlining, which aren't accessible either as a Layout or as a Fonts option. If you know the appropriate setup code and want to use the feature, 1-2-3 can send it to the printer before printing begins.

The special capabilities and the setup codes necessary to instruct printers to perform them vary from printer to printer. You must check your printer's manual to see whether it is capable of performing a particular task and what setup code it requires.

In printer manuals setup codes are often given in several forms. Look for the "decimal equivalent form"—a backslash (\) followed by three digits (such as \015)—because this is the *only* form 1-2-3 can use to send setup codes to the printer.

For examples of setup codes, see Table 6–1. These are the setup strings for the Epson dot matrix printers. While they by no means provide a universal standard, Epson printers are popular and their setup codes are recognized by many other printers. Also, see the appendix of the Lotus 1-2-3 manual for a list of Lotus setup strings that correspond to all of the characters in the common control codes.

Example

To instruct an Epson or Epson compatible dot matrix printer to underline your printout, type

/PP	Selects the Print Printer command.
O	Selects the Options submenu.
S	Selects the Setup option from the submenu.
Enter setup string:	Asks for setup string.

\027\0451	Type the setup string that causes Epson and Epson compatible dot matrix printers to underline each cell in the print range.
ENTER	Completes setting the setup string.
Q	Quits the Options submenu.
AG	Align and Go; prints the worksheet assuming that the print range and any other options choices have been made.
Q	Leaves the Print command and returns to Ready mode.

Clearing Setup Specifications

Once a setup code has been sent to your printer, the printer is set up to perform in a particular way, printing in compressed type, for example. The printer continues to print in compressed type until you turn the printer off (which resets the printer to its default values), send the code that cancels the previous code, or send a code (such as enlarged type) that replaces the first code. This is true even if you erase the setup code from the Print command, erase the entire worksheet, or load another worksheet.

The easiest way to clear the setup codes from your printer is to turn it off and then on again. This returns the printer to its default settings.

Embedded Print Commands

In addition to using the Setup command to send printing codes to your printer, you can embed the setup strings directly in a worksheet. This way, you can print different sections of your worksheet with different type fonts. For example, you can print the title and subtitle of a table in expanded type and the body of the table in compressed type. Codes sent with the Setup command control the printing of the entire print range, so you can't mix type fonts in the same printing. This is also a convenient way to view the setup codes specified for a worksheet. However, when you use embedded print codes you must set the margins manually.

The key to using embedded Print commands is the same split vertical line character that introduced the forced page break discussed earlier in this chapter. However, to introduce an embedded Print command you must type *two* vertical line characters so that the second vertical line character appears on the screen.

Also, like the forced page break, anything else on the line beginning with the print code is *not* printed. To make room, insert a row at the

Table 6-1   Setup strings for Epson dot matrix printers.

SETUP STRING	FUNCTION
Type Fonts	
\015	Turns on compressed printing (doesn't work with emphasized printing)
\018	Turns off compressed printing
\014	Turns on double width printing (Line 1 of page only)
\020	Turns off double width printing
\069	Turns on emphasized printing
\070	Turns off emphasized printing
\071	Turns on double strike mode
\072	Turns off double strike mode
\052	Turns on italic printing
\053	Turns off italic printing
Line Spacing	
\048	Sets line spacing to 1/8"
\049	Sets line spacing to 7/72"
\050	Returns line spacing default 1/6"
\051N	Sets line spacing to N/216" where N is a number between 1 and 255
\065N	Sets line spacing to N/72" where N is a number between 1 and 85
Cancel All Special Settings	
\064	Resets all special modes to their power up default states

location where you want to embed a print code. The embedded setup code must also be in the cell at the left-hand column of the print range. Otherwise, it is printed as text.

To embed the Epson command to turn on compressed type, move the cursor to a cell in the left-hand column of the print range at the point where you want compressed type to begin. Type

/WIR	Selects Insert Row.
ENTER	Inserts a row in your worksheet.
UP	Positions cursor on cell in inserted row.
¦¦\015	Enters the code for compressed type. Note only the second ¦ appears on the screen.
ENTER	Enters the code into the cell.

As with other print options, you must experiment in order to have the printout appear as you want it, because changing type fonts usually means changing typesize as well. Expanded type, for example, is twice as wide as standard type, and you must consider this when you locate a title relative to the body of a table.

Other

When you select the Other command on the Options menu, the following submenu appears:

As-Displayed   Formulas   Formatted   Unformatted   Blank-Header

The first four options really give you two either/or choices. The last option expands the number of lines printed on a page by the number of lines used for the header and footer lines and for separating the header and footer from the body of the table—a total of six lines. Blank-Header only works when both the header and footer lines are blank. Otherwise, selecting it has no effect. The defaults for the first four choices are As-Displayed and Formatted.

As-Displayed or Formulas

You normally want your spreadsheet printed as it is displayed on the screen. This is the default setting, and choosing As-Displayed results in a normal printout with the information arranged in columns and rows.

If you choose the Formulas option, a laundry list of the contents of each cell is printed one cell to a line. The list begins with the first cell

THE PRINT COMMAND

containing an entry in row 1 and then continues from left to right down the worksheet until all cells containing entries have been listed. Column width and range formats are printed for each cell containing an entry. Blank cells are not printed. (Don't confuse Formulas with the Range and Worksheet Format Text commands, which are used to display the contents—numbers, formulas, or functions—in the worksheet cell into which they have been entered.)

Figure 6–8 is a printout of the formulas for the worksheet in Figure 6–2. Notice that the entries are decimals, even though in Figure 6–2 they were displayed as percentages under the percentage format. Decimals are what would appear on the Status line, so decimals are listed.

One use of the Formulas option is to audit the structure of a spreadsheet. If you have a Formula printout of a correct worksheet, lay it next

Figure 6–8 When you choose Formulas under the Other choice on the Print Options menu, you get a listing of the contents of each cell of the worksheet, beginning with cell A1. Blank cells are ignored in the listing. This sample listing is for the worksheet in Figure 6–2.

```
A:B2: [W8] "SELECTED HEALTH PRACTICES IN THE
A:B3: [W8] "     UNITED STATES: 1977
A:B4: [W8] "             by Sex
A:B6: [W8] "Total
A:C6: [W12] "Male
A:D6: "Female
A:A7: [W15] 'Hours of Sleep
A:A8: [W15] '   less than 7
A:B8: [W8] 0.217
A:C8: [W12] 0.233
A:D8: 0.204
A:A9: [W15] '   7
A:B9: [W8] 0.279
A:C9: [W12] 0.298
A:D9: 0.264
A:A10: [W15] '   8
A:B10: [W8] 0.378
A:C10: [W12] 0.358
A:D10: 0.395
A:A11: [W15] '   9 or more
A:B11: [W8] 0.125
A:C11: [W12] 0.111
A:D11: 0.137
A:A13: [W15] "Eats Breakfast
A:A14: [W15] '   Every day
A:B14: [W8] 0.581
A:C14: [W12] 0.573
A:D14: 0.587
A:A15: [W15] '   Sometimes
A:B15: [W8] 0.159
A:C15: [W12] 0.158
A:D15: 0.159
A:A16: [W15] '   Never
A:B16: [W8] 0.261
A:C16: [W12] 0.27
A:D16: 0.254
A:A19: [W15] "Source: Statistical Abstract of the United States, 1982-1983,
A:A20: [W15] "U.S. Government Printing Office, Washington, D.C., p. 125.
```

to a Formula printout of a worksheet whose structure you want to verify, and any differences in structure are readily apparent.

A Formulas printout can also be used as a hard copy backup of the structure of a worksheet, just as you use the File Save command to make a file backup copy.

Formatted or Unformatted

The other either/or choice—Formatted and Unformatted—refers to whether the headers, footers, and page length are to be used to format the printout. When you choose Unformatted, the top and bottom margins aren't used. No headers or footers are printed, and printing continues until every line in the print range has been printed. There are no page breaks; the table is printed across the perforations in continuous feed paper.

The Formatted setting is usually used, but in several instances the Unformatted option is better. When you are making a print file, for example, eliminate headers, footers, and page breaks, because you add them later to conform to the style of the document into which the text file is being imported.

The Unformatted command, in conjunction with Options Advanced Layout Pitch Compressed, enables you to print the maximum amount of information on a given page.

Name

With the Name option you can assign a name to the current print setting—range, fonts, color, layout, device, and so on—and then use the name to make future printouts under the same settings. See Figure 6-9 for the command tree.

Names are saved with individual worksheets so they can be used with only one file, but if you make several different printouts based on the same spreadsheet, this is a much more convenient way to perform that task than writing a macro to do it. Named print settings are also very useful when you frequently print on two or more devices. Perhaps you print final copies on a laser printer but drafts on a dot matrix printer. Do the setup for each printer once and name the settings, then it's easy to switch between them. Also, use the command to remember the settings for a remote device that you use to print encoded files.

To assign a name to a set of print settings, begin by making all of the Print command choices. Verify your choices by making a printout. If the

Figure 6-9 The Print Options Name command tree.

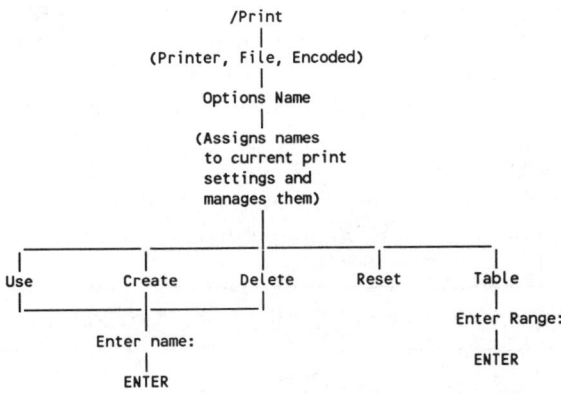

printout is correct, proceed. If not, correct any problems and do test prints until it is the way you want it. Then type

/PPO	Enters the Print Printer Options command.
Name	Select Name.
Create	Select Create.
Enter name:	Type a descriptive name.
ENTER	Accepts the name and records it.

To use a name, enter the command and select Use. To remove a name, select Delete. To get a table of named print settings, select Table and then point to a cell to tell 1-2-3 where to copy the range. Be careful. The command writes over the contents, if any, of the cells where the table is copied.

Beware: The Reset option on this command wipes out *all* named print settings as soon as you select it. Be certain you intend to take such a drastic action before selecting Reset. Use Delete to remove individually named print settings.

Remember to save the file containing the named print setting so you can use the name in the future.

The Options Advanced Commands

Release 3 introduces a new set of Print commands under the Advanced choice on the Options submenu. Some commands, such as Layout, Fonts, and Color, affect the appearance of your printed work. Others, such as Device, Priority, AutoLF, and Wait affect a grab bag of printer functions. Finally, Image leads to some very important graph print format options. Some printers aren't capable of using all of these options—particularly color and some of the fonts. Use the print sample to determine which options your printer can perform. See Figure 6–10 for a command tree.

Device

If you have only one print driver installed, you can ignore this option. When you have more than one driver, the Device option enables you to

Figure 6–10 The Print Printer or Encoded Options Advanced command tree.

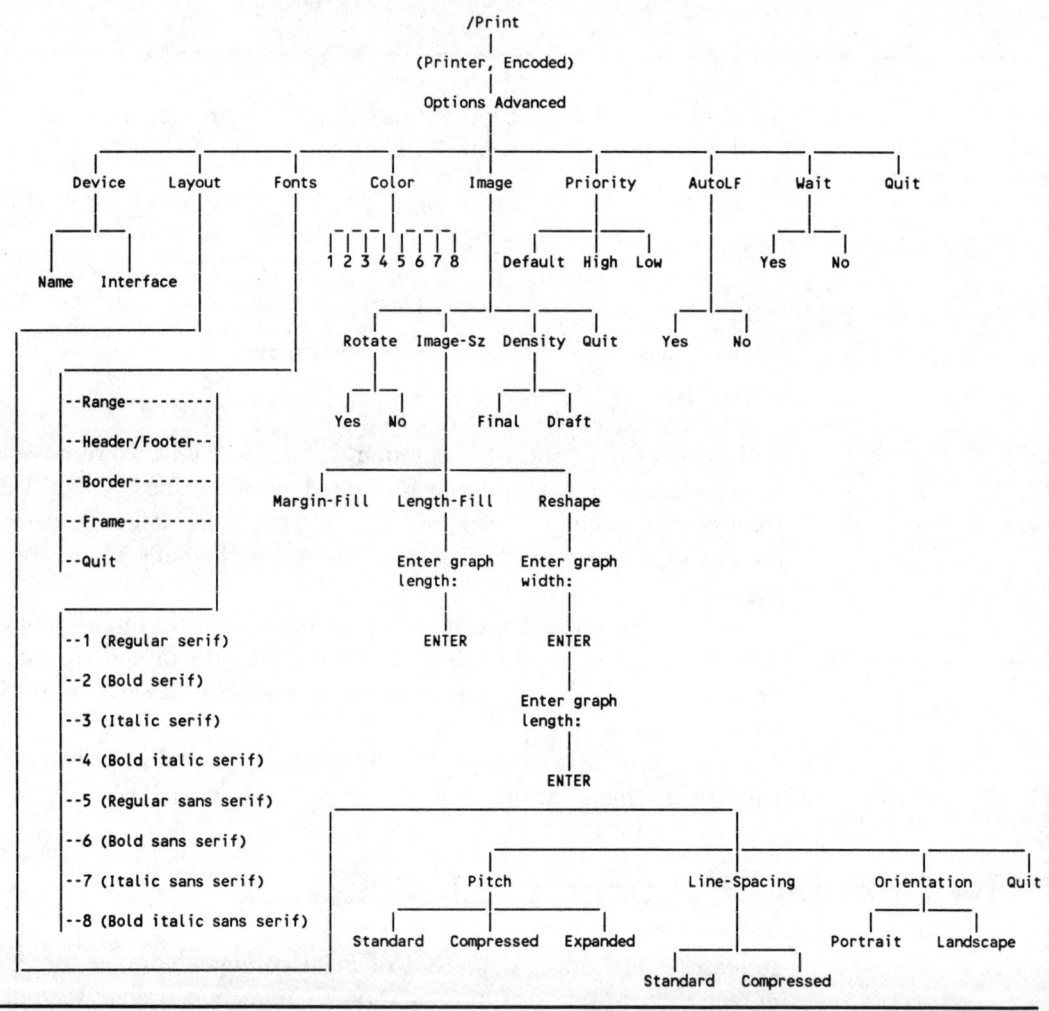

THE PRINT COMMAND

select which of the printers connected to your computer to send files to. Assuming you have the appropriate device drives installed, just select Device and the number of the particular printer you want to use. If you are using encoded files to print on a device not connected to your printer, be sure to switch to the appropriate device *before* creating the file.

Layout

Of all the Advanced options, this is the one you'll use most frequently. It was referred to several times earlier in this chapter. When you select Layout, you get the following choices:

Pitch	Options are Compressed, Standard (default), Expanded.
Line-Spacing	Options are Standard (default) and Compressed.
Orientation	Options are Portrait (default) and Landscape.
Quit	Leaves the Layout submenu.

Your printer may not be capable of performing all of these actions. Consult the print sample to discover which features your printer can handle.

Whenever you select Layout Pitch or Line-Spacing, 1-2-3 automatically adjusts the current setting for line length and page length to accommodate the new pitch or line-spacing. However, 1-2-3 continues to count the margins (top, bottom, left, and right) in standard characters and lines so your compressed pages have the same margins as your standard or expanded pages.

Warning: When you use the Layout options, do not use the Setup option. Mixing the two ways of selecting these features causes unpredictable results.

The orientation options, Portrait and Landscape, correspond to printing vertically (portrait) or horizontally (landscape) on each page. The Landscape option places more columns on a page, but your printer must be able to do it. Try it and see. Also, when printing landscape you may need to change the margin and page length settings.

Fonts

When you select Fonts, you are given the option of setting a different font for the print range, the header and footer, border rows and columns, and the frame. Select the section of the page in which you want to set a font and make your selection from the eight choices presented.

Note: Your printer may not be capable of printing some or all of the possible fonts. Consult the print sample to see which fonts your printer can print.

Color

If your output device supports color, you can choose to have the print range printed in one of eight colors. This option specifies only one color for each print range. To print ranges in different colors, specify the print range, its color, and print the range before specifying the next range and its color. Check the print sample to see which colors your output device supports.

Note: This option does not affect the colors in graphs.

Image

The Image choice is very important in determining the placement, size, and quality of the graphs you print with 1-2-3. As with other graph printing material, it is covered in Chapter 11.

Priority

When you select Advanced Priority, you are given the following three choices:

Default	Jobs are printed in the order received, unless a job is assigned a High or Low priority.
High	Current print job goes to the head of the queue. It is printed as soon as the current print job finishes.
Low	Current print job goes to the end of the queue. It is printed after all High priority and Default priority jobs.

Within each classification, jobs are printed on a first-submitted, first-printed basis. That is, if you have one high-priority job that hasn't been printed and you assign high priority to a second print job, the second job is not printed until after the first high-priority job has been printed.

Once you submit a print job, you can only cancel it by selecting Print Cancel. But, be warned, this cancels *all* of your print jobs. However, it doesn't cancel other users' print jobs when you are printing on a network.

AutoLF

After printing a line, most printers issue a line feed to move the print head to the next line before they resume printing. However, some printers expect the program using the printer to issue the line feed. If your printer prints the entire print job on one line, select the Advanced AutoLF option and select No. The No choice means that your printer doesn't automatically issue a line feed, so 1-2-3 needs to.

If you need to reset AutoLF here, use the Worksheet Global Default Printer command to change the AutoLF setting. Then select Update to make the change part of your startup routine so that every time you use 1-2-3 the AutoLF setting is correct.

Wait
This option determines whether 1-2-3 pauses after printing each page for a new sheet to be inserted in the printer. If you have a printer that requires single sheet feeding, select Advanced Wait Yes. Otherwise, ignore this option. Like AutoLF, this option can be set permanently with the Worksheet Global Default Printer command.

Quit
Selecting Quit returns you to the Options submenu. Pressing **ESC** does the same thing. Pressing **CTRL-BREAK**, however, cancels the Print command and returns you to the Ready mode.

THE PRINT FILE AND ENCODED COMMANDS

As noted in the introduction to this chapter, you can create three different types of output with the 1-2-3 Print command: printed worksheets, print files, and encoded files. Print files contain only plain text. All special print enhancements and graphs are lost when a print file is created. Print files can be exported to word processing programs where they can be edited, printed under special formatting, or combined with text in a document. Encoded files contain all of the print enhancements specified by 1-2-3, as well as the information for printing graphs. Encoded files can be printed with the operating system Print command.

Printing to a file to create either a print file or an encoded file is much like printing to paper, so most of the features and functions described earlier in this chapter apply to print files as well.

When 1-2-3 creates a print file, it automatically assigns it the .PRN filename extension. When 1-2-3 creates an encoded file it assigns the file the extension .ENC.

Creating an Encoded File

To create an encoded file, begin by typing

/P	Enters the Print Command.
E	Selects Encoded.

Enter name of encoded file:	Type the filename. The .ENC extension is added automatically.
ENTER	Accepts the filename. Enters Print command.

From here on, creating an encoded file is just like printing to a printer. Specify print ranges, select graphs to print, and choose options to be used. You can use all the Print command options just as if you were printing to your printer. However, be sure to select Options Advanced Device to specify the device on which the encoded file is to be printed if the device differs from your default printer.

When you have finished specifying options, print ranges, and graphs, type

A	Selects Align.
G	Selects G and creates the encoded file.
Q	Selects Quit to close the print job and returns to the Ready mode.

Encoded files may be quite large, because they contain a lot of printer instructions.

To print the encoded file, take it to a computer attached to the device you are going to use. Then use the operating system Print command to print the file. Consult your operating system manual for the exact operation of its Print command, including any parameters you must supply or syntax you must use.

Creating a Print File

Earlier in this chapter you printed the worksheet in Figure 6–2. To create a print file of that same worksheet, type

/P	Enters the Print Command.
F	Selects File to send output to a file.
Enter name of print file:	Type a filename. .PRN extension is assigned automatically.
ENTER	Accepts filename. As with the File Save command, if file already exists you are asked to Cancel, Replace, or Backup.
Range	Select Range. Specify which range of cells to print.

THE PRINT COMMAND

Enter range to print:	Move cursor to upper left cell of print range (A1 in Figure 6–2).
.	Tacks cursor to A1.
Arrow keys	Stretch cursor to highlight to lower right cell of print range (F20 in Figure 6–2).
ENTER	Specifies print range A1..F20.
Align	Very important: This tells 1-2-3 you are starting at the top of a page. Otherwise, page breaks may appear in unwanted locations.
Go	Begins creating the file.
Quit	Completes the print file, ends the Print command, and returns to Ready mode.

Opportunities and pitfalls are created by the fact that all but one of the Print command options can be used when you create a print file. The only command you can't use is the Setup command, because printing a print file is controlled by the program that ultimately uses the print file. Also, you can't include a graph image in a print file. If you try, 1-2-3 leaves the appropriate space in the file.

Print files are generally intended for use with a word processing or other application program. Keep the file's final use in mind, and you can avoid most print file problems. Here are some specific pitfalls to avoid.

Print Unformatted

Avoid page break problems by selecting Unformatted from the Options Other submenu. As described earlier, this choice suppresses the display of headers and footers and top and bottom margins. Your print file begins with the first row of the print range and continues to the last row with no page breaks in between. Page breaks, if necessary, are imposed by the program using the print file.

Remove Forced Page Breaks

If you have inserted forced page breaks in your print range, remove them before you create a print file. If you don't, at each forced page break 1-2-3 inserts into the print file the number of blank lines required to move to the top of the next page. Again, it is best to print unformatted and leave page breaks to the program using the print file.

Widen the Margins

Set the left margin to 0 and widen the right margin. By setting the left margin to 0, you avoid having four blank spaces placed at the beginning of each line. This lets your word processor determine the left margin. If you don't widen the right margin and the line length extends beyond it, 1-2-3 truncates the lines at the right margin and adds them to the print file, as illustrated in Figure 6–5. Reassembling the worksheet in your word processor can be tedious or impossible. With wider margins, each line prints without truncation, and the program using the print file can impose its own format on the information in the print file.

If your spreadsheet is very large, consider using the Borders option to place row labels and column headings on each page of a multiple-page printout.

Viewing a Print File

You can check to see whether the print file you created is the one intended by using the File Import command. Recall from Chapter 5 that with the File Import command you can read into a 1-2-3 worksheet a text file with the extension .PRN. The file is read in as a column of long labels starting at the current cursor location. Once a print file has been loaded, you can tell whether margins have been exceeded or page breaks occurred in the wrong places.

Even though you can view a print file with the File Import command, you should also save as a worksheet file any file from which you create a print file. It is much easier to modify a 1-2-3 worksheet than it is to change a print file.

HANDS ON: PRINTING IN COMPRESSED TYPE

Printing in compressed type is the most useful and most frequently used of all of the Print command options. If your printer can do it, and most dot matrix and laser printers can, printing a worksheet in compressed type is an excellent way to get the maximum amount of information on a single printed page.

Assume, for example, you'd like to add more information to Figure 6–2, the table on Selected Health Practices in the United States that illustrates printing under the default page parameters. You might want to show how eating and sleeping vary by income and age as well as by gender. This makes for a more interesting table, but it also adds several columns of information.

Without Compressed Type

Figure 6-11 shows how this expanded table would be printed under the default page parameters: Standard type on 8½ by 11-inch paper. As you can see, there are a number of problems with the way the table was printed.

First, the heading doesn't make much sense, because it is split between the first and second pages. Second, the columns for **55 and over** and those

Figure 6-11 When the expanded Selected Health Practices table is printed with the default settings, the table prints on two pages, and the long labels in the heading are truncated.

```
THE FOLLOWING COLUMNS ARE PRINTED ON THE FIRST PAGE:


                                                            SELECTED H
                                                                UNITE
                                                               by Age


                                              20-34       35-54
                  Total      Male    Female   years       years
  Hours of Sleep
    Less than 7   21.7%     23.3%    20.4%    20.2%       22.4%
    7             27.9%     29.8%    26.4%    28.9%       31.3%
    8             37.8%     35.8%    39.5%    38.2%       37.2%
    9 or more     12.5%     11.1%    13.7%    12.6%        9.0%

  Eats Breakfast
    Every day     58.1%     57.3%    58.7%    41.6%       55.5%
    Sometimes     15.9%     15.8%    15.9%    22.7%       16.2%
    Never         26.1%     27.0%    25.4%    35.8%       28.3%


  Source: Statistical Abstract of the United States, 1982-1983,
  U.S. Government Printing Office, Washington, D.C., p. 125.



THE FOLLOWING COLUMNS ARE PRINTED ON THE SECOND PAGE:

  EALTH PRACTICES IN THE
  D STATES: 1977
  , Sex, and Income

                  Less
    55 and        than     $5,000-   $15,000-  $25,000
    over         $5,000    $14,999   $24,999   and over

    22.7%         27.0%     21.4%     20.8%     19.3%
    23.2%         20.4%     26.6%     31.7%     33.6%
    38.0%         35.2%     38.8%     37.8%     38.0%
    16.1%         17.3%     13.2%      9.7%      9.2%


    80.1%         64.9%     58.0%     53.3%     56.5%
     7.5%         14.8%     16.0%     17.2%     15.3%
    12.4%         20.3%     26.0%     29.5%     28.1%
```

relating sleeping and eating to income appear on the second page. Only the first six columns of the table can be printed on the first page. To print more you would exceed the right margin, which 1-2-3 will not do.

Finally, it is difficult to make sense out of the information on the second page, because there are no row labels. You might be able to guess that as income goes up, the fraction of each income class getting nine or more hours of sleep a night declines rather rapidly. (The early bird does seem to get the worm!) But would you be able to tell that the older you are, the less likely you are to skip breakfast? The problem is that the row labels are all on the first page. They are entered in the first column, and the first column is only printed on the first page.

To correct these problems, you can use the Borders command to designate column A as a border column. The row labels then appear on both pages. If you do this, you need to redefine the print range to exclude column A. Otherwise, two sets of row labels appear on page 1. But there is a better way to solve the problem presented by the default page parameters. You can use compressed type to print the entire table on a single page.

Printing in Compressed Type

Assuming your printer can print in compressed type, you only have to choose one command to print Figure 6–11 on a single piece of paper. Select Options Advanced Layout Compressed.

Unlike in earlier versions of 1-2-3, now you don't have to adjust the right margin; 1-2-3 sets line widths in standard characters and automatically adjusts the number of characters printed within a given width whenever you select compressed type.

To print the worksheet in Figure 6–11 in compressed type, type

/PP	Enters the Print Printer command.
R	Selects Range. Specify which range of cells to print.
Enter print range:	Move the cursor to upper left cell of print range (A1 for Figure 6–11).
.	Tacks the cursor to A1.
Arrow keys	Stretch cursor to highlight to lower right cell of print range (K24 in Figure 6–11).
ENTER	Specifies the print range A1..K24.

THE PRINT COMMAND

O	Selects Options.
A	Selects Advanced.
L	Selects Layout.
P	Selects Pitch: Choices are Standard, Compressed, and Expanded.
C	Selects Compressed.
QQQ	Selects Quit three times. Returns you to the main Print command menu.
A	Selects Align to tell 1-2-3 print head is at the top of the page.
G	Selects Go to begin printing.
Q	Selects Quit to end the Print command and return to Ready mode.

The resulting printout is shown in Figure 6–12.

Compressed type is very readable, and it is one of the best ways to print large tables.

Figure 6-12 The two-page table from Figure 6-11 printed in one page using compressed type.

SELECTED HEALTH PRACTICES IN THE
UNITED STATES: 1977
by Age, Sex, and Income

	Total	Male	Female	20-34 years	35-54 years	55 and over	Less than $5,000	$5,000-$14,999	$15,000-$24,999	$25,000 and over
Hours of Sleep										
Less than 7	21.7%	23.3%	20.4%	20.2%	22.4%	22.7%	27.0%	21.4%	20.8%	19.3%
7	27.9%	29.8%	26.4%	28.9%	31.3%	23.2%	20.4%	26.6%	31.7%	33.6%
8	37.8%	35.8%	39.5%	38.2%	37.2%	38.0%	35.2%	38.8%	37.8%	38.0%
9 or more	12.5%	11.1%	13.7%	12.6%	9.0%	16.1%	17.3%	13.2%	9.7%	9.2%
Eats Breakfast										
Every day	58.1%	57.3%	58.7%	41.6%	55.5%	80.1%	64.9%	58.0%	53.3%	56.5%
Sometimes	15.9%	15.8%	15.9%	22.7%	16.2%	7.5%	14.8%	16.0%	17.2%	15.3%
Never	26.1%	27.0%	25.4%	35.8%	28.3%	12.4%	20.3%	26.0%	29.5%	28.1%

Source: Statistical Abstract of the United States, 1982-1983,
U.S. Government Printing Office, Washington, D.C., p. 125.

Line-Spacing Compressed and Orientation Landscape

Compressed type can also be combined with two other print options: Line-Spacing Compressed and Orientation Landscape.

With Line-Spacing Compressed, you can print 74 lines on a formatted page that leaves 5 standard lines for a top margin and 5 standard lines for a bottom margin. If you have also selected Compressed for the Pitch, your page will be dense, containing lots of information. If you haven't selected Compressed for the Pitch, the result is hard to read.

With Orientation Landscape, the lines are printed down the length of the page (sideways or broadside). You can print more columns and about as many rows. When combined with the Pitch Compressed command, Landscape is the best way to get the maximum number of columns on a page.

TIPS & TRAPS

Tips

Printing by Trial and Error.
Accept the fact that printing is a trial-and-error proposition. No one gets printing right the first time. Start simple, then master the more complex Print commands.

Changing Default Settings.
If you always change the line margins or the setup code, you can make your desired setting the default settings 1-2-3 uses when you start the program. These defaults are set with the Worksheet Global Default Printer command. Select Update from that command submenu to create a new configuration file for use each time you begin a 1-2-3 work session.

Forced Page Breaks.
Lotus normally prints 56 rows on each printed page. If you want 1-2-3 to stop before row 56, advance to the top of the next page, and continue printing, what you need is a forced page break. Insert one directly by entering |:: into the cell in the left-hand column of the print range when

you want a page break or use the Worksheet Page command to insert a row and the |::.

Printing Named Ranges.
When you are making a printout that includes ranges from different locations on a sheet or in a stack, make the designation of the print range easier by assigning range names to each print range. Then use the **NAME/F3** key to display the range name when you are specifying a print range, highlight the appropriate one with the arrow keys, and select it with the **ENTER** key.

Printing Column Headings and Row Labels on Every Page.
With the Option Borders command, you designate a set of columns (Border Rows) and/or a set of rows (Border Columns) to print to the left of each row or above each column. Use Border Rows for the columns containing the row labels. Use Border Columns for the rows containing the column headings. Once specified, the headings and labels print on each page of a multiple page printout.

Traps

Beware Align!
Select Align immediately before you select the Go command to print. Align tells 1-2-3 to reset its internal line counter to zero because the paper in your printer is properly aligned. If you use either the form feed button or the knob on your printer to move to the next page, your printer and 1-2-3 will be out of alignment. The result can be blank rows in the middle of printed pages and printing across the perforations on continuous feed paper. Failure to select Align before Go is the most common (and most frustrating) Lotus 1-2-3 printing error.

Forced Page Break Doesn't Work.
Check whether the Page Break indicator, |::, is entered into the left-hand column of the print range. If it is in any other column, the indicator isn't interpreted as a page break instruction. Rather, it is printed just like any other spreadsheet entry.

Can't Get the Page to Eject from Your Laser Printer?
If your print range contains less than 56 lines, the laser printer waits for you to specify another print range. To tell the laser printer you have finished with the page, select the Page command from the Print menu.

The same problem arises with laser printers and multiple page printouts. Everything is fine until the last page, which stays in the printer until you issue a Page command.

Footer Doesn't Print on Last Page.

The footer is only printed when the line counter reaches the bottom of the page. If the last page isn't a full page, the line counter never reaches the bottom. To print the last footer, select Page from the Print menu. This command, in effect, fills out the last page with blank lines and prints the footer.

Two Copies of Border Rows and/or Border Columns Appear on the First Page.

When you use Border Rows or Border Columns, do not include the designated rows or columns in the print range. If you do, material from the designated rows or columns appears twice—once from the print range and once from the Border Row or Border Column designation.

7

1-2-3's Built-In Functions and the Add-In Command

OBJECTIVES

After mastering the content of this chapter, you will be able to

☐ construct effective worksheets using values, formulas, and 1-2-3's extensive list of built-in functions.

☐ use built-in functions, operators, and formulas.

☐ employ @IF functions to give your spreadsheets intelligence.

☐ paste function names and range names with the NAME/F3 key.

☐ create @VLOOKUP and @HLOOKUP functions that span sheets, active files, and even lookup information in files stored on disk.

☐ use the Add-in command to load, invoke, remove, and otherwise manage add-in programs that attach to 1-2-3 to provide additional @ functions, macro commands, and applications.

INTRODUCTION

The preceding chapters introduced all of the Slash commands available to construct 1-2-3 worksheets. By now you know the difference between value and text entries and how to make and edit each type of entry. You can construct and manage stacks of worksheets and can set formats and label prefix characters. You can copy and move the contents of cells from one place to another on a worksheet or in a stack. You know how to use the File command to save and retrieve worksheets and how to use the

Print command to print worksheets and to create print and encoded files. With all that you know, you have only begun to tap your computer's calculating ability.

Electronic spreadsheets are constructed by defining the contents of rows and columns with labels, by entering values, and by defining the *relationships* between the cells of the worksheet. This "relationship" is how 1-2-3 taps your electronic computer's ability to do thousands and thousands of calculations each second.

The features that define the relationships between worksheet cells are the *operators* and the *built-in functions*.

Operators

Operators define a relationship between two cells, between two built-in functions, or between a built-in function and a cell. The simplest operators are the *arithmetic operators* (+, –, /, *, and ^ for exponentiation, or raising to a power). Other operators are *logical operators,* such as > for greater than, and the *string operators,* such as & for join, which is similar to the addition operator except that it applies to cells containing text strings.

Built-In Functions

Built-in functions instruct 1-2-3 to perform routine, though often very complex, computational tasks such as adding, averaging, or converting numbers to sines or cosines.

Once a cell's specific formula is defined, the value resulting from the formula is calculated and displayed in the cell in which it is entered.

Cell References

The cells referred to in functions and formulas can be on the same sheet, in the same active file, or in another file (active or inactive). Where a particular cell is located relative to the cell containing the formula or function determines how much information must be provided to 1-2-3 in the cell reference.

The following list shows the different forms of cell references and the situations under which they must be used. Each example assumes that the formula containing the reference is on Sheet A in the current file.

1-2-3'S BUILT-IN FUNCTIONS AND THE ADD-IN COMMAND

Current sheet: A1 or A1..A10

Current file, but on a different sheet: A:A1 or A:A1..A:A10

Different file: <<DIVSALES.WK3>>A:A1 or <<DIVSALES.WK3>>A:A1..A:A10

Different file in a different directory: <<C:\SALES\DIVSALES.WK3>>A:A1 or <<C:\SALES\DIVSALES.WK3>>A:A1..A:A10

You can always be more specific than required. For example, you can specify A:A1 when the cell containing the reference is also on sheet A. If you do, 1-2-3 drops the extra information when accepting the formula. Most of the examples in this chapter use references to cells on the sheet containing the formula or function. This simplifies the examples by eliminating the need for sheet letters or filenames, but you should remember that a 1-2-3 Release 3 function can refer to cells and ranges of cells in a wide variety of locations.

If you use the cursor to point, information about sheets and files appears automatically on the entry line as you cross the boundary between sheets and between active files. You can't point to a cell in an inactive file; you must type in the references. When you do, include the full pathname if the file isn't in the current directory.

"What If . . ." Analysis

After you have constructed a worksheet and defined the relationships, you can leave the task of calculating quick, error-free results to your computer. Thus, you can easily change an assumption about relationships to see what happens to the values on the worksheet under a large number of different assumptions.

The ability to quickly and accurately examine alternative assumptions is at the heart of the microcomputer revolution. It is called "What If . . ." or "sensitivity" analysis, and it is one of the most important things you can do with an electronic spreadsheet. In fact, this technique alone is why an electronic spreadsheet *is* an entirely new mousetrap rather than just a better way to do the same old things.

The following discussion of Lotus 1-2-3's 17 operators and 103 built-in functions is divided into ten parts:

Arithmetic operators

Logical operators

String operators

Statistical functions

Logical functions

Time and Date functions

Financial functions

Arithmetic and Trigonometric functions

Special functions

String functions

ARITHMETIC OPERATORS

The simplest operators are those that perform basic arithmetic operations on value entries. Table 7-1 lists the arithmetic operators and what operations they do. Value entries must begin with either a number (0 to 9) or one of the following characters: +, -, . (period), (, @, $, or #.

You can use the operators to add, subtract, multiply, divide, or raise to a power *any* 1-2-3 value. The value may be a number, a cell reference containing a value, or a built-in function. It may even be a cell on an inactive, saved file. The arithmetic operators can combine numbers, cell references, and built-in functions to form mathematical formulas exactly as you use the operators to define these relationships with a pencil and paper. The only difference is that 1-2-3 performs the calculations defined by the operators instantly and without error.

Table 7-1 Arithmetic operators.

FUNCTION	DESCRIPTION
+	Addition
-	Subtraction
*	Multiplication
/	Division
^	Exponentiation

Order of Operations

Use parentheses to determine the order in which to perform several operations in a formula. For example, use parentheses to tell 1-2-3 whether you want a formula to be evaluated as (1+2)*2 or as 1+(2*3). Use parentheses carefully to give clear instructions to 1-2-3 so you won't be surprised by an answer. If there is any doubt about groupings and the sequence of operations, use parentheses to declare the order of operation.

Be sure to pair each left parenthesis with a corresponding right parenthesis. If you don't, 1-2-3 refuses to accept your entry. Also, notice you must always supply the arithmetic operator. You cannot enter 3(2+3) to indicate implied multiplication.

Examples of Arithmetic Operators

Here are some examples of the arithmetic operators in action:

Function	Operators Used
5+7	+
B:B12*INTEREST	*
<<DIVSALES.WK3>>A:A45^.7	^
@SUM(A1..A8)/25	/
((B2−C8)+(N267*G37))^Y18	−, +, *, ^

Only the result of a formula (12, in the case of 5+7) is displayed in the cell containing the formula. Formulas can refer to any cell address, range, or named range (such as INTEREST in the previous list) on any sheet in any file. To inspect a formula, move the cursor to the cell and view its contents on the Status line. Alternatively, you can use the Worksheet or Range Format Text command to display formulas in their cells.

The operators are the workhorses of worksheet construction. The only limitations on the expressions you can create with them are your courage and 512, the number of characters that can be entered into a single 1-2-3 cell.

However, to work with a long or complicated formula it is best to break it into smaller parts and then combine the parts. This technique makes it much easier to find and correct any errors you make as you enter the formula.

LOGICAL OPERATORS

The logical operators are used to compare two values by asking a question that can only be answered as either true or false. A typical logical operator is >, the greater than logical operator. In the formula +A:A1>B:A1 it asks the question, "Is the value in cell A1 on sheet A greater than the value in cell A1 on sheet B?" When an expression containing a logical operator evaluates to true, a **1** is displayed in the cell. When it evaluates to false, a **0** is displayed. Table 7–2 lists 1-2-3's logical operators.

The last three logical operators—#AND#, #OR#, and #NOT#—are used to combine two logical expressions. For example, +A1>A2#AND#B1>B2 entered into a cell is true if and only if A1 is greater than A2 *and* at the same time B1 is greater than B2.

Logical operators frequently specify criteria in database commands and are often used with the built-in logical functions discussed later in this chapter. Logical operators can also be used directly on a spreadsheet. For example, on a stock portfolio spreadsheet you can use the greater than operator to determine how many times IBM's stock closed higher than it had closed on the previous day over 125 trading days in 1987.

In Figure 7–1, column A contains closing stock prices for IBM. Column B contains formulas that calculate the day-to-day change in IBM's price. The first formula, the one in cell B17, is +A17−A16. The remaining columns contain logical expressions to answer the particular question presented in the column heading. In column C, for example, the question is

Table 7–2   Logical operators.

OPERATOR	DESCRIPTION
<	Less than
<=	Less than or equal to
>	Greater than
>=	Greater than or equal to
<>	Not equal
#NOT#	Logical not (not A or B or C . . .)
#AND#	Logical and (A and B and C . . .)
#OR#	Logical or (A or B or C . . .)

1-2-3'S BUILT-IN FUNCTIONS AND THE ADD-IN COMMAND

Figure 7-1   Logical operators in action.

```
|    A              B           C         D          E           F
|1
|2  Number of Up Days:         62   <-- @SUM(C16..C141)
|3
|4  Number of Down Days:       59   <-- @SUM(D16..D141)
|5
|6  Number of Unch Days:        3   <-- @SUM(E16..E141)
|7
|8  Number of times Up
|9  Day follows Down Day       25   <-- @SUM(F16..F141)
|10
|11                Change
|12    IBM          From       Up       Down       Un-         Up after
|13   Closing     Previous   Day ???   Day ???   changed        Down
|14  Price in $     Day       +B17>0   +B17<0    +B17=0    +B18>0#AND#B17<0
|15 =================================================================
|16   $148.000
|17   $149.500    $1.50         1         0         0
|18   $149.375   ($0.13)        0         1         0             0
|19   $146.500   ($2.88)        0         1         0             0
|20   $147.625    $1.13         1         0         0             1
|21   $144.000   ($3.63)        0         1         0             0
|22   $145.000    $1.00         1         0         0             1
|23   $147.625    $2.63         1         0         0             0
|24   $148.125    $0.50         1         0         0             0
|25   $150.875    $2.75         1         0         0             0
|26   $150.000   ($0.88)        0         1         0             0
|27   $150.000    $0.00         0         0         1             0
|28   $157.000    $7.00         1         0         0             0
```

whether this was an "up day." The logical expression +B17>0 is true when an up day occurs and false when it doesn't. When the logical expression is true, a **1** is displayed. When it is false, a **0** is displayed. To find the number of times a stock closed above its previous close, you only need to add the contents of column C. This is done at the top of the table in cell C2.

In column D, an additional logical expression asks whether it was a "down day," and in column E the expression asks whether it was an "unchanged" day. Finally, in column F the logical operator, #AND#, is used to join two logical expressions to answer whether today was an "up after down" day.

STRING OPERATORS

The ampersand (&) can join the contents of two cells containing text in much the same way the addition operator joins two cells containing numbers. The ampersand also joins string functions such as @UPPER or @STRING (discussed later) to text. In addition, two of the logical operators, <>, and =, can be used to compare the contents of two cells containing text strings. Table 7-3 lists the 1-2-3 string operators.

You can also combine text with cell references and special string formulas to create "live" numbers in a memo or report. The numbers are linked to spreadsheet cells and change when the underlying numbers change. Text strings can also be used in conventional 1-2-3 functions such as @IF and @VLOOKUP to return words rather than numbers.

Finally, string functions have many applications in keyboard macros. They are especially useful in creating macros that vary their actions based on changes in the content of cells in the underlying worksheet. See Chapter 12.

Simple String Functions

One of the features labels share with values is that they can both be referred to in functions. The simple function +A1, for example, displays the contents of cell A1, regardless of whether the cell contains a label or a value. When cell A1 contains the text **Lotus 1-2-3**, a reference to cell +A1 displays on the screen

Lotus 1-2-3

The ampersand is used to join the contents of two text cells. Thus, when cell A2 contains the words **Release 3**, the formula +A1&A2 returns

Lotus 1-2-3Release 3

Table 7-3 String operators.

OPERATOR	DESCRIPTION
&	Join operator. Joins two cells containing strings or joins a string to a string function
=	Equal. Compares two strings, returning true if identical, false if not identical
<>	Not equal to. Compares two strings, returning true if not identical, false if identical
+	Begins a label entry that contains a string function
" "	Encloses text in a string function or expression

Using Quotation Marks in String Functions

So far, so good, but you undoubtedly noticed that there is no space between **1-2-3** and **Release**. This problem can be handled in several ways. A lagging space can be added to A1 or a leading space to cell A2. You can also solve the problem directly by including the space in the function.

To include any text (yes, a space is text!) in a string function, enclose the text characters in *quotation marks*. To include a space between Lotus and Release 3, modify the original function, +A1&A2, so that it reads

+A1&" "&A2

The function now returns

Lotus 1-2-3 Release 3

Note that an ampersand must be used to join the inserted text to *both* the first and the second cell references.

Writing Sentences with String Functions

In the preceding example, a single space was added between two words, but using quotation marks you can include longer pieces of text in your string functions. For example, when A1 contains **Lotus 1-2-3** and A2 contains **Release 3**, the function

+"The new "A1& &A2&" thinks in 3-D!"

generates and displays

The new Lotus 1-2-3 Release 3 thinks in 3-D!

The key to writing sentences containing string functions is to begin the sentence with a plus sign (+). This signals 1-2-3 to treat what follows as a string function and not as text. Without the plus sign everything, including the ampersands and the cell references, appears as text.

In practice, you may have to edit a function like this several times before the display is correct.

Combining Numbers and Text

You cannot directly combine references to cells containing numbers with references to cells containing text. That is, if cell A1 contains the text

Megan is number and cell A2 contains the number **1**, the formula +A1+A2 displays **1** instead of **Megan is number 1**. When formulas refer to cells that contain both values and text, the text cells are treated as if they had the value 0 (zero). Alternatively, when you use the ampersand to try to combine two cells, one containing numbers and the other text, the result is an **ERR** message.

To combine text with numbers you must use the @STRING function discussed later in this chapter.

Tips

The key to using string functions successfully is to remember that *all* text must be enclosed in quotation marks. A common error is to leave a space between a quotation mark and the ampersand that joins the text to a function. Another common error is to place a trailing blank after the last quotation mark. This can be done when you accidentally strike the SPACE BAR at the end of an entry. In both these cases 1-2-3 refuses to accept your entry.

Verify that your text string uses ampersands in all the appropriate places. In particular, ampersands must be used both before and after a cell reference or @STRING function when either of these is used in a text string.

If you have trouble creating a long text string, try creating just the first element of the string. When 1-2-3 accepts that, add the next element. This way you can build up the entire string element by element, and you can easily identify which element contains an error.

GENERAL RULES FOR USING BUILT-IN FUNCTIONS

Built-in functions are the computational workhorses of 1-2-3. There are more than 100 such functions, and they can do everything from adding or averaging the values in a range to finding the internal rates of return of a set of values. Familiarize yourself with all of 1-2-3's built-in functions. You never know when one can solve a particularly difficult problem.

Before turning to the discussion of specific built-in functions, you must be aware of the general principles that apply to all built-in functions.

Begin with @

Every 1-2-3 built-in function must begin with the at symbol, @, as in @SUM or @ROUND. If you don't begin with @, 1-2-3 enters what you type as text. Because built-in functions always begin with @ symbols, they are often called "@ functions."

Use NAME/F3 to Paste Function Names

You'll soon learn the names of the most commonly used built-in functions such as @SUM and @AVG, but there are many whose names you won't remember. Don't worry—as soon as you type @, press **NAME/F3** twice. The screen displays all of 1-2-3's built-in functions. Move the cursor to the function you want to use and press **ENTER** to paste it onto the entry line.

Arguments

In most cases you must tell each built-in function what to act on. The elements to act on—such as cell references and numbers—are called *arguments*. Some built-in functions require two or more arguments; eight of the functions don't require any arguments at all. The arguments for functions come in many different forms. Arguments can be a number, cell address, range of cells, named range, or a list combining these elements. They can even be other built-in functions. You can also use text as arguments in some functions. When this is allowed, you must enclose the text in double quotes.

Use HELP/F1 to Get Information About Arguments

Some functions require two or more arguments to be entered in the built-in function in a precise order. If you can't remember which arguments are required for a particular function or in which order they must be entered, press **HELP/F1** after you have typed or pasted the function name onto the entry line. When you do, the help screen describing that particular function appears on the screen. Get your information and return to the function by pressing **ESC**.

Point to Arguments

After you know which arguments belong in a function, you are ready to specify them. The best way to specify arguments is to point to the appropriate cells. As when you supply ranges for commands, you can use all the cursor control commands to point to cells and ranges of cells. The **END**+arrow key combination is particularly useful for specifying a column or row of cells as an argument for a function. When you point, 1-2-3 adds the sheet letter and, if necessary, the filename to the arguments as the cursor passes across sheet and file boundaries.

Remember also that when you specify a range of cells, the addresses of the first and last cell in the range must be separated by 1-2-3's range operator: two dots (..). In Point mode, the period you type to tack the anchor cell automatically supplies the two dots. The free cell is then ready to stretch the cursor over the desired range. When you are typing the cell addresses, instead of pointing to them, you must supply at least the first dot.

Use Range Names

If you have named the ranges you want to use as arguments, you can use them in any of the built-in functions or in formulas. Use the names anywhere you can use a cell reference. If you remember it, type the range name. If you don't, complete the formula or function up to the point where you need the range name, then press **NAME/F3**. The first four range names on the current sheet appear in the control panel. Press **NAME/F3** again and the screen is filled with range names. Highlight the one you need and press **ENTER** to paste it into the formula or function you are creating.

If more than one file is active, the names of other active files appear in the name list when you press **NAME/F3**. Select a filename; all of the named ranges in that file appear on the screen ready to paste into your formula or function. Pasting range names is the easiest and surest way to refer to ranges in other files, because 1-2-3 automatically adds the path and filename information to the cell reference.

Multiple Arguments

Whenever you use two or more arguments in a single built-in function, separate the individual parts of the argument with commas or semicolons. Note the semicolons in @SUM(C:D18;<<BUDGET.WK3>>M:G56; B1..B10). In this example, the values in cells C:D18 and <<BUDGET.WK3>>G56 are added to the sum of the values in the range of cells B1..B10. The result is displayed in the cell containing the function.

Correct Mistakes as You Go

If you make a mistake entering a function, 1-2-3 beeps, changes to Edit mode, and waits for you to correct your mistake. A very common mistake is forgetting to type the final parenthesis before pressing the ENTER key to complete the function.

You can edit any formula in any cell. Just move the worksheet cursor to that cell, press the **EDIT/F2** key, and make the changes. You can even change a formula into text by editing one of the label alignment characters before the entry.

If you begin to enter a formula into a cell and discover you have placed the cursor on the wrong cell, press **ESC** to cancel the entry. Move the cursor to the correct cell and enter your formula again.

Close All Open Parentheses

When parentheses are required to enclose the arguments of a built-in function or when you use parentheses to determine the order in which operations take place, make sure every left parenthesis has a corresponding right parenthesis later in the formula. If you do leave an unmatched parenthesis, 1-2-3 stubbornly refuses to accept your formula until each pair of parentheses is complete.

STATISTICAL FUNCTIONS

Now that you know about the general requirements of @ functions—arguments, range names, and so on—you are ready to get down to business. The place to begin is with the statistical functions, because they perform some of the most frequently used operations such as summing, counting, averaging, and finding the largest and smallest numbers in a list. Table 7–4 lists 1-2-3's statistical functions; Figure 7–2 shows some of them in action. In Figure 7–2, the formulas are shown to the right of the cells into which they are entered.

Among other statistics, the functions in Figure 7–2 calculate the total, maximum, minimum, and average monthly rainfall in San Francisco over the 30-year period 1951–1980.

To use a statistical function, move the cursor to the cell where you want the result to appear, enter the function, and then point to the arguments. It is as simple as that. Try it. To create the @SUM function in cell D8 of Figure 7–2, position the cursor on cell D8 and type

Table 7-4 Statistical functions. A "list" may be a cell, a range, a block, a formula, a range name, or a combination of these separated by commas.

FUNCTION	DESCRIPTION
@AVG(*list*)	Average value
@COUNT(*list*)	Number of arguments
@SUM(*list*)	Sum of values
@SUMPRODUCT(*list*)	Multiplies values and sums resulting products
@MIN(*list*)	Minimum value
@MAX(*list*)	Maximum value
@STD(*list*)	Standard deviation
@STDS(*list*)	Sample standard deviation
@VAR(*list*)	Variance
@VARS(*list*)	Sample variance

Figure 7-2 Statistical functions in action.

```
|A           A         B              C           D       E        F         |
|1 |
|2 |                            SAN FRANCISCO
|3 |                         AVERAGE MONTHLY RAINFALL
|4 |                        30 YEAR PERIOD: 1951 - 1980
|5 |
|6 |                               STATISTICS
|7 |
|8 |        January    4.65         Total       19.71 <-- @SUM(B8..B19)
|9 |        February   3.23
|10|        March      2.64         Average      1.64 <-- @AVG(B8..B19)
|11|        April      1.53
|12|        May        0.32         Maximum      4.65 <-- @MAX(B8..B19)
|13|        June       0.11
|14|        July       0.03         Minimum      0.03 <-- @MIN(B8..B19)
|15|        August     0.05
|16|        September  0.19   Standard Deviation 1.57 <-- @STD(B8..B19)
|17|        October    1.06
|18|        November   2.35         Variance     2.37 <-- @VAR(B8..B19)
|19|        December   3.55
|20_|
```

@SUM(	Provides the @ symbol, the function name, and the left parenthesis.
Arrow keys	Move cursor to cell B8. Entry line shows @SUM(B8.

.	Tacks cursor to cell B8. Entry line shows @SUM(B8..B8.
END DOWN	Moves the cursor to the cell B19 and highlights range B8..B19. Entry line shows @SUM(B8..B19.
)	Type closing parenthesis. Cursor jumps back to cell D8, the cell in which formula will be entered.
ENTER	Enters @SUM(B8..B19) in cell D8. Result, 19.71, displayed on the screen.

LOGICAL FUNCTIONS

The logical functions are listed in Table 7-5. Most of the logical functions return a 1 when a logical comparison is true and a 0 when it is false. Among other things, they can be used to test whether a cell displays a value, string, **ERR**, or NA. The most important logical function is @IF. This function gives your spreadsheet "intelligence."

The @IF Function

The @IF function chooses between two alternatives, depending on whether the first part of the @IF function evaluates to true or false. The true/false test is usually performed with the help of logical operators, but other logical functions such as @ISNUMBER or @ISRANGE can also be used.

A typical use of the @IF function is to test whether a cell contains a value other than zero. Whenever you define a division function where the cell containing the denominator is blank, the function displays **ERR**. This often happens when you create a number of functions on a worksheet and intend to enter information into the appropriate cells later. The result is a sprinkling of **ERR**s throughout your worksheet, which always provoke the question "What's wrong with your spreadsheet?"

To prevent this potentially embarrassing question, you can use the @IF function to display a zero, a blank, or a message instead of ERR. A typical example is @IF(A1<>0,B1/A1,"A1 IS ZERO").

The three arguments in this @IF function are

Function	@IF(
Logical comparison	A1<>0,

Table 7–5 Logical functions.

FUNCTIONS	DESCRIPTION[1]
@FALSE	Value is 0 (FALSE)
@TRUE	Value is 1 (TRUE)
@IF(*cond,x,y*)	*x* if cond is TRUE (non-zero); *y* if cond is FALSE (zero)
@ISNA(*x*)	Value is 1 (TRUE) if *x* = NA
@ISERR(*x*)	Value is 1 (TRUE) if *x* = ERR
@ISNUMBER(*x*)	Value is 1 (TRUE) if *x* = Number
@ISSTRING(*x*)	Value is 1 (TRUE) if *x* = String
@ISRANGE(*x*)	Value is 1 (TRUE) if *x* = Range name

[1]Logical Functions (1-2-3 considers any nonzero value to be true. Only 0 itself is false).

```
IF TRUE, DO            B1/A1,
IF FALSE, DO           "A1 IS ZERO")
```

Note: Do not leave blanks between the arguments when you enter @IF functions.

The first part of an @IF function is a *logical comparison*. It compares two values or two text strings and returns either a true or a false answer. In this example, the logical comparison asks, "Is the value in A1 different from zero?"

The value in the logical comparison section of the @IF function can be generated in several ways. The direct way is to use a logical comparison entered into the @IF function (as in the example). Alternatively, a reference to another cell containing a logical comparison can be used. Finally, you can use a formula or expression involving cell references and numbers, which may or may not involve logical operators. If your expression evaluates to zero, the @IF function considers it to be false. If it evaluates to any nonzero value, it is considered to be true.

If the answer to the logical comparison is true, the @IF function executes the argument in the second part of the function, the IF TRUE, DO argument. In this example, the logical comparison is true whenever A1 is not equal to zero. When this is the case, the @IF function executes B1/A1 and displays the results in the cell containing the @IF function.

If the answer to the logical comparison is false, the @IF function executes the third argument in the function, the IF FALSE, DO, and displays the results. In this example, if A1 is not different from zero (so A1<>0 is false), the @IF function displays the text string **A1 IS ZERO** in the cell rather than the **ERR** message that would appear when division by zero is attempted.

Nested Functions

You can combine @IF functions with other built-in functions, and you can nest @IF functions within one another to create a function with more than two branches.

Here is an example.

Function	@IF(
Logical comparison	A1<>0,
IF TRUE, DO	@IF(D25=10,@SUM(B2..K2),0),
IF FALSE, DO	@AVG(B2..K2))

This example contains as its IF TRUE, DO part another @IF function, which in turn contains an @SUM function. The last part, IF FALSE, DO, contains the @AVG function (to find the average for a range of cells). It is executed whenever the logical comparison is false. (Note the use of commas to set off each part of the @IF function.)

By combining built-in functions and by nesting @IF functions, you can create "smart" worksheets that do one thing in one situation and something different in another. You can also use text strings to give your @IF functions a "voice" so they can respond with the appropriate word or phrase. Be sure to remember to enclose text strings in quotation marks when using them as arguments for @IF functions.

For simplicity, the foregoing examples have not contained references to cells on other sheets or in other files. However, references like those could have been made and would have been incorporated into the functions in the normal way.

TIME AND DATE FUNCTIONS

The time and date functions are listed in Table 7–6. Lotus keeps track of dates and times by assigning a unique number to each day from January

Table 7-6 Time and Date functions.

FUNCTION	DESCRIPTION
@NOW	Serial number for current date and time
@TODAY	Value of current date
DATE FUNCTIONS	
@DATE(*yr,mth,day*)	Date number of specified date
@DATEVALUE(*x*)	Date number of date string *x*
@DAY(*date number*)	Day (1-31) of specified date
@MONTH(*date number*)	Month (1-12) of specified date
@YEAR(*date number*)	Year (00-199) of specified date
@D360(*start-date, end-date*)	Days between two date numbers, based on a 360-day year
TIME FUNCTIONS	
@TIME(*hr,min,sec*)	Time number of specified time
@TIMEVALUE(*x*)	Time number of time string *x*
@HOUR(*time number*)	Hour number of time number
@MINUTE(*time number*)	Minute number of time number
@SECOND(*time number*)	Second number of time number

1, 1900, to December 31, 2099, and a unique number to each moment of the day.

Date/time numbers are of the form 33486.43419. In a date/time number, numbers to the left of the decimal represent the date and those to the right represent the time of day. In this case, the date/time number is for the instant 10:25 AM on September 5, 1991.

Entering a Specify Date

Release 3 accepts entries in standard date or time format and places the corresponding date or time number in the cell. For example, entering 1-Jan-90 enters 32874 into the cell, whereas 10:00 PM enters 0.916667.

To enter dates from the current year, omit the year (so your entry appears something like 1-Jan); to enter a date in the next century enter the full year (such as 1-Jan-2001).

Date/time numbers can also be generated using the @TODAY, @NOW, @DATE, or @TIME functions. When you use the @DATE function to enter a particular date, your entry should be in the Year-Month-Day form. To enter years in the next century, add 100 to the last two digits of the year. That is, 2090 would be entered as 190. As with all built-in functions, the arguments can be values or cell references or named ranges containing values.

However you generate date or time numbers, they must be converted to readable form with one of the Worksheet or Range Date formats. (See Chapters 2 and 3 for these commands.) If you plan ahead, you can use the Automatic format (either Global or Range) to prepare cells to accept dates or times. After you set the Automatic format, when you make an entry in one of 1-2-3's standard date or time formats (such as 25-AUG-78 or 10:45 AM) 1-2-3 accepts the entry as a date or time, enters the appropriate value, and formats the cell appropriately. (See Table 2–1 in Chapter 2 for a complete list of date and time formats.)

Finally, you can use the Data Fill command described in the next chapter to fill a range of cells with dates or times. You can specify the increment for dates in days, weeks, months, quarters, or years and the increment for time in hours, minutes, or seconds.

Attributes of Date/Time Numbers

To pull a particular piece of information out of a date/time number use the @DAY, @MONTH, @YEAR, @HOUR, @MINUTE, and @SECOND functions. They return the number corresponding to the unit of time (such as 1 to 31 for @DAY, 1 to 12 for @MONTH) from a particular date/time number.

Using Date/Time Numbers

All the date numbers can be used in formulas such as @DATE(91,2,25)-@DATE(90,7,20), which determines the number of days between July 20, 1990, and February 25, 1991. They can be used to do financial calculations where the exact number of days between dates can be important for figuring holding periods for capital assets or in calculating rates of return. Dates are very useful in databases, where they can be used to date entries. The time part of the date/time number can be used to calculate the elapsed time of computer operations or phone calls. To date stamp each of your printouts, enter @NOW into a cell and format it to a date format.

Because each @DATE function requires typing a number of characters—and characters that change little from entry to entry—automating at least part of the process of entering a date is useful. If your worksheets include a lot of @DATE functions, check the short macro for entering dates given in Chapter 12.

FINANCIAL FUNCTIONS

Lotus' financial functions, listed in Table 7–7, provide simple, efficient ways to calculate specialized numbers such as the internal rate of return or the net present value of a stream of payments.

Uses of Financial Functions

Anyone who evaluates real estate investments or who deals with other problems involving cash flows over a number of periods will find the financial functions invaluable. See Table 7–7 for the arguments required by each of the financial functions.

When you use functions that calculate values for annuities, be aware that 1-2-3 calculates values for *simple* annuities. That is, payments are assumed to be made at the end of each period. This is sometimes called an annuity with "payment in arrears."

Calculating Your Mortgage Payment

Thinking of buying a house or financing a yacht? A simple spreadsheet has been set up in Figure 7–3 to solve the mathematical part of that problem. (Unfortunately, 1-2-3 doesn't have an @ function to handle the *cash* part of problems like buying a boat!) The spreadsheet uses the @PMT function to calculate the monthly payment required to fully amortize (pay off) a loan of a given principal, at a given interest rate, over a given number of periods. Figure 7–3 also contains formulas that calculate the total payments you make over the term of the loan and the total interest you pay.

The principal, interest, and term parameters are entered in cells B4, B5, and B6. Because mortgages are paid off by the month but interest

Table 7–7   Financial functions.

FUNCTION	DESCRIPTION
@IRR(*guess,range*)	Internal rate of return
@NPV(*x,range*)	Net present value at discount rate of x over range
@FV(*payment,interest,n*)	Future value of n payments at a specified interest rate
@PV(*payment,interest,n*)	Present value of an ordinary annuity of n payments at a specified interest rate
@PMT(*principal,interest,n*)	Mortgage payment per period for n periods of a given principal at a given interest
@RATE(*fv,pv,term*)	Periodic interest rate to grow present value, *pv*, into future value, *fv*, in term
@TERM(*pmt,int,fv*)	Number of payment periods necessary to grow to future value, *fv*, with periodic payments, *pmt*, and interest rate, *int*
@CTERM(*int,fv,pv*)	Number of compounding periods for an investment of present value, *pv*, to grow to future value, *fv*, earning a fixed periodic interest rate, *int*
@DDB(*cost,salvage life, period*)	Double-declining depreciation allowance for an asset
@SLN(*cost, salvage, life*)	Straight line depreciation for one period
@SYD(*cost, salvage, life, period*)	Sum-of-years-digits depreciation
@VDS(*cost,salvage,life start-period,end-period* [*depreciation-factor*], [*switch*])	Double-declining balance depreciation for an asset for length of time specified by start-period and end-period. Optional depreciation factor allows percentage of straight-line depreciation to vary. Optional switch to straight-line when straight line is greater than double-declining balance

Figure 7-3 @PMT function in action.

```
        A                  B           C      D       E
 1  USING THE @PMT FUNCTION
 2
 3      ASSUMPTIONS
 4
 5         Principal:    $100,000
 6    Interest Per Annum:   10.25%
 7       Term in Years:       30
 8
 9
10         RESULTS                    Formulas in column B
11
12      Monthly Payment:    $896.10   <-- @PMT(B5,B6/12,B7*12)
13
14       Total Payments: $322,596.47  <-- +B12*B7*12
15
16 Total Interest Payments: $222,596.47 <-- +B14-B5
17
18
19
20
```

rates are normally quoted on a per annum basis, the @PMT function entered into cell B12 contains some modifications. It is @PMT(B4, B5/12,B6*12).

The interest rate (from B5) is converted to a monthly interest rate by dividing by 12. The term of the loan in B6 is in years. The term is converted into months by multiplying by 12. The resulting *monthly* payment displayed in cell B12 is the amount required 12 times a year to pay off a loan with the characteristics in cells B4 through B6. Range formats have been set to display currency and percentages in the appropriate form.

With the worksheet in Figure 7-3 it is a simple matter to substitute different assumptions about the principal, term, and interest rate and then have 1-2-3 instantly calculate a new monthly payment.

MATHEMATICAL FUNCTIONS

The mathematical functions, described in Table 7-8, calculate values such as sines, cosines, and logarithms to various bases. Other functions supply the value of pi (@PI), take the absolute value of a number (@ABS), and generate a random number between 0 and 1 (@RAND). Use the trigonometric functions whenever you need one of those values. Use @RAND to generate a random number. Scale it up by 10, 100, or another multiple to give a random number between 0 and 10, between 0 and 100, and so on. Trigonometric functions require degrees to be expressed in radians.

Table 7–8 Mathematical and trigonometric functions. (Angles must be in radians.)

FUNCTION	DESCRIPTION
@ABS(x)	Absolute value of x
@ACOS(x)	Arc cosine
@ASIN(x)	Arc sine
@ATAN(x)	2-quadrant arc tangent
@ATAN2(x,y)	4-quadrant arc tangent of y/x
@COS(x)	Cosine
@EXP(x)	Exponential (e to the x power)
@INT(x)	Integer part
@LN(x)	Log base e
@LOG(x)	Log base 10
@MOD(x,y)	x mod y
@PI	3.141592653589794
@RAND	Random number between 0 and 1
@ROUND(x,n)	Round number x to n decimal places (+n to the right of decimal, –n to the left)
@SIN(x)	Sine
@SQRT(x)	Square root
@TAN(x)	Tangent

To convert degrees to radians, multiply the number of degrees by @PI/180.

Using the @MOD Function

The @MOD(x,y) function returns the remainder of a division of x by y. For example, @MOD(10,3) would be 1 (remainder of 10/3). The function has some specialized uses. For example, suppose you have a worksheet that calculates the number of employees required to do a task. Because you can't hire a fractional worker, you must adjust the number of workers upward by one whenever the requirement is fractionally higher than an integer. Rounding won't work, because values less than halfway to the next integer round down. The key is to combine the @MOD function with the @IF function and to add one worker whenever @MOD returns a value greater than 0.

Assume the required number of workers is calculated in cell G10. You can make the following entry in G11 to calculate the number of workers to be hired.

@IF(@MOD(G10/@INT(G10)>0),@INT(G10+1),G10)

If the result of G10/@INT(G10) is greater than zero (as it would be when the requirement calls for an additional fraction of a worker), 1 is added to the @INT of the calculated requirement. If the result isn't greater than zero, no remainder is detected by @MOD and the labor requirement can be used as calculated. For example, when G10 contains 4.3, the formula returns 5; when G10 contains 4.0, the formula returns 4.

Using the @ROUND Function

Recall that Format commands display a rounded result, but Lotus uses the actual value in a cell in all its calculations. The presence of extra decimal places can sometimes cause what are called "rounding errors," in which the displayed result appears to be in error.

For example, two cells each containing the number 0.004 would display and print as $0.00 under the Currency Format, two decimal places. But when these cells are added together, the result displays and prints as $0.01 because 0.004 + 0.004 adds to 0.008, which rounds to $0.01 under the specified format. If you are an accountant, or if for any other reason you need to avoid rounding errors, you can use the @ROUND function to round the actual contents of cells (which are used in calculations) to the desired number of decimal places. In the preceding example, when $0.004 is rounded to two decimal places the result in each cell is $0.00 and the sum of the cells is $0.00.

When you use the @ROUND function, you must supply two arguments. The first is the value to be rounded. This argument may be a number, a cell reference, or a function. The second argument is the number of decimal places to round to. If you specify a positive number such as 2, the number is rounded to the right of the decimal point. If you specify a negative number, −2, the number is rounded to the left of the decimal.

For example,

Function	Rounds to
@ROUND(1295.028,2)	1295.03
@ROUND(1295.028,1)	1295.0
@ROUND(1295.028,−2)	1300.0

SPECIAL FUNCTIONS

The special functions, listed in Table 7–9, are a grab bag of functions that don't fit neatly into any other category. You can use the @CHOOSE function to select any entry from a list. Use @ERR and @NA to display ERR or NA in cells and dependent cells. They are useful for signaling missing information or an error condition on a worksheet. The functions @COLS, @ROWS, and @SHEETS count the number of columns, rows, or sheets in a range and are useful for calculating the size of a named range. Finally, @INFO provides information about the current work session, such as the amount of memory available or the number of active files in memory.

Far and away the most important of these special functions are the two lookup functions: @HLOOKUP and @VLOOKUP. Lookup functions are always paired with lookup tables. A typical example of a lookup table is an income tax table, in which one value—taxable income—is used to look up a related value, tax due. Sales tax tables, commission or discount schedules, even calendars where dates are used to look up appointments are other examples of lookup tables.

In the following discussion, lookup tables and the functions are assumed to be entered into cells on the same sheet. This prevents cell references in the example from getting too complicated. In practice, however, it is often convenient to place the lookup tables on different sheets or even in entirely different files. The information is readily accessible yet doesn't take up space on the main sheet. Separate storage may make the tables easier to maintain and update. In fact, the other file doesn't even need to be in memory!

Constructing Lookup Tables and @LOOKUP Functions

Lookup tables can be used in any worksheet requiring different values based on the levels of other values. Examples are tax tables, commission tables, and discount tables.

Table 7–9 Special functions.

FUNCTION	DESCRIPTION
CELL AND RANGE INFORMATION	
@@(*cell address*)	The contents of the cell referenced by cell address
@CELL(*attribute, range*)	The code representing the attribute of range
@CELLPOINTER(*attribute*)	The code representing the attribute of the highlighted cell
@COORD(*worksheet, column, row, absolute*)	The absolute, mixed, or relative cell address created from values provided as arguments. Worksheet and column, 1–256, row 1–8,192, and absolute 1–8 as code for each combination of relative and absolute sheet, row, and column possible
@COLS(*range*)	The number of columns in a range
@ROWS(*range*)	The number of rows in a range
@SHEETS(*range*)	The number of worksheets in a range

continued

The lookup table is constructed by entering numbers or text strings into a vertical or horizontal matrix. The topmost row of a horizontal table and the leftmost row of a vertical table contain the numbers or words to be looked up. The remaining rows (or columns for a vertical table) contain the values or words to be returned by the lookup function.

Most lookup table applications use numbers (tax tables, for example), but you can also use words and phrases in your lookup tables. You can even mix the two. Words can be used in conjunction with date functions to find and display the name of the day of the week or the month of the year. Or you can use text strings to look up and return the appropriate word or phrase to insert in a macro based on entries elsewhere on the worksheet.

Figure 7–4 contains a vertical lookup table and several @VLOOKUP functions. Your first task is to create the lookup table in cells B8 through

Table 7–9 *Continued*

FUNCTION	DESCRIPTION
ERROR TRAPPING	
@ERR	The value ERR (error)
@NA	The value NA (not available)
LOOKUP CALCULATIONS	
@CHOOSE(*x*,v0,v1,...vn)	The *x*th value in list v0,v1,...,vn
@HLOOKUP(*x*,range,row number)	The contents in the cell that is the specified row number from the cell in the top row of range that matches *x*
@INDEX(range,column, row)	The value of the cell located at the intersection of column and row in range
@VLOOKUP(*x*,range, column number)	The contents in the cell that is the specified column number from the cell in the left column of range that matches *x*
SYSTEM AND SESSION INFORMATION	
@INFO(*attribute*)	System information for the current session

C13. To use the table, you enter a lookup function such as the one in cell D19 in Figure 7–4: @VLOOKUP(B19,B8..C13,1).

The three parts of every lookup function are the search value, the table range, and the offset.

Function	@VLOOKUP(
Search value	B19,
Table range	B8..C13,
Offset	1)

Note: Do not leave blanks between the arguments when you enter @VLOOKUP functions.

Figure 7-4 Vertical lookup table.

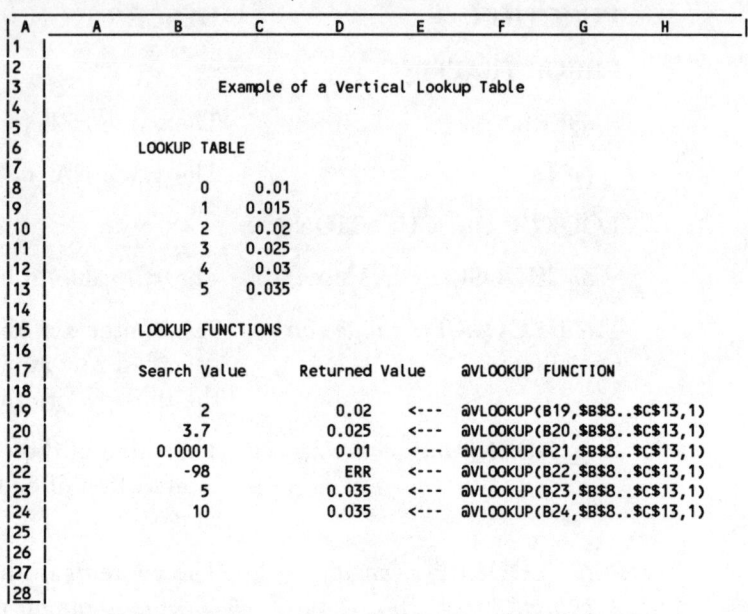

The *search value* is the first part of a lookup function and represents the value to be looked up. It is usually supplied by a reference to a cell (B19 in the example). The search value can be either a value or text, but when it is text it must *exactly* match the value in the table range. If it doesn't, a match won't be found.

The second part of a lookup function is the *table range.* It is the block of cells containing both the cells to be searched (the search range) and the cells containing the values to be returned. In the example, the table range is the block B8..C13.

The search range is always the leftmost column (for @VLOOKUP) or topmost row (for @HLOOKUP) of the table range. The values in the search range must be arranged from *smallest to largest,* and they must not contain any *duplicate values.* The search range can contain text strings. And it can even contain a mixture of values and text strings. Unlike earlier versions of 1-2-3, the text string in a lookup function does not need to be enclosed in quotation marks.

The third part of a lookup function is the *offset.* This number tells the lookup function where to find the value or word it is looking for *relative* to the top row or left column of the range. In the example, the offset is 1, and the lookup function returns a value or matching word from the column that is 1 column to the right of the search range.

The table range and the search range for the lookup function can be on the same sheet, different sheets, or even in different files.

How the Lookup Function Works

Here is how the lookup function works. It begins with the topmost (or leftmost) cell in the search range. When the search value is a value, 1-2-3 searches the range until it finds the largest value that is less than or equal to the search value. It then returns the corresponding value in the column (or row) given by the Offset and displays the result in the cell containing the lookup function.

When the search value is a text string, 1-2-3 searches the search range until it finds a text string that *exactly* matches the search string as to case as well as characters. It then returns the corresponding value (text string or value) in the column (or row) given by the Offset and displays the result in the cell containing the lookup function.

The function displays **ERR** whenever the search value is smaller than the smallest value in the search range. The function displays the largest value in the search range for all search values greater than the largest value in the search range. For example, in Figure 7–4, a search value of –98, smaller than the smallest value in the search range, causes the function in cell D22 to display **ERR**. When the search value is 10, larger than the largest value in the search range, it causes the function in D24 to display 0.035, the largest value in the search range.

When the search value is a text string, 1-2-3 returns **ERR** when it fails to find a text string in the search range that exactly matches the search string.

To test your understanding of lookup functions, cover the values in the Returned Value column in Figure 7–4 with a sheet of paper and, from the search values, predict the value that should be returned by the lookup function. Check your predictions against the table.

Always Test Your Lookup Functions

A final point. After creating a lookup table, test it. Do this by entering a lookup function into a cell near the table. Be sure you can see both the returned value and the lookup table. Then look up several values and verify that the value returned is the value you expected to be returned. Be sure to choose values larger and smaller than the largest and smallest value in the lookup range. That way you know what is returned when an

Table 7–10 Attribute codes for @CELL and @CELLPOINTER.

ATTRIBUTE	RESULT
"address"	Current cell address, column letter and row number only (for example, $B$7 or B7)
"row"	Current row number (between 1 and 8192)
"col"	Current column number (between 1 and 256)
"contents"	Current cell contents
"type"	Type of data in the cell: b if blank v if numeric or formula l if label
"prefix"	Current label prefix: ' if left-aligned " if right-aligned ^ if centered \ if repeating label ¦ if nonprinting label blank (no symbol) if the cell is empty or contains a value
"protect"	Current protection status: 1 if protected 0 if not protected

continued

out-of-range value is looked up. You can then decide how to handle that occurrence in your worksheet.

Using @CELL, @CELLPOINTER, and @INFO

Three other special functions provide information about a designated cell, @CELL; the cell currently under the worksheet cursor, @CELL-POINTER; or the current work session, @INFO. Each of these functions requires as an argument the word describing the desired attribute. These words are string functions and must be enclosed in quotation marks. See

Table 7–10   *Continued*

ATTRIBUTE	RESULT
"width"	Current column width (between 1 and 240)
"format"	Current numeric format: C0 to C15 for Currency F0 to F15 for Fixed G for General, label, or blank P0 to P15 for Percent S0 to S15 for Scientific ,0 to ,15 for Comma + for +/− D1 for DD-MM-YY D2 for DD-MM D3 for MM-YY D4 for MM/DD/YY D5 for MM/DD D6 for HH:MM:SS AM/PM D7 for HH:MM AM/PM D8 for HH:MM:SS (24 hour) D9 for HH:MM (24 hour)
"parentheses"	Current parentheses status: 0 if formatted for parentheses 1 if not formatted for parentheses
"worksheet"	Worksheet letter as a value from 1 to 256

Table 7–10 for a list of the attribute codes used with @CELL and @CELLPOINTER.

The @INFO function provides useful information about different attributes of the current work session such as the amount of memory currently available, the number of active files, and the current directory. To use the function you supply a string argument that refers to an attribute such as "memavail" for memory available or "directory" for current directory. The function returns the information requested about the attribute. See Table 7–11 for a list of arguments and what they return.

Table 7–11   Arguments and key to returned values for the @INFO function.

ARGUMENT	RETURNS
"memavail"	Current amount of available memory
"mode"	Current mode: 0 Wait 1 Ready 2 Label 3 Menu 4 Value 5 Point 6 Edit 7 Error 8 Find 9 Files 10 Help 11 Stat 12 Frmt 13 Names 99 All other modes (such as LEAF and user-defined)
"numfile"	Current number of active files
"origin"	Cell address of first cell in window that contains the worksheet cursor
"osreturncode"	Value returned by most recent /System command or {SYSTEM} advanced macro command
"osversion"	Current operating system version
"path"	Current path
"recalc"	Current recalculation mode as one of the two strings "automatic" or "manual"
"release"	Release of 1-2-3 being used. Consists of three parts: major release number, upgrade level, and revision number
"system"	Name of the operating system
"totmem"	Total memory available

STRING FUNCTIONS

In addition to the string operators introduced earlier in this chapter, 1-2-3 has a library of built-in functions capable of performing a number of different actions on text strings. Some of these built-in functions have very specialized uses. For example, @CHAR returns the ASCII character corresponding to a particular code number, whereas @CODE performs the reverse operation by specifying the ASCII code that corresponds to a particular character. Table 7–12 summarizes the 1-2-3 string functions.

One of these string functions may be just what you need to solve a particularly difficult problem. Functions with potentially wide applications are @PROPER, @LOWER, @UPPER, and @TRIM. They perform text processing functions. Use @PROPER to convert text to initial capital letters (what is called "proper" case). @UPPER converts text to all capitals; @LOWER converts text to all lowercase letters; and @TRIM removes leading, trailing, and intermediate blanks in excess of those needed to divide words. These four functions have important uses in conforming entries in a database to a standard format.

If you use one of these functions to modify a text entry, you can "freeze" your results using the Range Values command (See Chapter 3) to convert the formulas to their displayed values.

Combining Text and Values with the @STRING Function

In addition to the simple combinations achieved using the ampersand described earlier in this chapter, 1-2-3 has a special @ function for combining text and values in the same string. Values combined in this way are "live," so they change each time the values in the underlying worksheet change.

The technique is to use the @STRING function to convert a value into a string so it can be combined with other text. For example, in a worksheet where cell A43 contains a projection for 1991 sales growth, you can create a simple sales report by entering the following into a single cell:

+"Division sales are expected to grow to $"&@STRING(A43,0)&" in 1991."

When cell A43 contains the figure for projected 1991 sales, for example, $83,402.29, the function evaluates to

Division sales are expected to grow to $83402 in 1991.

Table 7–12 String functions.

FUNCTION	DESCRIPTION
@CHAR(*x*)	LMBCS character that corresponds to code number *x*
@CODE(*string*)	LIMBS code number for the first character in string
@EXACT(*string1,string2*)	1 (true) if string 1 and string 2 are exactly alike; otherwise, it returns 0 (false)
@FIND(*search string start number, string*)	Position at which the first occurrence of search string begins in string
@LEFT(*string,n*)	First *n* characters in string
@LENGTH(*string,n*)	Number of characters in string
@LOWER(*string*)	All letters in string in lowercase
@MID(*string, start number,n*)	*n* characters from string, beginning with the character at start number
@N(*range*)	Numeric value in the upper left corner cell in range
@PROPER(*string*)	All words in string with the first letter in uppercase and the rest in lowercase
@REPEAT(*string,n*)	String, duplicated *n* times
@REPLACE(*original string, start number,n, new string*)	*n* characters removed from original string, beginning at start number, and inserts new string in the same place
@RIGHT(*string,n*)	Last *n* characters in string
@S(*range*)	String value in the upper left corner
@STRING(*x,n*)	Numeric value *x* as a string, with *n* decimal places
@TRIM(*string*)	String with no leading or trailing spaces, and no consecutive spaces
@UPPER(*string*)	All letters in string in uppercase
@VALUE(*string*)	String that looks like a number in its actual numeric value

There are several things to note about the @STRING function.

First, it has two arguments. The first tells the function what to convert to a string character. As in the example, this argument is often a reference to a worksheet cell, but it can also be a formula or functions.

The second argument, 0 in the example, specifies the number of decimal places to be used. Unfortunately, you cannot automatically embed commas in the number and display the result with dollar signs. The dollar sign is easy to add as part of the text string. But displaying commas requires a fairly intricate use of the other string functions, particularly @LENGTH, @RIGHT, and @LEFT, to take the number apart in the right places so that commas can be inserted as text characters.

Tips for Including @STRING Functions in Paragraphs

String functions can be combined with normal text to create paragraphs where the numbers are live numbers. However, the task is made more difficult by the fact that you can't reformat string functions with the Range Justify command as you can regular long labels.

To embed string functions in paragraphs, begin by creating all of the text as long labels. Whenever you come to a point where an @STRING function goes, substitute place-holding characters such as question marks equal in number to the largest number of digits you expect to be called from the underlying worksheet. Then reformat the long labels with the Range Justify command.

Only after you are completely satisfied with the text should you convert those lines of text containing the question mark place holders to string functions. Do the conversion by editing in the plus sign to begin a string function. Then enclose the appropriate sections of text in quotation marks and add the necessary ampersands. Substitute the @STRING function for the question marks you used to hold their places in the text. When the editing is complete, press **ENTER**, and the new text function with its embedded @STRING functions is entered in your paragraph.

RELATIVE AND ABSOLUTE CELL REFERENCES

Relative (adjusting) and absolute (nonadjusting) cell references have already been discussed in connection with the Copy command in Chapter

4. See that chapter for more issues involved with relative and absolute cell references.

For this chapter's purposes it is sufficient to note that there are several ways to insert the dollar signs that designate cell references as absolute.

If you are typing a formula or function, you can type the dollar signs in the appropriate places. If you are using the pointing-with-the-cursor technique to designate a cell address or range, press the **ABS/F4** key to insert the dollar signs. Pressing the **ABS/F4** key converts A1 on sheet D, for example, into $D:$A$1. Pressing the key again causes the dollar signs to cycle through their possible locations, providing all possible combinations of relative and absolute references to rows, columns, and sheets.

If the function or formula has already been constructed, use the **EDIT/F2** key to shift to Edit mode. Once there, position the cursor under the cell reference you want to make absolute and press the **ABS/F4** key to make the dollar signs appear.

Absolute Named Ranges

Named ranges present a particular problem. When assigned, they are the equivalent of *relative* cell addresses. There is no way to make the assignment absolute. However, you frequently want named ranges used in formulas and functions to be absolute so that when the formula or function is copied the named range doesn't adjust. (See Chapter 3 for a discussion of using the Range Name Create command.)

To convert a named range to an absolute reference, type a dollar sign before the range name as you enter it into the formula (for example, **$COST**). To change a relative range name in an existing formula to an absolute one, use the **EDIT/F2** key. Position the cursor before the range name and type a dollar sign. Then press **ENTER** to return the formula to the cell.

Remember that an absolute (nonadjusting) cell reference is only an issue when you use the Copy command. If you aren't going to copy a formula, the references it contains can be either relative or absolute.

THE LOTUS ADD-IN COMMAND

Add-ins are a special advanced feature of Lotus 1-2-3; a feature that extends the power of 1-2-3 in almost unlimited directions.

Add-ins can be special @ functions; macro commands; or Lotus 1-2-3 applications that attach to 1-2-3 and work as an integral part of the program to enhance printing, graphics, or other functions. Adding an add-in to 1-2-3 is just like adding more RAM to your computer or adding a modem; it extends your computing power with a minimum of complications.

Add-ins are created with the Lotus Add-In Toolkit by vendors or advanced users comfortable with computer programming languages. Add-ins created for earlier versions of 1-2-3 do not work with Release 3, but most vendors are bringing out Release 3 versions of their popular add-ins. If you need more information about the Lotus Developer's Toolkit, contact Lotus Development Corporation. For a complete catalog of add-ins, call 1-800-635-6887 (United States and Canada only) during business hours.

The Add-in Menu

Before you can use an add-in you must attach it to 1-2-3 by pressing **ALT-F10** to display the Add-in command menu. See Figure 7–5 for the command tree.

The Add-in command menu's main menu choices are

Load	Reads an add-in into memory.
Remove	Removes an add-in and frees up memory.
Invoke	Runs an attached add-in.
Table	Writes a table of applications, @ functions, or macro add-ins to the worksheet.
Clear	Removes *all* add-in files from memory.
Settings	Specifies add-in files to automatically read into memory and/or add-ins to automatically invoke at startup.
Quit	Returns to Ready mode.

Loading an Add-in

To use an add-in, it must be in a directory on your hard disk. To load it, select Load and 1-2-3 displays all files in the current directory with the extension .PLC. To load an add-in stored in another directory, press **ESC**

Figure 7-5 Add-in command tree.

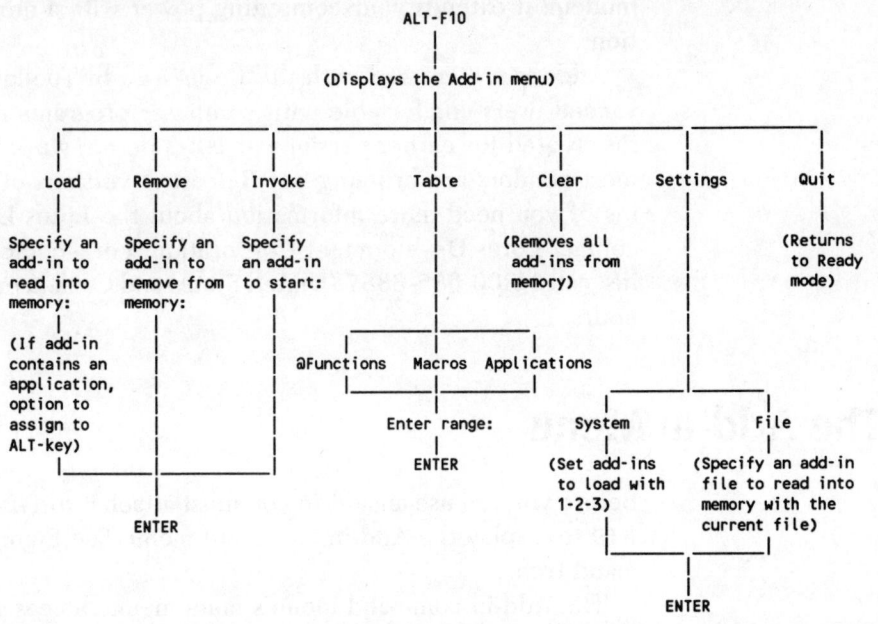

and edit the path and/or directory name. When the filename of the desired add-in appears in the control panel, highlight it and press **ENTER**.

You are then given the choice to assign the add-in to one of the APP keys—ALT-F7, ALT-F8, or ALT-F9—if they haven't already been assigned to other add-ins. Make your selection or select No-Key to run the add-in with the Invoke command.

Running an Add-in

If you assigned the add-in to one of the APP keys, press the appropriate key to run the program. If you selected No-Key, you must select Invoke from the Add-in menu to run the add-in. Even if you did select an APP key, you can also run the add-in with Invoke. When you select Invoke, highlight the desired add-in and press **ENTER** to run it.

Add-in Types

Lotus recognizes three types of add-ins: @ functions, macro commands, and applications. Applications are programs that enhance or extend 1-2-3 features such as the Print, Graph, or Data commands. The Allways® print enhancement add-in, for example, lets you produce desktop publishing-quality output from your 1-2-3 worksheets.

The @ function and macro command add-ins supplement 1-2-3's existing library of built-in functions and advanced macro commands. For example, there is no 1-2-3 function for determining the median or mode of a range of values. Someone using the Developer's Toolkit could create @MEDIAN and @MODE functions as add-ins that could then be used just like any other built-in function. Likewise, additional macro commands can be created and added to extend 1-2-3's existing library of advanced macro commands.

To use an add-in @ function, the add-in must be loaded into 1-2-3. If it isn't, 1-2-3 refuses to accept the function when you type it. If you load a worksheet that uses an add-in @ function that hasn't been loaded, **ERR** displays.

Because macros are entered as text (see Chapter 12), you can create a macro containing an add-in macro command, and 1-2-3 accepts it. However, you receive an error message if you try to run the macro before you load the add-in.

When you are using add-in @ functions or macro commands, you can use the Setting command on the Add-in menu to create a link between a file and a particular add-in so that the appropriate add-ins are loaded whenever the file that requires them is loaded with the File Retrieve command.

Conclusions

Add-ins are advanced 1-2-3 features. You don't need to use or even know about them to have access to the tremendous analytical powers of Release 3. But, in many cases the special features available with add-ins are just what you need to customize 1-2-3 so it works exactly the way you do—with enhanced @ functions, special macro commands, or extended Print, Data, or Graph commands.

Each add-in works a little differently, so be sure to carefully review the documentation accompanying the add-in. Also, be sure to obtain a version of a particular add-in that is designed to work with Release 3. As noted earlier, add-ins created for Release 2.0, 2.01, or 2.2 won't work with Release 3.

TIPS & TRAPS

Tips

Split the Screen.
When you are constructing a formula by referring to cells far from the cell that is to contain the formula, split the screen before you start to construct the function. Then use the **WINDOW/F6** key to move back and forth between windows. This technique is particularly helpful when you refer to cells on a different sheet in a stack.

Point, Point, and Point Again.
The pointing-with-the-cursor technique is the safest, fastest way to construct formulas and functions. Whenever a built-in function requires a range, point to it with the cursor and verify its correctness visually.

To tack the cursor to a cell, use the period key. Think of it as the "point" of a tack. To untack the cursor, use either the **ESC** key or the **BKSP** key. To view each corner of a highlighted range, press the period key to move the free cell to another corner.

What's Logical About 0 and 1?
Logical functions created with the logical operators evaluate to and display on the screen either a 0 (false) or a 1 (true). If you need to know how many entries in a range meet a certain criterion (say, sales exceeding $10,000), use a logical function to test each entry and then add up the resulting 1s. (You can also use the @DCOUNT function described in Chapter 9.)

Don't Forget ABS/F4.
Whenever you point to create a function or formula and you want the cell reference to be absolute or nonadjusting, press the **ABS/F4** key. The dollar signs signaling an absolute reference appear. The **ABS/F4** key also works when you press **EDIT/F2** to enter Edit mode.

Paste Range Names with NAME/F3.
When you want to use a named range (cell or group of cells) in a formula or function, press **NAME/F3**, and the first four named ranges on your

worksheet appear at the top of the screen. A second press displays all of the names simultaneously. Highlight the name you want to use, and press **ENTER** to paste it into your function.

This technique is particularly useful when you name the cells containing assumptions in the assumption space. Then, whenever you need to use an assumption in a formula, it is an easy matter to paste it into the formula.

Traps

What Are All Those ERRs?

ERR appears whenever you define a function that contains division by zero. This can happen when the denominator of a fraction contains a reference to a cell and that cell is blank. Division by zero is undefined, and 1-2-3 displays **ERR**. **ERR** also appears when a formula or function contains an undefined range name.

Move the cursor to the cell displaying the message. If there is no **ERR** in the formula when it displays on the Status line, there is no need to change the formula. Make an entry in the cell referred to in the denominator. Or you can wrap an @IF function around the formula to display a blank when the cell is empty and the result when it contains a valid entry. If the error occurs because of an undefined range name, define the range name, and **ERR** is replaced by the results.

If you check a formula and **ERR** appears in the formula, the **ERR** has probably been caused by deleting a row or column to which the formula referred. When **ERR** appears in the formula, you must correct it by supplying the correct cell reference.

The Case of the Missing Quotation Mark.

When you use string functions, all text must be enclosed in beginning and ending double quotation marks. The function isn't accepted or generates an **ERR** if any of the quotation marks are missing.

Named Ranges Are Relative References.

When you paste a range name into a formula or function, the reference represented by the named range is a relative cell reference. It adjusts whenever you copy the formula or function with the Copy command.

Usually, references to named cells in the assumption space are absolute, nonadjusting references. To convert a range name to an absolute cell reference, use the **EDIT/F2** and **ABS/F4** keys to edit dollar signs into the appropriate places in your functions.

8 Data Fill and Data Table Commands

OBJECTIVES

After mastering the content of this chapter, you will be able to

☐ use the Data Fill command to enter lists of numbers, dates, or times.

☐ construct and use One-, Two-, and Three-Way Data Tables to display the results of different assumptions.

☐ construct and use Labeled Data Table to do advanced sensitivity analysis.

INTRODUCTION

The two commands discussed in this chapter can add greatly to your ease of use with 1-2-3. The Data Fill command is just what's needed to fill a range with numbers, dates, or times that ascend or descend by regular intervals. Use it to label columns by months or years, to assign numbers to entries in a database, or to enter ranges in Data Table commands and the Data Distribution command (discussed in the next chapter).

The Data Table commands are your gateway to one of the most useful things you can do with an electronic spreadsheet: "What If . . ." analysis. In What If . . . analysis you change the assumptions behind a worksheet and then see what happens to key results. Keeping track of the results of different assumptions would be a serious problem were it not for the Data Table command. With this command you can instruct 1-2-3 to substitute many assumptions into a spreadsheet and collect the results in an easy-to-read table. The One-, Two-, and Three-Way Data Tables help you change one, two, or three assumptions simultaneously. The fourth type of data table, Labeled, provides great power and flexibility in constructing data tables in which any number of assumptions can change in any number of formulas.

THE DATA FILL COMMAND

Lotus 1-2-3's Data Fill command fills a range of cells with consecutive, equally incremented increasing or decreasing series of numbers, dates, or times. You must specify the *fill range*, the *Start* value, the *Step* increase (or decrease), and the *Stop* value. It's not really important to specify the exact ending value as long as it is larger than (or smaller, if the Step is negative) than the largest (or smallest) value to be generated in a specified range. See Figure 8–1 for the Data Fill command tree.

The Data Fill command has many uses. Whenever you want to use years (such as 1986 to 1987) as column headings, simply enter the Data Fill command, specify the range to be filled, specify the starting year as

Figure 8–1 Data Fill command tree.

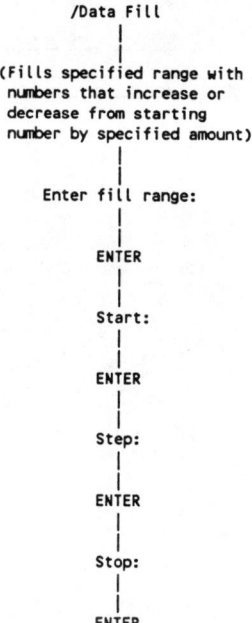

the starting number, and accept the default Step of 1. Press **ENTER**, and the columns are labeled with successive years. If you want to enter a list of dates, specify the first date and then, in response to the Step prompt, tell 1-2-3 to increment the date by days, weeks, months, quarters, or years. If you have a list and want to number the entries, use the Data Fill command. As you will see in the next section, the Data Fill command also speeds the construction of Data Tables.

The Start, Step, and Stop parameters are usually entered in the Data Fill command as numbers or as dates or times in one of 1-2-3's date/time formats. However, you can also enter formulas for these parameters or references to cells elsewhere on your spreadsheet. Using a formula enables you to control the Data Fill command with parameters generated by your spreadsheet.

For example, if you want to number each row in a named range but don't know how many rows it contains, enter **@ROWS**(*range name*) as the Stop parameter. @ROWS returns the number of rows in the range and stops the Data Fill command at that number.

Figure 8–2 shows several examples of the Data Fill command. Note that you can specify negative as well as positive Step settings. If you do use negative numbers, be sure to change the default ending value to one that's *smaller* than the smallest number in the range. The range can be a block of cells as well as a row or a column.

Figure 8–2   Data Fill command in action.

	A	B	C	D	E	F	G	H
1								
2			EXAMPLES OF THE DATA FILL COMMAND				
3								
4	32509	<-- Start:	1-Jan-89					
5	32540	Step:	1m					
6	32568	Stop:	1-Dec-89					
7	32599	Range:	A4..A20					
8	32629							
9	32660		50	150	250	350	450	<-- Start: 50
10	32690							Step: 100
11	32721							Stop: 450
12	32752							Range: B9..F9
13	32782							
14	32813		1	-4	-9	-14	-19	<-- Start: 1
15	32843		0.5	-4.5	-9.5	-14.5	-19.5	Step: -.5
16			0	-5	-10	-15	-20	Stop: -50
17			-0.5	-5.5	-10.5	-15.5	-20.5	Range: B14..F23
18			-1	-6	-11	-16	-21	
19			-1.5	-6.5	-11.5	-16.5	-21.5	
20			-2	-7	-12	-17	-22	
21			-2.5	-7.5	-12.5	-17.5	-22.5	
22			-3	-8	-13	-18	-23	
23			-3.5	-8.5	-13.5	-18.5	-23.5	
24								
25								
26								

Using the Data Fill Command

To fill the range A4 to A20 in Figure 8–2 with the dates incremented by months begin by positioning the cursor on cell A4 and type

/DF	Enters the Data Fill command.
Enter fill range:	Asks for the range of cells to fill.
.	Tacks cursor to cell A4.
DOWN	Stretches the cursor down to cell A20. Alternatively, if range is named, press **NAME/F3** to select named range.
ENTER	Accepts A4..A20 as the Fill Range.
Start: 0	Prompts to start at 0.
1-JAN-89	Type the starting date in any of 1-2-3's date formats.
ENTER	Accepts the starting date, 1-JAN-89.
Step: 1	Prompts to Step by 1.
1m	Type 1 followed by m to increment by months.
ENTER	Accepts 1m as the Step.
Stop: 8192	Prompts to stop at 8192.
1-DEC-89	Type the Stop date in a 1-2-3 date format or specify a number larger than the date number for 1-DEC-89 (32,843).
ENTER	Accepts the Stop date and executes the Data Fill command.

The Fill Range is filled with date numbers beginning with 32,509, the date number for 1-JAN-89. The date numbers increase by steps of one month and end when the range is full or the Stop date number—32,843 for 1-DEC-89—is reached. Note that the Stop date, 1-DEC-89, and the one month Step mean that only 12 dates are entered, even though the Fill Range, A4..A20 contains more than 12 cells. Use the Range Format Date command to format the date numbers to display in readable form.

Warning: Data Fill Overwrites Cells in Fill Range

The Data Fill command replaces the contents of any cell in the range with the appropriate data fill number, date, or time. Be sure not to accidentally write over existing entries. Also, note that cells in the fill range not filled by the command are *erased*.

Filling Ranges with Dates and Times

When you use the Data Fill command to fill a range with dates or times you must specify the Start and Stop values in an acceptable 1-2-3 Date or Time format. See Table 2–1 for a list of formats. The Step value is specified as an integer, and you indicate the size of the Step value in days, months, weeks, quarters, years, seconds, minutes, or hours by appending the appropriate code.

For example, if your Start value is a date and you enter the Step value as 3d, the date is incremented by 3 days. The following codes are available:

Step Code	Increases Start value by
d	days.
w	weeks.
m	months.
q	quarters.
y	years.

For time intervals the codes are

Step Code	Increases Start value by
s	seconds.
min	minutes.
h	hours.

Canceling Proposed Fill Ranges

The Data Fill command remembers the fill range you last used, as do most other 1-2-3 Data commands. This makes it easy to refill the same range. But unlike many other commands that remember ranges, the Data Fill command has no Reset option. So once you have used the command on a spreadsheet, 1-2-3 continues to suggest the specified range.

Use the **BKSP** key to cancel the proposed range and return the cursor to its location before entering the command. Use the **ESC** key to cancel the proposed range and leave the cursor in the anchor cell of the proposed range. The key you press depends on where you want to place the cursor after you cancel the proposed fill range.

Once you have repositioned the cursor and are ready to highlight a new fill range, press the period key to tack the cursor to the cell. Use the cursor movement keys to highlight the new fill range, then complete the specification of the command as described earlier.

THE DATA TABLE COMMAND

A very common operation with an electronic worksheet is to vary the level of one or two assumptions or parameters underlying the worksheet and to observe what this does to the levels of key variables. This is called doing What If . . . or sensitivity analysis, and it is one of the most wonderful features of electronic spreadsheet programs. However, the ability to quickly calculate a large number of alternative assumptions generates its own problems.

The most serious problem is keeping track of the results of multiple rounds of What If . . . analysis. Fortunately, 1-2-3 has just what you need, a special feature that makes tables of the results of multiple recalculations where each recalculation is performed with a different level of a key variable. The tools that do this are the One-, Two-, and Three-Way Data Tables and the Data Table Labeled command. See Figure 8–3 for the command tree.

This chapter discusses using data tables to do sensitivity analysis where you change one or more of the underlying assumptions, recalculate the worksheet, and table the results. In the next chapter the Data Table command is used in conjunction with a 1-2-3 database to provide a table of summary statistics for a database. Both uses require you to lay out the data table before using it. You learn how to do that in this chapter. In the next chapter you learn how to use data tables with databases.

The Assumption Space

The Data Table command can only be used with worksheets where the parameter or assumption you want to vary is entered into a single cell.

Figure 8–3   Data Table command tree.

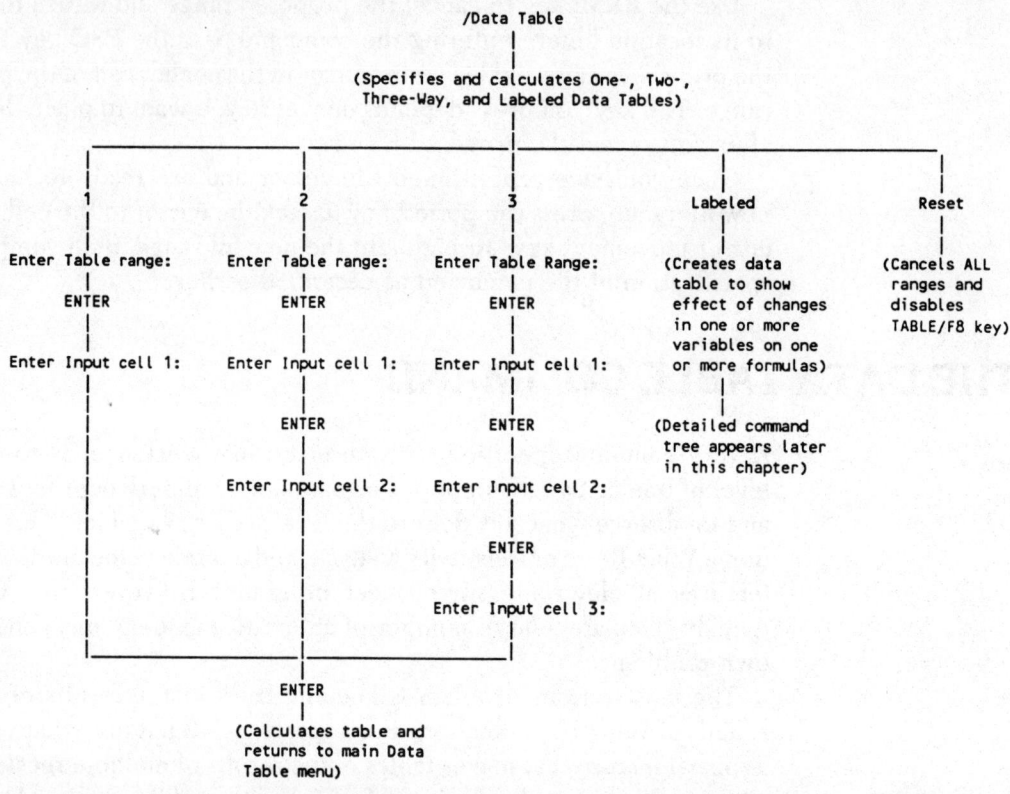

Figure 8–4   @PMT function worksheet.

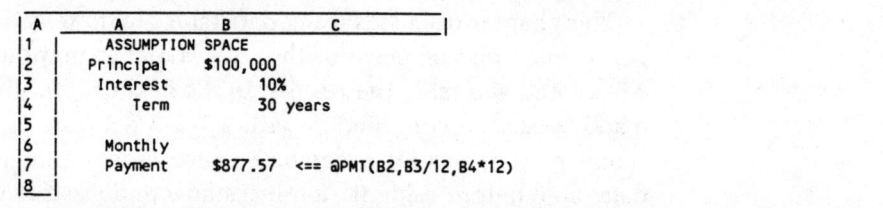

On a properly constructed worksheet the assumptions are often contained in the area at the top of the worksheet such as the area labeled **ASSUMPTION SPACE** in Figure 8–4. On that worksheet each assumption is entered into the worksheet only once—in its appropriate cell in the assumption space. Each time a formula uses one of the assumptions, it does so by referring to the appropriate cell in the assumption space.

Advantages of Assumption Spaces

The use of an assumption space is the single most important technique in constructing effective electronic spreadsheets. Besides enabling you to use data tables, a separate space offers several significant advantages over spreadsheets in which the assumptions are a part of the formulas.

The greatest advantage of a worksheet with an assumption space is that you can easily and quickly change your assumptions by changing only one number in one cell. Thus, you can test a large number of alternative assumptions easily and quickly.

When assumptions are actually part of the formulas in each cell, changing an assumption is a slow, tedious process. You must find and change each formula or function containing the assumption. Not only does this discourage you from trying different assumptions, but you may very well introduce errors into your spreadsheet as you try to change the formulas. You may forget to change an assumption in all of its locations, or you may corrupt a formula when adding new assumptions.

Having the assumptions explicitly stated in an assumption space also makes it easy to see the set of assumptions on which the current values in the spreadsheet depend. Without this information, discovering the assumptions behind a particular printout can be difficult or impossible.

Finally, with an assumption space on your worksheet, you are ready to construct data tables. Without an assumption space you simply can't take advantage of one of 1-2-3's most powerful and useful features.

ONE-WAY DATA TABLE

The worksheet in Figure 8–4 contains three parameters and an @PMT function to calculate the monthly payment necessary to amortize a loan of the given principal, interest rate, and term. Construct your own worksheet by entering the information from Figure 8–4 in the appropriate cells. Then use the Range Format commands to set the appropriate formats and the Worksheet Global Col-Width command to set column widths to 12 characters to accommodate all of the entries. Note in the @PMT function that the interest rate is divided by 12 to convert the annual percentage rate into a monthly rate and that the term is multiplied by 12 to convert the term in years into a term in months. Without these modifications, the formula would calculate the annual payment, not the desired monthly payment.

Once you have constructed the table in Figure 8–4, you may want to know the monthly payment at an interest rate of 8 or 11 or 9.375 percent.

You could substitute the appropriate percentage into cell B3 and read the result, but it would be hard to compare the results under alternative assumptions. But that is exactly what a data table can do.

Constructing a One-Way Data Table

As with other 1-2-3 features, all column headings, formulas, and values must be entered before entering the Data Table command. Once you enter the command, you define the range of cells containing the table and designate the cell (in the case of a One-Way Data Table) or two or three cells (in the case of Two- and Three-Way Data Tables) that are used as input cells. To repeat, the data table and the worksheet it is used with *must* be constructed before entering the Data Table command.

Figure 8–5 shows a diagram of a One-Way Data Table constructed on the same electronic worksheet as the cells shown in Figure 8–4. It is often useful to place the data table on its own sheet, but for simplicity the example continues with the worksheet and the data table on the same sheet. There are three important elements in all One-Way Data Tables.

- The cells in the first column contain the values that are substituted into the worksheet. In this case they are 8 to 12 percent. The Data Fill command is an easy way to enter these values; the Start is 8%, the Step .5%, and the Stop 12%. The cells are formatted with the Range Format Percent, 2 places.

Figure 8–5 Diagram of One-Way Data Table.

```
  A         A              B            C
 1       ASSUMPTION SPACE
 2       Principal       $100,000
 3       Interest            10%
 4       Term             30 years
 5
 6       Monthly
 7       Payment         $877.57    <== @PMT(B2,B3/12,B4*12)
 8
 9       Interest        Payment
10                       $877.57    <== +B7
11          8.00%
12          8.50%
13          9.00%
14          9.50%
15         10.00%
16         10.50%
17         11.00%
18         11.50%
19         12.00%
20
```

- The first cell of the first row must be left blank.
- Successive cells in the first row contain the formulas that are evaluated in each column. In Figure 8–5 the formula +B7 has been entered into cell B10. Column headings are not part of the range of the data table, but they are important for understanding the tabled results.

Table Range

The *table range* is the block of cells beginning with the blank cell in the upper left corner and extending down to the cell at the intersection of the row containing the last value and the column containing the last formula. In Figure 8–5 the table range is A10..B19. Note that the column headings are not included in the table range. Don't forget that you can use any of the cursor control keys to point to the table range.

The data table process erases the cells to the right of the first column and below the first row. You should, however, set the appropriate range format so the results display in an easily readable form. In the example, the Range Format Currency, 2 decimal places has been set for cells B10 through B19.

Input Cell

The *input cell* (1 in this case) is the cell on the worksheet where 1-2-3 enters successive values from the first column of the data table. In the example, you are going to vary the interest rate so input cell 1 is B3, the cell at the top of the spreadsheet labeled **Interest** in Figure 8–5. Use the cursor control keys when you point to input cell 1.

Using the One-Way Data Table Command

After you have entered the values in the first column, typed the formulas in the first row, labeled the columns, and applied the appropriate Range Formats, you are ready to enter the Data Table command and to instruct 1-2-3 to create a One-Way Data Table. Position the cursor on cell A10 in Figure 8–5 and type

/DT	Enters the Data Table command.
1 2 3 Labeled Reset	1, 2, and 3 are for One-, Two-, and Three-Way Data Tables. Labeled is for a Labeled Data Table, and Reset cancels all data table settings.

1	Selects a One-Way Data Table.
Enter table range:	Stretch the cursor over the range A10..B19.
ENTER	Accepts table range.
Enter input cell 1:	Asks for cell on worksheet to substitute the values from the leftmost column of the table range.
Arrow keys	Move the cursor to cell B2, the cell on the worksheet containing the interest rate assumption.
ENTER	Accepts input cell 1 and executes the command.

The Mode indicator flashes, and 1-2-3 recalculates the worksheet the required number of times. After a few seconds, the results appear in the appropriate cells of the data table, as Figure 8-6 shows.

Cell B10 in the first row of the data table contains the value, $877.57, which is calculated using the parameters actually entered in the worksheet. To eliminate confusion, use the Range Format Hidden command discussed in Chapter 3 to suppress the display of numbers generated by the formulas at the top of each column of a One-Way Data Table.

TWO-WAY DATA TABLE

The One-Way Data Table just described helps you see how sensitive your worksheet is to variations in a single variable (the interest rate in the

---

Figure 8-6   Completed One-Way Data Table.

```
| A |       A         B          C       |
|1  |    ASSUMPTION SPACE
|2  |   Principal   $100,000
|3  |   Interest        10%
|4  |      Term      30 years
|5  |
|6  |    Monthly
|7  |    Payment    $877.57
|8  |
|9  |   Interest    Payment
|10 |               $877.57
|11 |     8.00%     $733.76
|12 |     8.50%     $768.91
|13 |     9.00%     $804.62
|14 |     9.50%     $840.85
|15 |    10.00%     $877.57
|16 |    10.50%     $914.74
|17 |    11.00%     $952.32
|18 |    11.50%     $990.29
|19 |    12.00%   $1,028.61
|20 |
```

example). You may also want to know what happens when two variables, Interest and Term, change simultaneously. This calls for a Two-Way Data Table. It helps you to discover the effect of different terms and different interest rates on your monthly payment. With it you can answer the question of how much more you have to pay per month to pay off a shorter loan, or how much more you save per month if you can find a loan at a lower rate for a longer period.

Constructing a Two-Way Data Table

The structure of a typical Two-Way Data Table is illustrated in Figure 8-7. The interest rate again varies from 8% to 12%, and the term varies from 25 to 35 years.

To construct the table, enter the first value (interest rate) into the cells of the first column (cells A11..A19) and values for the second variable (term) into the cells of the first row (cells B9..D9). The Data Fill command can be used for these tasks. Add any column headings or titles required to make the table easier to understand, and apply the appropriate Range Formats from Figure 8-7.

Now, instead of leaving the first cell in the first row blank, as you did in the One-Way Data Table, enter into that cell a formula to define the values you want displayed in the body of the data table. In the example, the formula in cell A11 in Figure 8-7 is simply a reference to B7, the cell in which the monthly payment is calculated. However, any formula

Figure 8-7   Diagram of Two-Way Data Table.

```
| A |         A         |    B     |    C         |   D   |
|1  |   ASSUMPTION SPACE                                   |
|2  |   Principal       $100,000                           |
|3  |   Interest            10%                            |
|4  |      Term          30 years                          |
|5  |                                                      |
|6  |   Monthly                                            |
|7  |   Payment         $877.57                            |
|8  |                                                      |
|9  |   Interest                    Term in Years          |
|10 |    $877.57     |    25    |    30        |   35   |
|11 |     8.00%      |          |              |        |
|12 |     8.50%      |          |              |        |
|13 |     9.00%      |          |              |        |
|14 |     9.50%      |          |              |        |
|15 |    10.00%      |          |              |        |
|16 |    10.50%      |          |              |        |
|17 |    11.00%      |          |              |        |
|18 |    11.50%      |          |              |        |
|19 |    12.00%      |          |              |        |
|20 |                                                      |
```

relating to this worksheet can be entered into cell A10, and the results of the changing assumption on that formula will be displayed in the cells of the Two-Way Data Table.

Using the Two-Way Data Table Command

Once you have specified the formula and the values, you are ready to enter the Data Table command. Position the cursor on cell A10 (in the table shown in Figure 8–7) and type

/DT	Enters the Data Table command.
2	Selects a Two-Way Data Table.
Enter table range:	Stretch the cursor over the range A10..D19.
ENTER	Accepts table range.
Enter input cell 1:	Asks for cell in the assumption space to substitute the values from the leftmost column of the table range.
Arrow keys	Move the cursor to cell B3, the cell on the worksheet containing the Interest Rate.
ENTER	Accepts input cell 1.
Enter input cell 2:	Asks for cell in the assumption space to substitute values from the top row of the table range.
Arrow keys	Move cursor to cell B4, cell in assumption space containing the Term.
ENTER	Accepts input cell 2 and executes the Data Table command.

The Wait indicator flashes for a few moments, and the results of the operation are written into the data table. See Figure 8–8. The value displayed in the cell containing the formula, A10 in Figure 8–8, displays the value for the formula based on the parameters as actually entered in the worksheet. Again, you can use the Range Format Hidden command to suppress its display.

THREE-WAY DATA TABLE

Because 1-2-3 Release 3 can create three-dimensional stacks of worksheets, you can construct a Three-Way Data Table that spreads across

DATA FILL AND DATA TABLE COMMANDS

Figure 8-8 Completed Two-Way Data Table.

```
|  A  |      A          B         C          D        |
| 1   |   ASSUMPTION SPACE
| 2   |   Principal    $100,000
| 3   |   Interest        10%
| 4   |      Term        30 years
| 5   |
| 6   |   Monthly
| 7   |   Payment      $877.57
| 8   |
| 9   |   Interest              Term in Years
|10   |    $877.57       25        30         35
|11   |    8.00%      $771.82   $733.76    $710.26
|12   |    8.50%      $805.23   $768.91    $746.86
|13   |    9.00%      $839.20   $804.62    $783.99
|14   |    9.50%      $873.70   $840.85    $821.61
|15   |   10.00%      $908.70   $877.57    $859.67
|16   |   10.50%      $944.18   $914.74    $898.13
|17   |   11.00%      $980.11   $952.32    $936.96
|18   |   11.50%    $1,016.47   $990.29    $976.11
|19   |   12.00%    $1,053.22 $1,028.61  $1,015.55
|20   |
```

several sheets in the current file. This table enables you to perform sensitivity analysis where three variables change across a predetermined range of values. In the example you have been using, the third variable would be the Principal, cell A:A2.

The construction of a Three-Way Data Table is very much like the construction of a Two-Way Data Table except that multiple copies of the table are placed on consecutive sheets in the current file.

Constructing a Three-Way Table

To construct a Three-Way Data Table, begin by constructing the first table in exactly the same way you constructed the Two-Way Data Table. The results are shown in Figure 8-9. Place the first variable, the Interest rate, in the first column of the table and the second variable, the Term, in the first row of the table. Now, instead of placing a formula in the upper left-hand cell (cell A:A9 in Figure 8-9) you use that location for different values of the third variable, Principal.

So far, you have one copy of the data table on one sheet. The next step is to copy the data table you have just created to additional sheets. If necessary, use the Worksheet Insert Sheet command to insert some sheets after the current sheet. In this example you'll need two more sheets.

To copy the headings along with the body of the table in Figure 8-9, position the cursor on cell A:A10 and type

Figure 8–9   Diagram of Three-Way Data Table.

```
   A         A           B            C          D
 1 |    ASSUMPTION SPACE
 2 |    Principal    $100,000
 3 |    Interest       10%
 4 |       Term       30 years
 5 |
 6 |    Monthly
 7 |    Payment     $877.57
 8 |
 9 |                           Term in Years
10 | $50,000.00 |     25    |     30     |    35   |
11 |    8.00%   |           |            |         |
12 |    8.50%   |           |            |         |
13 |    9.00%   |           |            |         |
14 |    9.50%   |           |            |         |
15 |   10.00%   |           |            |         |
16 |   10.50%   |           |            |         |
17 |   11.00%   |           |            |         |
18 |   11.50%   |           |            |         |
19 |   12.00%   |           |            |         |
20 |
```

/C	Enters the Copy command.
Arrow keys	Use the arrow keys to highlight the rectangle A:A10..A:D19.
ENTER	Accepts the FROM range.
.	Tacks cursor to cell A:A10.
CTRL-PGUP	Press the next sheet key twice.
ENTER	Completes the Copy command.

You now have three copies of the basic data table. Each copy has the same variables in the top row and the left column, and each table has a blank cell in the upper left corner of the table area.

Entering the Third Variable

You are now ready to enter the third variable, Principal. Move the cursor to A:A10 and enter $50,000. Press **CTRL-PGUP**; the cursor moves to B:A10. Enter $100,000 and press **CTRL-PGUP** to move the cursor to C:A10. Then enter $150,000. When the third variable increases or decreases by uniform steps, you can use the Data Fill command to enter it.

Specifying the Formula

You must determine one final piece of information before you can use your Three-Way Data Table—the location of the formula into which the three variables are to be substituted. In the One- and Two-Way Data Tables, the formula is part of the data table, so you don't have to specify it as a separate step. For a Three-Way Data Table, the formula you are analyzing lies *outside* the data table and must be specified as a separate step.

In the example, you want to examine the monthly payment required for each loan. The formula displaying that information is in cell B6, so B6 is the cell you refer to for the location of the cell formula to be analyzed.

Using the Three-Way Data Table Command

You are ready to enter the Data Table command. Position the cursor on cell A10 and type

/DT	Enters the Data Table command.
3	Selects a Three-Way Data Table.
Enter table range:	Stretch the cursor over the range A:A10..A:D19 and then use **CTRL-PGUP** to stretch the cursor over the additional sheets in the table range.
ENTER	Accepts table range.
Enter formula cell:	Asks for the cell containing the formula to analyze.
Arrow keys	Move the cursor to cell B6, the cell containing the formula to be tabled.
ENTER	Accepts it.
Enter input cell 1:	Asks for the cell in the assumption space to substitute values from the leftmost column of the table range.
Arrow keys	Move the cursor to cell B3, the cell containing the interest rate assumption.
ENTER	Accepts input cell 1.

Enter input cell 2:	Asks for cell to substitute values from the top row of the table range.
Arrow keys	Move the cursor to cell B4, the cell containing the Term assumption.
ENTER	Accepts input cell 2.
Enter input cell 3:	Asks for the cell in the assumption space to substitute values from the top left cell of table range.
Arrow keys	Move cursor to cell B2, the cell containing the Principal assumption.
ENTER	Accepts input cell 3 and executes the Data Table command.

Each cell in the body of the data table on each sheet shows the results of the three assumptions:

Input 1: Interest Rate (left-hand column)

Input 2: Term in Years (top row)

Input 3: Principal (upper left corner)

See Figure 8–10 for the results from sheet A.

Figure 8–10   Completed Three-Way Data Table.

```
 A        A            B            C            D
 1     ASSUMPTION SPACE
 2     Principal    $100,000
 3     Interest         10%
 4         Term     30 years
 5
 6     Monthly
 7     Payment      $877.57
 8
 9                             Term in Years
10     $50,000.00         25           30           35
11           8.00%    $771.82      $733.76      $710.26
12           8.50%    $805.23      $768.91      $746.86
13           9.00%    $839.20      $804.62      $783.99
14           9.50%    $873.70      $840.85      $821.61
15          10.00%    $908.70      $877.57      $859.67
16          10.50%    $944.18      $914.74      $898.13
17          11.00%    $980.11      $952.32      $936.96
18          11.50% $1,016.47      $990.29      $976.11
19          12.00% $1,053.22    $1,028.61    $1,015.55
20
```

TIPS FOR USING DATA TABLES

Canceling Remembered Ranges

Lotus remembers the location of the table range and each input cell for each type of data table you specify and proposes that you use it each time you enter the command. Often this is a benefit. But sometimes you want to specify an entirely different table range or input cell. To cancel *all* proposed cells and ranges for *all* specified data tables type

/DTR   Selects the Data Table Reset command.

If you don't want to cancel all input cells and table ranges, you can change a specified input cell or table range by selecting the table type that contains it. When 1-2-3 proposes the input cell, just move the cursor to highlight the new input cell and press **ENTER**. To specify a new table range, press the **BKSP** or **ESC** key to unstick a proposed range. Then move the cursor to the beginning of the new table range. Stick the cursor to the first cell of the table range with the period key and proceed to highlight the new table range.

Modifying a Data Table

Once you have created a data table, you may want to modify it to display the results of different formulas or to use different values for the input cells. Such changes are easy to make because data tables are defined in terms of *location*, not in terms of the content of the cells.

The simplest way to change a data table is to replace existing entries with new values or formulas. In the case of the Two-Way Data Table in Figure 8–7, you could change the formula in cell A:A10, and that would change what is displayed in the cells when you next calculate the table. You could also use the Data Fill command to place a different range of annual contributions in the first row or different interest rates in the first column.

You can also expand the size of a data table using the Worksheet Insert command to insert additional rows or columns. If you are using a Three-Way Data Table, use the Worksheet Group command to insert rows or columns in all of the sheets in the current file at one time. When you use this technique, be sure you insert the rows or columns between the first and last rows or first and last columns. If you don't, the newly inserted space will be outside the table range.

Sometimes, when the data table is on the same sheet as the worksheet or Group mode is active, inserting rows or columns changes material elsewhere on your worksheet or on other sheets in the current file. The One- and Two-Way Data Tables described in this chapter are placed below the rest of the table on the same sheet, so inserting columns into these tables inserts new columns into other areas of the worksheet as well. Because you don't want to do this, use the Move command to move part of a data table over the required number of columns. Remember to leave either the upper left or the lower right corner of the table in place so the range of the data table expands automatically. You could also place the data table on its own sheet and then you'd be free to use the Insert and Delete commands.

If you want to calculate a previously specified data table, you must reenter the command and respecify the table range and input cells. If 1-2-3 proposes an appropriate table range or input cell, press **ENTER** to accept it. If it is inappropriate or 1-2-3 does not propose a range or cell, point to the correct table range or input cell.

However you modify a table, always verify that the correct ranges are specified by entering the command and checking each corner of the proposed table range. Remember that you can move the cursor from corner to corner of the proposed range by pressing the period key.

The TABLE/F8 Key

Once you have modified a data table, you are ready to recalculate it. Simply press the **TABLE/F8** key. This is much faster and easier than entering the Data Table command and accepting all the proposed responses. You can use the **TABLE/F8** key at any time to calculate the effects of any change to the worksheet itself or to the data table.

When you have defined more than one data table in the current file, the **TABLE/F8** key recalculates only the most recently used table. For example, to calculate the One-Way Data Table in Figure 8–6 after defining the Two-Way Data Table in Figure 8–8 when both data tables are in the same file, you must go back and cycle through the redefinition of the One-Way Data Table. You can do this by pressing **ENTER** at each proposed range or input cell.

Using Range Names

To make the use of multiple data tables easier, assign a range name to each table range and to the input cells. You can then use the **NAME/F3** function key to paste in the names for the ranges and input cells in response to the Data Table command prompts.

DATA TABLE LABELED COMMAND

With the Data Table Labeled command, you can construct Labeled Data Tables that are just like the One-, Two-, or Three-Way data tables you just learned to construct, but with greater power and flexibility of layout. You can also use the Data Table Labeled command to create what amounts to N-dimensional tables, in which any number of assumptions can be substituted in formulas and the results presented in table form. See Figure 8–11 for the command tree.

Figure 8–11   Data Table Labeled command tree.

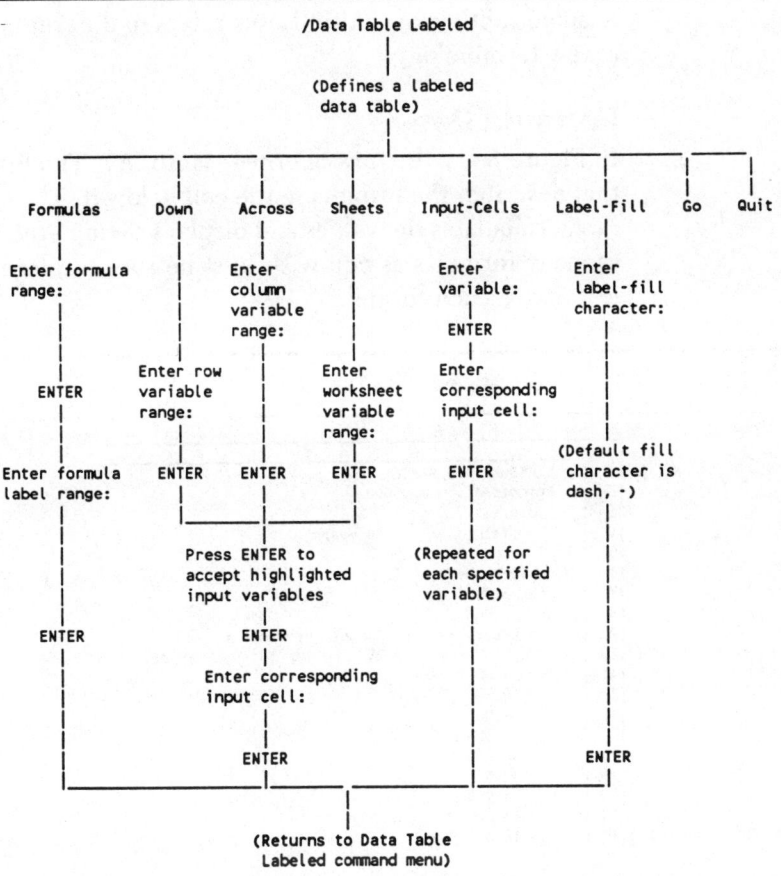

Because of its power, learning to use the Data Table Labeled command can present a formidable challenge, but one that you can overcome by building on your knowledge of One-, Two-, and Three-Way Data Tables. Your first task is to reconstruct the Two-Way Data Table discussed earlier using the Data Table Labeled command. If necessary, reread and review the material presented earlier in this chapter, because as new concepts are introduced, they are compared and contrasted to earlier concepts.

Terminology

The Data Table Labeled command makes use of some special terminology you must learn. Though the names are different, many of the concepts are familiar to you from your knowledge of other types of data tables.

Figure 8–12 contains a worksheet with a simple Labeled Data Table. It looks very much like the Two-Way Data Table, but it has been changed in some subtle ways. Also, Lotus refers to different parts of the table with a new terminology.

Formula Range

In Figure 8–12 the *formula range* is A6..A7. The first cell contains a label that describes the formula in the cell below it. The formula in the formula range calculates the values and displays them in the table. You can specify as many formulas as you wish; just be sure to place a *unique* label in the cell above each formula.

Figure 8–12   Layout of Labeled Data Table.

```
      A              B           C            D
1         ASSUMPTION SPACE
2     Principal     $50,000
3     Interest        10%
4       Term         30 years
5
6   Monthly Payment
7      $438.79
8
9     Interest ---------Monthly Payment------------
10                   25          30          35
11       8.00%
12       8.50%
13       9.00%
14       9.50%
15      10.00%
16      10.50%
17      11.00%
18      11.50%
19      12.00%
20
```

Formula Label Range

The labels from the first row of the formula range (cell A6) are going to be copied to other cells on your worksheet to indicate where the results of the formula are going to be tabled. The *formula label range* in Figure 8-12 is B9..D9.

Label-Fill Character

The default *label-fill character* is the dash, -. The labels in the formula label range *must* extend across all of the columns to be included in the table. In Figure 8-12 the formula label is too short to do that, so dashes (the label-fill character) have been added to cover the entire table width of cells. The text is entered only into cell B9, but the label-fill characters make it appear as if the formula label extends over the range B9..D9. If you don't like dashes, any character can be designated as the label-fill character.

Row Variable Range

The *row variable range* contains input values for each row of the table. In typical Lotus fashion, the row variable is a column of cells. The row variable range can be one or more columns to the left or the right of the table, as long as the columns are next to one another and each column contains a separate set of input values. In Figure 8-12 the row variable range is A11..A19 in column A.

Column Variable Range

The *column variable range* contains input values for each column of the table. It appears in one or more rows above or below the table. Again, each row must contain a separate variable and all of the columns in the column variable range must be next to one another. In Figure 8-12 the column variable range is B10..D10 in row 10.

Worksheet Variable Range

The *worksheet variable range* contains input values for each sheet of a 3-D table. It is displayed in one or more corresponding cells on each sheet. There is no worksheet variable range in Figure 8-12 because the data table is contained entirely on one sheet. But a worksheet variable range could be included to generate tables with different assumptions about the Principal in a fashion that is exactly like its use in the Three-Way Table discussed earlier.

As with row and column variable ranges, the sheet variable range can contain more than one cell. However, each cell must represent a different sheet variable, and all of the cells must be next to one another and in corresponding locations on each sheet. If they are not adjacent, you won't be able to highlight all of them at one time when you specify the sheet variables.

Table Range

In stark contrast with the other types of data tables, a Labeled Data Table *doesn't* require you to specify a table range. Instead, the table range is *implied* by the interaction of the location of the formula label range, and the location of the row variable range and the column variable range.

In essence, the table range for a Labeled Data Table is made up of those cells at the *intersection* of the columns covered by the formula label range and the rows covered by the row variable range. In Figure 8–12, the implied table range is B10..D19. Because of the implied nature of the table range, blank cells, formulas, and text can all be included within the implied table range.

Because cells at the *intersection* of row, column, and sheet variable ranges are tabled, these ranges can be anywhere in the current file. Though they are often close to the tabled cells, they don't need to be anywhere near the cells that are actually tabled.

Using the Data Table Labeled Command

To construct a Two-Way table based on the @PMT function using the Data Labeled Table command, construct the following ranges (cell references are to Figure 8–12):

Formula Range	Formula label(s) over formula(s): A6..A7.
Formula Label Range	Contains formula label(s) and label-fill characters. Use Copy command and edit in label-fill characters to span all columns in table: B9..D9.
Row Variable Range	Contains row(s) input variable(s) organized by column(s): A11..A19.
Column Variable Range	Contains column(s) input variable(s) organized by row(s): B10..D10.
Sheet Variable Range	Contains the sheet(s) input variable(s) organized by sheets; not shown in Figure 8–12.

Once these ranges have been constructed, begin the Data Table Labeled command by typing

DATA FILL AND DATA TABLE COMMANDS

/DT	Enters the Data Table command.
L	Selects Labeled.
Formulas	Selects Formulas.
Enter formula range:	Asks for range containing formulas and labels. Point to A6..A7.
ENTER	Accepts formula range.
Enter formula label range:	Asks for range above table containing formula label(s). Point to B9..D9.
ENTER	Accepts formula label range.
DOWN	Select Down for row variable input range.
Enter row variable range:	Asks for range containing variable to use in each row. Point to A11..A19.
ENTER	Accepts row variable range.
Press ENTER to accept highlighted input values.	Highlights row variable range.
ENTER	Confirms row variable range.
Enter corresponding input cell:	Asks for cell to substitute values from row variable range. Point to B3.
ACROSS	Select Across for column variable input range.
Enter column variable range:	Asks for range containing variable to use in each column. Point to B10..D10.
ENTER	Accepts column variable range.
Press ENTER to accept highlighted input values.	Highlights column variable range.
ENTER	Confirms column variable range.
Enter corresponding input cell:	Asks for cell to substitute values from column variable range. Point to B4.

GO   Executes Data Table Labeled command.

The result appears in Figure 8–13.

Verifying Variable Ranges and Input Cells

Because there can be many variable ranges and input cells, the Data Table Labeled command has an option that makes it easy to verify, and, if necessary, change variable ranges and input cells. The option is Input-Cells. Select it and 1-2-3 highlights the first row variable range. Verify it or change it and press **ENTER**. Then 1-2-3 shows you the input cell to which the first row variable range is assigned. Verify it or change it and press **ENTER**. You next see the subsequent row variable range. The process continues until you have been shown all of the variable ranges and their corresponding input cells.

If your Labeled Data Table fails to work as expected or you get an error message, use the Input-Cells option to verify and, if necessary, correct any range or input cell assignments.

Advanced Labeled Data Tables

If you have gotten this far, you may be asking yourself whether the journey has been worth the effort. After all, you have just created the same Two-

---

Figure 8–13   Completed Labeled Data Table.

```
|A          A              B           C             D         |
|1              ASSUMPTION SPACE
|2           Principal    $50,000
|3           Interest        10%
|4             Term        30 years
|5
|6       Monthly Payment
|7          $438.79
|8
|9           Interest ---------Monthly Payment------------
|10                           25          30            35
|11           8.00%       $385.91     $366.88      $355.13
|12           8.50%       $402.61     $384.46      $373.43
|13           9.00%       $419.60     $402.31      $392.00
|14           9.50%       $436.85     $420.43      $410.81
|15          10.00%       $454.35     $438.79      $429.84
|16          10.50%       $472.09     $457.37      $449.07
|17          11.00%       $490.06     $476.16      $468.48
|18          11.50%       $508.23     $495.15      $488.05
|19          12.00%       $526.61     $514.31      $507.77
|20 |
```

DATA FILL AND DATA TABLE COMMANDS

Way data table you constructed earlier in the chapter, but by using more complicated and confusing commands. The answer to your question lies both in pedagogy and potential.

The pedagogy was to mimic the Two-Way table as a device to introduce you to the commands and features of Labeled tables within a familiar and (I hope) comfortable environment. Now that you know the basics, you are ready to see the potential by looking at some of the tasks that can be done with a Labeled table that can't be done with the simpler Data Table commands.

Nontabled Cells in Table

Figure 8-14 contains a modified version of the @PMT Labeled Table. Columns and rows have been inserted into the table and dashes and vertical line characters have been added to improve the appearance of the table. Because the cells containing these characters are *not* at the intersection of a cell containing both a Down and an Across variable, nothing is calculated in these cells. This is also true of the text at the top of the table. Cells that are in the body of a Labeled Data Table but that aren't at the intersection of Across or Down variable cells can also contain built-in functions or formulas.

Multiple Row or Column Variables

To increase the power and flexibility of Labeled Data Tables, you can work with more than one set of row or column variables. However, they

Figure 8-14   Labeled Data Table containing multiple Down variables and noncalculating rows and columns.

```
| A  |    A        B         C          D         E         F         G        H         I        J          K          L          M         N         O          P  |
| 1  |                             ASSUMPTION SPACE                                                                                                                    |
| 2  |                             Principal    $100,000                                                                                                               |
| 3  |                             Interest         10%                                                                                                                |
| 4  |                             Term              30 years                                                                                                          |
| 5  |                                                                                                                                                                  |
| 6  | Monthly Payment Interest Paid                                                                                                                                    |
| 7  |     $877.57  $215,925.77                                                                                                                                         |
| 8  |                                                                                                                                                                  |
| 9  | |--------------------------------|---------------------------------------------|----------------------------------------------|                                    |
|10  | |       ASSUMPTIONS              |-------------Monthly Payment-----------------|--------------Interest Paid-------------------|                                    |
|11  | |                                |     Due Each Month for Given Term           |      Over Life of Loan for Given Term        |                                    |
|12  | |   Principal     Interest       |       25           30           35          |        25           30           35          |                                    |
|13  | |--------------------------------|---------------------------------------------|----------------------------------------------|                                    |
|14  | |   $50,000.00       8.00%|         $385.91      $366.88      $355.13    |    $65,772.43    $82,077.62    $99,154.78   |                                    |
|15  | |                    8.50%|         $402.61      $384.46      $373.43    |    $70,784.06    $88,404.43   $106,840.72   |                                    |
|16  | |                    9.00%|         $419.60      $402.31      $392.00    |    $75,879.45    $94,832.07   $114,638.52   |                                    |
|17  | |                    9.50%|         $436.85      $420.43      $410.81    |    $81,054.50   $101,353.76   $122,538.44   |                                    |
|18  | |--------------------------------|---------------------------------------------|----------------------------------------------|                                    |
|19  | |  $100,000.00       8.00%|         $771.82      $733.76      $710.26    |   $131,544.87   $164,155.25   $198,309.57   |                                    |
|20  | |                    8.50%|         $805.23      $768.91      $746.86    |   $141,568.13   $176,808.85   $213,681.44   |                                    |
|21  | |                    9.00%|         $839.20      $804.62      $783.99    |   $151,758.91   $189,664.14   $229,277.05   |                                    |
|22  | |                    9.50%|         $873.70      $840.85      $821.61    |   $162,109.00   $202,707.51   $245,076.87   |                                    |
|23  | |--------------------------------|---------------------------------------------|----------------------------------------------|                                    |
```

must be in adjacent rows or columns so that when you specify the Down or Across variables you can specify the *entire block*.

For example, in Figure 8–14 both column B and column C contain Down variables so when you select Down, highlight the range B14..C22. After you press **ENTER**, Lotus highlights only column B and asks you to verify column B as the first row variable. After you press **ENTER** to verify it, 1-2-3 then asks for its input cell. Point to cell E1 and press **ENTER**. Then 1-2-3 highlights the values in column C and asks you to verify them as the next row variable.

Hint: When you construct multiple Across or Down variables, place the variable that changes the most in the rightmost column or bottom row, the variable that changes less frequently in the next column to the left or row above. In Figure 8–13, Principal is the grouping variable, so it goes in the leftmost column. Interest changes more frequently so it goes in the column to the right of Principal.

Additional Hint: Cells B18 and C18 are left blank, so every cell in the table in row 18 is left uncalculated. If you enter anything (even a label that evaluates to zero) in B18 or C18, a value is calculated for the corresponding intersections in the table.

The table in Figure 8–14 has only two Down variables, but it could have as many as you wanted to include in the table. Each intersection in the table would be calculated using the appropriate values from the Across and Down variables that are in force at that intersection.

Multiple Sheet Labeled Tables

You can use the Sheet variable command to specify three-dimensional Labeled Tables. The principle is the same; input values that intersect in a cell on a sheet are the input values used in that cell.

Conclusion

The Data Table Labeled command provides almost unlimited power and flexibility in designing data tables. Just remember, the values that are calculated and filled in the table are cells at the intersection of Across and Down variables.

If you need this extra power, Lotus has it for you. If your work only requires One-, Two-, or Three-Way Data Tables, you don't need to bother learning the ins and outs of Labeled Data Tables.

TIPS & TRAPS

Tips

The Tip of Tips: The Assumption Space.
The single most important worksheet construction technique is to place each assumption in a single cell and then refer to that cell in any formula or function that requires the assumption. Changing assumptions is easy when you use an assumption space, because you only need to change the assumption in one cell. Also, when you print the assumption space along with the worksheet, you have a record of the assumptions behind the worksheet.

If you don't use an assumption space, changing assumptions can be time consuming and difficult, because every formula containing the assumption must be changed. Embedding the assumptions in the formulas denies you one of the most important features of 1-2-3: quick, easy ability to change assumptions. Furthermore, when you attempt to modify the formulas to reflect new assumptions you run a serious risk of introducing difficult-to-find structural errors into your spreadsheet.

Do I Need to Use Labeled Data Tables?
You only need the power and flexibility of Labeled Data Tables when you can't do what you need to do with a One-, Two-, or Three-Way Data Table.

The Information Meets at the Intersection.
The key to understanding Labeled Data Tables is that the tabled values occur at the *intersection* of cells in the row variable range and the column variable range. If a worksheet variable range has been used, values are tabled at the intersection of all three ranges.

Remember to Change the Stop Value When You Count Backward.
When using negative Steps in the Data Fill command, you must specify a Stop value that is *smaller* than the smallest value you want to fill. The default Stop value is 8192. If you accept it when the Step Value is negative, the command places nothing in the fill range because the Stop value is "reached" before the first value is entered.

Traps

Automatic Format Fails with Data Fill.
Don't set the Automatic format (Global or Range) when you use the Fill command to place date or time numbers into cells. Instead of recognizing the numbers as dates or times, 1-2-3 sees them as numbers and assigns the Fixed format with the appropriate number of decimal places.

Data Fill Doesn't Work with Dates.
Be sure to specify an ending value that is large enough to accommodate the largest date number that will be generated. In particular, don't press **ENTER** to accept the default Stop value, 8192, because it corresponds to June 4, 1922. Supply as the Stop value a date after the last date you want filled. Use one of 1-2-3's standard Date formats, such as 1-Jan-90.

9 | The Database Commands

OBJECTIVES

After mastering the content of this chapter, you will be able to

☐ use the commands and features of Lotus 1-2-3's database function.

☐ define and sort a database.

☐ set criteria to query a database to find or extract entries.

☐ use 1-2-3's special built-in database statistical functions.

☐ use the Data Distribution command to prepare a frequency distribution.

INTRODUCTION

Lotus 1-2-3's great strength as an analytical, problem-solving tool is that it successfully integrates into one package the powerful electronic worksheet described in the preceding chapters with a set of database commands for sorting and querying, and a set of graphics commands for displaying information graphically. This combination gives you immediate access to three powerful analytical tools: the spreadsheet, the database, and the graph.

The basic database commands are discussed in this chapter. With them you can sort, find, and extract information from the cells of your worksheet or from databases located in other 1-2-3 files. The next chapter shows how to use these commands on an external database created by a standalone program such as R:BASE®; Paradox®; or dBASE III,® dBASE III

Plus,® or dBASE IV.® Also discussed in this chapter are database statistical functions (special built-in functions for use with databases), and the Data Distribution command, which is used to create frequency distributions. The Graphics command is discussed in Chapter 11. It is used to display and print information in graphic form.

Two Data commands, Table and Fill, were discussed in the previous chapter because they have many uses on nondatabase worksheets. Those commands also have powerful database applications, which are discussed in this chapter. If you need more detailed information about constructing data tables or using the Data Fill command, see the discussion in Chapter 8. Three other specialized Data commands—Regression, Parse, and Matrix—are discussed in Chapter 10, along with the discussion of multiple input ranges and the Data External command. (See Figure 9–1 for the command tree for the Data commands discussed in this chapter.)

OVERVIEW

What Is a Database?

The first thing you need to know is that any *database* is a collection of information organized alphabetically, numerically, or by some other sys-

Figure 9–1 Data command tree.

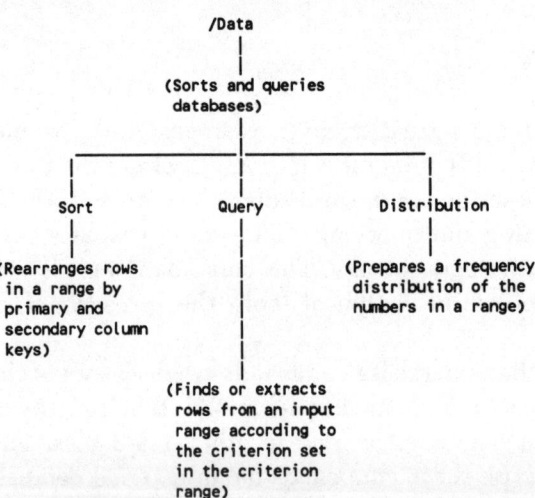

THE DATABASE COMMANDS

tem that helps you find individual entries quickly. Your home and office have many databases. An address book and a dictionary are databases, arranged alphabetically. A cookbook is a database arranged by type of meal, ethnic origin, or main ingredient. Calendars are databases arranged by dates, whereas your checkbook is a database arranged by check number. In business, lists of clients, manufacturing parts, suppliers, or creditors are databases. So are the Rolodex® and card files on your desk and the file cabinets in your office.

Figure 9–2 contains a small database of all-time batting leaders in professional baseball. It has the two characteristics of any database: it contains information, and it's organized. This database is used throughout this chapter to illustrate the features of 1-2-3's Data command.

Field Names

Figure 9-3 shows the general structure of a 1-2-3 database table (or simply database). The first row of the database must contain *field names*. The field names are like the column headings on an ordinary worksheet; they tell what type of information is entered into each column. In Figure 9–2 the field names tell you the columns containing information about such things as Games, At Bats, and Hits.

Figure 9–2 Database of All-Time Batting Leaders.

```
         A              B       C        D        E       F       G
 1
 2
 3                          ALL-TIME BATTING LEADERS
 4                             Ten or more seasons
 5
 6   PLAYER'S NAME        YEARS   GAMES   AT BATS   RUNS    HITS   AVERAGE
 7   ======================================================================
 8         Ty Cobb          24    3,033   11,429   2,244   4,191   0.367
 9   Rogers Hornsby         23    2,256    8,173   1,576   2,930   0.358
10      Joe Jackson         13    1,330    4,981     873   1,772   0.356
11    Pete Browning         13    1,180    4,839     867   1,716   0.355
12      Ed Delahanty        16    1,825    7,493   1,596   2,591   0.345
13     Willie Keeler        19    2,124    8,564   1,720   2,955   0.345
14   William Hamilton       14    1,578    6,262   1,694   2,157   0.344
15      Tris Speaker        22    2,789   10,208   1,881   3,515   0.344
16      Ted Williams        19    2,292    7,706   1,798   2,654   0.344
17      Dan Brouthers       19    1,665    7,493   1,596   2,591   0.343
18     Harry Heilmann       18    2,146    7,787   1,291   2,660   0.342
19         Babe Ruth        22    2,503    8,389   2,174   2,873   0.342
20      Jesse Burkett       16    2,063    8,389   1,708   2,872   0.341
21         Bill Terry       14    1,721    6,428   1,120   2,193   0.341
22         Lou Gehrig       17    2,164    8,001   1,888   2,721   0.340
23      George Sisler       15    2,055    8,267   1,284   2,812   0.340
24
25
```

Figure 9-3 All 1-2-3 databases are made up of fields and records. The first row of any database must contain field names. Successive rows contain records.

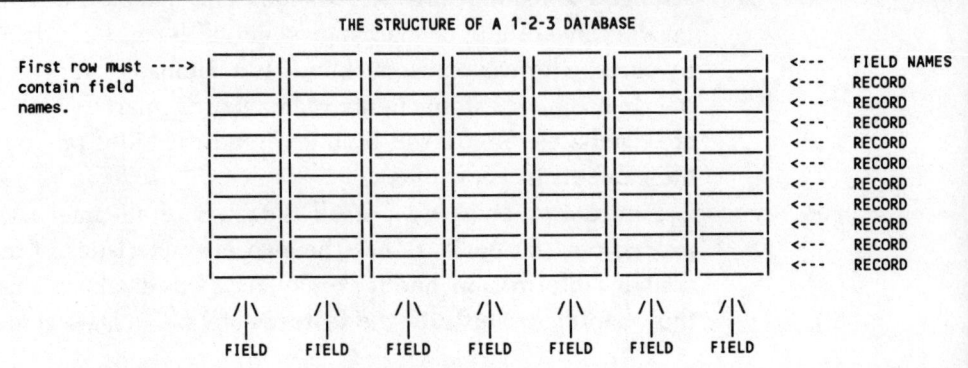

Records

Successive rows of the database table contain *records*. Records contain all the information about a single entry. If, for example, an entry is a player, as it is in Figure 9-2, each record (or row) contains all the information about a particular player.

Fields

Finally, cells containing individual pieces of information (Ty Cobb's Average, for example) are called *fields*. Sometimes the word *field* refers to an entire column as in "The At Bats field is next to the Runs field." Other times, *field* refers to a single cell in a record, "The number 11,429 is in Ty Cobb's At Bats field." Whether *field* refers to a column or a cell within a column will be clear from the context in which it is used.

The most important thing to remember about the structure of a 1-2-3 spreadsheet database is that the rows are the records and the columns or cells are the fields. External databases also contain fields and records, and when they are used by 1-2-3 the fields are in columns and the records in rows.

What Can You Do with a Database?

You can perform two general types of operations on a database: either *sort* it or *query* it. To sort a database is to rearrange the records. The batting database, Figure 9-2, is sorted by batting average in descending order. Ty Cobb is first because he is the player in the database with the highest life-time batting average. You can re-sort Figure 9-2 by number of hits, or years played, or alphabetically by players' last names.

To query a database is to ask to see those records meeting a particular set of criteria. Querying is a two-part process. The first, and most important, part is establishing the *criteria* for the records to be selected.

In Figure 9-2 you might establish a criterion to view the records for those hitters who had an average of at least 0.350 or who played in at least 1500 games. Or you might want to discover whether any players in the database averaged less than 0.345, played for at least 15 years, and got fewer than 1900 runs.

After you have established a query criterion, there are two different ways to view records that meet it. First, you can ask 1-2-3 to *find* those records. Lotus does this by highlighting in turn each record meeting your criterion. Alternatively, you can ask 1-2-3 to *extract* the selected records and place them in an output range.

Once in the output range, you can print extracted records, or you can copy the records into a separate file with the File Xtract command. Extracted records can also be used to generate graphs that display the information for those records meeting your criteria. They can even be used as additional databases.

Lotus also has two Data commands for managing your databases. The Delete command removes records from the database that match your criteria. The Modify command extracts records so you can modify them, then returns the modified records to the database.

THE DATA SORT COMMAND

The Data Sort command, whose command tree appears in Figure 9-4, is the simplest operation you can perform on a database. You use it to arrange data. Alphabetical order is common, but other orders are possible. "Reverse" telephone directories, for example, are ordered by area code or street address.

You will also want to sort data for analytical purposes. In the All-Time Batting Leaders database, sorting by different columns provides insight into who really was the best baseball player of all time. The rankings differ substantially when the players are arranged by Runs (Babe Ruth is second; Lou Gehrig is third) as compared to Average (Ruth is 12th; Gehrig is 15th), or by At Bats (where Pete Browning is last instead of fourth when the ranking is by Average). Re-sorting is one of the easiest ways to analyze information in a database.

Figure 9–4   Data Sort command tree.

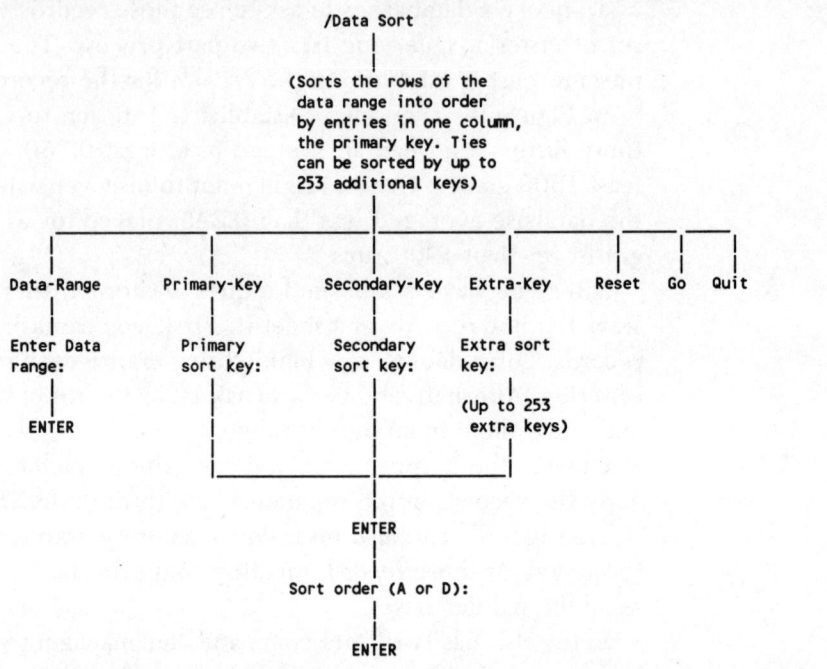

You can use the Data Sort command to sort any range of cells on your worksheet. Thus, you can enter row labels and use the command to alphabetize them. If you have a budget, you can sort it by amount to rank the entries. However, if the range you are sorting contains formulas, see the caution under Formulas and Functions.

Using the Data Sort Command

After you have entered the information to be sorted, you must respond to the prompts listed here. Extra sort keys are optional.

1. Data-Range.

2. Primary Key.

3. Sort Order (Ascending or Descending).

4. Extra Keys (optional).

Data-Range

The first parameter you must supply is the data range. It is the range of cells containing the records to be sorted. It includes *only* the records to be sorted. In particular, it must not include the field names at the top of the database. If it does, the field names are sorted into the database along with the records.

Figure 9–5 contains a 1-2-3 screen displaying the All-Time Batting Leaders database. Look at the control panel. Note that the Data Sort command has been entered and the prompt on the prompt line is asking for the data range. The correct data range, A8..H23, is highlighted. (Note that both the field names in row 6 and the double dashes in row 7 are omitted from the data range.)

As with any 1-2-3 range, you can either type in the addresses, point to the range, or supply a range name. Lotus remembers the last specified data range and proposes it the next time you enter the Data Sort command. Lotus also saves the data range as part of each worksheet file. After you have specified the data range, Lotus does not return to the Ready mode but continues to display the Sort command submenu so you can specify the other parameters.

Primary Key

Next, you must designate one column of the data range as the *primary key*. This is the column on which the rows (records) of the data range are

Figure 9–5   Database that is ready to sort, with the data range being specified.

```
A:A8: "Ty                                                         POINT
Enter data range: A8..H23

   A         B              C       D        E        F       G       H
|1 |
|2 |
|3 |                       ALL-TIME BATTING LEADERS
|4 |                         Ten or more seasons
|5 |
|6 | PLAYER'S NAME         YEARS   GAMES   AT BATS   RUNS    HITS   AVERAGE
|7 | ========================================================================
|8 |      Ty Cobb            24    3,033   11,429   2,244   4,191   0.367
|9 |   Rogers Hornsby        23    2,256    8,173   1,576   2,930   0.358
|10|      Joe Jackson        13    1,330    4,981     873   1,772   0.356
|11|    Pete Browning        13    1,180    4,839     867   1,716   0.355
|12|      Ed Delahanty       16    1,825    7,493   1,596   2,591   0.345
|13|     Willie Keeler       19    2,124    8,564   1,720   2,955   0.345
|14|   William Hamilton      14    1,578    6,262   1,694   2,157   0.344
|15|      Tris Speaker       22    2,789   10,208   1,881   3,515   0.344
|16|      Ted Williams       19    2,292    7,706   1,798   2,654   0.344
|17|     Dan Brouthers       19    1,665    7,493   1,596   2,591   0.343
|18|     Harry Heilmann      18    2,146    7,787   1,291   2,660   0.342
|19|        Babe Ruth        22    2,503    8,389   2,174   2,873   0.342
|20|      Jesse Burkett      16    2,063    8,389   1,708   2,872   0.341
17-Apr-90 11:01 AM
```

to be sorted. If, for example, you want to sort an address database alphabetically by last name, you would designate the column containing the last names as the primary key. To select the primary key, move the cursor to any cell in the desired field (it doesn't need to be in the data range) and press **ENTER**.

To sort the players in Figure 9–5 by the number of career hits, move the worksheet cursor to any cell in column G and press **ENTER**. That designates the Hits field as the primary key.

Ascending or Descending

Finally, you must decide whether you want the database sorted in ascending or descending order. Ascending order is 1, 2, 3, . . . or A, B, C, . . . Descending order is the opposite, such as when you "count down" or recite the alphabet backward. Descending is the proposed order (1-2-3 places **D** on the prompt line). You can select it by pressing **ENTER**. In the example in Figure 9–5, you'd probably like the player with the greatest number of hits to appear as the first record, so choose descending by typing a **D** or accept the proposed order by pressing the **ENTER** key.

Secondary Key and Extra Keys

The preceding three pieces of information (data range, primary key, and ascending or descending) are the only inputs required to perform a data sort, but you do have the option of specifying additional sort keys. You can select another field as the secondary key to sort any ties that result from the primary key sort. If one tie breaker isn't enough, you can specify additional columns as sort keys, up to a total of 255 sort keys (including the primary and secondary sort keys.)

Imagine, for example, a mailing list containing a Last Name field, a Zip Code field, and a field with a code for size of previous order. You might want to sort the mailing list with the Zip Code field as the primary key. Then the secondary key could be the code for order size so that all people in the same zip code would be sorted by size of their orders. The final key, the first extra key, could then sort all people in the same Zip Code with the same order size alphabetically by last name. Each time you specify a sort key you must also specify whether the sort is to be ascending or descending.

There aren't likely to be any ties in the number of Hits over a career in Figure 9–5, so it is only necessary to specify a primary key.

Go

After you have designated the data range, the primary key, the optional secondary and extra keys, and specified whether the sort is to be ascending

THE DATABASE COMMANDS

or descending, you are ready to sort the data range. To execute the Sort command, select Go from the command line of the Data Sort submenu. Lotus enters the Wait mode, the indicator light flashes, and in a few moments (depending on the size of the data range) the rearranged records are displayed.

Using the Data Sort Command

To sort the database in Figure 9–5 by Hits in descending order, position your cursor on cell A8 and type

/DS	Enters the Data Sort command.
D	Selects data range.
Enter data range:	Asks for range of cells to sort.
.	Tacks the cursor to cell A8.
Arrow keys	Expand data range to cover A8..H23.
ENTER	Sets data range.
P	Selects primary key.
Primary sort key:	Asks for column to use as the key to sort the data range.
Arrow keys	To sort on the Hits field, move the cursor to any cell in column G.
ENTER	Selects column G as the primary key.
Sort order (A or D): D	Asks for ascending or descending sort. Proposes descending sort.
ENTER	Accepts proposed sort order, descending.
G	Selects Go to execute the Data Sort command.

See Figure 9–6 for the result of your instructions to sort the Batting Leaders database on the Hits column in descending order.

Problems with Blanks, Brackets, and Formulas

While the Data Sort command is simple to use, you do need to know the order in which 1-2-3 places items so you won't be surprised by the results. Unless you changed the initial setting for the sort order (also called the

Figure 9-6 Database sorted on the Hits field, descending order.

```
      A         B         C       D         E        F       G      H
 1
 2
 3                      ALL-TIME BATTING LEADERS
 4                         Ten or more seasons
 5
 6   PLAYER'S NAME      YEARS   GAMES    AT BATS   RUNS    HITS   AVERAGE
 7   =====================================================================
 8         Ty Cobb        24    3,033   11,429   2,244   4,191   0.367
 9      Tris Speaker      22    2,789   10,208   1,881   3,515   0.344
10     Willie Keeler      19    2,124    8,564   1,720   2,955   0.345
11    Rogers Hornsby      23    2,256    8,173   1,576   2,930   0.358
12         Babe Ruth      22    2,503    8,389   2,174   2,873   0.342
13     Jesse Burkett      16    2,063    8,389   1,708   2,872   0.341
14     George Sisler      15    2,055    8,267   1,284   2,812   0.340
15        Lou Gehrig      17    2,164    8,001   1,888   2,721   0.340
16    Harry Heilmann      18    2,146    7,787   1,291   2,660   0.342
17      Ted Williams      19    2,292    7,706   1,798   2,654   0.344
18     Dan Brouthers      19    1,665    7,493   1,596   2,591   0.343
19      Ed Delahanty      16    1,825    7,493   1,596   2,591   0.345
20        Bill Terry      14    1,721    6,428   1,120   2,193   0.341
21   William Hamilton    14    1,578    6,262   1,694   2,157   0.344
22       Joe Jackson      13    1,330    4,981     873   1,772   0.356
23     Pete Browning     13    1,180    4,839     867   1,716   0.355
```

collating sequence) by using the Change Selected Equipment option in the Install program, 1-2-3 uses the sort order Numbers First, as described in Table 9-1.

Spaces

The space character (produced by pressing the SPACE BAR) can introduce the most perplexing problems, because to 1-2-3 a space is as much a character as an *A* or a 1. Spaces appear before letters in an ascending sort and after them in a descending sort. Spaces are sometimes placed before an entry (such characters are called *leading blanks*) to position a label in a cell. Sorting labels containing leading blanks usually produces unexpected results. For example, " **Zebra**" appears before "**Apple**" in an ascending sort!

To make matters worse, it is often difficult to tell whether a label's position is due to leading blanks or to the label-alignment character. 1-2-3 ignores the label-alignment character but uses the space as a character when sorting. To check for leading blanks, move the worksheet cursor to the cell and view the contents on the status line.

Empty cells (as opposed to cells containing the space character) are sorted together. They appear before nonblank records in an ascending sort and after them in a descending sort.

Table 9-1	Collating sequence with a default sort order of Numbers First.
Collating Sequence	**Sort Order (Ascending); Opposite for Descending**
Numbers First	1. Blank cells 2. Labels beginning with a space 3. Labels beginning with numbers in numerical order 4. Labels beginning with letters in alphabetical order 5. Labels beginning with other characters 6. Values Lowercase letters precede uppercase letters
Numbers Last	1. Blank cells 2. Labels beginning with a space 3. Labels beginning with letters in alphabetical order 4. Labels beginning with numbers in numerical order 5. Labels beginning with other characters 6. Values Lowercase letters precede uppercase letters
ASCII	1. Blank cells 2. All labels, using their ASCII values 3. Values Uppercase letters precede lowercase letters

Upper- and Lowercase Characters

Upper- and lowercase letters are different characters to 1-2-3, but it doesn't group all upper- and lowercase letters together. Instead, uppercase letters appear before the corresponding lowercase letter in a descending sort (*A* before *a*) and afterward in an ascending sort (*a* before *A*). Both *A* and *a* are sorted before any *b* in an ascending sort and vice versa for a descending sort. In any case, carefully verify any sort that contains a mixture of upper- and lowercase letters.

Forced Text Entry

When constructing your database, you must use forced text entry to enter numbers as text. Times when you want to treat numbers this way include entries of telephone numbers, zip codes, or part numbers or other codes containing letters but beginning with a number. But sorting these entries can cause problems because numbers as text appears before letters in an ascending sort (values appear after). Thus, a 1 as a forced text entry appears before *Alphabet* or *Apple,* both of which appear before 1 as a value entry. This may not be what you expect. In particular, be consistent when you enter zip codes. If any zip code in your database begins with a zero, enter all zip codes as forced text entries.

Formulas

Entries containing formulas or functions are sorted by their *displayed value,* even if that value changes after the formula is sorted into its new location.

To avoid problems as you sort formulas, follow these two simple rules.

- References to cells in the database should only refer to cells in the same record as the formula. Make the references relative, and they adjust as the formula (and the rest of the cells in the record) moves to a new location.

- Make all references to cells outside the database absolute references. Then when the formula is sorted to a new location the reference does not adjust.

In summary, make references to cells in the database relative and only to cells in the same record. Make references to cells outside the database absolute. If you don't follow these rules, sorting changes the displayed value.

When you are sorting in order to produce a printout and the records contain formulas with references to other records in your database, use the Range Values command to copy the displayed values to another area of your worksheet or to another sheet. Then sort and print the copied values.

Restoring the Original Order

Immediately after you have sorted a database, you can use 1-2-3's Undo command (if the Enable option is active) to return the database to its previous order, which may or may not be the original order. But once

THE DATABASE COMMANDS

you have taken one additional action, it isn't possible to undo the sort and return to the previous order.

If the original order was itself the result of a sort, you can sort the database to the original order. The Batting Leaders database, for example, was originally arranged by Average (descending order), so you can return to that order by sorting on the Average column.

There may be times, however, when the original database was not sorted. For example, you may have a database in which you record invoices as they come into your office. If your database doesn't include the date the invoice arrives, there may be no way to sort the database into the order in which the requests were received after it has been sorted into some other order.

If you need to be able to sort by order entered, use the Data Fill command to create a long column of consecutive numbers immediately to the right or left of the records. Include this column of numbers in the data range. It provides an "index" corresponding to the order in which the records were entered into the database. As you add new entries, expand the data range to include both new index numbers and new records. Whenever you want the database sorted by the sequence in which invoices were entered, sort on the index column.

SETTING UP THE DATA QUERY COMMAND

Sorting is a useful command, but the heart of 1-2-3's database feature is the Data Query commands. These specify criteria and then *find* or *extract* only those records that satisfy your requirements. See Figure 9–7 for the Data Query command tree.

To use the Data Query Command you must go through five steps:

1. Construct the database.

2. Construct the criteria.

3. Specify the input range.

4. Specify the criteria range.

5. Use the Data Query command to find or extract records meeting your criteria.

Other Query command options can be used to eliminate entries from a database (Delete); extract only one example of multiple entries (Unique); extract, modify, and replace records (Modify); erase range specifications (Reset); and exit the command (Quit).

Figure 9–7   Data Query command tree.

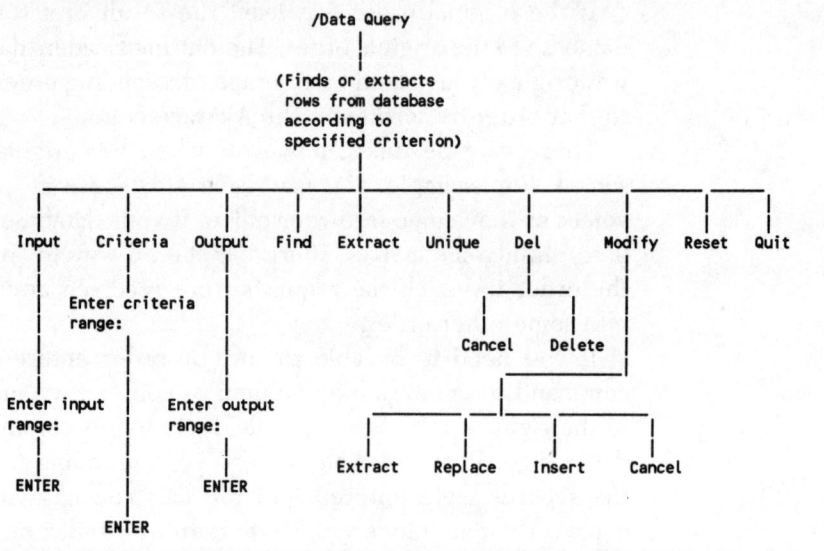

Lotus 1-2-3 Release 3 introduces the ability to work with multiple database tables at the same time. With multiple database tables you can construct sophisticated relational databases. This advanced feature is discussed in the next chapter, but it builds squarely on the knowledge of single-table databases you are acquiring in this chapter.

Construct the Database

Begin by constructing your database table. Recall the database structure illustrated in Figure 9–3. Place the field names at the top of the columns. If you use multiple-row field names, remember that only text in the single row directly above the database is used as field names by the database function. Be particularly careful not to include two identical field names. Once the field names have been specified, enter records one to a row.

As you create the database you have all 1-2-3's worksheet construction tools at your disposal. In particular, you can use the Worksheet Insert and Delete commands to insert or delete rows and columns. You can use the Copy and Move commands to rearrange entries, and you can use the Format commands to determine the appearance of the database.

Database Construction Hints

Figure 9-8 contains a 1-2-3 screen displaying the familiar Batting Leaders database. Notice that several "tricks" were used when constructing this database. First, the field names **Player's** and **Name** are actually entered into separate columns, column A and column B. The first names, in column A, are right aligned. The last names, in column B, are left aligned. By placing the last names in a separate column, it is possible to sort or query on the last name. You couldn't do that had you entered the first and last names into a single column unless you had entered them last name first.

Also, notice that row 7—the "first record"—is a row of double dashes (actually, equal signs). This separates the field names from the records and makes the database easier to read. Text evaluates to zero. So a criterion that is true for zero values, such as selecting players who have played fewer than 1500 games, also selects this row. When selected, the double dashes are either the first matching record or the first row of the output range. In either case, selecting them causes no problem.

Construct the Criteria Range

Assuming you have constructed your database along the lines just described, you are now ready to query the database for those records that

Figure 9-8 The 1-2-3 screen displaying the Batting Leaders database.

```
A:C1:                                                            READY

    A           B          C       D        E       F      G       H
1
2
3                    ALL-TIME BATTING LEADERS
4                    Ten or more seasons
5
6  PLAYER'S    NAME        YEARS   GAMES    AT BATS RUNS   HITS    AVERAGE
7  ========================================================================
8       Ty    Cobb          24     3,033    11,429  2,244  4,191   0.367
9    Rogers   Hornsby       23     2,256     8,173  1,576  2,930   0.358
10      Joe   Jackson       13     1,330     4,981    873  1,772   0.356
11     Pete   Browning      13     1,180     4,839    867  1,716   0.355
12       Ed   Delahanty     16     1,825     7,493  1,596  2,591   0.345
13   Willie   Keeler        19     2,124     8,564  1,720  2,955   0.345
14  William   Hamilton      14     1,578     6,262  1,694  2,157   0.344
15     Tris   Speaker       22     2,789    10,208  1,881  3,515   0.344
16      Ted   Williams      19     2,292     7,706  1,798  2,654   0.344
17      Dan   Brouthers     19     1,665     7,493  1,596  2,591   0.343
18    Harry   Heilmann      18     2,146     7,787  1,291  2,660   0.342
19     Babe   Ruth          22     2,503     8,389  2,174  2,873   0.342
20    Jesse   Burkett       16     2,063     8,389  1,708  2,872   0.341
17-Apr-90 11:15 AM
```

meet a particular criterion. To do this you must construct a criteria range to communicate your criteria to 1-2-3. The criteria range is made up of two parts:

- The criteria range field names
- One or more criteria

As with the database, the criteria range must be constructed *before* you enter the Data command.

Criteria Range Field Names

The criteria range is constructed in some out-of-the-way portion of your worksheet. It is now convenient to place the criteria range on a separate sheet. Wherever it is placed, the first row consists of the criteria range field names. These field names must be *exactly* the same as the field names in the input range; otherwise, the query does not work.

To ensure that the field names are the same in both ranges, use the Copy command to copy the field names from the input range to the criteria range. By using the Copy command you can be sure that leading and trailing blanks, capitalization, and spelling are the same in both places.

Figure 9–9 shows the field names from the database in Figure 9–8 copied into row 31 beginning with cell A31. All of the field names have been copied, but that is not necessary. Only field names for which you are going to establish a criterion need be copied.

Creating Criteria

To complete the construction of the criteria range, one or more items are entered into the rows immediately below the criteria range field names. An entry in a cell below a particular field name establishes a criterion with respect to that field. A record in the database is only selected when its entry satisfies the criterion in the corresponding field in the criteria range. An empty cell below a field name establishes no criterion for that field.

Figure 9–9 Criteria range, in which row 31 contains the field names and row 32 the criteria.

A	A	B	C	D	E	F	G	H
30								
31	PLAYER'S NAME		YEARS	GAMES	AT BATS	RUNS	HITS	AVERAGE
32			16					
33								
34								

THE DATABASE COMMANDS

Criteria can be divided into three categories: exact, relative, and multiple.

With *exact criteria* you can find those players in the Batting Leaders database who have played for exactly 16 years. With *relative criteria* you can find all the players who have played for at least 20 seasons. With *multiple criteria* you can find those players who have played for at least 16 years and who have a batting average greater than 0.344.

Exact Criteria

The place to begin setting criteria is with exact criteria, because they are the most straightforward criteria. You use exact criteria when you want to view only those records that meet your requirements exactly, such as when you want only Babe Ruth's record or just the records for players who have played for 19 years.

To specify an exact criterion, simply enter it into the cell below the appropriate field name. If the field contains text, the criterion must be a label. If the field contains values, the criterion must be a value.

Figure 9–10 shows several examples of exact criteria. The first criterion contains only the word **Ruth** beneath the criteria range field name **NAME**. This criterion selects only records with **Ruth** in the **NAME** field. The blank cells below the other criteria range field names indicate that any entry in those cells of a record is acceptable.

Study each criterion in Figure 9–10 and predict how each would be applied to the database. In every case, only records that satisfy a criterion exactly are selected. All other records in the database are passed over by the query operations.

Relative Criteria

In many situations an exact criterion is too restrictive. You may not want to see those batting leaders who have played exactly 19 seasons. Rather, you may want to see those who have played for at least 19 seasons. Or you might be interested in all players whose last names begin with the letter *B*, but who have any other letters in the rest of their names. The criteria that would find these records are called *relative criteria*, because the criteria are specified relative to a particular value such as 19 or *B*.

Lotus has different tools for specifying relative criteria depending on whether the field contains values or labels.

Value Fields

When a field contains values, you create relative criteria by creating formulas using the logical operators:

> Greater than

>= Greater than or equal to

< Less than

<= Less than or equal to

You can also use the special logical functions:

#AND# Logical AND: True only if A and B and C, and so on, are true.

#OR# Logical OR: True if either A or B or C, and so on, are true.

Function or Text

You can use the logical operators to form functions for cells in the first record of the input range. For example, to find players who have played for more than 19 years, enter the formula **+YEARS>19** under Years in the criteria range. Note that a plus sign, +, must precede the field name to

Figure 9-10 Four different criteria ranges, each with a different exact criterion.

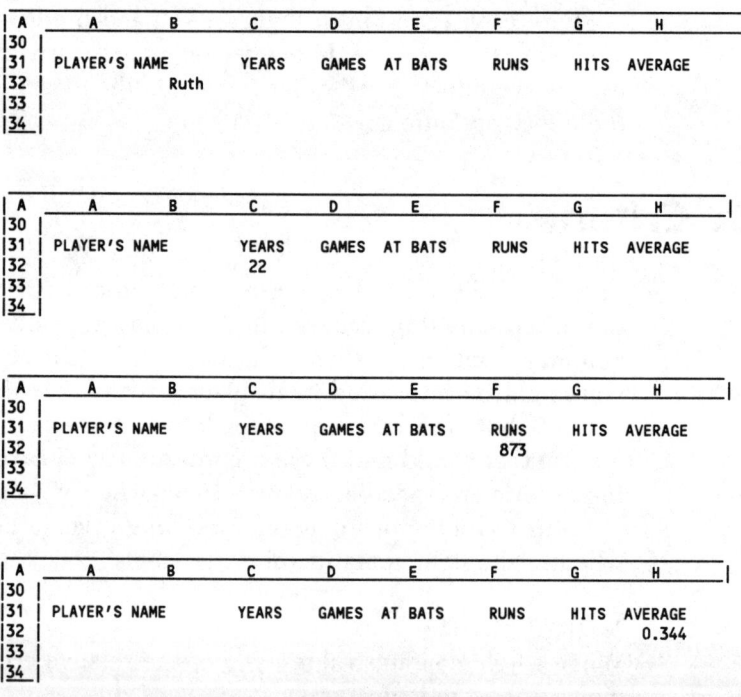

THE DATABASE COMMANDS

declare the entry a formula. An **ERR** appears on the screen because **YEARS** isn't really a range name. Using **YEARS** in a formula is like using an unassigned range name, which causes the formula to evaluate to **ERR**. Use the Range Format Text command to format the cell so you can see the contents, **+YEARS>19**, rather than the result, **ERR**. For the purposes of the Data Query command what 1-2-3 has done is act *as if* the input range field names are assigned to the cells in the record immediately below each field name.

This technique doesn't work when you have already used the Range Name Create command to assign the name to some other cell. In that case, either use the method described in the next paragraph or substitute the cell address in the first record for the implied range name. For example, if YEARS is already used as a range name elsewhere in the current file, make the criterion +C7>19.

In Release 3 (but not previous versions) there is an alternative way to achieve the same effect as the formula just described, with much less fuss. Just enter >19 in the cell below **Years** in the criteria range. The greater than symbol is accepted as a label and **>19** appears in the cell. Lotus views this exactly the way it does the formulas +YEARS>19 or its equivalent, +C7>19. It is easier to enter and appears on the screen. All around a better way to go. Figure 9–11 shows the Batting Leaders database with a relative criterion entered into cell C32. The criterion is the formula >19. Other criteria that produce the same result are +YEARS>19 and +C7>19.

But there are three catches. First, for some reason the less than symbol, <, is used in Release 3 as an alternative way to bring up the Main menu! If you want to use a formula that begins with the less than symbol, use forced text entry and begin by typing one of the label alignment characters.

Second, don't type embedded commas into numbers. The criterion >2,000 fails. What 1-2-3 needs is >2000.

Finally, you can't use this technique when you want to create criteria using the #OR# and #AND# operators. You must use an actual formula made up of field names or the appropriate cell addresses.

Figure 9–11   Criteria range with relative criterion entered into cell C32.

```
|A      A           B      C       D      E        F      G      H       |
|30|
|31|   PLAYER'S NAME        YEARS   GAMES  AT BATS  RUNS   HITS   AVERAGE
|32|                        >19
|33|
|34|
```

If you don't use the short form (such as >=16), it is very important to note that the cell reference in a criterion must be to the first record (the second row) in the input field. The formulas that establish a relative criterion in values fields must be defined relative to fields in the first record of the database. Lotus searches down the Years column applying the criterion to each entry. As it does, 1-2-3 adjusts the references in the criterion to each new row. Here, when a value is greater than or equal to 16, the record is selected. When a value is less than 16, the record is rejected.

Figure 9–12 contains a number of examples of relative criteria applied to value entries. Study the figure and predict how each criterion would be applied to the database in Figure 9–8.

Label Fields

In additional to the logical operators =, >, <, >=, <=, and <> discussed above, 1-2-3 has three special characters or *wildcards* that can be used to establish relative criteria for label fields. The characters are the question mark,

Figure 9–12 Criteria ranges containing different relative criteria.

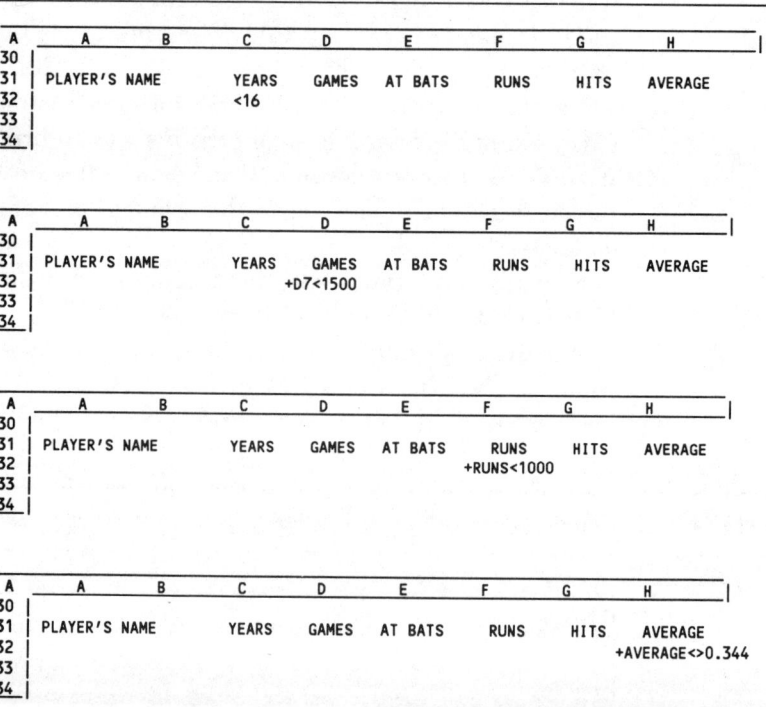

THE DATABASE COMMANDS

?, the asterisk, *, and the tilde, ~. Each character can be used to define criteria that accept a range of label entries. Here is how they work.

?   Any character may occupy the spot occupied by the question mark. The criterion **?at,** for example, selects bat, cat, rat, and hat. It would not accept brat, frat, or scat.

*   Any character may occupy the spot occupied by the asterisk, and any number of characters may appear after the asterisk. The asterisk is a very powerful wildcard. The criterion **B***, for example, selects any word beginning with a capital *B*. Better, Both, Baltimore, and Bolivia would all be selected by the **B*** criterion.

~   Any entry, except entries that match what follows the tilde, is selected. The tilde is a "negative" wildcard. For example, the criterion **~Ruth** selects all players whose last name is not Ruth.

You can combine wildcards in the same criterion. For example **~B*** accepts any entry that doesn't begin with a *B*, whereas **?a*** accepts any entry whose second letter is an *a*.

When you use the wildcards, be careful to avoid criteria that select records you don't want selected. Lotus follows your instructions to the letter (and the character), so make sure the criteria you establish are really the ones that select what you want to select. It is always good practice to check the selected records for entries you didn't intend to select and for the absence of records you expected to select. If there is a problem, redefine your criteria and repeat the query operation.

The use of logical operators in label criteria is a new feature of Release 3, and it greatly improves use of the Query command on label fields. They work in the natural way. For example, the criterion **>MEGAN** matches all entries that begin with any letter between N and Z. (You would need **>= MEGAN** to select Megan as well.)

Multiple Criteria

In many situations you will want to specify criteria that apply to several fields at one time. These are called *multiple criteria*, and they fall into two general categories. You may want the records that satisfy every criterion you establish, or you may want the records that satisfy any one of the criteria. These two ways to specify criteria are called **AND** and **OR** criteria, respectively.

In the Batting Leaders database, the **AND** criteria might be used to select all players who have played in at least 2000 games AND who have at least 2500 hits AND whose last names begin with B. Only those players who satisfied *all* the criteria would be selected. Failure to satisfy any one of the criteria causes the record to be rejected.

The **OR** criteria selects any player who has played in at least 2000 games, OR who has at least 2500 hits, OR whose last name begins with *B*. Meeting *any* one of the three criteria qualifies a record for selection. Only records that fail to meet all the criteria are rejected.

The key to instructing 1-2-3 to treat your criteria as **AND** criteria or **OR** criteria is the way you construct the criteria range. Each criterion in a *single row* of the criteria range is treated as **AND**. Criteria in *different rows* are treated as **OR**.

Figure 9–13 shows criteria required to find the records meeting the two criteria discussed in the preceding paragraphs. The first criteria range has the criteria entered into a single row, therefore, all the criteria must be satisfied by any record selected. The second criteria range contains three rows of criteria, therefore, a record can be selected by meeting the criteria in row 32, or row 33, or row 34.

You can combine **AND** criteria and **OR** criteria in the same criteria range. For example, you might want players whose last names begin with C or R, whose Average is at least 0.345, and whose Years are less than 23. In Figure 9–14 the C and R criteria are in different rows while the 23 and 0.345 criteria are in the same row.

Figure 9–13 When the criteria are in the same row (AND criteria), all the criteria must be met by a selected record. When the criteria are in different rows (OR criteria), a record can be selected by meeting all the criteria in any one row.

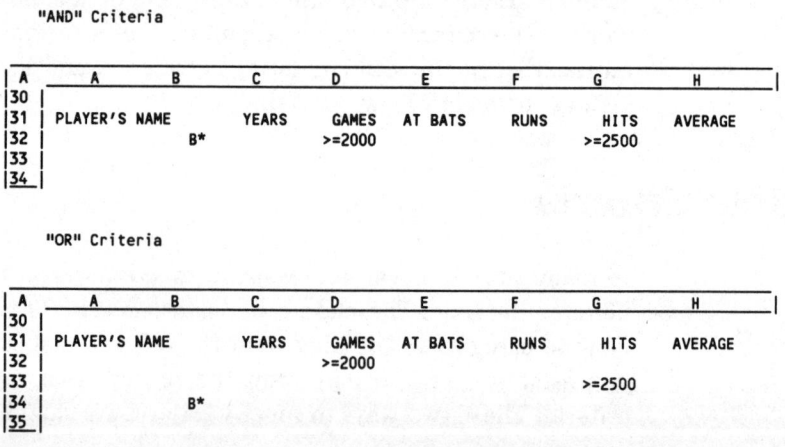

Figure 9-14 AND and OR criteria combined in the same criteria range.

```
     A              B       C      D       E       F       G       H
|30 |
|31 | PLAYER'S NAME        YEARS   GAMES   AT BATS RUNS    HITS    AVERAGE
|32 |                C*    <23                                     >=0.345
|33 |                R*    <23                                     >=0.345
|34 |
```

Blank Criteria Range

When you specify a criteria range that contains *only* blank cells you are, in essence, establishing criteria that accept *all* of the records in the Input range. There are times you will want to set criteria that select everything, and it is good to know there is a simple way to do this.

In earlier releases of 1-2-3, any blank row in the criteria range would select all records. In Release 3, the entire criteria range must be blank to select all records. If you have a row containing criteria and one or more blank rows, 1-2-3 ignores the blank rows and applies the criteria.

Make Absolute Reference to Cells Outside the Database

Whenever you use a formula in a criterion, be sure that cell references to fields within the database are relative, whereas references to cells outside the database are absolute. This requirement is easy to understand when you recall how 1-2-3 applies a criterion. It begins with the first record and evaluates the criterion for that field. It selects the record if the result is true (recall that true formulas evaluate to 1); it rejects the record if the formula evaluates to false (zero).

After testing the first record 1-2-3 moves down one record and tests the next record by adjusting the cell references so that they apply to that row. You usually want references to cells within the database to adjust, but you would want to use the same value for each record from a cell somewhere else on the worksheet. Keep references to cells within the database relative, and those to cells outside the database absolute.

Place the Criteria Range on a Separate Sheet

The next point has to do with the location of the criteria range. It may be anywhere on the worksheet. But because formulas are typically wider than value entries, you need extra column width to view the formulas under the Text format. So locate the criteria range in a place where you can expand the columns without disturbing either the database or any other entries. You can use the Worksheet Window command to display both sheets on the screen at the same time and the **WINDOW/F6** key to move between them.

Changing a Criterion

A criterion can be changed by simply editing the old criterion or by typing a new criterion and entering it into the appropriate cell in the criteria range. As with all changes, these changes must be made outside the Data Query command. You cannot change criteria from inside the command. To change criteria and requery the database efficiently, see the discussion of the **QUERY/F7** key later in the chapter.

Removing a Criterion

Always use the Range Erase command to remove a criterion. *Never* use the SPACE BAR to "blank" a cell, because the SPACE BAR is a character that establishes a space in the field as an exact criterion. The result is usually that no matching records are found and there is great confusion as to the reason the command "isn't working."

To check for misplaced space characters, move the cursor from cell to cell in the criteria range and check the Status line for the presence of a label alignment character.

Other Hints

Contrary to the examples in this chapter, when the criteria range is on the same sheet as the database the best location for the criteria range is to one side of the database, rather than below it. A far better solution is to use the Worksheet Insert command to insert a new sheet and place the criteria range on it.

In the preceding examples, the entire row of field names was copied as the first row of the criteria range. This isn't necessary. You only need the field names for the fields in which you intend to specify criteria. You can omit the other field names. The entire list of field names does serve to remind you of the possible fields in which a criterion may be specified and, for that reason, you may want to include all field names in your criteria ranges.

Summary

You now know about the three types of criteria you can use with 1-2-3 databases: exact, relative, and multiple. Establishing the criteria is the hardest part of using the Data Query command. Until you become comfortable specifying criteria, test each criterion by identifying a record you expect to be selected. Then specify the criterion in the command and verify that the record is, indeed, selected. (The Find command, discussed later in this chapter, is the easiest way to perform this task.)

If you have trouble specifying a criterion, write out in words what you want to use and then translate it into formulas 1-2-3 understands. When you first specify criteria, enter individual elements of multiple criteria and then test each element. (The **QUERY/F7** key, discussed later in this chapter, can be a great aid with this.)

Finally, it is quite easy to specify criteria that none of the records in your database satisfies. When this happens, you hear a "beep" to indicate that none of the entries in the input range has been selected. Begin relaxing your requirements until 1-2-3 selects the records you are looking for.

THE DATA QUERY FIND COMMAND

The hard work is over. You have created the database table and entered the criteria. You are now ready to learn how to use the Data Query command.

There are five ways to query a 1-2-3 database; you can use Find, Extract, Unique, Modify, or Delete.

Find	The Find command locates and highlights in the database each record meeting your criteria. Typically you use the Find command with a telephone database to find someone's telephone number. You don't need a copy of the record; you just want to view it on the screen while placing a call.
Extract	This command copies all matching records to an area of your worksheet designated as the output range. You can print, sort, or otherwise use the extracted records selected with Extract.
Unique	The Unique command is like the Extract command, except that where multiple, identical copies would be extracted, Unique extracts only one copy of each result. the extracted copies are automatically sorted in ascending order on the leftmost field in the output range. Use the Unique command to generate a list of clients from an invoice database or a list of salespersons from a sales record database.

Modify	This command inserts or replaces records in the input range with records from the output range. Modify is the easiest way to add records to an existing database and the most efficient way to modify a large group of records.
Delete	The Delete command (Del) removes all matching records from your database. Use Del to remove unneeded entries, but be very careful when using this command not to remove important data. Once a record is deleted, you cannot recover it with 1-2-3.

The following discussion begins with the Data Find command, because it requires the smallest amount of additional information. The discussion then adds the specifications necessary to perform the other Data Query commands.

To use any of the Data Query commands, begin by telling 1-2-3 the location of two pieces of information:

Input Range	This is your database. It *must* include as its first row the input range field names.
Criteria Range	The two or more rows containing your criteria. It *must* include as its first row the criteria range field names.

The Data Extract, Unique, and Modify commands also require you to designate an area of your spreadsheet as the output range. These commands and their associated output range are discussed later in this chapter.

Specifying the Input Range

The first range to specify after you have created the criteria range and entered your criteria is the input range.

Assume that you have entered the criterion >**7000** in the At Bats field. Now to find those players in the All-Time Batting Leaders database (Figure 9–8) who have had more than 7000 at bats, place your cursor on cell **A6** and type

/DQ	Enters the Data Query command.
I	Selects input range.
Enter input range:	Asks for range of cells containing the database.

THE DATABASE COMMANDS

.	Tacks cursor to cell A6.
Arrow keys	Stretch cursor over range A6..H23.
ENTER	Accepts input range and returns you to the Data Query submenu.

If you have already specified an input range, 1-2-3 proposes it. (The last input range is also stored with the worksheet.) If you want to accept the proposed range, press **ENTER**; otherwise, supply your own.

Specifying the Criteria Range

The next range to specify is the criteria range. It must include at least two rows, one of field names and at least one row below the field names containing criteria.

Continuing the example, the Data Query command submenu is still displayed. To specify the criteria range, type

C	Selects Criteria.
Enter criteria range:	Asks for range of cells containing criteria.
Arrow keys	Move cursor to cell A29.
.	Tacks cursor to cell A29.
Arrow keys	Stretch cursor over range A29..H30.
ENTER	Accepts criteria range and returns you to the Data Query command submenu.

You have now told 1-2-3 the location of the database (the input range) and the location of the criteria (the criteria range). You are now ready to use the Data Find command to locate those records that meet your criteria.

Using the Data Find Command

The Data Query command submenu is still displayed. To apply the specified criteria to the specified database, type

F	Selects the Find command.

In Figure 9–15 Lotus finds and highlights the first record in your database that has more than 7000 in its At Bats field. In the Batting Leaders database

Figure 9–15 The Find command locates and highlights those records in the input range that satisfy the criteria in the criteria range.

```
           A              B        C        D       E       F       G        H

  1
  2
  3                    ALL-TIME BATTING LEADERS
  4                       Ten or more seasons
  5
  6    PLAYER'S NAME      YEARS    GAMES   AT BATS  RUNS    HITS   AVERAGE
  7    ==============================================================================
  8          Ty Cobb       24      3,033   11,429   2,244   4,191   0.367
  9    Rogers Hornsby      23      2,256    8,173   1,576   2,930   0.358
 10       Joe Jackson      13      1,330    4,981     873   1,772   0.356
 11     Pete Browning      13      1,180    4,839     867   1,716   0.355
 12       Ed Delahanty     16      1,825    7,493   1,596   2,591   0.345
 13      Willie Keeler     19      2,124    8,564   1,720   2,955   0.345
 14   William Hamilton     14      1,578    6,262   1,694   2,157   0.344
 15       Tris Speaker     22      2,789   10,208   1,881   3,515   0.344
 16       Ted Williams     19      2,292    7,706   1,798   2,654   0.344
 17      Dan Brouthers     19      1,665    7,493   1,596   2,591   0.343
 18      Harry Heilmann    18      2,146    7,787   1,291   2,660   0.342
 19         Babe Ruth      22      2,503    8,389   2,174   2,873   0.342
 20      Jesse Burkett     16      2,063    8,389   1,708   2,872   0.341
 21        Bill Terry      14      1,721    6,428   1,120   2,193   0.341
 22        Lou Gehrig      17      2,164    8,001   1,888   2,721   0.340
 23      George Sisler     15      2,055    8,267   1,284   2,812   0.340
 24
 25
 26
 27
 28                  **************CRITERIA RANGE******************
 29    PLAYER'S NAME      YEARS    GAMES   AT BATS  RUNS    HITS   AVERAGE
 30                                         >7000
 31
 32
 33
```

that would be Ty Cobb's record. Can you predict which record will be selected when you press the **DOWN** arrow key? And the next?

Notice that the leftmost cell in the highlight record contains a flashing underline character. This character indicates the "active field." Use the **RIGHT** and **LEFT** arrow keys to move the underline character to the left or the right. As you do, you can scroll the screen to display all fields of a record that is too wide to view on the screen at one time.

To display other records meeting your criteria, press the appropriate key:

DOWN   Next matching record.

UP   Previous matching record.

END   Last record in database regardless of whether it matches or not.

THE DATABASE COMMANDS

HOME   First record in database regardless of whether it matches or not.

Editing a Found Record

A frequent use of the Find command is to locate a record that needs to be modified. To edit a record highlighted by the Find command press the **LEFT** or **RIGHT** arrow key to position the flashing underline character on the cell containing the field you want to edit. When the underline character is positioned, press the **EDIT/F2** key. The content of the cell then appears in the control panel where you can edit it.

When you are finished editing, press either the **ENTER** key or the **UP** or **DOWN** arrow key to transfer the edited material into the record and to continue viewing selected records.

Ending the Find Command

To end the Find command, press the **ESC** key to return to the Query submenu. From there you can perform other Data Query operations or exit the Data command altogether.

To exit the Data command, select Quit from the Query submenu. As you know, you can also always terminate a command by pressing **CTRL-BREAK** or by pressing the **ESC** key a sufficient number of times.

THE QUERY/F7 FUNCTION KEY

To change a criterion, you must leave the Data Query command and enter the new criterion from the Ready mode. You might think that to perform the query operation again, you'd have to reenter the Data Query command and make the selections all over again. Luckily, there is a keystroke saving alternative. You can press the **QUERY/F7** function key to repeat the most recently performed Data Query operation.

When you use the **QUERY/F7** key, 1-2-3 remains in Ready mode. You can enter new criteria into the appropriate cells in the criteria range and press **QUERY/F7** to have the criteria applied to the most recently defined Data Query command.

In a telephone number database, for example, you can enter one name, find it, then enter another and find it. You don't have to type the several keystrokes required to enter and exit the Data Query command itself.

Important: When you use the **QUERY/F7** key, you must define all the ranges required for the particular query operation, and you must also perform the operation at least one time from the Data Query command submenu.

If you want to perform a different Data Query operation, you must reenter the command and select the new operation from the menu. After you have selected it once, you can then use the **QUERY/F7** key to repeat that query operation.

THE DATA QUERY DELETE COMMAND

The Data Query Delete command (Del on the command menu) removes from the database all the records that meet your criteria. It is used to clean up a database by removing records that are no longer needed. Records appearing below those deleted move up to fill the space so no blank rows remain in the database. To prevent accidental use of this command, you must confirm your intention to use it by selecting Delete from the menu that appears when you select the Data Delete command. However, you don't get a chance to confirm each deletion—one confirmation and *everything* meeting your criteria is history.

Specifying the Range for Deletion

To use the Delete command you only need to specify two ranges, the input range and the criteria range. Once they are specified, select Delete and confirm your intention to have 1-2-3 remove the matching records from the input range. The Data Query Delete command can only be used with single-table input ranges.

Caution: Exercise care when you use the Delete command. Be particularly careful if you specify relative criteria or use wildcards, because Delete takes out every record meeting your criteria—whether you intended it to or not.

To avoid deleting the wrong records, first use your criteria to perform the Extract command (discussed below) on the database. Then check the extracted records to verify that none are records you want to keep. Only use the Delete option when you are satisfied that the criteria has selected only those records you wish to erase.

To avoid unpleasant surprises later, use the File Xtract command to save the extracted (and soon to be deleted) records into their own file, as described in Chapter 5. Should you later need a deleted record, you can find it in that file.

Undoing the Delete Command

When the Undo command is enabled, you can press Undo, **ALT-F4**, to restore all deleted records. However, you must do so *immediately* after executing the Delete command. If you don't notice your mistake before you perform any other operation, the Undo command won't work. In that case, your only hope is that you have a stored copy of the database. If you do, retrieve it to reverse the damage.

THE DATA QUERY EXTRACT COMMAND

The Data Extract command copies into an area called the output range those records that meet your criteria. It is the most useful of all the Data Query commands. With it you can extract information from one or more input ranges. See Chapter 10 for instructions about using the Data Extract command with more than one input range.

After you have extracted the records they can be printed or saved into their own worksheet file with the File Xtract command. You can also sort or analyze the extracted records, or you can graph them to display the information visually.

Using the Extract command is much like using the Find command except that the selected records are copied to the output range rather than highlighted in place in the database.

Constructing the Output Range

To use the Extract command, you must first create an output range. Once it has been constructed, you use the Output option on the Query command submenu to define its location.

If you are already in the Data command, you must return to the Ready mode to construct the output range.

Like the other two ranges the output range begins with a row of field names. The rows below the field names are where the extracted records are copied. Once again, the field names in the output range must be identical to the field names above the input range, so use the Copy command to copy them to their new location.

The output range can be on the same worksheet as the input and criteria ranges, and that is where it is for convenience in the examples presented in the text. But it is often much better to locate it on its own sheet in the current file where column widths can be expanded. Use the Worksheet Insert Sheet command to add an additional sheet to contain the output range.

Figure 9–16 contains an output range constructed below the criteria range on the Batting Leaders database you have been using. The field names in row 34 were copied from the field names in row 29, which had previously been copied from the input range field names at the top of the database, row 6.

Specifying the Output Range

You can specify the output range in two ways.

The easiest is to only specify the row of cells containing the output field names as the output range. Lotus then uses as many rows below the field names as necessary to copy the extracted records. However, 1-2-3 automatically erases everything in the columns below the output field names down to the bottom edge of the worksheet at row 8192. If you choose the first option, be certain there is nothing below the output field names that would be erased.

The alternative is to specify the output range as a rectangle of cells. When you do, Lotus only erases the entries in the specified rectangle and does not erase the entries below the rectangle. If the output range is too small to accommodate all the selected records, you receive a **Too many records for Output Range** error message. Respond to the message by pressing the **ENTER** key, and 1-2-3 fills the output range with as many selected records as will fit. To extract all the selected records, return to the Data Query command, expand the size of the output range, and repeat the extract operation.

Figure 9–16 The output range is required whenever the Extract command is used.

A	A	B	C	D	E	F	G	H
27								
28			************CRITERIA RANGE****************					
29	PLAYER'S NAME		YEARS	GAMES	AT BATS	RUNS	HITS	AVERAGE
30					>8500			
31								
32								
33			************OUTPUT RANGE****************					
34	PLAYER'S NAME		YEARS	GAMES	AT BATS	RUNS	HITS	AVERAGE
35								
36								
37								
38								
39								

THE DATABASE COMMANDS

When the output range is the only thing on its own sheet, simply designate the row of output range field names as the output range.

Extracting Records

To use the Extract command you must tell 1-2-3 the location of three ranges: the input range, the criteria range, and the output range. You can specify multiple input ranges, but see the next chapter for the correct techniques for working with them.

Assume you have already used the Copy command to copy the input range field names to row 34 beginning with cell A34. See Figure 9–16. Also assume you have performed the foregoing exercises with the Data Find command during which you specified the input range and the criteria range.

To extract copies of all records in the database that have more than 8500 in the At Bats field (see criteria range, Figure 9–16) move the cursor to cell A34 and type

/DQ	Enters the Data Query command.
I	Selects Input.
Enter input range: A6..H23	Asks for range of cells containing the database and highlights the last specified input range.
ENTER	Accepts proposed input range and returns you to the Data Query submenu.
C	Selects Criteria.
Enter criteria range: A29..H30	Asks for range of cells containing criteria and highlights the last specified criteria range.
ENTER	Accepts proposed criteria range and returns you to the Data Query command submenu.
O	Selects Output.
Enter output range:	Asks for the output range.
.	Tacks cursor to cell A34.
Arrow keys	Highlight the output range field names, A34..H34.

ENTER   Accepts the output range. Each time the command is used it erases everything between this range and the last row on the worksheet. Optionally, you can highlight down the number of rows you want to reserve for the output range.

E   Selects Extract and executes the command.

Lotus enters the Wait mode, the mode indicator flashes, and in a few moments the records for those players who have had more than 8500 at bats appear below the output range field names. See Figure 9–17.

If you know that the input and criteria ranges are correctly specified from a previous Data Query operation, you do not need to respecify them to use the Extract command.

Also note that the records in the output range do not contain any formulas or functions that may have been part of the database's structure. Only displayed values are copied to the output range.

Select Quit from the Data command submenu to return to the ready mode.

Calculated Fields

In the example the entries in the output range are the corresponding entries from the selected records in the input range. Selecting a field name selects the contents of that field. However, if you want an output that isn't in the database but that can be calculated from information in the database you can have it by specifying the appropriate formula or function as the output range field name. You can use any formula or built-in function except @@, @CELL, @HLOOKUP, @INDEX, @INFO,

Figure 9–17   Result of Extract command.

	A	B	C	D	E	F	G	H
27								
28			************CRITERIA RANGE*****************					
29	PLAYER'S NAME		YEARS	GAMES	AT BATS	RUNS	HITS	AVERAGE
30					>8500			
31								
32								
33			************OUTPUT RANGE*****************					
34	PLAYER'S NAME		YEARS	GAMES	AT BATS	RUNS	HITS	AVERAGE
35	Ty Cobb		24	3,033	11,429	2,244	4,191	0.367
36	Willie Keeler		19	2,124	8,564	1,720	2,955	0.345
37	Tris Speaker		22	2,789	10,208	1,881	3,515	0.344
38								
39								

@IRR, @N, @NPV, @ROWS, @S, @SHEETS, @STD, @STDS, @VAR, @VARS, @VLOOKUP, and the built-in database statistical functions discussed later in this chapter. For computing values, the most useful functions are @AVG, @COUNT, @MAX, @MIN, and @SUM.

For example, in Figure 9–18, the output range contains a formula in E36 that calculates the average number of games each player played in each year of his career. This information isn't in the database, but it is simply the number in the Games field divided by the number in the Years field. The formula entered into cell E36 is +D7/C7 and the resulting entries are the number of games per year for each record selected. Note that the entry in cell E36 is not text, but a formula. Cell E36 has been formatted as Text with the Range Format command, so the formula appears on the screen.

Omitted Field Names

The field names in the output range are often of the same number and in the same order as the field names in the input range. However, you can omit field names from the output range. If you do, the omitted fields do not appear. (See Figure 9–18 for an example.) You can use this technique to eliminate unnecessary or unwanted information from the selected records.

Rearranged Field Names

You can also rearrange the order in which the fields appear in the output range simply by rearranging the order of the output range field names.

Figure 9–18 Formulas used as output range field names result in calculated fields in the output range.

```
|A     A            B       C       D      E       F       G      H     |
|29 |
|30 |                        ************CRITERIA RANGE****************
|31 | PLAYER'S NAME          YEARS   GAMES  AT BATS RUNS    HITS   AVERAGE
|32 |                         19
|33 |
|34 |
|35 |                        ************OUTPUT RANGE******************
|36 | PLAYER'S NAME          YEARS   GAMES  +D7/C7
|37 |       Willie Keeler     19     2,124   112
|38 |        Ted Williams     19     2,292   121
|39 |        Dan Brouthers    19     1,665    88
|40 |
```

Figure 9–19 provides an example. This technique can be used on a database to restructure the order of the presentation of the fields. It can also be used on regular 1-2-3 worksheets when you want to reorganize the sequence in which the columns appear in a printout.

For example, assume your report only requires columns A, C, F, N, P, and X from a larger worksheet, and you'd like the columns to appear in the order P, X, F, N, C, A. You could use the Range Values command to copy the columns in the new order, or you could turn the worksheet into a database, extract the columns with the field names in the desired order, and print the results. Using the Data Extract command is faster for a large number of columns, and it has the added advantage that you can easily repeat the operation whenever the numbers in your spreadsheet change and you want to make a new printout.

If necessary, insert one or more rows at the top of your spreadsheet. Then, in the row immediately above the table, enter letters or, better yet, descriptive field names. Continue and create the criteria range by copying the field names to an unused portion of your spreadsheet or to another sheet. Finally, enter the output range field names in the order you want the extracted columns to appear.

Define your entire worksheet (including the field names) as your input range. Then specify the criteria range by specifying the criteria range field names and a *blank* row. The blank row accepts all records and extracts everything in each column. Finally, specify the output range and select Extract.

Remember, that only values and not formulas or functions are copied to the output range. Extracting a worksheet to reorder its columns destroys the structure behind the worksheet. But this is not a problem if you do the extraction just before you print the worksheet. Be sure to keep a copy

Figure 9–19   You can rearrange the order of the columns in the output range by rearranging the order of the field names.

	A	B	C	D	E	F	G	H
27								
28				************CRITERIA RANGE*****************				
29	PLAYER'S NAME		YEARS	GAMES	AT BATS	RUNS	HITS	AVERAGE
30					+E7>8500			
31								
32								
33				************OUTPUT RANGE*****************				
34	NAME	PLAYER'S	AVERAGE	RUNS	HITS	GAMES	AT BATS	YEARS
35	Cobb	Ty	0.367	2,244	4,191	3,033	11,429	24
36	Keeler	Willie	0.345	1,720	2,955	2,124	8,564	19
37	Speaker	Tris	0.344	1,881	3,515	2,789	10,208	22
38								
39								
40								

THE DATA QUERY UNIQUE COMMAND

of the worksheet with its formulas and functions intact in a file elsewhere on the same worksheet or on another sheet in a stack.

The Data Query Unique command works like the Extract command just discussed, except that when two records would result in identical output only one copy is extracted into the output range and the records are sorted in ascending order based on the content of the leftmost field.

For the Batting Leaders database, for example, you might want to know which batting averages are represented by the players. (Note that several players share various averages.) To get this information, define the output range field names to be only the field named Average. Be sure there is only a blank row in the criteria range so that all of the records in the database are selected. Then use the Unique command. The result is one and only one copy of each unique batting average and one copy of the double dashes (equal signs), which are also an entry in the Average field. Figure 9-20 shows the result.

Note that the Unique command also extracted one copy of the dashed lines at the top of the database. The Unique command can be used to obtain a list of states or cities represented in an address database or to obtain a unique list of field names as part of the input to a Data Table.

Figure 9-20   Result of Data Query Unique command.

```
| A              B        C         D        E      F     G     H     |
|29|
|30|                      ************CRITERIA RANGE****************
|31|  PLAYER'S NAME       YEARS    GAMES   AT BATS   RUNS   HITS  AVERAGE
|32|
|33|
|34|
|35|                      ************OUTPUT RANGE*****************
|36|  AVERAGE
|37|  =========
|38|    0.340
|39|    0.341
|40|    0.342
|41|    0.343
|42|    0.344
|43|    0.345
|44|    0.355
|45|    0.356
|46|    0.358
|47|    0.367
|48|
```

THE DATA QUERY MODIFY COMMAND

Data Query Modify is a new Lotus 1-2-3 Release 3 command. It enables you to add records to an existing database or to extract a set of records, modify them, and then return the modified records to the database. See Figure 9–21 for the command tree.

As for the other Data Query commands, you must have an input range (the database), a criteria range, and an output range to use Data Query Modify. Because the command is a database maintenance command, these ranges have probably been created for other database purposes. You simply appropriate them for use with the Modify command.

There are, however, some restrictions. The Data Query Modify command only works with a single input range. If you have multiple tables, the Modify command can only be used with one of them at a time. If you are using the Modify command to insert new records, the output range *must* be specified as a rectangle. If you are using it to Extract and Replace, you can specify a single row output range. Also, *do not* create the output range under the input range if you are going to use Modify to insert records into the input range. If you do, the insertion writes over the output range. Again, the best approach is to place the input and output ranges on separate sheets.

Once you have the ranges, you are ready to use the command.

Figure 9–21   Data Query Modify command tree.

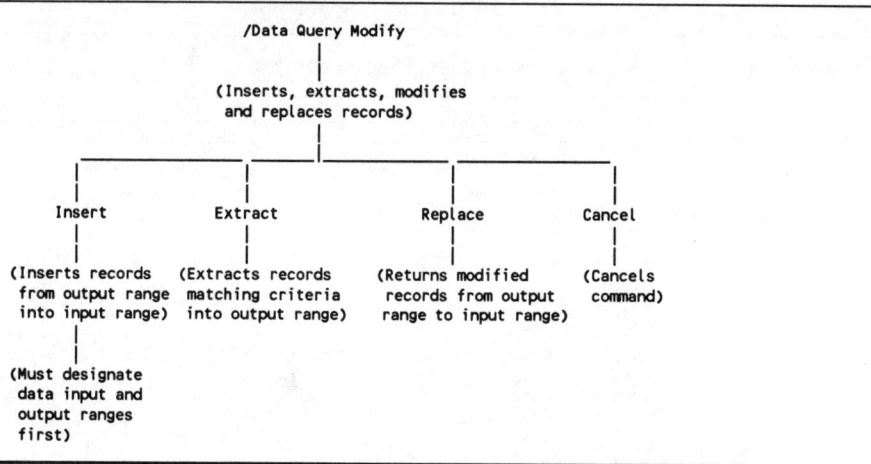

Inserting New Records

Perhaps the most powerful use of the Modify command is to insert new records in an existing database. From the Ready mode, enter the records to be inserted below the appropriate field names in the output range. You don't need to worry about the criteria range. It isn't relevant to the Modify Insert command.

To use the Modify Insert command, begin by selecting the Data Query command and type

/DQ   Enters the Data Query command. If necessary, specify the input range and the output range.

M   Selects Modify.

I   Selects Insert. Command executes and records in the output range are inserted into the input range.

Q   Returns to Ready mode.

The new records are added to the specified database below the existing records. The size of the input range is adjusted to accommodate the larger number of records. If the input range has been sorted, you must re-sort it to place the new records in their proper order.

Modifying Existing Records

The Data Query Modify Extract and Replace commands are what you need when you are modifying a group of records from a database. Before you enter the command, specify the criteria that selects the records you are interested in modifying. Then begin by typing

/DQ   Enters the Data Query command. If necessary, specify the input range, the criteria range, and the output range.

M   Selects Modify.

E   Selects Extract. The command executes and the records meeting the criteria are copied to the output range.

Q   Returns to Ready mode.

Note that you must select Quit (or press **ESC** several times) to return to the Ready mode. There you can use any of the tools at your disposal to modify the records in the output range. You can use the **EDIT/F2** key to edit entries, or you can retype them. You can completely erase entries or use the Worksheet Delete Row command to delete them. You can even replace existing information in a record to construct an entirely new record. However, don't add a new record below the extracted records. Use the Modify Insert command to add records to an existing database.

When you have finished modifying the records in the output range, type

/DQM   Enters the Data Query Modify command.

R   Selects Replace.

When you select Replace, the modified records are read back into the database, where they replace the previous records.

Canceling the Data Query Modify Command

To cancel the Modify command without updating the records in the input range, select Data Query Modify Cancel. This cancels the command and causes 1-2-3 to forget where the records in the output range came from. Use the Cancel command whenever you perform a Modify Extract command and discover that the criteria used were incorrect. Alternatively, change the criteria and select Modify Extract to replace the previous records with records that meet the new criteria.

THE DATABASE STATISTICAL FUNCTIONS

Lotus has seven special built-in statistical functions for use with databases. They are listed in Table 9–2. The functions are designated as database functions by a *D* before the function name (such as @DSUM). They perform the same type of statistical operation (summation, for example) as the regular built-in functions. The difference is that the database statistical functions only operate on designated fields in those records selected by your criteria.

For example, in the Batting Leaders database you can have @DSUM calculate the total number of hits by players who have played 15 or more seasons. Or you can have @DMAX find the player with the highest batting average among those players who have played less than 18 years and who have played in more than 1600 games. You can also use the database statistical functions to create tables of statistics on the selected records.

THE DATABASE COMMANDS

Table 9–2 Database statistical functions, each with three arguments: the location of the input range, the offset, and the location of the criteria range.

Function	Description
@DAVG	Averages values in the offset field of selected records
@DCOUNT	Counts number of nonblank cells in the offset field of selected records
@DGET	Returns the current value or string in a field
@DMAX	Finds maximum value in the offset field of selected records
@DMIN	Finds minimum value in the offset field of selected records
@DQUERY	Performs a function from an external database
@DSTD	Calculates standard deviation of values in the offset field of selected records
@DSTDS	Calculates standard deviation of sample values in the offset field of selected records
@DSUM	Sums values in the offset field of selected records
@DVAR	Calculates variance of values in the offset field of selected records
@DVARS	Calculates sample variance of values in the offset field of selected records

The database statistical functions can also be combined with the Data Table command discussed in Chapter 8 to produce Data Tables where several successive criteria are used to select the records. An example of these functions is presented in the Hands On section at the end of this chapter.

Using Database Statistical Functions

Database statistical functions are used much like their nondatabase counterparts, except that you must supply *three* separate pieces of information.

(Note that each of the three arguments is separated from the others by a comma.)

A typical database statistical function has the form

@FUNCTION NAME *(input range, offset, criteria range)*

You are already familiar with the input range and the criteria range. They have exactly the same meaning here as they do when used with other Data Query commands. The input range is the database (including the field names) and the criteria range is the range of cells containing field names and the criteria established for querying a particular input range.

The new piece of information required by the database statistical functions is the *offset*. An offset is how you specify the column containing the fields for which you want the statistics calculated. Lotus designates the leftmost column in the input range as offset 0, the second column as offset 1, the third, offset 2, and so on.

Figure 9–22 shows the offsets for the Batting Leaders database at the top of the input range, row 7. When specifying an offset number, remember to begin counting at zero with the leftmost column of the input range. Other than the need to specify the input range, the offset, and the criteria range, the database statistical functions can be used like any other built-in function.

A typical database statistical function is

@DAVG(A8..H25,3,A29..H30)

When linked with the All-Time Batting Leaders database, this function calculates and displays the average number of games played by players who met whatever criteria you've established.

Figure 9–22 "Offset" in a database statistical function is the column containing the fields on which the function operates. The first column in the input range is offset zero.

```
|   A       A           B           C         D         E        F       G       H     |
|1 |
|2 |                            ALL-TIME BATTING LEADERS
|3 |                               Ten or more seasons
|4 |
|5 |                     OFFSET is given by number above field name
|6 |
|7 |        0           1           2         3         4        5       6       7
|8 |    PLAYER'S NAME               YEARS   GAMES    AT BATS   RUNS    HITS  AVERAGE
|9 |    ===============================================================================
|10|         Ty Cobb                 24     3,033    11,429   2,244   4,191   0.367
|11|      Rogers Hornsby             23     2,256     8,173   1,576   2,930   0.358
|12|       Joe Jackson               13     1,330     4,981     873   1,772   0.356
|13|      Pete Browning              13     1,180     4,839     867   1,716   0.355
```

You will find, however, that it's much easier to use range names, as in @DAVG($INPUT,3,$CRITERIA), than the range addresses in this function example. Whenever you are basing several database statistical functions on the same input and criteria ranges, simplify your task by naming the appropriate ranges.

Database statistical functions can be copied with the Copy command, but if you do intend to copy one of the functions, be sure to designate the input and criteria ranges as absolute; otherwise, they adjust when the copies are made. You must do this regardless of whether you are using range names or cell addresses to specify the ranges.

Just like any other built-in functions, the database statistical functions recalculate whenever a change that affects the value of the function takes place. This even includes changes in the criteria and in the criteria range referred to by the database statistical function. Of course, when recalculation is set to Manual, the functions only recalculate when you press the **CALC/F9** key.

Database Statistical Functions in Action

Figure 9–23 contains several database statistical functions. The function is displayed as text immediately to the right of the cell containing the function. Note the use of absolute range names in the functions.

THE DATA DISTRIBUTION COMMAND

The Data Distribution command is used to create a count of values falling within specified ranges in a distribution. This count is called a *frequency distribution*; it is often graphed as a bar graph. See Figure 9–24 for the command tree.

The command requires you to specify two ranges. The first is the *bin range*. It is a range you construct, and it is where the output of the Data Distribution command is written. The second is the *values range*. It is the range of cells containing the values to be tallied into the bin range by the Data Distribution command.

Constructing the Bin Range

Assume you'd like to create the frequency distribution for the At Bats column data from the information in the Batting Leaders database. The

Figure 9-23 The database statistical functions at the bottom of this table calculate the specified statistics for those records selected by the criteria in the criterion range.

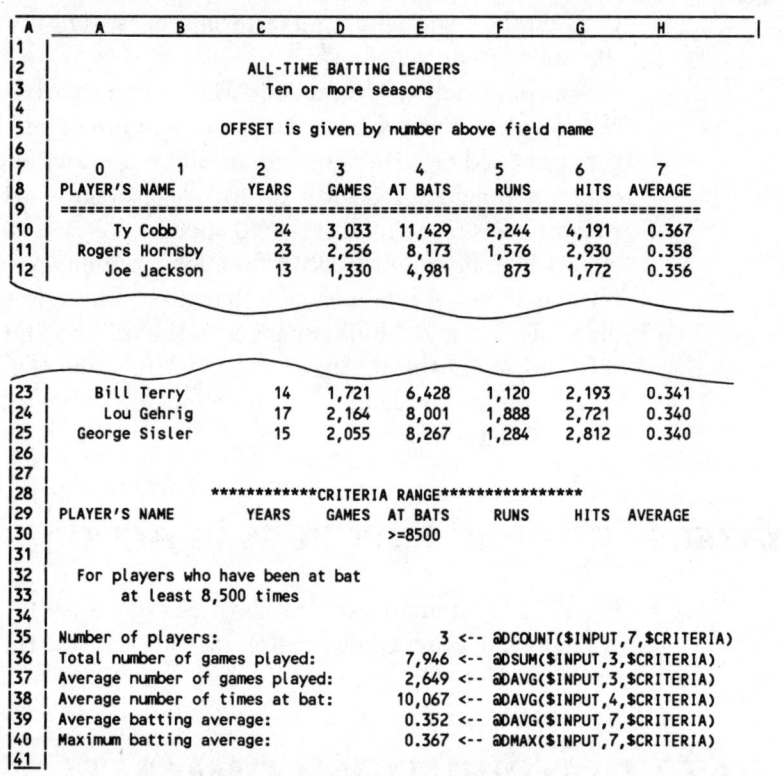

Figure 9-24 Data Distribution command tree.

THE DATABASE COMMANDS

first step in using the Data Distribution command is to construct the bin range.

The bin range is a column of values that determines the intervals into which the numbers from the At Bats field will be counted. It is called the *bin range* because each number serves as a "bin" into which to count the values.

The values that define the bins must be in strictly increasing order. If the intervals in the bin range are regular (as they often are), you can use the Data Fill command to specify them.

You must leave a blank column of cells immediately to the right of the bin range. Furthermore, these blank cells must extend one row below the last value in the bin range. This column of cells is where Lotus places the "count." The last cell (the one below the last cell in the bin range) is where 1-2-3 places the count for all values that are larger than the largest value in the bin range. All values smaller than the smallest value in the bin range (the value in the first cell) are counted in the first cell. See Figure 9–25 for an example of the bin and count ranges for the Data Distribution command.

The labels in rows 5 through 9 in Figure 9–25 are not required by the command, but have been entered to make the results easier to understand.

Figure 9–25 Data Distribution command used to generate a frequency distribution of the At Bats field in the Batting Leaders database.

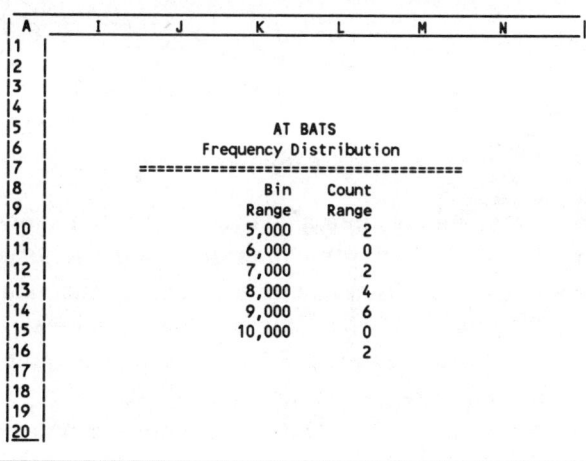

Using the Data Distribution Command

Once you have specified the values in the bin range, you are ready to use the Data Distribution command. To obtain a distribution of the At Bats field in the All-Time Batting Leaders database, begin by typing

/DD	Enters the Data Distribution command.
Enter values range:	Asks for the range of cells containing values to be counted.
Arrow keys	Position the cursor on cell E10 in the Batting Leaders database (first cell of At Bats field).
.	Tacks the cursor to cell E10.
Arrow keys	Highlight the range E10..E25.
ENTER	Accepts E10..E25 as the values range.
Enter bin range:	Asks for the range containing the bins.
Arrow keys	Position the cursor on cell K10 (first cell of the bin range).
.	Tacks the cursor to cell K10.
Arrow keys	Highlight the range K10..K16.
ENTER	Accepts K10..K16 as the bin range and executes the Data Distribution command, returning you to the Ready mode. (See Figure 9–25 for the results.)

Lotus remembers the values range and bin range so you can easily repeat the Data Distribution operation. You can, for example, change the intervals in the bin range and then recount the values into different intervals. Should you need to, the bin range can be expanded or contracted with the Worksheet Insert and Delete commands and with the Move command, or the bin range can be respecified.

An obvious use of the Data Distribution command is to create a frequency distribution, which is then graphed to create a histogram. Chapter 11 shows how to construct 1-2-3 graphs, but it should come as no surprise that the range of cells into which the count is placed can be used as the input range for a bar graph. You can also use the numbers in the bin range as the labels for the bars.

THE DATABASE COMMANDS

HANDS ON: USING THE DATA COMMAND

Many of the Data command features—input range, criteria range, data tables, and database statistical functions—can be combined to perform powerful data summary and analysis functions.

Figure 9-26 contains a small database of expense records. Each row contains an entry for the month, the person, and the expense. In the current form of the database, it is difficult to tell what expenses have been incurred by each person each month. The information would be easier to understand and use if it were summarized as a table. The summary is particularly useful when there are hundreds of records in the database.

A data table can be used to obtain the desired summary statistics. Chapter 8 explained the application of data tables to regular 1-2-3 worksheets. From that discussion, you know that a data table works by substituting successive entries from the data table into specified cells (input cells). Lotus then recalculates the worksheet and displays the results in the data table. (See the discussion in Chapter 8 for the details of constructing and using data tables.)

Data tables can be constructed for use with databases, but instead of substituting successive values, the data table can substitute successive *criteria*. The criteria can be values or, as in the following example, labels. Database statistical functions can then be used to calculate summary statistics for those records selected by each criteria.

Figure 9-26 Sample database of expenses by person and month for June, July, and August.

	A	B	C	D	E	F	G
1							
2	***INPUT RANGE***					**CRITERIA RANGE**	
3	Month	Person	Expenses			Month	Person
4	============================						
5	June	Jones	$36.15				
6	July	Smith	$29.54				
7	August	Jones	$15.47				
8	July	Smith	$161.00				
9	June	Smith	$115.31				
10	August	Smith	$87.69				
11	August	Jones	$13.45				
12	June	Smith	$251.78				
13	July	Jones	$0.36				
14	July	Jones	$147.98				
15	August	Smith	$36.25				
16	June	Smith	$12.54				
17	June	Jones	$98.73				
18	August	Smith	$64.12				
19	July	Jones	$91.54				
20	July	Jones	$125.79				
21							
22							
23							

Constructing the Data Table

Figure 9–27 shows a Two-Way Data Table constructed to the right of the database. From the discussion of data tables, recall that the formula to be evaluated in each cell of a Two-Way table is entered into the upper left cell of the data table range. In Figure 9–27, the cell is E10. The formula in E10 is @DSUM(A3..C20,2,F3..G4). Also recall that the first argument of the @DSUM function is the location of the input range. The next argument is the offset, which is the column in the input range to be summed. Finally, the last argument is the location of the criteria range.

The entries in the first column of the data table—June, July, and August—are the three months for which expense records have been collected, whereas the entries in row 10—Smith and Jones—are the salespersons. When the data table is calculated, labels for the months are substituted into cell F4 and those for the persons into G4 of the criteria range.

Using the Data Table

Once the database, criteria range, and data table have been constructed, position the cursor on cell E10 (in Figure 9–27) and type

Figure 9–27 A Two-Way Data Table used to summarize expenses for each month for each person in the input range.

```
| A      A         B        C         D      E         F         G         H        |
|1 |
|2 |         ***INPUT RANGE***                     **CRITERIA RANGE**
|3 |      Month    Person  Expenses               Month       Person
|4 |      ==========================
|5 |      June     Jones    $36.15
|6 |      July     Smith    $29.54
|7 |      August   Jones    $15.47                ***TWO-WAY DATA TABLE***
|8 |      July     Smith    $161.00                    MONTHLY EXPENSES
|9 |      June     Smith    $115.31
|10|      August   Smith    $87.69      1287.7    Smith       Jones      Totals
|11|      August   Jones    $13.45                June
|12|      June     Smith    $251.78               July
|13|      July     Jones    $0.36                 August
|14|      July     Jones    $147.98
|15|      August   Smith    $36.25                Total
|16|      June     Smith    $12.54
|17|      June     Jones    $98.73
|18|      August   Smith    $64.12       Formula in cell E10: @DSUM(A3..C20,2,F3..G4)
|19|      July     Jones    $91.54
|20|      July     Jones    $125.79
|21|
|22|
|23|
```

/DT	Enters the Data Table command.
2	Selects a Two-Way Data Table.
Input cell 1:	Asks for cell in which to substitute labels from left-hand column of data table (Months).
Arrow keys	Point to cell F3 in criteria range.
ENTER	Sets input cell 1 as F3.
Input Cell 2:	Asks for cell in which to substitute labels from top row of data table (Persons).
Arrow keys	Point to cell G3 in criteria range.
ENTER	Sets input cell 2 as G3 and executes Data Table command.

Each cell in the data table is at the intersection of a name and a month; therefore, the value in that cell shows the total expenses claimed by each person for each month—just the information you were looking for.

Note that the value displayed in cell E10 is the value of the formula @DSUM(A3..C20,2,F3..G4) when both cells in the criteria range are blank. Further, recall that the value displayed in the upper left cell is the value for the formula evaluated under the entries that have been made into the input cells on the worksheet—not the values that are substituted into those cells by executing the Data Table command. If you wish, you can suppress the display of this value using the Range Format Hidden command on cell E10. See Figure 9–28 for the completed Data Table.

The totals in column H and in row 15 that provide total expenses by month and by person are calculated by the familiar @SUM functions.

Extensions

The Two-Way Data Table just described can be used as a model for other combinations of data tables and database statistical functions. Substitute the @DAVG or @DMAX function in cell E10 for the @DSUM function, and you have the average monthly expenditure or the maximum monthly expenditure for each person for each month.

If you wanted these figures for each person over all three months, you could have the information by constructing a One-Way Data Table. The persons' names would be entered into the cells in the first column, and the required database statistical functions would be entered into the appropriate cells of the first row.

In the example the names and the months were entered directly. You could also use the Data Query Unique command to extract copies of each

Figure 9–28 Completed data table.

```
      A          B         C       D       E          F          G          H
 1
 2         ***INPUT RANGE***               **CRITERIA RANGE**
 3     Month    Person   Expenses          Month     Person
 4     ============================
 5     June     Jones    $36.15
 6     July     Smith    $29.54
 7     August   Jones    $15.47                    ***TWO-WAY DATA TABLE***
 8     July     Smith    $161.00                        MONTHLY EXPENSES
 9     June     Smith    $115.31
10     August   Smith    $87.69          1287.7      Smith      Jones     Totals
11     August   Jones    $13.45           June      $379.63    $134.88    $514.51
12     June     Smith    $251.78          July      $190.54    $365.67    $556.21
13     July     Jones    $0.36            August    $188.06    $28.92     $216.98
14     July     Jones    $147.98
15     August   Smith    $36.25           Total     $758.23    $529.47   $1,287.70
16     June     Smith    $12.54
17     June     Jones    $98.73
18     August   Smith    $64.12         Formula in cell E10: @DSUM(A3..C20,2,F3..G4)
19     July     Jones    $91.54
20     July     Jones    $125.79
21
22
23
```

month and each name in your database. The months could then be copied into the left-hand column of the data table. The Range Transpose command could be used to copy and transpose the names into the top row of the data table.

Conclusions

Data tables used with databases are as easy to construct as the data tables used with regular electronic spreadsheets. In conjunction with database statistical functions, data tables become powerful tools for expanding the analysis and presentation of information stored in 1-2-3 databases.

Remember to use the Copy command to enter the criteria in the appropriate cells of the data table. As for all criteria, 1-2-3 considers spelling, punctuation, and leading and trailing blanks when searching for matches. The only way to be sure the criteria you specify in the data table are the same as the entries in the database is to use the Copy command to copy them from the database to the cells of the data table.

TIPS & TRAPS

Tips

Editing Found Records.
Once you have found a record with the Data Find command, use the **RIGHT** and **LEFT** arrow keys to position the flashing underline character on the cell in the record you want to edit. Then press the **EDIT/F2** key to edit the record. Press either the **UP** or **DOWN** arrow key to move to another matching record or press **ENTER** to leave the Find command.

Leaving the Cursor on a Found Record.
When you use the **QUERY/F7** key to perform the Find command from the Ready mode, you can leave the cursor on the found record and return to the Ready mode by pressing the **QUERY/F7** key a second time. If you press the **ENTER** key, the cursor is returned to its location before you originally pressed the **QUERY/F7** key.

Sorting Formulas: Relative References and Absolute References.
You won't have any trouble sorting records containing formulas as long as the formulas only contain references to cells in the record containing the formula or to cells entirely outside of the database. References to cells in the record must be relative; references to cells outside the database must be absolute.

In general, do not sort records containing formulas that refer to cells in the database that are not in the record containing the formula. If you do, the formula in its newly sorted location typically refers to the wrong cells.

Use the Range Format Text Command to See Your Relative Criteria.
Relative criteria evaluate to either 0 or 1. To see the criteria rather than a 0 or 1, format the cells in the criteria range with the Range Format Text command. This format displays on the screen the content of each cell, not the result of the formula.

Traps

The Nonempty "Empty" Cell.
Some people are in the habit of using the SPACE BAR to insert a space character to "erase" a cell. In general this is a bad technique, and you must never do it in a criteria range. The "blank" cell actually contains a criterion, the space character. It doesn't display, so the cell appears empty, but 1-2-3 only matches records that have a space character in the designated field.

Always use the Range Erase command to remove unneeded criteria from the criteria range.

The Dangers of Multiple-Row Field Names.
The database field names must be in the single top row of the data range. You can get longer, more descriptive field names by stacking them in several rows at the top of the database, but remember, 1-2-3 uses only the single row at the top of the data range.

If you use this technique, be careful not to inadvertently create two identical field names. For example, stacking **First Name** and **Last Name** into two rows puts **First** and **Last** in the first row and **Name** and **Name** in the second row. The second row is actually the row containing the field names—which are identical.

Relative Criteria Don't Work.
The formulas you use to specify relative criteria must refer to cells in the record immediately below the row containing the database field names. If your criteria do not refer to cells in this row, make the reference absolute.

Try replacing your formula with the short form for specifying relative criteria. For example, type >**16** instead of the formula +C7>16. When you use the short form, 1-2-3 always applies it to the correct cell.

If your criteria still won't work, try relaxing the boundaries of the selection. It is possible that your criteria are so restrictive that none of the records in your database meet them.

10 Multiple Input Ranges and External Databases

OBJECTIVES

After mastering the content of this chapter, you will be able to

☐ construct and use databases with multiple input ranges.

☐ use a key field to join two or more input ranges.

☐ use the Data External command to connect to and use an external database.

☐ use the Data External command to create a new table in an external database.

INTRODUCTION

In the last chapter you learned how to use 1-2-3's Data commands to construct, sort, query, and modify a spreadsheet database. In that chapter all of your databases were single-table databases where the input, output, and criteria ranges all resided on 1-2-3 worksheets. In this chapter, you extend your knowledge of 1-2-3's database commands to include systems of databases made up of two or more input ranges and to the use of external databases constructed by standalone database programs such as R:BASE, Paradox, or dBASE III, dBASE III Plus, or dBASE IV.

These are advanced topics, so before you begin learning about them you must have read and understood the material in Chapter 9. In particular, you must be familiar with the concepts of records and fields in a 1-2-3 database. You must also be comfortable with the specification of different types of criteria in the criteria range and the specification and purpose of the output range. If you need additional information about any of these concepts, review the material in Chapter 9.

The first part of this chapter deals with the topic of using multiple input ranges (databases) with the Data Query Extract and Data Query Unique commands. These are the only database commands that can use multiple input ranges. The second part deals with the Data External command, which is used to access, query, manage, and create external databases in conjunction with standalone database programs.

USING MULTIPLE INPUT RANGES

As you know, the database feature in 1-2-3 is made up of three elements: the input range; the criteria range; and, for those commands that extract information from a database, the output range. In the input range, each column is a field and each row is a record. The top row contains input range field names that label each field and that are used extensively in the database commands. (See Figure 9–3 for the general structure of all 1-2-3 input ranges.)

In many situations, a single input range (or database) is all that is needed. In other situations, two or more input ranges can greatly improve the maintenance and management of database information. For example, if you have a database of invoices of sales to customers, you could include in each record all of the information you have about each customer. This might include a full address, contact name, telephone number or numbers, notes, special shipping or handling requirements, and possibly several other pieces of information. This information would have to be repeated each time a sale was made to a particular customer, so the information might appear many times in your invoice database. Approaching database construction in this way adds many fields to the database, involves multiple entries of the same information, and, in general, makes the sales database more difficult to understand and use.

An alternative way is to create two different databases (or input ranges). One can contain the information about your customers where each customer's data occupies only one record. The other can contain the information about the sale, which includes one field that identifies the customer. The customer identifier could be the customer's name, a code number, or an abbreviation. The customer field takes up very little space in the sales database, but it enables you to join the information in the customer database to information in the sales database. The result is access to all of the information in the single-table database, but with the economy and elegance of smaller, easier-to-use tables. A group of related tables is often called a *relational* database, because information in each table relates to information in other tables and because one query can be used to extract information from several related tables at one time.

To understand how 1-2-3 uses multiple tables and to highlight the crucial concepts involved, it is useful to work through a very simple example. Figure 10-1 contains two databases: Numbers and Letters. Each database contains only one field, and each field contains only three records. In Figure 10-1 a criteria range and an output range have also been constructed. The input range, the criteria range, and the output range have been assigned range names with the Range Name Create command.

The Implied Database

When two or more input ranges are specified for use with the Extract or Unique commands the result is an "implied database table" or "implied database," for short. The database is "implied" in the sense that you can form a mental picture of the fields and records in this database even though the database table really doesn't exist. Most importantly, the criteria you specify are applied against the records in the implied database.

The records in the implied database are made up of *all possible* combinations of the records from the specified input ranges. The resulting number of records grows very quickly to very large numbers. For example, the implied database made up of the Numbers and Letters databases in

Figure 10-1   Two simple databases used to create an implied database.

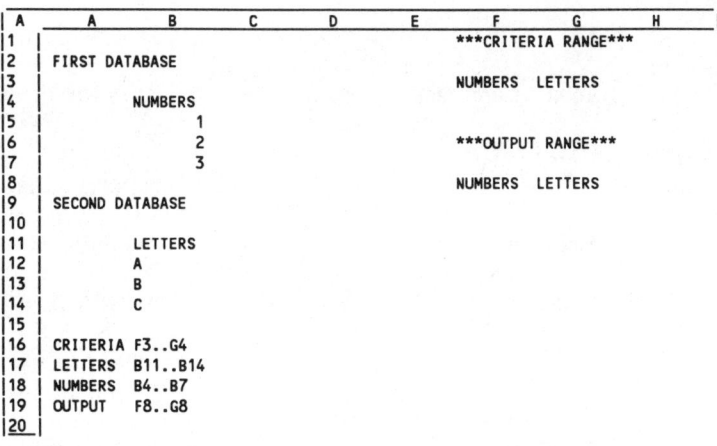

Figure 10-1 has nine records (3 × 3). If there were 10 records in each database, the resulting implied database would have 100 records. If you are using three databases, each with 100 records, the implied database associated with those 300 records in the three databases is 100 × 100 × 100, or 1,000,000 records!

It is easy to view the database that is implied when you use two or more databases, though you may not have enough space to write the records to a spreadsheet with *only* 8192 rows. To generate the implied database, all you need to do is use all of the field names from all of the input ranges as your output range field names. Then specify a blank criteria range. This selects *all* of the records in the implied database and writes them to the output range.

If you have a computer handy, create the spreadsheet shown in Figure 10-1 and actually perform the exercises described here. Once you have created the table in Figure 10-1, to generate the implied database for the two input ranges, type

/DQ	Selects the Data Query command.
Input	Selects Input to specify the input ranges.
Enter input range:	Asks for the input ranges.
NUMBERS,LETTERS	Type the name of each input range. Separate the ranges with a comma.
ENTER	Accepts the input ranges.
C	Selects Criteria.
Enter criteria range:	Asks for the criteria range.
CRITERIA	Type the name assigned to the criteria range.
ENTER	Accepts criteria range.
Output	Asks for the output range.
OUTPUT	Type the name assigned to the output range.
ENTER	Accepts the output range.

MULTIPLE INPUT RANGES AND EXTERNAL DATABASES

E	Selects Extract to extract all records from the implied database.
Quit	Returns to the Ready mode.

Note: An easier way to specify the named ranges in the preceding example is to press the **NAME/F3** key each time you are prompted for a range. Then highlight the appropriate range name and press **ENTER** to paste it into the command. When you specify the two input ranges, be sure to type the comma that separates one input range from the other.

The result of applying a blank criteria range when both the Numbers and Letters databases are specified as input ranges appears in Figure 10–2. This is the implied database, and, as promised, it contains nine records, 1A, 2A, and so forth, which are all of the possible combinations of the three fields (1, 2, 3 and A, B, C) from the two input ranges.

When you enter a criterion after both input ranges have been specified, you are, in essence, applying the criterion against the implied database in Figure 10–2. To see how this works, enter a 1 under Numbers in the criteria range and press the **QUERY/F7** key. The result appears in Figure 10–3.

Note that three records from the implied database meet the criterion. To select a single record from the implied database you must specify a criterion under each of the field names in the criteria range. With this qualification firmly in mind, you can specify any of the different types of

Figure 10–2 The implied database.

```
| B    E        F        G       H     |
|1  |          ***CRITERIA RANGE***
|2  |
|3  |          NUMBERS  LETTERS
|4  |
|5  |
|6  |          ***OUTPUT RANGE***
|7  |
|8  |          NUMBERS  LETTERS
|9  |             1 A
|10 |             2 A
|11 |             3 A
|12 |             1 B
|13 |             2 B
|14 |             3 B
|15 |             1 C
|16 |             2 C
|17 |             3 C
|18 |
|19 |
|20 |
```

Figure 10–3 Criteria applied against the implied database.

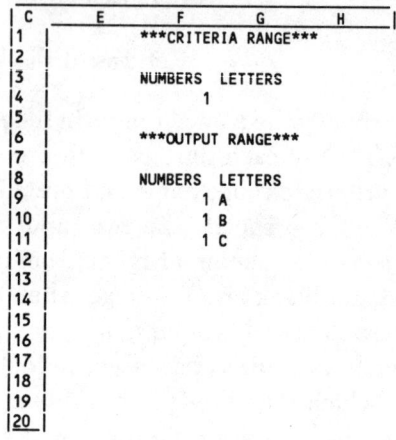

criteria discussed in Chapter 9 against the implied database in order to select the appropriate records.

Joining Input Ranges

The preceding example illustrates how two or more input ranges can be specified to create an implied database that contains every possible combination of the records from each database. The result, unfortunately, contains a great deal of garbage (a pseudotechnical term for *nonsense*), in the sense that the implied database combines completely inappropriate material. To understand this problem and to learn how to overcome it, construct the two simple databases shown in Figure 10–4, the criteria range and the output range. Name the ranges as shown in Figure 10–4.

The criteria range contains only the field name Customer; all that is left to do is to generate the implied database. Repeat the steps described earlier for the implied database to extract all the records from the databases in Figure 10–4. When you are finished, the implied database shown in Figure 10–5 appears.

There are nine records in the implied database in Figure 10–5, because there were three records in each of two original input ranges. Look closely at the records. The first three records are identical through the State field, but after that the Date, Customer, and Amount fields differ for each record. This result occurs because 1-2-3 treats each possible combination

Figure 10-4   Sample databases.

```
   A         B            C           D         E          F          G
1
2         ***ORDERS DATABASE***                ***CRITERIA RANGE***
3
4         DATE      CUSTOMER      AMOUNT      CUSTOMER
5         01-Apr         Tom      $54.32
6         05-Apr        Dick      $24.89
7         07-Apr       Harry      $12.56
8
9        ***CUSTOMER DATABASE***                  ***RANGE NAMES***
10
11   PERSON    STREET        CITY        STATE       CRITERIA    F4..F5
12   Tom       1 North St.   Boston      MA          CUSTOMERS   A11..D14
13   Dick      2 South St.   New York    NY          ORDERS      A4..C7
14   Harry     3 East St.    Berkeley    CA          OUTPUT      A18..G18
15
16                           ***OUTPUT RANGE***
17
18   PERSON    STREET        CITY        STATE       DATE    CUSTOMER   AMOUNT
19
20
```

Figure 10-5   Implied database from the two sample databases in Figure 10-4.

```
     A          B            C          D         E         F         G
15
16                           ***OUTPUT RANGE***
17
18   PERSON     STREET       CITY       STATE    DATE     CUSTOMER   AMOUNT
19   Tom        1 North St.  Boston     MA       01-Apr   Tom        $54.32
20   Tom        1 North St.  Boston     MA       05-Apr   Dick       $24.89
21   Tom        1 North St.  Boston     MA       07-Apr   Harry      $12.56
22   Dick       2 South St.  New York   NY       01-Apr   Tom        $54.32
23   Dick       2 South St.  New York   NY       05-Apr   Dick       $24.89
24   Dick       2 South St.  New York   NY       07-Apr   Harry      $12.56
25   Harry      3 East St.   Berkeley   CA       01-Apr   Tom        $54.32
26   Harry      3 East St.   Berkeley   CA       05-Apr   Dick       $24.89
27   Harry      3 East St.   Berkeley   CA       07-Apr   Harry      $12.56
28
29
```

of a record from the Customer database with *each* record in the Orders database as a record in the implied database.

Nonsense Records

Look at the first three records again. Of those three records, only the first makes any sense. The other two are nonsense because they pair Tom's address with orders for Dick and Harry. Only the first pairs Tom's address with Tom's order. Look at the other two groups of three records. In each, one record pairs a person's address with his order. The other two records in each group are nonsense. The existence of these nonsense records makes using a set of joined input ranges difficult because lots of garbage gets extracted for most criteria.

What you really need is some way to limit the implied database to those records that make analytical sense—in this case, to limit the database to records containing both a person's order and his address. Luckily, there is an easy solution to this problem.

The Key Field

The key to splicing two or more input ranges together in the proper fashion is using a *key field*—a field (or set of fields) in each input range that contains the same information. In the last chapter, the primary key told 1-2-3 how to sort a database. In this chapter, the key field tells 1-2-3 how to join or link one database table to another database table.

Examine the Orders and the Customer databases in Figure 10–4. Notice that the field named Customer in the Orders database contains the same information as the Person field in the Customer database. These are the key fields. (In a moment you'll find out why the same field name wasn't used for both fields.)

To tell 1-2-3 that the Person and Customer fields are the key fields, all you have to do is enter the following formula into any cell in the criteria range:

+CUSTOMER=PERSON

In essence, you are setting a criterion that says to select a record from the implied database *only* if it meets the criterion that the entry in the Customer field of Orders is identical to the entry in the Person field of Customer. With this formula in the criteria range of Figure 10–4, using the Extract command results in the display shown in Figure 10–6.

These are the only records from Figure 10–5 that make any sense. The join formula eliminated the nonsense records, which were those in which one person's address was paired with another person's order.

Figure 10–6 Records selected from implied database after using join formula +CUSTOMER= PERSON.

```
|C       A           B           C           D       E       F           G       |
|15 |
|16 |                           ***OUTPUT RANGE***
|17 |
|18 |    PERSON      STREET      CITY        STATE   DATE    CUSTOMER    AMOUNT
|19 |    Dick        2 South St. New York    NY      05-Apr  Dick        $24.89
|20 |    Harry       3 East St.  Berkeley    CA      07-Apr  Harry       $12.56
|21 |    Tom         1 North St. Boston      MA      01-Apr  Tom         $54.32
|22 |
|23_|
```

MULTIPLE INPUT RANGES AND EXTERNAL DATABASES

In Figure 10-7, several changes have been made to the basic spreadsheet from Figure 10-4. The criteria and output ranges have been moved to a separate sheet. Additional field names have been added to the criteria range, including the entirely bogus field name Join Formula. The join formula (displayed under the Range Format Text) is entered in the cell below this field name. The criteria range (B32..F34) covers the field names and the two additional rows. The field name Customer has been eliminated from the output range, because it duplicates the Person field. To check your understanding of the purpose of these fields, place a sheet of paper over Figure 10-7, uncover a criterion, and try to predict the record or records it selects. Then check your answer.

Figure 10-7 Use of join formula in sample criteria and the records selected.

```
| F        A              B              C          D         E         F       |
|30 |             ***CRITERIA RANGE***
|31 |
|32 |             JOIN FORMULA   AMOUNT     CITY       DATE      PERSON
|33 |             +PERSON=CUSTOMER  HARRY
|34 |
|35 |
|36 |                            ***OUTPUT RANGE***
|37 |
|38 | PERSON         STREET         CITY       STATE     DATE      AMOUNT
|39 |    Harry 3 East St.        Berkeley    CA        07-Apr    $12.56
|40 |
|41 |
```

```
| F        A              B              C          D         E         F       |
|30 |             ***CRITERIA RANGE***
|31 |
|32 |             JOIN FORMULA   AMOUNT     CITY       DATE      PERSON
|33 |             +PERSON=CUSTOMER           B*
|34 |
|35 |
|36 |                            ***OUTPUT RANGE***
|37 |
|38 | PERSON         STREET         CITY       STATE     DATE      AMOUNT
|39 |    Harry 3 East St.        Berkeley    CA        07-Apr    $12.56
|40 |    Tom   1 North St.       Boston      MA        01-Apr    $54.32
|41 |
```

```
| F        A              B              C          D         E         F       |
|30 |             ***CRITERIA RANGE***
|31 |
|32 |             JOIN FORMULA   AMOUNT     CITY       DATE      PERSON
|33 |             +PERSON=CUSTOMER  >25
|34 |
|35 |
|36 |                            ***OUTPUT RANGE***
|37 |
|38 | PERSON         STREET         CITY       STATE     DATE      AMOUNT
|39 |    Tom   1 North St.       Boston      MA        01-Apr    $54.32
|40 |
|41 |
```

The criteria illustrated in Figure 10–7 contain formulas, strings, and so on, and they all establish an AND relationship with the join formula. So far no OR criteria have been established, because no entries have been made into row 34 in the criteria range. In Figure 10–8, an entry has been made into row 34 to establish an OR relationship between the criteria in the second and third rows of the criteria range. When the OR criteria are applied to the input ranges, the result is Figure 10–8.

The criteria are <30 in the amount field in the first row and Tom in the second row. Presumably, the criteria select those records with Tom in the Person field or a number less than 30 in the Amount field. The result is not what was expected. There are three records for Tom, but two of them are the nonsense records that you got before you used the +PERSON=CUSTOMER formula to join the two databases on their key fields.

The problem can be traced to the lack of a join formula in row 34. Without the formula the second criteria (Tom) selects all of the possible combinations of Tom in the Customer database with all of the records in the Orders database. To avoid this problem, include a join formula in *each* row of each criteria you establish. That is, be sure to always establish an AND relationship between each of your criteria and the join formula. See Figure 10–9 for the proper criteria.

Using Identical Field Names

In the previous example, the key field in each database was given a different field name—Customer in the Orders database and Person in the Customer database. This was done to avoid the confusion that would have

Figure 10–8   OR criteria.

```
|F        A              B             C           D         E         F        |
|30 |            ***CRITERIA RANGE***
|31 |
|32 |            JOIN FORMULA   AMOUNT      CITY        DATE      PERSON
|33 |            +PERSON=CUSTOMER <30
|34 |                                                             TOM
|35 |
|36 |                           ***OUTPUT RANGE***
|37 |
|38 | PERSON         STREET        CITY        STATE     DATE      AMOUNT
|39 | Tom         1 North St.      Boston      MA        01-Apr    $54.32
|40 | Tom         1 North St.      Boston      MA        05-Apr    $24.89
|41 | Tom         1 North St.      Boston      MA        07-Apr    $12.56
|42 | Dick        2 South St.      New York    NY        05-Apr    $24.89
|43 | Harry       3 East St.       Berkeley    CA        07-Apr    $12.56
|44 |
|45 |
|46 |
```

Figure 10-9   OR criteria with join formula in each row of criteria range.

```
     A            B              C          D         E         F
|30|              ***CRITERIA RANGE***
|31|
|32|              JOIN FORMULA   AMOUNT     CITY      DATE      PERSON
|33|              +PERSON=CUSTOMER <30
|34|              +PERSON=CUSTOMER                              TOM
|35|
|36|                             ***OUTPUT RANGE***
|37|
|38| PERSON       STREET         CITY       STATE     DATE      AMOUNT
|39| Tom          1 North St.    Boston     MA        01-Apr    $54.32
|40| Dick         2 South St.    New York   NY        05-Apr    $24.89
|41| Harry        3 East St.     Berkeley   CA        07-Apr    $12.56
|42|
|43|
|44|
|45|
```

occurred had the same field name existed in two or more active databases. When such duplicates occur, 1-2-3 displays the error message **Ambiguous field reference in query -- Press HELP (F1)** and refuses to proceed.

There are two ways to avoid this problem. The easiest is to assign unique field names to each field in all of the input ranges you intend to use together. The technique used here was to use synonyms: Person and Customer. Alternatively, each field name can be qualified in some way that makes it unique. For example, CUSTOMER_1 and CUSTOMER_2 can be used as field names in the Orders and Customer input ranges.

Alternatively, you can assign identical field names, but then you *must* include information about the input range whenever you use the field name in either the criteria range or the output range. The technique is to precede the field name with the name assigned to the table and to separate the two with a period. For example, when CUSTOMER is a field name in both databases, you refer to the CUSTOMER field in the Orders input range as ORDERS.CUSTOMER and the CUSTOMER field in the Customer input range as CUSTOMER.CUSTOMER.

Note: When the argument separator is a period (as it often is in European countries) use a comma to separate the table name from the field name. Use the Worksheet Global Default Status command to check the current argument separator. Use the Worksheet Global Default Other International Punctuation command to change the current argument separator.

USING EXTERNAL DATABASES

As you saw in the last chapter 1-2-3's Data command provides many powerful and flexible tools for creating and using spreadsheet-based databases. Earlier in this chapter you learned how two or more input ranges are used to form a relational database. Now you will learn how to use the Data External command to connect to and work with external database tables that have been created by standalone database programs such as dBASE III or R:BASE. This features gives 1-2-3 users instant access to corporate databases created by these programs and maintained on data processing networks. See Figure 10–10 for the Data External command tree.

The Database Driver

Before you can use the Data External commands on a database created by a standalone program you must have the appropriate *database driver*. The database driver is a program that allows 1-2-3 to read data from and send data to external tables. If you do not have the required database driver, you must obtain it from the manufacturer of the database you wish to use. A sample database driver (named SAMPLE) for accessing database tables created with dBASE III is supplied with 1-2-3 Release 3. It is used in the examples throughout the rest of this chapter. Call 1-800-343-5414 during East Coast business hours for an updated list of available database drivers.

Database drivers for other standalone database programs operate in a similar fashion, but you must carefully read the documentation supplied with each driver for information specific to that driver. In addition, if you are using the Data External commands on a network, you may need specific passwords or other "permissions" to use or modify the data-

Figure 10–10 Data External command tree.

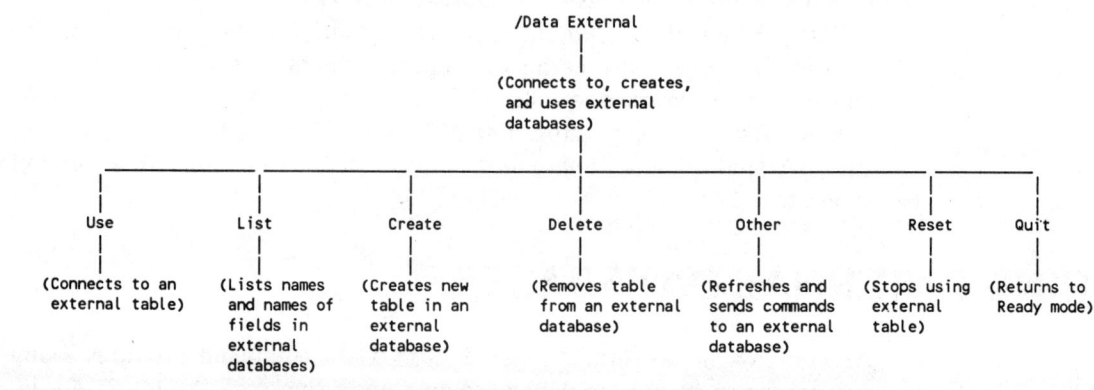

base. Check with the database administrator for additional information about the types of actions permissible for each database you intend to access.

If you are using the database driver on a database you have created that runs only on your microcomputer, you are the database administrator and you will know whether passwords are required for access to your database tables.

Databases, Tables, and External Tables

From earlier discussions of 1-2-3 database commands you know that a database table is made up of rows (records) and columns (fields). Every external database table is also made up of records and fields. You can think of the records and fields as being arranged in rows and columns and as corresponding to the input range for the typical 1-2-3 Data command. However, external databases frequently contain more than one table. Therefore, external databases are often like the multiple input range databases discussed earlier in this chapter. You can use only one of several tables or you can join tables together with join functions in order to create implied tables as described above.

Because external databases usually contain more than one table, *database* is the term used in the rest of this chapter to describe the entire collection of tables; *database table*, *table*, or *input range* describe a single table in a database.

Database Driver Commands

The functions—query, modify, delete, and create—that you can perform on an external table are just like the corresponding actions for a 1-2-3 input range. In fact, after you are connected to the external database, using it is exactly like using an input range stored on a disk. You'll establish a criteria range, specify criteria, and have selected records copied to an output range.

Some actions may not be permitted by the database driver you have, or the action may require special passwords or permissions. For example, with the sample database driver supplied with 1-2-3 you can't delete or modify existing records in an external table, delete the table entirely, or send commands or creation strings to an external table. Consult the documentation that comes with your database driver and consult the database administrator to find out what restrictions, if any, there are on the actions for each database.

Connecting to an External Database

Your first task is to use the Data External Use command to establish a connection between 1-2-3 and the external database. See Figure 10–11 for the command tree.

To use an external table you must have the required database driver, and you must tell 1-2-3 the *full table name* of each external table you wish to use. A full table name contains three parts:

Database driver	The database driver 1-2-3 needs to use the specific database. The driver name is Sample in the following example.
Name of external database	The full pathname into the subdirectory containing the database files. This name is C:\123R3 in the next example.
Owner name	If you are required to supply a password to use a particular table, specify it after the name of the external database (optional).
Name of external table within external database.	You connect to specific tables. Must specify the name of the table within the database. This is EMPFILE in the next example.

Figure 10–11   Data External Use command tree.

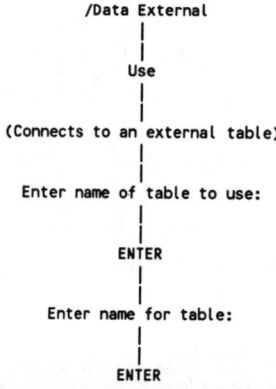

MULTIPLE INPUT RANGES AND EXTERNAL DATABASES

The full table name required to use the dBASE III table EMPFILE.DBF with the Sample database driver when the file is located in the C:\123R3 subdirectory is SAMPLE C:\123R3 EMPFILE. If an owner's name is required, it appears after C:\123R3. When you establish a connection, 1-2-3 prompts you through the creation of the full table name for each table you connect to.

Once you have established a connection to an external database table, you can use it as the input range to Data Query commands and you can extract records from it. You can also modify or delete records, or delete the entire table, provided those actions are allowed by your particular database driver.

Hint: You must tell 1-2-3 the full path to the subdirectory containing the database files. To make specifying the full table name easier, use the File Dir command to make the subdirectory containing the database files the default subdirectory. When you do, 1-2-3 proposes it at the appropriate point in connecting to the database.

To connect to the dBASE III database table named EMPFILE with the Sample driver when the files are in the default subdirectory, C:\123R3, type

/D	Enters the Data command.
E	Selects External.
U	Selects Use.
Enter name of table to use:	Asks for the name of the database driver to use. All available drivers appear at the top of the screen. Unless you have installed additional drivers, Sample is the only name listed.
Arrow keys	Highlight desired database driver.
ENTER	Selects Sample.
C:\123R3	You must provide the full pathname into the subdirectory containing the tables you are going to use. The current default subdirectory is displayed.
ENTER	Selects C:\123R3.
EMPFILE	Names of tables in C:\123R3 that can be used with the driver Sample appear in the control panel. Unless you have additional dBASE III files in the C:\123R3 subdirectory, only the sample file EMPFILE appears.

ENTER	To accept EMPFILE.
Enter range name for table: **EMPFILE**	You must assign a range name to each external table. Proposes name of external table as range name. Accept or change it. You *must* change the name if it has already been used or looks like a cell address (such as FY89). Lotus doesn't display a default range name when the external table name begins with a $ or an !, or contains a period (.).
ENTER	Accepts EMPFILE as range name for external table. Completes connection and returns to Data External menu.

Repeat the previous steps for each external table you wish to connect to with the Data External command. Remember, you can use the **NAME/F3** key to get a full-screen display of driver names and table names whenever they are displayed.

When you are asked to assign a range name to the external table, 1-2-3 proposes you use the name of the file containing the external table. If possible, accept it to maintain a close connection between the range name and the underlying external table. After connecting to the external table, you always refer to the table by its range name whenever you use the table in a Data Query command, in a database statistical function, or with a data table.

You can't use the proposed range name when it has already been used as a range name in the current file or when it would be confused with a cell address. In that case, assign a name that is close to the filename so you can maintain a close connection between the two. For example, if the external table is in a file named BUDGET and that name has already been used in the current file, use a name like BUDGET_DB to maintain the connection between the external table and its range name. Also, when the filename of an external database file begins with a dollar sign ($) or an exclamation point (!), or contains a period (.), 1-2-3 does not propose a range name. Again, select your own range name and make it as close to the filename as possible.

Data External List

You can use the Data External List command before connecting to a table to discover the names of the tables in the current subdirectory that can be used with a particular database driver. If you don't have a list, the first

MULTIPLE INPUT RANGES AND EXTERNAL DATABASES

thing you want to do after connecting to an external database is use the External List command to list the tables in the external database and the fields in each table. See Figure 10–12 for the command tree.

Data External List Tables

To get a list of the tables in the Sample database you must supply the name of the database driver and the name of the database. Type

/DE	Enters the Data External command.
Tables Fields	Select Tables.
Enter name of database whose tables are to be listed:	Asks for database driver name. Driver names are displayed on the screen. If necessary, supply full path to subdirectory containing database.
Arrow keys	Highlight SAMPLE.
ENTER	Select SAMPLE.

Figure 10–12 Data External List command tree.

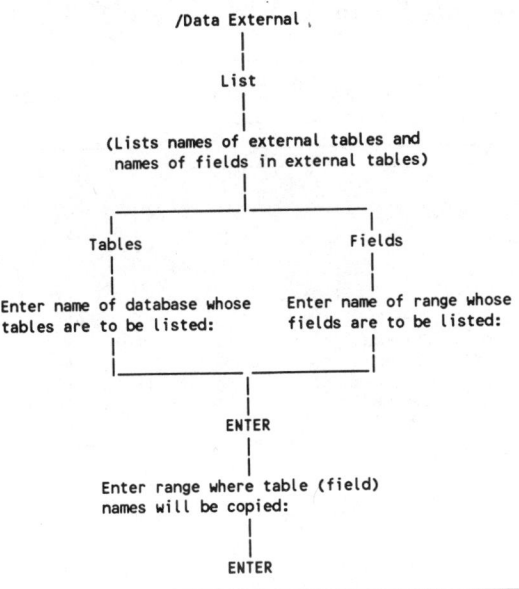

Enter range where table names will be copied:	Asks for location on sheet where information can be tabled.
Arrow keys	Move cursor to A3, the location where a three-column table can be written. Number of rows in table corresponds to number of tables in database.
ENTER	Executes the List Tables command. Leaves program in Data External menu.

The External List Tables command lists all database tables of the type supported by the specified driver in the specified subdirectory. See rows 3 and 4 in Figure 10–13. In addition to the EMPFILE.DBF file, it also contains a .DBF file named EXPORTER, which is listed below EMPFILE.

The table contains two columns. The first column contains the filename of the table. When the particular external database includes table descriptions, they are listed in the second column. When no table description is included (as in the example in Figure 10–13) **NA** is displayed. Remember, you can use the External List Tables command to find out which database files are in a particular subdirectory even when you haven't connected to any external database tables.

Data External List Fields

The External List Fields command lists only the fields in those tables that have been attached to 1-2-3 by the Data External Use command. Because

Figure 10–13   Result of using Data External List Tables and List Fields on EMPFILE.

	A	B	C	D	E	F
1						
2						
3	EMPFILE	NA				
4	EXPORTER	NA				
5						
6						
7						
8	EMPID	Numeric	5,0	NA	NA	NA
9	LASTNAME	Character	12	NA	NA	NA
10	FIRSTNAME	Character	12	NA	NA	NA
11	DOH	Date	8	NA	NA	NA
12	SALARIED	Logical	1	NA	NA	NA
13	DEPTNUM	Numeric	5,0	NA	NA	NA
14						
15						
16						
17						
18						
19						
20						

MULTIPLE INPUT RANGES AND EXTERNAL DATABASES

the EXPORTER file hasn't been attached, you can't use the List Fields command to obtain information about the fields in that database.

To get a table listing the fields in the EMPFILE database, type

/DE	Enters the Data External command.
L	Selects List.
F	Selects Fields.
Enter name of range whose fields are to be listed:	Asks for name assigned to external file during Use command.
Arrow keys	Highlight EMPFILE.
ENTER	Selects EMPFILE.
Enter range where filenames will be copied:	Asks for location to write table six columns wide and as deep as number of field names in database table. Move cursor to A8.
ENTER	Executes command, writes table, and leaves program at Data External menu.

Refer again to Figure 10–13, rows 8 through 13, for the result of the List Fields command. Reading from left to right in the figure, the columns in the table contain the following information:

Field Name	Name used to identify field. Identical in function to input range field name. (required)
Data Type	Type of entry in the field: Numeric, Character, Date, Logical, and so on. (required)
Field Width	Number of characters allowed in field. Comma followed by digit signifies number of decimal places. (required)
Field Label	Alternate version of Field Name. Used to identify abbreviated field names. (optional)
Field Description	Short description of contents of field. (optional)

| Field Creation String | Special information used by database to specify a field. (optional) |

Whenever a Field Label, Field Description, or Field Creation String is omitted, an **NA** appears in its place.

Using an External Database Table

The information you just obtained with the List Fields command is invaluable for understanding and using external tables. In particular, the list of field names in the first column can easily be used to construct criteria and output ranges so you can query the external table.

Data Query Extract

Before you can query any 1-2-3 database table, you must construct a criteria range and an output range. To query the EMPFILE table, use the Range Transpose command to transpose the field names in the range A8..A13 to A:21. The Range Transpose command is used instead of the Copy command because the field names in the criteria range must be in a row. Then copy the field names from A:21..F21 into A24..F24. See Figure 10-14.

The field names in rows 21 and 24 become the criteria and output ranges. External databases can contain many thousands of records, but when they don't, you can view all of the records at one time by extracting them into the 1-2-3 spreadsheet. To extract all of the records from the EMPFILE table into the output range on the spreadsheet in Figure 10-4, return to the Ready mode and type

| /DQ | Enters the Data Query command. |
| I | Selects Input. |

Figure 10–14 Criteria and output ranges for querying EMPFILE.

	A	B	C	D	E	F
21	EMPID	LASTNAME	FIRSTNAME	DOH	SALARIED	DEPTNUM
22						
23						
24	EMPID	LASTNAME	FIRSTNAME	DOH	SALARIED	DEPTNUM
25						
26						
27						

MULTIPLE INPUT RANGES AND EXTERNAL DATABASES

NAME/F3	Displays named ranges, including range name EMPFILE assigned to external table as part of the External Use command.
Arrow keys	Highlight EMPFILE.
ENTER	Selects EMPFILE as input range.
ENTER	Specifies input range.
C	Selects Criteria.
Arrow keys	Move cursor to first cell of criteria range, A21.
.	Tacks cursor to cell A21.
Arrow keys	Highlight A21..F22.
ENTER	Accepts criteria range.
O	Selects Output.
Arrow keys	Move cursor to first cell of output range, A24.
.	Tacks cursor to cell A24.
Arrow keys	Highlight A24..F24.
ENTER	Accepts output range.
E	Selects Extract to execute the command.

The result appears in Figure 10–15. You could also have selected Unique. Because the criteria range is blank, all of the records would be extracted,

Figure 10–15   All records from EMPFILE extracted into output range.

```
|   A             A          B           C         D        E        F     |
|21 |  EMPID       LASTNAME    FIRSTNAME   DOH       SALARIED DEPTNUM
|22 |
|23 |
|24 |  EMPID       LASTNAME    FIRSTNAME   DOH       SALARIED DEPTNUM
|25 |        67543 Mordocs     William     06/03/87         1    2323
|26 |        65437 Gordon      Elisabeth   10/10/88         0    3434
|27 |        43546 Minon       Margo       01/01/86         1    7456
|28 |        32355 Wall        Jonathan    12/14/87         0    3299
|29 |        87548 Peters      Donald      04/23/87         1    2323
|30 |        43357 Wiseman     Marcus      09/29/83         0    2323
|31 |        11241 Thomason    Andrea      04/12/80         1    1122
|32 |        78950 Kilbean     Harrison    11/23/83         1    2223
|33 |        66357 Youngman    Jane        08/09/86         1    1122
|34 |        19941 Stevenson   Kimberly    09/24/87         0    7456
|35 |
|36 |
|37_|
```

but they would be sorted in ascending order with the first column as the primary key.

Summary

To work easily and effectively with a database driver and external tables, use the following commands:

File Dir	Changes the default directory to the directory containing the database files you are going to use. (optional)
Data External List Tables	Obtains a list of all database files in the designated subdirectory that can be used with the chosen database driver. (optional)
Data External Use	Establishes a connection to an external database and assigns a range name to it for use in Data commands. (required)
Data External List Fields	Used to obtain a list of field names and other information about the fields in an external table. Table must have been connected to 1-2-3 with the External Use command. (optional)
Data External Reset	Disconnects 1-2-3 from an external database table. (required)

Whether you can use the Delete or Modify commands to delete records or to extract, modify, and return records to an external database depends on the features included with a particular database driver. The Sample driver included with the 1-2-3 Release 3 package does not delete or modify records in external databases. When you attempt to use one of these database commands, you receive the error message **Driver cannot perform this database operation -- Press HELP (F1)**.

Whereas the Sample database driver doesn't use the Modify command to modify existing records in an external table, it does use the Data Modify Insert command to insert new records into an existing external database. The operation is the same as described in Chapter 9, except that the input range is the name assigned to the external table. Step-by-step instructions for using the Data Modify Insert command appear later in this chapter.

Because the external table is on disk, you cannot use the Data Find command because that command can only be applied to input ranges that reside on sheets currently in memory.

CREATING A NEW TABLE IN AN EXTERNAL DATABASE

The Sample database driver uses the External Create command to create entirely new tables in the external database. See Figure 10–16 for the command tree. The key to creating a new external table is a *table definition*. You have already seen an example of a table definition, but you know it as the results of the External List Fields command. In that table (Figure 10–13) each row completely defines one field in the external table. Taken together, they define the entire table.

Several different ways can be used to generate a table definition. The simplest uses an existing 1-2-3 input range or an existing external database table as a template. In the following example, an existing 1-2-3 input range is turned into an external table.

Figure 10–16 Data External Create command tree.

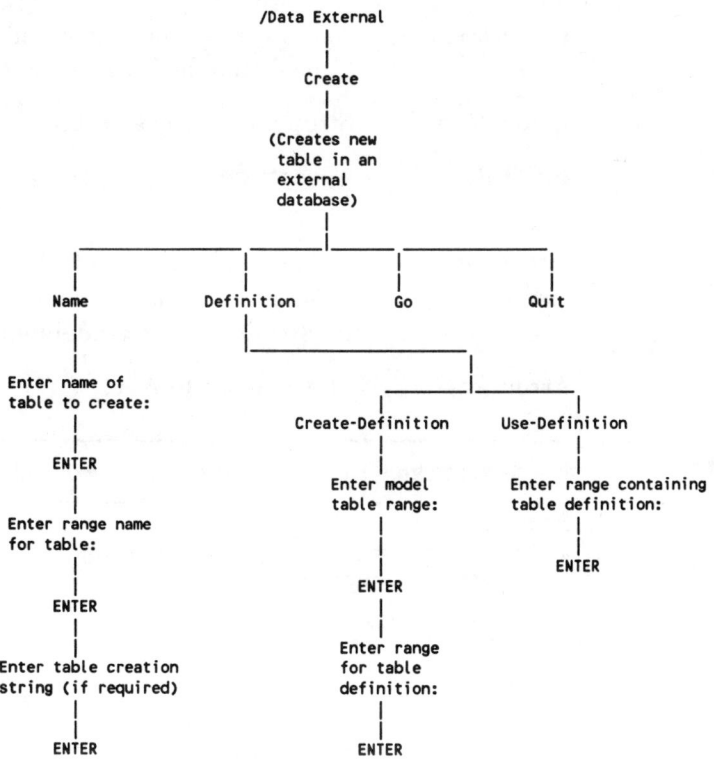

Figure 10-17 contains the Orders database from Figure 10-4. You can use the structure of the Orders database to define the structure of an external database table under the control of the Sample database driver. The external table is a dBASE III database table, and once created it can be used just like any other external table.

Creating the Table Definition

The first step in using the table in Figure 10-17 as a model for a new external table is to use the existing database in cells A4..C7 as a template to create a table definition. To specify the table definition, type

/DE	Enters the Data External command.
C	Selects Create.
D	Selects Definition.
C	Selects Create-Definition to use an existing table to define the external table.
Enter model table range:	Asks for row containing field names *and* the row immediately below containing one record.
Arrow keys	Stretch cursor over A4..C5.
ENTER	Accepts field names and one record as model table range.
Enter range for table definition:	Asks for area to write table definition. Must be six columns wide and as many rows deep as there are field names in the model table range.
Arrow keys	Move cursor to A10.

Figure 10-17 Orders database from Figure 10-4 as model for external table.

```
| A     A         B           C        |
|1 |
|2 |         ***ORDERS DATABASE***
|3 |
|4 |        DATE     CUSTOMER     AMOUNT
|5 |        01-Apr        Tom     $54.32
|6 |        05-Apr       Dick     $24.89
|7 |        07-Apr      Harry     $12.56
|8 |
|9 |
|10|
```

MULTIPLE INPUT RANGES AND EXTERNAL DATABASES

ENTER	Writes the table definition to cells beginning in A10. Returns to Create submenu.

See Figure 10–18 for the way the screen looks after the External Create Definition command has been used to create the table definition based on the Orders database.

Naming the External Database Table

Before you can use a table definition, you must use the External Create Name command to name the table to be created. This opens the database file into which the definition is written.

After using the Definition command, 1-2-3 leaves you in the Create submenu. The following instructions assign the name ORDERS to a new external table in the subdirectory C:\123R3 under the control of the Sample database driver. To assign the name, type

N	Selects Name.
Enter name of table to create:	Asks for *full table name*.
Arrow keys	Highlight appropriate database driver. Use Sample.
ENTER	Selects Sample.
C:\123R3	Must specify path to subdirectory where new external table is to be created.
ENTER	To select C:\123R3.

Figure 10–18 Result of External Create Definition Create-Definition command.

```
| A      A          B         C         D        E         F       |
|1 |
|2 |         ***ORDERS DATABASE***
|3 |
|4 |      DATE      CUSTOMER    AMOUNT
|5 |      01-Apr         Tom    $54.32
|6 |      05-Apr        Dick    $24.89
|7 |      07-Apr       Harry    $12.56
|8 |
|9 |
|10 | DATE      Date                            NA       NA        NA
|11 | CUSTOMER  Character         13            NA       NA        NA
|12 | AMOUNT    Numeric                         NA       NA        NA
|13 |
|14 |
```

ORDERS	Type name of new database. This name is assigned as a filename to the database file.
ENTER	To accept name ORDERS.
Enter range name for table: ORDERS	External table must have a range name. Lotus suggests using the name you just assigned to the external table.
ENTER	Accepts ORDERS.
Enter table creation string (if required):	Consult documentation accompanying database driver to determine whether creation string is required. None required by Sample.
ENTER	Ends process of assigning a name to the database to be created.

The preceding steps are much like the steps you go through to use an external database table. You have to specify the full table name, which includes the name of the database driver, the location where the file is to be created, and the filename to be assigned. Also specify the range name to be used with the table in other Data commands.

Caution: Do not leave the Create submenu after you have specified the table name, because 1-2-3 *does not remember* your specification. If you do leave the submenu for the Data External command menu or the main menu, you *must* repeat the preceding steps and reassign the name to your new database table.

Creating the External Table

You have created a table definition and you have assigned a name to your new external table. Lotus remembers the range containing the table definition you just created and uses it when defining the external table. You are now ready to complete the process.

The last step is to type

G	Selects Go. Uses the table definition to create a dBASE III table with the name Orders.

A new database table in a file named ORDERS.DBF is created. The file contains only field names and the information about field types and field widths from the definition range. However, the database driver automatically adds default values for the field width for Date and Amount because none were specified.

MULTIPLE INPUT RANGES AND EXTERNAL DATABASES

Verifying Field Information

The Order table is automatically attached to 1-2-3 just as if you had gone through the External Use process described earlier. To verify the attachment and find out what default values Sample assigned, from the Ready mode type

/DEL	Selects the Data External List command.
F	Selects Fields.
Enter name of range whose fields are to be listed:	Asks for name assigned to Order external database table.
Arrow keys	Highlight Order.
ENTER	Selects Order.
Enter range where field names will be copied:	Asks for location to copy information about fields.
Arrow keys	Move cursor to A15.
ENTER	Executes command.
Q	Returns to Ready mode.

See Figure 10–19 for the results. Note that the Sample database driver assigned eight characters as the field width for the DATE field and nine

Figure 10–19 Rows 15 to 17 contain result of using External List Fields on newly created database table.

```
    A          B           C        D       E       F
 1
 2        ***ORDERS DATABASE***
 3
 4      DATE      CUSTOMER      AMOUNT
 5      01-Apr         Tom      $54.32
 6      05-Apr        Dick      $24.89
 7      07-Apr       Harry      $12.56
 8
 9
10  DATE     Date                        NA      NA      NA
11  CUSTOMER Character           13      NA      NA      NA
12  AMOUNT   Numeric                     NA      NA      NA
13
14
15  DATE     Date                 8      NA      NA      NA
16  CUSTOMER Character           13      NA      NA      NA
17  AMOUNT   Numeric            9,0      NA      NA      NA
18
19
20
```

characters, zero decimal places as the field width and number of decimal places for the AMOUNT field.

The default currency field specification cuts off the digits to the right of the decimal. When amounts are read into the ORDERS table, they are rounded to zero decimal places.

Create-Definition Versus Use-Definition

The two commands, Create-Definition (just described) and Use-Definition, are alternative ways of telling 1-2-3 the location of the cells containing the table definition. When you use Create-Definition, the range containing the table definition it creates is remembered and used by the Go command to create the external table. When you don't use the Create-Definition command to create the table definition, you must use the Use-Definition command to tell 1-2-3 which cells contain the table definition. The Use-Definition command is used with the alternative ways to create a table definition, which is discussed next.

Modifying a Table Definition

Before you created the ORDERS table you could have edited the table definition to restore the decimal places in the currency field. The technique is to enter a digit—9 is the default—followed by a comma and the number of decimal places. So 9,2 would define a nine-digit field with two places to the right of the decimal. To get 1-2-3 to accept 9,2 either format the cell to Range Format Other Label before you enter 9,2, or begin the entry with a label alignment character to accomplish the forced text entry.

External Delete

Once the table definition is satisfactory, proceed to create the table. If you have already created the external table, and then wish to modify it, you must first delete the file containing the external table and then repeat the creation process already described. See Figure 10–20 for the Data External Delete command tree.

If your database driver can delete external tables, type

/DED   Selects the Data External Delete command.

Enter name of   Select database driver, Sample in this example.
table to delete:

Figure 10-20   Data External Delete command tree.

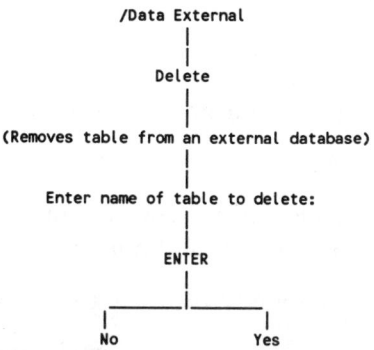

        C:\123R3   Selects path to external table file.

        ORDERS   Selects name of external table file.

        ENTER   Completes specification of full table name: SAMPLE C:\123R3 ORDERS.

        No Yes   Select Yes to delete the table.

The Sample database driver won't delete an external table. Instead, you can use the File Erase Other command to erase the file named ORDERS.DBF. You can also use the operating system command Erase to erase the file from the operating system.

Alternate Ways to Generate a Table Definition

In the preceding example a 1-2-3 database table was used as a model for the table definition that was used to generate a new table in the external database. There are two other ways to generate a table definition.

If the external table you want to create is to have a structure similar to an existing external table, use the Data External List Fields command discussed earlier in this chapter. Select the external table you want to use as a model for the new external table and the command writes a definition to your spreadsheet. This becomes the table definition for the new external table. Return to the Ready mode and edit in changes to field names, field types, and so on, until each row provides a correct definition for each field in the new external table.

The other way to create a table definition is to type it directly into a range of cells. The range must be arranged in the pattern of a table definition, which is

Column	Contents
1	Field names (required)
2	Data type (required)
3	Field width (required for label fields, may be optional for value fields)
4	Column labels (may be optional)
5	Field description (may be optional)
6	Field creation strings (may be optional)

Whether a particular element in the table definition is required or optional depends on the requirements of the particular database program you are using. Check the manuals for the database program and the database driver you are using. Alternatively, use the External List Fields command to examine the structure of some existing tables to determine which fields are optional. When an entry in a particular field is optional, it contains NA in the list table whenever nothing is specified for that field.

After you have generated the table definition from an existing 1-2-3 database table, an external table, or by entering it directly, use the External Create command to assign a name to the new table and use the External Create Definition Use-Definition command to create the new table. The steps are identical to the steps described in the preceding section.

Adding Records to an External Table

You can use either the Extract command or the Modify Insert command to add records to an existing external database table. Whether you can add records to particular external tables depends on the permissions you have from the database administrator and the features of the database driver you are using.

To use the Extract command, designate the external table as the output range and the table supplying the new records as the input range. The input range may be in a current active file, a closed file on disk, or it may be another external database table. When it is another external database table, you must use the Data External Use command to connect to it before

MULTIPLE INPUT RANGES AND EXTERNAL DATABASES

you can use that table as an input range. Set the appropriate criteria and then perform the Extract command. Unlike an Extract command used on a 1-2-3 output range, the command adds selected records to the external table and *doesn't* erase the existing records in the table.

Hint: When you are using a criterion to pass selected records from the input range to the external table, perform the extraction to an output range somewhere on an active sheet. Then inspect the selected records to ensure that they are the ones you intend to add to the external table. This is particularly important with the Sample database driver, because you can't remove records from an external table.

The Data Modify Insert command can also be used to add records to an external table. To use the command, remember that the input range is where the modified records are inserted, whereas the output range is where the records are coming from. See Chapter 9 for a complete discussion of the Data Modify command.

To add the records from the database in cells A4..C7 in Figure 10–21 to the external table named ORDERS, begin by selecting Data Query Reset to cancel any previously specified ranges.

After selecting Reset you are left in the Data Query menu. Then type

I	Selects input range.
Enter input range:	Asks for input range.
NAME/F3	Display named ranges. Highlight ORDERS, the name of the external database.
ENTER	Selects ORDERS.
ENTER	Confirms ORDERS as the input range.
C	Selects Criteria.

Figure 10–21 Output and criteria ranges for use with Data Query Modify command.

```
     A         B          C         D      E      F
1
2            ***ORDERS DATABASE***
3
4         DATE      CUSTOMER     AMOUNT
5         01-Apr         Tom     $54.32
6         05-Apr        Dick     $24.89
7         07-Apr       Harry     $12.56
8
9
10        DATE      CUSTOMER     AMOUNT
11
12
13
```

Arrow keys	Place cursor on cell A10.
.	Tacks cursor to A10.
Arrow keys	Stretch cursor over A10..C11.
ENTER	Accepts criteria range.
O	Selects output range.
Enter output range:	Asks for output range.
Arrow keys	Position cursor on A4.
.	Tacks cursor to A4.
Arrow keys	Stretch cursor over A4..C7.
ENTER	Accepts output range.
M	Selects Modify.
I	Selects Insert. Copies records from output range to the input range.
Q	Quit. Returns to Ready mode.

The records from A5..C7 are inserted into the external database table named ORDERS in the file ORDERS.DBF.

OTHER DATA EXTERNAL COMMANDS

There are three additional commands listed under Data External Other. Depending on your situation, you may never need to use any of these commands. See Figure 10-22 for the command tree.

Refresh

You may be using an external table that is on a network, and other users may be making additions or deletions to that table. You can use the Refresh command to execute Data Query and Data Table commands and to update worksheet formulas and database statistical functions at the interval you specify. This guarantees your worksheet is using and displaying the most up-to-date information.

MULTIPLE INPUT RANGES AND EXTERNAL DATABASES

Figure 10-22 Data External Other command tree.

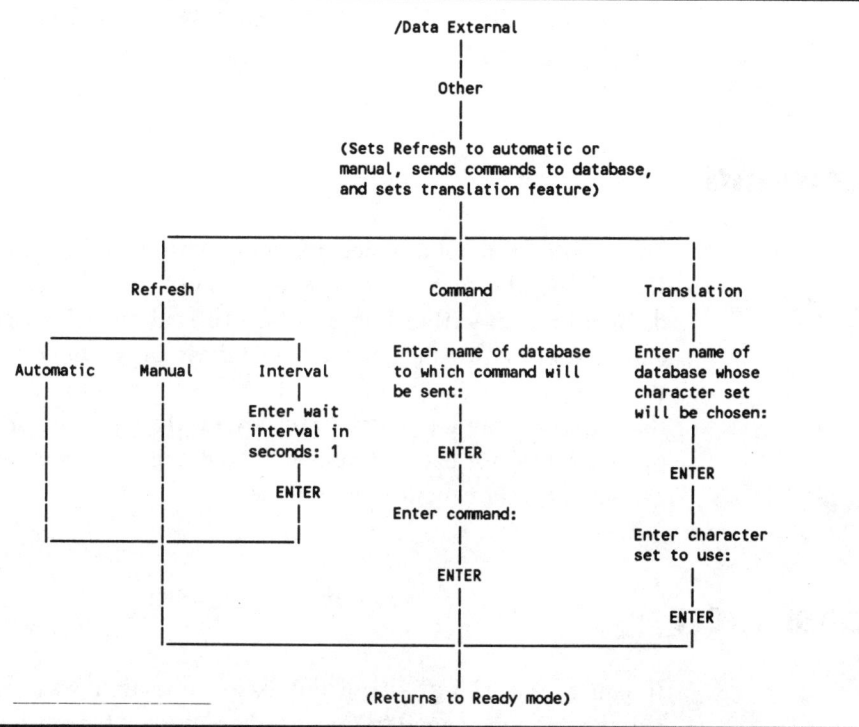

Before you set Refresh to automatic, select Interval to set the interval. The default is one second, which means that 1-2-3 is updating continuously. Once the interval is set, 1-2-3 returns you to the Ready mode. To enable automatic refreshing, you must again enter the External Other command and select Automatic. Your database commands are then automatically repeated at the designated interval, and formulas and functions depending on those commands are updated with current information from the external database.

Warning: When you enable automatic refreshing, the Data Table and Data Query commands are disabled. To change any of these commands or to specify new ones, you must reenter the External Other command and turn off automatic refreshing by selecting Manual.

Manual is the default setting for refresh. With Manual refreshing, actions are only executed on command. For example, if you have defined a Data Extract operation where records are extracted from an external table into a range on a worksheet, that extraction only takes place when you type **/DQE** or press the **QUERY/F7** key after having performed the command from within the Data command. If you think the external database may have changed since you last entered the command, and Manual is the current setting for Refresh, you must either repeat the command or press **QUERY/F7** to repeat the command.

Command

Some external databases accept commands from the 1-2-3 database driver. If available, this feature can greatly expand your ability to manage external databases from within Lotus 1-2-3. To find out which commands, if any, can be used with your particular database program you must consult both the manual that came with the database program and the documentation that accompanied the database driver. Pay particular attention to the proper syntax for each command. The database driver supplied with 1-2-3 cannot directly execute commands.

Translation

If you are working with a database table that was created in another country, you may need to select a character set to translate the information in the table so it can be used with your particular hardware configuration.

To see if you need to change the translation table 1-2-3 is currently using, perform a Data Query Extract on the external table. If the extracted records contain nonstandard characters, use the External Translation command to specify another character set and then repeat the operation.

ENDING THE CONNECTION TO AN EXTERNAL TABLE

When you have finished using an external table, use the External Reset command to disconnect from it. See Figure 10-23 for the command tree.

Assuming you have connected to the EMPFILE file used earlier in this chapter, to disconnect from it type

/DE	Enters the Data External command.
R	Selects Reset.

Figure 10-23 Data External Reset command tree.

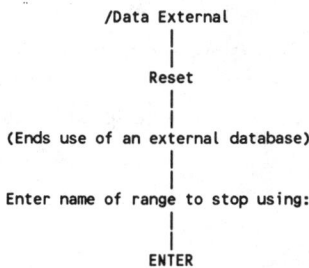

Enter name of range to stop using:	Asks for the name assigned to the external table. Names assigned to external tables are listed.
NAME/F3	Optional. Displays names of all connected tables.
Arrow keys	Highlight EMPFILE.
ENTER	Executes command, disconnects EMPFILE, and leaves you in External menu.

The Reset command closes the external table and ends all data exchange between 1-2-3 and the external table. When the table you closed is the only one in use in a particular external database, 1-2-3 ends its connection to that database. When the table is the only one used with a particular database driver, 1-2-3 removes the driver from memory.

Caution: As you know you can leave 1-2-3 by selecting Quit from the Main menu, and you can leave the program "ungracefully" by simply turning off your computer. Both of these methods abruptly disconnect 1-2-3 from any external databases that are in use at the time. Some database drivers may not close the external database files when you sever your connection by leaving 1-2-3 by either quitting the program or turning off the power. So, to avoid corrupting database files, *always* use the Data External Reset command to sever your connection to any external database before you leave 1-2-3.

THE DATA REGRESSION, PARSE, AND MATRIX COMMANDS

Three Data commands—Regression, Parse, and Matrix—provide advanced features and extended functions for users who need these special tools.

Unfortunately, it is beyond the scope of this book to go into the uses of these commands in detail. If you need to use the Regression or Matrix commands, it is assumed that you either know how to use these techniques or that you can consult a statistics textbook to obtain the required knowledge. With that qualification, the following description of the Regression, Parse, and Matrix commands give a knowledgeable user access to these 1-2-3 features.

The Data Regression Command

Regression analysis is a statistical technique for extracting from historical information the way one variable is related to another. Many problems call for this type of analysis. Lotus 1-2-3 can perform simple and multiple regression on up to 75 independent or explanatory variables with up to 8191 observations for each variable. Once the regression has been calculated, it is possible to use the results for prediction.

To use the Data Regression command, you must give 1-2-3 the location of three ranges. The ranges may be in the current file or in any other active files.

X range — The range containing the independent variable or variables.

Y range — The range containing the dependent variable.

Output range — The range of cells where the results of the Data Regression command are written. Like the output range for the Data Query Extract command discussed in the last chapter, this is the place where the output of the command appears. Lotus uses a rectangle at least four columns wide and nine rows deep. You only supply the upper left cell of the range.

See Figure 10–24 for the command tree.

Constructing the Spreadsheet

As with the other Data commands, you must construct the spreadsheet you are going to use with the Regression command *before* you enter the command. There are several important things to observe when constructing the spreadsheet.

1. Both X and Y ranges must be in columns.

Figure 10-24   Data Regression command tree.

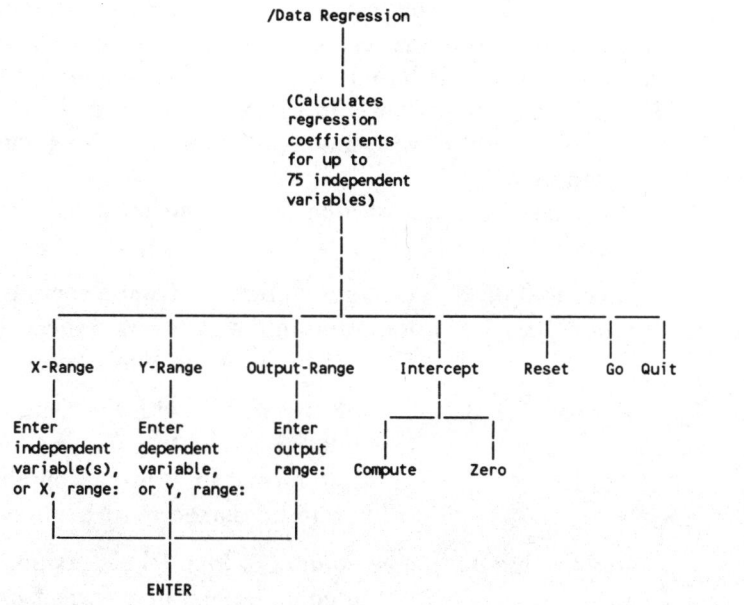

2. All X variables must be in consecutive columns.

3. The number of observations (rows) in the X range and the Y range must be the same. If they aren't, 1-2-3 refuses to calculate the regression. The ranges can be on different sheets in the current file, but they must contain the same number of rows, up to 8191.

4. There cannot be any blank cells in either range. Lotus cannot deal with missing information. Remove both X and Y observations when one is missing.

5. The area designated as the output range can be in any active file, but it must be empty because 1-2-3 erases it just before writing the results to the worksheet.

The Data Parse Command

The Data Parse command is the answer to the problem of importing into a 1-2-3 worksheet information that has been downloaded from a mainframe computer or captured from a remote database. You can also import and parse information that has been typed on a word processor or printed to a disk by another program.

The Data Parse command takes long labels (the form in which information is most often received from a remote source), and "chops" them into individual cells based on a format line generated by the command. The parsed information is in the form of either labels or values and is immediately usable with any 1-2-3 function. See Figure 10–25 for the command tree.

To parse a column of long labels, you must have the following four elements:

A column of long labels	Generally obtained from a remote computer and imported into a 1-2-3 worksheet. (See Chapter 5 for details about the File Import command.)
Format line(s)	Templates created with the Data Parse command that tell 1-2-3 how to parse the long labels. Multiple format lines are acceptable, but the column to be parsed *must* begin with a format line.
Input column	The column of long labels. As noted, the first entry in the column must be a format line.
Output range	The range of cells into which the parsed lines are to be written.

Figure 10–25 Data Parse command tree.

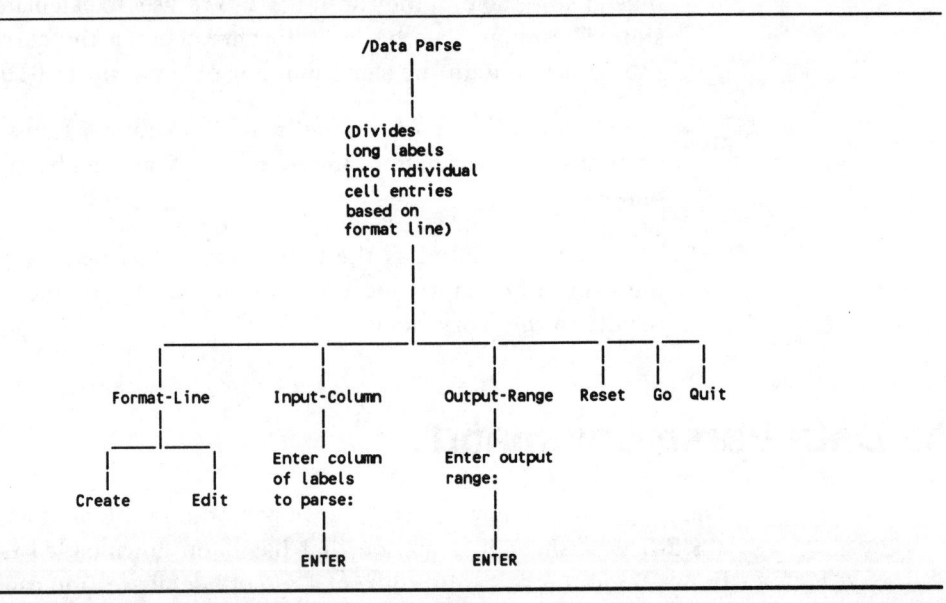

Once you import the text into your spreadsheet with the File Import command, specify a format line, designate the input column, and specify the upper left corner of the output range, select Go to parse the input column. Inspect the results carefully. To correctly parse the input column you will probably have to edit the format line and, possibly, insert additional format lines. Several trials are often required to correctly parse the text.

The Data Matrix Command

The Data Matrix command is an advanced 1-2-3 command with special features for solving problems in matrix algebra. A "matrix" is a fancy name for a rectangular set of numbers. A 1-2-3 range on a single sheet is a matrix. Once you have one or more matrices the command can perform two matrix algebra operations: matrix multiplication and matrix inversion.

Matrix multiplication is just multiplication of two matrices. But to be multiplied together, matrices must meet special qualifications. Matrix multiplication is only possible when the first matrix has the same number of columns as the second matrix has rows. If this requirement isn't met, the matrices are said to be "incompatible" and matrix multiplication cannot be performed. When two compatible matrices are multiplied together, the result is a third matrix that has the same number of rows as the first matrix and the same number of columns as the second matrix.

Matrix inversion is the process of finding an "inverse" for a matrix. An inverse of a number has the mathematical property that when a number and its inverse are multiplied together the product is always 1. Thus ⅙ is the inverse of 6 and vice versa. When a matrix is multiplied by its inverse, the result is a matrix containing only 1s. Inverse matrices are the key to solving systems of simultaneous linear equations. Inverses only exist for square matrices.

Release 3 of 1-2-3 can multiply matrices up to 256 rows by 256 columns and invert square matrices up to 80 rows by 80 columns. To fully understand and apply these operations, you have to study statistics and linear algebra. Consult a textbook of your choosing. See Figure 10–26 for the Data Matrix command tree.

Figure 10-26   Data Matrix command tree.

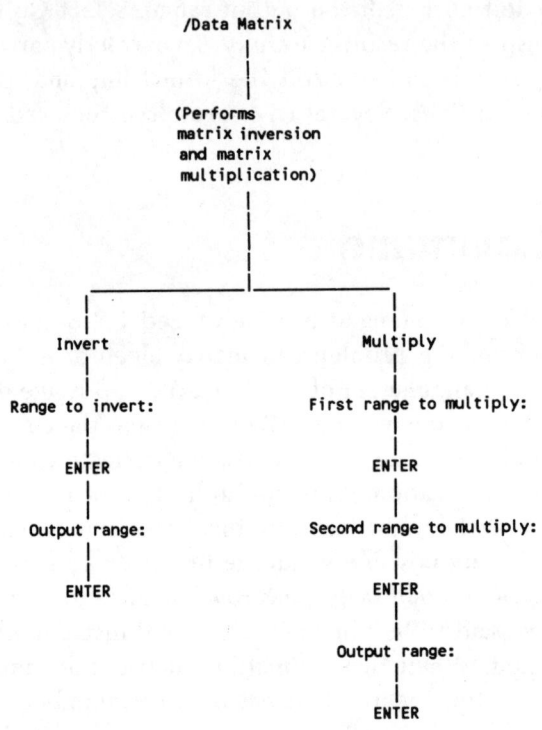

TIPS & TRAPS

Tips

When Using Multiple Input Ranges Use Unique Field Names.
When two or more input ranges are specified, field names used in criteria or output ranges must be unique, or you must precede each field name that occurs in two or more tables with the range name assigned to the input range. Be sure to separate the table name from the field name by a period, as in ORDERS.CUSTOMER. It's easier to use synonyms.

What Is This "Implied Database" Stuff?
Whenever two or more input ranges are specified for a Data Query command, 1-2-3 creates an implied database, which is composed of all possible

combinations of all the records from all of the input ranges. The number of records in the implied database can get very large very quickly. For example, specifying three input ranges each containing 100 records generates an implied database containing 100 × 100 × 100 records or 1,000,000 records.

When two or more input ranges are specified for a Data Extract or Data Unique command, the criteria specified are applied against the implied database and the records selected are from that database.

Use File Dir Before Data External Use.
When you link to an external database, Lotus proposes the current subdirectory as the location of database files. To have the appropriate subdirectory proposed, use the File Dir command to change the default directory to the directory containing the database files you are going to use.

Use a Model to Create a New External Table.
The easiest way to generate a table definition for a new external table is to construct a 1-2-3 spreadsheet table using the field names you want assigned to the external table. Be sure to enter at least one record immediately below the field names. Then use the Data External Create-Definition command to create a table definition that is based on your 1-2-3 spreadsheet table. Edit field types, character width, and number of decimal places, and supply any additional information required by the database driver you are using.

Traps

Where Did All Those Crazy Records Come from?
Whenever you specify two or more input ranges, 1-2-3 creates an implied database, in which each record in each database is combined with every other record in every other database. The number of records in the implied database is the product of the number of records in each database. Many of these records are complete nonsense. When there are identical fields in two or more input ranges, those fields (often called *key fields*) can be used to join the input ranges. This often eliminates many of the nonsense records from the implied database.

I Selected Refresh Automatic and Now I Can't Do Anything.
When Refresh Automatic is selected, *all* Data Query and Data Table commands are disabled. To use one of these commands you must enter the

Data External Other Refresh command and select Manual to turn off Automatic refreshing.

Lotus Forgot the Name of the External Table I Was Creating.

When you use the Data External Create Name command and then leave that submenu, 1-2-3 forgets the name you have assigned to the external table. To avoid this problem, perform the task of assigning a name to your external table just before you select Go to create it.

11 The Graph Commands

OBJECTIVES

After mastering the content of this chapter, you will be able to

- create any one of 1-2-3's seven basic graph types.
- title, rotate, scale, format, and use other options to enhance the display of 1-2-3 graphs.
- use the GRAPH/F10 key and the Group command to specify all of the data ranges for a graph at one time.
- create and manage a library of named graphs based on ranges in the current file.
- display a spreadsheet and a graph on the screen at the same time.
- print the current graph or a named graph.
- print graphs and spreadsheet cells on the same page.
- use the GRAPH/F10 key to display the current graph at any time.

INTRODUCTION

The 1-2-3 Graph command can create seven basic graph types: line, bar, XY, stacked-bar, pie, high-low-close, and mixed. In addition, most graph types can be rotated. For example, bar graphs can be rotated to display as horizontal bar graphs. On several graph types the right- and left-hand

Y scales can be specified, and either the X or Y scale (or both) can be expressed in logarithms.

What are the characteristics of these graphs?

- The *line*, *bar*, and *stacked-bar charts* compare relative magnitudes. In each of these graphs, magnitudes are plotted along the vertical axis and categories (months, quarters, divisions, and so on) are presented along the horizontal axis.

- *Pie charts* (sometimes called *pie graphs*) display the relationship between a whole and its parts.

- The *XY graph* displays the relationship between two or more numerical magnitudes, one on the x-axis and the other on the y-axis.

- The *high-low-close graph* displays information about securities transactions and includes a range to show volume as well as high, low, and closing prices.

- The *mixed graph* combines bar and line graphs. It plots different types of data on the same graph.

Each graph type is illustrated later in this chapter.

When you first encounter the 1-2-3 Graph command (see Figure 11-1 for the command tree), you may be overwhelmed by its large number of

Figure 11-1 The Graph command tree.

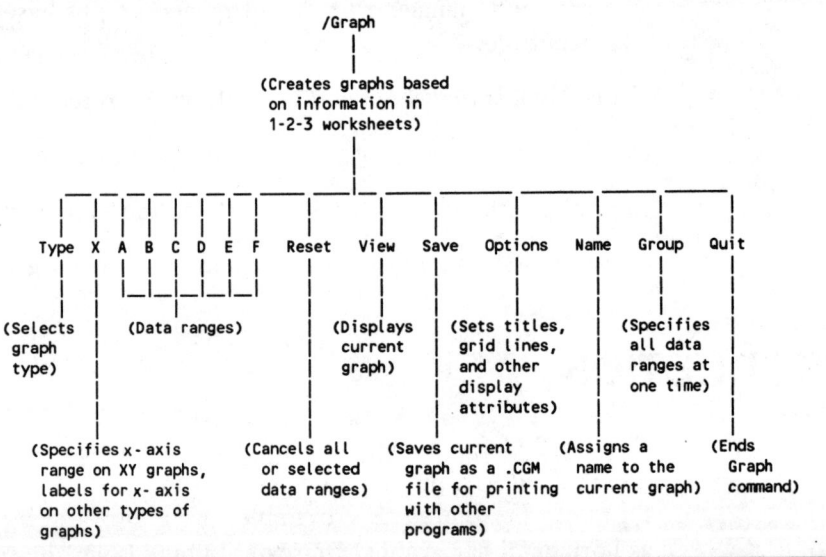

THE GRAPH COMMANDS

choices. Don't worry. Creating a 1-2-3 graph actually requires only three menu choices and, if you wish, 1-2-3 can supply one by default. In fact, 1-2-3 can automatically graph the information in a spreadsheet, but before you learn that option, it is important to understand exactly how the Graph command works when you specify each element directly.

When you construct a graph by specifying the information the three required choices are

T	Selects a graph type or accepts the line graph, 1-2-3's default graph type.
A B C D E F	Specify at least one data range (listed as A through F on the Graph command menu).
V	Selects Views (or press **GRAPH/F10**) to see your graph displayed on your screen.

That is all. Just a graph type and at least one data range. All other choices on the Graph command menu are options—options you exercise only when you need a special feature.

A Word About Hardware

In a moment you will go through the steps required to create your first 1-2-3 graph, but first a word about hardware. Most personal computers that can run Lotus 1-2-3 Release 3 can display both text and graphics. However, if you specify a graph and it doesn't appear when you select View, check the following.

First, can your computer display graphics? A few personal computer configurations may not have a graphics-capable video display. If your system is one of them, you won't be able to view graphs on your screen, though you may still be able to print your graphs.

Second, have you installed the appropriate graphics driver for your computer? To check, start 1-2-3 by typing **LOTUS** to enter the Access System, then select **Install**. Follow the steps for Change Selected Equipment and select Modify Current DCF. You don't actually have to modify anything, but that choice lets you see what has been specified as the display driver for your system. If it isn't what you are using, change it and save the changes. Otherwise, your system isn't capable of displaying graphics.

To get a printed version of a 1-2-3 graph, you need a graphics-capable printer such as one of the Epson brand dot matrix printers, a laser printer, or a plotter such as Hewlett-Packard's HP7440A plotter. If you don't have a graphics-capable monitor but do have a printer capable of printing 1-2-3 graphs, you can still specify and print graphs. You won't be able to view the graphs before printing, but you do have available the full range of printing options.

THE ABC'S OF CREATING A 1-2-3 GRAPH

Assuming your monitor is capable of displaying graphs and your printer can print them, you are ready to create your first graph. This section describes the steps for defining a graph in the order you perform them.

Create the Worksheet First

A 1-2-3 graph cannot exist independently of the worksheet that contains the information to be graphed. Thus, the first step in creating a 1-2-3 graph is to create the worksheet. Pay particular attention to the row labels and column headings, because you have the option of using the text from these cells as labels for your graph. To be effective, labels should be short, because the space around a graph is at a premium.

You can also use the worksheet title and subtitle to title your graphs, but if you used leading blanks to center the titles on the worksheet, these blanks cause the automatic centering feature of the Graph command to incorrectly align the titles.

Each of the six data ranges can come from different sheets in a stack, or, once specified, from a file stored on disk. In fact, a data range can extend across one or more sheets in a stack. However, if one or more of your graph ranges extends across separate sheets in a stack, be sure the range you intend to graph is located in the *same cell* on each sheet. For example, if you want a graph of total sales by region when your stack contains sheets for each region, construct each sheet so that regional sales appear in the same cell, such as A:G49, B:G49, and C:G49.

The following example assumes you have constructed the worksheet in Figure 11-2.

Specify the Graph

To use the information in Figure 11-2 to specify a bar chart of the total doctorate degrees conferred in each year, begin by typing

Figure 11-2 Doctorate Degrees Conferred worksheet.

```
 A      A         B      C      D      E      F      G
|1 |
|2 |
|3 |                    Doctorate Degrees Conferred
|4 |                         1960 to 1985
|5 |  (In Thousands)
|6 |
|7 |              1960   1965   1970   1975   1980   1985
|8 |
|9 |  Total       9.8    18.7   29.9   34.1   32.6   32.9
|10|  Male        8.8    14.7   25.9   26.8   22.9   21.7
|11|  Female      1.0    4.0    4.0    7.3    9.7    11.2
|12|
|13|
|14|
|15|
|16|
```

/G	Enters the Graph command.
T	Selects Type.
B	Selects Bar from the Type submenu.
A	Selects the A Data Range.
Arrow keys	Position the cursor on cell B9, the first cell of the row containing the total doctorate degrees.
.	Tacks cursor to cell B9.
Arrow keys	Highlight B9..G9.
ENTER	Accepts the A Data Range.
V	Selects View to display bar chart of total doctorate degrees conferred.

Figure 11-3 shows the resulting graph. It is a "bare bones" graph. It is enough for a quick graphic look at the data, and for some purposes that is enough; for others, it isn't. In any case, you'll soon learn how to enhance this graph's appearance through the various Graph command options. When you have finished viewing the graph, press any key to return to the Graph command menu.

Before you examine the other Graph command options, take a moment to compare a few more basic elements of all 1-2-3 graphs.

Graph Type

Experiment with graph types to find the type that best displays the information you are currently graphing. The line graph is 1-2-3's default

Figure 11–3 Unadorned bar graph of total doctorates conferred 1960 to 1985.

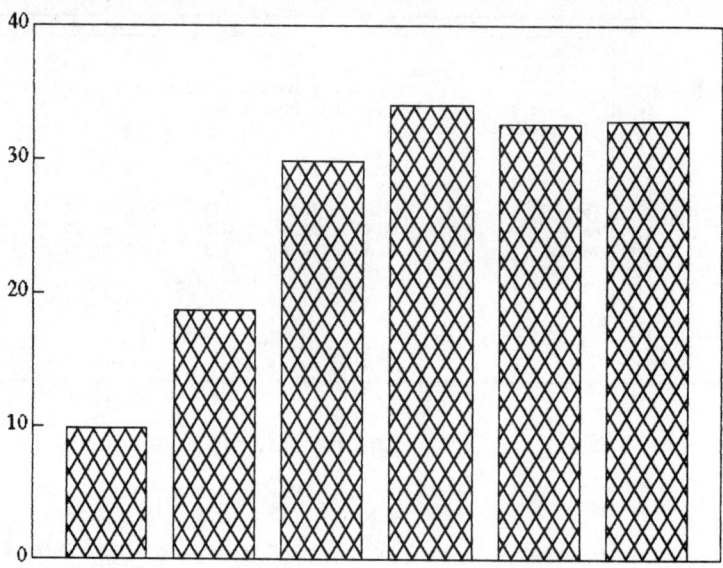

graph type. It is a good, all-purpose choice. But another graph type may present your information more clearly or more dramatically.

To choose a different graph type, select Type from the main Graph command menu and make your choice. Then select View and the current data ranges are regraphed in the new type.

Data Range

Lotus graphs display information located in ranges of cells on 1-2-3 worksheets. The ranges can be on the same sheet, on different sheets in a stack, across sheets in a stack, or even in files stored on disk.

You can add a range to an existing graph by selecting an unused data range (A through F). If the range is already specified, 1-2-3 highlights it. Remember that you can move the active cell designated by the flashing-underline cursor from one end of a range to the other by pressing the period key. Don't leave a blank data range between two other data ranges. To remove a data range, select Reset and the letter of the range you want to remove.

Some graph types place special requirements on the data ranges.

Pie charts, for example, only display data specified in the A data range. Information in other data ranges is used to control aspects of the display of the pie chart. For this reason, switching to a pie chart may produce unexpected results when you have specified data ranges other than the A data range. Graphs of the XY type require you to specify the data to be plotted along the x-axis as the X data range. Other graph types do not use the X range as a data range.

View the Graph

The View Command

You can view your graph in two ways. If you are still at the main Graph command menu, select View and the graph appears. Alternatively, press the **GRAPH/F10** key. This key can be used at any time, even when you are half way through the specification of another command such as the Print command. It also has some important uses in specifying graphs automatically. Those features are described later in this chapter.

When you construct a graph, take the time to view it every time you add a data range, change graph types, modify a feature, or in any other way change your graph. Viewing graphs frequently tells you which options enhance the graph and which muddle your point. If you specify several options before viewing the graph, you may not be able to tell which is causing a problem.

After you have selected View or pressed **GRAPH/F10** and examined your graph, press any key to remove the graph from your screen and return to the spreadsheet.

Understand the X Range

The X range can cause some confusion because the type of information specified as the X range on most graph types isn't a data range at all. On bar charts (including multiple bar charts), line, stacked-bar, high-low-close, and mixed graphs, the content of the X range—as in the example just discussed—is used to *label* the divisions along the horizontal axis. On pie charts, the X range supplies a label for each segment of the chart.

Only on an XY graph is the X range a true data range. Graphs of the XY type plot numerical values on both axes, and the x-axis data on an XY graph is specified under the X data range. You must specify data for the X range of an XY graph and that range must not contain any labels.

On any other type of graph, you can enter any information you desire into a range of the appropriate size and use the X range to designate it as labels for the divisions. When you create labels in this way, the label range must contain the same number of cells as there are cells in the other data ranges. If it doesn't, the labels won't correspond to the correct divisions.

As you can see from Figure 11-3, the absence of x-axis labels makes it difficult to make the connection between the bars and the categories being graphed. Without this information many graphs are almost impossible to understand. Figure 11-4 shows Figure 11-3 with the column headings—1960 to 1985—from cells B7..G7 used as x-axis labels.

Crowded X-Axis Labels

In Figure 11-4 there is plenty of room to label each division, but this is not always the case. Had data been graphed for every year between 1940 and 1985, 45 bars would have been plotted and there would not have been room to display forty-five x-axis labels. In fact, the x-axis labels would have written over each other, becoming impossible to read.

The solution to this problem is to use the Options Scale Skip command to designate how many divisions to skip between x-axis labels. See the discussion of that command later in this chapter.

THE ABC'S OF PRINTING A 1-2-3 GRAPH

You have just seen how easy it is to turn data from your spreadsheet into a graph displayed on the screen. It is equally easy to turn a graph displayed

Figure 11-4   Bar graph of total doctorate degrees conferred with x-axis labels.

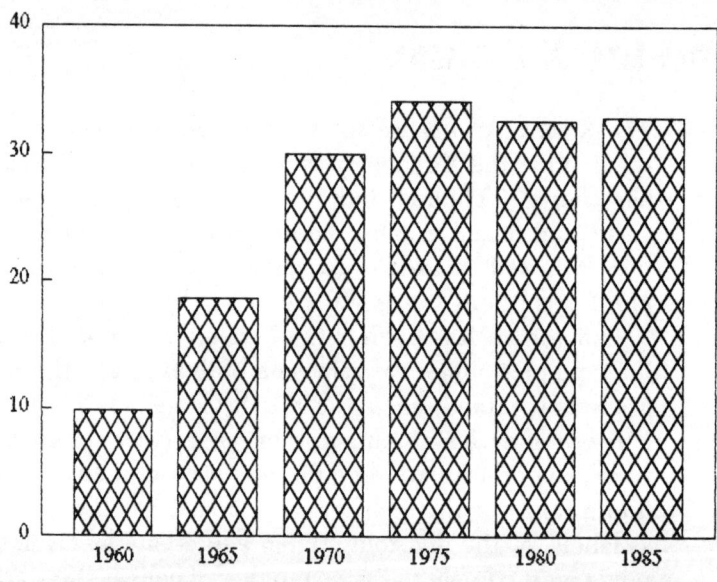

THE GRAPH COMMANDS 423

on your screen into a printed copy of the graph. There are several ways to print a graph, but the following step-by-step instructions show you the easiest way to get a printed copy of your graphs.

The rest of the exercises in this chapter assume you have a printer capable of printing graphs and that it is on line and the print head is positioned at the top of a page. To create Figure 11-4, the printed copy of the graph you just specified, begin by pressing **GRAPH/F10** to display the graph on the screen. Once you have verified that it is the *current graph*, press any key to redisplay the worksheet. Then type:

/PP	Enters the Print Printer command.
I	Selects Image.
C	Selects Current.
AG	Selects Align and Go, and the current graph begins printing.
Q	Selects Quit to return to the Ready Mode.

It takes a few moments to print the current graph, but printing takes place in the background so you can continue to work with 1-2-3. The result is the graph in Figure 11-4.

TITLES AND LEGENDS

Once you have chosen a graph type and specified at least one data range, you are ready to add additional features to your graph. Many of the enhancements are added by selecting the appropriate choice from the Graph Options menu. Each option you add should enhance the appearance and clarity of your graph. If an option doesn't improve the layout of the graph, abandon it and try another. See Figure 11-5 for a command tree of the Graph Options.

Many options are available to enhance the appearance and impact of your 1-2-3 graphs, but two—Legends and Titles—are particularly important and frequently used. They are discussed in this section. The other options—Format, Grid, Scale, Color, B&W, Data-Labels, and Advanced—are of less general importance and are, therefore, discussed later in this chapter.

Legends

Each bar, line, stacked-bar, or XY graph assigns a different symbol, cross-hatching pattern, or color (if you are displaying the graph in color) to

Figure 11-5 Graph Options command tree.

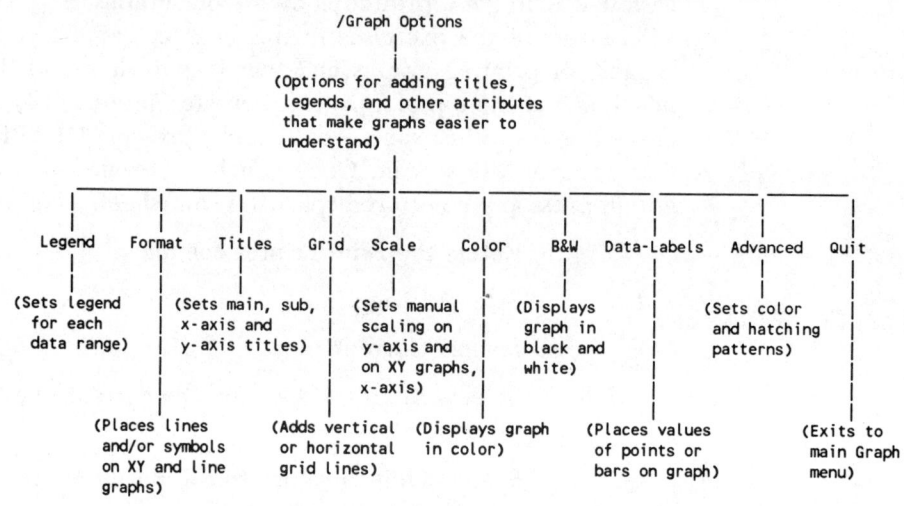

each data range. The Legend option labels each symbol, pattern, or color. Legends are displayed along the bottom of the graph and are essential for comprehending a multiple-bar, stacked-bar, or line graph.

Figure 11-6 shows the Degrees Conferred multiple-bar chart with legends specified for each data range. Cover the legends with a sheet of paper to see how difficult it is to tell which bar goes with which data range when the legends aren't available. When your graph contains several data ranges or when the legends are long, 1-2-3 displays the legends on two lines. When a legend is too long to display, it is truncated. When this happens, edit the legend until it fits in the allotted space.

You can use two methods to specify legends. One is to specify the legend as part of the Option Legends command. The other is to use text from the spreadsheet. The first method is discussed here, the second, in the next section.

To specify a legend for the A data range in Figure 11-6 (which is based on the spreadsheet in Figure 11-2), recall that the A data range contains the data for total doctorates conferred. You must have this information before you enter the Legend subcommand, because there is no way to obtain it once you are there. If necessary, select the A data range and 1-2-3 highlights the range of cells assigned to that range.

To enter a legend from the Ready mode begin by typing

/GO   Enters the Graph Options command.

L   Selects the Legend option.

THE GRAPH COMMANDS

Figure 11-6 Multiple bar graph with legends.

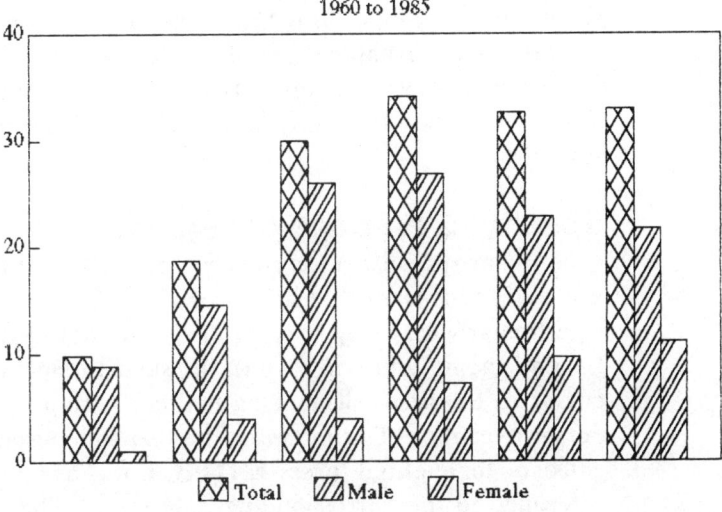

A	Selects the A data range as the range to be assigned the legend.
Enter legend for A range:	Asks for A range legend.
Total	Type the A range legend.
ENTER	Enters A range legend and returns you to the Graph Command submenu.

Continue to specify legends for the other two data ranges. When you are finished, the result is as shown in Figure 11-6.

Using Text from the Sheet as a Legend

As you have just seen, you can specify a legend by typing letters or numbers in response to the Legend prompt. There is, in fact, an easier way to specify legends when the legend text already appears on a spreadsheet: Refer to a cell on the worksheet. To specify a cell address as the location of a legend, precede the cell address with the backslash character (\). For example, to use the contents of cell A9 as a legend, type \A9 in response to the Legend prompt.

Unlike previous versions of 1-2-3, you can point to the cell containing the legend by pressing the **UP** or **DOWN** arrow key to move 1-2-3 into Point mode. Also, in Release 3, cell addresses supplied as legends now automatically adjust to any change you make in the structure of the spreadsheet with the Move, Insert, or Delete command.

The major advantages of using text from the worksheet are that it is fast, establishes a close link between the graph and the underlying worksheet, and is easy to modify by just changing the contents of a cell on the spreadsheet.

Specifying a Range of Legends

When your spreadsheet is constructed so that all of the text you want to use as legends is located in consecutive cells, you can take advantage of a particularly easy way to specify legends. Select Range from the Options Legend menu, and when you are asked to **Enter legend range:**, move the cursor to the first cell, tacking it there with a period. Then stretch the cursor over the cells containing the text to be used as legends. When the cells are highlighted, press **ENTER**. Lotus assigns each cell as a legend reference to the corresponding data range. That is, the first cell is the legend for the A data range, and so on. You can use this technique with the spreadsheet in Figure 11–2, because all of the text you would use for legends is contained in consecutive cells in the range A9..A11.

Titles

The other option you use with most graphs is the Titles option. This option lets you specify the text that appears around the graph. Your choices are

First	Main title. Appears centered above the graph.
Second	Subtitle. Appears centered under the main title.
X-Axis	Appears below the graph, but above the legends.
Y-Axis	Appears vertically, to the left of the graph.
2Y-Axis	Appears vertically, to the right of the graph.
Note	First line of footnote. Appears in lower left corner. Can extend to the right corner of graph area.
Other-Note	Second line of footnote. Appears below the first line of footnote. Can extend to the right corner of graph area.

THE GRAPH COMMANDS

The main title is centered above the worksheet, and the subtitle is centered under it. Subject to the capabilities of your printer, you can control the typeface and typesize used for each of these titles. The typesize changes on the screen, but the font does not. See the discussion of Options Advanced later in this chapter. Figure 11–7 illustrates the placement of titles.

Like legends, titles can be typed in response to the prompt, or they can be supplied by referring to a spreadsheet cell. Again, if you refer to a cell, precede the reference with a backslash and use the arrow keys to point.

To specify the main title for the Degrees Conferred graph, begin by typing

/GO	Enters the Graph Options command.
T	Selects the Titles option.
F	Selects First title.

Figure 11–7 Graph with all titles and notes designated.

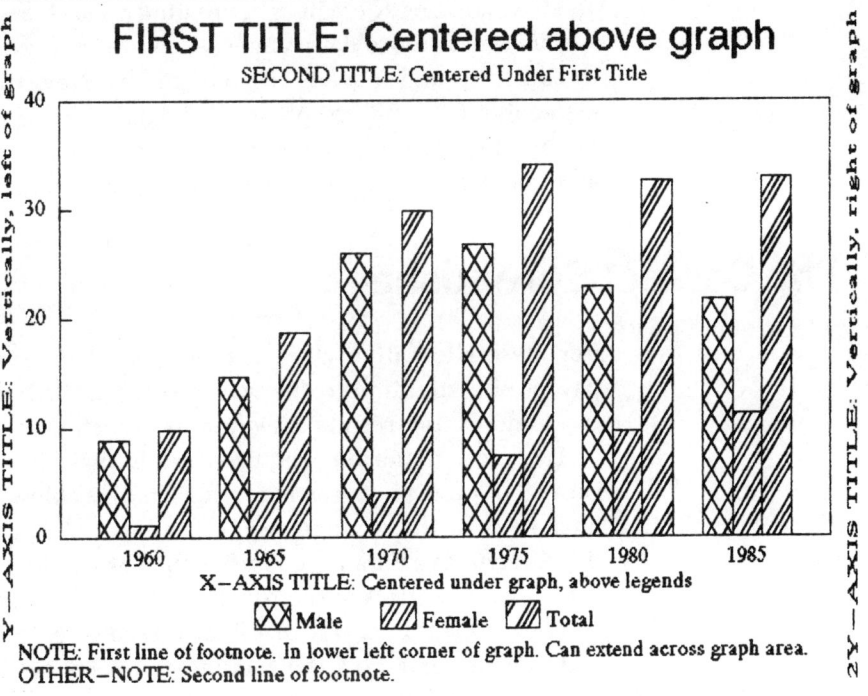

Enter graph title, top line:	Asks for the main title.
\	Indicates you are going to use a cell reference.
Arrow keys	Move the cursor until cell D3 is highlighted.
ENTER	To accept the text in \D3 as the main title.

You are returned to the Options submenu, where you can continue to specify other titles and/or options.

Automatic "Thousands" and "Millions"

If the data on your worksheet is measured in thousands or millions, you don't need to supply the words *Thousands* or *Millions* as y-axis or second y-axis titles. Lotus automatically labels the axis with the appropriate word whenever it rounds the numbers. On the other hand, if the numbers on the worksheet are already rounded, as they are in the Degrees Conferred graph, you need to supply the appropriate y-axis label.

ALTERNATIVE WAYS TO SPECIFY DATA RANGES

You have learned the ABC's of creating a 1-2-3 graph: select a graph type, specify one or more data ranges, and view your graph. You also know how to add titles and legends to your graphs. Now that you know the basic elements of a 1-2-3 graph and how they go together, you are ready to begin adding to your graphic tool kit. The place to begin is with two additional ways to specify data ranges, and, hence, to create a graph.

The Correct Spreadsheet

For these alternative ways of specifying data ranges to work, you must pay careful attention to the way you create the table you want graphed. If you don't, the results are often unexpected and unusable.

The most important requirement is that the data ranges—X and A through F—must be arranged in consecutive columns or rows. The X range must be first, the A range second, and so on. To avoid having 1-2-3 treat the X range as a data range rather than as labels for the x-axis tick marks, use only text entries in the row or column that contains the X range. That is, use forced text entry for 1985 instead of entering it as a value.

The cells containing the X range can either be directly above or to the left of the cells containing the A through F data ranges. They should be

THE GRAPH COMMANDS

above the cells when the data ranges are arranged in rows, and they should be to the left when the data ranges are arranged in columns. Always include an X range when using the Group command discussed in the next section. If you don't, 1-2-3 treats the top row or left column of the range you specify as the X range even when you intend it to be the A data range.

Finally, the X range may be separated from the A through F data ranges by a single blank row or column. When the X data range is a row across the top of the A through F data ranges, it may be separated from the A through F data ranges by either a blank row or a row of repeating text labels.

The spreadsheet in Figure 11–2 meets these requirements.

Group

If necessary, select Graph Reset Graph to clear any current graph settings. If you don't do this and a current graph has been specified, the following technique only replaces the data ranges in the current graph with those specified by the Group command.

After you have cleared the current graph, to specify all of the data ranges in Figure 11–2 at one time, begin by typing

/G	Enters the Graph command.
G	Selects Group.
Enter group range:	Asks for the range of cells to assign to the X and A through F data ranges.
Arrow keys	Position cursor on B7.
.	Tacks cursor to B7.
Arrow keys	Stretch cursor over B7..G11.
ENTER	Accepts Group range.
R	Selects Rowwise to designate the rows of the Group range as data ranges.
ENTER	Completes command.
V	Selects View to view the group range graphed as a line graph.

The result appears in Figure 11–8. You can add titles, legends, or any other options or features to complete the graph.

Figure 11-8 Data from Figure 11-2 graphed with the Graph Group command.

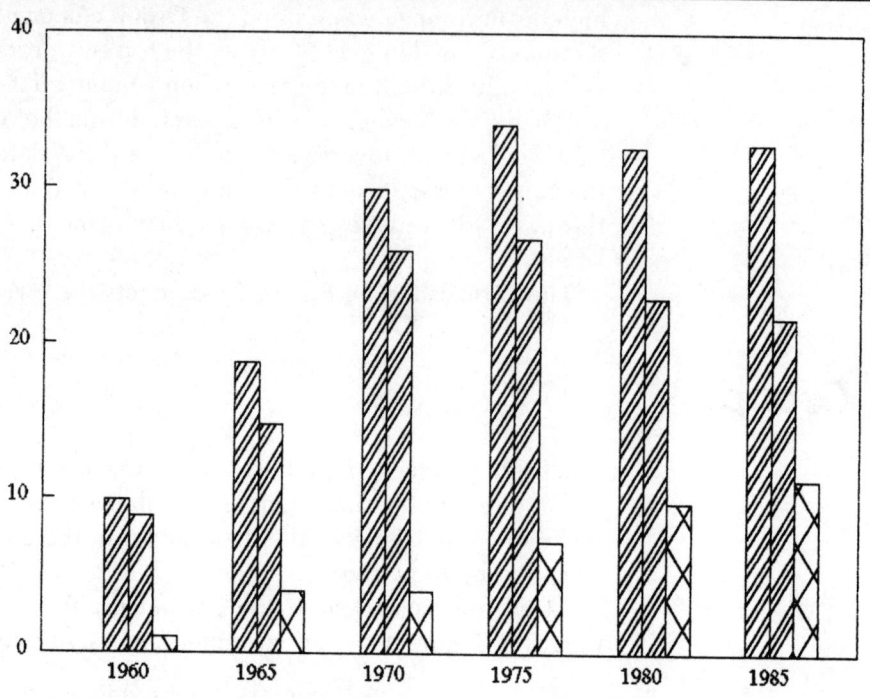

Automatic Graphing

The Group command speeds the specification of the data ranges, but 1-2-3 can, in fact, assign the data ranges for you automatically. However, to use the automatic assignment of data ranges you must use extra care in laying out the spreadsheet. You must follow all of the rules specified under Group: data ranges in consecutive columns or rows, X range containing only text as the first row or first column. But you must separate the material to be graphed automatically from all other material (including titles) by *at least* two blank rows or two blank columns.

When the material you want to graph automatically meets the foregoing requirements, position the cursor anywhere in the range and press **GRAPH/F10**. If the result is garbled, verify that the material to be graphed is separated from *all* other material by at least two blank rows and two blank columns. If it is, consider the next possibility.

Columnwise or Rowwise

How 1-2-3 treats data ranges for automatic graphing depends on the *Worksheet* setting for Columnwise or Rowwise. The default is Columnwise, which means that graph ranges X and A through F are assigned to *columns*. In the worksheet in Figure 11-2, the data is entered in rows. An automatic graph based on that spreadsheet makes no sense when the data ranges are columns. To change the way 1-2-3 treats ranges, type

/WGD   Enters the Worksheet Global Default command.

G   Selects Graph.

R   Selects Rowwise to change the orientation for automatic graphing.

QQ   Returns to the Ready Mode.

You don't need to return to the Ready mode to use the GRAPH/F10 key, so as soon as you change the orientation, press **GRAPH/F10** to see if it improved the graph.

Assuming you have changed the automatic graphing direction to Rowwise from Columnwise, the spreadsheet shown in Figure 11-2 is a candidate for automatic graphing. But you may also run into some problems getting the X range to line up with the correct points. The solution requires some trial and error work. For example, position the cursor in the middle of the block, say on D10, then press **GRAPH/F10**. The data ranges appear, but the X range isn't assigned. Now move the cursor to D8 and press **GRAPH/F10** again. This time, it picks up the row of column labels as the X range. Several trials are often necessary to get the automatic specification of the data ranges to come out correctly.

Selecting View when no data ranges have been specified is just like selecting **GRAPH/F10**. The same rules apply, and the same automatic assignment of the X range and the A through F data ranges takes place. The only drawback View has compared with using **GRAPH/F10** from the Ready mode is that you can't move the cursor to adjust its position when the assignment doesn't come out right.

Changing Automatic Graph Types

The default automatic graph type is Line, but you can use any of the other graph types by simply entering the Graph command, selecting Type, and making your choice.

GRAPH TYPES

Lotus 1-2-3 can create and print seven basic graph types and a number of variations on the basic graph types. This section contains an example and a discussion of each graph type. Legends, titles, and other labels have been added to the figures to make them easier to understand.

The best way to familiarize yourself with the variety of Lotus graph types is to view each graph you create using each of the graph types. You quickly learn what each does and which is best for a particular application.

Line Graph

The line graph, 1-2-3's default graph type, is an all-purpose graph. It displays information as a series of data points connected by lines. Each data point represents the level of a variable measured on the y-axis across categories, such as divisions, regions, days, months, years, or quarters displayed on the x-axis. A line graph is much like a bar chart, and anything that can be presented as a line graph can also be presented as a horizontal or vertical bar chart. Figure 11–9 presents an example of a typical line graph.

The most important addition you can make to a line graph is to label the divisions along the x-axis. Otherwise, you can't tell which information belongs to each division, product, month, year, and so on. To label the divisions, specify as the X data range the cells on your spreadsheet that contain the information you want displayed along the horizontal axis of the graph.

The Option Format command can suppress the display of connecting lines, symbols at the data points, or both lines and symbols. Suppress the lines to display the information as a scatter diagram. Suppress the symbols when the number of observations grows large and the symbols crowd together. Suppress both when you want to simplify a graph by displaying fewer data ranges.

Bar Charts: Horizontal, Vertical, and Multiple

The Type selection Bar produces several distinct graph types, depending on the number of data ranges specified and whether the graph is displayed

Figure 11-9   Line graph.

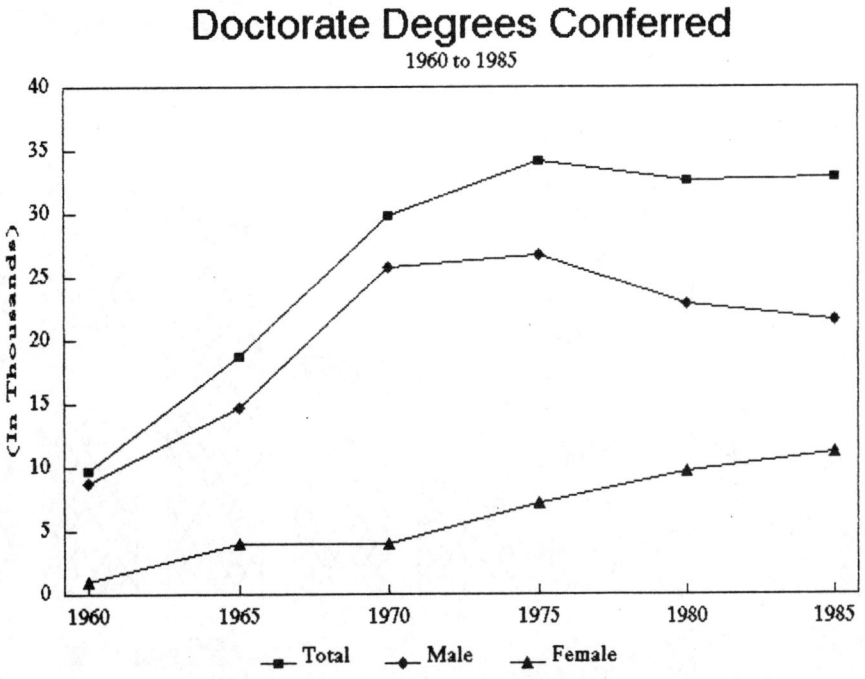

horizontally or vertically. But no matter what type of illustration you specify, all bar charts show relative performance such as sales, employment, or expenses, over categories such as regions, products, years, industries, or quarters. In this way, bar charts are similar to line graphs, but they can be displayed either vertically (Figure 11-10) or horizontally (Figure 11-11).

When two or more data ranges are specified, a bar chart automatically becomes a multiple-bar chart, a sample of which appears in Figure 11-12. This is not a separate graph type, but an extension of the horizontal and vertical bar charts.

As with the line graph, the X range is used to specify the labels to be displayed at the divisions along the x-axis of horizontal and the y-axis of vertical bar charts.

Figure 11–10 Bar chart.

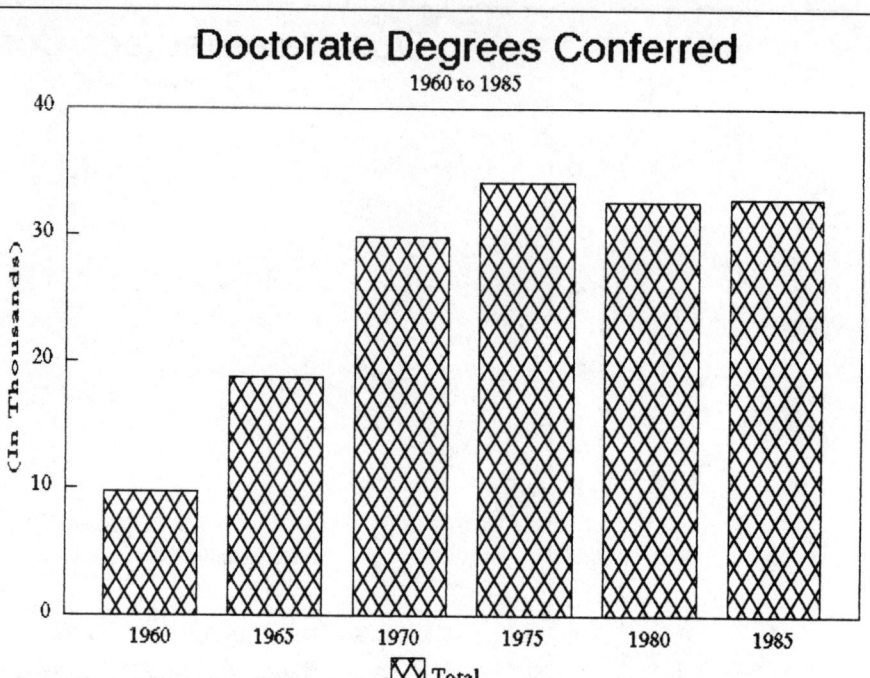

Stacked-Bar Chart

The stacked-bar chart shows the relationship between parts and wholes across categories such as regions, products, or years. See Figure 11–13 for an example.

Information such as male and female recipients of doctorate degrees in Figure 11–13 that graphs well as a stacked-bar chart can also be graphed as a bar or line graph. However, bar and line graphs often make no sense when redisplayed as a stacked-bar chart. The key to these graph types is the part:whole relationship. If the information in each data range adds up to a whole, then a stacked-bar chart is appropriate. Otherwise, it isn't.

As with the line and bar charts, the X range specifies the location of x-axis labels for a stacked-bar chart.

Figure 11-11   Horizontal bar chart.

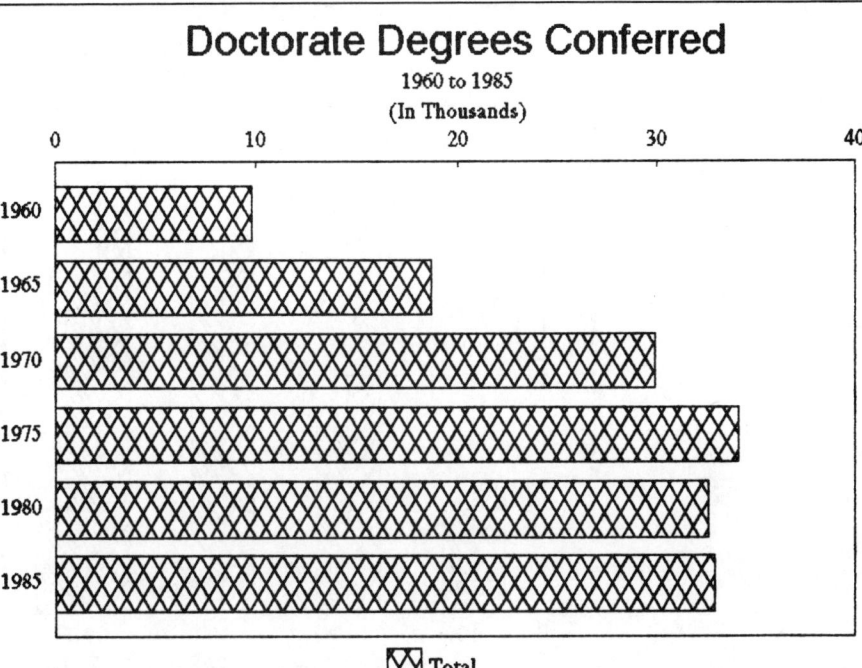

Mixed Graph

The Mixed graph type is a combination of bar chart and line graph. See Figure 11-14. You can specify up to three ranges (A, B, and C) to be plotted as bars and three additional ranges (D, E, and F) to be plotted as lines. In Figure 11-14 the detail—number of male and female recipients of doctorate degrees—is presented as bars to emphasize the absolute increase in female recipients of degrees and the absolute decline in degrees conferred on males. The line graph shows what has been happening to the total degrees conferred.

In Figure 11-14 both the line and the bars use the scale on the left y-axis. When they represent completely different types of information such as doctorate degrees conferred and total population, you can use the second y-axis (discussed later under Features) to scale either the bars or the line on the right y-axis.

Figure 11–12 Multiple-bar chart.

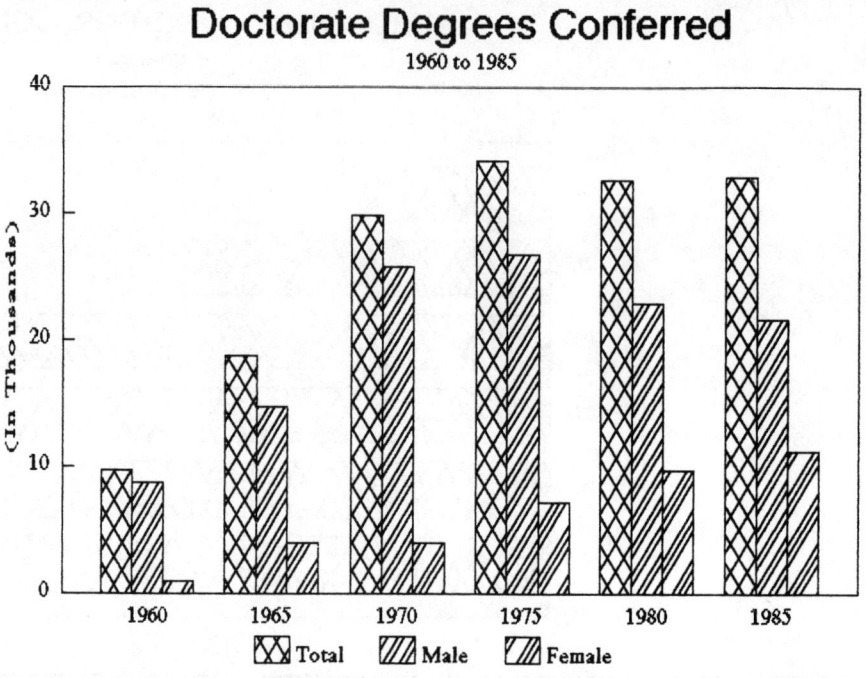

High-Low-Close Graph

The high-low-close graph is used to plot stock, bond, or other security prices where information is typically given as the high price for the period, the low price for the period, and the closing price for the period. The upper and lower ends of the line plot the high and low prices. Tick marks to the right indicate the closing price and tick marks to the left show the opening price. You don't need to specify all of this information, but you must specify data in ranges A and B. The data ranges contain the following information:

- A   High price. Indicates top of bar. (required)
- B   Low price. Indicates bottom of bar. (required)
- C   Closing price. Right-pointing tick mark. (optional)
- D   Opening price. Left-pointing tick mark. (optional)
- E   Volume. Plotted as a vertical bar chart along the bottom of the graph. (optional)

Figure 11-13   Stacked-bar chart.

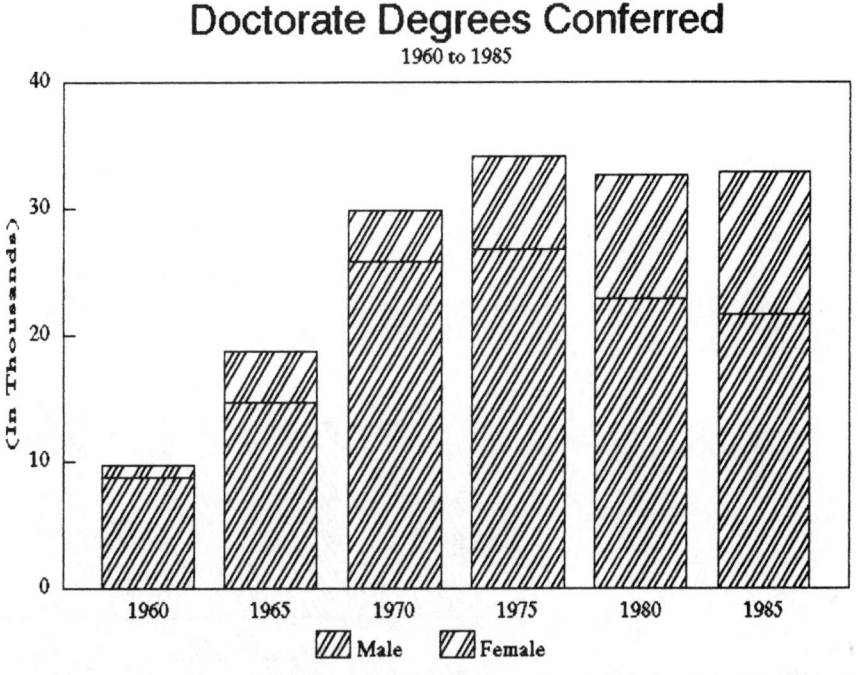

F   Line through high-low-close graph. (optional)

See Figure 11-15 for an example. All ranges have been specified except range D, opening price, and range F, line through graph.

As in the bar, line, stacked bar, and mixed graphs, the X range is used to specify the x-axis labels for the high-low-close chart.

XY Graph

An XY graph is like a line graph, except that the x-axis represents a real data range rather than arbitrary divisions such as months, regions, or sales territories. The numbers on the y-axis are said to be a function of the values on the x-axis.

To construct an XY graph you specify the values for the x-axis as the X data range. This range must contain only values. Any labels in the X range are evaluated as zero, and the result is usually a strange-looking graph. See Figure 11-16 for an example of an XY graph.

Figure 11-14   Mixed graph combining a bar chart and a line graph.

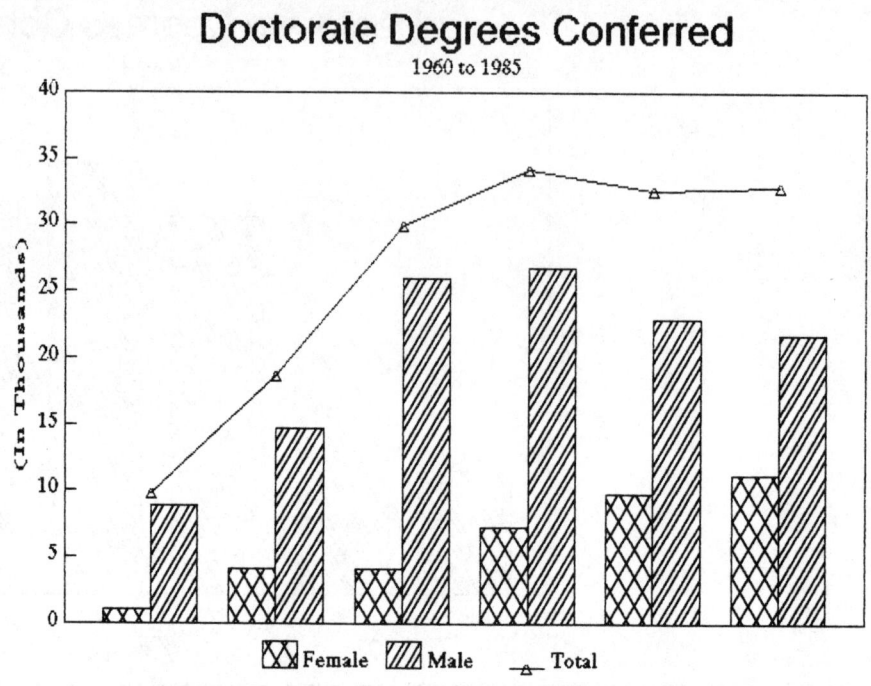

Pie Charts

Like the stacked-bar chart, the pie chart displays the relationship between a whole and its parts, but for only *one* period or division. Therefore, a pie chart uses only one data range, the A range. However, entries in the B data range control display attributes (color, hatching, and exploding), and entries in the C range suppress the display of the percentage attributable to each segment. You can also use the Options Advanced commands Color and Hatches to specify the color or hatching pattern for the entire A range. A pie chart ignores anything in data ranges D through F. A pie chart is typically used to show such things as the relative sizes of categories in a budget, regional sales in total sales, or sources of revenue by product line.

See Figure 11-17 for an example of a pie chart.

As noted, the pie chart uses the A range for data but the B range to specify the type of crosshatching or the color used to fill a segment and whether to "explode," or offset, the segment for emphasis. The C range

Figure 11-15   High-low-close graph.

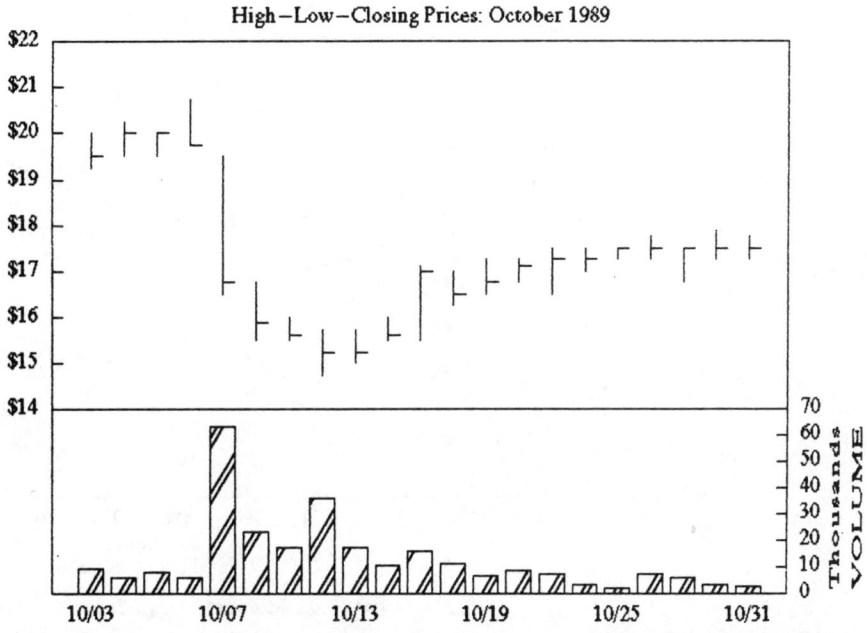

determines whether the percentage of the total represented by the segment is displayed.

The numbers 1 to 14 in the B range indicate the different fill patterns. Adding 100 to a number (such as 101, 102) specifies that the segment is to be exploded. Figure 11-18 shows a 15-sector pie chart with each sector exploded. Segment 1 contains the crosshatching patterns that result from the Code 101, segment 2 the Code 102, and so forth. The last segment, segment 15, contains a negative code. This causes that segment to disappear from the pie chart. Note that segment 1 (the first entry in the B range) appears at the "three o'clock" position. Successive segments are displayed counterclockwise from segment 1. Also in Figure 11-18 the C range has been specified. It contains only zeros, which signal 1-2-3 to suppress the display of the percent associated with each segment.

If you want the segments labeled, specify the labels as the X range in the same way you specified the X range as the labels for the x-axis in a line, bar, or stacked-bar chart.

| Figure 11-16 | XY graph. |

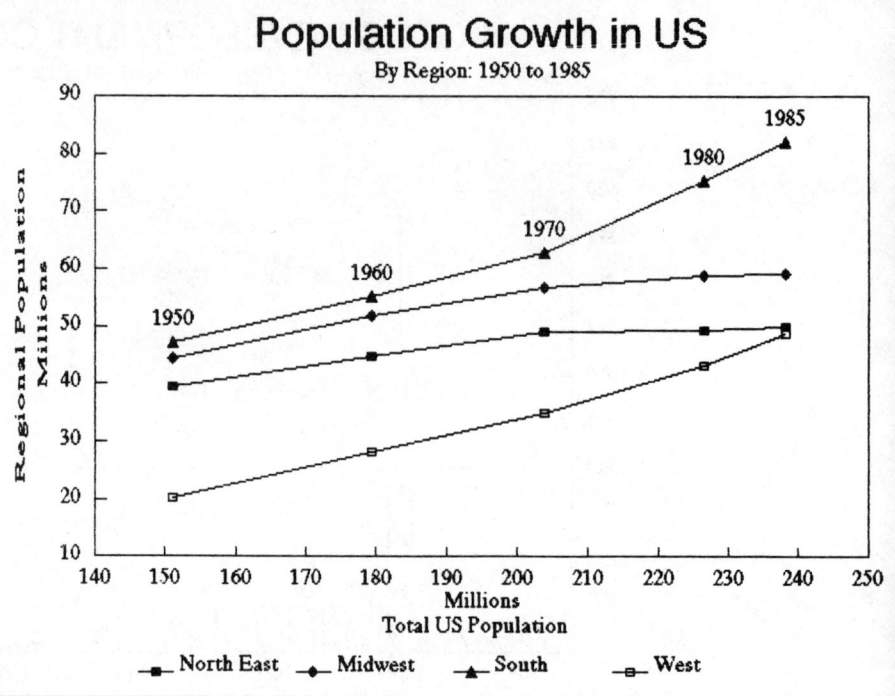

FEATURES

One of the choices under Type is Features. This option modifies the display of many of the graphs in ways that almost result in entirely new graph types.

Features Options

When you select Features you are given the following choices:

Vertical	Displays graph vertically. Default display.
Horizontal	Used with all graph types except pie. Displays graph horizontally with x-axis along left edge of screen.

THE GRAPH COMMANDS

Figure 11-17   Pie chart.

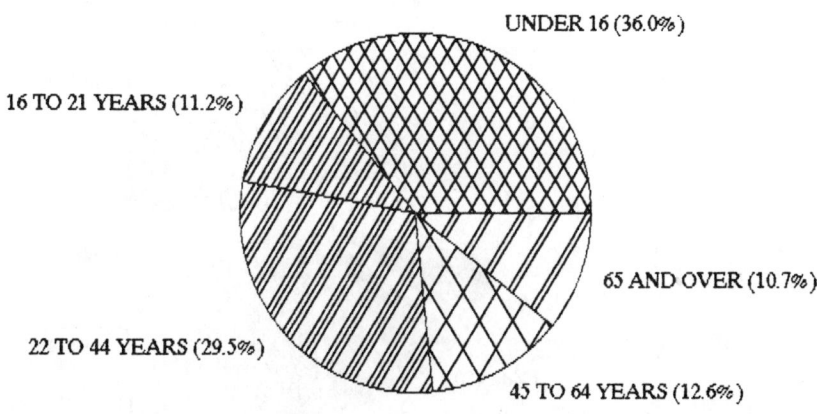

Stacked	Choices: Yes No. Used with line, bar, mixed, and XY with two or more data ranges. Each range is added to the range below it.
100%	Choices: Yes No. Used with line, bar, mixed, stacked bar, and XY graphs with two or more data ranges. Displays corresponding data range values as percentages of their total value.
2Y-Ranges	Choices: Graph A B C D E F Quit. Assigns all (Graph) or selected data ranges to the right-hand (or second) y-axis.
Y-Ranges	Choices: Graph A B C D E F Quit. Assigns all (Graph) or selected data ranges to the left-hand y-axis. Default is to assign all data ranges to the left-hand y-axis.

Horizontal and Vertical

Vertical is the default orientation. Use it to restore a graph that is currently displayed horizontally to vertical display. Horizontal rotates the graph 90 degrees and places the x-axis along the left edge of the screen. The original y-axis now appears across the top of the graph and, if one has been spec-

Figure 11-18 Crosshatching codes for pie chart.

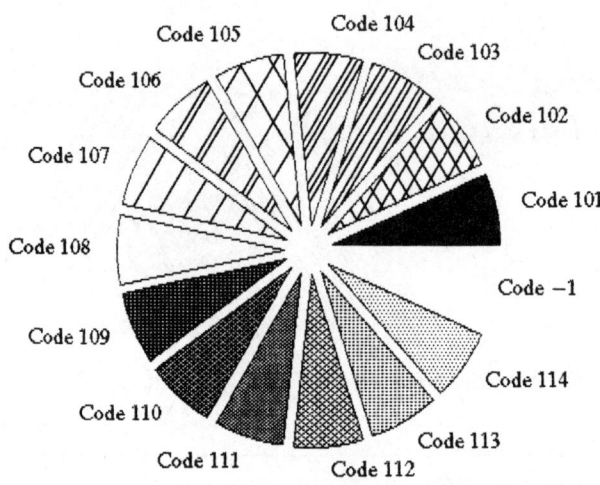

ified, the second y-axis is displayed along the bottom of the graph. Any titles that have been assigned to an axis rotate with the corresponding axis. Refer again to Figure 11-11 for an example of a bar chart displayed horizontally.

Stacked

Selecting Stacked is the equivalent of selecting Stack Bar as the type. In fact, if you originally have a bar chart with multiple bars the result is exactly the same as selecting Stack Bar as the graph Type. But you can also stack line, mixed, and XY graphs to create the equivalent of a stacked-bar chart with those graph types. In Figure 11-19, the two data ranges are the number of doctorate degrees conferred on males and on females. When the Features Stacked option is selected, each line is added to the preceding line. In this way, the distance to the top line is total doctorate degrees conferred, whereas the distance between the two lines is the number of female doctorate holders.

100%

This option conveys the part:whole relationship of a pie chart, but for each x-axis division on a line, bar, mixed, stacked bar, or XY graph. Under

Figure 11-19 Line graph with data ranges stacked. Top line shows total doctorate degrees conferred, and distance between lines shows number of degrees conferred on women.

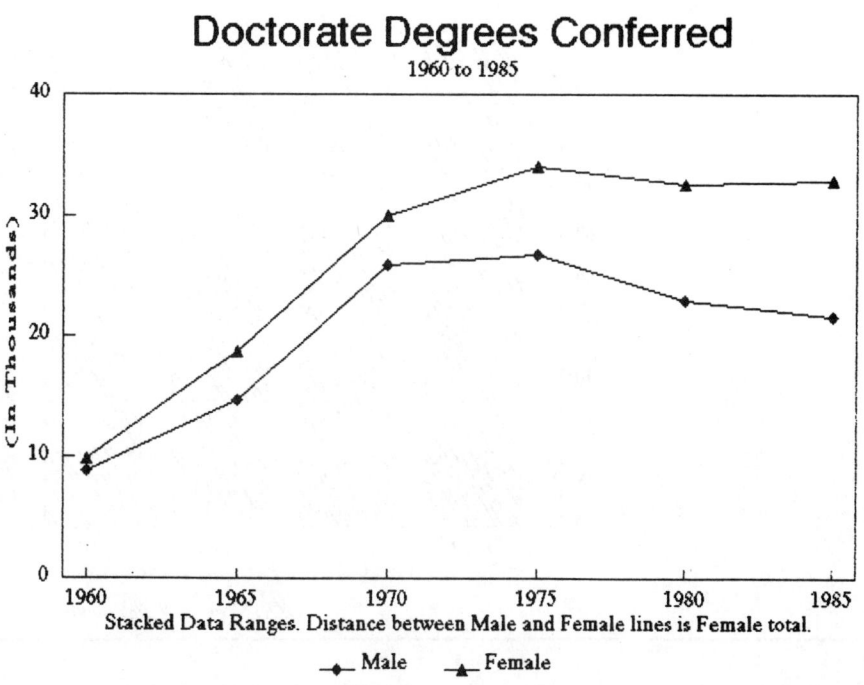

the 100% option, each data point on one of these graphs is presented as a percentage of the total data points for a particular month, year, sales territory, or other division. See Figure 11-20 for an example of a line graph after the 100% option is used.

2Y-Ranges and Y-Ranges

These two options shift data ranges back and forth between the left and right vertical axes. The default is to assign all data ranges to the left vertical axis (the normal y-axis). When you select 2Y-Ranges you can assign individual ranges to the right-hand axis, or you can select Graph to assign all of the ranges at one time. The Y-Ranges option transfers back to the left vertical axis specified ranges that were assigned to the second y-axis by the 2Y-Ranges option. The second y-axis is often used when there is a large difference between the magnitudes graphed on each axis or the items represented by each axis are totally different. See Figure 11-21 for an example of a graph with two Y ranges.

Figure 11-20 Figure 11-19 graphed as a 100% bar chart.

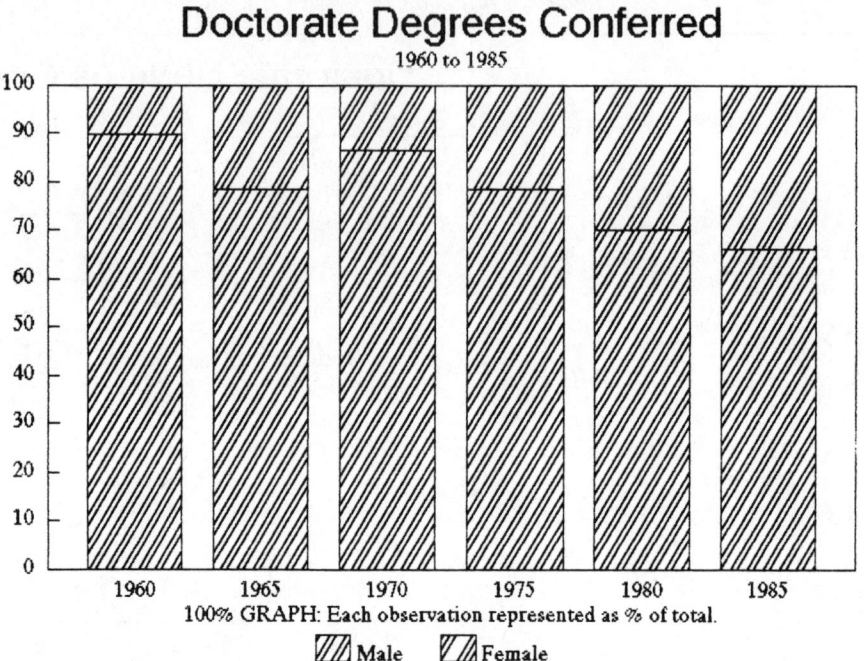

Logarithmic Scaling

Logarithmic scaling of the x-, y-, or second y-axis isn't part of the Features command discussed in this section. Still it is a way to modify your graph almost to the point of making it into a new graph type, so it should be treated here along with the other Type Features options. Besides, the command is buried in such an obscure place you'll probably never find it on your own.

When an axis is scaled logarithmically each division represents 10 times the previous division (1, 10, 100, 1000, and so on), rather than an equal absolute number of units. Logarithmically scaled axes are useful when a data range increases or decreases by a great amount.

The command that scales an axis logarithmically is under Options Scale Y-Scale (X-Scale or 2Y-Scale) Type. When you finally get that deep in the command tree, you have the option of selecting Standard (equal absolute units between tick marks) or Logarithmic.

Figure 11-21 Graph with both left and right y-axes.

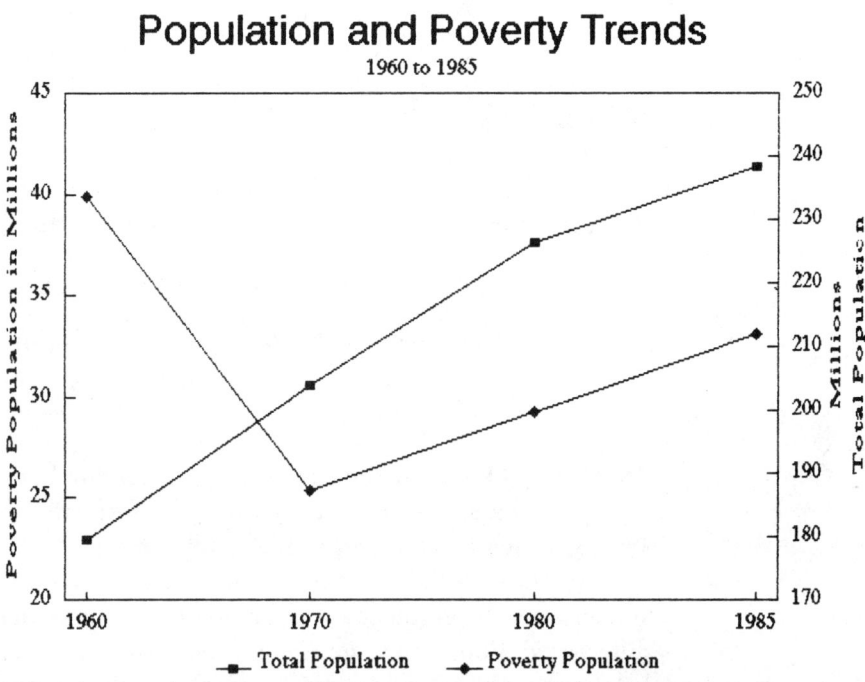

DISPLAYING GRAPHS AND SPREADSHEETS SIMULTANEOUSLY

Although it is not part of the Graph command, you know from Chapter 2 that the Worksheet Window command can be used to split the screen into two parts where the right side displays the current graph and the left side displays part of the worksheet. For this feature to work, your monitor and display driver must be capable of displaying both text and graphics at the same time. If they aren't capable of such a display, the graph side of the screen appears as a blank. To find out whether your system can display both graphs and text simultaneously, try it.

Before you split the screen, press **GRAPH/F10** to verify that a graph is currently specified. If the screen comes up blank, specify a graph before splitting the window. Alternatively, you can specify a graph after splitting, and the specified graph appears in the window. If, however, you select a named graph after you split the window, the named graph fills the entire screen. When you press a key to return to the spreadsheet, the graph is displayed in the graph window and the spreadsheet in the left-hand text window.

As with all Worksheet Window commands, the location of the cursor before entering the command determines where the split takes place. If the cursor isn't in the correct cell, you must return to the Ready Mode and correctly position it before entering the Worksheet Window command.

To split the screen and display a graph in the right-hand window, position the cursor in the column where you want the split and type

/WW   Enters the Worksheet Window command.

G   Selects Graph to divide the screen vertically at the current cursor location. You are immediately returned to the Ready mode.

See Figure 11–22 for the split screen containing both a spreadsheet and a graph. The spreadsheet contains the information to generate Figure 11–18, which is displayed in the graph window.

Once the screen is split, when you change anything in the underlying spreadsheet the graph changes automatically. In particular, you can select different options from the Graph command menu (graph types, crosshatching patterns, color assignments, or other options) and watch the

Figure 11–22   Screen split showing graph in right-hand window and spreadsheet in left-hand window.

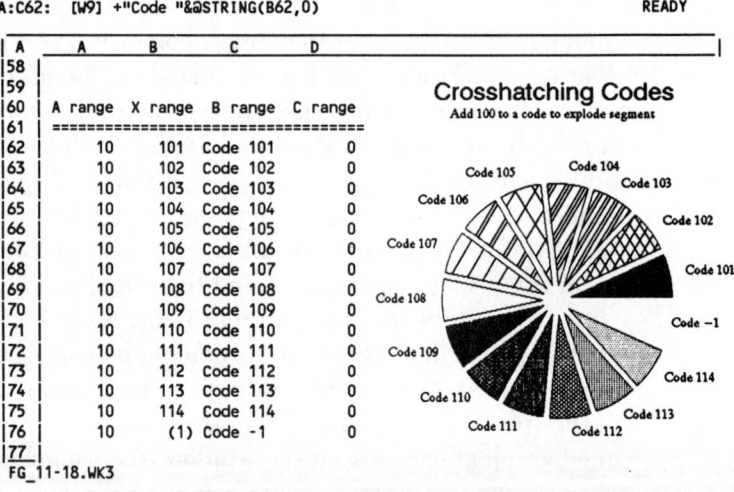

THE GRAPH COMMANDS 447

graph change. This is a particularly useful technique for getting the correct details for a graph.

To remove the split, type

/WW   Enters the Worksheet Window command.

C   Selects Clear. You are returned to the Ready mode.

BUILDING A LIBRARY OF NAMED GRAPHS

You can create many different graphs based on the information in one spreadsheet or on multiple spreadsheets in a stack. But each time you create a new graph it becomes the current graph, and the graph that was the current graph is lost. To save the current graph for viewing later, use the Graph Name command to assign it a name. In this way you can build a library of named graphs. See Figure 11–23 for the command tree.

Graph names, like range names, can be up to 15 characters long and can use all of the characters on the keyboard, including the SPACE BAR character. Graph names are saved with the worksheet and can be used any time the worksheet is loaded into memory.

Figure 11–23   Graph Name command tree.

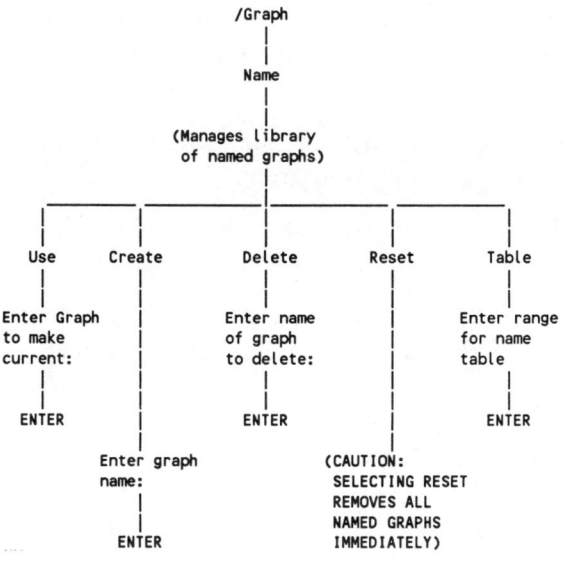

Names are assigned to the current graph. If you need to verify the current graph, select View or press **GRAPH/F10** before you assign the name. To assign a name to the current graph, type

/G	Enters the Graph command.
N	Selects Name from the main Graph command menu.
C	Selects Create.
Enter graph name:	Asks for name to assign to graph.
doc_degree_bar	Type in name for the graph.
ENTER	Assigns specified name to current graph.

Graph names must be unique, but more than one name can be assigned to the same graph.

Using Named Graphs

To use a named graph, type

/GN	Enters the Graph Name command.
U	Selects the Use option.
NAME/F3	Optionally displays all named graphs on the screen at one time. Otherwise, only the first four names appear at the top of the screen.
Arrow keys	Highlight the name of the graph to be made the current graph.
ENTER	Makes the highlighted graph name the current graph. Graph is displayed.

The **NAME/F3** key makes it particularly easy to find a graph when many graphs have been named on the same spreadsheet.

Removing Named Graphs

There are two ways to remove named graphs; one is simple, the other *drastic*.

THE GRAPH COMMANDS 449

Graph Name Delete

Because the Graph Name Delete command removes one graph at a time, it is the preferred way to remove names of graphs you no longer want to keep in your library.

To use the command, type

/GND	Enters the Graph Name Delete Command.
NAME/F3	Optionally displays all named graphs on the screen at one time.
Arrow keys	Highlight name of graph to be deleted.
ENTER	Deletes the highlighted graph name.

Graph Name Reset

As with most 1-2-3 Reset commands, this command removes *all* graph names *instantly*. You are not given a chance to reconsider once you touch the **R** key or press **ENTER** when Reset is highlighted.

Be extremely cautious when using the Reset command. Only do it when you are certain you want to wipe out all graph names. Remember, the Delete option is the preferred alternative, because it removes named graphs one at a time.

Modifying Named Graphs

When you make a named graph the current graph, you can add data ranges, change titles, change graph types, and make any other modification you desire. However, those changes don't *automatically* become part of the specifications of the named graph. In fact, if you were to use the Graph Name Use command to select the named graph again, you would find the graph returned to its original state minus all of your modifications.

To save the modifications made to a named graph, you *must* rename the graph. This is the same as when modifying a worksheet. Loading a worksheet and modifying it doesn't save the modifications. You must go one step farther and use the File Save command to save the worksheet.

You can assign a new name to the modified graph or you can reassign its previous name to replace the previous specification with the modified specification.

Tabling Named Graphs

When you create several named graphs in the same active file, go one further step: create a table of named graphs. The table includes the name you assigned, the type of graph, and the text assigned as the First Title (the main graph title). Like many other 1-2-3 commands of this type, the output writes over the current cell contents, so make your life easier (and safer) by using the Worksheet Insert Sheet command to add a new sheet to the current file, then place the table of graph names on that sheet.

To create a table of named graphs in the current file, type

/GN	Enters the Graph Name command.
T	Selects Table.
Enter range for name table:	Asks for upper left hand of range of cells in which to write table.
Arrow keys	Position the cursor.
ENTER	Executes the command and writes a table of graph names, types, and titles.

See Figure 11–24 for a table of graph names for some of the graphs used in this chapter.

Figure 11–24   Result of Graph Name Table command.

A	Z	AA	AB	AC	AD	AE	AF	AG
1	FIGURE 11-10	Bar	Doctorate Degrees Conferred					
2	FIGURE 11-11	Bar	Doctorate Degrees Conferred					
3	FIGURE 11-12	Bar	Doctorate Degrees Conferred					
4	FIGURE 11-13	Stack-Bar	Doctorate Degrees Conferred					
5	FIGURE 11-14	Mixed	Doctorate Degrees Conferred					
6	FIGURE 11-15	HLC	LOTUS DEVELOPMENT CORP.					
7	FIGURE 11-17	Pie	PERSONS BELOW THE POVERTY LINE IN THE UNITED STATES					
8	FIGURE 11-18	Pie	Crosshatching Codes					
9	FIGURE 11-19	Line	Doctorate Degrees Conferred					
10	FIGURE 11-20	Line	Population and Poverty Trends					
11	FIGURE 11-24	Line	Doctorate Degrees Conferred					
11	FIGURE 11-25	Line	Doctorate Degrees Conferred					
13	FIGURE 11-26	Bar	CROSSHATCHING PATTERNS FOR ADVANCED HATCHES					
14	FIGURE 11-3	Bar						
15	FIGURE 11-4	Bar						
16	FIGURE 11-6	Bar	Doctorate Degrees Conferred					
17	FIGURE 11-7	Bar	FIRST TITLE: Centered above graph					
18	FIGURE 11-8	Bar						
19	FIGURE 11-9	Line	Doctorate Degrees Conferred					
20								

CANCELING GRAPH SETTINGS

The Graph Reset command removes specified ranges from the current graph, options from the current graph, or the entire graph. Unlike most other 1-2-3 Reset commands, this command doesn't execute as soon as you select it. Instead, the following submenu appears:

Graph A B C D E F Ranges Options Quit

Reset Graph

Select Graph to cancel the current graph. No ranges, options, or other choices survive this Reset operation. The graph type is returned to line, the default graph type.

Reset Data Range

To remove a particular data range from the current graph, select the letter of the range. All other ranges, options, and so on, remain unaffected.

You can continue to remove ranges. When you are finished, select Quit to return to the main Graph command menu.

Reset Ranges

This option clears all data ranges—A through F and the X data range. It leaves intact the graph Type and any options or other settings you have selected.

Use this option when you want to use a particular graph setting with an entirely different set of data ranges. If you want to add the new graph to your library, assign it a name. Use the old name if you want to replace the old graph specification; use a new name if you want to keep the old graph specification in your library.

Reset Options

This choice clears all of the choices you have made under the Options submenu. Legends, titles, scaling, and so on, are cleared. Make this choice when you want to assign completely new options to the current graph type and data ranges.

OPTIONS

Earlier in this chapter you were introduced to the two most important Graph options: Legend and Titles. The other choices under Options are more specialized (refer again to Figure 11–5 for the command tree) and thus are used less frequently.

B&W and Color

Two options, B&W and Color, switch the display between black and white and color. Black and white graphs use different crosshatching patterns to separate different bars; color graphs use different colors for this purpose.

If your printer cannot print or plot in color, the crosshatching patterns are substituted for the colors when you print your graph. Color is the initial default setting for color monitors except for Color Graphic Adapter (CGA) monitors. B&W is the initial default setting for monochrome and CGA monitors. Lotus assigns default colors and hatching patterns, but you can change them with the Graph Options Advanced commands Color and Hatches, discussed below.

Whenever you select B&W or Color you are left in the Options submenu.

Data Labels

Data labels are values placed on a graph to give the exact value for a bar; a segment of a stacked-bar chart; a high, low, or close on a high-low-close graph; or a data point on a line, area, or XY graph. Because it is often hard to read exact values from a graph, data labels are used to provide the information directly.

To place the total above the data points in a line graph of the Degrees Conferred worksheet in Figure 11–2, from the Ready mode type

/GO	Enters the Graph Options command.
D	Selects the Data-Labels option.

THE GRAPH COMMANDS

A	Selects A as the data range to be assigned data labels.
Enter data-label range for first data range:	Asks for the location of the A (or first) data range data labels.
Arrow keys	Position the cursor on B9, the first cell of the range containing total doctorates.
.	Tacks cursor to cell B9.
Arrow keys	Highlight range B9..G9.
ENTER	Sets range.
A	Selects Above as position for data labels.
QQ	Returns to main Graph menu.
V	Selects View to view the graph.

The result appears in Figure 11–25.

Skipping Data Labels

Use data labels sparingly, because their number and position can clutter a graph to the point where it is very difficult to read. If this happens, reposition the data labels or eliminate some or all of them.

Skipping data labels can present a problem, because the information most often used as data labels is the same as information used in the corresponding data range. To eliminate some of the information, use the Range Values command to make a copy of the data range. Then erase from the copied range those data points you do not want displayed. When the range containing the values is specified, only those cells containing entries are displayed as data points. Be sure to specify the entire range so the remaining data labels line up with the correct data points.

Canceling a Data Label Range

To cancel a data label assignment, use the Reset command and select the data range to which the labels were assigned. This cancels both the data range and the data labels assigned to that range. Then reassign the data range you just canceled to restore it to your graph.

There are two other ways you can cancel a data label range. If the data label range and the data range aren't the same cells, just erase the cells designated as the data range. The data labels are still assigned, but because there is nothing in the cells it appears as if there are no data labels.

Figure 11–25 Data labels above A data range.

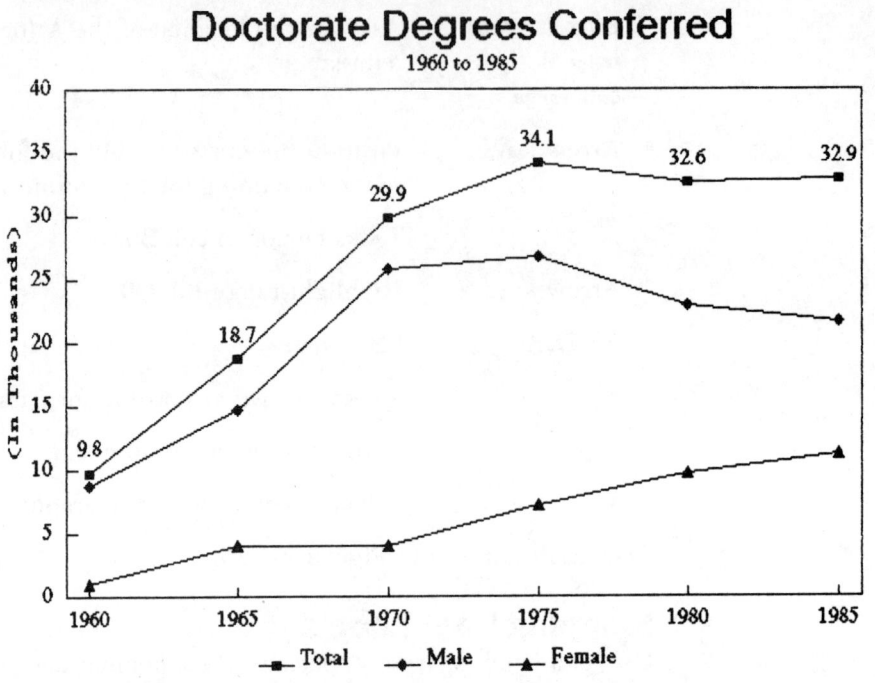

Alternatively, if you have used a data range for data labels, reassign that data label range to a blank cell. The blank cell makes it appear as if no data label range has been assigned.

Grid

The grid option serves some of the same functions as data labels and has some of the same drawbacks. With the grid option, you specify either horizontal or vertical lines (or both) to form a grid.

Grids make it easier to estimate the value of a data point or the height of a bar and therefore are a substitute for data labels. Again, the rule is to use grids when they help and not to use them when they make your graph harder to understand.

When you select Y-Axis you are given the choice of having the grid come from the left y-axis (the Y option), the right y-axis (the 2Y option), or from both axes.

See Figure 11–26 for Figure 11–25 displayed with grid lines.

Figure 11-26 Figure 11-25 displayed with grid lines.

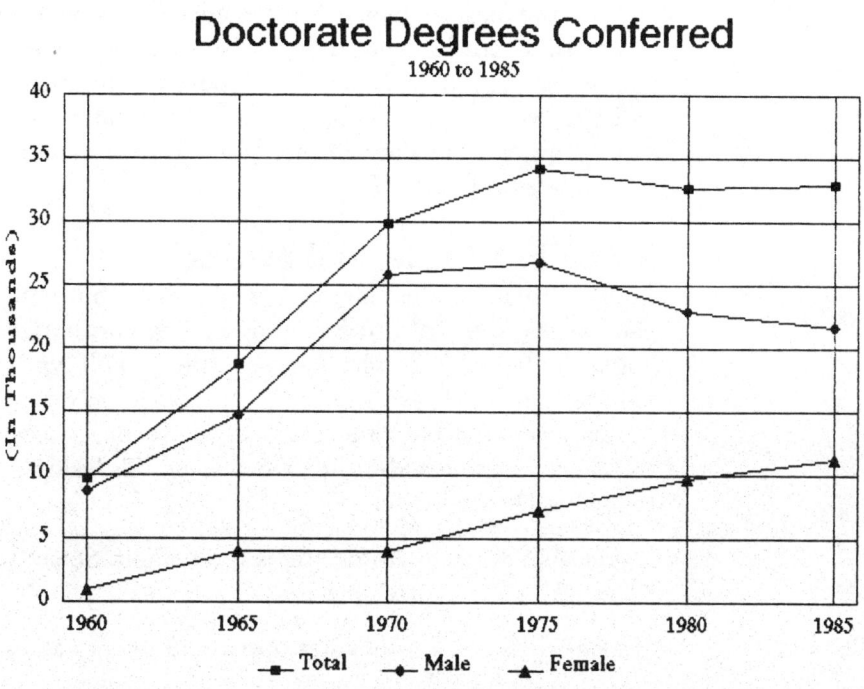

Scale

The Scale option contains a number of choices that have to do with the way 1-2-3 treats the horizontal and vertical axes. When you select the Graph Options Scale command the following submenu appears:

Y Scale   X Scale   Skip   2Y-Scale

The three scale choices enable you to change from automatic to manual scaling, suppress scale indicators, and change the display format of values used to label divisions on the axis. The Skip option in the command is the most frequently used of the Scale command options.

Skip

When there are relatively few x-axis labels, 1-2-3 displays them by each division on a single line below the x-axis. When there are more, 1-2-3 uses two lines to display them. When there are many, 1-2-3 reduces the size of each x-axis label to the point of unreadability. The Skip command restores readability or simply clears out the clutter that can occur where there are many x-axis labels.

With the Skip command you can choose to have every other (2), every third (3), fourth (4), and so on, divisions labeled while skipping the label for the intervening divisions. The skip factor ranges from 1 (every division) to 8192. When you choose a skip factor greater than 1, intervening divisions appear, but they are not labeled. Experiment to arrive at the appropriate skip factor.

X-Scale, Y-Scale, and 2Y-Scale

Lotus normally scales the axis automatically, but with these options you can specify the scale to be used. Scaling the horizontal axis manually applies only to XY graphs, because other graph types don't use the horizontal scale to display values. The 2Y-Scale only applies when you have assigned some of the data ranges to the second y-axis.

When you select X-Scale, Y-Scale, or 2Y-Scale, a submenu with the following choices appears:

Automatic	Automatic is the default. Select to cancel manual scaling.
Manual	Activates upper and lower values.
Lower	Sets lower value. You must select Manual to activate it.
Upper	Sets upper value. You must select Manual to activate it.
Format	Sets Standard 1-2-3 numerical display formats (Percent, Currency, and so on). General is the default format.
Indicator	Turns On (default) or Off or sets Manually the scale indicator (for example, Thousands) displayed along an axis. With Manual you can specify any text up to 512 characters long.
Type	Choices are Standard (default) and Logarithmic. Choose Logarithmic to divide axis evenly between progressive orders of magnitude (powers of 10).
Exponent	Choices are Automatic (default) or Manual. Choose Manual to specify the order of magnitude of the scaling.

THE GRAPH COMMANDS

Width   Choices are Automatic (default) or Manual. Manual sets the maximum width for scale numbers. Asterisks are displayed if maximum is exceeded.

Quit   Returns to Options submenu.

The default for each of the axes is automatic scaling, but Manual has some important uses. When the bars are tall and all of the interesting variation occurs at the top, use the Manual option for scale to begin the bar chart near the top instead of at zero. For an XY graph in which you want to focus in on just one part of the graph, set both the X and Y scales to include just the section you are interested in.

Format

Format is a confusing name for this command, because this "format" is not the same as the "format" just discussed under the Scale option, which is the typical use of the word in 1-2-3 (as in Range Format). This format doesn't affect the display of values. Rather, it sets certain attributes for the lines and data points on line, area, and XY graphs. It has no effect on bar charts, pie charts, or high-low-close graphs.

When you select the Graph Options Format command, the following submenu appears:

Graph   A   B   C   D   E   F   Quit

Select either the entire Graph or the appropriate data range and the following submenu appears:

Lines   Symbols   Both   Neither   Area

The default is Both, which displays both symbols and their connecting lines.

Lines suppress the display of symbols that mark each data point. This option is useful when there are so many data points that the graph is difficult to read.

Selecting Symbols suppresses the display of the connecting lines. The result is a scatter plot.

Selecting Both restores the display to its default status—both lines and symbols.

The Neither choice causes the line to disappear from the screen. When there are several data ranges on a graph, this is a quick way to eliminate some of the clutter in order to focus on one or two lines. To restore a line to display, select its letter and specify one of the other choices. If you select Graph, then Neither, the entire graph disappears from the screen. To restore the display of the graph, select Graph and then specify one of the other choices.

When you select Graph and then Area, the areas between the lines are filled with a color or a hatch pattern, depending on whether you are displaying your graphs in color or monochrome. If you select a single data range, 1-2-3 fills the area between that data range and the x-axis with either color or a hatch pattern.

Advanced

With the Option Advanced you can specify the following attributes on the current graph:

Colors	Sets one of eight colors for each data range, hides a data range, or specifies a range that contains a code to assign colors to individual data points.
Text	Sets color, font, and/or size for different blocks of text (first title, legends, and so on).
Hatches	Sets hatch patterns for data ranges.

These choices affect both the appearance of the graph on your display screen and the way the graph is printed with your printer.

Colors

The Colors option lets you set the colors in which each data range is displayed and in which each is printed, if your printer is capable of printing colors. If your printer can't print in color, printing reverts to black and white settings even when you have selected options under this command. When you select Colors and specify the data range, A through F, you are presented with the following submenu:

1 2 3 4 5 6 7 8 Hide Range

The numbers represent different assignments. Unfortunately, the colors assigned to the numbers vary depending on the type of monitor you have. Furthermore, the colors that are printed for each number depend on the capabilities of your printer and, in any case, may not match the colors displayed on the screen!

The only way to make sense out of this is to do some tests with your particular system. To see which colors appear on your screen when you select a particular number, create a simple bar graph with six data ranges

THE GRAPH COMMANDS

and assign the numbers 1 through 6 to the ranges A through F. Make a note of the results for future reference. You still have two more numbers (colors) to check. Create another bar chart with two data ranges and assign the remaining two numbers, 7 and 8, to those two ranges. Add the resulting information to your notes about colors.

It is easier to discover the abilities of your printer. Just select the Sample option from the Print command menu, and 1-2-3 generates a sample printout that lists the colors available with your printer and the numbers to which the colors are assigned. (See Chapter 6 for a discussion of the print sample.)

The Hide option hides the selected data range. Watch out here. You can also hide a data range with the Options Format Neither command. Try to remember which way you have performed this action, because "unhiding" a data range one way doesn't unhide it when it was hidden the other way.

Use the Range option to assign different colors to each data point, bar, or segment in a pie chart. The technique is to construct a range the same size as the data range you want to color, and then enter numbers from 1 to 14 into corresponding cells in the range. As a bonus, if you enter a zero or a negative number, the associated observation is suppressed from the screen. As with all other 1-2-3 ranges this range must be constructed *before* you enter the Advanced Colors Range command.

Depending on your monitor, you can display up to 14 colors. This is more than you could display by simply using the 1 to 8 color numbers discussed earlier. If you assign the same number to all of the observations in a data range, the entire range displays in the assigned color. The real use for this feature, however, is to use color to point out either similar observations or extreme observations. In this application, use an @IF function or other appropriate formula or function to generate the number to assign to each observation. A similar feature is available under the Hatches option discussed later in the chapter. See that discussion for an illustration of the Range option.

Text

The Advanced Text option lets you set color, font, and size for different groups of text around your graph. The groups are

First	First line of graph title.
Second	Second line of graph title, axis titles, and legends.
Third	Scale indicators, axis labels, data labels, and footnotes.

After you select a group, you have the following choices:

Color	Choices are 1 2 3 4 5 6 7 8 Hide. The same color assignments apply here as for the Colors option, discussed earlier.
Font	Choices are Default 1 2 3 4 5 6 7 8.
Size	Choices are Default 1 2 3 4 5 6 7 8 9.

Your Font and Size choices are limited by the capabilities of your printer. The default Font setting is 1 for the first group and 3 for the second and third groups. The default Size is 7 for the first group, 4 for the second group, and 2 for the third group. Lotus does not change the font on the screen, only in the printed version. It does change the size, but the size change is limited to small (choices 1 through 3), medium (choices 4 through 6), and large (choices 7 through 9). To determine the capabilities of your printer and the corresponding Font and Size number assignments, print the sample described in Chapter 6.

Hatches

Hatches is to monochrome graphs as Colors is to colored graphs. When you select Hatches and specify one of the data ranges A through F, you get to specify a crosshatching pattern for the data range. The eight choices and their corresponding patterns are

1	Solid
2	Fine crosshatching
3	Fine double hatching
4	Fine triple hatching
5	Coarse crosshatching
6	Coarse double hatching
7	Coarse single hatching
8	Hollow

As with the Colors option, you can also specify a range that can assign any of up to 14 different hatching patterns to individual observations. See Figure 11–27 for a graph where each bar represents one of the 14 different patterns. Also notice that by specifying a zero or a negative number you can cause the corresponding observation to disappear. The hatching pattern appearing on the screen is the same as the hatching pattern that will appear when the graph is printed.

Figure 11-27   Hatching codes for use with Advanced Hatches Range command.

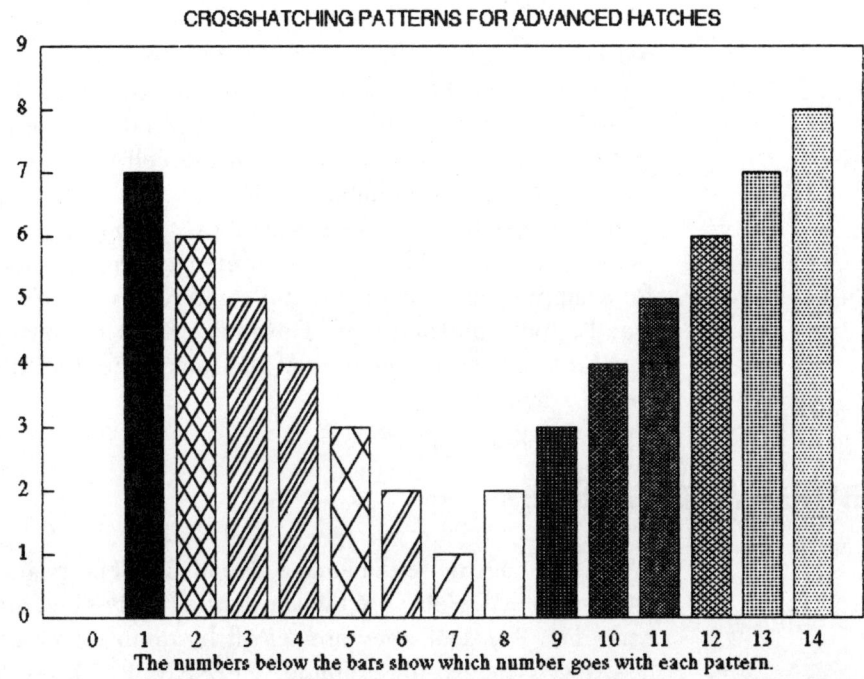

Quit

Quit, the last choice on the Options submenu, returns you to the Graph command main menu. Once there, you can select View to see the effect of choices made while in the Options submenu. You can also return to the Graph command main menu by pressing the ESC key once.

USING GRAPHS WITH MULTIPLE ACTIVE FILES

There are a few special considerations to keep in mind as you use the Graph command when there is more than one active worksheet in memory. The most important have to do with specifying ranges in other files, using the Graph Name command across files, and with the concept of the current graph.

Whatever the complications with multiple active files, remember this. Each graph resides with its own worksheet and its specifications are saved with that worksheet.

Data Ranges

The data ranges (A through F) that a graph uses can be taken from anywhere. They can be in other active files or in files stored on disk. When the range is in another active file, you can use the cursor and sheet movement keys to point to the range. When you do, the full path and filename to the cells are provided as part of the cell reference. However, the X data range must be in an active file.

References to cells containing titles, footnotes, or other text must be in currently active files. If you do refer to a cell in another file for a title, for example, and then save that file and remove it from memory, the title won't appear on the graph. However, if you retrieve the second file so that both files are in memory at the same time, the title will be restored to the graph.

Names Across Files

When you have more than one active file in memory and you select Graph Name Use or Delete, the filenames of all active files appear in the graph name list. As usual, they are set off by double greater than and double less than symbols, for example, <<FINANCE.WK3>>. Selecting the filename causes all the named graphs in the selected file to appear. You can then either use or delete named graphs in the other file. Luckily, the devastating Graph Name Reset only works its dastardly deeds on the named graphs in the current file.

Current Graph

Each active file has its own current graph. Therefore, the graph that is displayed when you press **GRAPH/F10** changes as you move from active file to active file. Furthermore, the current graph for one file may actually be a graph from another file. This can happen when the technique described for names across files is used to select a named graph from another active file. When you do, that graph becomes the current graph for the file where the cursor currently resides.

You can even go so far as to name the current graph when the current graph is based entirely on data ranges and settings in another active file. However, when you save either the current file or the file providing the information, the specifications are lost. The graph name still appears when you select Name Use, but a blank screen appears when you select it.

Other than these few qualifications, using graphs when more than one file is active is as easy as creating formulas or copying information across files.

USING GRAPHS WITH OTHER PROGRAMS

Many other microcomputer programs—word processors, graphic enhancement programs, and so on—can use graphs created by Lotus 1-2-3. To transfer a graph to these programs, you usually must save the graph into a picture file with a .PIC extension or into a graph metafile with a .CGM extension. The type of file saved depends on the current global setting. The default is metafile (.CGM), but you can change it by selecting Worksheet Global Default Graph and choosing PIC. The type of file you save depends on the requirements of the program that is going to use the file. Consult the manual for that program.

Saving a graph file is much like saving any 1-2-3 file. First, the graph you want to save must be the current graph. Verify this by pressing **GRAPH/F10**. The graph that appears on the screen is the graph that is saved.

To save the current graph type

/G	Enters the Graph command.
S	Selects Save.
Enter graph file name:	Asks for filename. Type a filename.
ENTER	Accepts the filename and saves the graph into file.

The saved graph contains all the titles, legends, and other features of the current graph. Like other Save commands, if you later modify the current graph, you must repeat the above steps to add your changes to the .CGM or .PIC file.

PRINTING GRAPHS

Most of this chapter has been devoted to the options and techniques used to create 1-2-3 graphs, but an important part of 1-2-3's graphics function is the ability to print your graphs on printers and plotters. There are three ways to print a graph: printing the current graph, printing a named graph, and printing a named graph in between ranges of spreadsheet cells.

Printed graphs are created through the Print command, but before you can print a graph you must have a printer or plotter capable of printing graphics. Also, you must have told 1-2-3 about your particular printer or plotter during the installation procedure. If you haven't, if you have changed devices since installation, or if you try to print and get a message saying that no device drive has been installed, return to the Access system and select Install. When you get to the main Install menu, select Change Selected Equipment followed by Modify Current DCF and Change Selected Printer. At this point you can specify the printer or plotter you are using. Complete the Install procedure by following the directions as they appear on the screen.

Some warnings are in order before you learn each of the three methods of printing a 1-2-3 graph.

What You See May Not Be What You Get

Like printing worksheets, printing graphs may require that you adopt a trial and error approach. A little patience doesn't hurt, either.

Many problems occur because printing a graph involves an interaction between settings selected with the Graph command and settings selected with the Print command. Thus, you can specify typefaces and typesizes with the Graph Options Advanced Text command, but none of the typefaces and only a few of the typesizes appear on the screen. Of particular concern is the fact that a typesize may be small enough to display a note or title on the screen, but too large to print the corresponding text on the graph. Either change the size with the Graph Options Advanced Text command or edit the text so that it fits on the graph in its current size.

If you change the margin settings with the Print Options Margin Left or Print Options Margin Right command, you effectively change the size of the graph. Lotus tries to adapt its typesize to these changes, but if it can't it truncates the labels. Again, there is no substitute for a little trial and error work. When you make a test print, be sure to select Printer Options Advanced Image Density Draft to save your ribbon and to speed up the printing process.

Defaults

Several Print command settings affect the printing of graphs. These commands are discussed in detail later in this section, but for now you just need to know the default settings for these options. They are

Option	Default
Rotate	Portrait: Across the page.
Image-Sz	Margin-Fill: From left to right margin.
Density	Final: Highest quality available from printer.

Note that Image-Sz is determined by the setting for the Left and Right margin under the Margins choice in the Print command Options submenu. If only part of your graph prints on a page, check the margin settings. Perhaps you have set the right margin beyond 80 for 8½-inch-wide paper or 135 for 15-inch-wide paper.

Printer or Encoded

One final choice must occur before you print your graph. As you enter the Print command menu, you can select either Printer or Encoded as the destination for your printed graph. Printer sends the output to the printer or plotter connected to your computer. Encoded prints the graph to a file. The file can then be taken or sent to a remote device, where it can be printed with the operating system Print command. Encoded files are frequently used when one high-quality graphic device such as a plotter or a laser printer must be shared by several people.

When you are using encoded files, be sure to use the Options Advanced Device command to select the appropriate device driver for the output device you are using if it is different from the one you normally use. For more information on creating encoded print files, see Chapter 6.

Printing the Current Graph

Printing the current graph under the default settings for size, density, and orientation is the easiest method available for printing a 1-2-3 graph. Instructions for printing the current graph were presented earlier in this chapter in The ABC's of Printing a 1-2-3 Graph. Consult that section if you need more information.

Briefly, the graph that appears when you press **GRAPH/F10** or select View is the current graph. It may be the graph you've just constructed or one you have selected from your library with the Name Use command.

To print the current graph, simply select Print Printer (or Encoded) Image, Current, Align, and Go. When you do, an image of the current graph is sent to your printer or written to an encoded file.

Printing a Named Graph

Printing a named graph is as easy as printing the current graph. In addition, it enables you to specify several graphs to be printed one after the other. The one drawback of printing named graphs is that you don't get to view the graph before you print it. If you are not sure whether all the titles, legends, and other features of a graph you want to print have been properly specified, select Graph Name Use to make the graph in question the current graph. Once you have verified the construction of the graph, you can proceed to print it either as the current graph or as a named graph.

To print a named graph under the default settings for size, orientation, and density type

/P	Enters the Print command.
Printer Encoded	Select either Printer or Encoded.
I	Selects Image.
N	Selects Named-Graph.
NAME/F3	Optional. Displays all named graphs on the screen. If other files are active, their filenames appear and can be selected.
Arrow keys	Highlight name of graph to print.
ENTER	Selects named graph for printing. Returns to main Print command menu.
G	Selects Go to print the graph. Specify options or select Image to specify another named graph for printing. Repeat as needed.
Q	Returns to Ready mode.

Note: You *must* select Go after you specify each graph. You can't select several graphs and then give one Go to print them all. If you forget to select Go, that graph isn't printed. Also, Lotus prints as many graphs as will fit on each page. The graph size is controlled by the placement of the left and right margins. At the default margin settings, 1-2-3 prints one graph on each 8½ by 11-inch page.

Combining Graphs with Other Print Ranges

Finally, you can specify one or more graphs as part of the Range option in the print command. The key points here are to use a semicolon or a

THE GRAPH COMMANDS

comma to separate the print ranges from the graph ranges and to precede each graph name with an asterisk.

For example, to include a graph named REVENUE between two print ranges named LAST_YEAR and NEXT_YEAR, you would specify the following in the Print Range command:

Enter print range: LAST_YEAR,*REVENUE,NEXT_YEAR

Unfortunately, pressing the **NAME/F3** key while you use the Range command only displays a list of named ranges. You can use it to specify the named print ranges, but you can't use it to specify the names of named graphs. You must remember the names you assigned to your graphs and type them in response to the **Enter print range:** prompt.

To combine the spreadsheet material underlying the doctorate degrees conferred example that has been used throughout this chapter with the graph in Figure 11-25, load the file containing the spreadsheet (Figure 11-2) and type

/PP	Enters the Print command and selects Printer.
R	Selects Range.
Arrow keys	Position the cursor on cell A3.
.	Tacks cursor to cell A3.
Arrow keys	Stretch cursor over A3..H15.
,	Inserts the argument separator.
*Figure 11-25	Names the graph to be printed, beginning with an asterisk.
ENTER	Accepts print range and named graph.
AG	Selects Align and Go to print the print range followed by the named graph.
Q	Selects Quit to return to the Ready mode.

The graph and its accompanying spreadsheet cells appear in Figure 11-28.

Hints

Because you cannot select named graphs from a list with the **NAME/F3** key as you specify graphs to print through the Range command, do the next best thing. Use the Graph Name Table command to write a table of named graphs to empty cells on your spreadsheet. Then, before you begin

Figure 11-28   Result of specifying both a print range and a graph with the Print Printer Range command.

```
                           Doctorate Degrees Conferred
                                 1960 to 1985
     (In Thousands)

                  1960    1965    1970    1975    1980    1985
     Total         9.8    18.7    29.9    34.1    32.6    32.9
     Male          8.8    14.7    25.9    26.8    22.9    21.7
     Female        1.0     4.0     4.0     7.3     9.7    11.2
```

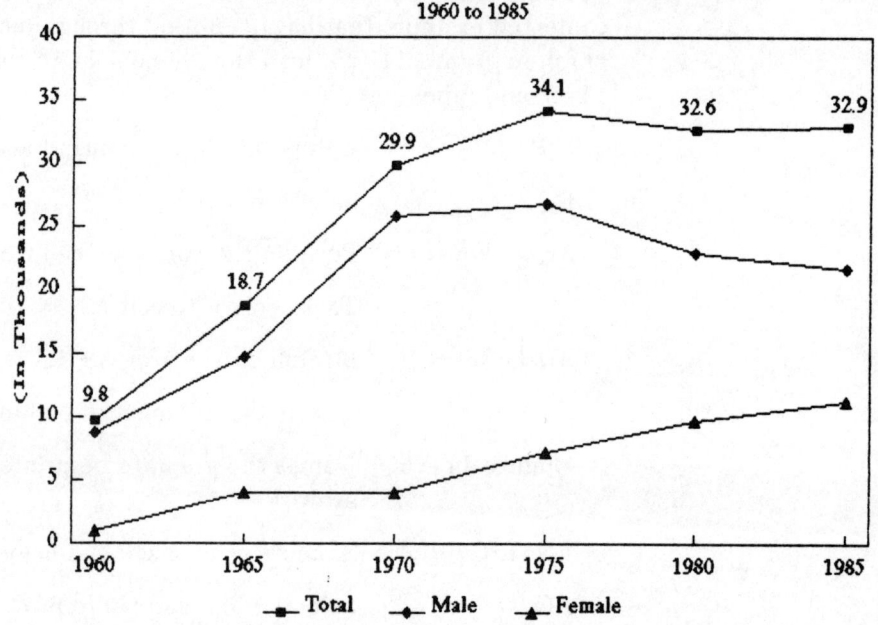

the Print command, position the cursor so that the table is on the screen. This way you can copy the named graph names as you need them.

Lotus provides no way to adjust the spacing between the spreadsheet cells and the graph. To add additional lines, specify the spreadsheet ranges to include the required number of blank lines either before or after the print range, as appropriate. Naturally, several trials may be necessary to establish the required size of each print range.

The default image size is determined by the location of the left and right margins. These must also be set to determine the width of the print range. If you don't want a graph that fills the margin from left to right, select Options Advanced Image Image-Sz Reshape, and you can specify the width and height of your graph in standard characters. Unfortunately, you can't mix graph sizes, because the size setting controls the size of all graphs printed under the current Range command. If you do change the graph size and 1-2-3 can fit more than one graph on a page, it will. If you want only one graph printed per page, select the Page command after you select Go to print the graph.

Finally, you can specify named graphs through the Range command without specifying any spreadsheet cells. When you do you can see a list of all of the graphs you wish to print. Unfortunately, you can't paste graph names into the Range command to specify the graphs to print.

Options Advanced Image

As noted earlier in this section, the Print command option Options Advanced Image controls certain aspects of graph printing. See Figure 11–29 for the command tree.

When you select Advanced Image, the following options appear:

Rotate	Choices are No for horizontal (default) or Yes for vertical.
Image-Sz	Choices are Margin-Fill (default), Length-Fill, or Reshape.
Density	Choices are Final (default) or Draft.
Quit	Leaves the Image option.

Lotus' default graph print settings are to print graphs horizontally across the page and within the current margins. Graphs are printed with a 4 to 3 ratio (4 units of width to 3 units of length). With the standard margins the default graph takes up about half of an 8½ by 11-inch page. When you select Rotate Yes, the graph is printed vertically and takes up the entire page.

When you select Image-Sz, you choose among the Margin-Fill, Length-Fill, or Reshape options. Under Margin-Fill (the default) 1-2-3 prints the largest graph possible between the current margin settings. Margin settings are in standard characters for a horizontal graph and standard lines for a vertical graph. Thus, changing the left and right margins changes the size of a graph printed across the page, whereas changing the top and bottom margins changes the size of a graph printed vertically.

Figure 11–29 Print Printer Options Advanced Image command tree.

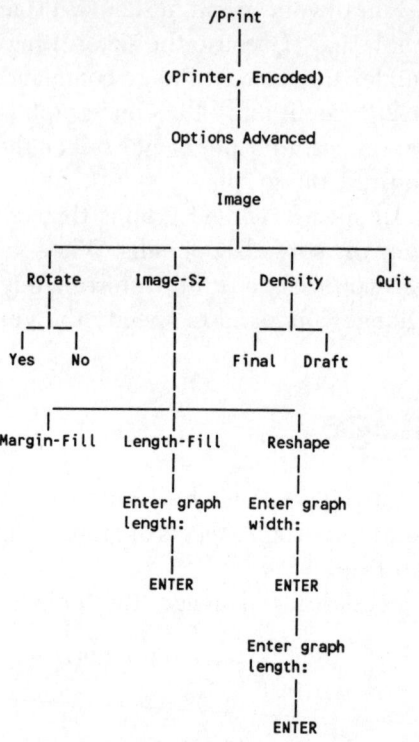

When you select Length-Fill, you are determining how many standard lines the graph occupies. In everyday terms you are determining the *height* of the graph, except that the ratio of 4 to 3 width to length may override your selection. The default Length-Fill is 66 lines (the entire standard page), but the number of lines a graph uses is really determined by the left and right margins and the 4 to 3 ratio for width to length. If you want to squeeze a graph in from the margins without actually resetting the margins, reduce the length with the Reshape option to 25 lines or so and a smaller graph is printed, centered between your existing margins.

The Reshape option specifies the image's width (in standard characters) and length (in standard lines). The default for width is 76 characters, and the default for length is 66 lines. You can select any combination of width and length to size a graph into a particular area. However, reshaping only affects the graphs—the type used for titles, legends, and other features of a graph *is not* resized. When you are trying to reshape a graph, there is simply no substitute for a lot of trial and error printing.

THE GRAPH COMMANDS

The final choice on the Image submenu is Density. Your choices are between Final and Draft. Most dot matrix printers print Draft graphs much faster than Final graphs, so if you use such a printer select Draft whenever speed is most important. The Final option (the default) prints your graphs with the highest possible quality. Use it to make your best impression.

Conclusion

Printing graphs with 1-2-3 requires that you manage the interaction between choices made in the Graph command to specify and augment a graph and choices made in the Print command to specify print settings for a particular graph. Until you are familiar with the interaction of these features, the easiest thing to do is to use the Print Printer Image Current method of printing graphs. You can press **GRAPH/F10** before printing to see how your specifications look on the screen. Then select Align and Go to print the graph. Finally, compare the result to the image on the screen and make any adjustments that are required. With a little bit of experience you will be able to use all of the Graph command features to get good-looking printouts of your graphs.

HANDS ON: USING THE GRAPH COMMAND

In the first 10 chapters you mastered many of the commands and features of Lotus 1-2-3. You know how to use 1-2-3's many tools to construct and use electronic spreadsheets. You know how to create a database and get the most out of the Query, Find, and Data Table commands. In this chapter you have learned to use the 1-2-3 Graph command to create and print graphs. You now have a formidable tool kit with which to solve almost any problem involving information or numbers and to print your conclusions as professional reports, memos, and presentations.

The Worksheet

Lotus' individual elements are certainly powerful tools, but when combined, their usefulness is much more than the sum of their parts. The following Hands On exercise uses a graph to present the information generated by the database and the data table constructed in the Hands On section of Chapter 9 (reproduced here as Figure 11–30). If you need to

Figure 11-30   Worksheet and data table.

```
    A         B       C       D       E           F          G          H
 1
 2        ***INPUT RANGE***                   **CRITERION RANGE**
 3      Month    Person Expenses              Month     Person
 4      ============================
 5      June     Jones    $36.15
 6      July     Smith    $29.54
 7      August   Jones    $15.47                ***TWO-WAY DATA TABLE***
 8      July     Smith   $161.00                      MONTHLY EXPENSES
 9      June     Smith   $115.31
10      August   Smith    $87.69           1287.7       Smith      Jones    Totals
11      August   Jones    $13.45            June      $379.63    $134.88   $514.51
12      June     Smith   $251.78            July      $190.54    $365.67   $556.21
13      July     Jones     $0.36            August    $188.06     $28.92   $216.98
14      July     Jones   $147.98
15      August   Smith    $36.25            Total     $758.23    $529.47 $1,287.70
16      June     Smith    $12.54
17      June     Jones    $98.73
18      August   Smith    $64.12       Formula in cell E10: @DSUM(A3..C20,2,F3..G4)
19      July     Jones    $91.54
20      July     Jones   $125.79
21
22
23
```

review the details of this table's construction see the Hands On section in Chapter 9.

Creating a Horizontal Bar Chart

To create a horizontal bar chart of the information in Figure 11-30, begin by typing

/G	Enters the Graph command.
T	Selects Type.
F	Selects Features.
H	Selects Horizontal.
Q	Selects Quit. Returns to main Graph command menu.
A	Selects the A data range.
. Arrow keys and ENTER	Use the period key and the arrow keys to specify Smith's expenses, F11..F13, as the A data range.
B	Selects B data range.

THE GRAPH COMMANDS

. Arrow keys
and **ENTER**   Use the period key and the arrow keys to specify Jones' expenses, G11..G13, as the B data range.

C   Selects C data range.

. Arrow keys
and **ENTER**   Use the period key and the arrow keys to specify Total expenses, H11..H13, as the C data range.

V   Selects View to view the graph to this point.

The horizontal bar chart in Figure 11–31 appears on the screen. The basic graph is here, but division labels for the y-axis, legends, and titles still must be added.

Adding Titles

You are still using the Graph command so to add the titles, continue typing

O   Selects the Options command.

T   Selects the Titles option.

Figure 11–31   Horizontal bar chart.

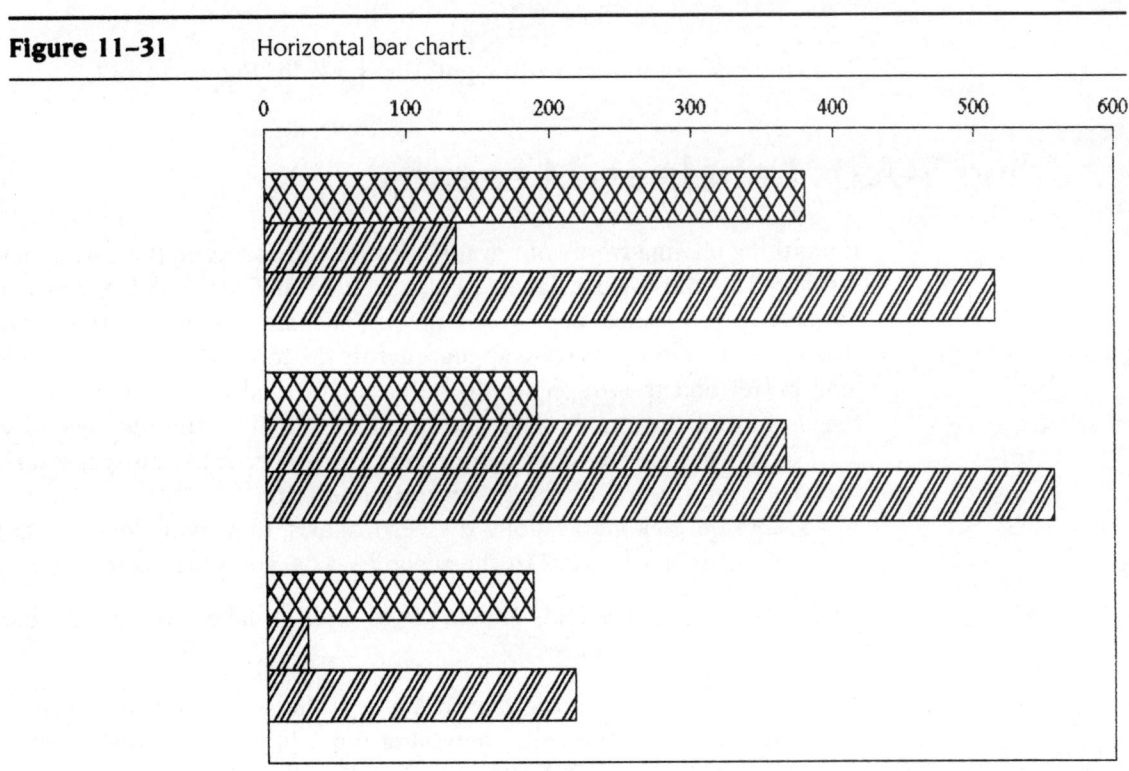

F	Selects First title.
Enter graph title, line:	Asks for the text for the main top title.
\G8	Type reference to cell containing MONTHLY EXPENSES on worksheet.
ENTER	Accepts First title.
S	Selects Second title.
Enter graph title, second line:	Asks for the text for the subtitle.
June, July, and August	Type the text.
ENTER	Accepts Second title.
Q	Selects Quit to return to main Graph command menu.
V	Selects View.

The result of your work to this point is shown in Figure 11–32.

Adding Y-Axis Labels and Legends

Is anything missing from your graph? Yes. The divisions on the x-axis (now displayed as the y-axis) haven't been labeled and without legends it is difficult to tell which bar represents which piece of information. Furthermore, the old y-axis scale appears across the top of the graph. It would look better and the graph would be easier to read if it appeared along the bottom of the graph. The bottom of the graph is the old second y-axis, so reassigning the data ranges to the second y-axis causes the scale to move from the top of the graph to the bottom.

To label the tick marks along the vertical axis, to provide legends, and to reassign the data ranges to the second y-axis, continue typing

X	Selects X data range, used to label divisions on bar charts.
. Arrow keys and ENTER	Use the period key and the arrow keys to specify the cells containing June, July, and August E11..E13 as the X data range.

THE GRAPH COMMANDS 475

Figure 11-32 Figure 11-31 with titles added.

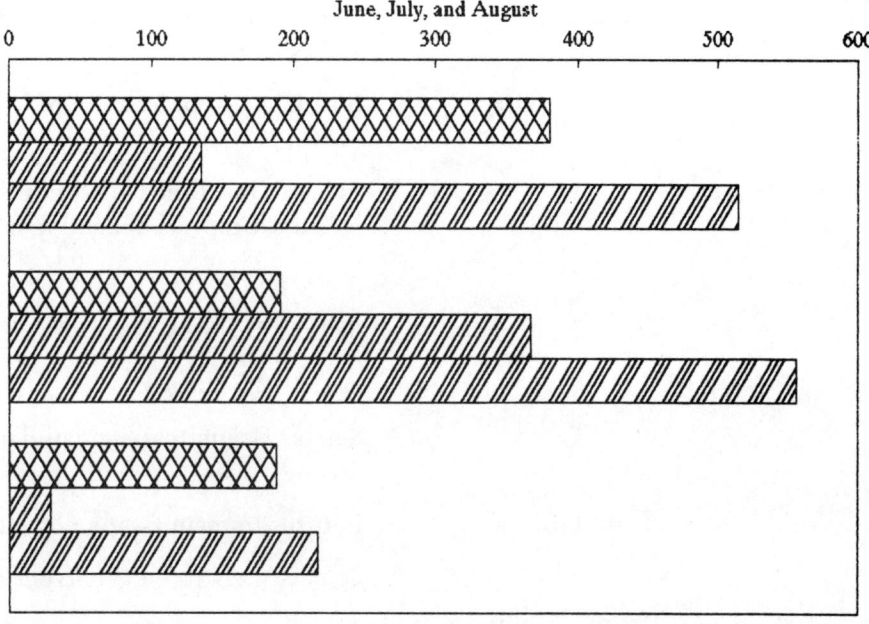

O	Selects Options.
L	Selects Legends.
A	Selects legend for A data range.
Enter legend for A range:	Asks for legend for A data range.
\F10	Type reference to cell containing Smith on the worksheet.
ENTER	Sets F10 as the location of legend for A data range.
LB	Selects Legend option, B data range.
Enter legend for B range:	Asks for legend for B data range.
\G10	Type reference to cell containing Jones on the worksheet.

ENTER	Sets G10 as the location of legend for B data range.
LC	Selects Legend option, C data range.
\E15	Types reference to cell containing Total on the worksheet.
ENTER	Sets E15 as the location of legend for C data range.
Q	Selects Quit to leave Option submenu and return to main Graph command menu.
T	Selects Type.
F	Selects Features.
2	Selects 2Y-Ranges.
G	Selects Graph to assign all data ranges to the second y-axis.
QQ	Returns to main Graph command menu.
V	Selects View to view current graph.

Figure 11–33 displays your completed graph.

Is there anything else you would like to add? The numbers on the second y-axis (the horizontal axis in Figure 11–32), for example, could be formatted to dollars, or the actual expenses for each person for each month could be added to the bars as data labels. You could also try some other graph types to see if one of them displays the information more clearly or dramatically. Try as many options as you like. View the graph after each choice. Retain an option when it improves your graph; drop it when it makes the graph cluttered or otherwise difficult to read or understand.

Naming the Graph

Once you have arrived at a satisfactory graph specification, use the Name option from the Graph command menu to assign a name to your graph to preserve the graph specifications for viewing later. Type

N	Selects the Name option.
C	Selects Create.

Figure 11-33 Figure 11-32 with legends, x-axis tick marks, and y-axis reassigned to second y-axis.

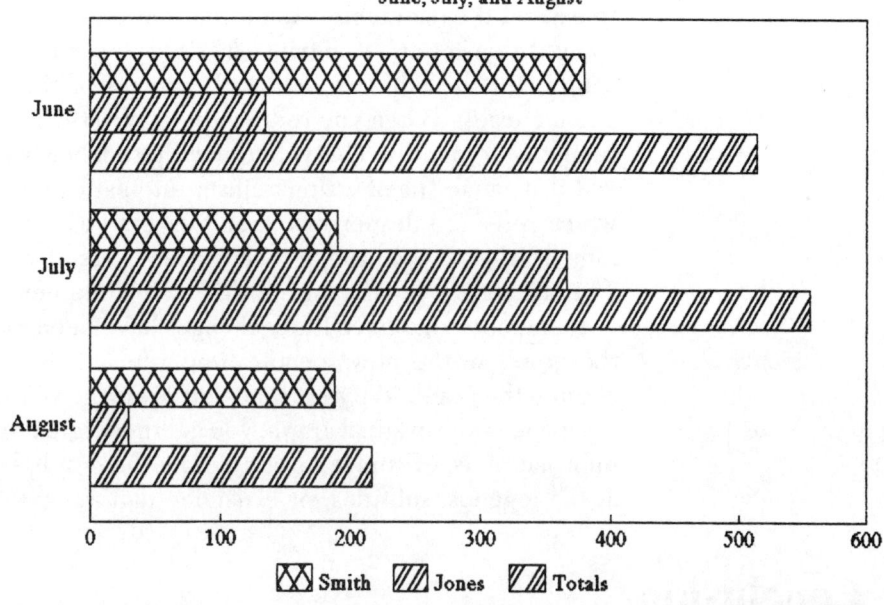

Enter graph name:	Asks for name for graph.
EXPENSES/MONTH	Type name.
ENTER	Adds EXPENSES/MONTH as a named graph to the library of named graphs stored with this worksheet.

You can now print your graph and save the worksheet with this graph specified and ready for use the next time you retrieve this file.

Modifying the Database and Redrawing the Graph

To insert additional information in your database, use the Move command or the Worksheet Insert Row command to move the last entry (row 20 in Figure 11-29) down the necessary number of rows. Using either command automatically adjusts the range specifications in the @DSUM function (cell

E10) to the enlarged input range. After you have entered the new expenses, press **TABLE/F8**, and the data table is recalculated. Next press **GRAPH/F10**, and your bar chart is redrawn to reflect the additional information.

To add additional months or salesperson names, use the Move command to expand the data table. (You can also use the Insert command, provided using it doesn't affect entries elsewhere on the worksheet.) The specifications for the table as well as the ranges of the other functions adjust automatically. When you redraw the graph, the x-axis labels (the months) reflect new months. This is because those labels were entered as a range and that range specification adjusts automatically. However, the legends, which refer to salespersons, aren't entered as a range. They are entered individually, so you have to specify a new legend for each new salesperson. The last step is to edit the subtitle to include new months.

Remember that once these changes have been made, you must rename the graph so the new specifications replace the old ones. If you don't rename the graph, the next time you press the **GRAPH/F10** key or select the name of the original graph, you get the original specifications. Updated information is, of course, used to draw the graph, but new elements such as the legends, subtitles, or expanded data ranges are not included.

Conclusion

In this Hands On section you have seen the easy, natural integration of the graphics, database, and spreadsheet functions of 1-2-3. As you become familiar with these three functions, you will find many opportunities for creating worksheets that integrate different features. In fact, you will soon find the distinction between spreadsheet, database, and graphics receding into the background as Lotus becomes an integrated decision-making support tool, an easy-to-use aid that is a natural extension of your analytical mind. Use this tool to organize information, analyze problems, and prepare the results for display and distribution. At that point, doing your job with Lotus 1-2-3 becomes as easy as . . . well . . . 1, 2, 3.

TIPS & TRAPS

Tips

Trial and Success and View Often.
Construct your graphs step-by-step and use the **GRAPH/F10** key to view each option immediately after you select it. If you specify several options, you may not be able to tell which enhances your graph and which makes it difficult or impossible to read.

Sometimes Reset Is Okay!
Unlike several other 1-2-3 commands the Reset command on the main Graph command menu is not a disaster waiting to happen. When you select Reset you get to specify whether to cancel the current graph or individual data ranges.

So You Can't Read the X-Axis Labels Because There Are Too Many Divisions.
Use the Options Scale Skip command to suppress every other (enter 2), every third (enter 3), and so on, x-axis label. Sometimes several trials are required to find the correct skip factor.

Traps

Lost Update of Named Graph.
When you call up a named graph and modify it, the changes you make are not incorporated in the named graph specification until you reenter the Graph Name Create option and rename the graph. You can reassign the previous name, or you can give it a new name.

The Data Labels Won't Go Away.
Once you have specified a range of data labels, you are stuck with the specification. You can only cancel the data label specification by canceling the entire graph or the data range to which the labels were assigned. The alternative is to reassign the no-longer-wanted data labels to a blank cell somewhere on your spreadsheet.

When Format Doesn't Mean Format.

The word *format* as applied to the Option Format command has a different use than Range or Worksheet Format. The Graph Option Format command controls the lines and symbols used on line, area, and XY graphs. It doesn't control the display format of the numbers along the x- and y-axes. To apply the familiar "format" options to those numbers select Options Scale and either X-Axis or Y-Axis. There you see a Format option you can use to set the standard 1-2-3 display formats (Fixed, Currency, and so on).

12 Macros: The Hidden Power of 1-2-3

OBJECTIVES

After mastering the content of this chapter, you will be able to

☐ automate repetitive worksheet tasks.

☐ use special macro keywords for ENTER, the arrow keys, and the other noncharacter keys on the keyboard.

☐ use special advanced macro commands in macros.

☐ create macros using the keystroke recorder.

☐ create and use custom menus.

☐ manage macros when several files are active.

☐ create a macro library for use with all your spreadsheets.

INTRODUCTION

Lotus 1-2-3 has an advanced feature that can automate repetitive typing tasks, generate custom menus, and create sophisticated templates. This feature goes by several names: the *typing alternative*, *keyboard macros*, or *macros*, for short. It's a feature many users never learn about. That is most unfortunate—keyboard macros are easy to construct and use. If you'll take the time to master a few easy-to-learn principles you'll have access to one of the most useful and powerful features of Lotus 1-2-3.

WHAT IS A KEYBOARD MACRO?

In its simplest form, a *keyboard macro* is a series of characters that 1-2-3 interprets as keypresses from your keyboard. It is an automatic way of typing. There are two important advantages to having Lotus enter the keystrokes: First, your computer and Lotus can enter them much faster than you can. Second, once you store the keystrokes correctly, your computer and 1-2-3 enter them without ever making an error.

An example of a simple keyboard macro is the text "LOTUS IS POWERFUL." Whenever you use this macro, 1-2-3 types LOTUS IS POWERFUL. The Mode indicator changes to Label, and the text appears in the control panel as if you had typed it. When you press the **ENTER** key, 1-2-3 enters the text into the current active cell. While macros can be used to type frequently used words and phrases, they can also press the keys that select 1-2-3's commands—/C for Copy, for example—or that create built-in functions such as @DATE(91,11,25) for the date 25-Nov-91.

1-2-3 also has a large library of special programming commands that can be used only within keyboard macros. Among other actions, commands include {BRANCH}, which passes control to subroutines; {BEEP}, which beeps the speaker on your computer to tell you when a long calculation is finished; and {INDICATE}, which changes the display in the Mode indicator to **HELLO**. There is also a command for creating data input forms, {FORM}, and one for adding new records to a database, {APPENDBELOW}. The most powerful of the built-in commands are the ones that create custom menus, {MENUCALL} and {MENUBRANCH}. These menus display and function just like regular 1-2-3 menus, except that you specify the menu choices and the actions that occur when a choice is selected.

Whereas the things you can do with a keyboard macro are, in fact, greater than the things you can do with 1-2-3 itself, the actual creation of a keyboard macro is a simple process. It's so simple, in fact, that you create small macros "on the fly" as you construct your spreadsheets. Whenever you repeat an action the third time—setting a format, widening a column, copying the same range—consider writing a macro to automate the action.

SIX RULES FOR CREATING AND USING KEYBOARD MACROS

You can create and use any keyboard macro, from the simplest to the most complex, by following just six simple rules. These rules apply whether you enter the keystrokes directly or perform the action and paste the results from the keystroke recorder into your worksheet.

A typical macro is displayed in Figure 12-1. This macro prints a range named REPORT in compressed type. It illustrates the general rules for creating and running any keyboard macro. The six rules are as described in this section.

Rule 1: Text Only

When you create macros directly, you can use *only* text characters or string formulas. No formulas, functions, values, or commands are allowed.

You must use forced text entry for any cell entry beginning with a slash or the greater than symbol, both of which bring up the menu, the @ symbol to start a built-in function, or any other character that 1-2-3 interprets as a command, function, or value. In Figure 12-1, forced text entry must be used in cell P66 to get 1-2-3 to accept /pp as text instead of entering the Print command.

Information recorded by the keystroke recorder is recorded as text, so you don't need to worry about forced text entry.

Figure 12-1   Typical keyboard macro to print a range named REPORT in compressed type.

A	O	P	Q	R	S	T
58						
59						
60						
61						
62						
63						
64			MACRO TO PRINT RANGE NAMED "REPORT" IN COMPRESSED TYPE			
65						
66		\P	/pp	Enters the print command, selects printer		
67			ca	Clears all previous settings		
68			rREPORT~	Selects Range and specifies REPORT		
69			oalpc	Selects Options Advanced Layout Pitch Compressed		
70			qqq	Three Quit commands required to return to main Print command menu		
71			lll	Issues command to move paper ahead three lines		
72			ag	Selects Align then Go to print REPORT range		
73			p	Selects Page to advance to next page		
74			q	Selects Q to end Print command		
75						

Your macro can be located anywhere in the current file or in any active file. However, the best place for macros in the current file is on their own sheet, usually the last sheet in the file. If the file contains only one sheet or if you want to place a macro on a sheet with other entries, place it below and to the right of the lower right corner of your spreadsheet. In this location, you can insert and delete rows in the spreadsheet and not accidentally affect your macro.

Rule 2: Use a Single Column

The macro must be entered as text into a single, consecutive column of cells. There must be no blank or value cells in the column, because a macro stops executing when it encounters something other than a label cell. Note in Figure 12–1 how each logical step of the Print command is entered into consecutive cells beginning with cell P66.

Rule 3: Name the First Cell

Use the Range Name Create command to name the first cell of the column that contains the text of your macro. In Figure 12–1, this is cell P66.

You have two choices when assigning the range name. You can assign a descriptive range name such as \SAVE or \MONTHLY_UPDATE. The backslash is not required, but make it a habit to start all macro range names with it so you can easily distinguish range names assigned to macros from other range names. Alternatively, you can assign a name made up of a backslash followed by a letter, such as \A or \Z. A good descriptive name for the macro in Figure 12–1 would be \PRINT, whereas a good backslash letter name would be \P. The choice you make depends on how you want to run your macro. Running the macro is discussed under Rule 6. In the figure the characters \P have been entered as text into cell O66, the cell immediately to the right of cell P66, the first cell of the macro. This construction makes it easy to tell what name was assigned to the macro. It also has the added advantage of making it possible to use the Range Name Label command. Position the cursor on O66 and type

/RN	Enters the Range Name Command.
L	Selects the Labels option.
R	Selects Right, because P66 (first cell of macro) is to the *right* of O66, the cell containing \P.

Enter label range:	Asks for range of cells containing labels.
ENTER	Accepts cell under worksheet cursor, O66, as label range, executes the command and assigns the label in O66, \P, to the first cell of the macro, P66.

For more information about using the Range Name Label command, see Chapter 3.

Once you have entered text into a column of consecutive cells and assigned a name to the first cell, your macro is complete. You are ready to use it.

Rule 4: Turn Off Automatic Recalculation

To execute your macros as quickly as possible, use Worksheet Global Default Recalc Manual to turn off automatic recalculation. Unlike normal operation, where recalculation takes place in the background, during macro operation it takes place in the foreground. That means 1-2-3 pauses to recalculate the *entire* worksheet *each* time a macro makes a change to the worksheet. The wait is minimal with small macros, but very noticeable with larger ones.

You can make one of the early instructions in each macro one to turn on manual recalculation and then, if necessary, make one of the last instructions the instruction to turn automatic recalculation back on. If you need a recalculation during the course of a macro, you can use either {RECALC} or {CALC}, discussed later in this chapter.

Rule 5: Position the Cursor

To use a macro, you must begin by positioning the cursor on the cell where you want the action to start.

Because most 1-2-3 actions take place relative to the current location of the worksheet cursor, it is very important either to position the cursor manually before running the macro or to have the first action in the macro be the proper positioning of the cursor.

The Print command macro in Figure 12-1 is an exception to this rule, because the Print command functions regardless of the worksheet cursor location.

Rule 6: Run the Macro

There are two ways to run a macro. If you have assigned one of the \ letterkey names, you can run the macro by pressing and holding down the **ALT** key followed by the letterkey. This is called the "speed method," because it requires the fewest keystrokes, and macros given backslash letterkey names are called *speed macros*.

When you use the speed method, Lotus runs the designated speed macro no matter where it is located in the stack. However, if the same backslash letterkey name exists in two or more active files, 1-2-3 only executes the select speed macro when it is located in the current file. Otherwise, you receive an error message.

The second method of running a macro is to press the **ALT-F3** combination (what Lotus calls the macro key) and then select the appropriate range name from the list that appears on the screen. You can use this method with any macro, including speed macros, but you must use it to run a macro whenever

- you haven't assigned a \ letterkey name.

- you want to use a speed macro in another active file and the same speed name exists in the current file.

- the same speed name exists in two or more active files, neither of which is the current active file.

The macro key is somewhat slower, but it does enable you to use the Range Name Create command to assign descriptive names to your macros, which you can annotate and table. (See Chapter 3.)

When you press **ALT-NAME/F3**, only the named ranges in the current file appear, along with the file names of other active files. Highlight the name of the macro you want to run and press **ENTER**. All range names are listed, so you can also run speed macros this way. If the macro is in another active file, highlight its name and press **ENTER**. Then select the named macro you want to run. (See the discussion of working with multiple active files later in this chapter.)

With either of these methods, macro execution begins immediately.

HOW A MACRO WORKS

Lotus begins processing a macro by executing the first character in the cell to which the macro range name was applied. This character is executed as if the corresponding key on the keyboard were pressed. If the first character is an A, for example, Lotus begins a label entry by typing an A.

When the first character is a slash, 1-2-3 presses the slash key, which causes the menu to appear. Subsequent letters are interpreted as selecting commands and subcommands by the speed-typing method. In Figure 12–1, for example, **/pp** in cell P66 begins the macro by pressing the slash key and entering the Print Printer command.

When 1-2-3 runs out of characters to process in the first cell, it automatically drops down to the next cell in the column and looks for more characters to process. For example, in Figure 12–1 after processing the **/pp** in cell P66, 1-2-3 moves down to cell P67, where it finds **ca**. Pressing C followed by A selects Clear All to clear any previous print command settings.

Processing continues down the cells in the column until 1-2-3 either encounters a nonlabel cell (a blank cell or a value cell) or an explicit command to quit. When 1-2-3 finds such a cell, macro execution stops and control returns to the operator.

THE SINGLE STEP COMMAND

Everyone makes errors when constructing macros, so don't be surprised when your macro doesn't run perfectly the first time you try it. Also, don't be surprised if the source of your error isn't obvious, because 1-2-3 executes keystrokes at breakneck speed and only stops when it reaches a set of characters it simply cannot process.

To regain control of 1-2-3 when an error occurs, press either the **ESC** key or the **ENTER** key to acknowledge the **ERROR** message in the Mode indicator. The next step in finding the error is to look over your macro. Sometimes, you can find a misplaced or missing character by simple examination.

However, if your macro is long and complicated or the error subtle, you probably can't find it by just looking at the macro. In that case, you can call on a special 1-2-3 feature called the Single Step command. It enables you to execute a macro one character at a time.

To use the Single Step command, press the **ALT-EDIT/F2** key combination and select Step. When you do, the word **STEP** appears at the bottom of your screen. Now when you start a macro in the normal way, the word **STEP** changes to a flashing **SST** (for Single Step). The macro executes one character at a time each time you press a key on the keyboard. (The other choices that appear when you press **ALT-EDIT/F2**—

Playback, Copy, and Erase—are discussed under the Keystroke Recorder topic later in this chapter.)

When you discover an error, press the **CTRL-BREAK** keys to exit from the macro. Correct the error you have identified, start the macro, and single step through it again.

Note that when **STEP** is displayed at the bottom of the screen, the Single Step command only affects the execution of macros. When you are not executing a macro, the Single Step command has no effect on 1-2-3's operation. You can perform all customary actions as if the Single Step command were turned off.

If you still can't identify the cause of an error, try going back to the actual keystrokes you are trying to program into your macro. You may have overlooked a key or two. The keys that produce actions, such as ENTER or RIGHT, but that don't cause a character to appear on the screen are particularly easy to miss, so check each keystroke carefully. If necessary, print out your macro and compare the instructions to the keystrokes as you perform them. As you discover your errors, modify and test the macro until it runs perfectly.

Once you have corrected all the errors in a macro and are ready to leave the Single Step command, press the **ALT-EDIT/F2** key and once again select Step. The word **STEP** disappears from the bottom of your screen, and your macro is once again executed at its normal breakneck speed. You can also turn Single Step on and off any time during the execution of a macro when 1-2-3 waits for input during an interactive command such as {MENUCALL}, {MENUBRANCH}, {GETLABEL}, {GET-NUMBER}, or {?}.

SPECIAL KEY NAMES

You know that when you construct macros you use characters to represent the keys you want 1-2-3 to press. Unfortunately, there are a number of keys on your keyboard that you certainly want to use in macros but that don't produce characters on the screen when pressed. The most frequently used of these keys is the ENTER key (discussed in the next section), but the ESC key, the arrow keys, the BKSP key, and many other keys produce actions instead of characters. The character-for-keystroke rule doesn't work in these cases. Fortunately, there is a way to use these keys in macros.

What 1-2-3 does is to recognize action key names enclosed in *curly brackets* (braces) as an instruction to press the designated key. Thus, the instruction to press the RIGHT arrow key in a macro is {RIGHT} or simply

{R}; the ESC key is {ESC}; and so on. See Table 12–1 for a list of action keys and their macro equivalents.

You can also instruct 1-2-3 to press the arrow keys, the ESC key, and the BKSP key multiple times by including a number after the key name. For example, {RIGHT 5} or {R 5} presses the RIGHT arrow key five times while {ESC 8} presses the ESC key eight times. Be sure to include a space between the key name and the number when you indicate multiple keystrokes.

The ENTER Key

Because the ENTER key is so frequently used, it is an exception to the curly braces rule. It is assigned a special character all its own: the tilde, ~. Whenever 1-2-3 encounters a tilde in a macro, it executes the same code as for the ENTER key.

Should you need to include a tilde or the bracket character as a character in a macro, enclose it in braces. Use {~} for the tilde and {{} and {}} for the braces.

In Figure 12–1 note that the tilde is used in cell P68 where the **ENTER** key is required after you have specified the name of the range to print.

ADVANCED MACRO COMMANDS

So far in this chapter you have learned to create macros out of characters and the special key names that mimic the keystrokes of nondisplaying keys. You can create powerful and useful macros with these simple tools, but 1-2-3 has some very elegant features in its macro tool kit. These features are a group of 51 advanced macro commands that can be used only from within a keyboard macro. They are your key to the real power of 1-2-3.

A complete list of Release 3 advanced macro commands is given in Table 12–2.

The Pause Command

The most useful advanced macro command is Pause, {?}. Whenever a Pause command is encountered in a macro, execution stops. The letters **CMD** appear at the bottom of the screen to indicate that 1-2-3 is still operating under the command of a macro. When the macro is paused, you can type,

Table 12–1 Designations for action keys for use in keyboard macros.

ACTION KEY NAME	KEYBOARD KEY/ DESCRIPTION
~ (tilde)	ENTER
{ESCAPE} or {ESC}	ESC
{UP}	UP
{DOWN} or {D}	DOWN
{RIGHT} or {R}	RIGHT
{LEFT} or {L}	LEFT
{HOME}	HOME
{END}	END
{PGUP}	PGUP
{PGDN}	PGDN
{BACKSPACE} or {BS}	BKSP
{DELETE} or {DEL}	DEL
{BIGLEFT}	CTRL-LEFT
{BIGRIGHT}	CTRL-RIGHT
{FILE}	CTRL-END
{FIRST CELL} or {FC}	CTRL-HOME
{FIRST FILE}, {FF} or {FILE} {HOME}	CTRL-END HOME
{INSERT} or {INS}	INS
{LASTCELL} or {LC}	END CTRL-HOME
{LASTFILE}, {F} or {FILE} {END}	CTRL-END END
{NEXTFILE}, {NF} or {FILE} {NS}	CTRL-PGUP
{PREVFILE}, {PF} or {FILE} {PS}	CTRL-END CTRL-PGDN
{EDIT}	EDIT/F2

continued

Table 12-1 Continued

ACTION KEY NAME	KEYBOARD KEY/ DESCRIPTION
{NAME}	NAME/F3
{ABS}	ABS/F4
{GOTO}	GOTO/F5
{WINDOW}	WINDOW/F6
{QUERY}	QUERY/F7
{TABLE}	TABLE/F8
{CALC}	CALC/F9
{GRAPH}	GRAPH/F10
{MENU}	/ (slash to bring up command menu)
{?}	Pause for manual input until user presses ENTER
{~}	To have tilde appear as ~
{{} and {}}	To have braces appear as { and }

use the cursor movement keys, and perform any other action *except* press the ENTER key. Pressing ENTER tells 1-2-3 to stop pausing and resume macro execution.

The Pause command has many uses for expanding 1-2-3's power, because information such as a date or a name is easy for you to supply interactively but may be entirely beyond the ability of 1-2-3 to obtain directly.

Note that if you use the Single Step command described earlier with a macro containing Pause commands, you must press the **ENTER** key at the point in the macro required by the Pause command. This makes it somewhat more difficult to use the Single Step command to find errors in macros that use the Pause command.

Table 12-2 Advance macro commands.

ADVANCED MACRO COMMAND	ACTION
{?}	Halts macro execution temporarily, allowing user to type and move around; macro continues when user presses ENTER
{routine-name arg1, arg2,...}	Calls a subroutine, optionally with arguments
{BEEP number}	Sounds the computer's bell or tone
{BLANK location}	Erases the entries from a specified cell or range
{BRANCH location}	Continues macro execution at a different cell
{BREAKON} and {BREAKOFF}	Enables and disables the use of the BREAK key to interrupt macro execution
{CLOSE}	Closes a file that has been opened with the {OPEN} command
{CONTENTS destination-location,source-location,width-number, format-number}	Places the contents of one cell in another cell as a label, optionally formatting the result using a particular column width and numeric display format
{DEFINE location 1:type 1, location 2:type 2,...}	Specifies cells that will store arguments specified in a subroutine call
{DISPATCH location}	Branches to destination specified at location

continued

Table 12–2 *Continued*

ADVANCED MACRO COMMAND	ACTION
{FILESIZE *location*}	Determines number of bytes in currently open file and records finding in cell specified by location
{FOR *counter-location, start-number,stop-number,step-number,starting-location*}	(FOR-NEXT loop) Repeatedly executes the macro that begins at a particular location
{FORBREAK}	Cancels execution of current FOR loop. 1-2-3 continues executing at the next character after the currently executing FOR command
{GET *location*}	Halts macro execution for one keystroke and stores the character or special key the user presses as a label in a specified cell
{GETLABEL *prompt-string,location*}	Halts macro execution temporarily, prompts the user to type, and stores the characters as a label in a specified cell
{GETNUMBER *prompt-string,location*}	Halts macro execution temporarily, prompts the user to type a number or numeric expression, and creates a number in a specified cell
{GETPOS *location*}	Determines current position in open file, and displays it in location cell
{IF *true-false-expression*}	Conditionally executes the statement(s) and keystroke(s) that follow the IF command in the same cell

continued

Table 12-2 *Continued*

ADVANCED MACRO COMMAND	ACTION
{INDICATE string}	Specifies up to 72 characters to replace the standard 1-2-3 indicator in the upper right corner of the screen; without argument restores the standard indicator
{LET location,number} {LET location,string}	Stores a label or number in a specified cell. You can specify a string-valued expression as the string argument
{LOOK location}	For characters entered, places the first character typed at the specified location cell. If the user has not typed anything, erases the location cell. In either case, macro execution continues
{MENUBRANCH menu-location}	Halts macro execution temporarily, prompts the user to make a menu choice, then calls a subroutine based on the choice
{MENUCALL menu-location}	Halts macro execution temporarily, prompts the user to make a menu choice, then calls a subroutine based on the choice
{ONERROR branch-location,message-location}	Continues execution at a specified branch-location if a 1-2-3 error occurs. Optionally stores the error message that 1-2-3 would have displayed at message-location
{OPEN filename, access-mode}	Opens a specified file for reading, writing, or both

continued

Table 12–2 *Continued*

ADVANCED MACRO COMMAND	ACTION
{PANELOFF}	Suppresses redrawing of the control panel during macro execution
{PANELON}	Restores standard control panel redrawing, undoing a PANELOFF command
{PUT *location, col-number, row-number, number* or *string*}	Stores a label or number in one of the cells of a specified range. You can specify a string-valued expression as the string argument
{QUIT}	Terminates macro processing, returning control to keyboard
{READ *bytecount, location*}	Reads characters from a file into the cell specified to location
{READLN *location*}	Copies a line of characters from the currently open file into the specified location
{RECALC *location*}	Recalculates the formulas in a specified range, proceeding row-by-row
{RECALCCOL *location*}	Recalculates the formulas in a specified range, proceeding column-by-column
{RESTART}	Continues macro execution at the next character or cell as if at the beginning of a new macro
{RETURN}	(Subroutine return) Continues macro execution just after the location of the last {*routine-name*} or MENUCALL statement

continued

Table 12-2   Continued

ADVANCED MACRO COMMAND	ACTION
{SETPOS position-number}	Sets a new position in the currently open file
{WAIT time-serial-number}	Suspends macro execution until a specified time
{WINDOWSOFF}	Suppresses redrawing the windows area of the display screen during macro execution
{WINDOWSON}	Restores standard window redrawing, undoing a WINDOWSOFF command
{WRITE string}	Copies characters into an open file
{WRITELN string}	Adds a carriage return-line feed sequence to a string of characters and writes the string to a file

The /X Commands

Earlier versions of 1-2-3 had a limited group of commands, called /X commands. Table 12–3 displays the set of special /X commands for use within keyboard macros. All /X commands were available in Release 1A, so any macro created with that program works with Release 3. Furthermore, if you know how to use these /X commands, you can continue to use them with Release 3 even though they are all duplicated with advanced macro commands. In Table 12–3 the equivalent advanced macro command is listed under the description of each /X command.

CUSTOM MENUS

The most powerful and elegant advanced macro commands are the ones that create custom menus. With these commands not only can you au-

Table 12-3 /X commands from Lotus 1-2-3 Release 1A.

/X COMMAND	DESCRIPTION
/XI*formula*~	Evaluates logical comparison in formula. If the comparison is TRUE, continue processing on the same line; if FALSE, move down one line and continue processing. Equivalent: {IF}
/XG*location*~	Transfers processing within the keyboard macro to the specified location. Doesn't move the worksheet cursor. Equivalent: {BRANCH}
/XQ	Terminates execution of the keyboard macro. Equivalent: {QUIT}
/XC*range*~	Transfers processing to a subroutine in the specified range. Equivalent: {*routine-name*}
/XR	Returns processing to the main keyboard macro after transfer to a subroutine. Equivalent: {RETURN}
/XN*message*~*range*~	Displays a message in the control panel and accepts a number input that is placed in the range. Equivalent: {GETNUMBER}
/XL*message*~*range*~	Displays a message in the control panel and accepts a label input that is placed in the range. Equivalent: {GETLABEL}
/XM*range*~	Displays a user-defined menu from the specified location in the control panel. Equivalent: {MENUBRANCH}

tomate your spreadsheet, but you can display alternative actions in the easy-to-understand and familiar format of a 1-2-3 menu.

Three commands create menus. They are the /XM command and the two advanced macro commands {MENUBRANCH} and {MENUCALL}. The /XM command and {MENUBRANCH} are equivalent functions. The difference between the two keywords is subtle.

When they are executed, both {MENUBRANCH} and {MENUCALL} create a menu that appears at the top of the screen, where it functions like a typical 1-2-3 menu. The difference between the two keywords comes after a choice is executed. With {MENUBRANCH}, macro execution ends after the choice is executed. With {MENUCALL}, macro execution continues in the cell that is immediately below the cell containing {MENUCALL} in the main macro.

Each custom menu has two parts:

Menu Text   Text used to create the menu. It must be entered into spreadsheet cells in a particular pattern.

Menu Macro   Either {MENUCALL} or {MENUBRANCH} must be executed to use the menu text to create a menu.

The best way to learn to use custom menus is to work through a detailed example. In the following example you'll go through the steps to construct a menu that solves a problem many people have when they want to print different sections of the same worksheet. In this example, one printout summarizes the worksheet and is distributed to department heads. Another section supplies special detailed information for the accounting division. A third prints the entire worksheet for the files. Additional subsections could be printed, and you can easily add options for printing them to the menu you are about to create.

Creating the Menu Text

The first step in creating a custom menu is to enter the text in the cells of your worksheet for the menu items and prompts to be displayed in the control panel. In a completed menu, each column contains three distinct elements: a menu item, a prompt, and a macro.

Refer to Figure 12–2 for an illustration of the layout of the three elements of each menu item.

Top Row: Up to eight menu items in the top row, one to a
Menu Item   cell.

   Leave a blank cell to the right of the last menu item. The total number of characters in all your menu items cannot exceed the width of the screen—72 characters. Characters exceeding the limit are not displayed, but within the 72-character limit, multiple-word menu items are allowed.

Second Row: Enter the prompt for each menu item into the cell
Prompt   *directly below* the menu item.

   Each prompt may be up to 72 characters long and *must* be entered as a long label in the single

MACROS: THE HIDDEN POWER OF 1-2-3

Figure 12-2   Structure of a typical entry in a custom menu.

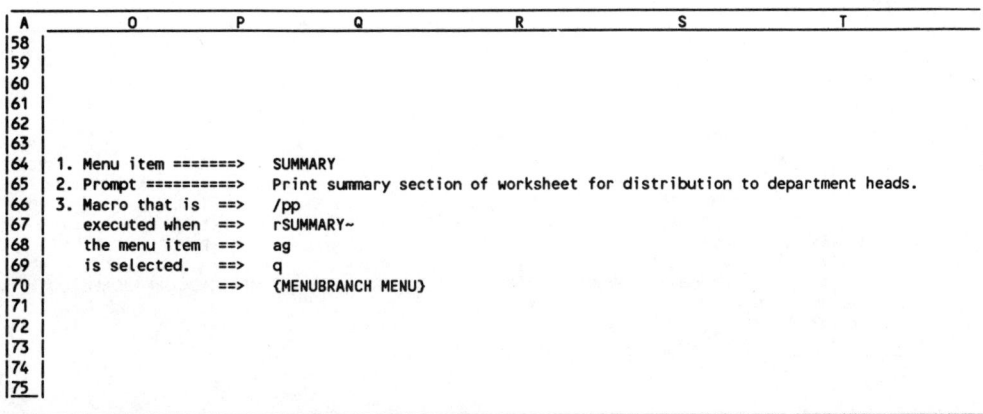

	cell immediately below the menu item it describes. After you enter the prompts the line below the menu items is impossible to read, because the long labels are truncated where there are entries in the cells to the right. To view a prompt, place the worksheet cursor on it and read the prompt on the Status line.
Remaining Rows: Macro	Enter macro to be executed by each menu item into cells immediately below the prompt for that item. In addition to typical macro commands, the macro can contain the command to call another menu (a submenu) or a command to branch to a subroutine to be executed as the menu choice.

Figure 12-3 contains all of the text necessary to form a menu that prints different parts of a worksheet depending on the menu item chosen. Note the relationship between a menu item, its prompt, and the macro executed when the item is selected.

The prompts in row 62 of Figure 12-3 can't be read on the screen because they appear on the screen as truncated long labels. To read a prompt, position the cursor on its cell and read it on the Status line. The actual contents of each cell in row 62 are

Cell	Contents
Q62	Print summary section of worksheet for distribution to department heads.

Figure 12–3 Completed custom menu and the menu macro that invokes it.

```
   A     P        Q              R              S              T              U
55 |
56 |
57 |
58 | \M    {MENUCALL MENU}
59 |
60 |
61 | MENU  SUMMARY          DETAIL          FILE COPY        SAVE             QUIT
62 |       Print summary sectiPrint detail sectioPrint entire workshSave worksheet undeLeave menu.
63 |       /pp              /pp             /pp              /fs              {QUIT}
64 |       rSUMMARY~        rDETAIL~        rFILE~           {ESC}
65 |       ag               ag              ag               REPORT~
66 |       q                q               q                r
67 |       {MENUBRANCH MENU} {MENUBRANCH MENU} {MENUBRANCH MENU} {MENUBRANCH MENU}
68 |
69 |
70 |
71 |
72 |
73 |
```

R62 Print detail section of worksheet for distribution to field reps.

S62 Print entire worksheet for file.

T62 Save worksheet under original filename.

U62 Leave menu.

Along with the text that becomes the menu, you must also enter into cell Q58 in Figure 12–3 the following macro code:

{**MENUCALL MENU**}

The advanced macro command, {MENUCALL}, actually creates the menu from the text entered into spreadsheet cells beginning with the cell named MENU.

So far, you have only entered the text for the menu and associated macros. Now enter the text you'll use with the Range Name Create command, \M and MENU, into the cells P58 and P61, immediately to the left of the cells to which they will be assigned as range names.

The final step in creating the menu macro of Figure 12–3 is to assign \M and MENU as range names to the appropriate cells. Move the cursor to cell P58 and type

/RNL   Enters the Range Name Labels command.

R   Selects Right as the location of the cells to be named relative to the cells containing the labels.

Enter label range:	Asks for location of labels to be used as range names.
.	Tacks cursor to cell P58.
Arrow keys	Highlight the range P58..P61.
ENTER	Assigns \M to Q58 and MENU to Q61.

Note: Blank cells in the label range do not create range names.

Using a Custom Menu

You are now ready to use your menu. To do so, press **ALT-M** or press the macro key and type \M. When you do, the menu appears in the control panel at the top of the screen, as shown in Figure 12–4.

The menu you just created works just like any 1-2-3 menu. Use the arrow keys to highlight menu choices, and, as you do, the highlight moves from choice to choice and the associated prompt appears in the control panel. You can select a menu item by pressing **ENTER** to select the highlighted choice, or you can type the first letter of your choice.

If you use the typing method and if two choices begin with the same letter, 1-2-3 selects the first occurrence. Therefore, try to specify menu choices that begin with different characters. When you do make a menu choice, 1-2-3 executes the instructions in the macro under that choice.

Modifying a Menu

Adding to a Menu

If your original menu has fewer than eight items, you can add additional choices to it by simply placing additional menu choices in cells immedi-

Figure 12–4   Screen as it appears when you run the menu macro from Figure 12–3.

```
A:A43:                                                          MENU
SUMMARY   DETAIL   FILE COPY   SAVE   QUIT
Print summary section of worksheet for distribution to department heads.
| A         A           B           C           D           E      |
|43 |
|44 |
|45 |
|46 |
|47 |
```

ately to the right of the last menu choice. Lotus automatically includes the material in the menu.

When you need more than eight choices, make one of your choices "OTHER" and have it execute another menu macro with additional menu choices. With this technique, you can have as many menu choices as you want by simply creating the required number of submenus.

Redisplaying a Menu

If you want your menu to redisplay after each choice, end each macro in the menu with the advanced macro command that generated the menu in the first place. In the example, end each menu choice with {MENU-BRANCH MENU}. Now the last action taken by each macro is to redisplay the menu so you can make additional choices. If you don't regenerate the menu, it disappears after each menu choice macro is executed.

Quitting a Menu

You can always stop a macro's execution by pressing **CTRL-BREAK**, pressing **ESC**, or by letting execution stop at the end of a menu choice. However, menus are easier to use when you include QUIT as one of the options. The macro under the QUIT option can be the explicit Quit command—{QUIT}—or it can simply be a blank cell since macro execution stops whenever a nonlabel cell is encountered.

Suggestion for Additional Menu Macros

If you use a hard disk and store worksheets in various subdirectories, you must use the File Dir or the Worksheet Global Default Dir command to change the subdirectory Lotus uses each time you move from one project to another. You can simplify this task by including a worksheet file in each directory containing a macro that is just a menu of all your subdirectories. When you are ready to switch from budget files to revenue files, for example, call up the file containing the subdirectory menu and select your new subdirectory.

The macro associated with each choice enters the Worksheet Global Default Dir command and resets the default directory to the desired subdirectory. You can also add the keystrokes required to enter the File Retrieve command in the new directory so that you'll be ready to select the file you want to load.

This same subdirectory menu can be used when several people share a hard disk and each person stores his or her worksheet files in a different subdirectory. Here the menu gives each user quick and easy access to specific files. If each user has multiple subdirectories, each subdirectory can have its own menu. Instructions for creating a subdirectory macro are contained in the Hands On section at the end of this chapter.

Full-Screen Prompts

Menu prompts are usually long enough to describe an action, but if you want a longer description, you can use the {GOTO} keyword to position the worksheet cursor in a particular cell. In this way text describing each menu option is displayed.

This technique can also be used to create help screens for specific tasks. To save a file, for example, the operator may have to insert a particular diskette in a disk drive and to supply a particular filename. This process can be described on the screen by making the first action in a Save menu macro a {GOTO} command that displays a section of your worksheet containing these detailed instructions. The pause keyword, {?}, stops the macro so the operator can read the screen, and a message at the bottom of the screen explains **Press ENTER to continue.**

ADDITIONAL MACRO COMMANDS, KEYWORDS, AND FEATURES

Automatic Macros: \0

It is often convenient to have a macro executed automatically when the worksheet containing it is loaded into 1-2-3. This way you can select from choices such as Update, Store, and Print as soon as the worksheet is loaded. This technique can also be used to automatically display the directory menus described in the Hands On section.

To create what is called an "auto-executing macro," just give the {MENUCALL} macro the name \0. Macros with the \0 name automatically execute when the worksheet they are on is loaded into memory. If you wish to execute the macro from within an already-loaded worksheet, give the macro a conventional backslash letterkey name (**ALT-0** won't work) or use the macro key **ALT-NAME/F3** to run \0.

Note: You can disable automatic execution with the Worksheet Global Default Autoexec command. Do this if your macro adds to the stack a file containing a \0 macro. Otherwise, the macro in the file executes automatically when it is loaded.

Autoloading Worksheets

Worksheets with the AUTO123 filename automatically load into memory when 1-2-3 is loaded. You can combine a \0 macro with an AUTO123 worksheet to get a completely automatic macro. (See Chapter 5 for more details.) The autoloading and autoexecuting features are particularly powerful when you combine them with the subdirectory macros described in the Hands On section. The combination gives the operator the opportunity to choose the subdirectory in which to work each time the 1-2-3 spreadsheet program is loaded into memory.

Branching Commands

Among the other frequently used command keywords is {BRANCH}. This command sends the execution of a macro to a designated cell where macro processing continues. To use the command to branch to a subroutine named OPTIONS you would enter {BRANCH OPTIONS}. When 1-2-3 encounters this command, it stops processing macro instructions in the current cell, and goes to the cell named OPTIONS, where it continues executing characters as keystrokes.

Here is a simple example of the {BRANCH} command.

```
\A {?}
  {DOWN}
  {BRANCH \A}
```

This is a data entry macro that moves the cursor down each time you press **ENTER** to accept what you have just typed. The macro's name is \A, and {BRANCH \A} just reruns it endlessly. When you are ready to stop the macro, press **CTRL-BREAK**.

Do not confuse {BRANCH} with the {GOTO} keyword, which moves the cursor to a new location. {BRANCH} doesn't move the cursor, it just transfers macro processing to a new cell.

An alternative to the {BRANCH} command is to enclose the range name assigned to the subroutine in braces. The command {OPTIONS} branches to the subroutine named OPTIONS. The difference is that you can pass arguments to the subroutine with a range name keyword, whereas you can't do so with a {BRANCH} keyword.

When passing arguments such as {OPTIONS 35,25}, you must begin the subroutine (OPTIONS in this case) with a {DEFINE} command. For example,

{DEFINE N26:Value,G45:String}

accepts argument 1, 35 in {OPTIONS 35,25} as a value and stores it in cell N26. The second argument, 25, is accepted as a label and is stored in cell G45. You can omit the Value and String qualifiers, and you can abbreviate them to V and S.

Input Commands

Other frequently used advanced macro commands are the two input commands {GETLABEL} and {GETNUMBER}. Both pause macro execution and display a user-defined message. For example, if you enter

{GETNUMBER Enter your age: ,A1}

1-2-3 displays the prompt **Enter your age:** in the control panel and waits for a response. When you respond to the message and press the **ENTER** key, the response is stored in the designated cell, A1, and the macro continues processing instructions. The difference between the two input commands is that {GETNUMBER} accepts a value input (number) while {GETLABEL} accepts a label input.

If/Then Command

Another useful command is the keyword {IF}. This command is a branching function that can be used to send macro execution in one direction or another depending on the outcome of a logical comparison. The form of the command is

{IF formula}

The formula is a logical comparison that evaluates to 1 when true and 0 when false or a reference to a cell containing a logical function. When the comparison is true, macro execution continues in the same cell. When it is false, macro execution ceases in the cell and continues in the cell immediately below it.

In the following example, the {IF} command is used in conjunction with the {QUIT} command:

{IF TEST>0}TEST IS GREATER THAN ZERO.~{QUIT}
TEST IS NOT GREATER THAN ZERO.~
{QUIT}

The logical comparison **TEST>0** asks whether the value in TEST is greater than zero. If the answer is yes, 1-2-3 types **TEST IS GREATER THAN ZERO**, enters it, and continues processing keystrokes in the same cell, which is the {QUIT} command to end macro execution.

If, however, the answer is no, then 1-2-3 stops processing keystrokes in the cell and drops down to the cell below. There it finds the text, TEST IS NOT GREATER THAN ZERO, which it types and enters. Then it executes {QUIT}. Try this macro out. Enter the text, name it \A, and name a cell TEST. Then enter a number into TEST and execute the \A macro.

Additional Advanced Macro Commands

Lotus has many more advanced macro commands. Some—such as {PANELON}, {PANELOFF}, {WINDOWSON}, and {WINDOWSOFF}—control the display. The first two keywords turn on and off redrawing the control panel during macro execution. The second two perform the same action for the part of the displaying screen's worksheet. In addition to suppressing the "light show" that accompanies macro execution, these commands can speed up macro execution by a factor of four or five by eliminating the need to repaint the screen.

Provided you haven't disabled it with the Worksheet Global Default Other Beep, you can use the {BEEP} keyword to sound your computer's "bell" to signal the end of a long operation or to call attention to your worksheet at a particular level of a parameter. You can even program the bell in four different tones by including the numbers 1 to 4 in the keyword, as in {BEEP 4}. If you are particularly talented, you can write a macro to play "Twinkle, Twinkle Little Star!"

The {INDICATE} advanced macro command lets you determine the text displayed in the Mode indicator. Enclose the text in quotation marks, such as in the command line

{INDICATE "PLEASE WAIT FOR WORKSHEET UPDATE"}

or use a range name to refer to a cell containing the prompt. You can even make the Mode indicator disappear by placing nothing between the quotation marks, as in

{INDICATE ""}

The Mode indicator is restored to its original function by {PROMPT} without an argument or the end of macro execution.

Lotus also has a number of keywords for opening, reading, and writing to a file. These commands include {OPEN} and {CLOSE}, to open and close the file; and {READ}, {WRITE}, and {WRITELN}, to read and write to a file. {WRITELN} adds a carriage return-line feed to the end of the sequence of characters written to the file.

WORKING WITH SEVERAL ACTIVE FILES

Macros are particularly powerful tools when they are combined with Release 3's ability to store multiple files in memory. You can use macros from one file on cells in another, and you can design macros to operate across files and even on files stored on disk. Finally, you can set aside a file as a library of your most frequently used macros and read that file into memory whenever you need to use one of those macros. However, you must be aware of several potential problems when you use macros with several active files in memory.

Range Names

To begin with, you must understand how 1-2-3 interprets range names in macros when they aren't preceded by filenames. Range names used in commands and formulas that aren't preceded by filenames are assumed to refer to the current file. For example, the macro command

/cINTEREST~~

copies the contents of the range named INTEREST into the current cursor location. Because there is no filename before INTEREST, 1-2-3 looks for that range name in the current file. On the other hand, the macro command

/c<<C:\FINANCE\BUDGET.WK3>>INTEREST~~

looks for the range named interest in a file named BUDGET.WK3, which may or may not be active.

When range names are used in flow control commands within macros, 1-2-3 assumes that the named range is in the file containing the macro. For example, {PRINT} is a subroutine call to a range named PRINT. Because no filename precedes the range name, 1-2-3 assumes that the subroutine is on the worksheet containing the macro. If there is any possibility of confusion, provide a filename for range names.

Running Macros Across Active Files

Macros can only be run when they are in active files, but you can start a macro in one active file while the cursor is in another.

You can always use the macro key, **ALT-NAME/F3**, to run macros in any active file. When you press the macro key, the range names in the current file appear on the screen. Highlight the desired macro name (even a \ letterkey name) and press **ENTER** to run it. The filenames of other active files are also displayed on the screen. To run a macro in one of them, highlight the desired filename and press **ENTER** to display the range names in that file. Then proceed to select a macro range name to run.

Macros named with \ letterkey names can present some problems. To run a macro that has a \ letterkey name when the cursor is in any active file, press **ALT** and the letterkey. No problems arise when only one macro in all of the active files is assigned to the particular letterkey name. However, if more than one macro has the same letterkey, 1-2-3 has to resolve the conflict. Here is how 1-2-3 does it. If a macro with the letterkey name exists in the current file, that macro is executed. If no macro with the letterkey name exists in the current file, but two or more exist in other active files, 1-2-3 refuses to execute the macro. In that case, use **ALT-NAME/F3** to run the macro.

Creating a Macro Library

To create a macro library, collect your frequently used macros in a separate file. Macros that add columns or rows of numbers, enter dates, enter repetitively typed text, or append data to databases are among the many candidates for the library.

When you create the macros, pay particular attention to the range name issues discussed here.

Name each of the macros in your library with two names. Make one a \ letterkey name that uses a letter that is suggestive of the action. For example, use \A for a macro that adds a column of numbers. Make the other name a descriptive range name beginning with a backslash. Use the **ALT** letterkey method of running macros when there are no other letterkey names in active files. Use the macro key when there are such names or when you can't remember which letterkey was assigned to a particular macro.

Finally, you can use a custom menu to display long prompts and to choose many of your library macros. To get macros such as the macro to

MACROS: THE HIDDEN POWER OF 1-2-3

add a column of numbers to work in a menu, you must use the {?} command to pause the macro at the appropriate spot while the cursor is properly positioned. A little bit of experience, and you will be able to fine tune your macros to perform optimally in the spreadsheets you construct.

USING THE KEYSTROKE RECORDER

Release 3 contains a keystroke recorder that automatically records each keystroke you make. The recorder has a relatively small memory, 512 bytes, but that is enough to record about 500 characters—more than are required for most 1-2-3 operations. When the memory is full, it adopts a first-in, first-out rule. That is, it drops the oldest recorded keystroke as it adds newer ones to memory.

The keystroke recorder has two main purposes. First, you can copy the recorded keystrokes into a range on your spreadsheet. The recording is in macro form ({D} for DOWN arrow) so all you need to do is name the first cell and you have a macro. This is a particularly easy way to get the instructions for an action-based macro like printing a range or saving a file. But because you don't type the advanced macro commands, you can't use the recorder to create macros that use them. However, you can edit changes, including adding the advanced macro commands, to make the recorded keystrokes fully operational as a macro.

The second use of the keystroke recorder is to play back the recorded keystrokes. If you want to repeat an operation several times but don't want to write a macro to do it, just do the operation once and play back the keystrokes. As they are played back the keystrokes function just like a macro; they enter the codes of the keys listed in the recorder.

The keystroke recorder has a simple command tree, which is shown in Figure 12–5. You are already familiar with the use of the Step option to execute macros in Single Step mode. The other three options—Playback, Copy, and Erase—are the keystroke recorder part of ALT-EDIT/F2.

Warning: Although the keystroke recorder records in macro form, it records *cell addresses* as the arguments for formulas and functions even when you use the arrow keys to point to ranges. This means the action recorded is for a *specific* set of cells and not for a general action. For example, if you created an @SUM function in cell A7 to add together the contents of cells A1 through A6, the recorder records @SUM(A:A1..A:A6) even if you typed @SUM({UP}.{END}{UP}), which specifies the range with the cursor keys. To convert the recorded keystrokes to the general actions that would be useful in a macro, you must edit in the appropriate changes. See the Playback and Copy examples that follow.

Figure 12-5 ALT-EDIT/F2 command tree.

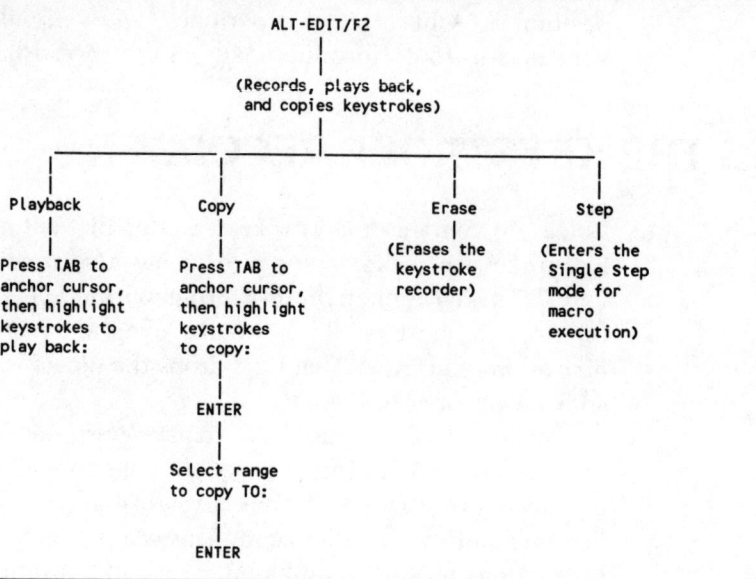

Erase

The Erase option clears the keystroke recorder. Use this option before you perform an action you want to play back or copy and you won't have to contend with a display containing a lot of irrelevant keystrokes.

Playback

When you select either the Playback or Copy option, the control panel expands to nine lines and displays the most recently entered keystrokes. The limit, as was noted, is 512 keystrokes, and the control panel expands to display up to that many. See Figure 12-6 for the way the screen looks when you select Playback.

The keystrokes that appear on the third line of the control panel in Figure 12-6 have been recorded in macro form with a {D} for **DOWN** arrow key, and with other mnemonic names. **ENTER** keystrokes have been recorded as tildes and, had you pressed a function key during the macro execution, the appropriate key name would have been recorded in braces.

Figure 12-6 Control panel expands to nine lines after you select Playback.

```
A:A7:    [W12] @SUM(A1..A6)                                    EDIT
Press TAB to anchor cursor, then highlight keystrokes to play back:
\=~{D}@SUM(A:A1..A:A6)~
```

	A	B	C	D	E	F	G
1	$1,452.00						
2	$1,626.00						
3	$1,562.00						
4	$1,789.00						
5	$1,467.00						
6	============						
7	$7,896.00						
8							

You can move the cursor through the keystrokes until it is positioned at the beginning or end of the group of keystrokes you want to play back. Then press the **TAB** key to anchor the cursor to that cell. You can't use the period because it is a character, and, as the Mode indicator shows, you are using Edit mode. Once the cursor is anchored, use the arrow keys to highlight the keystrokes to play back and press **ENTER** to repeat the action.

The recorder records every action you take. Unless you're superhuman that means it records lots of mistakes, though you can correct typing mistakes with the **BKSP** key before pressing **ENTER**. So before you select keystrokes to replay move the cursor through the text and make any corrections required to keep 1-2-3 from repeating your mistakes. If you are going to play back the keystrokes in a cell other than A7, you'll need to change the specific range, A:A1..A:A6, to general cursor movements.

Copy

The Copy option copies designated keystrokes from the recorder to cells in your spreadsheet, beginning with the current cursor location. In its operation the Copy option resembles the Playback option just discussed. When you select Copy, the most recent keystrokes are displayed, and you are invited to use the TAB key to anchor the cursor. Move the cursor to the appropriate spot and press **TAB**. Then highlight the keystrokes you want to copy to the worksheet. You can edit the keystrokes before you use the TAB key or after they are copied into your spreadsheet.

After you press **ENTER** to select the keystrokes to copy, the command prompts you to select a range. Move the cursor to the first cell of the location where you want the copy to appear and press **ENTER**. Lotus copies the recorded keystrokes into the spreadsheet, beginning with the cursor location. It divides instructions so they occupy the current column width but doesn't divide any instructions in a way that would make them unusable as macro commands. You can control the width into which 1-2-3 writes keystrokes by changing the column width before you enter the command. Also, when you are prompted to select the range to copy to, specify more than one column; 1-2-3 creates long labels of that width.

Using Copy to Create a Macro

In Figure 12–7 **ALT-EDIT/F2** has been pressed and Copy selected. Note that the keystrokes necessary to place a row of equal signs or double dashes (\=) under a column of numbers and then create an @SUM function to add the numbers are shown at the top of the screen.

Before the recorded text can be used as a macro that enters a row of double dashes and totals the column anywhere on your spreadsheet, you must convert the specific range reference in the @SUM function to the appropriate cursor movement keys. Or you can copy the specific information into the sheet and then edit the results. To change the recorded information in the example, use the **LEFT** arrow key to position the cursor after the left parenthesis. Type{UP}.{END}{UP}Then use the **DEL** key to remove A:A1..A:A6. The screen now looks like Figure 12–8.

When you are satisfied that the text you want to copy to the spreadsheet is correct, press **HOME** to move the cursor to the beginning of the recorded text. Then press **TAB** to anchor the cursor and **END** to highlight

Figure 12–7 Screen appearance after you select Copy.

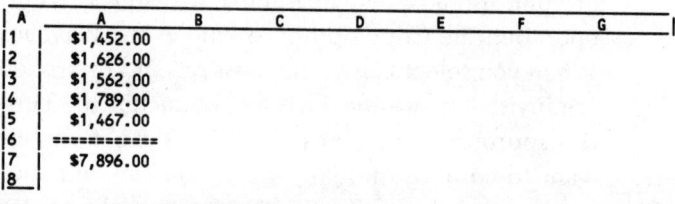

MACROS: THE HIDDEN POWER OF 1-2-3

Figure 12-8   Contents of memory buffer after you change cell addresses to cursor movements.

```
A:A7:  [W12] @SUM(A1..A6)                                        EDIT
Press TAB to anchor cursor, then highlight keystrokes to copy:
\=~{D}@SUM({UP}.{END}{UP})~
```

```
  A           A           B       C       D       E       F       G
 |1 |    $1,452.00
 |2 |    $1,626.00
 |3 |    $1,562.00
 |4 |    $1,789.00
 |5 |    $1,467.00
 |6 |   ============
 |7 |    $7,896.00
 |8 |
```

Figure 12-9   Text of memory buffer copied to cells in column D.

```
A:D1:  '\=~{D}                                                   EDIT
```

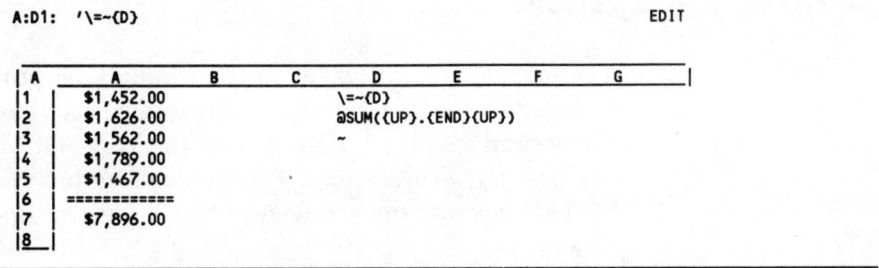

to the end of the recorded text. Press **ENTER** to complete the selection process. The prompt **Enter cell to copy TO:** appears. Move the cursor to cell D1 and press **ENTER**. The result is Figure 12-9. To finish, use the Range Name Create command to assign a macro range name to cell D1. Test your macro with the Single Step command and correct any errors you find.

MACRO HINTS

Here are some hints to help you get the most out of your macros.

Always Use Range Names in Macros

One of the most important hints is to always use range names in macros rather than references to cell addresses. If you don't, using the Insert,

Delete, or Move commands can cause changes in the addresses of cells in which information is located. These changes usually cause your macro not to work.

For example, if your macro uses a reference to cell A5 and you insert a row above row 5, the contents of cell A5 shift downward one row. With A5 in your macro, the reference would still be to cell A5, even though the information is no longer in that cell.

On the other hand, had you assigned a name such as INDEX to cell A5 and then used INDEX in your macro, it would still pick up the value from the cell named INDEX, no matter where the cell was moved to by an Insert, Delete, or Move command.

In essence, references to named ranges in macros are relative, or adjusting, cell references. References to actual cell addresses, even when they do not include dollar signs (such as A5), are treated in a macro as absolute cell references.

Know Your Action

The most important hint is to run through the process you are going to make into a macro. If necessary, write down each key you press to perform the desired operation. Until you get the hang of it, you may have to repeat the process several times. Pay particular attention to keys such as the **ENTER** key and the arrow keys that do not produce a character on the screen.

Place Logically Separate Actions in Separate Cells

Keep the number of characters entered in a single cell to a minimum. Do this by entering logically separate parts of your macro in separate cells. Macros are very cryptic, and the more characters you place in a single cell, the harder it is to understand what the macro does and the harder it is to find and correct the inevitable errors.

Figure 12-10 illustrates two different ways of writing a macro to enter a date, format the cell with the date format, and copy the entry into a range named TARGET. Though the methods are equivalent in the top and bottom macros, the bottom macro is much easier to understand.

Figure 12–10 Alternative ways to write the same keyboard macro.

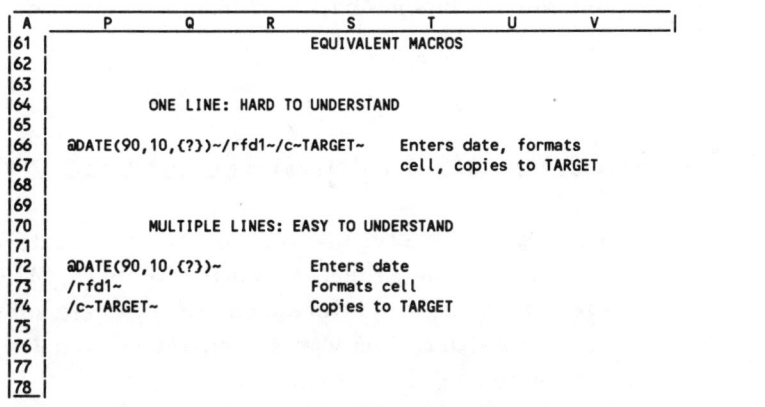

Easy HELP

To get information about advanced macro commands, type just a left brace, {, and press **HELP/F1**. Lotus displays a list of all the advanced macro commands. Select the one you need help with and press **ENTER**.

Use Subroutines

Use subroutines to break a large macro up into its logical parts. Subroutines are easier to understand, troubleshoot, and modify than one long macro. In many situations you can save time, because often one subroutine can be used by many different macros.

Call the subroutine into the main macro with the {BRANCH LOCATION} or {ROUTINE-NAME} advanced macro command. If you use {ROUTINE-NAME} to call the subroutine, you can use {RETURN} to return to the main macro when the subroutine is finished.

Give All Macros Titles

Annotate your macros by placing a descriptive title above every macro you create. If it's feasible, also place a brief description of the action performed to the right of each row of the macro. See Figure 12–1 for an example.

Annotating is particularly important when someone other than the creator of the macro will use it or modify it. It is also a very useful memory jog when you come back to a macro several weeks or months after you have created it.

Place All Macros on a Separate Sheet

The best way to organize your macros is to locate all of those created for a file on their own sheet. This makes them easy to find and gives you lots of room for titles and comments. Also, you are not going to inadvertently destroy a macro this way as you insert or delete columns or rows or otherwise modify a spreadsheet.

Use Uppercase Only for Range Names and Advanced Macro Commands

Follow the convention of placing range names and advanced macro commands in uppercase and all other characters in a macro in lowercase. This helps distinguish between specific macro commands and other characters in a macro. The only exception to this rule is any text you wish to have typed in uppercase.

Select Easy-to-Remember Names for Macros

If your worksheet contains only one or two speed macros, use \A and \Z as macro names. They are close to the **ALT** key on most keyboards and are therefore easy to remember and easy to use. When you use more than one or two speed macro names, select something that is easily associated with the function, such as \P for the print macro and \S for the save macro.

If you have several named macros, assign longer, descriptive names, such as \PRINT_MACRO or \MENU_MACRO, and use the macro execution key to run them. Start each macro name with a backslash so you can tell them apart from other range names. Also, all of the names beginning with a backslash conveniently appear together at the end of the name list.

Enter Macro Name as Text to Left of Macro

Whatever you name your macro, enter the name to the left of the first cell. This way, you immediately know the range name assigned to each macro. You can also use the Range Name Labels Right command to assign the text as a range name to the cell immediately to its right.

Use Custom Menus

When you have several macros on a single worksheet, place them in a custom-designed menu. The menu can be called by **ALT** and a single key (often *M* for Menu), or you can assign a descriptive name such as \PRINT_MENU to the menu and use the macro key to run it.

Menus are much easier to use than trying to remember the letters assigned to several macros, because each choice in a menu is assigned a full-word name and is described in a long prompt.

Test Macros for Errors

Macros are a cryptic programming language, and everyone makes errors in creating them. So you must always test your macros, because many errors can only be discovered when the macro is actually run. If necessary, use the Single Step command for this "debugging" phase.

Use Blank Cells for Macro Testing

Always move the cursor to a blank cell when you test a macro. If you leave the cursor on your macro and the macro enters information in the cell under the worksheet cursor, the entry replaces your macro. Avoid this problem by checking that the cursor is in a blank cell before you test a macro. Follow this hint even with macros that you don't expect to make an entry, because errors often cause entries in the cell under the worksheet cursor.

SUMMARY

Keyboard macros add a powerful dimension to 1-2-3's basic spreadsheet, database, and graphics functions. This dimension of 1-2-3 automates routine tasks and creates custom worksheets where the user interacts with specialized menus and prompts.

The uses to which you can put macros are almost limitless. Printing several sections of the same worksheet, using the File Combine command to link worksheets and controlling data input with the Range Input command are obvious situations in which a keyboard macro can make your work quicker and more accurate.

Macros that mimic keystrokes are easy to use, and you can create them whenever you encounter a repetitive task in the construction or use of a worksheet. The advanced macro commands enable you to create the custom menus and other special features needed to construct easy-to-use worksheets.

No matter how simple or complicated the macros you are constructing are, be sure to keep in mind the rules spelled out in this chapter. Be sure to label your macros and provide descriptive text to explain how they work. Otherwise, it may be extremely difficult to correct or modify a macro at a later date.

HANDS ON: SELF-MODIFYING MACROS

The string functions discussed in Chapter 7 can be used to create many kinds of self-modifying macros. In the following exercise you'll learn how to create a "full-screen" menu to choose which of several subdirectories to make current. One of the advantages of this technique is that to modify a menu choice you don't have to change the underlying macro.

Constructing the Menu Screen

Figure 12–11 displays the full-screen menu to be used in this exercise. Column A contains the full names to the subdirectories. This way you don't have to worry about where the target subdirectory is relative to the current subdirectory.

The text to the right of the subdirectory names describes the contents of each subdirectory. The line at the top of the screen, **Move your cursor to the desired directory and press ENTER** tells you how to use the full-screen menu.

Constructing the Macro

Your first step is to construct the screen that contains your subdirectory names and a brief description of the contents of each subdirectory. Start

MACROS: THE HIDDEN POWER OF 1-2-3

Figure 12–11   Text to form full-screen menu.

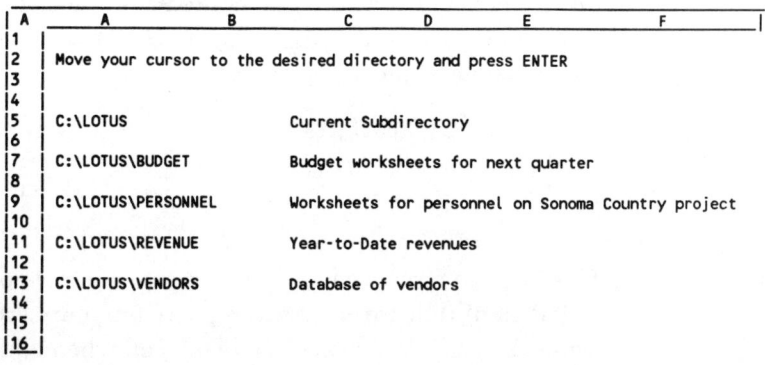

Figure 12–12   Macros that use text in Figure 12–11 to change directories.

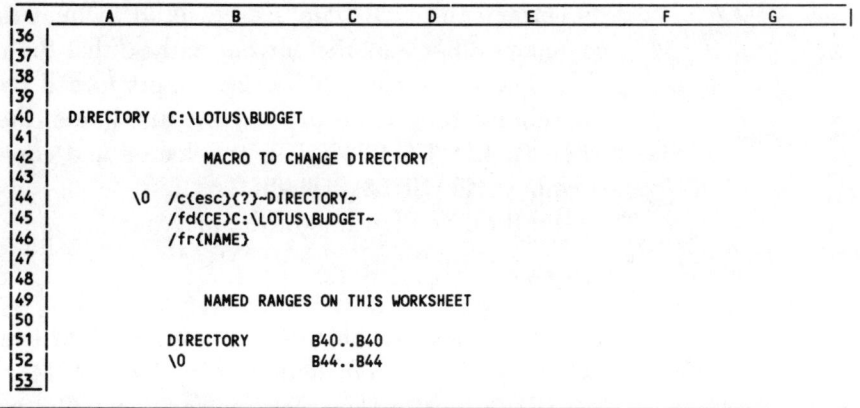

with the current, default subdirectory (LOTUS in Figure 12–11). Later you can add or modify subdirectories by editing the text on this screen.

Once you have laid out the menu screen, you are ready to construct the macro in Figure 12–12, which operates this worksheet.

Going from top to bottom, cell B40, to the right of the Range name **DIRECTORY**, is the cell into which different subdirectory names are copied. The macro itself begins in cell B44. It is made up of four lines.

The first line is

/c{ESC}{?}~DIRECTORY~

This instruction enters the Copy command. The cursor is tacked to the current cell when you enter the command. The {ESC} keyword unsticks the cursor so it can be moved around the screen. The {?} pauses the macro. When you have highlighted your choice, press **ENTER** to execute the Copy command and copy the contents of the cell under the cursor to the cell named DIRECTORY.

The second line is:

+"/fd{CE}"&DIRECTORY&"~"	Actual contents
ERR	What appears on the screen when B40 is empty

This line is a string function. The actual contents of the cell (the first line just shown) differ from what appears on your screen because the range name DIRECTORY refers to a blank cell when you first create the macro. The result is the **ERR** that appears on the screen. When a subdirectory name is copied to B40, the string function evaluates to the proper description of that subdirectory.

The initial plus sign declares this line to be a string function. The text **/fd{CE}** and the final tilde are enclosed in quotation marks. The macro command **{CE}** clears the current path so that the new path can be specified. The range name **DIRECTORY** refers to cell B40 where the name of the subdirectory was copied by the first line of the macro. For example, when C:\LOTUS\REVENUE is selected and copied into B40, this line becomes **/fdC:\LOTUS\REVENUE~**.

The third and last line of the macro is

/fr{NAME}

This is the instruction to enter the File Retrieve command (after you switch to the selected subdirectory). The {NAME} command presses the **NAME/F3** function key to display all of the filenames in the current subdirectory on the screen at one time.

You have now finished constructing your macro.

Name the Ranges

Your next task is to assign range names to the appropriate cells. This is simple, because during the construction process the appropriate range names have been entered in column A, next to the cells to which they are to be assigned. You can, therefore, use the Range Name Labels command to assign all of the range names at one time.

Begin by placing the cursor on cell A40 and typing

/RNL	Enters the Range Name Labels command.
R	Selects Right, because the cells to be labeled are to the right of the cells containing the text to be used as labels.
Enter label range:	Asks for location of labels to be used as range names.
.	Tacks cursor to cell A40.
Arrow keys	Highlight the range A40..A44.
ENTER	Completes the command.

The name assigned to the macro itself is \0. This is the special macro name for an autoexecuting macro. Whenever this worksheet is loaded, this macro executes automatically. Use the **ALT-NAME/F3** key to run the macro from within an active worksheet.

To completely automate this worksheet, place the cursor on cell A5 so the menu screen appears when the file is retrieved. Then save it with the filename **AUTO123**. Now, whenever you begin a 1-2-3 work session this worksheet loads automatically and the macro executes automatically (provided you haven't turned autoexecution off with the Worksheet Global Default Autoexec command).

To work properly, the AUTO123 worksheet must be saved into the subdirectory 1-2-3 defaults to when you first load it each work session. That is usually the subdirectory containing the program files. You can verify this by using the Worksheet Global Default Directory command to display the current default directory.

TIPS & TRAPS

Tips

Place Macros on Their Own Sheet.

Reserve a separate sheet in each stack for macros. The last sheet in the current file is often the most convenient choice, because it is both out of the way and can be reached easily by pressing **END CTRL-HOME** to move the last active cell on the last worksheet. And then pressing **HOME** moves the cursor to A1 on that sheet. By placing all macros together on a separate sheet, you'll know where to find your macros, and you won't inadvertently destroy them when you insert or delete rows or columns on your other worksheets.

Place Macro Names to the Left of Macros.
Use the column immediately to the left of each macro as a place to put macro names. Doing this clearly documents the name of each macro and makes it easy to use the Range Name Labels command to assign the text as a range name to the adjacent cell.

Edit Recorded Macros.
After you paste text from the keystroke recorder into your worksheet to use as a macro, be sure to edit the record material for mistyped keystrokes. The recorder keeps track of every key you press, and some of the keys may represent mistakes and the keystrokes necessary to correct them. Removing these extra keystrokes makes your macro easier to understand and modify. It also means that the macro runs faster.

Use the Slow-Motion Key.
To find mistakes in a macro, press **ALT-EDIT/F2** and select Step to single step your macro and pinpoint errors. The word **STEP** appears at the bottom of the screen. Any macro you now run runs in Single Step mode. That is, each time you press one of the keys, a character in the macro executes. Everything is slowed down so you can tell exactly what is happening at each step.

Whenever Possible, Use Range Names.
Informative, carefully chosen range names are one of the few ways you can make your macro code easier to understand. Also, range names adjust to modifications in the spreadsheet while references to specific cells or ranges of cells are absolute. They don't adjust to any change you might make to the worksheet.

Lotus assumes range names without filenames refer to named ranges in the current file. However, range names without filenames that are part of macro flow control commands such as {BRANCH} are assumed to refer to named ranges in the file containing the macro.

Traps

Watch Out for Blanks!
Misplaced blanks in macros can be a most frustrating source of error, because 1-2-3 reads each character as a press of the designated key. In

particular, watch out for trailing blanks, because they are very difficult to detect on the screen.

Self-Destroying Macros.
Position the cursor on an empty cell before you test a macro. Don't position the cursor on the text of a macro when you run the macro. Even if you don't intend to enter characters in cells with your macros, mistakes in macros often create entries in the cell under the worksheet cursor. Therefore, whenever the action programmed into the macro allows it, position the cursor on an empty cell before you test or run a macro.

Pitfalls in Single Step Mode.
When you use the **ALT-EDIT/F2** Step command, pay particular attention to the Pause command ({?}), menus, and other points in a macro where you have to provide keyboard input. If you don't provide an appropriate response, the Single Step command can hang up. You can avoid some of these problems by pressing **ENTER** to move from one step to the next.

To execute the rest of your macro at normal speed, press **ALT-EDIT/F2** again and select Step. Then press any key. To cancel your macro and return to the Ready mode, press **CTRL-BREAK** and then **ENTER**.

I Can't Tell Macro Names from Range Names.
When you use the **ALT-NAME/F4** key to run a macro, all range names are displayed. To tell macro names from other range names, begin each macro name with a backslash. Thus, \PRINT is a macro, whereas PRINT is some other named range.

Index

@CELL, 280
@CELL POINTER, 280
@IF, 265-267
@INFO, 280
@MOD, 273
@PMT, 270-272
@ROUND, 274
@STRING, 283
@SUM, 264-265
@VLOOKUP, 275-279

A

absolute cell reference, 146-149
  Copy command and, 146-149
  creation of, 146
  database and, 332, 343, 371
  functions, 285-286
absolute named ranges, functions of, 286
active cell, 5
  indicator, 9
adding files to stack, 185
adding sheets to stack, 58
add-ins
  attaching, 287-288
  menu, 287
  running, 288
  types, 288-289

advanced macro commands, 482, 496-498, 503-507. *See also* macros
align before printing, 214, 249
alignment of labels. *See* label alignment characters
all modified files, saving, 172
anchor cell, 93
  repositioning, 95
AND criteria in database, 342
arithmetic operators, 254. *See also* operators
arrow keys. *See* cursor control keys
assumption space, 297-299
  importance of, 319
asterisk, 38-39, 86
AUTO123 filename, 163, 504

B

BKSP (backspace key), 23, 95
backup copies of diskettes, 164, 203
bin range, 363. *See also* Data Distribution command
blank characters, Data Sort command and, 329-330, 372
borders and multi-page printouts, 230
built-in (@) functions
  arguments, 261
  database statistical, 360-363
  financial, 270-272

general rules, 260–263
logical, 265–267
mathematical, 272–275
multiple arguments, 262
nested, 267
parenthesis using, 263
pasting range names, 261
point to arguments, 261–262
range names, 262
relative and absolute cell
 references, 285–286
special, 275–283
statistical, 263–265
string, 283
time and date, 267

C

calculated fields in output range, 355.
 See also database querying
canceling
 proposed data table ranges, 309
 proposed print range, 214
cautions
 align when not used in printing,
  249
 Automatic format and Data Fill
  command, 320
 blanks in criteria range, 372
 borders and correct print range,
  230
 Copy command, 143
 Data Fill command, 296
 Data Query Delete command, 350
 extracting formulas, 181
 File Combine Copy command, 184
 File Retrieve command, 178–179
 Global command, 37–38
 Graph Name Reset command, 449
 implied database, 379–380, 413
 lost update of named graph, 479
 macros, self-destroying, 523
 Move command, 153–154
 open parenthesis, 263
 Range Erase command, 101–102
 Range Name Reset command, 133
 refresh automatic, 413
 Single Step mode, 523

space character in macros, 522–523
System command, 155–156
testing macros, 485
turn off automatic recalculation in
 macros, 485
Undo limits to, 53–54
Worksheet Delete command, 61–62
Worksheet Window command, 79
cell(s)
 active, 5
 address, 4
 anchor, 93, 95
 entries in, 20
 expanding cursor and, 93–96
 Range commands and, 92–93
cell references
 Copy command and, 144–149
 database and, 332, 343, 371, 372
 in functions, 252–253
centering long labels, 130
CIRC (circular reference)
 finding, 80–81, 87
 indicator, 8
clearing print settings, 223
column variable labeled data table,
 313
columns
 displaying, 64
 hiding, 64
 width all, 45–46
 width one, 63
 width range, 65
command trees, 25
 Add-in, 288
 Copy, 137
 Data, 322
 Data Distribution, 364
 Data External, 384
 Data External Create, 395
 Data External Delete, 401
 Data External Other, 405
 Data External Reset, 407
 Data External Use, 386
 Data Fill, 293
 Data Matrix, 412
 Data Parse, 410
 Data Query, 334
 Data Regression, 409
 Data Table, 298
 Data Table Labeled, 311

INDEX 527

Data Sort, 94
File Admin, 191
File Combine, 182
File Dir, 199
File Erase, 197
File Import, 190
File List, 198
File New, 186
File Open, 186
File Retrieve, 170
File Save, 170
File Xtract, 180
Graph, 416
Graph Name, 447
Graph Options, 424
Keystroke Recorder, 510
Move, 152
Print, 206
Print Options, 225
Print Options Advanced, 238
Print Options Advanced Image, 470
Print Options Name, 237
Quit, 156
Range, 89
Range Erase, 101
Range Format, 97
Range Input, 123
Range Justify, 114
Range Label, 100
Range Name, 103
Range Prot, 119
Range Search, 121
Range Transpose, 152
Range Unprot, 119
Range Value, 152
Slash, 26
Worksheet, 34
Worksheet Column, 62
Worksheet Delete, 59
Worksheet Erase, 66
Worksheet Global, 36
Worksheet Global Col-Width, 46
Worksheet Global Default, 50
Worksheet Global Format, 39
Worksheet Global Label, 44
Worksheet Global Protection, 49
Worksheet Global Recalculation, 47
Worksheet Insert, 57
Worksheet Status, 80
Worksheet Titles, 67

Worksheet Window, 71
commands
  Add-In, 286–290
  Copy, 135–149
  Data Distribution, 363–366
  Data External Create, 396–398
  Data External Delete, 401
  Data External List, 388–395
  Data External Other, 404–406
  Data External Reset, 406–407
  Data External Use, 386–388
  Data Fill, 293–297
  Data Matrix, 411–412
  Data Parse, 409–411
  Data Query, 333–360
  Data Query Delete, 350–351
  Data Query Extract, 351–357
  Data Query Find, 345–349
  Data Query Modify, 358–360
  Data Query Unique, 357
  Data Regression, 408–409
  Data Sort, 325–333
  Data Table, 297–319
  Data Table Labeled, 311–318
  File Admin, 190–196
  File Combine, 181–184
  File Dir, 198–199
  File Erase, 196–197
  File Import, 188–190
  File List, 197–198
  File New, 187–188
  File Open, 185–187
  File Retrieve, 176–178
  File Save, 171–176
  File Xtract, 179–181
  Graph Name, 415–480
  Graph Name Reset, 449
  Graph Options, 423–428, 452–461
  Graph Options Advanced, 458–461
  Graph Options Legends, 423–426
  Graph Options Titles, 426–428
  Graph Reset, 451–452
  Keystroke Recorder, 509–513
  Move, 151–154
  Print, 207–250
  Print Options, 224–241
  Print Options Advanced, 237–241
  Print Options Advanced Image, 469–471
  Print Options Name, 205–250

INDEX

Quit, 30, 156–157
Range, 88–133
Range Erase, 101–102
Range Format, 96–100
Range Input, 123–125
Range Justify, 113–118
Range Label, 100–101
Range Name, 102–103
Range Prot, 119
Range Search, 120–123
Range Transpose, 150–151
Range Unprot, 119
Range Value, 149–150
System, 154–156
Undo, 29, 52–53
Worksheet, 33–87
Worksheet Column, 62–65
Worksheet Delete, 59–62
Worksheet Erase, 65–67
Worksheet Global, 36–38
Worksheet Global Col-Width, 45–46
Worksheet Global Default, 50–56
Worksheet Global Format, 38–43
Worksheet Global Label, 43–45
Worksheet Global Recalculation, 46–48
Worksheet Global Protection, 48–50
Worksheet Insert, 56–59
Worksheet Page, 81–82
Worksheet Status, 79–80
Worksheet Titles, 67–70
Worksheet Window, 70–79
compressed type printing in, 219, 244–248
control panel, 8–10
controlling the spreadsheet display
  moving between windows, 72
  perspective view, 74–75
  title locking, 67–70
  unsynchronizing windows, 73–74
  windows, 70–74
  ZOOM to full size, 72–73
copying, 136–137
  absolute cell references, 146–149
  formulas and functions, 143–144
  multiple copies made easy, 161
  named ranges, 148–149

  relationship between FROM and TO ranges, 139–140
  relative cell references, 144–146
  stored files, 142–143
  techniques, 138–139
  three-dimensional ranges, 140
  using split screen, 139, 160
correcting mistakes, 23–24
  erased cells, 185
  ESC, 28
  Undo, 29
criteria, 335–336. *See also* database querying
criteria range, 347. *See also* database querying
CTRL-BREAK, 110, 123, 183
currency. *See* Range and Worksheet Format commands
current file, 13
current worksheet, 14
cursor
  expanding, 93–96
  unsticking, 57–58, 138
  worksheet, 5
cursor control keys, 15–19
  arrow keys, 15
  big move keys, 16
  file to file, 18
  sheet to sheet, 17
  single worksheet, 16

D

data tables
  hands on exercise, 367–370
  labeled, 311–318
  one-way, 299–302
  three-way, 304–308
  tips, 309–311
  two-way, 302–304
database defined, 323–324
database, external, 383–406
  adding records to, 402–404
  connecting to, 386
  creating new tables in, 395–399
  database drivers, 384
  deleting table in, 400–401
  ending connection to, 406–407

INDEX 529

external tables, 385
  listing fields, 390–392
  listing tables, 388–390
  naming table, 397
  using, 392–395
database querying. *See also* Data
    Query command
  adding records to database, 359
  AND criteria, 342
  blank criteria range, 343
  calculated fields in output range,
    354–355
  changing criteria, 344
  criteria range, 335–336, 347
  deleting records, 350–351
  exact criteria, 337
  extracting records, 351–357
  finding records, 345–349
  input range, 334–335, 346–347
  modifying records, 359–360
  multiple criteria, 341–342
  omitted fields in output range, 355
  OR criteria, 342
  output range, 351–353
  QUERY/F7, 349–350
  rearranged fields in output range,
    355
  relative criteria, 337–341
  removing criteria, 344
database, sorting. *See also* Data Sort
    command
  case, 331
  data range, 327
  extra keys, 328
  formulas, 332
  primary key, 327
  problems with, 329–332
  restoring original order, 332–333
  secondary key, 328
  sort order, 328, 331
  spaces, 330
dates. *See also* Worksheet and Range
    Format commands
  Automatic format and, 269
  Data Fill command with, 296
  entering, 268–269
  format, 41
  functions, 267–270
default print parameters, 215–218
  dealing with problems, 215–221

default settings for commands, 35–36.
    See also Worksheet Status
    command
  making permanent, 56
deletions
  cell. *See* Range Erase command
  column, 59–60
  file, 61
  row, 59–60
  sheet, 60–61
dollar sign, absolute cell reference
    and, 146

E

edit line, 9
editing records, 371. *See also* Data
    Find command
encoded files, creating, 208, 241–242
ending a work session, 30. *See also*
    System command
entries
  label, 20
  value, 20
entry line, 9
entry line cursor, 20
erasing
  files in stack, 61
  files on disk, 196
  ranges, 101
  worksheets, 60, 65–67
ERR, 291
  using @IF to prevent display, 265
  when using Worksheet Delete, 62
ESC (escape key), 28, 94–95
expanding cursor, 93
external database. *See* database
    external
extracting records. *See* database
    external and database querying

F

field. *See also* database sorting and
    database querying
  defined, 324
  field names, 323

INDEX

field names in database, 323
file-and-clock indicator, 6, 52
files
  correcting erased cells, 185
  extracting formulas, cautions, 181
  filename extensions, 167–168
  filenames, 166
  NAME/F3 in saving, 173
  need to save, 163–164
  options, File Combine, 183–184
  organizing, 169
  password-protected files, 193
  positioning cursor before, File Combine, 183
  positioning cursor before File Import, 189
  reservations on network, 191–193
  retrieving, 177
  retrieving into stack. *See* File New and File Open commands
  retrieving read only files, 177
  saving, 111
  saving as password-protected, 175
  saving in Release 2 format, 175
  saving read only files. *See* File Admin command
  sealing files, 193–194
  using File Combine, 184, 201
  using File Import, 190
  using File Open, 185–186
  using File Retrieve, 177
  using File Save, 171–172
filling ranges. *See also* Data Fill command
  date and time, 296
  using Data Fill, 295
footer last page, 228
forced page break, 81–82, 221
  when it doesn't work, 86
forced text entry, 23, 45
formatting headers and footers, 228
formatting value cells
  Global, 38–43
  Range, 96–100
formula range, 312–313. *See also* Data Table Label command
formulas
  add-in, 288–289
  built-in types, 253–254
  copying, 143–144

  Data Sort command and, 332
  displaying, 42
  File Xtract command and, 181
  linking across sheets and files, 4–5, 252
  names in, 111, 262
  printing and, 234–236
  string, 258–260
free cell, 93
freezing values. *See* Range Value command
function keys, 20, 21
  ABS/F4, 148, 290
  CALC/F9, 7–8, 21, 47–48
  EDIT/F2, 9, 23–24, 49, 118, 286
  GOTO/F5, 16, 18
    range names and, 103, 107
    sheet-to-sheet, 18
  GRAPH/F10, 431
  HELP/F1, 24
  NAME/F3
    and File commands, 173
    in function, 261
    print range, 213
    and Range names, 105–106
  QUERY/F7, 349–350
  TABLE/F8, 310
  WINDOW/F6, 72
  ZOOM, ALT-F6, 72–73
functions. *See* built-in functions

G

Getting back to 1-2-3. *See* System command
graphs. *See also* Graph command
  2Y-ranges, 441, 443–444
  ABC's of creating, 418–422
  ABC's of printing, 422–423
  advanced options, 458–461
  canceling graph settings, 451–452
  color, 452, 458–459
  crosshatching bars, 460–461
  crosshatching pie segments, 438–439
  crowded x-axis labels, 422, 455–456
  current graph, 462–463

INDEX

data labels, 452–454
data range, 428–431
exploding pie segments, 438–439
features, 440–445
format, 457–458
GRAPH/F10, 431
grid, 454–455
group, 428–431
hardware, 417–418
hatching. *See* graphs crosshatching
horizontal graph, 435, 440, 441–442, 472–476
legends, 423–426
library of named graphs, 447–450
logarithmic scaling, 442
multiple active files, 461–463
name reset, 449
naming, 447–448
options, 452–461
printing. *See* printing graphs
removing named graphs, 448–449
saving graphs, 463
scale, 455–457
spreadsheets and graph on screen, 445–447
stacked ranges, 441–442
table of named graphs, 450
titles, 426–428
types, 415–416, 431–445
using named graphs, 448
using with other programs, 463
x range for regression, 408–409
x range option, 421–422
xy graph, 421–422
Graph windows, 75
Group mode, 29–30
  indicator, 8
  Range commands and, 132
  Worksheet commands and, 37, 87

H

Help feature. *See* function keys

I

Input cell, 301, 304, 308
input range, database construction and, 346. *See also* database querying

insertions
  column, 56, 58
  file, 185–188
  row, 56–58
  sheet, 58–59
installing 1-2-3, 2
inverting matrices. *See* Data Matrix command

J

joining input ranges, 378. *See also* multiple input ranges

K

key field, 380. *See also* multiple input ranges
keyboard macros. *See* macros
keystroke recorder, 509
  copying, 511–512
  creating macros, 512–513
  playback, 510–511
  using, 509

L

label alignment characters, 22
  changing alignment, 43–45, 100
label entries, 20, 22–23
label-fill character, labeled data table, 313
landscape printing, 219
leaving 1-2-3. *See* Quit and System commands
logical operators, 256–257
lookup functions, 275–280
lookup table, 276. *See also* lookup functions

M

macros
  /X commands, 496
  action keys, 488–496

INDEX

table, 490–491
active files and, 507–509
advanced macro commands, 482, 492–496, 496–498, 503–507
autoexecuting, 503–504
autoloading worksheet and, 504–505
automatic recalculations, turn off, 485
branching commands, 504
custom menus, 496–503
   adding to, 501–502
   creating, 498–501
   modifying, 501–502
   quitting, 502
   redisplaying, 502
   using, 501
definition, 482
finding errors, 487–488
hands on, self-modifying macros, 518–521
hints, 513–517
how macro works, 486–487
if/then, 505–506
input commands, 505
keystroke recorder and, 509. *See also* keystroke recorder
library, 508–509
naming rules, 484–485
pause, 489–491
range name, importance of, 513–514
rules for creating, 483–486
running, 486
Single Step, 487–488
subroutines, 515
turn off automatic recalculation, 485
using Name Range Labels, 484–485
map view, 76
margins. *See* Print command
menu line, 9
mistake correcting. *See* correcting mistakes
mode indicators table, 9
moving cells
   named ranges, 153
   using Move command, 153

moving the cursor. *See* cursor control keys
multiple input ranges, 374–375. *See also* Data Query command
   implied database, 375–378
   joining input ranges, 378–382

N

named ranges. *See also* Range Name command
   making absolute, 148–149
   moving caution, 153–154
   naming cells with spreadsheet text, 110
   notes, adding to range names, 107
   using in commands, 109–110
   using in formulas, 261, 262
   verifying, 110
nonsense records, 379. *See also* multiple input ranges
numeric keypad, 15

O

offset, lookup function, 278
operators
   arithmetic, 254
   logical, 256
   range, 92
   string, 257
OR criteria in database, 341–342
order of operations, 255
output range, 351. *See also* database querying

P

page breaks
   forced, 81–82, 221, 248, 249
   removing, 243
parentheses in formulas, 255
parsing long labels. *See* Data Parse command
password-protected files, 175, 193–194

INDEX

pointing-with-the-cursor, 93, 261
  functions, 290
PR on status line, 49
primary sort key, 327. *See also*
  database sorting
printing
  align, 214
  borders, 230
  canceling proposed ranges, 214, 223
  compressed type, 219, 239, 244–248
  date stamp, 228–229
  default page layout, 215–218
  to encoded, 208, 241–242
  to file, 207
  fonts, changing, 239
  footers, 227
  formatting headers and footers, 228
  frame, 230–231
  graphs, 223
  headers, 227
  landscape, 239
  margins, 226
  naming print settings, 236
  page numbers, 228
  page-length, 226
  pitch, changing, 239
  print sample, 210–211
  to printer, 207
  priority, changing, 240
  problems with default settings, 218–221
  set up strings, 231
  under default settings, 2
printing graphs, 463–471. *See also*
  Print Options Other Image command
  advanced options, 469–471
  combining with spreadsheet, 466–467
  current graph, 465
  defaults, 464–465
  encoded, 465
  hints, 467–469
  named graph, 466
prompt line, 9
proposed range
  canceling, 309
  print command, 142

unsticking cursor, 138
viewing, 162
protecting files. *See* File Admin Seal command

Q

quitting 1-2-3. *See* ending a work session

R

ranges. *See also* Range commands
  absolute range names, 148–149
  assigning names to, 102–113
  canceling proposed, 296–297, 309
  changing formats, 99–100
  defined, 90–91
  deleting range names, 111
  format on Status line, 99
  functions in, 261
  limitations on range names, 104
  notes added to range names, 107–108
  operator, 92
  pasting named ranges into commands and functions, 105–107
  printing and, 213
  proposed by 1-2-3, 214
  Range Uprot with Range Input command, 123
  specifying, 89–96, 115
  tabling range names, 108–109
  undefined range names, 113
  using across files, 107
  using name ranges in commands, 109–110
  using named ranges in formulas, 111
  using Range Justify command, 114–115
  using Range Unprot command, 120
  using text on spreadsheet to name ranges, 110–111

record defined, 324. *See also* database sorting and database querying
reformatting long labels. *See* Range Justify command
regression. *See* Data Regression command
relative cell references, 144–145
   Copy command and, 144–146
   database and, 332, 343, 371
   functions, 285–286
retrieving information from disk. *See* File Retrieve command
RO, 8, 204. *See also* File Admin Reservation command
rounding errors, 41, 274–275
row variable labeled data table, 313

S

sample printout, 210–211. *See also* printing
saving worksheets, 111. *See also* files, saving
screen tour, 3–10
scrolling the screen, 19
search value in lookup function, 278
setup strings, 231–234
   clearing, 232
   embedded, 232
   entering, 231, 234
Sheet Indicator, 4
simultaneous equations solving. *See* Data Matrix command
slash (/) key, 25
slash commands, 25–26
   command tree, 26
   using a command menu, 26–28
soft cell boundaries, 114
sorting. *See* database sorting
stack, 10–14
   moving around, 17–18, 85
stars. *See* asterisks
starting 1-2-3, 3. *See also* installing 1-2-3
statistical functions, built-in. *See* built-in (@) functions
status indicators, 7
status line, 9

string functions, 258–260
   creating, 283
   text and numbers, 283–285
summary space worksheet construction and, 159
suspending printing, 209
System command when not to use, 155

T

table range
   data table, 301
   data table labeled, 314
   lookup function, 273
tabling features
   active files, 195
   filenames, 194–196
   files linked to current file, 195
   range names and notes, 108–109
text files, imported into 1-2-3 worksheets. *See* File Import command
three-dimensional ranges
   adding files, 185–188
   adding sheets, 58
   copying, 140–142
   current file, 13
   data table three way, 304–308
   group, 129–130. *See also* Group mode
   macros, active files and, 507–509
   macros, location of, 516
   moving from sheet to sheet, 17–19
   perspective view, 74
   ranges, 91
   removing files, 61
   removing sheets, 60
   saving all modified files, 171
   stack, 10
   windows, 73
   working in, 10–14
tilde as ENTER in macros, 16, 489. *See also* macros
time, entering, 268–269
transposing cells. *See* Range Transpose command

INDEX

U

Undo command limits, 53
user-defined formulas, 254–256

V

value entries defined, 22
values range, 363. *See also* Data Distribution command.
viewing cell content, 132

W

warnings. *See* cautions
wild cards in database, 341. *See also* database querying
word processing with 1-2-3, 117–118. *See also* Range Search command
worksheet commands
   asterisks displayed under Worksheet Format command, 38–39
   changing column width for a range of columns, 65
   circular references, finding, 80–81
   clearing titles, 70
   clearing windows to return to normal display, 78–79
   columns, inserting, 56
   contrasted to Range commands, 34
   default settings, 35
   deleting columns or rows, 59–60
   deleting files, 61
   deleting sheets, 60–61
   expanding window to full screen, 72–73
   formats, table of, 40
   graph window, 75–76
   hide and display columns, 64
   for inserting files. *See* File Open and File New commands
   for inserting forced page breaks, 81
   map window, 76
   moving between windows, 72
   perspective view, 74–75
   protecting worksheets, 48–50. *See also* File Admin Seal command
   recalculation manual in macros, 47
   removing forced page breaks, 82
   rows, inserting, 56
   saving Worksheet command default settings, 56
   set and reset column width, 63
   sheets inserting, 58
   synchronized windows, 73–74
   Undo and Worksheet commands, 52–54
worksheet default settings, 51
worksheet variable labeled data table, 313

X

X option under Graph command, 421–422
X range for regression, 408–409

Y

Y range for regression, 408–409

Z

ZOOM, ALT-F6, 72–73